# The WMD Mirage

# THE
# WMD
## MIRAGE

Iraq's Decade of Deception
and America's False Premise for War

•

*Featuring the Report to the President from
the Commission on the Intelligence Capabilities
of the United States Regarding Weapons
of Mass Destruction*

EDITED AND WITH AN INTRODUCTION BY

## Craig R. Whitney

of *The New York Times*

PublicAffairs

NEW YORK

BOOK DESIGN AND COMPOSITION BY JENNY DOSSIN

ISBN 1–58648–361–7

FIRST EDITION
10 9 8 7 6 5 4 3 2 1

# Contents

## PART IV

# Part V

# Introduction

When the United States went to war against the dictatorship of Saddam Hussein in Iraq on the night of March 19–20, 2003, President George W. Bush told the American people that the objectives were "to disarm Iraq, to free its people and to defend the world from grave danger."

Two years and tens of thousands of Iraqi casualties later, the United States had captured Saddam Hussein and Iraq had held its first free elections. But American forces had suffered more than 1,500 combat deaths and were engaged in a deadly struggle with an insurgency that had spread across the country, and questions were being asked.

Before the war, there were few Americans who doubted that Iraq would be better off without Saddam Hussein, whether or not they believed that military action to overthrow him was justified. But there were more than a few who questioned its basic premise. Saddam was a "grave danger" to the United States, the president and other administration officials kept insisting, because he had illegally reconstituted programs to develop biological, chemical, and nuclear weapons of mass destruction and could provide these weapons to the terrorists who had shown their lethal hatred of America on September 11, 2001.

At the administration's insistence, the United Nations had agreed to send inspectors with an ultimatum, but when the inspectors said they could work their way through the inspection sites and prove true or false Saddam's claims that he had no more weapons, not only the president and the secretary of state, but also U.S. intelligence did not believe these assurances. "When these inspections did not find evidence of active Iraqi WMD programs and in fact, even refuted some aspects of the [intelligence community's] nuclear and biological assessments, many analysts did not regard this information as significant," a critical U.S. Senate Select Committee on Intelligence report, included in this book, noted in 2004.

But now the world knows that the analysts were wrong and that the basic premise of the war was false. Saddam had no weapons of mass destruction in 2003, as the American military teams sent in after his removal discovered after they began scouring the country— just as the French and other opponents of the war had predicted the United Nations inspectors would have discovered if only the United States had given them time to complete their work.

Dr. David A. Kay, an American who had been chief U.N. nuclear weapons inspector in Iraq, was named a special advisor to the director of central intelligence in 2003 and sent back in to look for any hidden evidence and to make a definitive postmortem report on all of Iraq's weapons programs. Charles A. Duelfer, the American (and former deputy chief of UNSCOM) named to succeed Kay in January of 2004, called an end to the search in December, after concluding in an exhaustive report first published in October 2004 (excerpted in these pages) that Iraq had ended its nuclear, chemical, and biological weapons programs long before the American invasion. Duelfer found no actual weapons, though he did find evidence that Saddam had tried to preserve expertise and equipment that could be used to resume weapons production if sanctions against Iraq were lifted and inspections ceased. Saddam had blustered and behaved belligerently and defiantly because he was Saddam, Duelfer concluded. Saddam ran his police state on fear, and he himself feared dangerous adversaries, Iran and Israel, in a part of the world where the weapons his enemies thought he had were almost as good as any weapons he actually had. Like other dictators before him, Saddam was his own worst enemy.

.    .    .

Why the United States went to war on a false premise will long be debated. Was the Bush administration simply wrong, misled by intelligence that was also wrong, or did the government deliberately "cook" the intelligence to mislead, and to justify a war it was determined to wage for other reasons? Bitter partisan arguments rage, here and in Iraq, about these questions, about whether the United States was really determined to seize control of the Iraqi oilfields or whether George W. Bush was following some Oedipal urge to finish the job his father had left undone at the end of Operation Desert Storm, the Gulf War, in 1991. This book is not an attempt to resolve these questions, whose answers may have to wait until future historians have access to all the internal administration debates.

The administration had broader aims for the war from the beginning, and said that a principal goal was to liberate and bring democracy to Iraq, and to tip the strategic balance in the whole Middle East toward freedom.

But that was not the main justification the president gave for waging the war—that Iraq's weapons of mass destruction were an unacceptable danger to the United States and to the world at a time of global terrorism. To understand how the United States could be so wrong about Saddam's weapons programs and go to war on a false premise is the object here. This book collects basic documents that chart, step by step, what the United Nations inspectors knew and what they did not know about Iraq's weapons of mass destruction capabilities, what the U.S., President Bush and Secretary of State Colin L. Powell thought they would find in Iraq in 2003, and what Duelfer actually found there after the war—nothing.

The story of the failure of American intelligence in Iraq is fully summarized in the report of an investigative body named by the president himself: the Commission on the Intelligence Capabilities of the United States Regarding Weapons of Mass Destruction. This, the "WMD commission," headed by a Republican former federal appeals court judge, Laurence H. Silberman, and a Democratic former governor and senator from Virginia, Charles S. Robb, told the president in its report March 31 that the intelligence he had received on Iraq had been "dead wrong." The findings of that report are published here. The commission's charge was to recommend ways of avoiding similar debacles in other places in the future. "We were not authorized to investigate how policymakers used the intelligence assessments they received from the Intelligence Community," the commission reported. "Accordingly, while we interviewed a host of current and former policymakers during the course of our investigation, the purpose of those interviews was to learn about how the Intelligence Community reached and communicated its judgments about Iraq's weapons programs—not to review how policymakers subsequently used that information."

The commission recommended dozens of organizational changes: more reliable human sources of information about weapons programs in hostile countries and terrorist networks, better outside supervision and control of coordination among the 15 intelligence agencies, a new, streamlined national counter proliferation center to manage intelligence collection and analysis of weapons of mass destruction across the spectrum, and more authority for the new director of national intelligence, John D. Negroponte, whose new position Congress created in a sweeping reorganization at the end of 2004 after the extent of the intelligence disaster in Iraq had become clear.

The fears that underlay the false premise of the war in Iraq were very real and had long been widely shared. The United Nations Security Council had set up a special commission, UNSCOM, in 1991, after Operation Desert Storm which drove Saddam's forces out of Kuwait. UNSCOM was to supervise the dismantling of weapons that no one doubted Iraq had, or was trying to develop, then: nuclear, chemical, and biological weapons of mass destruction and missiles with a range of 150 kilometers or more that could deliver such weapons. It was also given the mandate of making sure that Iraq could not reconstitute such weapons in the future, and until UNSCOM could certify that there were no more such weapons and no ways of making any, the economic sanctions imposed against Iraq because of its invasion of Kuwait would remain in effect.

And Saddam had actually used weapons of mass destruction—not only in the war against Iran that began when Iraq invaded in 1980, but against his own people. Iraq used mustard gas and Tabun, a chemical nerve agent, against Iranian human wave attacks in 1983 and 1984 and used chemical weapons to put down a Kurdish revolt in the city of Halabja in 1988. In all, Iraq later declared to the U.N., it had used 19,500 chemical-weapons bombs, more than 54,000 chemical artillery shells and 27,000 short-range chemical rockets during the war with Iran, and gone through 1,800 tons of mustard gas, 140 tons of Tabun, and more than 600 tons of Sarin, all deadly weapons prohibited by international conventions.

Saddam publicly boasted of the chemical weapons in Iraq's arsenal in 1990, deployed them to his troops in the field before Operation Desert Storm, and may have credited to their existence the American decision not to press the offensive to Baghdad then. When Shiite uprisings threatened him in the wake of Iraq's defeat, in March of 1991, he used tear gas as well as nerve agents (which apparently malfunctioned) in Najaf and Karbala.

American aircraft had bombed the sites where the United States believed Iraqi scientists were working on biological and nuclear as well as chemical weapons before and during the war. When the U.N. inspections began in the spring of 1991, Saddam tried to hide the weapons his scientists had developed and the facilities for making them.

But the international inspectors—armed in many cases with intelligence information provided by the United States—were more thorough than he had expected. Dr. Kay tried to take an International Atomic Energy Agency inspection team into nuclear sites at Abu Ghuraib and Falluja at the end of June 1991, but was blocked by Iraqi troops who fired warning shots over the inspectors' heads. The team brought back videos and photographs indicating that Iraq was hiding undeclared uranium enrichment equipment, and the international inspections were toughened even more.

When they found incontrovertible evidence of the regime's illegal activities, UNSCOM inspectors destroyed them, but they were met with defiance and obstruction at every turn. Iraq denied ever having worked on the prohibited nerve agent VX, a chemical so deadly that a tiny drop of it on the skin can kill, but UNSCOM discovered documents indicating that Iraq had been making VX, and forced the regime to admit that it had manufactured 200 liters of it. Later, in 1995, UNSCOM forced Iraq to own up to having made 3,900 liters, four tons' worth.

Biological weapons inspections were the same story. Iraq denied it had any in 1991, but at the same time, it was secretly destroying its stocks and trying to preserve dual-capability research facilities. Only in 1995, confronted by U.N. inspectors' discovery of large quantities of bacteriological growth media that had no practical civilian use, did Iraq finally admit to having used it to develop botulinum toxin and anthrax spores for military purposes—

8,500 liters of anthrax. The inspectors calculated that it could have produced much more; confronted with this information, Iraq said it had destroyed all it had in the summer of 1991, but could produce no documentation for the claim.

After Saddam's son-in-law Lieutenant General Hussein Kamil, in charge of the weapons programs, defected to Jordan in August 1995 and revealed secrets UNSCOM had not yet uncovered, Iraqi officials tried to pin responsibility for the chemical program—and for the denial of its existence—on him. (He was later lured back to Baghdad and executed.) A trove of documents about the nuclear program that had been hidden on his property also fell into UNSCOM's hands and forced Saddam to disclose more details. After determining that a biochemical complex at Al Hakam, southwest of Baghdad, was actually part of the weapons development program, U.N. inspectors demolished dozens of buildings at the complex in 1996.

Saddam had also been developing the means to put his weapons into warheads that could be delivered by artillery, specially-adapted aircraft, and long-range missiles, programs the U.N. inspectors also systematically probed despite Iraqi denials, protests, obstructionism and obfuscation.

The United Nations inspections went on, at first under Rolf Ekeus, a Swedish civil servant, and later under Richard Butler, an Australian diplomat, both working closely with the IAEA, led by Mohamed ElBaradei of Egypt. Though they had initially expected their work to take months, they were unable to certify Iraqi compliance even after years of inspections. Between the inspections and coalition bombs in Operation Desert Storm, hundreds of tons of weaponry and manufacturing equipment had been destroyed in hundreds of sites all around the country, but, as Butler wrote in a book published in 2001, Iraq was also thwarting UNSCOM's work by destroying some weapons and equipment itself.

Iraq could have destroyed the weapons under U.N. supervision to demonstrate compliance, but instead of that, it hid much of what it was doing. "The unilateral destruction of materials by Iraq was a second major problem," Butler wrote in 2000. "The Security Council resolutions specify that all destruction of illegal weapons must be conducted under international supervision. Iraq ignored this requirement. Beginning in 1991, Iraq destroyed significant quantities of prohibited weapons in total secrecy. Missiles were cut up, chemical weapons and warheads were exploded, and the shattered fragments were buried in pits in the desert."*

Saddam, as Duelfer concluded after the war from interviews with captured officials, was balancing two conflicting aims in his mind: the need to get rid of international economic sanctions, which could only be done if he got rid of the prohibited weapons, and the need to keep Iran and, to a lesser extent, Israel off balance by allowing them to think he still had them. Perhaps he thought the United States would never make good on threats to intervene with military force to make him disarm.

To the inspectors on the ground, Iraq seemed to become steadily less cooperative, declaring some facilities "presidential sites" in 1997 and barring the inspectors from them; then barring all American inspectors on the UNSCOM team (among them at the time was Duelfer) and, finally, at the end of 1998, saying he would have nothing more to do with UNSCOM on the grounds that it was a creature of the CIA and the Pentagon.

Unable to do their work, UNSCOM and the IAEA pulled out of Iraq at the end of 1998, and soon after the United States and Britain conducted four days of intense bombing raids in an operation dubbed Desert Fox. The raids, aimed at 100 industrial and military factories thought to be involved in Iraq's weapons programs, did extensive damage. But there were no more inspections on the ground in Iraq until 2002.

.    .    .

So from 1998 to 2002, both the United Nations and the United States had no effective way of assessing what Saddam was doing except electronic intercepts of communications, intelligence satellites, and reports from defectors. U.S. intelligence was mostly blind, with few human agents on the ground inside Iraq, and even those few it misused, the Senate committee found in 2004: "None of the guidance given to human intelligence collec-

*Richard Butler, *The Greatest Threat: Iraq, Weapons of Mass Destruction, and the Growing Crisis of Global Security.* New York: PublicAffairs, 2000, pp. 51–52.

tors suggested that collection be focused on determining *whether* Iraq had WMD. Instead, the requirements assumed that Iraq had WMD, and focused on uncovering those activities and collecting against the extent of Iraq's WMD production and the locations of hidden stocks of weapons," the Senate report said.

United States intelligence, to borrow a phrase from Secretary of Defense Donald H. Rumsfeld, did not distinguish between what it knew and what it only thought it knew about Iraq. Because Saddam undeniably had WMD capabilities before the 1991 war, and because he had lied and tried to mislead inspectors after the war, he must be trying to rebuild the WMD capabilities the inspectors had destroyed now that they were gone, American intelligence analysts assumed. Defectors with political agendas of their own eagerly confirmed this assumption.

From 1998 to 2002, American intelligence analysts had no way of testing this assumption, and apparently persuaded themselves that they did not need to test it. Yet it was wrong.

President Bush was not the only policymaker who followed the reasoning that led to it. President Bill Clinton explained his bombing order in 1998 with a warning about Saddam: "Mark my words, he will develop weapons of mass destruction. He will deploy them, and he will use them. Because we're acting today, it is less likely that we will face these dangers in the future."

Unlike his successor, Clinton did not conclude that sending in American troops to overthrow Saddam was the solution, though his secretary of state, Madeleine K. Albright, had said in a speech at Georgetown University earlier that year that the United States would quickly develop normal relations with a successor to Saddam if "a coherent and united Iraqi opposition" could put one in power.

But Saddam crushed all opposition, as he had done after the Gulf War. As to what he was doing with his weapons programs, and what his relationships might be with Al Qaeda and other international terrorist groups, recognized as a grave and global threat after suicide bombings that destroyed the American embassies in Tanzania and Kenya in August 1998, the Clinton administration remained largely in the dark. It focused mostly on Afghanistan, where the Taliban regime allowed Osama bin Laden to set up training camps.

In Iraq, the United States would not let the United Nations lift international sanctions until the WMD question was resolved. Iraq's protests that innocent women and children were starving as a result produced the United Nations oil for food program, which enriched Saddam and his cronies while only slightly alleviating civilian suffering, and brought about more diplomatic maneuvering, notably by Russia, to set up a new inspection program that might prove more acceptable to Saddam.

The result, at the end of 1999, was the creation of the United Nations Monitoring, Verification, and Inspection Commission (UNMOVIC), established under bureaucratic rules that gave it less autonomy from the U.N. bureaucracy than UNSCOM had. It was given the same seemingly impossible task of getting Iraq to disclose all of its weapons and arms development programs and to allow the inspectors to render them harmless.

After Russia and France vetoed Secretary-General Kofi Annan's initial choice of Rolf Ekeus as executive chairman, Annan named another Swedish diplomat, Dr. Hans Blix, former head of the IAEA. Iraq nonetheless vowed to have nothing to do with UNMOVIC.

So, into the new millennium, the stalemate continued, with Saddam acting belligerently and refusing all cooperation with international arms inspections—giving skeptics like Richard Butler and intelligence analysts in Washington every reason to believe that because he could, Saddam must be doing everything possible to rebuild his arsenal of weapons of mass destruction. "He clearly continues to have the motive and means to threaten great danger, and now the opportunity for renewed weapons development, given the extended absence of international arms control in Iraq," Butler wrote at the time.

Wrangling with sanctions and allies at the United Nations was a complicated and frustrating business. Iraqi propaganda about the effect of sanctions on innocent civilians chipped steadily away at the resolve the Clinton administration had urged on Russia and its European and Arab allies. Hans Blix slowly assembled his team of weapons inspectors, but Saddam kept refusing to have anything to do with them. As the 2000 presidential election campaign heated up, Governor Bush's team began accusing Vice President

Al Gore and the Clinton administration of paralysis while Iraq openly restarted ballistic-missile tests.

Former Secretary of Defense Dick Cheney, campaigning in Albuquerque that September, said, "For a period of time there, in the aftermath of the Gulf War, we had a very robust inspection regime under way. We had people in there all the time, checking out, making certain that he wasn't going back trying to rebuild his biological and chemical capabilities. Now we've seen a situation develop in which he's kicked out all the inspectors and this administration appears to be helpless to do anything about it."

Influential Republicans like Senator John McCain had long been urging the Clinton administration to take stronger action. "Air attacks will do limited damage," Senator McCain had said before Clinton ordered the bombing in 1998. "But following that, there has to be this effort to destabilize and overthrow [Saddam]. Otherwise we'll end up in the same situation a year or two years or three years from now." Another Bush supporter, Paul D. Wolfowitz, told Eric Schmitt of *The New York Times* then, "Getting rid of Saddam is not a fairy tale. It's doable."

Until September 11, 2001, Cheney, Wolfowitz, and others in the Bush administration seemed convinced that Iraq, not Al Qaeda, was the deadliest terrorist threat to the United States, according to former White House terrorism adviser Richard A. Clarke, who tried unsuccessfully to focus the new president's aides' attention on Osama bin Laden before the September 11 attacks.

They assumed the worst about Saddam even more after September 11 than before. If there was a possibility that Saddam could be rebuilding his weapons of mass destruction, in their view, then he must be rebuilding . To assume that Saddam might actually have destroyed his own capability in hopes of lifting the international sanctions would have seemed wildly irresponsible to them even before September 11. After that, for the Bush administration, such an assumption was out of the question. Iraq became a problem that could wait no longer. The president and those who had his ear were persuaded not only that Iraq had far deadlier weapons than the fully-fueled airplanes that Al Qaeda had used to destroy the World Trade Center and wreck the Pentagon, but was linked to Al Qaeda and could provide the weapons to terrorists to use in future attacks against the United States.

Bush administration officials began talking openly about eliminating the threat from Iraq soon after American forces went into Afghanistan to eliminate Al Qaeda sanctuaries there and to depose bin Laden's Taliban protectors. President Bush described Iraq, North Korea, and Iran an "axis of evil" in his 2002 State of the Union address. "With respect to Iraq, it has long been, for several years now, a policy of the United States government that regime change would be in the best interests of the region, the best interests of the Iraqi people. And we are looking at a variety of options that would bring that about," Colin Powell said in Senate testimony on February 12, 2002.

Though administration officials said then that the final decision to invade had not been made and the military plans had not yet been worked out, the United States and Britain, which saw the Iraqi threat the same way, were already laying down a strategy of working through the United Nations to issue an ultimatum that would force Iraq to let the weapons inspectors come back in. Inevitably, Washington seemed to assume, there would be another impasse with Saddam, but it would be the last one.

As Michael R. Gordon and David E. Sanger wrote in *The New York Times* of February 13, 2002: "Several senior administration officials have begun to talk privately about a two-track approach to deposing Mr. Hussein that would balance military and diplomatic planning. The first steps, which could take five months or more, involve working through the United Nations to develop tighter but more focused sanctions against Iraq and demand that it allow nuclear inspectors unfettered access to the country. But senior administration officials say they fully expect that such an effort would fail, which would lay the base for a military campaign, one in which the United States would both encourage internal rebellions against the Iraqi leader's rule and use American military power."

"Senior officials said a consensus was emerging that it is important to take on the Iraqi leader, with the help of allies if possible, and without them if necessary," Gordon and Sanger wrote. The actions of the administration over the next year followed this script to the letter, and its assertions became steadily more insistent.

Donald Rumsfeld organized his own Pentagon special intelligence group of analysts who looked for evidence overlooked by other agencies of ties between Saddam and the terrorists. There was no doubt in his mind that Iraq was building up its arsenal. "If you want to know a world-class liar, it's Saddam Hussein," Rumsfeld told American sailors and marines in Bahrain on June 10, 2002. "They have them, and they continue to develop them, and they have weaponized chemical weapons," he said in Kuwait the same day. "They've had an active program to develop nuclear weapons. It's also clear that they are actively developing biological weapons."

By September, the Pentagon was assembling the forces it would need in the Gulf region to move into Iraq and eliminate the threat it saw.

The Bush administration never laid out convincing evidence of links between Saddam Hussein and Al Qaeda, but kept insisting that they existed. Secretary Powell, in a speech to the United Nations in early 2003, emphasized the presence in Iraq of Abu Musaab al-Zarqawi, the terrorist who later took over the leadership of the insurrection that has killed thousands of Iraqi civilians and hundreds of American soldiers there. But, though Powell said Zarqawi had established a training camp under Saddam, the camp was located in a Kurdish area of northern Iraq that had not been under Saddam's control since the Gulf War in 1991, and the administration never showed that Zarqawi had ever met or coordinated any of his activities with Saddam.

The bipartisan National Commission on Terrorist Attacks Upon the United States found, in a staff report issued in June 2004, no evidence of a "collaborative relationship" between Saddam's regime and Al Qaeda. Vice President Dick Cheney insisted even then that this did not mean there were no links between them.

But in any case, Saddam Hussein could not have provided terrorists with weapons of mass destruction after the mid–1990s, because he did not have any then. It was the American military overthrow of Saddam that made Iraq into the terrorist threat the administration said it had invaded to prevent. Porter J. Goss, the CIA director, said as much in February 2005 when he told Congress that Islamic extremists were using the anti-American insurgency in Iraq as a recruiting ground for global terrorist activities.

The president conjured up the specter of an even more devastating terrorist threat from Saddam's Iraq in a speech to the General Assembly on September 12, 2002, a speech that set the stage for the confrontations with both Iraq and the United Nations itself that followed. "Iraq has made several attempts to buy high-strength aluminum tubes used to enrich uranium for a nuclear weapon," he said; in October, the president got the congressional authorization he had asked for to use military force to confront the threat. Based on the intelligence he and his advisers chose to use, it did appear necessary. But the intelligence about almost everything, including the aluminum tubes, had been wrong.

.    .    .

U.S. intelligence agencies had agreed in October 2002 on a secret document that summarized what they thought they knew about Iraq—a national intelligence estimate, or NIE, whose summarized unclassified major findings are included in this volume.

The facts American troops and weapons inspectors found in Iraq after the invasion so completely contradicted the assertions made in the NIE (many of them repeated over the following year in speeches and testimony by the president, the secretary of state, and their advisers) that it became a central focus in the reappraisal of American intelligence capabilities that followed the September 11 disasters.

As the Senate Select Committee on Intelligence report of July 2004 makes clear, nearly every finding in the NIE had been wrong. "The major key judgments in the NIE, particularly that Iraq 'is reconstituting its nuclear program,' 'has chemical and biological weapons,' was developing an unmanned aerial vehicle (UAV) 'probably intended to deliver biological warfare agents,' and that 'all key aspects—research & development (R&D), production, and weaponization—of Iraq's offensive biological weapons (BW) program are active and that most elements are larger and more advanced than they were before the Gulf War,' either overstated, or were not supported by, the underlying intelligence," the committee found.

The reason was not simply bad luck in what is recognized to be a difficult and risky business—intelligence has to try to uncover secrets adversaries do their best to conceal. The intelligence failures in Iraq stemmed, the committee found, from something more fundamentally wrong, a lack of rigorous questioning of the inherited conventional wisdom on Iraq, assumptions, taken as facts, that went beyond the facts. Since the intelligence community was telling the administration what it wanted to hear, there was apparently no pressure from the White House to question the intelligence findings, or to "cook" the intelligence—the CIA and other agencies had done that by themselves.

Even the title—"National Intelligence Estimate on Iraq's Continuing Programs for Weapons of Mass Destruction"—was in error, since it would turn out that the only continuing program Iraq had was to develop long-range missiles the United Nations had forbidden it to have since the Gulf War. "Baghdad has chemical and biological weapons as well as missiles with ranges in excess of UN restrictions; if left unchecked, it probably will have a nuclear weapon during this decade," the estimate stated. "Most agencies believe that Saddam's personal interest in and Iraq's aggressive attempts to obtain high-strength aluminum tubes for centrifuge rotors—as well as Iraq's attempts to acquire magnets, high-speed balancing machines, and machine tools—provide compelling evidence that Saddam is reconstituting a uranium enrichment effort for Baghdad's nuclear weapons program."

Though the NIE did not suppress the dissenting views—"most agencies" did not include the Department of Energy or the State Department's Bureau of Intelligence and Research—the president and his advisers chose to ignore those agencies' warnings that Iraq did not want the aluminum tubes for use in uranium enrichment at all, but for rocket motors.

The State Department bureau also described as "highly dubious" a claim given credence in the NIE, and later cited by the president in his State of the Union address, that Iraq was trying to get uranium from Africa to use in nuclear weapons. The uranium acquisition assertion turned out to come from a fraudulent document (CIA Director George Tenet later apologized for letting this information get into the president's speech), and the INR view on the aluminum tubes proved correct.

Mohamed ElBaradei of the IAEA publicly reported both these errors to the United Nations ten days before the president took the United States to war, but in the ultimatums he gave as he moved closer to the showdown with Saddam, President Bush brushed that aside. And, even though the NIE consensus had been that American intelligence had only "low confidence" in their judgment that Saddam in desperate circumstances might make biological or chemical weapons available to terrorists, the president continued to emphasize this threat and made it a main point of his "declaration of war" on March 19, 2003.

Itself misled (and accused of misleading readers) in some of its own prewar reporting on Iraq's presumed weapons buildup, *The New York Times* described in a long article called "The Nuclear Card" in October 2004 how National Security Adviser Condoleezza Rice and other advisers to the president had rejected dissenting warnings from within the government bureaucracy about the nuclear intelligence. Powell, whom Rice succeeded as secretary of state in President Bush's second term, publicly criticized intelligence that had led him to make a vivid description in his United Nations speech of "mobile biological weapons laboratories" in Iraq which turned out to be hydrogen generators for balloons. "I looked at the four elements that they gave me for that one, and they stood behind them," he said in April 2004. "Now it appears not to be the case that it was that solid." Later newspapers reported that some of the information in Powell's speech had come from a defector code-named Curve Ball whose dubious reliability at least one intelligence official had tried to warn his superiors about; another claim in the speech, that Saddam had offered to train Al Qaeda operatives to use chemical and biological weapons, reportedly came from a false confession tortured out of a captured associate of bin Laden.

·    ·    ·

As Charles Duelfer found later in his report describing postwar interviews with captured Iraqi officials and other evidence, the real WMD threat from Saddam in early 2003 was intention, not capability—his hope of one day reconstituting the weapons he had destroyed and the programs he had dismantled when the United Nations lifted all sanctions and withdrew its inspectors.

Under Hans Blix, the inspectors were operating under very different assumptions than the United States was making. "UN-MOVIC, for its part, is not presuming that there are proscribed items and activities in Iraq, but nor is it . . . presuming the opposite, that no such items and activities exist in Iraq," Dr. Blix told the United Nations on January 28, 2003. "Presumptions do not solve the problem. Evidence and full transparency may help."

Four months earlier, challenging the General Assembly to enforce its many resolutions on Iraq, President Bush had used completely different logic: "We know that Saddam Hussein pursued weapons of mass murder even when inspectors were in his country," he said. "Are we to assume that he stopped when they left? The history, the logic, and the facts lead to one conclusion: Saddam Hussein's regime is a grave and gathering danger. To suggest otherwise is to hope against the evidence."

Almost at the last moment before the bombs started to fall, Saddam's regime finally started being cooperative, Dr. Blix reported on March 7, 2003. "Even with a proactive Iraqi attitude, induced by continued outside pressure, it would still take some time to verify sites and items, analyze documents, interview relevant persons, and draw conclusions. It would not take years, nor weeks, but months," he told the United Nations. But the United States had no more patience for inspections; with war imminent, the United Nations pulled out of Iraq on March 18, after having inspected 411 sites and found no new hidden weapons or production plants.

Even after American troops went in and could find no weapons, Rumsfeld and others said they were confident that they were hidden somewhere and would eventually turn up. But even if they didn't, the president himself appeared to be unfazed. "So what's the difference?" he asked when Diane Sawyer pressed him in an interview on ABC News in December 2003; Saddam's evil intentions were threat enough.

·    ·    ·

"We were almost all wrong," David Kay confessed to Congress in January 2004, as he turned over the Iraq inspections job to Charles Duelfer to complete. Seven months later, the Senate Select Committee threw salt in the CIA's wounds by scoring the agency's numerous intelligence failures, after it had already been thoroughly thrashed by the September 11 Commission. Congress then approved the wholesale reorganization that subordinated the CIA to a new director of national intelligence, and President Bush named John D. Negroponte to the job in February 2005.

Just how extensive the failures had been in Iraq was left to Duelfer to detail in his monumental report. "Iraq did not possess a nuclear device, nor had it tried to reconstitute a capability to produce nuclear weapons after 1991," the Iraq Security Group he led found. "While a small number of old, abandoned chemical munitions have been discovered, ISG judges that Iraq unilaterally destroyed its undeclared chemical weapons stockpile in 1991," it said; "ISG found no direct evidence that Iraq, after 1996, had plans for a new [biological weapons] program or was conducting BW-specific work for military purposes." It reached these conclusions even though it also found that many weapons sites or suspected dual-use facilities, left unguarded by the occupiers, had been looted of explosives and equipment—90 of the places the United Nations had inspected, in fact, were "stripped or razed," UNMOVIC reported in early 2005.

Duelfer's team found "an extensive, yet fragmentary and circumstantial body of evidence suggesting that Saddam pursued a strategy to maintain a capability to return to WMD production after sanctions were lifted by preserving assets and expertise." A state drug plant in Samarra, the ISG found, could have been converted within weeks in 2003 to produce biological warfare weapons using anthrax spores. Other facilities could have produced mustard gas within the same time period, but not nerve gas.

So Saddam schemed and plotted to have weapons and retained a limited "break-out" capability of duplicating one day some of those he had been forced to destroy. But after 1996, he had none.

Readers will no doubt draw their own conclusions about the lessons to be learned from a war the United States said it needed to fight, for a reason that turned out to be specious. As debate intensifies in the United States, the United Nations, and the world about what to do about weapons of mass destruction that both Iran and North Korea make no bones about wanting to develop and, unlike Saddam Hussein in early 2003, may actually have, the quality of intelligence is crucial.

The documents included here show that a rigorous system of weapons inspections, led by competent inspectors and backed by the credible threat of international sanctions, was far more effective in Iraq than skeptics in Washington believed it was. American insistence on making the system tough had led to the establishment of UNMOVIC, yet key American policymakers apparently did not have enough confidence in Hans Blix as its leader, or in the United Nations as an institution, to believe its assurances that getting to the bottom of Iraq's weapons programs was only a matter of time. But Blix and the United Nations were right and Washington was wrong.

For all the "freedom fries," for all the rivers of Beaujolais that ran down gutters all over the United States after France and Germany opposed the American and British decision to go to war in 2003, it is now clear that it was entirely reasonable, even if irritating, for Dominique de Villepin, the French foreign minister, to ask at the United Nations then, "Why should we today engage in a war with Iraq? Why should we wish to proceed at any price by force when we can succeed peacefully?"

Success without war in ensuring that Iraq had no weapons of mass destruction, and in keeping things that way, might have taken years and would have required indefinite continuation of rigorous inspections. That would have left Saddam in power with the risk of violence, cruelty, and aggressive behavior that reasonable minds might well find, as the president did, less acceptable than the American and Iraqi deaths and terrorist violence that were the price of bringing democracy to Iraq. But it is now clear that the war cannot be justified as having been necessary to eliminate Saddam's weapons of mass destruction.

Some may draw a different lesson from the documents in this book, not about the past but about the future. Some may conclude that the cooperation and advice of allies unafraid to tell the United States when they think it is wrong, along with a properly safeguarded inspection mechanism backed by the United Nations, can help Washington, not hinder it, in dealing with the threat of weapons of mass destruction in the hands of countries like Iran and North Korea.

Once again, in mid–2005, U.S. intelligence believes, but apparently has little evidence for the belief, that there is a real WMD threat, this time from Iran and North Korea. Once again, the United States is skeptically playing along with its European allies' efforts to deal with it peacefully, this time by trying to get Iran to be cooperative, while efforts the United States and its Asian allies are making to try to rein in North Korea appear ineffectual. Once again, the United States does not have full confidence in the head of the lead international agency on nuclear arms, the IAEA, and is lobbying for the replacement of Mohamed ElBaradei. And once again, there are press reports of U.S. military preparations if force is needed to deal with the problem.

The ability of the United States to lead its allies and the United Nations depends not only on its unquestioned military power but on its trustworthiness. U.S. intelligence on Iran and North Korea is one of the subjects of the report of the bipartisan presidential WMD commission. It may well be the most important part of the report, but its findings on those countries remain classified, except for this one clue: "We found," the WMD commission reported in discussing American intelligence on unconventional weapons programs in Iran, North Korea, China, and Russia, "that we have only limited access to critical information about several of these high-priority intelligence targets."

The ability of the United States to lead its allies and the United Nations depends not only on its unquestioned military power but on its trustworthiness. U.S. intelligence on Iran and North Korea is one of the subjects of the report of the bipartisan Presidential Commission on the Intelligence Capabilities of the United States Regarding Weapons of Mass Destruction. It may well be the most important.

# PART I

The Bush administration began setting out reasons for removing Saddam Hussein's regime with military force in speeches in the late summer and early fall of 2002.

The intelligence findings that underlay the administration's rationale were not publicly announced, but they were summarized in a National Intelligence Estimate that was presented to high administration officials and to Congress on October 1, 2002. Called "Iraq's Continuing Programs for Weapons of Mass Destruction," the 93-page document, a synthesis of the views of six intelligence agencies, is mostly still secret today. The government released the excerpts reproduced here in July 2003, after it had become clear that American troops in Iraq were not going to find the weapons that the estimate, and the presidential speeches built on its assumptions, had said Saddam was amassing.

There is one notable difference between the two Bush speeches given in this volume and the publicly known parts of the intelligence estimate. While the estimate was mostly wrong, it did allow for some of the uncertainty that is inherent in all intelligence—it was, in fact, an "estimate" that turned out to be wrong, as detailed in the postmortem reports by the Senate Select Committee on Intelligence and by the director of central intelligence's Iraq Survey Group also published in this volume. The presidential speeches, designed to convince a skeptical world audience and a less skeptical audience at home, express little uncertainty at all about the extent and the nature of the threat. In the president's mind, that was clearly linked to terrorism after September 11, and waiting for proof to be nailed down, as he said in Cincinnati on October 7, 2002, could mean waiting for a mushroom cloud.

The NIE and the president's speeches were both wrong in a

more fundamental and disturbing sense as well. The conclusions the intelligence paper reached and that the president relied on were not supported by the underlying intelligence reports they were based on, as the Senate committee reported in the summer of 2004.

The NIE was produced in some haste in mid- to late September 2002 as the administration was asking Congress to give the president authority to go to war in Iraq if he thought it necessary. Members of the Senate Select Committee on Intelligence "expressed concerns that they would be expected to vote on an Iraq Resolution shortly and had no NIE on which to base their vote," the committee reported in 2004 (the heavily-censored conclusions of its report are also published in this book).

The estimate came not at the beginning but closer to the end of a secret debate among government agencies about what to make of the contradictory fragments of knowledge they had about what Iraq was doing. What is known now about two of the most embarrassing errors in the estimate—the aluminum tubes it said Saddam wanted to use in high-speed centrifuges to enrich uranium to weapons grade, and supplies of uranium it said he was trying to acquire in Africa—shows how politics worked inside and outside the world of intelligence to produce flawed results.

Saddam's regime did in fact shop for 60,000 precision-engineered, high-strength aluminum tubes from Hong Kong in early 2001, a move that set off alarm bells in the British and American agencies that learned about it at the time.

According to the Senate committee report and a *New York Times* article published in October 2004 that was drawn from it, an analyst in the CIA's center for Weapons Intelligence, Nonproliferation and Arms Control who had been involved in work on centrifuges at the government nuclear laboratories in Oak Ridge, Tennessee, in the late 1970s and early 1980s concluded that the tubes had "little use other than for a uranium enrichment program." The CIA reported as much to top administration officials on April 10, 2001.

But the very next day, other experts at the Department of Energy, which runs the government weapons complex and actually builds nuclear centrifuges, contested this assessment and said that the tubes Saddam was shopping for were the wrong size and shape for a uranium centrifuge. On May 9, 2001, according to *The New York Times*, the department's "Daily Intelligence Highlight" stated that Iraq wanted the tubes to use in rocket engines, for which it had manufactured aluminum tubes of precisely the same dimensions in the 1990s. Energy Department experts spelled out their findings in more detail in an additional secret Technical Intelligence Note on August 17, 2001, and the State Department's intelligence arm, the Bureau of Intelligence and Research, sided with them later.

After September 11, President Bush, Vice President Dick Cheney, and their advisers began taking renewed interest in intelligence reports about Saddam's weapons capabilities. But they got their briefings from the CIA, whose analyses kept citing the aluminum tubes as evidence that Saddam was again trying to develop nuclear weapons. According to government officials cited by the *Times*, and according to the Senate intelligence committee report, the Energy Department dissent got short shrift from the CIA.

"He is actively pursuing nuclear weapons at this time," Cheney said in March 2002, and at the end of August, in an address to the Veterans of Foreign Wars in Nashville, he went farther: "We now know Saddam has resumed his efforts to acquire nuclear weapons."

A week later, on September 8, 2002, another *New York Times* article made the first public mention of the administration's concern (though no mention of the internal debate) about the aluminum tubes: "In the last 14 months, Iraq has sought to buy thousands of specially designed aluminum tubes, which American officials believe were intended as components of centrifuges to enrich uranium. American officials said several efforts to arrange the shipment of the aluminum tubes were blocked or intercepted but declined to say, citing the sensitivity of the intelligence, where they came from or how they were stopped.

"The diameter, thickness and other technical specifications of the aluminum tubes had persuaded American intelligence experts that they were meant for Iraq's nuclear program, officials said, and that the latest attempt to ship the material had taken place in recent months."

Vice President Cheney, on "Meet The Press" that day, confirmed that the tubes "raised our level of concern," and said he knew "for sure" and "in fact" and "with absolute certainty" that Saddam was buying equipment to built a nuclear bomb, the *Times* reported. Condoleezza Rice, then the president's national security adviser, also told CNN that the tubes were "only really suited for nuclear weapons programs."

On September 12, President Bush challenged the United Nations to enforce its ban on Saddam's weapons of mass destruction: "Iraq has made several attempts to buy high-strength aluminum tubes used to enrich uranium for a nuclear weapon," he said. "Should Iraq acquire fissile material, it would be able to build a nuclear weapon within a year. And Iraq's state-controlled media has reported numerous meetings between Saddam Hussein and his nuclear scientists, leaving little doubt about his continued appetite for these weapons."

Thus did the public learn about the aluminum tubes in September of 2002, just before the secret National Intelligence Estimate summarized the state of knowledge, and the debate about them, in these words: "Most agencies believe that Saddam's personal interest in and Iraq's aggressive attempts to obtain high-strength aluminum tubes for centrifuge rotors—as well as Iraq's attempts to acquire magnets, high-speed balancing machines, and machine tools—provide compelling evidence that Saddam is reconstituting a uranium enrichment effort for Baghdad's nuclear weapons program," the NIE said.

The document highlighted (or quarantined) separately, in boxes typographically set apart from the main body of the report, the dissenting views from the State Department's Bureau of Intelligence and Research and from the Department of Energy: "In INR's view Iraq's efforts to acquire aluminum tubes is central to the argument that Baghdad is reconstituting its nuclear weapons program, but INR is not persuaded that the tubes in question are intended for use as centrifuge rotors. INR accepts the judgment of technical experts at the U.S. Department of Energy (DOE) who have concluded that the tubes Iraq seeks to acquire are poorly suited for use in gas centrifuges to be used for uranium enrichment and finds unpersuasive the arguments advanced by others to make the case that they are intended for that purpose. INR considers it far more likely that the tubes are intended for another purpose, most likely the production of artillery rockets."

For the State Department's intelligence arm, there was no convincing evidence that Saddam was trying to build nuclear weapons, and the NIE said so. Cheney's spokesman later told the *Times* that the vice president learned about disagreement within the intelligence community only when the NIE was distributed. That was a year and a half after the debate had begun—and at least a year after Cheney and intelligence officials in the Defense Department had been relentlessly pushing every government agency for everything it knew about Iraq, its weapons programs, and its support of terrorism.

As the estimate said, although the Department of Energy did not believe that the tubes were evidence of a reconstituted Iraqi nuclear weapons program, it concurred in the general view that there was one. Part of the evidence it relied on was the second most publicly contested part of the NIE—reports, mainly from British intelligence, that Saddam had been trying to acquire uranium for weapons from Africa:

- A foreign government service reported that as of early 2001, Niger planned to send several tons of "pure uranium" (probably yellowcake) to Iraq. As of early 2001, Niger and Iraq reportedly were still working out arrangements for this deal, which could be for up to 500 tons of yellowcake. We do not know the status of this arrangement.

- Reports indicate Iraq also has sought uranium ore from Somalia and possibly the Democratic Republic of the Congo.

"We cannot confirm whether Iraq succeeded in acquiring uranium ore and/or yellowcake from these sources," the NIE concluded. Separately, it reported the State Department's view of the report: "The claims of Iraqi pursuit of natural uranium in Africa are, in INR's assessment, highly dubious."

Only a day after the document was officially circulated, the Deputy Director of Central Intelligence was skittish about how solid the agency actually considered the evidence for uranium acquisition from various African countries. The British "stretched a little bit beyond where we would stretch," he testified to the Senate intelligence committee on October 2.

A week later, an Italian journalist brought documents to the U.S. Embassy in Rome that purported to buttress the reports of uranium dealings between Niger and Iraq. A State Department analyst who saw them found them suspect: "You'll note that it bears a funky Emb. of Niger stamp (to make it look official, I guess)," the analyst wrote, according to the Senate intelligence committee. The committee also reported that a Department of Energy analyst sent an e-mail reflecting strong skepticism to a State Department counterpart who was complaining about the department's views being excluded from an interagency assessment in late 2002 of Iraq's official WMD denials to the United Nations. "There are some very strong points to be made in respect to Iraq's arrogant non-compliance with the UN sanctions," this analyst noted, warning prophetically: "However, when individuals attempt to convert those 'strong statements' into the 'knock out' punch, the Administration will ultimately look foolish—i.e. the tubes and Niger!"

On October 4, 2002, the CIA published an unclassified white paper based on the NIE that left out all mention of attempts by Saddam to procure uranium in Africa. But it said that "Baghdad could produce a nuclear weapon within a year if it were able to procure weapons-grade fissile material abroad." The white paper acknowledged the existence of reservations about the aluminum tubes, but it said "All intelligence experts agree that Iraq is seeking nuclear weapons." The overall impression the white paper left was that Saddam was not just seeking nuclear weapons, hoping to be able to build them someday, but actively trying to do so.

On October 7, the president was to deliver the Cincinnati speech. His national security council staff had sent a draft to the CIA three days earlier containing the line "and the regime has been caught attempting to purchase up to 500 metric tons of uranium oxide from Africa—an essential ingredient in the enrichment process." The CIA urged that the line be deleted because of growing doubts about the claim, and because it had already told Congress that the British might have exaggerated the amount.

The president made no mention of it in his speech. But he did use another piece of intelligence that later turned out to be equally dubious, saying that "we've learned that Iraq has trained Al Qaeda members in bomb making and poisons and gases." The basis for this statement was a confession obtained from an Al Qaeda leader captured in Pakistan in December 2001. Sometime after the Cincinnati speech, the terrorist, Ibn al-Shaykh al-Libi, recanted his confession and administration officials stopped making the claim.

On October 11, the Senate voted 77–23 to give President Bush the authority he had sought to invade Iraq. The resolution said that one of the reasons Iraq posed a threat to the United States was that it was "actively seeking a nuclear weapons capability."

The U.S. experts in the Iraq Survey Group sent in after Saddam's regime was overthrown in the spring of 2003 found no evidence at all of uranium centrifuges, but they did find 13,000 rockets, all produced with the aluminum tubes Iraq had bought from abroad. Rockets were, in fact, the only weapons of mass destruction American inspectors would find in Iraq after the war.

George Tenet, the CIA director in 2003, issued a statement in August of that year noting that intelligence was "an iterative process" and repeating that "we stand by the judgments in the NIE."

The NIE, he said, had not based the finding that Iraq had resumed its nuclear weapons program on the reports that it was trying to acquire uranium. "Not surprisingly, the Iraqis went to great lengths to mask their intentions across the board, including in their efforts to acquire tubes with increasingly higher sets of specifications," Tenet wrote. "Thus, the fact that we had alternative views on the issue would be expected. But the NIE went to great lengths to spell out those views. Many reading these alternative views, however, almost certainly recalled how far Iraq had come in the early 1990s toward a nuclear weapon without our knowledge, making all the factors leading us to the reconstitution judgment more important."

And he insisted, responding to charges that officials of the Bush administration had told the agencies to give them the intelligence about Iraq that they wanted to hear, "No one outside the

Intelligence Community told us what to say or not to say in this Estimate."

In another attempt to defend the estimate, given in a speech at Georgetown University in February 2004, he pointed out, "The question being asked about Iraq in the starkest of terms is: were we 'right' or were we 'wrong.' In the intelligence business, you are almost never completely wrong or completely right."

"On missiles, we were generally on target," Tenet said.

# President George W. Bush's Speech to the United Nations General Assembly

•

# September 12, 2002

[. . . ]

Our common security is challenged by regional conflicts—ethnic and religious strife that is ancient, but not inevitable. In the Middle East, there can be no peace for either side without freedom for both sides. America stands committed to an independent and democratic Palestine, living side by side with Israel in peace and security. Like all other people, Palestinians deserve a government that serves their interests and listens to their voices. My nation will continue to encourage all parties to step up to their responsibilities as we seek a just and comprehensive settlement to the conflict.

Above all, our principles and our security are challenged today by outlaw groups and regimes that accept no law of morality and have no limit to their violent ambitions. In the attacks on America a year ago, we saw the destructive intentions of our enemies. This threat hides within many nations, including my own. In cells and camps, terrorists are plotting further destruction, and building new bases for their war against civilization. And our greatest fear is that terrorists will find a shortcut to their mad ambitions when an outlaw regime supplies them with the technologies to kill on a massive scale.

In one place—in one regime—we find all these dangers, in their most lethal and aggressive forms, exactly the kind of aggressive threat the United Nations was born to confront.

Twelve years ago, Iraq invaded Kuwait without provocation. And the regime's forces were poised to continue their march to seize other countries and their resources. Had Saddam Hussein been appeased instead of stopped, he would have endangered the peace and stability of the world. Yet this aggression was stopped—

by the might of coalition forces and the will of the United Nations.

To suspend hostilities, to spare himself, Iraq's dictator accepted a series of commitments. The terms were clear, to him and to all. And he agreed to prove he is complying with every one of those obligations.

He has proven instead only his contempt for the United Nations, and for all his pledges. By breaking every pledge—by his deceptions, and by his cruelties—Saddam Hussein has made the case against himself.

In 1991, Security Council Resolution 688 demanded that the Iraqi regime cease at once the repression of its own people, including the systematic repression of minorities—which the Council said, threatened international peace and security in the region. This demand goes ignored.

Last year, the U.N. Commission on Human Rights found that Iraq continues to commit extremely grave violations of human rights, and that the regime's repression is all pervasive. Tens of thousands of political opponents and ordinary citizens have been subjected to arbitrary arrest and imprisonment, summary execution, and torture by beating and burning, electric shock, starvation, mutilation, and rape. Wives are tortured in front of their husbands, children in the presence of their parents—and all of these horrors concealed from the world by the apparatus of a totalitarian state.

In 1991, the U.N. Security Council, through Resolutions 686 and 687, demanded that Iraq return all prisoners from Kuwait and other lands. Iraq's regime agreed. It broke its promise. Last year the Secretary General's high-level coordinator for this issue reported that Kuwait, Saudi, Indian, Syrian, Lebanese, Iranian, Egyptian, Bahraini, and Omani nationals remain unaccounted for—more than 600 people. One American pilot is among them.

In 1991, the U.N. Security Council, through Resolution 687, demanded that Iraq renounce all involvement with terrorism, and permit no terrorist organizations to operate in Iraq. Iraq's regime agreed. It broke this promise. In violation of Security Council Resolution 1373, Iraq continues to shelter and support terrorist organizations that direct violence against Iran, Israel, and Western governments. Iraqi dissidents abroad are targeted for murder. In 1993, Iraq attempted to assassinate the Emir of Kuwait and a former American President. Iraq's government openly praised the attacks of September the 11th. And al Qaeda terrorists escaped from Afghanistan and are known to be in Iraq.

In 1991, the Iraqi regime agreed to destroy and stop developing all weapons of mass destruction and long-range missiles, and to prove to the world it has done so by complying with rigorous inspections. Iraq has broken every aspect of this fundamental pledge.

From 1991 to 1995, the Iraqi regime said it had no biological weapons. After a senior official in its weapons program defected and exposed this lie, the regime admitted to producing tens of thousands of liters of anthrax and other deadly biological agents for use with Scud warheads, aerial bombs, and aircraft spray tanks. U.N. inspectors believe Iraq has produced two to four times the amount of biological agents it declared, and has failed to account for more than three metric tons of material that could be used to produce biological weapons. Right now, Iraq is expanding and improving facilities that were used for the production of biological weapons.

United Nations' inspections also revealed that Iraq likely maintains stockpiles of VX, mustard and other chemical agents, and that the regime is rebuilding and expanding facilities capable of producing chemical weapons.

And in 1995, after four years of deception, Iraq finally admitted it had a crash nuclear weapons program prior to the Gulf War. We know now, were it not for that war, the regime in Iraq would likely have possessed a nuclear weapon no later than 1993.

Today, Iraq continues to withhold important information about its nuclear program—weapons design, procurement logs, experiment data, an accounting of nuclear materials and documentation of foreign assistance. Iraq employs capable nuclear scientists and technicians. It retains physical infrastructure needed to build a nuclear weapon. Iraq has made several attempts to buy high-strength aluminum tubes used to enrich uranium for a nuclear weapon. Should Iraq acquire fissile material, it would be able to build a nuclear weapon within a year. And Iraq's state-controlled media has reported numerous meetings between Saddam Hussein and his nuclear scientists, leaving little doubt about his continued appetite for these weapons.

Iraq also possesses a force of Scud-type missiles with ranges beyond the 150 kilometers permitted by the U.N. Work at testing and production facilities shows that Iraq is building more long-range missiles that it can inflict mass death throughout the region.

In 1990, after Iraq's invasion of Kuwait, the world imposed economic sanctions on Iraq. Those sanctions were maintained after the war to compel the regime's compliance with Security Council resolutions. In time, Iraq was allowed to use oil revenues to buy food. Saddam Hussein has subverted this program, working around the sanctions to buy missile technology and military materials. He blames the suffering of Iraq's people on the United Nations, even as he uses his oil wealth to build lavish palaces for himself, and to buy arms for his country. By refusing to comply with his own agreements, he bears full guilt for the hunger and misery of innocent Iraqi citizens.

In 1991, Iraq promised U.N. inspectors immediate and unrestricted access to verify Iraq's commitment to rid itself of weapons of mass destruction and long-range missiles. Iraq broke this promise, spending seven years deceiving, evading, and harassing U.N. inspectors before ceasing cooperation entirely. Just months after the 1991 cease-fire, the Security Council twice renewed its demand that the Iraqi regime cooperate fully with inspectors, condemning Iraq's serious violations of its obligations. The Security Council again renewed that demand in 1994, and twice more in 1996, deploring Iraq's clear violations of its obligations. The Security Council renewed its demand three more times in 1997, citing flagrant violations; and three more times in 1998, calling Iraq's behavior totally unacceptable. And in 1999, the demand was renewed yet again.

As we meet today, it's been almost four years since the last U.N. inspectors set foot in Iraq, four years for the Iraqi regime to plan, and to build, and to test behind the cloak of secrecy.

We know that Saddam Hussein pursued weapons of mass murder even when inspectors were in his country. Are we to assume that he stopped when they left? The history, the logic, and the facts lead to one conclusion: Saddam Hussein's regime is a grave and gathering danger. To suggest otherwise is to hope against the evidence. To assume this regime's good faith is to bet the lives of millions and the peace of the world in a reckless gamble. And this is a risk we must not take.

Delegates to the General Assembly, we have been more than patient. We've tried sanctions. We've tried the carrot of oil for food, and the stick of coalition military strikes. But Saddam Hussein has defied all these efforts and continues to develop weapons of mass destruction. The first time we may be completely certain he has a—nuclear weapons is when, God forbid, he uses one. We owe it to all our citizens to do everything in our power to prevent that day from coming.

The conduct of the Iraqi regime is a threat to the authority of the United Nations, and a threat to peace. Iraq has answered a decade of U.N. demands with a decade of defiance. All the world now faces a test, and the United Nations a difficult and defining moment. Are Security Council resolutions to be honored and enforced, or cast aside without consequence? Will the United Nations serve the purpose of its founding, or will it be irrelevant?

The United States helped found the United Nations. We want the United Nations to be effective, and respectful, and successful. We want the resolutions of the world's most important multilateral body to be enforced. And right now those resolutions are being unilaterally subverted by the Iraqi regime. Our partnership of nations can meet the test before us, by making clear what we now expect of the Iraqi regime.

If the Iraqi regime wishes peace, it will immediately and unconditionally forswear, disclose, and remove or destroy all weapons of mass destruction, long-range missiles, and all related material.

If the Iraqi regime wishes peace, it will immediately end all support for terrorism and act to suppress it, as all states are required to do by U.N. Security Council resolutions.

If the Iraqi regime wishes peace, it will cease persecution of its civilian population, including Shi'a, Sunnis, Kurds, Turkomans, and others, again as required by Security Council resolutions.

If the Iraqi regime wishes peace, it will release or account for all Gulf War personnel whose fate is still unknown. It will return the remains of any who are deceased, return stolen property, accept liability for losses resulting from the invasion of Kuwait, and fully cooperate with international efforts to resolve these issues, as required by Security Council resolutions.

If the Iraqi regime wishes peace, it will immediately end all illicit trade outside the oil-for-food program. It will accept U.N. administration of funds from that program, to ensure that the money is used fairly and promptly for the benefit of the Iraqi people.

If all these steps are taken, it will signal a new openness and accountability in Iraq. And it could open the prospect of the United Nations helping to build a government that represents all Iraqis— a government based on respect for human rights, economic liberty, and internationally supervised elections.

The United States has no quarrel with the Iraqi people; they've suffered too long in silent captivity. Liberty for the Iraqi people is a great moral cause, and a great strategic goal. The people of Iraq deserve it; the security of all nations requires it. Free societies do not intimidate through cruelty and conquest, and open societies do not threaten the world with mass murder. The United States supports political and economic liberty in a unified Iraq.

We can harbor no illusions—and that's important today to remember. Saddam Hussein attacked Iran in 1980 and Kuwait in 1990. He's fired ballistic missiles at Iran and Saudi Arabia, Bahrain, and Israel. His regime once ordered the killing of every person between the ages of 15 and 70 in certain Kurdish villages in northern Iraq. He has gassed many Iranians, and 40 Iraqi villages.

My nation will work with the U.N. Security Council to meet our common challenge. If Iraq's regime defies us again, the world must move deliberately, decisively to hold Iraq to account. We will work with the U.N. Security Council for the necessary resolutions. But the purposes of the United States should not be doubted. The Security Council resolutions will be enforced—the just demands of peace and security will be met—or action will be unavoidable. And a regime that has lost its legitimacy will also lose its power.

Events can turn in one of two ways: If we fail to act in the face of danger, the people of Iraq will continue to live in brutal submission. The regime will have new power to bully and dominate and conquer its neighbors, condemning the Middle East to more years of bloodshed and fear. The regime will remain unstable—the region will remain unstable, with little hope of freedom, and isolated from the progress of our times. With every step the Iraqi regime takes toward gaining and deploying the most terrible weapons, our own options to confront that regime will narrow. And if an emboldened regime were to supply these weapons to terrorist allies, then the attacks of September the 11th would be a prelude to far greater horrors.

If we meet our responsibilities, if we overcome this danger, we can arrive at a very different future. The people of Iraq can shake off their captivity. They can one day join a democratic Afghanistan and a democratic Palestine, inspiring reforms throughout the Muslim world. These nations can show by their example that honest government, and respect for women, and the great Islamic tradition of learning can triumph in the Middle East and beyond. And we will show that the promise of the United Nations can be fulfilled in our time.

Neither of these outcomes is certain. Both have been set before us. We must choose between a world of fear and a world of progress. We cannot stand by and do nothing while dangers gather. We must stand up for our security, and for the permanent rights and the hopes of mankind. By heritage and by choice, the United States of America will make that stand. And, delegates to the United Nations, you have the power to make that stand, as well.

Thank you very much. (Applause.)

# The National Intelligence Estimate

•

## October 2002

•

### Iraq's Continuing Programs
### for Weapons of Mass Destruction

## Key Judgments

*[This document is given as declassified and released by the Bush administration in June, 2004, including the dissenting view about whether Iraq was developing nuclear weapons from the State Department's Bureau of Intelligence and Research (INR), also given as published.—ed.]*

We judge that Iraq has continued its weapons of mass destruction (WMD) programs in defiance of UN resolutions and restrictions. Baghdad has chemical and biological weapons as well as missiles with ranges in excess of UN restrictions; if left unchecked, it probably will have a nuclear weapon during this decade. (See INR alternative view at the end of these Key Judgments.)

We judge that we are seeing only a portion of Iraq's WMD efforts, owing to Baghdad's vigorous denial and deception efforts. Revelations after the Gulf war starkly demonstrate the extensive efforts undertaken by Iraq to deny information. We lack specific information on many key aspects of Iraq's WMD programs.

Since inspections ended in 1998, Iraq has maintained its chemical weapons effort, energized its missile program, and invested more heavily in biological weapons; in the view of most agencies, Baghdad is reconstituting its nuclear weapons program.

• Iraq's growing ability to sell oil illicitly increases Baghdad's capabilities to finance WMD programs; annual earnings in cash and goods have more than quadrupled, from $580 million in 1998 to about $3 billion this year.

• Iraq has largely rebuilt missile and biological weapons facilities damaged during Operation Desert Fox and has expanded its chemical and biological infrastructure under the cover of civilian production.

• Baghdad has exceeded UN range limits of 150 km with its ballistic missiles and is working with unmanned aerial vehicles (UAVs), which allow for a more lethal means to deliver biological and, less likely, chemical warfare agents.

• Although we assess that Saddam does not yet have nuclear weapons or sufficient material to make any, he remains intent on acquiring them. Most agencies assess that Baghdad started reconstituting its nuclear program about the time that UNSCOM inspectors departed—December 1998.

How quickly Iraq will obtain its first nuclear weapon depends on when it acquires sufficient weapons-grade fissile material.

• If Baghdad acquires sufficient fissile material from abroad it could make a nuclear weapon within several months to a year.

• Without such material from abroad, Iraq probably would not be able to make a weapon until 2007 to 2009, owing to inexperience in building and operating centrifuge facilities to produce highly enriched uranium and challenges in procuring the necessary equipment and expertise.

– Most agencies believe that Saddam's personal interest in and Iraq's aggressive attempts to obtain high-strength aluminum tubes for centrifuge rotors—as well as Iraq's attempts to acquire magnets, high-speed balancing machines, and machine tools—provide compelling evidence that Saddam is reconstituting a uranium enrichment effort for Baghdad's nuclear weapons program. (DOE agrees that reconstitution of the nuclear program is underway but assesses that the tubes probably are not part of the program.)

- Iraq's efforts to re-establish and enhance its cadre of weapons personnel as well as activities at several suspect nuclear sites further indicate that reconstitution is underway.

- All agencies agree that about 25,000 centrifuges based on tubes of the size Iraq is trying to acquire would be capable of producing approximately two weapons' worth of highly enriched uranium per year.

• In a much less likely scenario, Baghdad could make enough fissile material for a nuclear weapon by 2005 to 2007 if it obtains suitable centrifuge tubes this year and has all the other materials and technological expertise necessary to build production-scale uranium enrichment facilities

We assess that Baghdad has begun renewed production of mustard, sarin, GF (cyclosarin), and VX; its capability probably is more limited now than it was at the time of the Gulf war, although VX production and agent storage life probably have been improved.

• An array of clandestine reporting reveals that Baghdad has procured covertly the types and quantities of chemicals and equipment sufficient to allow limited CW agent production hidden within Iraq's legitimate chemical industry.

• Although we have little specific information on Iraq's CW stockpile, Saddam probably has stocked at least 100 metric tons (MT) and possibly as much as 500 MT of CW agents—much of it added in the last year.

• The Iraqis have experience in manufacturing CW bombs, artillery rockets, and projectiles. We assess that they possess CW bulk fills for SRBM warheads, including for a limited number of covertly stored Scuds, possibly a few with extended ranges.

We judge that all key aspects—R&D, production, and weaponization—of Iraq's offensive BW program are active and that most elements are larger and more advanced than they were before the Gulf war.

- We judge Iraq has some lethal and incapacitating BW agents and is capable of quickly producing and weaponizing a variety of such agents, including anthrax, for delivery by bombs, missiles, aerial sprayers, and covert operatives.

  - Chances are even that smallpox is part of Iraq's offensive BW program.

  - Baghdad probably has developed genetically engineered BW agents.

- Baghdad has established a large-scale, redundant, and concealed BW agent production capability.

  - Baghdad has mobile facilities for producing bacterial and toxin BW agents; these facilities can evade detection and are highly survivable. Within three to six months [Corrected per Errata sheet issued in October 2002] these units probably could produce an amount of agent equal to the total that Iraq produced in the years prior to the Gulf war.

Iraq maintains a small missile force and several development programs, including for a UAV probably intended to deliver biological warfare agent.

- Gaps in Iraqi accounting to UNSCOM suggest that Saddam retains a covert force of up to a few dozen Scud-variant SRBMs with ranges of 650 to 900 km.

- Iraq is deploying its new al-Samoud and Ababil–100 SRBMs, which are capable of flying beyond the UN-authorized 150-km range limit; Iraq has tested an al-Samoud variant beyond 150 km—perhaps as far as 300 km.

- Baghdad's UAVs could threaten Iraq's neighbors, U.S. forces in the Persian Gulf, *and if brought close to, or into, the United States, the U.S. Homeland.*

  - An Iraqi UAV procurement network attempted to procure commercially available route planning software and an associated topographic database that would be able to support targeting of the United States, according to analysis of special intelligence.

  - The Director, Intelligence, Surveillance, and Reconnaissance, U.S. Air Force, does not agree that Iraq is developing UAVs *primarily* intended to be delivery platforms for chemical and biological warfare (CBW) agents. The small size of Iraq's new UAV strongly suggests a primary role of reconnaissance, although CBW delivery is an inherent capability.

- Iraq is developing medium-range ballistic missile capabilities, largely through foreign assistance in building specialized facilities, including a test stand for engines more powerful than those in its current missile force.

We have low confidence in our ability to assess when Saddam would use WMD.

- Saddam could decide to use chemical and biological warfare (CBW) preemptively against U.S. forces, friends, and allies in the region in an attempt to disrupt U.S. war preparations and undermine the political will of the Coalition.

- Saddam might use CBW after an initial advance into Iraqi territory, but early use of WMD could foreclose diplomatic options for stalling the US advance.

- He probably would use CBW when be perceived he irretrievably had lost control of the military and security situation, but we are unlikely to know when Saddam reaches that point.

- We judge that Saddam would be more likely to use chemical weapons than biological weapons on the battlefield.

- Saddam historically has maintained tight control over the use of WMD; however, he probably has provided contingency instructions to his commanders to use CBW in specific circumstances.

Baghdad for now appears to be drawing a line short of conducting terrorist attacks with conventional or CBW against the United States, fearing that exposure of Iraqi involvement would provide Washington a stronger cause for making war.

Iraq probably would attempt clandestine attacks against the U.S. Homeland if Baghdad feared an attack that threatened the survival of the regime were imminent or unavoidable, or possibly for revenge. Such attacks—more likely with biological than chemical agents—probably would be carried out by special forces or intelligence operatives.

- The Iraqi Intelligence Service (IIS) probably has been directed to conduct clandestine attacks against US and Allied interests in the Middle East in the event the United States takes action against Iraq. The US probably would be the primary means by which Iraq would attempt to conduct any CBW attacks on the US Homeland, although we have no specific intelligence information that Saddam's regime has directed attacks against US territory.

Saddam, if sufficiently desperate, might decide that only an organization such as al-Qa'ida—with worldwide reach and extensive terrorist infrastructure, and already engaged in a life-or-death struggle against the United States—could perpetrate the type of terrorist attack that he would hope to conduct.

- In such circumstances, he might decide that the extreme step of assisting the Islamist terrorists in conducting a CBW attack against the United States would be his last chance to exact vengeance by taking a large number of victims with him.

# State/INR Alternative View of Iraq's Nuclear Program

The Assistant Secretary of State for Intelligence and Research (INR) believes that Saddam continues to want nuclear weapons and that available evidence indicates that Baghdad is pursuing at least a limited effort to maintain and acquire nuclear weapons-related capabilities. The activities we have detected do not, however, add up to a compelling case that Iraq is currently pursuing what INR would consider to be an integrated and comprehensive approach to acquire nuclear weapons. Iraq may be doing so, but INR considers the available evidence inadequate to support such a judgment. Lacking persuasive evidence that Baghdad has launched a coherent effort to reconstitute its nuclear weapons program, INR is unwilling to speculate that such an effort began soon after the departure of UN inspectors or to project a timeline for the completion of activities it does not now see happening. As a result, INR is unable to predict when Iraq could acquire a nuclear device or weapon.

In INR's view Iraq's efforts to acquire aluminum tubes is central to the argument that Baghdad is reconstituting its nuclear weapons program, but INR is not persuaded that the tubes in question are intended for use as centrifuge rotors. INR accepts the judgment of technical experts at the U.S. Department of Energy (DOE) who have concluded that the tubes Iraq seeks to acquire are poorly suited for use in gas centrifuges to be used for uranium enrichment and finds unpersuasive the arguments advanced by others to make the case that they are intended for that purpose. INR considers it far more likely that the tubes are intended for another purpose, most likely the production of artillery rockets. The very large quantities being sought, the way the tubes were tested by the Iraqis, and the atypical lack of attention to operational security in the procurement efforts are among the factors, in addition to the DOE assessment, that lead INR to conclude that the tubes are not intended for use in Iraq's nuclear weapon program.

# Confidence Levels for Selected Key Judgments in This Estimate

## *High Confidence*

* Iraq is continuing, and in some areas expanding, its chemical, biological, nuclear and missile programs contrary to UN resolutions.

* We are not detecting portions of these weapons programs.

* Iraq possesses proscribed chemical and biological weapons and missiles.

* Iraq could make a nuclear weapon in months to a year once it acquires sufficient weapons-grad fissile material

## *Moderate Confidence*

* Iraq does not yet have a nuclear weapon or sufficient material to make one but is likely to have a weapon by 2007 to 2009. (See INR alternative view, page 84).

## *Low Confidence*

* When Saddam would use weapons of mass destruction.

* Whether Saddam would engage in clandestine attacks against the US Homeland.

- Whether in desperation Saddam would share chemical or biological weapons with al-Qa'ida.

*[NIE page 24]*
[ . . . ]
**Uranium Acquisition.** Iraq retains approximately two-and-a-half tons of 2.5 percent enriched uranium oxide, which the IAEA permits. This low-enriched material could be used as feed material to produce enough HEU for about two nuclear weapons. The use of enriched feed material also would reduce the initial number of centrifuges that Baghdad would need by about half. Iraq could divert this material—the IAEA inspects it only once a year—and enrich it to weapons grade before a subsequent inspection discovered it was missing. The IAEA last inspected this material in late January 2002.

Iraq has about 500 metric tons of yellowcake [a refined form of natural uranium] and low enriched uranium at Tuwaitha, which is inspected annually by the IAEA. Iraq also began vigorously trying to procure uranium ore and yellowcake; acquiring either would shorten the time Baghdad needs to produce nuclear weapons.

- A foreign government service reported that as of early 2001, Niger planned to send several tons of "pure uranium" (probably yellowcake) to Iraq. As of early 2001, Niger and Iraq reportedly were still working out arrangements for this deal, which could be for up to 500 tons of yellowcake. We do not know the status of this arrangement.

- Reports indicate Iraq also has sought uranium ore from Somalia and possibly the Democratic Republic of the Congo.

We cannot confirm whether Iraq succeeded in acquiring uranium ore and/or yellowcake from these sources. Reports suggest Iraq is shifting from domestic mining and milling of uranium to foreign acquisition. Iraq possesses significant phosphate deposits, from which uranium had been chemically extracted before Operation Desert Storm. Intelligence information on whether nuclear-related phosphate mining and/or processing has been reestablished is inconclusive, however.

[ ... ]

*[NIE page 84]*

# Annex A

*Iraq's Attempts to Acquire Aluminum Tubes*

*[This excerpt from a longer view includes INR's position on the African uranium issue]*

## INR's Alternative View: Iraq's Attempts to Acquire Aluminum Tubes

Some of the specialized but dual-use items being sought are, by all indications, bound for Iraq's missile program. Other cases are ambiguous, such as that of a planned magnet-production line whose suitability for centrifuge operations remains unknown. Some efforts involve non-controlled industrial material and equipment—including a variety of machine tools—and are troubling because they would help establish the infrastructure for a renewed nuclear program. But such efforts (which began well before the inspectors departed) are not clearly linked to a nuclear end-use. Finally, the claims of Iraqi pursuit of natural uranium in Africa are, in INR's assessment, highly dubious.

*[The Defense Intelligence Agency also declassified part of a report it completed in September 2002 entitled "Iraq—Key WMD Facilities— An Operational Support Study," which DIA described as "a planning document produced in support of United States Central Command," which oversaw the military operations in Iraq. Excerpts, as given at http://www.dia.mill/Public/Press/press12.pdf:]*

## Defense Intelligence Agency

- This study was not a DIA assessment of Iraq's weapons of mass destruction program or capability. It addressed issues related to Iraq's chemical, biological, and nuclear program infrastructure.

- DIA stands solidly behind the Intelligence Community's assessment that Iraq had an on-going chemical weapons program that was in violation of United Nations sanctions.

- The following is the declassified section on Iraq's chemical warfare program from the classified DIA study:

## Chemical Warfare (CW) Program

A substantial amount of Iraq's chemical warfare agents, precursors, munitions, and production equipment were destroyed between 1991 and 1998 as a result of Operation DESERT STORM and UNSCOM actions. Nevertheless, we believe Iraq retained production equipment, expertise and chemical precursors and can reconstitute a chemical warfare program in the absence of an international inspection regime. Iraq's successful use of chemical weapons in the past against Iranian troops and Kurdish civilians increases the likelihood of a chemical warfare reconstitution. Iraq has not signed the Chemical Weapons Convention (CWC).

There is no reliable information on whether Iraq is producing and stockpiling chemical weapons, or where Iraq has—or will—establish its chemical warfare agent production facilities. Unusual munitions transfer activity in mid–2002 suggests that Iraq is distributing CW munitions in preparation for an anticipated US attack. Iraq retains all the chemicals and equipment to produce the blister agent mustard but its ability for sustained production of G-series nerve agents and VX is constrained by its stockpile of key chemical precursors and by the destruction of all known CW production facilities during Operation Desert Storm and during subsequent UNSCOM inspections. In the absence of external aid, Iraq will likely experience difficulties in producing nerve agents at the rate executed before Operation Desert Storm.

Iraq is steadily establishing a dual use industrial chemical infrastructure that provides some of the building blocks necessary for production of chemical agents. In addition, Iraq has renovated and added production lines at two facilities formerly associated with Baghdad's chemical warfare program—Habbaniyah I and Habbaniyah II. Activities include building reconstruction, salvage operations, and equipment movement and deliveries in the months that followed the 1998 expulsion of United Nations inspectors. Baghdad is rebuilding portions of its chemical production infrastructure under the guise of a civilian need for pesticides, chlorine, and other legitimate chemical products, giving Iraq the potential for a small "breakout" production capability.

Although we lack any direct information, Iraq probably possesses CW agent in chemical munitions, possibly including artillery rockets, artillery shells, aerial bombs, and ballistic missile warheads. Baghdad also probably possesses bulk chemical stockpiles, primarily containing precursors, but that also could consist of some mustard agent or stabilized VX.

Iraqi doctrine for the use of chemical weapons evolved during the Iran-Iraq war, and was fully incorporated into Iraqi offensive operations by the end of the war in 1988. Iraq demonstrated its ability to use chemical weapons during that conflict in the following roles: in a defensive role to disrupt or halt an overwhelming enemy offensive; as a preemptive weapon to disrupt staging areas before an offensive attack; and as an offensive weapon during well-staged attacks to regain territory. Authority for use of chemical weapons during that war eventually became delegated to corps commanders. The Iraqis delivered chemical agents with artillery, multiple rocket launchers, mortars, and aerial bombs dropped by fixed wing aircraft and helicopters. Iraq also used chemical agents against Kurdish civilians in 1988. Historical precedent suggests Saddam already may have deployed chemical weapons to western Iraq, as he did during Operation DESERT STORM, to be used against Israel in the event of coalition military action that threatens the regime.

Iraq will develop various elements of its chemical industry to achieve self-sufficiency in producing the chemical precursors required for CW agent production. Iraq might construct a new dedicated CW facility or facilities at remote sites to avoid detection or, alternatively, upgrade the production capabilities at its Habbaniyah I and II facilities to produce the agent mustard and binary components necessary for the production of nerve agents.

# President George W. Bush's Speech
# at Cincinnati Museum Center

•

# October 7, 2002

[. . .]

Tonight I want to take a few minutes to discuss a grave threat to peace, and America's determination to lead the world in confronting that threat.

The threat comes from Iraq. It arises directly from the Iraqi regime's own actions—its history of aggression, and its drive toward an arsenal of terror. Eleven years ago, as a condition for ending the Persian Gulf War, the Iraqi regime was required to destroy its weapons of mass destruction, to cease all development of such weapons, and to stop all support for terrorist groups. The Iraqi regime has violated all of those obligations. It possesses and produces chemical and biological weapons. It is seeking nuclear weapons. It has given shelter and support to terrorism, and practices terror against its own people. The entire world has witnessed Iraq's eleven-year history of defiance, deception and bad faith.

We also must never forget the most vivid events of recent history. On September the 11th, 2001, America felt its vulnerability—even to threats that gather on the other side of the earth. We resolved then, and we are resolved today, to confront every threat, from any source, that could bring sudden terror and suffering to America.

Members of the Congress of both political parties, and members of the United Nations Security Council, agree that Saddam Hussein is a threat to peace and must disarm. We agree that the Iraqi dictator must not be permitted to threaten America and the world with horrible poisons and diseases and gases and atomic weapons. Since we all agree on this goal, the issues is : how can we best achieve it?

Many Americans have raised legitimate questions: about the nature of the threat; about the urgency of action—why be concerned now; about the link between Iraq developing weapons of terror, and the wider war on terror. These are all issues we've discussed broadly and fully within my administration. And tonight, I want to share those discussions with you.

First, some ask why Iraq is different from other countries or regimes that also have terrible weapons. While there are many dangers in the world, the threat from Iraq stands alone—because it gathers the most serious dangers of our age in one place. Iraq's weapons of mass destruction are controlled by a murderous tyrant who has already used chemical weapons to kill thousands of people. This same tyrant has tried to dominate the Middle East, has invaded and brutally occupied a small neighbor, has struck other nations without warning, and holds an unrelenting hostility toward the United States.

By its past and present actions, by its technological capabilities, by the merciless nature of its regime, Iraq is unique. As a former chief weapons inspector of the U.N. has said, "The fundamental problem with Iraq remains the nature of the regime, itself. Saddam Hussein is a homicidal dictator who is addicted to weapons of mass destruction."

Some ask how urgent this danger is to America and the world. The danger is already significant, and it only grows worse with time. If we know Saddam Hussein has dangerous weapons today—and we do—does it make any sense for the world to wait to confront him as he grows even stronger and develops even more dangerous weapons?

In 1995, after several years of deceit by the Iraqi regime, the head of Iraq's military industries defected. It was then that the regime was forced to admit that it had produced more than 30,000 liters of anthrax and other deadly biological agents. The inspectors, however, concluded that Iraq had likely produced two to four times that amount. This is a massive stockpile of biological weapons that has never been accounted for, and capable of killing millions.

We know that the regime has produced thousands of tons of chemical agents, including mustard gas, sarin nerve gas, VX nerve gas. Saddam Hussein also has experience in using chemical weapons. He has ordered chemical attacks on Iran, and on more than forty villages in his own country. These actions killed or injured at least 20,000 people, more than six times the number of people who died in the attacks of September the 11th.

And surveillance photos reveal that the regime is rebuilding facilities that it had used to produce chemical and biological weapons. Every chemical and biological weapon that Iraq has or makes is a direct violation of the truce that ended the Persian Gulf War in 1991. Yet, Saddam Hussein has chosen to build and keep these weapons despite international sanctions, U.N. demands, and isolation from the civilized world.

Iraq possesses ballistic missiles with a likely range of hundreds of miles—far enough to strike Saudi Arabia, Israel, Turkey, and other nations—in a region where more than 135,000 American civilians and service members live and work. We've also discovered through intelligence that Iraq has a growing fleet of manned and unmanned aerial vehicles that could be used to disperse chemical or biological weapons across broad areas. We're concerned that Iraq is exploring ways of using these UAVS for missions targeting the United States. And, of course, sophisticated delivery systems aren't required for a chemical or biological attack; all that might be required are a small container and one terrorist or Iraqi intelligence operative to deliver it.

And that is the source of our urgent concern about Saddam Hussein's links to international terrorist groups. Over the years, Iraq has provided safe haven to terrorists such as Abu Nidal, whose terror organization carried out more than 90 terrorist attacks in 20 countries that killed or injured nearly 900 people, including 12 Americans. Iraq has also provided safe haven to Abu Abbas, who was responsible for seizing the Achille Lauro and killing an American passenger. And we know that Iraq is continuing to finance terror and gives assistance to groups that use terrorism to undermine Middle East peace.

We know that Iraq and the al Qaeda terrorist network share a common enemy—the United States of America. We know that Iraq and al Qaeda have had high-level contacts that go back a decade. Some al Qaeda leaders who fled Afghanistan went to Iraq. These include one very senior al Qaeda leader who received medical treatment in Baghdad this year, and who has been associated with planning for chemical and biological attacks. We've learned that Iraq has trained al Qaeda members in bomb-making and poisons and deadly gases. And we know that after September the 11th, Saddam Hussein's regime gleefully celebrated the terrorist attacks on America.

Iraq could decide on any given day to provide a biological or chemical weapon to a terrorist group or individual terrorists. Alliance with terrorists could allow the Iraqi regime to attack America without leaving any fingerprints.

Some have argued that confronting the threat from Iraq could detract from the war against terror. To the contrary; confronting the threat posed by Iraq is crucial to winning the war on terror. When I spoke to Congress more than a year ago, I said that those who harbor terrorists are as guilty as the terrorists themselves. Saddam Hussein is harboring terrorists and the instruments of terror, the instruments of mass death and destruction. And he cannot be trusted. The risk is simply too great that he will use them, or provide them to a terror network.

Terror cells and outlaw regimes building weapons of mass destruction are different faces of the same evil. Our security requires that we confront both. And the United States military is capable of confronting both.

Many people have asked how close Saddam Hussein is to developing a nuclear weapon. Well, we don't know exactly, and that's the problem. Before the Gulf War, the best intelligence indicated that Iraq was eight to ten years away from developing a nuclear weapon. After the war, international inspectors learned that the regime has been much closer—the regime in Iraq would likely have possessed a nuclear weapon no later than 1993. The inspectors discovered that Iraq had an advanced nuclear weapons development program, had a design for a workable nuclear weapon, and was pursuing several different methods of enriching uranium for a bomb.

Before being barred from Iraq in 1998, the International Atomic Energy Agency dismantled extensive nuclear weapons-related facilities, including three uranium enrichment sites. That same year, information from a high-ranking Iraqi nuclear engineer who had defected revealed that despite his public promises, Saddam Hussein had ordered his nuclear program to continue.

The evidence indicates that Iraq is reconstituting its nuclear weapons program. Saddam Hussein has held numerous meetings with Iraqi nuclear scientists, a group he calls his "nuclear mujahideen"—his nuclear holy warriors. Satellite photographs reveal that Iraq is rebuilding facilities at sites that have been part of its nuclear program in the past. Iraq has attempted to purchase high-strength aluminum tubes and other equipment needed for gas centrifuges, which are used to enrich uranium for nuclear weapons.

If the Iraqi regime is able to produce, buy, or steal an amount of highly enriched uranium a little larger than a single softball, it could have a nuclear weapon in less than a year. And if we allow that to happen, a terrible line would be crossed. Saddam Hussein would be in a position to blackmail anyone who opposes his aggression. He would be in a position to dominate the Middle East. He would be in a position to threaten America. And Saddam Hussein would be in a position to pass nuclear technology to terrorists.

Some citizens wonder, after 11 years of living with this problem, why do we need to confront it now? And there's a reason. We've experienced the horror of September the 11th. We have seen that those who hate America are willing to crash airplanes into buildings full of innocent people. Our enemies would be no less willing, in fact, they would be eager, to use biological or chemical, or a nuclear weapon.

Knowing these realities, America must not ignore the threat gathering against us. Facing clear evidence of peril, we cannot wait for the final proof—the smoking gun—that could come in the form of a mushroom cloud. As President Kennedy said in October of 1962, "Neither the United States of America, nor the world community of nations can tolerate deliberate deception and offensive threats on the part of any nation, large or small. We no longer live in a world," he said, "where only the actual firing of weapons represents a sufficient challenge to a nations security to constitute maximum peril."

Understanding the threats of our time, knowing the designs and deceptions of the Iraqi regime, we have every reason to assume the worst, and we have an urgent duty to prevent the worst from occurring.

Some believe we can address this danger by simply resuming the old approach to inspections, and applying diplomatic and economic pressure. Yet this is precisely what the world has tried to do since 1991. The U.N. inspections program was met with systematic deception. The Iraqi regime bugged hotel rooms and offices of inspectors to find where they were going next; they forged documents, destroyed evidence, and developed mobile weapons facilities to keep a step ahead of inspectors. Eight so-called presidential palaces were declared off-limits to unfettered inspections. These sites actually encompass twelve square miles, with hundreds of structures, both above and below the ground, where sensitive materials could be hidden.

The world has also tried economic sanctions—and watched Iraq use billions of dollars in illegal oil revenues to fund more weapons purchases, rather than providing for the needs of the Iraqi people.

The world has tried limited military strikes to destroy Iraq's weapons of mass destruction capabilities—only to see them openly rebuilt, while the regime again denies they even exist.

The world has tried no-fly zones to keep Saddam from terrorizing his own people—and in the last year alone, the Iraqi military has fired upon American and British pilots more than 750 times.

After eleven years during which we have tried containment, sanctions, inspections, even selected military action, the end result is that Saddam Hussein still has chemical and biological weapons and is increasing his capabilities to make more. And he is moving ever closer to developing a nuclear weapon.

Clearly, to actually work, any new inspections, sanctions or enforcement mechanisms will have to be very different. America wants the U.N. to be an effective organization that helps keep the peace. And that is why we are urging the Security Council to adopt a new resolution setting out tough, immediate requirements. Among those requirements: the Iraqi regime must reveal and destroy, under U.N. supervision, all existing weapons of mass destruction. To ensure that we learn the truth, the regime must allow witnesses to its illegal activities to be interviewed outside the country—and these witnesses must be free to bring their families with them so they all beyond the reach of Saddam Hussein's terror and murder. And inspectors must have access to any site, at any time, without pre-clearance, without delay, without exceptions.

The time for denying, deceiving, and delaying has come to an end. Saddam Hussein must disarm himself—or, for the sake of peace, we will lead a coalition to disarm him.

Many nations are joining us in insisting that Saddam Hussein's regime be held accountable. They are committed to defending the international security that protects the lives of both our citizens and theirs. And that's why America is challenging all nations to take the resolutions of the U.N. Security Council seriously.

And these resolutions are clear. In addition to declaring and destroying all of its weapons of mass destruction, Iraq must end its support for terrorism. It must cease the persecution of its civilian population. It must stop all illicit trade outside the Oil For Food program. It must release or account for all Gulf War personnel, including an American pilot, whose fate is still unknown.

By taking these steps, and by only taking these steps, the Iraqi regime has an opportunity to avoid conflict. Taking these steps would also change the nature of the Iraqi regime itself. America hopes the regime will make that choice. Unfortunately, at least so far, we have little reason to expect it. And that's why two administrations—mine and President Clinton's—have stated that regime change in Iraq is the only certain means of removing a great danger to our nation.

I hope this will not require military action, but it may. And military conflict could be difficult. An Iraqi regime faced with its own demise may attempt cruel and desperate measures. If Saddam Hussein orders such measures, his generals would be well advised to refuse those orders. If they do not refuse, they must understand that all war criminals will be pursued and punished. If we have to act, we will take every precaution that is possible. We will plan carefully; we will act with the full power of the United States military; we will act with allies at our side, and we will prevail. (Applause.)

There is no easy or risk-free course of action. Some have argued we should wait—and that's an option. In my view, it's the riskiest of all options, because the longer we wait, the stronger and bolder Saddam Hussein will become. We could wait and hope that Saddam does not give weapons to terrorists, or develop a nuclear weapon to blackmail the world. But I'm convinced that is a hope against all evidence. As Americans, we want peace—we work and sacrifice for peace. But there can be no peace if our security depends on the will and whims of a ruthless and aggressive dictator. I'm not willing to stake one American life on trusting Saddam Hussein.

Failure to act would embolden other tyrants, allow terrorists access to new weapons and new resources, and make blackmail a permanent feature of world events. The United Nations would betray the purpose of its founding, and prove irrelevant to the problems of our time. And through its inaction, the United States would resign itself to a future of fear.

That is not the America I know. That is not the America I serve. We refuse to live in fear. (Applause.) This nation, in world war and in Cold War, has never permitted the brutal and lawless to set history's course. Now, as before, we will secure our nation, protect our freedom, and help others to find freedom of their own.

Some worry that a change of leadership in Iraq could create instability and make the situation worse. The situation could hardly get worse, for world security and for the people of Iraq. The lives of Iraqi citizens would improve dramatically if Saddam Hussein were no longer in power, just as the lives of Afghanistan's citizens improved after the Taliban. The dictator of Iraq is a student of Stalin, using murder as a tool of terror and control, within his own cabinet, within his own army, and even within his own family.

On Saddam Hussein's orders, opponents have been decapitated, wives and mothers of political opponents have been systematically raped as a method of intimidation, and political prisoners have been forced to watch their own children being tortured.

America believes that all people are entitled to hope and human rights, to the non-negotiable demands of human dignity. People everywhere prefer freedom to slavery; prosperity to squalor; self-government to the rule of terror and torture. America is a friend to the people of Iraq. Our demands are directed only at the regime that enslaves them and threatens us. When these demands are met, the first and greatest benefit will come to

Iraqi men, women and children. The oppression of Kurds, Assyrians, Turkomans, Shi'a, Sunnis and others will be lifted. The long captivity of Iraq will end, and an era of new hope will begin.

Iraq is a land rich in culture, resources, and talent. Freed from the weight of oppression, Iraq's people will be able to share in the progress and prosperity of our time. If military action is necessary, the United States and our allies will help the Iraqi people rebuild their economy, and create the institutions of liberty in a unified Iraq at peace with its neighbors.

Later this week, the United States Congress will vote on this matter. I have asked Congress to authorize the use of America's military, if it proves necessary, to enforce U.N. Security Council demands. Approving this resolution does not mean that military action is imminent or unavoidable. The resolution will tell the United Nations, and all nations, that America speaks with one voice and is determined to make the demands of the civilized world mean something. Congress will also be sending a message to the dictator in Iraq: that his only chance—his only choice is full compliance, and the time remaining for that choice is limited.

Members of Congress are nearing an historic vote. I'm confident they will fully consider the facts, and their duties.

The attacks of September the 11th showed our country that vast oceans no longer protect us from danger. Before that tragic date, we had only hints of al Qaeda's plans and designs. Today in Iraq, we see a threat whose outlines are far more clearly defined, and whose consequences could be far more deadly. Saddam Hussein's actions have put us on notice, and there is no refuge from our responsibilities.

We did not ask for this present challenge, but we accept it. Like other generations of Americans, we will meet the responsibility of defending human liberty against violence and aggression. By our resolve, we will give strength to others. By our courage, we will give hope to others. And by our actions, we will secure the peace, and lead the world to a better day.

May God bless America. (Applause.)

# PART II

The president had told the United Nations and the world in September of 2002 that Saddam could avoid war if he opened the country to arms inspections and fully cooperated to allow the inspectors to verify that Iraq disclosed and destroyed all the arms that United Nations resolutions over the years had forbidden it to have.

With Britain as its principal ally, and with support from other countries, including France, the United States was able to persuade the United Nations Security Council on November 8 to approve Resolution 1441, requiring Iraq to make an "accurate, full and complete declaration of all aspects of its programs to develop chemical, biological, and nuclear weapons, ballistic missiles, and other delivery systems such as unmanned aerial vehicles and dispersal systems" within 30 days and allow inspectors to verify its declarations. It would face "serious consequences" if it did not comply, the resolution warned, but at French and German insistence, the Security Council did not agree to American proposals to make retaliation automatic in that case. Instead, it agreed that if push came to shove, it would reconvene and reconsider.

The chief United Nations weapons inspector, Hans Blix, reported to the Security Council on January 27, 2003, on the 12,000-page declaration Iraq had in fact made on December 7, 2002. "In the fields of missiles and biotechnology, the declaration contains a good deal of new material and information covering the period from 1998 and onward. This is welcome," he said, but he found much of the rest of the declaration wanting and leaving important issues unresolved.

The U.N. inspectors' reports "do not contend that weapons of mass destruction remain in Iraq, nor do they exclude that possibility," Blix said, an important difference with the Bush administration's operating assumption that if Iraq denied having weapons, it must be hiding them someplace, and inspectors could look forever without finding them. Blix's operating assumption was that thorough inspections could eventually verify whether Iraq was telling the truth.

The contradictions between the inspectors' questions and Iraq's denials, Blix told the Security Council, "point to lack of evidence and inconsistencies, which raise question marks, which must be straightened out, if weapons dossiers are to be closed and confidence is to arise. They deserve to be taken seriously by Iraq rather than being brushed aside as evil machinations of UNSCOM. Regrettably, the 12,000-page declaration, most of which is a reprint of earlier documents, does not seem to contain any new evidence that would eliminate the questions or reduce their number."

He also pointed out that between 1991 and 1998, United Nations inspectors had destroyed more of Iraq's weapons of mass destruction than Operation Desert Storm did, and had also dismantled its nuclear weapons infrastructure.

His report acknowledged that Iraq had let the inspectors back in, and said that "access has been provided to all sites we have wanted to inspect and with one exception it has been prompt." The rest of his presentation outlined the work ahead of the inspectors, who then numbered 100, plus another 160 support staff. "All serve the United Nations and report to no one else," Blix said.

The Bush administration was running out of patience. "To those who say, why not give the inspection process more time, I ask, how much more time does Iraq need to answer these questions?" Secretary of State Powell asked at the World Economic Forum in Davos on the eve of the president's January 28 State of the Union address.

"The world has waited 12 years for Iraq to disarm," the president told Congress then. "The United States will ask the U.N. Security Council to convene on February the fifth to consider the facts of Iraq's ongoing defiance of the world. Secretary of State Powell will present information and intelligence about Iraq's illegal weapons programs, its attempts to hide those weapons from inspectors and its links to terrorist groups. We will consult, but let there be no misunderstanding: If Saddam Hussein does not fully disarm, for the safety of our people and for the peace of the world, we will lead a coalition to disarm him."

But his confidence that Iraq had misled the United Nations and the world rested on a foundation of faulty intelligence. And for all the warnings in the intelligence community about the possible unreliability of its information about Iraq's alleged attempts to procure uranium for bomb-making in Africa, President Bush's advisers let the president use 16 words in his State of the Union address that they later came to regret.

The director of central intelligence at the time, George Tenet, and the deputy national security adviser to the president, Stephen J. Hadley, took the blame for a series of lapses that allowed the 16 words to appear in the speech: "The British government has learned that Saddam Hussein recently sought significant quantities of uranium from Africa." The British had published the claim in a white paper in the fall of 2002, and there were reports from French and other sources, some based on documents whose authenticity was questionable, of a uranium deal between Iraq and Niger. But the State Department's Bureau of Intelligence and Research had long been on record within the government with its view that claims that Iraq was trying to buy uranium in Africa were highly dubious. Even the Central Intelligence Agency had enough misgivings to ask a former American ambassador, Joseph Wilson, to go to Niger to find out what he could in early 2002. (He reported that he could not substantiate the reports, but information that his wife, Valerie Plame, was a CIA officer and had suggested his appointment was leaked to the conservative columnist Robert Novak and prompted a grand jury investigation into who had made this disclosure, possibly a crime under Federal law.)

In December 2002, the CIA asked the U.S. ambassador to the United Nations, then John D. Negroponte, to tone down a reference to the reports in a speech he made there on December 19. Negroponte's speech originally singled out Niger, and though the ambassador referred only to "Africa" when he delivered it, various bureaucratic lapses had left Niger in the fact sheet distributed with the speech. Niger's prime minister denied making any such deal on Christmas Eve, and the International Atomic Energy Agency asked the administration after the New Year what information it had to substantiate the claim.

Two weeks before the president's State of the Union speech, according to the Senate Select Committee on Intelligence, an INR nuclear analyst e-mailed other intelligence community analysts that he believed "the uranium purchase agreement probably is a hoax." But the CIA did not advise the president's staff to take the reference out of the speech, and Tenet, given a copy of the draft the day before the president's address, later told the committee he had not read it before it was delivered.

The IAEA received copies of the documents it had requested on February 4, and a month later, on March 3, reported to the United States that it had concluded from analysis of the documents and interviews with Iraqi officials that they were forgeries that did not substantiate the existence of any Iraq-Niger deal. By that time, the United States had also determined that French intelligence reports that had seemed to buttress the claim were based on the same forged documents, and a U.S. naval attaché in Ivory Coast had found only bales of cotton in two warehouses in Benin that had been suspected of storing uranium destined for Iraq, and on March 11 the CIA told policymakers the underlying documentation for the claim was fake. A British parliamentary investigation in mid–2004 into the British intelligence on Iraq found that its original report—which said that Iraq had been interested in acquiring uranium from Niger, not that it had actually obtained any—had not been based on the forged documents. The investigation also found that British intelligence had in general "inclined towards over-cautious or worst-case estimates" on Iraq, but less so than its American counterparts.

If the president was embarrassed, he was not deterred.

Secretary Powell made no reference to uranium from Africa in his presentation to the United Nations on February 5, a presentation he and the president wanted to use to make the case that Iraq had flagrantly violated all the resolutions barring it from developing or possessing weapons of mass destruction and was making fools of its inspectors. "Every statement I make today is backed up by sources, solid sources," he told the assembly. "These are not assertions. What we're giving you are facts and conclusions based on solid intelligence."

But many of the assertions proved to be not facts but flawed assumptions. Powell's speech dwelt at some length on the aluminum tubes, mistaking them as evidence of a nuclear weapons program. He dramatically recounted a captured Al Qaeda leader's information about cooperation with Iraq on poison-gas and chemical weapons, information that came from confessions that were later recanted and discounted by American intelligence. And Powell detailed the threat posed by more than a dozen mobile germ-warfare weapons factories he said four sources—two Iraqi defectors and two other people in a position to know—had given detailed reports about:

"We know that Iraq has at least seven of these mobile biological agent factories," Powell said. "The truck-mounted ones have at least two or three trucks each. That means that the mobile production facilities are very few, perhaps 18 trucks that we know of. There may be more, but perhaps 18 that we know of. Just imagine trying to find 18 trucks among the thousands and thousands of trucks that travel the roads of Iraq every single day. It took the inspectors four years to find out that Iraq was making biological agents. How long do you think it will take the inspectors to find even one of these 18 trucks without Iraq coming forward, as they are supposed to, with the information about these kinds of capabilities?"

Neither the United Nations nor, later, the Iraq Survey Group found any such trucks, because Saddam did not have any. Each of the four sources Powell cited turned out to be flawed, the Senate Select Intelligence Committee found later. One, an Iraqi major who had defected, was a "fabricator," a biological weapons expert for the Pentagon tried to point out before Powell gave his speech. Another, a defector code-named Curve Ball, was the source described by Powell as "an eyewitness, an Iraqi chemical engineer who supervised one of these facilities. He was actually present during biological agent production runs." But Curve Ball was aptly named, in the view of the Pentagon expert, the only American official who had actually met him. The analyst e-mailed the deputy chief of a CIA weapons task force the day before the speech, which he had read in draft form, and raised concerns about the reliability of all four of the sources. "I do have a concern with the validity of the information based on 'CURVE BALL' having a terrible hangover," the e-mail, parts of which were later published by the Senate committee, said, adding that there was concern about whether, "in fact, CURVE BALL was who he said he was."

"It was obvious to me that his case officer, for lack of better words, had fallen in love with his asset and the asset could do no wrong," this analyst told the committee's staff. "I was becoming frustrated, and when asked to go over Colin Powell's speech . . . and I went through the speech, and I thought, my gosh, we have got—I have got to go on record and make my concerns known. . . ." The CIA official he e-mailed replied, "Let's keep in mind the fact that this war's going to happen regardless of what Curve Ball said or didn't say, and that the Powers That Be probably aren't terribly interested in whether Curve Ball knows what he's talking about." The two analysts, who were personal friends, talked through the issues, the CIA official told the committee staff, but he concluded there was no need to take anything out of the speech.

He was not acting under pressure from policymakers to toe any line, the CIA man said. "I was reading the same newspapers you were. It was inevitable, it seemed to me at the time, and to most of us, that war was coming. I was not privy to any particular information including war plans or anything. My level was too low for that."

The committee concluded in its report in July 2004 (included in this volume) that "Much of the information provided or cleared by the Central Intelligence Agency for inclusion in Secretary Powell's speech was overstated, misleading, or incorrect."

Only the information on Iraq's missile programs in Powell's speech held up to any degree in the aftermath of the war. Powell was highly embarrassed and angry when it became clear after the war how misleading so much of his speech had been, and he urged the Presidential Commission on the Intelligence Capabilities of the United States Regarding Weapons of Mass Destruction, whose report is the last document in this volume, to find out "how we got ourselves into that position."

# United Nations Security Council Resolution 1441

•

# November 8, 2002

*The Security Council,*

*Recalling* all its previous relevant resolutions, in particular its resolutions 661 (1990) of 6 August 1990, 678 (1990) of 29 November 1990, 686 (1991) of 2 March 1991, 687 (1991) of 3 April 1991, 688 (1991) of 5 April 1991, 707 (1991) of 15 August 1991, 715 (1991) of 11 October 1991, 986 (1995) of 14 April 1995, and 1284 (1999) of 17 December 1999, and all the relevant statements of its President,

*Recalling also* its resolution 1382 (2001) of 29 November 2001 and its intention to implement it fully,

*Recognizing* the threat Iraq's non-compliance with Council resolutions and proliferation of weapons of mass destruction and long-range missiles poses to international peace and security,

*Recalling* that its resolution 678 (1990) authorized Member States to use all necessary means to uphold and implement its resolution 660 (1990) of 2 August 1990 and all relevant resolutions subsequent to resolution 660 (1990) and to restore international peace and security in the area,

*Further recalling* that its resolution 687 (1991) imposed obligations on Iraq as a necessary step for achievement of its stated objective of restoring international peace and security in the area,

*Deploring* the fact that Iraq has not provided an accurate, full, final, and complete disclosure, as required by resolution 687 (1991), of all aspects of its programs to develop weapons of mass destruction and ballistic missiles with a range greater than one hundred and fifty kilometers, and of all holdings of such weapons, their components and production facilities and locations, as well as all other nuclear programs, including any which it claims are for purposes not related to nuclear-weapons-usable material,

*Deploring further* that Iraq repeatedly obstructed immediate, unconditional, and unrestricted access to sites designated by the United Nations Special Commission (UNSCOM) and the International Atomic Energy Agency (IAEA), failed to cooperate fully and unconditionally with UNSCOM and IAEA weapons inspectors, as required by resolution 687 (1991), and ultimately ceased all cooperation with UNSCOM and the IAEA in 1998,

*Deploring* the absence, since December 1998, in Iraq of international monitoring, inspection, and verification, as required by relevant resolutions, of weapons of mass destruction and ballistic missiles, in spite of the Council's repeated demands that Iraq provide immediate, unconditional, and unrestricted access to the United Nations Monitoring, Verification and Inspection Commission (UNMOVIC), established in resolution 1284 (1999) as the successor organization to UNSCOM, and the IAEA, and regretting the consequent prolonging of the crisis in the region and the suffering of the Iraqi people,

*Deploring also* that the Government of Iraq has failed to comply with its commitments pursuant to resolution 687 (1991) with regard to terrorism, pursuant to resolution 688 (1991) to end repression of its civilian population and to provide access by international humanitarian organizations to all those in need of assistance in Iraq, and pursuant to resolutions 686 (1991), 687 (1991), and 1284 (1999) to return or cooperate in accounting for Kuwaiti and third country nationals wrongfully detained by Iraq, or to return Kuwaiti property wrongfully seized by Iraq,

*Recalling* that in its resolution 687 (1991) the Council declared that a ceasefire would be based on acceptance by Iraq of the provisions of that resolution, including the obligations on Iraq contained therein,

*Determined* to ensure full and immediate compliance by Iraq without conditions or restrictions with its obligations under resolution 687 (1991) and other relevant resolutions and recalling that the resolutions of the Council constitute the governing standard of Iraqi compliance,

*Recalling* that the effective operation of UNMOVIC, as the

successor organization to the Special Commission, and the IAEA is essential for the implementation of resolution 687 (1991) and other relevant resolutions,

*Noting* that the letter dated 16 September 2002 from the Minister for Foreign Affairs of Iraq addressed to the Secretary-General is a necessary first step toward rectifying Iraq's continued failure to comply with relevant Council resolutions,

*Noting further* the letter dated 8 October 2002 from the Executive Chairman of UNMOVIC and the Director-General of the IAEA to General Al-Saadi of the Government of Iraq laying out the practical arrangements, as a follow-up to their meeting in Vienna, that are prerequisites for the resumption of inspections in Iraq by UNMOVIC and the IAEA, and expressing the gravest concern at the continued failure by the Government of Iraq to provide confirmation of the arrangements as laid out in that letter,

*Reaffirming* the commitment of all Member States to the sovereignty and territorial integrity of Iraq, Kuwait, and the neighboring States,

*Commending* the Secretary-General and members of the League of Arab States and its Secretary-General for their efforts in this regard,

*Determined* to secure full compliance with its decisions,

*Acting* under Chapter VII of the Charter of the United Nations,

1. *Decides* that Iraq has been and remains in material breach of its obligations under relevant resolutions, including resolution 687 (1991), in particular through Iraq's failure to cooperate with United Nations inspectors and the IAEA, and to complete the actions required under paragraphs 8 to 13 of resolution 687 (1991);

2. *Decides*, while acknowledging paragraph 1 above, to afford Iraq, by this resolution, a final opportunity to comply with its disarmament obligations under relevant resolutions of the Council; and accordingly decides to set up an enhanced inspection regime with the aim of bringing to full and verified completion the disarmament process established by resolution 687 (1991) and subsequent resolutions of the Council;

3. *Decides* that, in order to begin to comply with its disarmament obligations, in addition to submitting the required biannual declarations, the Government of Iraq shall provide to UN-

MOVIC, the IAEA, and the Council, not later than 30 days from the date of this resolution, a currently accurate, full, and complete declaration of all aspects of its programs to develop chemical, biological, and nuclear weapons, ballistic missiles, and other delivery systems such as unmanned aerial vehicles and dispersal systems designed for use on aircraft, including any holdings and precise locations of such weapons, components, subcomponents, stocks of agents, and related material and equipment, the locations and work of its research, development and production facilities, as well as all other chemical, biological, and nuclear programs, including any which it claims are for purposes not related to weapon production or material;

4. *Decides* that false statements or omissions in the declarations submitted by Iraq pursuant to this resolution and failure by Iraq at any time to comply with, and cooperate fully in the implementation of, this resolution shall constitute a further material breach of Iraq's obligations and will be reported to the Council for assessment in accordance with paragraphs 11 and 12 below;

5. *Decides* that Iraq shall provide UNMOVIC and the IAEA immediate, unimpeded, unconditional, and unrestricted access to any and all, including underground, areas, facilities, buildings, equipment, records, and means of transport which they wish to inspect, as well as immediate, unimpeded, unrestricted, and private access to all officials and other persons whom UNMOVIC or the IAEA wish to interview in the mode or location of UNMOVIC's or the IAEA's choice pursuant to any aspect of their mandates; further decides that UNMOVIC and the IAEA may at their discretion conduct interviews inside or outside of Iraq, may facilitate the travel of those interviewed and family members outside of Iraq, and that, at the sole discretion of UNMOVIC and the IAEA, such interviews may occur without the presence of observers from the Iraqi Government; and instructs UNMOVIC and requests the IAEA to resume inspections no later than 45 days following adoption of this resolution and to update the Council 60 days thereafter;

6. *Endorses* the 8 October 2002 letter from the Executive Chairman of UNMOVIC and the Director-General of the IAEA to General Al-Saadi of the Government of Iraq, which is annexed

hereto, and decides that the contents of the letter shall be binding upon Iraq;

7. *Decides* further that, in view of the prolonged interruption by Iraq of the presence of UNMOVIC and the IAEA and in order for them to accomplish the tasks set forth in this resolution and all previous relevant resolutions and notwithstanding prior understandings, the Council hereby establishes the following revised or additional authorities, which shall be binding upon Iraq, to facilitate their work in Iraq:

- UNMOVIC and the IAEA shall determine the composition of their inspection teams and ensure that these teams are composed of the most qualified and experienced experts available;

- All UNMOVIC and IAEA personnel shall enjoy the privileges and immunities, corresponding to those of experts on mission, provided in the Convention on Privileges and Immunities of the United Nations and the Agreement on the Privileges and Immunities of the IAEA;

- UNMOVIC and the IAEA shall have unrestricted rights of entry into and out of Iraq, the right to free, unrestricted, and immediate movement to and from inspection sites, and the right to inspect any sites and buildings, including immediate, unimpeded, unconditional, and unrestricted access to Presidential Sites equal to that at other sites, notwithstanding the provisions of resolution 1154 (1998) of 2 March 1998;

- UNMOVIC and the IAEA shall have the right to be provided by Iraq the names of all personnel currently and formerly associated with Iraq's chemical, biological, nuclear, and ballistic missile programs and the associated research, development, and production facilities;

- Security of UNMOVIC and IAEA facilities shall be ensured by sufficient United Nations security guards;

- UNMOVIC and the IAEA shall have the right to declare, for

the purposes of freezing a site to be inspected, exclusion zones, including surrounding areas and transit corridors, in which Iraq will suspend ground and aerial movement so that nothing is changed in or taken out of a site being inspected;

- UNMOVIC and the IAEA shall have the free and unrestricted use and landing of fixed- and rotary-winged aircraft, including manned and unmanned reconnaissance vehicles;

- UNMOVIC and the IAEA shall have the right at their sole discretion verifiably to remove, destroy, or render harmless all prohibited weapons, subsystems, components, records, materials, and other related items, and the right to impound or close any facilities or equipment for the production thereof; and

- UNMOVIC and the IAEA shall have the right to free import and use of equipment or materials for inspections and to seize and export any equipment, materials, or documents taken during inspections, without search of UNMOVIC or IAEA personnel or official or personal baggage;

8. *Decides* further that Iraq shall not take or threaten hostile acts directed against any representative or personnel of the United Nations or the IAEA or of any Member State taking action to uphold any Council resolution;

9. *Requests* the Secretary-General immediately to notify Iraq of this resolution, which is binding on Iraq; demands that Iraq confirm within seven days of that notification its intention to comply fully with this resolution; and demands further that Iraq cooperate immediately, unconditionally, and actively with UNMOVIC and the IAEA;

10. *Requests* all Member States to give full support to UNMOVIC and the IAEA in the discharge of their mandates, including by providing any information related to prohibited programs or other aspects of their mandates, including on Iraqi attempts since 1998 to acquire prohibited items, and by recommending sites to be inspected, persons to be interviewed, conditions of

such interviews, and data to be collected, the results of which shall
be reported to the Council by UNMOVIC and the IAEA;

11. *Directs* the Executive Chairman of UNMOVIC and the Director-General of the IAEA to report immediately to the Council
any interference by Iraq with inspection activities, as well as any
failure by Iraq to comply with its disarmament obligations, including its obligations regarding inspections under this resolution;

12. *Decides* to convene immediately upon receipt of a report in
accordance with paragraphs 4 or 11 above, in order to consider
the situation and the need for full compliance with all of the relevant Council resolutions in order to secure international peace
and security;

13. *Recalls*, in that context, that the Council has repeatedly
warned Iraq that it will face serious consequences as a result of its
continued violations of its obligations;

14. *Decides* to remain seized of the matter.

## Annex

*[Text of Blix/El-Baradei letter]*

United Nations Monitoring,
    Verification and Inspection Commission
The Executive Chairman
International Atomic Energy Agency
The Director General

8 October 2002

Dear General Al-Saadi,
    During our recent meeting in Vienna, we discussed practical
arrangements that are prerequisites for the resumption of inspections in Iraq by UNMOVIC and the IAEA. As you recall, at the
end of our meeting in Vienna we agreed on a statement which
listed some of the principal results achieved, particularly Iraq's acceptance of all the rights of inspection provided for in all of the
relevant Security Council resolutions. This acceptance was stated
to be without any conditions attached.

During our 3 October 2002 briefing to the Security Council, members of the Council suggested that we prepare a written document on all of the conclusions we reached in Vienna. This letter lists those conclusions and seeks your confirmation thereof. We shall report accordingly to the Security Council.

In the statement at the end of the meeting, it was clarified that UNMOVIC and the IAEA will be granted immediate, unconditional and unrestricted access to sites, including what was termed "sensitive sites" in the past. As we noted, however, eight presidential sites have been the subject of special procedures under a Memorandum of Understanding of 1998. Should these sites be subject, as all other sites, to immediate, unconditional and unrestricted access, UNMOVIC and the IAEA would conduct inspections there with the same professionalism.

H.E. General Amir H. Al-Saadi
Advisor
Presidential Office
Baghdad
Iraq

We confirm our understanding that UNMOVIC and the IAEA have the right to determine the number of inspectors required for access to any particular site. This determination will be made on the basis of the size and complexity of the site being inspected. We also confirm that Iraq will be informed of the designation of additional sites, i.e. sites not declared by Iraq or previously inspected by either UNSCOM or the IAEA, through a Notification of Inspection (NIS) provided upon arrival of the inspectors at such sites.

Iraq will ensure that no proscribed material, equipment, records or other relevant items will be destroyed except in the presence of UNMOVIC and/or IAEA inspectors, as appropriate, and at their request.

UNMOVIC and the IAEA may conduct interviews with any person in Iraq whom they believe may have information relevant to their mandate. Iraq will facilitate such interviews. It is for UNMOVIC and the IAEA to choose the mode and location for interviews.

The National Monitoring Directorate (NMD) will, as in the past, serve as the Iraqi counterpart for the inspectors. The Baghdad Ongoing Monitoring and Verification Centre (BOMVIC) will be maintained on the same premises and under the same conditions as was the former Baghdad Monitoring and Verification Centre. The NMD will make available services as before, cost free, for the refurbishment of the premises.

The NMD will provide free of cost: (a) escorts to facilitate access to sites to be inspected and communication with personnel to be interviewed; (b) a hotline for BOMVIC which will be staffed by an English speaking person on a 24 hour a day/seven days a week basis; (c) support in terms of personnel and ground transportation within the country, as requested; and (d) assistance in the movement of materials and equipment at inspectors' request (construction, excavation equipment, etc.). NMD will also ensure that escorts are available in the event of inspections outside normal working hours, including at night and on holidays.

Regional UNMOVIC/IAEA offices may be established, for example, in Basra and Mosul, for the use of their inspectors. For this purpose, Iraq will provide, without cost, adequate office buildings, staff accommodation, and appropriate escort personnel.

UNMOVIC and the IAEA may use any type of voice or data transmission, including satellite and/or inland networks, with or without encryption capability. UNMOVIC and the IAEA may also install equipment in the field with the capability for transmission of data directly to the BOMVIC, New York and Vienna (e.g. sensors, surveillance cameras). This will be facilitated by Iraq and there will be no interference by Iraq with UNMOVIC or IAEA communications.

Iraq will provide, without cost, physical protection of all surveillance equipment, and construct antennae for remote transmission of data, at the request of UNMOVIC and the IAEA. Upon request by UNMOVIC through the NMD, Iraq will allocate frequencies for communications equipment. Iraq will provide security for all UNMOVIC and IAEA personnel. Secure and suitable accommodations will be designated at normal rates by Iraq for these personnel. For their part, UNMOVIC and the IAEA will require that their staff not stay at any accommodation other than those identified in consultation with Iraq.

On the use of fixed-wing aircraft for transport of personnel and equipment and for inspection purposes, it was clarified that aircraft used by UNMOVIC and IAEA staff arriving in Baghdad may land at Saddam International Airport. The points of departure of incoming aircraft will be decided by UNMOVIC. The Rasheed airbase will continue to be used for UNMOVIC and IAEA helicopter operations. UNMOVIC and Iraq will establish air liaison offices at the airbase. At both Saddam International Airport and Rasheed airbase, Iraq will provide the necessary support premises and facilities. Aircraft fuel will be provided by Iraq, as before, free of charge.

On the wider issue of air operations in Iraq, both fixed-wing and rotary, Iraq will guarantee the safety of air operations in its air space outside the no-fly zones. With regard to air operations in the no-fly zones, Iraq will take all steps within its control to ensure the safety of such operations.

Helicopter flights may be used, as needed, during inspections and for technical activities, such as gamma detection, without limitation in all parts of Iraq and without any area excluded. Helicopters may also be used for medical evacuation.

On the question of aerial imagery, UNMOVIC may wish to resume the use of U–2 or Mirage overflights. The relevant practical arrangements would be similar to those implemented in the past.

As before, visas for all arriving staff will be issued at the point of entry on the basis of the UN Laissez-Passer or UN Certificate; no other entry or exit formalities will be required. The aircraft passenger manifest will be provided one hour in advance of the arrival of the aircraft in Baghdad. There will be no searching of UNMOVIC or IAEA personnel or of official or personal baggage. UNMOVIC and the IAEA will ensure that their personnel respect the laws of Iraq restricting the export of certain items, for example, those related to Iraq's national cultural heritage. UNMOVIC and the IAEA may bring into, and remove from, Iraq all of the items and materials they require, including satellite phones and other equipment. With respect to samples, UNMOVIC and

IAEA will, where feasible, split samples so that Iraq may receive a portion while another portion is kept for reference purposes. Where appropriate, the organizations will send the samples to more than one laboratory for analysis.

We would appreciate your confirmation of the above as a correct reflection of our talks in Vienna.

Naturally, we may need other practical arrangements when proceeding with inspections. We would expect in such matters, as with the above, Iraq's co-operation in all respect.

Yours sincerely,

(*Signed*)
Hans Blix
Executive Chairman
United Nations Monitoring, Verification and
    Inspection Commission

(*Signed*)
Mohamed ElBaradei
Director General
International Atomic Energy Agency

# Security Council Update on WMD Inspection

•

# January 27, 2003

•

*by Dr. Hans Blix, Executive Chairman, UNMOVIC*

The resolution adopted by the Security Council on Iraq in November last year asks UNMOVIC and the IAEA to "update" the Council 60 days after the resumption of inspections. This is today. The updating, it seems, forms part of an assessment by the Council and its Members of the results, so far, of the inspections and of their role as a means to achieve verifiable disarmament in Iraq.

As this is an open meeting of the Council, it may be appropriate briefly to provide some background for a better understanding of where we stand today.

With your permission, I shall do so.

I begin by recalling that inspections as a part of a disarmament process in Iraq started in 1991, immediately after the Gulf War. They went on for eight years until December 1998, when inspectors were withdrawn. Thereafter, for nearly four years there were no inspections. They were resumed only at the end of November last year.

While the fundamental aim of inspections in Iraq has always been to verify disarmament, the successive resolutions adopted by the Council over the years have varied somewhat in emphasis and approach.

In 1991, resolution 687 (1991), adopted unanimously as a part of the cease-fire after the Gulf War, had five major elements. The three first related to disarmament. They called for:

- declarations by Iraq of its programs of weapons of mass destruction and long range missiles;

- verification of the declarations through UNSCOM and the IAEA;

- supervision by these organizations of the destruction or the elimination of proscribed programs and items.

After the completion of the disarmament :

- the Council would have authority to proceed to a lifting of the sanctions (economic restrictions); and

- the inspecting organizations would move to long-term ongoing monitoring and verification.

Resolution 687 (1991), like the subsequent resolutions I shall refer to, required cooperation by Iraq but such was often withheld or given grudgingly. Unlike South Africa, which decided on its own to eliminate its nuclear weapons and welcomed inspection as a means of creating confidence in its disarmament, Iraq appears not to have come to a genuine acceptance—not even today—of the disarmament, which was demanded of it and which it needs to carry out to win the confidence of the world and to live in peace.

As we know, the twin operation 'declare and verify', which was prescribed in resolution 687 (1991), too often turned into a game of 'hide and seek'. Rather than just verifying declarations and supporting evidence, the two inspecting organizations found themselves engaged in efforts to map the weapons programs and to search for evidence through inspections, interviews, seminars, inquiries with suppliers and intelligence organizations. As a result, the disarmament phase was not completed in the short time expected. Sanctions remained and took a severe toll until Iraq accepted the Oil for Food Program and the gradual development of that program mitigated the effects of the sanctions.

The implementation of resolution 687 (1991) nevertheless brought about considerable disarmament results. It has been recognized that more weapons of mass destruction were destroyed under this resolution than were destroyed during the Gulf War: large quantities of chemical weapons were destroyed under UNSCOM supervision before 1994. While Iraq claims—with little evidence—that it destroyed all biological weapons unilaterally in 1991, it is certain that UNSCOM destroyed large biological weapons production facilities in 1996. The large nuclear infrastructure was destroyed and the fissionable material was removed from Iraq by the IAEA.

One of three important questions before us today is how much might remain undeclared and intact from before 1991; and, possibly, thereafter; the second question is what, if anything, was illegally produced or procured after 1998, when the inspectors left; and the third question is how it can be prevented that any weapons of mass destruction be produced or procured in the future.

In December 1999—after one year without inspections in Iraq—resolution 1284 (1999) was adopted by the Council with 4 abstentions. Supplementing the basic resolutions of 1991 and following years, it provided Iraq with a somewhat less ambitious approach: in return for "cooperation in all respects" for a specified period of time, including progress in the resolution of "key remaining disarmament tasks", it opened the possibility, not for the lifting, but the suspension of sanctions.

For nearly three years, Iraq refused to accept any inspections by UNMOVIC. It was only after appeals by the Secretary-General and Arab States and pressure by the United States and other Member States, that Iraq declared on 16 September last year that it would again accept inspections without conditions.

Resolution 1441 (2002) was adopted on 8 November last year and emphatically reaffirmed the demand on Iraq to cooperate. It required this cooperation to be immediate, unconditional and active. The resolution contained many provisions, which we welcome as enhancing and strengthening the inspection regime. The unanimity by which it was adopted sent a powerful signal that the Council was of one mind in creating a last opportunity for peaceful disarmament in Iraq through inspection. [ . . . ]

I turn now to the key requirement of cooperation and Iraq's response to it. Cooperation might be said to relate to both substance and process. It would appear from our experience so far that Iraq has decided in principle to provide cooperation on process, notably access. A similar decision is indispensable to provide cooperation on substance in order to bring the disarmament task to completion through the peaceful process of inspection and to bring the monitoring task on a firm course. An initial minor step would be to adopt the long-overdue legislation required by the resolutions.

I shall deal first with cooperation on process.

## Cooperation on process

It has regard to the procedures, mechanisms, infrastructure and practical arrangements to pursue inspections and seek verifiable disarmament. While inspection is not built on the premise of confidence but may lead to confidence if it is successful, there must nevertheless be a measure of mutual confidence from the very beginning in running the operation of inspection.

Iraq has on the whole cooperated rather well so far with UNMOVIC in this field. The most important point to make is that access has been provided to all sites we have wanted to inspect and with one exception it has been prompt. We have further had great help in building up the infrastructure of our office in Baghdad and the field office in Mosul. Arrangements and services for our plane and our helicopters have been good. The environment has been workable.

Our inspections have included universities, military bases, presidential sites and private residences. Inspections have also taken place on Fridays, the Muslim day of rest, on Christmas day and New Years day. These inspections have been conducted in the same manner as all other inspections. We seek to be both effective and correct.

In this updating I am bound, however, to register some problems. Firstly, relating to two kinds of air operations.

While we now have the technical capability to send a U–2 plane placed at our disposal for aerial imagery and for surveillance during inspections and have informed Iraq that we planned to do so, Iraq has refused to guarantee its safety, unless a number of conditions are fulfilled. As these conditions went beyond what is stipulated in resolution 1441 (2002) and what was practiced by

UNSCOM and Iraq in the past, we note that Iraq is not so far complying with our request. I hope this attitude will change.

Another air operation problem—which was solved during our recent talks in Baghdad—concerned the use of helicopters flying into the no-fly zones. Iraq had insisted on sending helicopters of their own to accompany ours. This would have raised a safety problem. The matter was solved by an offer on our part to take the accompanying Iraq minders in our helicopters to the sites, an arrangement that had been practiced by UNSCOM in the past.

I am obliged to note some recent disturbing incidents and harassment. For instance, for some time farfetched allegations have been made publicly that questions posed by inspectors were of intelligence character. While I might not defend every question that inspectors might have asked, Iraq knows that they do not serve intelligence purposes and Iraq should not say so.

On a number of occasions, demonstrations have taken place in front of our offices and at inspection sites.

The other day, a sightseeing excursion by five inspectors to a mosque was followed by an unwarranted public outburst. The inspectors went without any UN insignia and were welcomed in the kind manner that is characteristic of the normal Iraqi attitude to foreigners. They took off their shoes and were taken around. They asked perfectly innocent questions and parted with the invitation to come again.

Shortly thereafter, we received protests from the Iraqi authorities about an unannounced inspection and about questions not relevant to weapons of mass destruction. Indeed, they were not. Demonstrations and outbursts of this kind are unlikely to occur in Iraq without initiative or encouragement from the authorities. We must ask ourselves what the motives may be for these events. They do not facilitate an already difficult job, in which we try to be effective, professional and, at the same time, correct. Where our Iraqi counterparts have some complaint they can take it up in a calmer and less unpleasant manner.

## Cooperation on substance

The substantive cooperation required relates above all to the obligation of Iraq to declare all programs of weapons of mass destruction and either to present items and activities for elimination or else to provide evidence supporting the conclusion that nothing proscribed remains.

Paragraph 9 of resolution 1441 (2002) states that this cooperation shall be "active". It is not enough to open doors. Inspection is not a game of "catch as catch can". Rather, as I noted, it is a process of verification for the purpose of creating confidence. It is not built upon the premise of trust. Rather, it is designed to lead to trust, if there is both openness to the inspectors and action to present them with items to destroy or credible evidence about the absence of any such items.

## The declaration of 7 December

On 7 December 2002, Iraq submitted a declaration of some 12,000 pages in response to paragraph 3 of resolution 1441 (2002) and within the time stipulated by the Security Council. In the fields of missiles and biotechnology, the declaration contains a good deal of new material and information covering the period from 1998 and onward. This is welcome.

One might have expected that in preparing the Declaration, Iraq would have tried to respond to, clarify and submit supporting evidence regarding the many open disarmament issues, which the Iraqi side should be familiar with. . . . While UNMOVIC has been preparing its own list of current "unresolved disarmament issues" and "key remaining disarmament tasks" in response to requirements in resolution 1284 (1999), we find the issues listed in the two reports as unresolved, professionally justified. These reports do not contend that weapons of mass destruction remain in Iraq, but nor do they exclude that possibility. They point to lack of evidence and inconsistencies, which raise question marks, which must be straightened out, if weapons dossiers are to be closed and confidence is to arise.

They deserve to be taken seriously by Iraq rather than being brushed aside as evil machinations of UNSCOM. Regrettably, the 12,000 page declaration, most of which is a reprint of earlier documents, does not seem to contain any new evidence that would eliminate the questions or reduce their number. Even Iraq's letter sent in response to our recent discussions in Baghdad to the President of the Security Council on 24 January does not lead us to the resolution of these issues.

I shall only give some examples of issues and questions that need to be answered and I turn first to the sector of chemical weapons.

# Chemical weapons

The nerve agent VX is one of the most toxic ever developed.

Iraq has declared that it only produced VX on a pilot scale, just a few [metric] tons and that the quality was poor and the product unstable. Consequently, it was said, that the agent was never weaponized. Iraq said that the small quantity of agent remaining after the Gulf War was unilaterally destroyed in the summer of 1991.

UNMOVIC, however, has information that conflicts with this account. There are indications that Iraq had worked on the problem of purity and stabilization and that more had been achieved than has been declared. Indeed, even one of the documents provided by Iraq indicates that the purity of the agent, at least in laboratory production, was higher than declared.

There are also indications that the agent was weaponized. In addition, there are questions to be answered concerning the fate of the VX precursor chemicals, which Iraq states were lost during bombing in the Gulf War or were unilaterally destroyed by Iraq.

I would now like to turn to the so-called "Air Force document" that I have discussed with the Council before. This document was originally found by an UNSCOM inspector in a safe in Iraqi Air Force Headquarters in 1998 and taken from her by Iraqi minders. It gives an account of the expenditure of bombs, including chemical bombs, by Iraq in the Iraq-Iran War. I am encouraged by the fact that Iraq has now provided this document to UNMOVIC.

The document indicates that 13,000 chemical bombs were dropped by the Iraqi Air Force between 1983 and 1988, while Iraq has declared that 19,500 bombs were consumed during this period. Thus, there is a discrepancy of 6,500 bombs. The amount of chemical agent in these bombs would be in the order of about

1,000 [metric] tons. In the absence of evidence to the contrary, we must assume that these quantities are now unaccounted for.

The discovery of a number of 122 mm chemical rocket warheads in a bunker at a storage depot 170 km southwest of Baghdad was much publicized. This was a relatively new bunker and therefore the rockets must have been moved there in the past few years, at a time when Iraq should not have had such munitions.

The investigation of these rockets is still proceeding. Iraq states that they were overlooked from 1991 from a batch of some 2,000 that were stored there during the Gulf War. This could be the case. They could also be the tip of a submerged iceberg. The discovery of a few rockets does not resolve but rather points to the issue of several thousands of chemical rockets that are unaccounted for.

The finding of the rockets shows that Iraq needs to make more effort to ensure that its declaration is currently accurate. During my recent discussions in Baghdad, Iraq declared that it would make new efforts in this regard and had set up a committee of investigation. Since then it has reported that it has found a further 4 chemical rockets at a storage depot in Al Taji.

I might further mention that inspectors have found at another site a laboratory quantity of thiodiglycol, a mustard gas precursor.

Whilst I am addressing chemical issues, I should mention a matter, which I reported on 19 December 2002, concerning equipment at a civilian chemical plant at Al Fallujah. Iraq has declared that it had repaired chemical processing equipment previously destroyed under UNSCOM supervision, and had installed it at Fallujah for the production of chlorine and phenols. We have inspected this equipment and are conducting a detailed technical evaluation of it. On completion, we will decide whether this and other equipment that has been recovered by Iraq should be destroyed.

## Biological weapons

I have mentioned the issue of anthrax to the Council on previous occasions and I come back to it as it is an important one.

Iraq has declared that it produced about 8,500 liters of this biological warfare agent, which it states it unilaterally destroyed in the summer of 1991. Iraq has provided little evidence for this production and no convincing evidence for its destruction.

There are strong indications that Iraq produced more anthrax than it declared, and that at least some of this was retained after the declared destruction date. It might still exist. Either it should be found and be destroyed under UNMOVIC supervision or else convincing evidence should be produced to show that it was, indeed, destroyed in 1991.

As I reported to the Council on 19 December last year, Iraq did not declare a significant quantity, some 650 kg, of bacterial growth media, which was acknowledged as imported in Iraq's submission to the Amorim panel in February 1999. As part of its 7 December 2002 declaration, Iraq resubmitted the Amorim panel document, but the table showing this particular import of media was not included. The absence of this table would appear to be deliberate as the pages of the resubmitted document were renumbered.

In the letter of 24 January to the President of the Council, Iraq's Foreign Minister stated that "all imported quantities of growth media were declared". This is not evidence. I note that the quantity of media involved would suffice to produce, for example, about 5,000 liters of concentrated anthrax.

# Missiles

I turn now to the missile sector. There remain significant questions as to whether Iraq retained SCUD-type missiles after the Gulf War. Iraq declared the consumption of a number of SCUD missiles as targets in the development of an anti-ballistic missile defense system during the 1980s. Yet no technical information has been produced about that program or data on the consumption of the missiles.

There has been a range of developments in the missile field during the past four years presented by Iraq as non-proscribed activities. We are trying to gather a clear understanding of them through inspections and on-site discussions.

Two projects in particular stand out. They are the development of a liquid-fueled missile named the Al Samoud 2, and a solid propellant missile, called the Al Fatah. Both missiles have been tested to a range in excess of the permitted range of 150 km, with the Al Samoud 2 being tested to a maximum of 183 km and the Al Fatah to 161 km. Some of both types of missiles have already been provided to the Iraqi Armed Forces even though it is stated that they are still undergoing development.

The Al Samoud's diameter was increased from an earlier version to the present 760 mm. This modification was made despite a 1994 letter from the Executive Chairman of UNSCOM directing Iraq to limit its missile diameters to less than 600 mm. Furthermore, a November 1997 letter from the Executive Chairman of UNSCOM to Iraq prohibited the use of engines from certain surface-to-air missiles for the use in ballistic missiles.

During my recent meeting in Baghdad, we were briefed on these two programs. We were told that the final range for both systems would be less than the permitted maximum range of 150 km.

These missiles might well represent *prima facie* cases of proscribed systems. The test ranges in excess of 150 km are significant, but some further technical considerations need to be made, before we reach a conclusion on this issue. In the mean time, we have asked Iraq to cease flight tests of both missiles.

In addition, Iraq has refurbished its missile production infrastructure. In particular, Iraq reconstituted a number of casting chambers, which had previously been destroyed under UNSCOM supervision. They had been used in the production of solid-fuel missiles. Whatever missile system these chambers are intended for, they could produce motors for missiles capable of ranges significantly greater than 150 km.

Also associated with these missiles and related developments is the import, which has been taking place during the last few years, of a number of items despite the sanctions, including as late as December 2002. Foremost amongst these is the import of 380 rocket engines which may be used for the Al Samoud 2.

Iraq also declared the recent import of chemicals used in propellants, test instrumentation and, guidance and control systems. These items may well be for proscribed purposes. That is yet to be determined. What is clear is that they were illegally brought into Iraq, that is, Iraq or some company in Iraq, circumvented the restrictions imposed by various resolutions.

Mr. President, I have touched upon some of the disarmament issues that remain open and that need to be answered if dossiers are to be closed and confidence is to arise. Which are the means at the disposal of Iraq to answer these questions? I have pointed to some during my presentation of the issues. Let me be a little more systematic. Our Iraqi counterparts are fond of saying that there are no proscribed items and if no evidence is presented to the contrary they should have the benefit of the doubt, be presumed innocent. UNMOVIC, for its part, is not presuming that there are proscribed items and activities in Iraq, but nor is it—or I think anyone else after the inspections between 1991 and 1998—presuming the opposite, that no such items and activities exist in Iraq. Presumptions do not solve the problem. Evidence and full transparency may help. Let me be specific.

# Find the items and activities

Information provided by Member States tells us about the movement and concealment of missiles and chemical weapons and mobile units for biological weapons production. We shall certainly follow up any credible leads given to us and report what we might find as well as any denial of access.

So far we have reported on the recent find of a small number of empty 122 mm warheads for chemical weapons. Iraq declared that it appointed a commission of inquiry to look for more. Fine. Why not extend the search to other items? Declare what may be found and destroy it under our supervision?

# Find documents

When we have urged our Iraqi counterparts to present more evidence, we have all too often met the response that there are no more documents. All existing relevant documents have been presented, we are told. All documents relating to the biological weapons program were destroyed together with the weapons.

However, Iraq has all the archives of the Government and its various departments, institutions and mechanisms. It should have budgetary documents, requests for funds and reports on how they have been used. It should also have letters of credit and bills of lading, reports on production and losses of material.

In response to a recent UNMOVIC request for a number of specific documents, the only new documents Iraq provided was a ledger of 193 pages which Iraq stated included all imports from 1983 to 1990 by the Technical and Scientific Importation Division, the importing authority for the biological weapons program. Potentially, it might help to clear some open issues.

The recent inspection find in the private home of a scientist of a box of some 3,000 pages of documents, much of it relating to the laser enrichment of uranium, support a concern that has long existed that documents might be distributed to the homes of private individuals. This interpretation is refuted by the Iraqi side, which claims that research staff sometimes may bring home papers from their work places. On our side, we cannot help but think that the case might not be isolated and that such placements of documents is deliberate to make discovery difficult and to seek to shield documents by placing them in private homes.

Any further sign of the concealment of documents would be serious. The Iraqi side committed itself at our recent talks to encourage persons to accept access also to private sites. There can be no sanctuaries for proscribed items, activities or documents. A denial of prompt access to any site would be a very serious matter.

# Find persons to give credible information: a list of personnel

When Iraq claims that tangible evidence in the form of documents is not available, it ought at least to find individuals, engineers, scientists and managers to testify about their experience. Large weapons programs are moved and managed by people. Interviews with individuals who may have worked in programs in the past may fill blank spots in our knowledge and understanding. It could also be useful to learn that they are now employed in peaceful sectors. These were the reasons why UNMOVIC asked for a list of such persons, in accordance with resolution 1441.

Some 400 names for all biological and chemical weapons programs as well as their missile programs were provided by the Iraqi side. This can be compared to over 3,500 names of people associated with those past weapons programs that UNSCOM either interviewed in the 1990s or knew from documents and other sources. At my recent meeting in Baghdad, the Iraqi side committed itself to supplementing the list and some 80 additional names have been provided.

## Allow information through credible interviews

In the past, much valuable information came from interviews. There were also cases in which the interviewee was clearly intimidated by the presence of and interruption by Iraqi officials. This was the background of resolution 1441's provision for a right for UNMOVIC and the IAEA to hold private interviews "in the mode or location" of our choice, in Baghdad or even abroad.

To date, 11 individuals were asked for interviews in Baghdad by us. The replies have invariably been that the individual will only speak at Iraq's monitoring directorate or, at any rate, in the presence of an Iraqi official. This could be due to a wish on the part of the invited to have evidence that they have not said anything that the authorities did not wish them to say. At our recent talks in Baghdad, the Iraqi side committed itself to encourage persons to accept interviews "in private", that is to say alone with us. Despite this, the pattern has not changed. However, we hope that with further encouragement from the authorities, knowledgeable individuals will accept private interviews, in Baghdad or abroad. [ . . . ]

# Excerpt from President George W. Bush's
# State of the Union Address

•

# January 28, 2003

[. . .]

Today, the gravest danger in the war on terror, the gravest danger facing America and the world, is outlaw regimes that seek and possess nuclear, chemical, and biological weapons. These regimes could use such weapons for blackmail, terror, and mass murder. They could also give or sell those weapons to terrorist allies, who would use them without the least hesitation.

This threat is new; America's duty is familiar. Throughout the 20th century, small groups of men seized control of great nations, built armies and arsenals, and set out to dominate the weak and intimidate the world. In each case, their ambitions of cruelty and murder had no limit. In each case, the ambitions of Hitlerism, militarism, and communism were defeated by the will of free peoples, by the strength of great alliances, and by the might of the United States of America. (Applause.)

Now, in this century, the ideology of power and domination has appeared again, and seeks to gain the ultimate weapons of terror. Once again, this nation and all our friends are all that stand between a world at peace, and a world of chaos and constant alarm. Once again, we are called to defend the safety of our people, and the hopes of all mankind. And we accept this responsibility. (Applause.)

America is making a broad and determined effort to confront these dangers. We have called on the United Nations to fulfill its charter and stand by its demand that Iraq disarm. We're strongly supporting the International Atomic Energy Agency in its mission to track and control nuclear materials around the world. We're working with other governments to secure nuclear materials in the former Soviet Union, and to strengthen global treaties banning the production and shipment of missile technologies and weapons of mass destruction.

In all these efforts, however, America's purpose is more than to follow a process—it is to achieve a result: the end of terrible threats to the civilized world. All free nations have a stake in preventing sudden and catastrophic attacks. And we're asking them to join us, and many are doing so. Yet the course of this nation does not depend on the decisions of others. (Applause.) Whatever action is required, whenever action is necessary, I will defend the freedom and security of the American people. (Applause.)

Different threats require different strategies. In Iran, we continue to see a government that represses its people, pursues weapons of mass destruction, and supports terror. We also see Iranian citizens risking intimidation and death as they speak out for liberty and human rights and democracy. Iranians, like all people, have a right to choose their own government and determine their own destiny—and the United States supports their aspirations to live in freedom. (Applause.)

On the Korean Peninsula, an oppressive regime rules a people living in fear and starvation. Throughout the 1990s, the United States relied on a negotiated framework to keep North Korea from gaining nuclear weapons. We now know that that regime was deceiving the world, and developing those weapons all along. And today the North Korean regime is using its nuclear program to incite fear and seek concessions. America and the world will not be blackmailed. (Applause.)

America is working with the countries of the region—South Korea, Japan, China, and Russia—to find a peaceful solution, and to show the North Korean government that nuclear weapons will bring only isolation, economic stagnation, and continued hardship. (Applause.) The North Korean regime will find respect in the world and revival for its people only when it turns away from its nuclear ambitions. (Applause.)

Our nation and the world must learn the lessons of the Korean Peninsula and not allow an even greater threat to rise up in Iraq. A brutal dictator, with a history of reckless aggression, with ties to terrorism, with great potential wealth, will not be permitted to dominate a vital region and threaten the United States. (Applause.)

Twelve years ago, Saddam Hussein faced the prospect of being the last casualty in a war he had started and lost. To spare himself, he agreed to disarm of all weapons of mass destruction. For the next 12 years, he systematically violated that agreement. He pursued chemical, biological, and nuclear weapons, even while inspectors were in his country. Nothing to date has restrained him from his pursuit of these weapons—not economic sanctions, not isolation from the civilized world, not even cruise missile strikes on his military facilities.

Almost three months ago, the United Nations Security Council gave Saddam Hussein his final chance to disarm. He has shown instead utter contempt for the United Nations, and for the opinion of the world. The 108 U.N. inspectors were sent to conduct—were not sent to conduct a scavenger hunt for hidden materials across a country the size of California. The job of the inspectors is to verify that Iraq's regime is disarming. It is up to Iraq to show exactly where it is hiding its banned weapons, lay those weapons out for the world to see, and destroy them as directed. Nothing like this has happened.

The United Nations concluded in 1999 that Saddam Hussein had biological weapons sufficient to produce over 25,000 liters of anthrax—enough doses to kill several million people. He hasn't accounted for that material. He's given no evidence that he has destroyed it.

The United Nations concluded that Saddam Hussein had materials sufficient to produce more than 38,000 liters of botulinum toxin—enough to subject millions of people to death by respiratory failure. He hadn't accounted for that material. He's given no evidence that he has destroyed it.

Our intelligence officials estimate that Saddam Hussein had the materials to produce as much as 500 tons of sarin, mustard and VX nerve agent. In such quantities, these chemical agents could also kill untold thousands. He's not accounted for these materials. He has given no evidence that he has destroyed them.

U.S. intelligence indicates that Saddam Hussein had upwards of 30,000 munitions capable of delivering chemical agents. Inspectors recently turned up 16 of them—despite Iraq's recent declaration denying their existence. Saddam Hussein has not accounted for the remaining 29,984 of these prohibited munitions. He's given no evidence that he has destroyed them.

From three Iraqi defectors we know that Iraq, in the late 1990s, had several mobile biological weapons labs. These are designed to produce germ warfare agents, and can be moved from place to a place to evade inspectors. Saddam Hussein has not disclosed these facilities. He's given no evidence that he has destroyed them.

The International Atomic Energy Agency confirmed in the 1990s that Saddam Hussein had an advanced nuclear weapons development program, had a design for a nuclear weapon and was working on five different methods of enriching uranium for a bomb. The British government has learned that Saddam Hussein recently sought significant quantities of uranium from Africa. Our intelligence sources tell us that he has attempted to purchase high-strength aluminum tubes suitable for nuclear weapons production. Saddam Hussein has not credibly explained these activities. He clearly has much to hide.

The dictator of Iraq is not disarming. To the contrary; he is deceiving. From intelligence sources we know, for instance, that thousands of Iraqi security personnel are at work hiding documents and materials from the U.N. inspectors, sanitizing inspection sites and monitoring the inspectors themselves. Iraqi officials accompany the inspectors in order to intimidate witnesses.

Iraq is blocking U–2 surveillance flights requested by the United Nations. Iraqi intelligence officers are posing as the scientists inspectors are supposed to interview. Real scientists have been coached by Iraqi officials on what to say. Intelligence sources indicate that Saddam Hussein has ordered that scientists who cooperate with U.N. inspectors in disarming Iraq will be killed, along with their families.

Year after year, Saddam Hussein has gone to elaborate lengths, spent enormous sums, taken great risks to build and keep weapons of mass destruction. But why? The only possible explanation, the only possible use he could have for those weapons, is to dominate, intimidate, or attack.

With nuclear arms or a full arsenal of chemical and biological weapons, Saddam Hussein could resume his ambitions of conquest in the Middle East and create deadly havoc in that region. And this Congress and the America people must recognize another threat. Evidence from intelligence sources, secret communications, and statements by people now in custody reveal that Saddam Hussein aids and protects terrorists, including members of al Qaeda. Secretly, and without fingerprints, he could provide one of his hidden weapons to terrorists, or help them develop their own.

Before September the 11th, many in the world believed that Saddam Hussein could be contained. But chemical agents, lethal viruses and shadowy terrorist networks are not easily contained. Imagine those 19 hijackers with other weapons and other plans—this time armed by Saddam Hussein. It would take one vial, one canister, one crate slipped into this country to bring a day of horror like none we have ever known. We will do everything in our power to make sure that that day never comes. (Applause.)

Some have said we must not act until the threat is imminent. Since when have terrorists and tyrants announced their intentions, politely putting us on notice before they strike? If this threat is permitted to fully and suddenly emerge, all actions, all words, and all recriminations would come too late. Trusting in the sanity and restraint of Saddam Hussein is not a strategy, and it is not an option. (Applause.)

The dictator who is assembling the world's most dangerous weapons has already used them on whole villages—leaving thousands of his own citizens dead, blind, or disfigured. Iraqi refugees tell us how forced confessions are obtained—by torturing children while their parents are made to watch. International human rights groups have catalogued other methods used in the torture chambers of Iraq: electric shock, burning with hot irons, dripping acid on the skin, mutilation with electric drills, cutting out tongues, and rape. If this is not evil, then evil has no meaning. (Applause.)

And tonight I have a message for the brave and oppressed people of Iraq: Your enemy is not surrounding your country—your enemy is ruling your country. (Applause.) And the day he and his regime are removed from power will be the day of your liberation. (Applause.)

The world has waited 12 years for Iraq to disarm. America will not accept a serious and mounting threat to our country, and our friends and our allies. The United States will ask the U.N. Security Council to convene on February the 5th to consider the facts of Iraq's ongoing defiance of the world. Secretary of State Powell will present information and intelligence about Iraqi's legal— Iraq's illegal weapons programs, its attempt to hide those weapons from inspectors, and its links to terrorist groups.

We will consult. But let there be no misunderstanding: If Saddam Hussein does not fully disarm, for the safety of our people and for the peace of the world, we will lead a coalition to disarm him. (Applause.)

Tonight I have a message for the men and women who will keep the peace, members of the American Armed Forces: Many of you are assembling in or near the Middle East, and some crucial hours may lay ahead. In those hours, the success of our cause will depend on you. Your training has prepared you. Your honor will guide you. You believe in America, and America believes in you. (Applause.)

Sending Americans into battle is the most profound decision a President can make. The technologies of war have changed; the risks and suffering of war have not. For the brave Americans who bear the risk, no victory is free from sorrow. This nation fights reluctantly, because we know the cost and we dread the days of mourning that always come.

We seek peace. We strive for peace. And sometimes peace must be defended. A future lived at the mercy of terrible threats is no peace at all. If war is forced upon us, we will fight in a just cause and by just means—sparing, in every way we can, the innocent. And if war is forced upon us, we will fight with the full force and might of the United States military—and we will prevail. (Applause.)

And as we and our coalition partners are doing in Afghanistan, we will bring to the Iraqi people food and medicines and supplies—and freedom. (Applause.)

Many challenges, abroad and at home, have arrived in a single season. In two years, America has gone from a sense of invulnerability to an awareness of peril; from bitter division in small matters to calm unity in great causes. And we go forward with confidence, because this call of history has come to the right country.

Americans are a resolute people who have risen to every test of our time. Adversity has revealed the character of our country, to the world and to ourselves. America is a strong nation, and honorable in the use of our strength. We exercise power without conquest, and we sacrifice for the liberty of strangers.

Americans are a free people, who know that freedom is the right of every person and the future of every nation. The liberty we prize is not America's gift to the world, it is God's gift to humanity. (Applause.)

We Americans have faith in ourselves, but not in ourselves alone. We do not know—we do not claim to know all the ways of Providence, yet we can trust in them, placing our confidence in the loving God behind all of life, and all of history.

May He guide us now. And may God continue to bless the United States of America. (Applause.)

# Secretary of State Colin L. Powell's Speech to the U.N. Security Council

•

# February 5, 2003

Mr. President, Mr. Secretary General, distinguished colleagues, I would like to begin by expressing my thanks for the special effort that each of you made to be here today. This is an important day for us all as we review the situation with respect to Iraq and its disarmament obligations under U.N. Security Council Resolution 1441.

Last Nov. 8, this Council passed Resolution 1441 by a unanimous vote. The purpose of that resolution was to disarm Iraq of its weapons of mass destruction. Iraq had already been found guilty of material breach of its obligations stretching back over 16 previous resolutions and 12 years.

Resolution 1441 was not dealing with an innocent party, but a regime this Council has repeatedly convicted over the years. Resolution 1441 gave Iraq one last chance, one last chance, to come into compliance or to face serious consequences.

No Council member present in voting on that day had any illusions about the nature and intent of the resolution or what serious consequences meant if Iraq did not comply. And to assist in its disarmament, we called on Iraq to cooperate with returning inspectors from UNMOVIC and IAEA. We laid down tough standards for Iraq to meet to allow the inspectors to do their job. This Council placed the burden on Iraq to comply and disarm and not on the inspectors to find that which Iraq has gone out of its way to conceal for so long. Inspectors are inspectors; they are not detectives.

I asked for this session today for two purposes: first, to support the core assessments made by Dr. Blix and Dr. ElBaradei. As Dr. Blix reported to this Council on Jan. 27, "Iraq appears not to have come to a genuine acceptance, not even today, of the disarmament which was demanded of it." And as Dr. ElBaradei reported, Iraq's declaration of Dec. 7 "did not provide any new information relevant to certain questions that have been outstanding since 1998."

My second purpose today is to provide you with additional information, to share with you what the United States knows about Iraq's weapons of mass destruction as well as Iraq's involvement in terrorism, which is also the subject of Resolution 1441 and other, earlier, resolutions.

I might add at this point that we are providing all relevant information we can to the inspection teams for them to do their work. The material I will present to you comes from a variety of sources. Some are U.S. sources, and some are those of other countries. Some of the sources are technical, such as intercepted telephone conversations and photos taken by satellites. Other sources are people who have risked their lives to let the world know what Saddam Hussein is really up to.

I cannot tell you everything that we know, but what I can share with you, when combined with what all of us have learned over the years, is deeply troubling. What you will see is an accumulation of facts and disturbing patterns of behavior. The facts and Iraq's behavior demonstrate that Saddam Hussein and his regime have made no effort, no effort, to disarm as required by the international community. Indeed, the facts and Iraq's behavior show that Saddam Hussein and his regime are concealing their efforts to produce more weapons of mass destruction.

Let me begin by playing a tape for you. What you're about to hear is a conversation that my government monitored. It takes place on Nov. 26 of last year, on the day before United Nations teams resumed inspections in Iraq. The conversation involves two senior officers: a colonel and a brigadier general from Iraq's elite military unit, the Republican Guard.

[Transcript of audiotape in Arabic, as translated by the State Department.]

COLONEL—Peace. We just have a small question.
GENERAL—Yeah.
COLONEL—About this committee that is coming—
GENERAL—Yeah, yeah.
COLONEL—with Mohamed ElBaradei.

GENERAL—Yeah, yeah.
COLONEL—Yeah.
GENERAL—Yeah?
COLONEL—We have this modified vehicle.
GENERAL—Yeah.
COLONEL—What do we say if one of them sees it?
GENERAL—You didn't get a modified—you don't have a modi-
   fied—
COLONEL—By God, I have one.
GENERAL—Which? From the workshop?
COLONEL—From the Al Kindi Company.
GENERAL—What?
COLONEL—From Al Kindi.
GENERAL—Yeah, yeah. I'll come to you in the morning. I have
   some comments. I'm worried you all have something left.
COLONEL—We evacuated everything. We don't have anything
   left.
GENERAL—I will come to you tomorrow.
COLONEL—O.K.

Let me pause and review some of the key elements of this conversation that you've just heard between these two officers.

First, they acknowledge that our colleague, Mohamed ElBaradei, is coming. And they know what he's coming for. And they
know he's coming the next day. He's coming to look for things
that are prohibited. He is expecting these gentlemen to cooperate
with him and not hide things.

But they're worried: We have this modified vehicle. What do
we say if one of them sees it? What is their concern? Their concern is that it's something they should not have, something that
should not be seen.

The general is incredulous: You didn't get a modified—you
don't have one of those, do you?

I have one.

Which? From where?

From the workshop. From the Al Kindi Company.

What?

From Al Kindi.

I'll come to see you in the morning. I'm worried you all have something left.

We evacuated everything. We don't have anything left.

Note what he says: We evacuated everything. We didn't destroy it. We didn't line it up for inspection. We didn't turn it in to the inspectors. We evacuated it to make sure it was not around when the inspectors showed up. I will come to you tomorrow.

The Al Kindi Company—this is a company that is well known to have been involved in prohibited weapons systems activity.

Let me play another tape for you. As you will recall, the inspectors found 12 empty chemical warheads on Jan. 16. On Jan. 20, four days later, Iraq promised the inspectors it would search for more. You will now hear an officer from Republican Guard headquarters issuing an instruction to an officer in the field. Their conversation took place just last week, on Jan. 30.

HEADQUARTERS—Sir.
FIELD—Yes.
H.Q.—There is a directive of the Guard Chief of Staff at the conference today.
FIELD—Yes.
H.Q.—They are inspecting the ammunition you have—
FIELD—Yes.
H.Q.—for the possibility there are forbidden ammo.
FIELD—Yes?
H.Q.—For the possibility there is, by chance, forbidden ammo.
FIELD—Yes.
H.Q.—And we sent you a message to inspect the scrap areas and the abandoned areas.
FIELD—Yes.
H.Q.—After you have carried out what is contained in the message, destroy the message.
FIELD—Yes.
H.Q.—Because I don't want anyone to see this message.
FIELD—O.K., O.K.

Let me pause again and review the elements of this message. They are inspecting the ammunition you have.

Yes, yes.

For the possibility there are forbidden ammo.

For the possibility there is by chance forbidden ammo?

Yes. And we sent you a message yesterday to clean out all of the areas, the scrap areas, the abandoned areas. Make sure there is nothing there.

Remember the first message: evacuate it. This is all part of a system of hiding things and moving things out of the way and making sure they have left nothing behind.

You go a little further into this message and you see the specific instructions from headquarters: After you have carried out what is contained in this message, destroy the message because I don't want anyone to see this message. O.K., O.K.

Why? Why? This message would have verified to the inspectors that they have been trying to turn over things; they were looking for things. But they don't want that message seen because they were trying to clean up the area, to leave no evidence behind of the presence of weapons of mass destruction. And they can claim that nothing was there and the inspectors can look all they want and they will find nothing.

This effort to hide things from the inspectors is not one or two isolated events.

Quite the contrary. This is part and parcel of a policy of evasion and deception that goes back 12 years, a policy set at the highest levels of the Iraqi regime.

We know that Saddam Hussein has what is called, "a higher committee for monitoring the inspection teams."

Think about that. Iraq has a high-level committee to monitor the inspectors who were sent in to monitor Iraq's disarmament. Not to cooperate with them; not to assist them, but to spy on them and to keep them from doing their jobs.

The committee reports directly to Saddam Hussein. It is headed by Iraq's vice president, Taha Yassin Ramadan. Its members include Saddam Hussein's son, Qusay. This committee also includes Lt. Gen. Amir al-Saadi, an adviser to Saddam. In case that name isn't immediately familiar to you, General Saadi has been the Iraqi regime's primary point of contact for Dr. Blix and Dr. ElBaradei.

It was General Saadi who last fall publicly pledged that Iraq was prepared to cooperate unconditionally with inspectors. Quite the contrary, Saadi's job is not to cooperate, it is to deceive; not to disarm, but to undermine the inspectors; not to support them, but to frustrate them and to make sure they learn nothing.

We have learned a lot about the work of this special committee. We learned that just prior to the return of inspectors last November, the regime had decided to resume what we heard called, "the old game of cat and mouse."

For example, let me focus on the now-famous declaration that Iraq submitted to this Council on Dec. 7. Iraq never had any intention of complying with this Council's mandate. Instead, Iraq planned to use the declaration to overwhelm us and overwhelm the inspectors with useless information about Iraq's permitted weapons so that we would not have time to pursue Iraq's prohibited weapons.

Iraq's goal was to give us in this room, to give those of us on this Council, the false impression that the inspection process was working. You saw the result. Dr. Blix pronounced the 12,200-page declaration rich in volume but poor in information and practically devoid of new evidence. Could any member of this Council honestly rise in defense of this false declaration?

Everything we have seen and heard indicates that, instead of cooperating actively with the inspectors to insure the success of their mission, Saddam Hussein and his regime are busy doing all they possibly can to ensure that inspectors succeed in finding absolutely nothing.

My colleagues, every statement I make today is backed up by sources, solid sources. These are not assertions. What we're giving you are facts and conclusions based on solid intelligence. I will cite some examples and these are from human sources.

Orders were issued to Iraq's security organizations as well as to Saddam Hussein's own office to hide all correspondence with the Organization of Military Industrialization. This is the organization that oversees Iraq's weapons of mass destruction activities. Make sure there are no documents left which would connect you to the O.M.I.

We know that Saddam's son Qusay ordered the removal of all

prohibited weapons from Saddam's numerous palace complexes. We know that Iraqi government officials, members of the ruling Baath Party, and scientists have hidden prohibited items in their homes. Other key files from military and scientific establishments have been placed in cars that are being driven around the countryside by Iraqi intelligence agents to avoid detection.

Thanks to intelligence they were provided, the inspectors recently found dramatic confirmation of these reports. When they searched the home of an Iraqi nuclear scientist, they uncovered roughly 2,000 pages of documents. You see them here being brought out of the home and placed in U.N. hands. Some of the material is classified and related to Iraq's nuclear program.

Tell me, answer me, are the inspectors to search the house of every government official, every Baath Party member and every scientist in the country to find the truth, to get the information they need to satisfy the demands of our Council?

Our sources tell us that in some cases the hard drives of computers at Iraqi weapons facilities were replaced. Who took the hard drives? Where did they go? What's being hidden? Why?

There's only one answer to the why: to deceive, to hide, to keep from the inspectors. Numerous human sources tell us that the Iraqis are moving not just documents and hard drives but weapons of mass destruction to keep them from being found by inspectors.

While we were here in this Council chamber debating Resolution 1441 last fall, we know—we know from sources that a missile brigade outside Baghdad was dispersing rocket launchers and warheads containing biological warfare agent to various locations, distributing them to various locations in western Iraq. Most of the launches and warheads had been hidden in large groves of palm trees and were to be moved every one to four weeks to escape detection.

We also have satellite photos that indicate that banned materials have recently been moved from a number of Iraqi weapons of mass destruction facilities.

Let me say a word about satellite images before I show a couple. The photos that I am about to show you are sometimes hard for the average person to interpret, hard for me. The painstaking work of photo analysis takes experts with years and years of experience poring for hours and hours over light tables. But as I show you these images, I will try to capture and explain what they mean, what they indicate to our imagery specialists.

Let's look at one. This one is about a weapons munitions facility, a facility that holds ammunition at a place called Taji. This is one of about 65 such facilities in Iraq. We know that this one has housed chemical munitions. In fact, this is where the Iraqis recently came up with the additional four chemical weapons shells.

Here you see 15 munitions bunkers in yellow and red outlines. The four that are in red squares represent active chemical munitions bunkers. How do I know that? How can I say that? Let me give you a closer look. Look at the image on the left. On the left is a close-up of one of the four chemical bunkers. The two arrows indicate the presence of sure signs that the bunkers are storing chemical munitions. The arrow at the top that says security points to a facility that is a signature item for this kind of bunker. Inside that facility are special guards and special equipment to monitor any leakage that might come out of the bunker. The truck you also see is a signature item. It's a decontamination vehicle in case something goes wrong. This is characteristic of those four bunkers. The special security facility and the decontamination vehicle will be in the area if not at any one of them or one or the other it is moving around those four. And it moves as it is needed to move as people are working in the different bunkers.

Now look at the picture on the right. You are now looking at two of those sanitized bunkers. The signature vehicles are gone. The tents are gone. It's been cleaned up. And it was done on the 22nd of December as the U.N. inspection team is arriving. And you can see the inspection vehicles arriving in the lower portion of the picture on the right. The bunkers are clean when the inspectors get there. They found nothing.

This sequence of events raises the worrisome suspicion that Iraq had been tipped off to the forthcoming inspections at Taji. As it did throughout the 1990's, we know that Iraq today is actively using its considerable intelligence capabilities to hid its illicit activities. From our sources, we know that inspectors are under constant surveillance by an army of Iraqi intelligence operatives. Iraq is relentlessly attempting to tap all of their communications, both voice and electronics. I would call my colleagues attention to the fine paper that the United Kingdom distributed yesterday, which describes in exquisite detail Iraqi deception activities.

In this next example you will see the type of concealment activity Iraq has undertaken in response to the resumption of inspections. Indeed, in November 2002, just when the inspections were about to resume, this type of activity spiked. Here are three examples:

At this ballistic missile site on Nov. 10, we saw a cargo truck preparing to move ballistic missile components.

At this biological weapons related facility on Nov. 25, just two days before inspections resumed, this truck caravan appeared, something we almost never see at this facility. And we monitor it carefully and regularly.

At this ballistic missile facility, again, two days before inspections began, five large cargo trucks appeared along with a truck-mounted crane to move missiles.

We saw this kind of housecleaning at close to 30 sites. Days after this activity, the vehicles and the equipment that I've just highlighted disappear and the site returns to patterns of normalcy. We don't know precisely what Iraq was moving, but the inspectors already knew about these sites. So Iraq knew that they would be coming.

We must ask ourselves, why would Iraq suddenly move equipment of this nature before inspections if they were anxious to demonstrate what they had or did not have? Remember the first intercept in which two Iraqis talked about the need to hide a modified vehicle from the inspectors. Where did Iraq take all of this equipment? Why wasn't it presented to the inspectors?

Iraq also has refused to permit any U–2 recognizance flights that would give the inspectors a better sense of what's being moved before, during and after inspections. This refusal to allow this kind of recognizance is in direct specific violation of operative Paragraph 7 of our Resolution 1441.

Saddam Hussein and his regime are not just trying to conceal weapons, they're also trying to hide people. You know the basic facts. Iraq has not complied with its obligation to allow immediate unimpeded, unrestricted and private access to all officials and other persons as required by Resolution 1441.

The regime only allows interviews with inspectors in the presence of an Iraqi official, a minder. The official Iraqi organization charged with facilitating inspections announced—announced publicly and announced ominously that, "Nobody is ready to leave Iraq to be interviewed."

Iraqi Vice President Ramadan accused the inspectors of conducting espionage, a veiled threat that anyone cooperating with U.N. inspectors was committing treason.

Iraq did not meet its obligations under 1441 to provide a comprehensive list of scientists associated with his weapons of mass destruction programs. Iraq's list was out of date. It contained only about 500 names, despite the fact that UNSCOM had earlier put together a list of about 3,500 names.

Let me just tell you what a number of human sources have told us. Saddam Hussein has directly participated in the effort to prevent interviews. In early December, Saddam Hussein had all Iraqi scientists warned of the serious consequences that they and their families would face if they revealed any sensitive information to the inspectors. They were forced to sign documents acknowledging that divulging information is punishable by death.

Saddam Hussein also said that scientists should be told not to agree to leave Iraq. Anyone who agreed to be interviewed outside Iraq would be treated as a spy. This violated 1441.

In mid-November just before the inspectors returned, Iraqi experts were ordered to report to the headquarters of the special security organization to receive counterintelligence training. The training focused on evasion methods, interrogation resistance techniques, and how to mislead inspectors.

Ladies and gentlemen, these are not assertions. These are facts corroborated by many sources, some of them sources of the intelligence services of other countries. For example, in mid-December, weapons experts at one facility were replaced by Iraqi intelligence agents who were to deceive inspectors about the work that was being done there. On orders from Saddam Hussein, Iraqi officials issued a false death certificate for one scientist, and he was sent into hiding.

In the middle of January, experts at one facility that was related to weapons of mass destruction, those experts had been ordered to stay home from work to avoid the inspectors. Workers from other Iraqi military facilities not engaged in illicit weapons projects were to replace the workers who had been sent home.

A dozen experts have been placed under house arrest, not in their own houses but as a group at one of Saddam Hussein's guest houses. It goes on and on and on.

As the examples I have just presented show, the information and intelligence we have gathered point to an active and systematic effort on the part of the Iraqi regime to keep key materials and people from the inspectors in direct violation of Resolution 1441. The pattern is not just one of reluctant cooperation, nor is it merely a lack of cooperation. What we see is a deliberate campaign to prevent any meaningful inspection work.

My colleagues, operative Paragraph 4 of U.N. Resolution 1441, which we lingered over so long last fall, clearly states that false statements and omissions in the declaration and a failure by Iraq at any time to comply with and cooperate fully in the implementation of this resolution shall constitute, the facts speak for themselves, shall constitute a further material breach of its obligation.

We wrote it this way to give Iraq an early test—to give Iraq an early test. Would they give an honest declaration? And would they early on indicate a willingness to cooperate with the inspectors? It was designed to be an early test. They failed that test. By this standard, the standard of this operative paragraph, I believe that Iraq is now in further material breach of its obligations.

I believe this conclusion is irrefutable and undeniable. Iraq has now placed itself in danger of the serious consequences called for in U.N. Resolution 1441. And this body places itself in danger of irrelevance if it allows Iraq to continue to defy its will without responding effectively and immediately.

The issue before us is not how much time we are willing to give the inspectors to be frustrated by Iraqi obstruction, but how much longer are we willing to put up with Iraq's noncompliance before we as a Council, we as the United Nations, say enough, enough?

The gravity of this moment is matched by the gravity of the

threat that Iraq's weapons of mass destruction pose to the world. Let me now turn to those deadly weapons programs and describe why they are real and present dangers to the region and to the world.

First, biological weapons. We have talked frequently here about biological weapons. By way of introduction and history, I think there are just three quick points I need to make. First, you will recall that it took UNSCOM four long and frustrating years to pry— to pry an admission out of Iraq that it had biological weapons. Second, when Iraq finally admitted having these weapons in 1995, the quantities were vast.

Less than a teaspoon of dry anthrax, a little bit, about this amount. This is just about the amount of a teaspoon, less than a teaspoon full of dry anthrax in an envelope shut down the United States Senate in the fall of 2001. This forced several hundred people to undergo emergency medical treatment and killed two postal workers, just from an amount just about this quantity that was inside of an envelope. Iraq declared 8,500 liters of anthrax. But UNSCOM estimates that Saddam Hussein could have produced 25,000 liters. If concentrated into this dry form, this amount would be enough to fill tens upon tens upon tens of thousands of teaspoons. And Saddam Hussein has not verifiably accounted for even one teaspoonful of this deadly material.

And that is my third point, and it is key. The Iraqis have never accounted for all of the biological weapons they admitted they had and we know they had. They have never accounted for all the organic material used to make them. And they have not accounted for many of the weapons filled with these agents, such as there are 400 bombs. This is evidence, not conjecture. This is true. This is all well-documented.

Dr. Blix told this Council that Iraq has provided little evidence to verify anthrax production and no convincing evidence of its destruction. It should come as no shock then that since Saddam Hussein forced out the last inspectors in 1998, we have amassed much intelligence indicating that Iraq is continuing to make these weapons.

One of the most worrisome things that emerges from the thick intelligence file we have on Iraq's biological weapons is the existence of mobile production facilities used to make biological agents. Let me take you inside that intelligence file and share with you what we know from eyewitness accounts.

We have firsthand descriptions of biological weapons factories on wheels and on rails. The trucks and train cars are easily moved and are designed to evade detection by inspectors. In a matter of months, they can produce a quantity of biological poison equal to the entire amount that Iraq claimed to have produced in the years prior to the gulf war. Although Iraq's mobile production program began in the mid–1990's, U.N. inspectors at the time only had vague hints of such programs.

Confirmation came later, in the year 2000. The source was an eyewitness, an Iraqi chemical engineer who supervised one of these facilities. He actually was present during biological agent production runs. He was also at the site when an accident occurred in 1998. Twelve technicians died from exposure to biological agents. He reported that when UNSCOM was in country and inspecting, the biological weapons agent production always began on Thursdays at midnight, because Iraq thought UNSCOM would not inspect on the Muslim holy day, Thursday night through Friday. He added that this was important, because the units could not be broken down in the middle of a production run, which had to be completed by Friday evening, before the inspectors might arrive again.

This defector is currently hiding in another country, with the certain knowledge that Saddam Hussein will kill him if he finds him.

His eyewitness account of these mobile production facilities has been corroborated by other sources. A second source, an Iraqi civil engineer in a position to know the details of the program, confirmed the existence of transportable facilities moving on trailers. A third source, also in a position to know, reported in summer 2002 that Iraq had manufactured mobile production systems mounted on road trailer units and on rail cars. Finally, a fourth source, an Iraqi major, who defected, confirmed that Iraq has mobile biological research laboratories, in addition to the production facilities I mentioned earlier.

We have diagrammed what our sources reported about these

mobile facilities. Here you see both truck- and rail-car-mounted mobile factories. The description our sources gave us of the technical features required by such facilities are highly detailed and extremely accurate. As these drawings based on their descriptions show, we know what the fermenters look like. We know what the tanks, pumps, compressors and other parts look like. We know how they fit together, we know how they work, and we know a great deal about the platforms on which they are mounted.

As shown in this diagram, these factories can be concealed easily, either by moving ordinary-looking trucks and rail cars along Iraq's thousands of miles of highway or track, or by parking them in a garage or a warehouse or somewhere in Iraq's extensive system of underground tunnels and bunkers.

We know that Iraq has at least seven of these mobile biological agent factories. The truck-mounted ones have at least two or three trucks each. That means that the mobile production facilities are very few, perhaps 18 trucks that we know of. There may be more, but perhaps 18 that we know of. Just imagine trying to find 18 trucks among the thousands and thousands of trucks that travel the roads of Iraq every single day. It took the inspectors four years to find out that Iraq was making biological agents. How long do you think it will take the inspectors to find even one of these 18 trucks without Iraq coming forward, as they are supposed to, with the information about these kinds of capabilities?

Ladies and gentlemen, these are sophisticated facilities. For example, they can produce anthrax and botulinum toxin. In fact, they can produce enough dry biological agent in a single month to kill thousands upon thousands of people. And dry agent of this type is the most lethal form for human beings. By 1998, U.N. experts agreed that the Iraqis had perfected drying techniques for their biological programs. Now Iraq has incorporated this drying expertise into these mobile production facilities.

We know from Iraq's past admissions that it has successfully weaponized not only anthrax, but also other biological agents, including botulinum toxin, aflatoxin and ricin. But Iraq's research efforts did not stop there. Saddam Hussein has investigated dozens of biological agents, causing diseases such as gas gangrine, plague, typhus, tetanus, cholera, camel pox and hemorrhagic fever. And he also has the wherewithal to develop smallpox.

The Iraqi regime has also developed ways to disperse lethal biological agents widely, indiscriminately, into the water supply, into the air. For example, Iraq had a program to modify aerial fuel tanks for Mirage jets. This video of an Iraqi test flight, obtained by UNSCOM some years ago, shows an Iraqi F–1 Mirage jet aircraft. Note the spray coming from beneath the Mirage. That is 2,000 liters of simulated anthrax that a jet is spraying.

In 1995, an Iraqi military officer, Mujaheed Salai Abdul Latif, told inspectors that Iraq intended the spray tanks to be mounted onto a MIG–21 that had been converted into an unmanned aerial vehicle, or a UAV UAV's outfitted with spray tanks constitute an ideal method for launching a terrorist attack using biological weapons. Iraq admitted to producing four spray tanks, but to this day, it has provided no credible evidence that they were destroyed, evidence that was required by the international community.

There can be no doubt that Saddam Hussein has biological weapons and the capability to rapidly produce more, many more, and he has the ability to dispense these lethal poisons and diseases in ways that can cause massive death and destruction.

If biological weapons seem too terrible to contemplate, chemical weapons are equally chilling. UNMOVIC already laid out much of this, and it is documented for all of us to read in UNSCOM's 1999 report on the subject.

Let me set the stage with three key points that all of us need to keep in mind. First, Saddam Hussein has used these horrific weapons on another country and on his own people. In fact, in the history of chemical warfare, no country has had more battlefield experience with chemical weapons since World War I than Saddam Hussein's Iraq.

Second, as with biological weapons, Saddam Hussein has never accounted for vast amounts of chemical weaponry: 550 artillery shells with mustard, 30,000 empty munitions, and enough precursors to increase his stockpile to as much as 500 tons of chemical agents. If we consider just one category of missing weaponry, 6,500 bombs from the Iran-Iraq war, UNMOVIC says the amount of chemical agent in them would be in the order of a thousand tons. These quantities of chemical weapons are now unaccounted for.

Dr. Blix has quipped that, "Mustard gas is not marmalade; you are supposed to know what you did with it." We believe Saddam Hussein knows what he did with it and he has not come clean with the international community. We have evidence these weapons existed. What we don't have is evidence from Iraq that they have been destroyed or where they are. That is what we are still waiting for.

Third point: Iraq's record on chemical weapons is replete with lies. It took years for Iraq to finally admit that it had produced four tons of the deadly nerve agent VX. A single drop of VX on the skin will kill in minutes. Four tons. The admission only came out after inspectors collected documentation as a result of the defection of Hussein Kamel, Saddam Hussein's late son-in-law. UNSCOM also gained forensic evidence that Iraq had produced VX and put it into weapons for delivery. Yet, to this day, Iraq denies it had ever weaponized VX. And on Jan. 27, UNMOVIC told this Council that it has information that conflicts with the Iraqi account of its VX program.

We know that Iraq has embedded key portions of its illicit chemical weapons infrastructure within its legitimate civilian industry. To all outward appearances, even to experts, the infrastructure looks like an ordinary civilian operation. Illicit and legitimate production can go on simultaneously; or on a dime, this dual-use infrastructure can turn from clandestine to commercial and then back again. These inspections would be unlikely: any inspections of such facilities would be unlikely to turn up anything prohibited, especially if there is any warning that the inspections are coming. Call it ingenious or evil genius, but the Iraqis deliberately designed their chemical weapons programs to be inspected. It is infrastructure with a built-in ally.

Under the guise of dual-use infrastructure, Iraq has undertaken an effort to reconstitute facilities that were closely associated with its past program to develop and produce chemical weapons. For example, Iraq has rebuilt key portions of the Tariq state establishment. Tariq includes facilities designed specifically for Iraq's chemical weapons program and employs key figures from past programs.

That's the production end of Saddam's chemical weapons business. What about the delivery end? I'm going to show you a small part of a chemical complex called Al Musayyib, a site that Iraq has used for at least three years to transship chemical weapons from production facilities out to the field.

In May 2002, our satellites photographed the unusual activity in this picture. Here we see cargo vehicles are again at this transshipment point, and we can see that they are accompanied by a decontamination vehicle associated with biological or chemical weapons activity. What makes this picture significant is that we have a human source who has corroborated that movement of chemical weapons occurred at this site at that time. So it's not just the photo, and it's not an individual seeing the photo. It's the photo and the knowledge of an individual being brought together to make the case.

This photograph of the site, taken two months later in July, shows not only the previous site, which is the figure in the middle at the top with the bulldozer sign near it; it shows that this previous site, as well as all of the other sites around the site, have been fully bulldozed and graded. The topsoil has been removed. The Iraqis literally removed the crust of the earth from large portions of this site in order to conceal chemical weapons evidence that would be there from years of chemical weapons activity.

To support its deadly biological and chemical weapons programs, Iraq procures needed items from around the world using an extensive clandestine network. What we know comes largely from intercepted communications and human sources who are in a position to know the facts.

Iraq's procurement efforts include equipment that can filter and separate microorganisms and toxins involved in biological weapons; equipment that can be used to concentrate the agent; growth media that can be used to continue producing anthrax and botulinum toxin; sterilization equipment for laboratories; glass-lined reactors and specialty pumps that can handle corrosive chemical weapons agents and precursors; large amounts of thionyl chloride, a precursor for nerve and blister agents; and other chemicals, such as sodium sulfide, an important mustard agent precursor.

Now of course, Iraq will argue that these items can also be used for legitimate purposes. But if that is true, why did we have to learn about them by intercepting communications and risking the lives of human agents? With Iraq's well-documented history on biological and chemical weapons, why should any of us give Iraq the benefit of the doubt? I don't, and I don't think you will either after you hear this next intercept.

Just a few weeks ago, we intercepted communications between two commanders in Iraq's Second Republican Guard Corps. One commander is going to be giving an instruction to the other. You will hear, as this unfolds, that what he wants to communicate to the other guy—wants to make sure the other guy hears clearly, to the point of repeating it, so that it gets written down and completely understood. Listen.

COLONEL—Captain Ibrahim?
CAPTAIN—I am with you, sir.
COLONEL—Remove.
CAPTAIN—Remove.
COLONEL—The expression.
CAPTAIN—The expression.
COLONEL—Nerve agents.
CAPTAIN—Nerve agents.
COLONEL—Wherever it comes up.
CAPTAIN—Wherever it comes up.
COLONEL—In the wireless instructions.
CAPTAIN—In the instructions.
COLONEL—Wireless.
CAPTAIN—Wireless.

Let's review a few selected items of this conversation. Two officers talking to each other on the radio want to make sure that nothing is misunderstood.
Remove.
Remove.
The expression.

The expression. I got it.

Nerve agents.

Nerve agents.

Wherever it comes up.

Got it. Wherever it comes up.

In the wireless instructions.

In the instructions.

Correction. No, in the wireless instructions.

Wireless. I got it.

Why does he repeat it that way? Why is he so forceful, making sure this is understood, and why did he focus on wireless instructions? Because the senior officer is concerned that somebody might be listening. Well, somebody was.

Nerve agents.

Stop talking about it. They are listening to us. Don't give any evidence that we have these horrible agents.

But we know that they do, and this kind of conversation confirms it.

Our conservative estimate is that Iraq today has a stockpile of between 100 and 500 tons of chemical-weapons agent. That is enough agent to fill 16,000 battlefield rockets. Even the low end of 100 tons of agent would enable Saddam Hussein to cause mass casualties across more than 100 square miles of territory, an area nearly five times the size of Manhattan.

Let me remind you that of the 122-millimeter chemical warheads that the U.N. inspectors found recently, this discovery could very well be, as has been noted, the tip of a submerged iceberg. The question before us all, my friends, is, when will we see the rest of the submerged iceberg?

Saddam Hussein has chemical weapons. Saddam Hussein has used such weapons. And Saddam Hussein has no compunction about using them again—against his neighbors and against his own people. And we have sources who tell us that he recently has authorized his field commanders to use them. He wouldn't be passing out the orders if he didn't have the weapons or the intent to use them.

We also have sources who tell us that since the 1980's, Saddam's regime has been experimenting on human beings to perfect its biological or chemical weapons. A source said that 1,600 death-row prisoners were transferred in 1995 to a special unit for such experiments. An eyewitness saw prisoners tied down to beds, experiments conducted on them, blood oozing around the victims' mouths, and autopsies performed to confirm the effects of the prisoners—on the prisoners. Saddam Hussein's inhumanity has no limits.

Let me turn now to nuclear weapons. We have no indication that Saddam Hussein has ever abandoned his nuclear-weapons program. On the contrary, we have more than a decade of proof that he remains determined to acquire nuclear weapons.

To fully appreciate the challenge that we face today, remember that in 1991, the inspectors searched Iraq's primary nuclear weapons facilities for the first time and they found nothing to conclude that Iraq had a nuclear-weapons program. But based on defector information, in May of 1991, Saddam Hussein's lie was exposed.

In truth, Saddam Hussein had a massive clandestine nuclear-weapons program that covered several different techniques to enrich uranium, including electromagnetic isotope separation, gas centrifuge and gas diffusion. We estimate that this illicit program cost the Iraqis several billion dollars. Nonetheless, Iraq continued to tell the IAEA that it had no nuclear weapons program. If Saddam had not been stopped, Iraq could have produced a nuclear bomb by 1993, years earlier than most worst-case assessments that have been made before the war.

In 1995, as a result of another defector, we find out that after his invasion of Kuwait, Saddam Hussein had initiated a crash program to build a crude nuclear weapon in violation of Iraq's U.N. obligations. Saddam Hussein already possesses two out of the three key components needed to build a nuclear bomb. He has a cadre of nuclear scientists with the expertise, and he has a bomb design. Since 1998, his efforts to reconstitute his nuclear program have been focused on acquiring the third and last component, sufficient fissile material to produce a nuclear explosion. To make the fissile material, he needs to develop an ability to enrich uranium.

Saddam Hussein is determined to get his hands on a nuclear

bomb. He is so determined that he has made repeated covert attempts to acquire high-specification aluminum tubes from 11 different countries, even after inspections resumed.

These tubes are controlled by the Nuclear Suppliers Group precisely because they can be used as centrifuges for enriching uranium. By now, just about everyone has heard of these tubes, and we all know that there are differences of opinion; there is controversy about what these tubes are for. Most U.S. experts think they are intended to serve as rotors in centrifuges used to enrich uranium. Other experts and the Iraqis themselves argue that they are really to produce the rocket bodies for a conventional weapon, a multiple rocket launcher.

Let me tell you what is not controversial about these tubes. First, all the experts who have analyzed the tubes in our possession agree that they can be adapted for centrifuge use. Second, Iraq had no business buying them for any purpose; they are banned for Iraq.

I am no expert on centrifuge tubes, but just as an old Army trooper, I can tell you a couple of things. First, it strikes me as quite odd that these tubes are manufactured to a tolerance that far exceeds U.S. requirements for comparable rockets. Maybe the Iraqis just manufacture their conventional weapons to a higher standard than we do, but I don't think so.

Second, we actually have examined tubes from several different batches that were seized clandestinely before they reached Baghdad. What we notice in these different batches is a progression to higher and higher levels of specification, including in the latest batch, an anodized coating on extremely smooth outer and inner surfaces. Why would they continue refining the specifications, go to all that trouble for something that, if it was a rocket, would soon be blown into shrapnel when it went off?

The high-tolerance aluminum tubes are only part of the story. We also have intelligence from multiple sources that Iraq is attempting to acquire magnets and high-speed balancing machines. Both items can be used in a gas centrifuge program to enrich uranium.

In 1999 and 2000, Iraqi officials negotiated with firms in Romania, India, Russia and Slovenia for the purchase of a magnet production plant. Iraq wanted the plant to produce magnets weighing 20 to 30 grams. That's the same weight as the magnets used in Iraq's gas centrifuge program before the gulf war. This incident, linked with the tubes, is another indicator of Iraq's attempt to reconstitute its nuclear weapons program.

Intercepted communications from mid–2000 through last summer show that Iraq front companies sought to buy machines that can be used to balance gas centrifuge rotors. One of these companies also had been involved in a failed effort, in 2001, to smuggle aluminum tubes into Iraq.

People will continue to debate this issue, but there is no doubt in my mind, these illicit procurement efforts show that Saddam Hussein is very much focused on putting in place the key missing piece from his nuclear weapons program, the ability to produce fissile material.

He also has been busy trying to maintain the other key parts of his nuclear program, particularly his cadre of key nuclear scientists. It is noteworthy that over the last 18 months, Saddam Hussein has paid increasing personal attention to Iraq's top nuclear scientists, a group that the government-controlled press calls openly, his "nuclear mujahedeen." He regularly exhorts them and praises their progress.

Progress towards what end? Long ago, the Security Council, this Council, required Iraq to halt all nuclear activities of any kind.

Let me talk now about the systems Iraq is developing to deliver weapons of mass destruction, in particular Iraq's ballistic missiles and unmanned aerial vehicles, UAV's.

First, missiles. We all remember that before the gulf war, Saddam Hussein's goal was missiles that flew not just hundreds, but thousands of kilometers. He wanted to strike not only his neighbors, but also nations far beyond his borders. While inspectors destroyed most of the prohibited ballistic missiles, numerous intelligence reports over the past decade from sources inside Iraq indicate that Saddam Hussein retains a covert force of up to a few dozen Scud-variant ballistic missiles. These are missiles with a range of 650 to 900 kilometers.

We know from intelligence and Iraq's own admissions that Iraq's alleged permitted ballistic missiles, the Al Samoud 2 and the

Al Fatah, violate the 150-kilometer limit established by this Council in Resolution 687. These are prohibited systems. UN-MOVIC has also reported that Iraq has illegally imported 380 SA–2 rocket engines. These are likely for use in the Al Samoud 2. Their import was illegal on three counts. Resolution 687 prohibited all military shipments into Iraq. UNSCOM specifically prohibited use of these engines in surface-to-surface missiles. And finally, as we have just noted, they are for a system that exceeds the 150-kilometer range limit. Worst of all, some of these engines were acquired as late as December, after this Council passed Resolution 1441.

What I want you to know today is that Iraq has programs that are intended to produce ballistic missiles that fly over 1,000 kilometers. One program is pursuing a liquid-fuel missile that would be able to fly more than 1,200 kilometers. And you can see from this map as well as I can who will be in danger of these missiles.

As part of this effort, another little piece of evidence, Iraq has built an engine test stand that is larger than anything it has ever had. Notice the dramatic difference in size between the test stand on the left, the old one, and the new one on the right. Note the large exhaust vent. This is where the flame from the engine comes out. The exhaust vent on the right test stand is five times longer than the one on the left. The one on the left was used for short-range missiles. The one on the right is clearly intended for long-range missiles that can fly 1,200 kilometers.

This photograph was taken in April of 2002. Since then, the test stand has been finished and a roof has been put over it, so it will be harder for satellites to see what's going on underneath the test stand.

Saddam Hussein's intentions have never changed. He is not developing the missiles for self-defense. These are missiles that Iraq wants in order to project power, to threaten, and to deliver chemical, biological and, if we let him, nuclear warheads.

Now, unmanned aerial vehicles, UAV's: Iraq has been working on a variety of UAV's for more than a decade. This is just illustrative of what a UAV would look like. This effort has included attempts to modify for unmanned flight the MIG–21 and, with greater success, an aircraft called the L–29. However, Iraq is now concentrating not on these airplanes but on developing and testing smaller UAV's, such as this.

UAV's are well-suited for dispensing chemical and biological weapons. There is ample evidence that Iraq has dedicated much effort to developing and testing spray devices that—being adapted for UAV's. And in the little that Saddam Hussein told us about UAV's, he has not told the truth.

One of these lies is graphically and indisputably demonstrated by intelligence we collected on June 27 last year. According to Iraq's Dec. 7 declaration, its UAV's have a range of only 80 kilometers. But we detected one of Iraq's newest UAV's in a test flight that went 500 kilometers, nonstop, on autopilot in the racetrack pattern depicted here. Not only is this test well in excess of the 150 kilometers that the United Nations permits, the test was left out of Iraq's Dec. 7 declaration. The UAV was flown around and around and around in this circle, and so that its 80-kilometer limit really was 500 kilometers, un-refueled and on autopilot, violative of all of its obligations under 1441.

The linkages over the past 10 years between Iraq's UAV program and biological and chemical warfare agents are of deep concern to us. Iraq could use these small UAV's, which have a wingspan of only a few meters, to deliver biological agents to its neighbors or, if transported, to other countries, including the United States.

My friends, the information I have presented to you about these terrible weapons and about Iraq's continued flaunting of its obligations under Security Council Resolution 1441 links to a subject I now want to spend a little bit of time on, and that has to do with terrorism.

Our concern is not just about these illicit weapons; it's the way that these illicit weapons can be connected to terrorists and terrorist organizations that have no compunction about using such devices against innocent people around the world.

Iraq and terrorism go back decades. Baghdad trains Palestine Liberation Front members in small arms and explosives. Saddam uses the Arab Liberation Front to funnel money to the families of Palestinian suicide bombers in order to prolong the intifada. And it's no secret that Saddam's own intelligence service was involved in dozens of attacks or attempted assassinations in the 1990's.

But what I want to bring to your attention today is the potentially much more sinister nexus between Iraq and the Al Qaeda terrorist network, a nexus that combines classic terrorist organizations and modern methods of murder. Iraq today harbors a deadly terrorist network, headed by Abu Musaab al-Zarqawi, an associate and collaborator of Osama bin Laden and his Al Qaeda lieutenants.

Zarqawi, a Palestinian born in Jordan, fought in the Afghan War more than a decade ago. Returning to Afghanistan in 2000, he oversaw a terrorist training camp. One of his specialties and one of the specialties of this camp is poisons.

When our coalition ousted the Taliban, the Zarqawi network helped establish another poison and explosive training center camp, and this camp is located in Northeastern Iraq. You see a picture of this camp. The network is teaching its operative how to produce ricin and other poisons. Let me remind you how ricin works. Less than a pinch—imagine a pinch of salt—less than a pinch of ricin, eating just this amount in your food would cause shock, followed by circulatory failure. Death comes within 72 hours and there is no antidote. There is no cure. It is fatal.

Those helping to run this camp are Zarqawi lieutenants operating in northern Kurdish areas outside Saddam Hussein's controlled Iraq, but Baghdad has an agent in the most senior levels of the radical organization Ansar al-Islam, that controls this corner of Iraq. In 2000, this agent offered Al Qaeda safe haven in the region. After we swept Al Qaeda from Afghanistan, some of its members accepted this safe haven. They remain there today.

Zarqawi's activities are not confined to this small corner of northeast Iraq. He traveled to Baghdad in May 2002 for medical treatment, staying in the capital of Iraq for two months while he recuperated to fight another day. During this stay, nearly two dozen extremists converged on Baghdad and established a base of operations there. These Al Qaeda affiliates, based in Baghdad, now coordinate the movement of people, money and supplies into and throughout Iraq for his network, and they've now been operating freely in the capital for more than eight months.

Iraqi officials deny accusations of ties with Al Qaeda. These denials are simply not credible. Last year, an Al Qaeda associate bragged that the situation in Iraq was "good," that Baghdad could be transited quickly.

We know these affiliates are connected to Zarqawi because they remain, even today, in regular contact with his direct subordinates, including the poison cell plotters. And they are involved in moving more than money and matériel. Last year, two suspected Al Qaeda operatives were arrested crossing from Iraq into Saudi Arabia. They were linked to associates of the Baghdad cell, and one of them received training in Afghanistan on how to use cyanide.

From his terrorist network in Iraq, Zarqawi can direct his network in the Middle East and beyond. We in the United States, all of us at the State Department, and the Agency for International Development, we all lost a dear friend with the cold-blooded murder of Mr. Lawrence Foley in Amman, Jordan, last October.

A despicable act was committed that day—the assassination of an individual whose sole mission was to assist the people of Jordan. The captured assassin says his cell received money and weapons from Zarqawi for that murder. After the attack, an associate of the assassin left Jordan to go to Iraq to obtain weapons and explosives for further operations.

Iraqi officials protest that they are not aware of the whereabouts of Zarqawi or of any of his associates. Again, these protests are not credible. We know of Zarqawi's activities in Baghdad. I described them earlier. And now, let me add one other fact. We asked a friendly security service to approach Baghdad about extraditing Zarqawi and providing information about him and his close associates. This service contacted Iraqi officials twice, and we passed details that should have made it easy to find Zarqawi. The network remains in Baghdad; Zarqawi still remains at large to come and go.

As my colleagues around this table and as the citizens they represent in Europe know, Zarqawi's terrorism is not confined to the Middle East. Zarqawi and his network have plotted terrorist actions against countries including France, Britain, Spain, Italy, Germany and Russia.

According to detainees, Abu Atiya, who graduated from Zarqawi's terrorist camp in Afghanistan, tasked at least nine North African extremists in 2001 to travel to Europe to conduct poison and explosive attacks. Since last year, members of this network have been apprehended in France, Britain, Spain and Italy. By our last count, 116 operatives connected to this global web have been arrested. The chart you are seeing shows the network in Europe.

We know about this European network, and we know about its links to Zarqawi, because the detainee who provided the information about the targets also provided the names of members of the network. Three of those he identified by name were arrested in France last December. In the apartments of the terrorists, authorities found circuits for explosive devices and a list of ingredients to make toxins. The detainee who helped piece this together says the plot also targeted Britain. Later evidence again proved him right. When the British unearthed a cell there just last month, one British police officer was murdered during the disruption of the cell.

We also know that Zarqawi's colleagues have been active in the Pankisi Gorge, Georgia, and in Chechnya, Russia. The plotting to which they are linked is not mere chatter. Members of Zarqawi's network say their goal was to kill Russians with toxins.

We are not surprised that Iraq is harboring Zarqawi and his subordinates. This understanding builds on decades-long experience with respect to ties between Iraq and al Qaeda. Going back to the early and mid–1990s, when bin Laden was based in Sudan, an al Qaeda source tells us that Saddam and bin Laden reached an understanding that al Qaeda would no longer support activities against Baghdad.

Early Al Qaeda ties were forged by secret high-level intelligence service contacts with Al Qaeda—secret Iraqi intelligence high-level contacts with Al Qaeda. We know members of both organizations met repeatedly and have met at least eight times at very senior levels since the early 1990's. In 1996, a foreign security service tells us that bin Laden met with a senior Iraqi intelligence official in Khartoum and later met the director of the Iraqi intelligence service.

Saddam became more interested as he saw Al Qaeda's appalling attacks. A detained Al Qaeda member tells us that Saddam was more willing to assist Al Qaeda after the 1998 bombings of our embassies in Kenya and Tanzania. Saddam was also impressed by Al Qaeda's attacks on the USS Cole in Yemen in October 2000.

Iraqis continued to visit bin Laden in his new home in Afghanistan. A senior defector, one of Saddam's former intelligence chiefs in Europe, says Saddam sent his agents to Afghanistan sometime in the mid–1990's to provide training to Al Qaeda members on document forgery. From the late 1990's until 2001, the Iraqi embassy in Pakistan played the role of liaison to the Al Qaeda organization.

Some believe—some claim these contacts do not amount to much. They say Saddam Hussein's secular tyranny and Al Qaeda's religious tyranny do not mix. I am not comforted by this thought. Ambition and hatred are enough to bring Iraq and Al Qaeda together, enough so Al Qaeda could learn how to build more sophisticated bombs and learn how to forge documents; and enough so that Al Qaeda could turn to Iraq for help in acquiring expertise on weapons of mass destruction.

And the record of Saddam Hussein's cooperation with other Islamist terrorist organizations is clear. Hamas, for example, opened an office in Baghdad in 1999, and Iraq has hosted conferences attended by Palestine Islamic Jihad. These groups are at the forefront of sponsoring suicide attacks against Israel.

Al Qaeda continues to have a deep interest in acquiring weapons of mass destruction. As with the story of Zarqawi and his network, I can trace the story of a senior terrorist operative telling how Iraq provided training in these weapons to Al Qaeda. Fortunately, this operative is now detained, and he has told his story. I will relate it to you now as he himself described it.

This senior Al Qaeda terrorist was responsible for one of al Qaeda's training camps in Afghanistan. His information comes first- hand from his personal involvement at senior levels of Al Qaeda. He says bin Laden and his top deputy in Afghanistan, deceased Al Qaeda leader Muhammad Atef, did not believe that Al Qaeda labs in Afghanistan were capable enough to manufacture these chemical or biological agents. They needed to go somewhere else; they had to look outside of Afghanistan for help. Where did they go, where did they look? They went to Iraq.

The support that Husseini describes included Iraq offering chemical or biological weapons training for two Al Qaeda associates beginning in December 2000. He says that a militant known as Abu Abdullah al-Iraqi had been sent to Iraq several times between 1997 and 2000 for help in acquiring poisons and gases. Abdullah al- Iraqi characterized the relationship he forged with Iraqi officials as "successful."

As I said at the outset, none of this should come as a surprise to any of us. Terrorism has been a tool used by Saddam for decades. Saddam was a supporter of terrorism long before these terrorist networks had a name, and this support continues. The nexus of poisons and terror is new; the nexus of Iraq and terror is old. The combination is lethal.

With this track record, Iraqi denials of supporting terrorism take their place alongside the other Iraqi denials of weapons of mass destruction. It is all a web of lies. When we confront a regime that harbors ambitions for regional domination, hides weapons of mass destruction, and provides haven and active support for terrorists, we are not confronting the past, we are confronting the present. And unless we act, we are confronting an even more frightening future.

My friends, this has been a long and a detailed presentation, and I thank you for your patience. But there is one more subject that I would like to touch on briefly, and it should be a subject of deep and continuing concern to this Council: Saddam Hussein's violations of human rights. Underlying all that I have said, underlying all the facts and the patterns of behavior that I have identified, is Saddam Hussein's contempt for the will of this Council, his contempt for the truth and, most damning of all, his utter contempt for human life.

Saddam Hussein's use of mustard and nerve gas against the Kurds in 1988—1988—was one of the 20th century's most horrible atrocities. Five thousand men, women and children died. His campaign against the Kurds from 1987 to '89 included mass summary executions, disappearances, arbitrary jailing, ethnic cleansing and the destruction of some 2,000 villages. He has also conducted ethnic cleansing against the Shiite Iraqis and the Marsh Arabs, whose culture has flourished for more than a millennium.

Saddam Hussein's police state ruthlessly eliminates anyone who dares to dissent. Iraq has more forced disappearance cases than any other country: tens of thousands of people reported missing in the past decade. Nothing points more clearly to Saddam Hussein's dangerous intentions and the threat he poses to all of us than his calculated cruelty to his own citizens and to his neighbors. Clearly, Saddam Hussein and his regime will stop at nothing until something stops him.

For more than 20 years, by word and by deed, Saddam Hussein has pursued his ambition to dominate Iraq and the broader Middle East using the only means he knows: intimidation, coercion and annihilation of all those who might stand in his way. For Saddam Hussein, possession of the world's most deadly weapons is the ultimate trump card, the one he must hold to fulfill his ambition.

We know that Saddam Hussein is determined to keep his weapons of mass destruction. He's determined to make more. Given Saddam Hussein's history of aggression, given what we know of his grandiose plans, given what we know of his terrorist associations and given his determination to exact revenge on those who oppose him, should we take the risk that he will not someday use these weapons at a time and a place and in a manner of his choosing, at a time when the world is in a much weaker position to respond? The United States will not and cannot run that risk to the American people. Leaving Saddam Hussein in possession of weapons of mass destruction for a few more months or years is not an option, not in a post-Sept. 11 world.

My colleagues, over three months ago, this Council recognized that Iraq continued to pose a threat to international peace and security, and that Iraq had been and remained in material breach of its disarmament obligations. Today, Iraq still poses a threat, and Iraq still remains in material breach. Indeed, by its failure to seize on its one last opportunity to come clean and disarm, Iraq has put itself in deeper material breach and closer to the day when it will face serious consequences for its continued defiance of this Council.

My colleagues, we have an obligation to our citizens, we have an obligation to this body, to see that our resolutions are complied with. We wrote 1441 not in order to go to war; we wrote 1441 to try to preserve the peace. We wrote 1441 to give Iraq one last chance. Iraq is not, so far, taking that one last chance. We must not shrink from whatever is ahead of us. We must not fail in our duty and our responsibility for the citizens of the countries that are represented by this body.

# PART III

The United Nations inspectors who went back into Iraq at the end of 2002 found the regime a bit more cooperative than it had been in the early to mid–1990s, but still recalcitrant, giving up secrets only reluctantly and not allowing the inspectors to speak privately with the weapons programs officials they demanded to see.

Hans Blix, the Swedish diplomat who headed UNMOVIC's team of several hundred inspectors and support staff, believed nevertheless that, given enough time, they would be able to verify Iraq's claims that it had done away with its weapons of mass destruction, or find and destroy any that it might have hidden.

But the inspectors' real problem was not in Baghdad. It was in Washington, where President Bush and the rest of his administration had run out of patience with Saddam even before the inspectors had gone in.

Blix's reports to the U.N. Security Council and American reactions to them show that he and Washington were not even on the same wavelength. For Washington, the inspectors were there to ratify the administration's claims that Iraq would never cooperate, as it had refused to do in the 1990s. For Blix, the inspectors were there to finish a job they had been prevented from completing in 1998.

"How much, if any, is left of Iraq's weapons of mass destruction and related proscribed items and programs? So far, UNMOVIC has not found any such weapons, only a small number of empty chemical munitions which should have been declared and destroyed," Blix told the Security Council on February 14, as 250,000 American and British troops massed in the Persian Gulf. "I must not jump to the conclusion that they exist," Blix said, but Washington had reached that conclusion months before. The inspectors did find some missiles and rocket engines that violated the prohibitions against Iraq, and even made Iraq start destroying them.

On February 13, administration officials said they were drafting a new proposed resolution for the Security Council to declare that Saddam had failed to disarm and must now face the "consequences." Standing in front of an aircraft carrier, the president challenged the United Nations to show some backbone: "The decision is this for the United Nations: When you say something does it mean anything?" Bush said; if Resolution 1441 meant anything, it meant that by now, Iraq was in breach of its obligation to cooperate fully and immediately and military action against it was justified.

Blix kept acting as if the inspections could work, further irritating Washington by criticizing part of the intelligence Secretary of State Powell had presented to the United Nations the previous week, satellite photos that he said showed Iraqi trucks cleaning up a weapons site in advance of an inspection.

"We have noted that the two satellite images of the site were taken several weeks apart," Blix said the same day as the president was suggesting United Nations spinelessness. "The report of movement of munitions at the site could just as easily have been a routine activity as a movement of proscribed munitions in anticipation of imminent inspection," Blix told the Security Council; "our reservation on this point does not detract from our appreciation of the briefing."

"We are facing a difficult situation," Powell replied. "More inspectors—sorry, it's not the answer. What we need is immediate cooperation." Three weeks later, speaking in Washington, he asked, "Has Saddam Hussein made a strategic, political decision to comply with the United Nations Security Council resolutions? that's the question. There is no other question."

Blix's reports to the Security Council were giving ambivalent answers to this question. "During the period of time covered by the present report, Iraq could have made greater efforts to find any remaining proscribed items or provide credible evidence showing the absence of such items," he said on February 28. "The results in terms of disarmament have been very limited so far. The destruction of missiles, which is an important operation, has not yet begun. Iraq could have made full use of the declaration, which was submitted on 7 December. It is hard to understand why a number of the measures, which are now being taken, could not have been initiated earlier."

President Bush, at a press conference March 6, was impatient: "It makes no sense to allow this issue to continue on and on, in the hopes that Saddam Hussein disarms. The whole purpose of the debate is for Saddam to disarm. We gave him a chance. As a matter of fact, we gave him 12 years of chances. But, recently, we gave him a chance, starting last fall. And it said, last chance to disarm. The resolution said that. And had he chosen to do so, it would be evident that he's disarmed.

So more time, more inspectors, more process, in our judgment, is not going to affect the peace of the world. So whatever is resolved is going to have some finality to it, so that Saddam Hussein will take us seriously."

Blix reported the next day that Iraq had begun destroying missiles the inspectors had discovered with longer than permissible range. "We are not watching the breaking of toothpicks. Lethal weapons are being destroyed," he said, but added, "It is obvious that, while the numerous initiatives, which are now taken by the Iraqi side with a view to resolving some long-standing open disarmament issues, can be seen as 'active', or even 'proactive', these initiatives 3–4 months into the new resolution cannot be said to constitute 'immediate' cooperation."

The bottom line was this, Blix said: "While cooperation can and is to be immediate, disarmament and at any rate the verification of it cannot be instant. Even with a proactive Iraqi attitude, induced by continued outside pressure, it would still take some time to verify sites and items, analyze documents, interview relevant persons, and draw conclusions. It would not take years, nor weeks, but months."

France and Germany, along with Russia and China, were willing to give the inspectors the time they said they needed. The United States and Britain, supported by Spain, thought Saddam had had enough time, and if left to his own devices, the president was prepared to go to war without United Nations approval. But Prime Minister Tony Blair, under tremendous political pressure at home, persuaded him to go to the Security Council one more time and ask for explicit authorization. With the French foreign minister, Dominique de Villepin, actively lobbying for votes against the resolution and France and Russia threatening to use their veto power against it, the resolution was withdrawn on March 17. The United States and Britain prepared to go to war together, with support and token contributions from others, notably Spain.

The president spoke that night on national television and betrayed his regret at having been talked into going to the U.N. in the first place the previous September, at the inspections process, at the American allies he felt had betrayed him.

"Today, no nation can possibly claim that Iraq has disarmed," he said. "And it will not disarm so long as Saddam Hussein holds power. For the last four-and-a-half months, the United States and our allies have worked within the Security Council to enforce that Council's long-standing demands. Yet, some permanent members of the Security Council have publicly announced they will veto any resolution that compels the disarmament of Iraq. These governments share our assessment of the danger, but not our resolve to meet it. Many nations, however, do have the resolve and fortitude to act against this threat to peace, and a broad coalition is now gathering to enforce the just demands of the world. The United Nations Security Council has not lived up to its responsibilities, so we will rise to ours."

Bombs began falling in Baghdad and the troops started pouring across the border on March 20. They would not find weapons of mass destruction in Iraq. What they would find is just how effective inspections and diplomatic pressure had been over the years, and how wrong the United States intelligence had been.

# UNMOVIC and IAEA Progress Reports on U.N. Inspections of Weapons of Mass Destruction Sites in Iraq

•

# February 14, 2003

## Hans Blix, executive chairman of UNMOVIC:

Mr. President, since I reported to the Security Council on 27th of January, UNMOVIC has had [. . . ]two further weeks of operational and analytical work in New York and active inspections in Iraq.

This brings the total period of inspections so far to 11 weeks.

Since then, we have also listened on the 5th of February to the presentation to the council by the U.S. secretary of State and the discussion that followed. Lastly, Dr. ElBaradei and I have held another round of talks in Baghdad with our counterparts and with Vice President Ramadan on the 8th and 9th of February.

[. . . ]

The number of Iraqi minders during inspections has often reached a ratio—had also reached a ratio as high as five per inspectors. During the talks in January in Baghdad, the Iraqi side agreed to keep the ratio to about one to one. The situation has improved.

Since we arrived in Iraq, we have conducted more than 400 inspections covering more than 300 sites. All inspections were performed without notice, and access was almost always provided promptly. In no case have we been—seen convincing evidence that the Iraqi side knew in advance that the inspectors were coming.

The inspections have taken place throughout Iraq at industrial sites, ammunition depots, research centers, universities, presidential sites, mobile laboratories, private houses, missile production facilities, military camps and agricultural sites.

At all sites which had been inspected before 1998, re-baselining activities were performed. These included the identification of the function and contents of each building, new or old, at a site. It also included verification of previously tagged equipment, application of seals and tags, taking samples, and discussions with the site's personnel regarding past and present activities. At certain sites, ground-penetrating radar was used to look for underground structures or buried equipment.

Through the inspections conducted so far, we have obtained a good knowledge of the industrial and scientific landscape of Iraq as well as of its missile capability, but, as before, we do not know every cave and corner. Inspections are effectively helping to bridge the gaps in knowledge that arose due to the absence of inspections between December 1998 and November 2002.

More than 200 chemical and more than 100 biological samples have been collected at different sites. Three-quarters of these have been screened using our own analytical laboratory capabilities at the Baghdad center. The results to date have been consistent with Iraqi declarations.

We have now commenced the process of destroying approximately 50 liters of mustard gas declared by Iraq that was being kept under UNMOVIC's seal at the Muthanna site. One-third of the quantity has already been destroyed. The laboratory quantity of thiodiglycol, a mustard gas precursor which we found at another site, has also been destroyed.

The total number of staff in Iraq now exceeds 250, 250 from 60 countries. This includes about 100 UNMOVIC inspectors, 15 IAEA inspectors, 15 air crew, and 65 support staff.

Mr. President, in my 27th of January update to the council, I said that it seemed from our experience that Iraq had decided in principle to provide cooperation on process, most importantly on prompt access to all sites and assistance to UNMOVIC in the establishment of the necessary infrastructure.

This impression remains, and we note that access to sites has, so far, been without problems, including those that have never been declared or inspected, as well as to presidential sites and private residences.

In my last updating, I also said that a decision to cooperate on substance was indispensable in order to bring, through inspection, the disarmament task to completion and to set the monitoring system on a firm course. Such cooperation, as I have noted, requires more than the opening of doors. In the words of Resolution 1441, it requires immediate, unconditional, and active efforts by Iraq to resolve existing questions of disarmament, either by presenting remaining proscribed items and programs for elimination, or by presenting convincing evidence that they have been eliminated.

In the current situation, one would expect Iraq to be eager to comply. While we were in Baghdad, we meet a delegation from the government of South Africa. It was there to explain how South Africa gained the confidence of the world in its dismantling of the nuclear weapons program by a wholehearted cooperation over two years with IAEA inspectors. I have just learned that Iraq has accepted an offer by South Africa to send a group of experts for further talks.

How much, if any, is left of Iraq's weapons of mass destruction and related proscribed items and programs? So far, UNMOVIC has not found any such weapons, only a small number of empty chemical munitions, which should have been declared and destroyed.

Another matter, and one of great significance, is that many proscribed weapons and items are not accounted for. To take an example, a document which Iraq provided suggested to us that some 1,000 tons of chemical agent were unaccounted for.

I must not jump to the conclusion that they exist. However, that possibility is also not excluded. If they exist, they should be presented for destruction. If they do not exist, credible evidence to that effect should be presented.

We are fully aware that many government and intelligence organizations are convinced and assert that proscribed weapons, items and programs continue to exist. The U.S. Secretary of State presented material in support of this conclusion. Governments have many sources of information that are not available to inspectors. The inspectors, for their part, must base their reports only on the evidence which they can themselves examine and present publicly. Without evidence, confidence cannot arise.

Mr. President, in my earlier briefings, I have noted that significant outstanding issues of substance were listed in two Security Council documents from early 1999, and should be well known to Iraq. I referred as examples to the issues of anthrax, the nerve agent VX and long-range missiles and said that such issues, and I quote myself, "deserve to be taken seriously by Iraq rather than being brushed aside," unquote.

The declaration submitted by Iraq on the 7th of December last year, despite its large volume, missed the opportunity to provide the fresh material and evidence needed to respond to the open questions. This is perhaps the most important problem we are facing. Although I can understand that it may not be easy for Iraq in all cases to provide the evidence needed, it is not the task of the inspectors to find it. Iraq itself must squarely tackle this task and avoid belittling the questions.

In my January update to the council, I referred to the Al-Samoud 2 and the Al-Fatah missiles, reconstituted casting chambers, a missile engine test stand, and the import of rocket engines, which were all declared to UNMOVIC by Iraq.

I noted that the Al-Samoud 2 and the Al-Fatah could very well represent prime facie cases of proscribed missile systems, as they had been tested to ranges exceeding the 150 kilometers limit set by the Security Council. I also noted that Iraq had been requested to cease flight test of these missiles until UNMOVIC completed a technical review.

Earlier this week UNMOVIC missile experts met for two days with experts from a number of member states to discuss these items. The experts concluded unanimously that based on the data provided by Iraq, the two declared variants of the Al-Samoud 2 missile were capable of exceeding 150 kilometers in range. This missile system is therefore proscribed for Iraq, pursuant to Resolution 687 and the monitoring plan adopted by Resolution 715.

As for the Al-Fatah, the experts found that clarification of the missile data supplied by Iraq was required before the capability of the missile system could be fully assessed.

With respect to the casting chambers, I note the following. UNSCOM ordered and supervised the destruction of the casting chambers, which had been intended for use in the production of the proscribed Badar 2000 missile system. Iraq has declared that it has reconstituted these chambers. The experts have confirmed that the reconstituted casting chambers could still be used to produce motors for missiles capable of ranges significantly greater than 150 kilometers. Accordingly, these chambers remain proscribed.

The expert also studied the data on the missile engine test stand that is nearing completion and had assessed it to be capable of testing missile engines with thrusts greater than that of the SA–2 engine. So far the test stand has not been associated with a proscribed activity.

On the matter of the 380 SA–2 missile engines imported outside of the export-import mechanism, and in contravention of Paragraph 24 of Resolution 687, UNMOVIC inspectors were informed by Iraq during an official briefing that these engines were intended for use in the Al- Samoud 2 missile system, which has now been assessed to be proscribed. Any such engines configured for use in this missile system would also be proscribed. I intend to communicate these findings to the government of Iraq.

At the meeting in Baghdad on the 8th and the 9th of February, the Iraqi side addressed some of the important outstanding disarmament issues and gave us a number of papers; for instance, regarding anthrax and growth material, the nerve agent VX, and missile production.

Experts who were present from our side studied the papers during the evening of 8th of February and met with Iraqi experts in the morning of 9 February for further clarifications. Although no new evidence was provided in the papers and no open issues were closed through them or the expert discussions, the presentation of the papers could be indicative of a more active attitude focusing on the important open issues.

The Iraqi side suggested that the problem of verifying the quantities of anthrax and two VX precursors, which had been declared unilaterally destroyed, might be tackled through certain technical and analytical methods. Although our experts are still assessing the suggestions, they are not very hopeful that it could prove possible to assess the quantities of material poured into the ground years ago. Documentary evidence and testimony by the staff that dealt with the items still appears to be needed.

Not least, against this background, a letter on the 12th of February from Iraq's National Monitoring Directorate may be of relevance. It presents a list of 83 names of participants, I quote, "in the unilateral destruction in the chemical field which took place in the summer of 1991." Unquote. As the absence of adequate evidence of that destruction has been and remains an important reason why quantities of chemicals had been deemed unaccounted for, the presentation of a list of persons who can be interviewed about the actions appears useful and pertains to cooperation on substance. I trust that the Iraqi side will put together a similar list of names of persons who participated in the unilateral destruction of other proscribed items, notably in the biological field.

The Iraqi side also informed us that the commission which had been appointed in the wake of our finding 12 empty chemical weapons warheads had its mandate expanded to look for any still existing proscribed items. This was welcomed. A second commission, we learned, has now been appointed with a task of searching all over Iraq for more documents relevant to the elimination of proscribed items and programs. It is headed by the former minister of Oil, General Amer Rashid, and is to have very extensive powers of search in industry, administration, and even private houses.

The two commissions could be useful tools to come up with proscribed items to be destroyed and with new documentary evidence. They evidently need to work fast and effectively to convince us and the world that it is a serious effort.

The matter of private interviews was discussed at length during our meeting in Baghdad. The Iraqi side confirmed the commitment which it had made to us on the 20th of January to encourage persons asked to accept such interviews, whether in or out of Iraq. So far, we have only had interviews in Baghdad. A number of persons have declined to be interviewed unless they were allowed to have an official present or were allowed to tape the interview. Three persons that had previously refused interviews on UNMOVIC's terms subsequently accepted such interviews just prior to our talks in Baghdad on the 8th and 9th of February.

These interviews proved informative. No further interviews have since been accepted on our terms. I hope this will change. We feel that interviews conducted with (sic) any third party present and without tape recording would provide the greatest credibility.

At the recent meeting in Baghdad, as on several earlier occasions, my colleague Dr. ElBaradei and I had urged the Iraqi side to enact legislation implementing the U.N. prohibitions regarding weapons of mass destruction. This morning we had a message that a presidential decree has now been issued containing prohibitions with regard to importation and production of biological, chemical and nuclear weapons. We have not yet had time to study the details of the text of the decree.

Mr. President, I should like to make some comments on the role of intelligence in connection with inspections in Iraq. A credible inspection regime requires that Iraq provide full cooperation on process, granting immediate access everywhere to inspectors; and on substance, providing full declarations supported by relevant information and material and evidence. However, with the closed society in Iraq of today and the history of inspections there, other sources of information, such as defectors and government intelligence agencies, are required to aid the inspection process.

I remember myself how in the 1991, several inspections in Iraq, which were based on the information received from a government, helped to disclose important parts of the nuclear weapon program. It was realized that an international organization authorized to perform inspections anywhere on the ground could make good use of the information obtained from governments, with eyes in the sky, ears in the ether, access to defectors and both eyes and ears on the market for weapons-related material. It was understood that the information residing in the intelligence services government could come to very active use in the international effort to prevent proliferation of weapons of mass destruction. This remains true, and we have by now a good deal of experience in the matter.

International organizations need to analyze such information critically and especially benefit when it comes from more than one source. The intelligence agencies, for their part, must protect their sources and methods. Those who provide such information must know that it will be kept in strict confidence and be known to very few people.

UNMOVIC has achieved good working relations with intelligence agencies, and the amount of information provided has been gradually increasing. However, we must recognize that there are limitations, that misinterpretations can occur.

Intelligence information has been useful for UNMOVIC. In one case, it led us to a private home where documents mainly relating to laser enrichment of uranium were found. In other cases, intelligence has led to sites where no proscribed items were found. Even in such cases, however, inspection of these sites were useful in proving the absence of such items and in some cases, the presence of other items, conventional munitions. It showed that conventional arms are being moved around the country and that movements are not necessarily related to weapons of mass destruction.

The presentation of intelligence information by the U.S. Secretary of state suggested that Iraq had prepared for inspections by cleaning up sites and removing evidence of proscribed weapons programs. I would like to comment only on one case which we are familiar with, namely, the trucks identified by analysts as being for chemical decontamination at the munitions depot. This was a declared site, and it was certainly one of the sites Iraq would have expected to be to inspect—us to inspect. We have noted that the two satellite images of the site were taken several weeks apart. The report of movement of munitions at the site could just as easily had been a routine activity as a movement of proscribed munitions in anticipation of imminent inspection.

Our reservation on this point does not detract from our appreciation of the briefing.

Yesterday UNMOVIC informed the Iraqi authorities of its intention to start the U–2 surveillance aircraft early next week, under arrangements similar to those UNSCOM had followed. We are also in the process of working out modalities for the use of the French Mirage aircraft, starting late next week, and for the Drones supplied by the German government. The offer from Russia of an Antonov aircraft with night vision capabilities is a welcome one and is next on our agenda for further improving UNMOVIC's and IAEA's technical capabilities. These developments are in line with suggestions made in a "non-paper" recently circulated by France suggesting a further strengthening of the inspection capabilities.

It is our intention to examine the possibilities for surveying ground movements, notably trucks. In the face of persistent intelligence reports—for instance, about mobile biological-weapons production units—such measures could well increase the effectiveness of inspections.

UNMOVIC is still expanding its capabilities, both in terms of numbers of staff and technical resources. On my way to the recent Baghdad meeting, I stopped in Vienna to meet 60 experts who just completed our general training course for inspectors. They came from 22 countries, including Arab countries.

Mr. President, UNMOVIC is not infrequently asked how much more time it needs to complete its task in Iraq. The answer depends upon which task one has in mind: the elimination of weapons of mass destruction and related items and programs, which were prohibited in 1991; the disarmament task; or the monitoring that no new proscribed activities occur.

The latter task, though not often focused upon, is highly significant and not controversial. It will require monitoring, which is ongoing—that is, open-ended—until the council decides otherwise.

By contrast, the task for disarmament foreseen in Resolution 687 and the progress on key remaining disarmament tasks, foreseen in Resolution 1284, as well as the disarmament obligations, which Iraq was given a final opportunity to comply with under Resolution 1441, were always required to be fulfilled in a shorter time span.

Regrettably, the high degree of cooperation required of Iraq for disarmament through inspection was not forthcoming in 1991.

Despite the elimination under UNSCOM and the IAEA supervision of large amounts of weapons, weapons-related items and installations over the years, the task remained incomplete when inspectors were withdrawn almost eight years later, at the end of 1998.

If Iraq had provided the necessary cooperation in 1991, the face of disarmament under Resolution 687 could have been short, and a decade of sanctions could have been avoided. Today, three months after the adoption of Resolution 1441, the period of disarmament through inspection could still be short, if, I quote, "immediate, active and unconditional cooperation," unquote, with UNMOVIC and the IAEA were to be forthcoming.

Thank you, Mr. President.

# Mohamed ElBaradei, director general of IAEA:

Mr. President, my report to the council today is an update on the status of IAEA's nuclear verification activities in Iraq, pursuant to Security Council Resolution 1441 and other relevant resolutions. Less than three weeks have passed since my last update to the council on 27 January, a relatively short period in the overall inspection process. However, I believe it is important for the council to remain actively engaged and fully informed at this critical time.

The focus of the IAEA inspection has moved from the reconnaissance phase into the investigative phase. The reconnaissance phase was aimed at reestablishing rapidly our knowledge base of Iraq's nuclear capabilities, ensuring that nuclear activities at known key facilities had not been resumed, verifying the location of nuclear material and relevant non-nuclear material and equipment, and identifying the current workplace of former key Iraqi personnel.

The focus of the investigative phase is achieving an understanding of Iraq's activities over the last four years, in particular in areas identified by states as being of concern, and those identified by the IAEA on the basis of its own analysis.

Since our 27 January report, the IAEA has conducted an additional 38 inspections at 19 locations, for a total of 177 inspections at 125 locations. Iraq has continued to provide immediate access to all locations. In the course of the inspections, we have identified certain facilities at which we will be establishing containment and surveillance systems in order to monitor on a continuous basis activities associated with critical, dual-use equipment. At this time, we are using recurrent inspections to ensure that this equipment is not being used for prohibited purposes.

As I mentioned in my last report to the council, we have a number of wide-area and location-specific measures for detecting indications of undeclared past or ongoing nuclear activities in Iraq, including environmental sampling and radiation-detection surveys.

In this regard, we have been collecting a broad variety of samples, including water, sediment and vegetation, at inspected facilities and at other locations across Iraq and analyzing them for signature of nuclear activities.

We have also resumed air sampling at key locations in Iraq. Three of the four air samplers that were removed in December 2002 for refurbishing have been returned to Iraq. One of these has been installed at a fixed location, and the other two are being operated from mobile platforms. We are intending to increase their number to make optimum use of this technique.

We are also continuing to expand the use of hand-held and car-borne gamma surveys in Iraq. The gamma survey vehicle has been used en route to inspections sites and within sites, as well as in urban and industrial areas. We will start helicopter-borne gamma surveys as soon as the relevant equipment receives its final certification for use on the helicopter model provided to us for use in Iraq.

The IAEA has continued to interview key Iraqi personnel. We have recently been able to conduct four interviews in private; that is, without the presence of an Iraqi observer. The interviewees, however, have tape-recorded their interviews.

In addition, discussion has continued to be conducted with Iraqi technicians and officials as part of inspection activities and technical meetings. I should note that during our recent meeting in Baghdad, Iraq reconfirmed its commitment to encourage its citizens to accept interviews in private both inside and outside of Iraq.

In response to a request by the IAEA, Iraq has expanded the list of relevant Iraqi personnel to over 300, along with the current work locations. The list includes the higher-level scientists known to the IAEA in the nuclear and nuclear-related areas.

We will continue, however, to ask for information about Iraqi personnel of lesser rank whose work may be of significance to our mandate.

I would like now to provide an update on a number of specific issues that we are currently pursuing.

I should mention that, shortly before our recent meeting in Baghdad, and based on our discussion with Iraqi counterpart, Iraq provided documentations related to these issues: the reported attempt to import uranium, the attempted procurement of aluminum tubes, the procurement of magnets and magnet production capabilities, the use of HMX and, those questions and concerns that were outstanding in 1998.

I will touch briefly on each of these issues.

Iraq continues to state that it has made no attempt to import uranium since the 1980s. The IAEA recently received some additional information relevant to this issue, which will be further pursued; hopefully, with the assistance of the African country reported to have been involved.

The IAEA is also continuing to follow up on acknowledged effort by Iraq to import high-strength aluminum tubes. As you well know, Iraq has declared these efforts to have been in connection with a program to reverse engineer conventional rockets. The IAEA has verified that Iraq had indeed been manufacturing such rockets.

However, we are still exploring whether the tubes were intended rather for the manufacture of centrifuges for uranium enrichment. In connection with this investigation, Iraq has been asked to explain the reasons for the high-tolerance specifications that it had requested from various suppliers.

Iraq has provided documentations related to the project of reverse engineering, and has committed itself to providing samples of tubes received from prospective suppliers. We will continue to investigate the matter further.

In response to the IAEA inquiries about Iraq's attempt to procure a facility for the manufacture of magnets and the possible link with a resumption of a nuclear program, Iraq recently provided additional documentations, which we are presently examining.

In the course of our inspection conducted in connection with aluminum tube investigation, the IAEA inspectors found a number of documents relevant to transactions aimed at the procurement of carbon fiber, the dual-use material used by Iraq in the past clandestine uranium enrichment program for the manufacture of gas centrifuge rotors.

Our review of these documents suggests that the carbon fibers sought by Iraq was not intended for enrichment purpose, as the specification of the material appear not to be consistent with those needed for manufacturing rotor tubes. In addition, we have carried out follow-up inspection, during which we have been able to observe the use of such carbon fibers in non-nuclear-related applications and to take samples. The IAEA will nevertheless continue to pursue this matter.

# UNMOVIC Executive Chairman Blix's Progress Report on U.N. Inspections of Weapons of Mass Destruction Sites in Iraq

•

## February 28, 2003

*[Excerpts]*
[. . . ]

## Declaration submitted by Iraq on 7 December 2002

Responding to the requirement in paragraph 3 of Security Council resolution 1441 (2002) to provide a "currently accurate, full and complete declaration of all aspects of its programs to develop chemical, biological, and nuclear weapons, ballistic missiles, and other delivery systems", on 7 December, Iraq submitted a declaration to UNMOVIC and the IAEA and, through its President, to the Security Council. The declaration, including supporting documents, comprised more than 12,000 pages.

On 19 December and again on 9 January, the Executive Chairman, in his informal briefings to the Council, presented an assessment of the information contained in the declaration. UNMOVIC experts have found little new significant information in the part of the declaration relating to proscribed weapons programs, nor much new supporting documentation or other evidence. New material, on the other hand, was provided concerning non-weapons-related activities during the period from the end of 1998 to the present, especially in the biological field and on missile development.

The part that covers biological weapons is, in UNMOVIC's assessment, essentially a reorganized version of a previous declaration provided by Iraq to the United Nations Special Commission (UNSCOM) in September 1997. In the chemical weapons area, the basis of the current declaration was a declaration submitted by Iraq in 1996 with subsequent updates and explanations. In the missile field, the declaration follows the same format, and has largely the same content as Iraq's 1996 missile declaration and updates.

However, some sections contained new information. In the chemical weapons field, Iraq further explained its account of the material balance of precursors for chemical warfare agents, although it did not settle unresolved issues on this subject.

In the missile area, there is a good deal of information regarding Iraq's activities in the past few years. A series of new projects have been declared that are at various stages of development.

As there is little new substantive information in the weapons part of Iraq's declaration, or new supporting documentation, . . . issues that were identified as unresolved . . . remain. In most cases, the issues remain unresolved because there is a lack of supporting evidence. Such supporting evidence, in the form of documentation, testimony by individuals who took part in the activities, or physical evidence, would be required.

## Inspections and inspection capabilities in Iraq

Since the arrival of the first inspectors in Iraq on 27 November 2002, UNMOVIC has conducted more than 550 inspections covering approximately 350 sites. Of these 44 sites were new sites. All inspections were performed without notice, and access was in virtually all cases provided promptly. In no case have the inspectors seen convincing evidence that the Iraqi side knew in advance of their impending arrival.

The inspections have taken place throughout Iraq at industrial sites, ammunition depots, research centers, universities, presidential sites, mobile laboratories, private houses, missile production facilities, military camps and agricultural sites. At all sites, which had been inspected before 1998, re-baselining activities were performed. This included the identification of the function and contents of each building, new or old, at a site. It also included verification of previously tagged equipment, application of seals and tags, evaluation of locations for the future installation of cameras and other monitors, as well as taking samples and discussions with the site personnel regarding past and present activities. At certain sites, ground-penetrating radar was used to look for underground structures or buried equipment. Similar activities were performed at new sites. Inspections are effectively helping to bridge the gap in knowledge that arose due to the absence of inspections between December 1998 and November 2002.

More than 200 chemical and more than 100 biological samples have been collected at different sites. Three quarters of these have been screened using UNMOVIC's own analytical laboratory capabilities at the Baghdad Ongoing Monitoring, Verification and Inspection Centre (BOMVIC). The results to date have been consistent with Iraq's declarations.

UNMOVIC has identified and started the destruction of approximately 50 liters of mustard declared by Iraq that had been placed under UNSCOM supervision and seal at the Muthanna site in 1998. This process will continue. A laboratory quantity (1 liter) of thiodiglycol, a mustard precursor, which had been found at another site, has also been destroyed.

Towards the end of February 2003, a juncture when rotation of inspectors is taking place, the number of UNMOVIC personnel in Iraq reached a total of 202 staff from 60 countries. This includes 84 inspectors. In addition, BOMVIC has a team of United Nations translators and interpreters and a logistics and administrative staff. A unit of 10 United Nations security officers ensures the security of BOMVIC offices 24 hours a day. Medical and communication staff has been provided by the Government of New Zealand as a contribution to UNMOVIC operations. The manpower required to refurbish BOMVIC office space at the Canal Hotel was provided by the Government of Switzerland.

UNMOVIC air operations are carried out by 1 airplane and 8 helicopters, with a total of 57 air staff. These operations are covered by contracts with four different companies. The L–100 plane, which flies between Larnaca and Baghdad, is under a contract with a South African company. Contracts with Canadian,

Russian and United Kingdom companies cover the helicopter assets.

With the exception of the crew of the aircraft and the helicopters and the staff provided by the Governments of New Zealand and Switzerland, all UNMOVIC employees of BOMVIC are United Nations staff recruited under the staff rules of the Organization.

A field office was opened in Mosul, in the north of Iraq, the first week in January, with the cooperation of Iraqi authorities. This operation base is temporarily located in a hotel with full communications capabilities. There are currently 28 staff at this location. Planning for the setting-up of prefabricated offices at Mosul airport is currently under way. There is a United Nations security team at the field office, and arrangements have been made to ensure medical assistance to the staff.

UNMOVIC is in the process of planning for a second field office in Basra, in the south of Iraq, in March. The Iraqi authorities are providing cooperation to this effect.

During the period from 1 December 2002 to 28 February 2003, inspectors have been provided with high technology, state-of-the-art equipment. This includes some 35,000 tamper-proof tags and seals for tagging equipment, 10 enhanced chemical agent monitors (ECAMS), 10 toxic industrial materials detectors (TIMs), 10 chemical monitors (APCC), nuclear, biological and chemical protection (NBC) suits, respirators, dosimeters with reader, a complete chemical laboratory with requisite laboratory supplies and equipment, ground-penetrating radars, 3 portable gas chromatograph-mass spectrometers, 12 ultrasonic pulse echo detectors to screen the inside of warheads, equipment for sampling warheads (MONIKA), 3 alloy analyzers, and biological detection and screening equipment to include PCR, ELISA, immunoassay and rapid screening technologies. Additionally, UNMOVIC has used its network of accredited laboratories to analyze a sample of missile propellant. Cameras and other surveillance systems are currently in Cyprus awaiting shipment to Baghdad.

The Commission's Larnaca field office has been expanded. It continues to provide essential logistics and other support.

# High-level meetings in Baghdad

On 19 and 20 January and on 8 and 9 February, the Executive Chairman, together with the Director General of the IAEA, visited Baghdad to discuss relevant inspection and cooperation issues. He was accompanied in these missions by a number of UNMOVIC senior staff and experts.

The first meetings in January between the Iraqi side and UNMOVIC and the IAEA were devoted to stocktaking of the inspections which had taken place so far and to resolving certain operational issues. This included the questions of the clarification of the 7 December declaration, provision of documents, the conduct of interviews, air operations, as well as access and Iraqi assistance to the logistic buildup. A joint statement was issued upon conclusion of the talks. While it recorded a number of matters which had been solved, some remained unresolved, such as flights by U–2 surveillance planes, the conduct of interviews, the enactment of national legislation.

At the meeting on 8 and 9 February, the Iraqi side addressed some of the important outstanding disarmament issues. A number of papers were handed over to UNMOVIC, regarding unresolved issues in all three disarmament fields. Expert discussions were held to clarify the contents of these papers. However, they did not contain new evidence, nor did they resolve any of the open issues.

Other matters discussed included the possibility of verifying, through technical and analytical methods, the quantities of biological agents and chemical precursors, which had been declared unilaterally destroyed; the establishment of Iraqi Commissions to search for proscribed items and relevant documents, the necessity of private interviews, and the enactment of national legislation in accordance with the monitoring plan approved by the Security Council in resolution 715 (1991).

# Interviews

In accordance with paragraph 5 of Security Council resolution 1441 (2002), UNMOVIC has the right to conduct, at its sole discretion, interviews with Iraqi officials and other persons with or without the presence of observers from the Iraqi Government, both inside and outside of Iraq. In the review period, UNMOVIC requested 28 individuals to present themselves for interviews in Baghdad (without the presence of observers). At first, none of them agreed. At the meeting on 19–20 January, the Iraqi side committed itself to "encourage" persons to accept interviews "in private". Immediately prior to the next round of discussions, Iraq informed UNMOVIC that three candidates, who had previously declined to be interviewed under UNMOVIC's terms, had changed their minds. UNMOVIC is currently examining the practical modalities for conducting interviews outside the territory of Iraq.

## Missile programs declared by Iraq

In its 7 December declaration and again in its semi-annual monitoring declaration, Iraq declared the development and production of two types of surface-to-surface missiles, which, according to the data presented, were capable of surpassing the range limit imposed on Iraq by Security Council resolution 687 (1991) and had indeed done so in a number of tests. Iraq also declared the acquisition of a large number of surface-to-air missile engines for use, after appropriate modification, in the production of these missiles. This import violates the arms embargo established by the Council in paragraph 24 of resolution 687 (1991).

UNMOVIC staff have evaluated and assessed these missile projects—the Al Samoud 2 and the Al Fatah. It has also sought the assessment of a panel of international experts on the matter. To that end, a meeting took place on 10–11 February at United Nations Headquarters with experts from China, France, Germany, the United Kingdom of Great Britain and Northern Ireland, Ukraine and the United States of America. The Russian expert nominated was unable to attend.

As a result of these assessments, it was concluded that all variants of the Al Samoud 2 missile were inherently capable of ranges of more than 150 kilometers and were therefore proscribed weapons systems.

The panel found that clarification of the Al Fatah missile data supplied by Iraq was required before the capability of the missile system could be assessed. UNMOVIC will request such clarification.

UNMOVIC inspection teams proceeded to tag the Al Samoud 2 missiles, as well as related missile components, such as engines.

The experts also reviewed the capabilities of casting chambers at the Al Mamoun facility. These had previously been destroyed under UNSCOM supervision since they were intended for use in the production of the proscribed Badr–2000 missile, but had subsequently been refurbished by Iraq. The experts concluded that these reconstituted chambers could still be used to produce motors for missiles capable of ranges significantly greater than 150 kilometers. Accordingly, these chambers remain proscribed.

On 21 February, UNMOVIC, in accordance with relevant resolutions, directed Iraq to destroy the proscribed missile system and the reconstituted casting chambers. The destruction process is to commence by 1 March.

## Aerial operations

Subsequent to the high-level discussions on 8 and 9 February, on 10 February, the Government of Iraq formally accepted UNMOVIC's use of aerial surveillance platforms and undertook to take the necessary measures to ensure their safety.

The first such flight was conducted by a high-altitude U–2 surveillance aircraft on 17 February. This aircraft has conducted further flights. The missions are flown by the United States on behalf of UNMOVIC. A Mirage IV medium-altitude surveillance aircraft, flown on behalf of UNMOVIC by the Government of France, undertook its first mission on 26 February. The two aircraft can provide a number of different types of imagery and both are able to provide digital imagery to UNMOVIC in New York within a few hours of the missions taking place. UNMOVIC is currently discussing the use of a Russian AN–30 surveillance aircraft and German unmanned aerial vehicles (UAV) to supplement its aerial surveillance platforms. UNMOVIC already has eight helicopters stationed in Iraq, as well as access to satellite imagery.

The increased capability for aerial surveillance through these new platforms provides UNMOVIC and the IAEA with additional tools to strengthen their operations and to verify Iraq's compliance with its obligations.

## Other developments

In December, UNMOVIC asked Iraq to provide, under the fourth subparagraph of paragraph 7 of resolution 1441 (2002), the names of all personnel currently or formerly associated with some aspects of Iraq's program of weapons of mass destruction and ballistic missiles. The Iraqi response was received at the end of December. However, it was deemed to be inadequate, as it did not even include all those who had been previously listed in Iraq's full, final and complete declaration. Iraq has since then supplemented its list of participants in the missile program, and has declared itself to be ready to do the same in the other disciplines. This matter is still being followed up.

On 14 January, UNMOVIC received from the National Monitoring Directorate Iraq's semi-annual monitoring declaration for the period from July 2002 to January 2003.

On 16 January, UNMOVIC chemical experts inspecting the Al Ukhaidhir military stores, discovered a number of empty 122-mm chemical munitions. The munitions have been tagged pending their destruction.

Following this discovery, Iraq appointed a commission of inquiry to undertake an investigation and comprehensive search for similar cases at all locations. One find of four more empty 122-mm chemical munitions was reported by that commission at Al Taji munitions stores. Subsequently, UNMOVIC inspectors found two more such munitions at the same site. These six munitions will also be destroyed.

Later in January, Iraq expanded the mandate of the commission to search for any remaining proscribed items on Iraqi territory. A second commission was appointed with the task of searching for any documents relevant to the proscribed items and programs. It is headed by the former Minister of Oil, General Amer Rashid, and has extensive powers of search in industry, administration and private houses.

On 21 and 25 February, Iraq informed UNMOVIC that two complete R–400 aerial bombs (one of which had liquid contents), plus remnants of what it states were 118 R–400 bombs, had been excavated at Azzizziyah, the declared unilateral destruction site of BW-filled aerial bombs, along with some related components and remnants of other destroyed munitions. UNMOVIC inspectors are currently investigating these finds.

In the course of February, the Iraqi side transmitted to UN-MOVIC lists of persons involved in the unilateral destruction during the summer of 1991 in the chemical, biological and missile fields.

After repeated requests by UNMOVIC and the IAEA for national implementing legislation, a presidential decree was issued in Baghdad on 14 February, containing prohibitions for persons and companies in the private and mixed sectors against the production or import of biological, chemical and nuclear weapons. UNMOVIC is requesting clarification of the decree and enquiring whether further legislative actions will follow.

# Staffing

As at the end of February 2003, UNMOVIC core staff in the Professional grades at Headquarters comprised 75 persons (of 30 nationalities). Thirteen members of the staff are women. [. . . ]

# Training

UNMOVIC conducted its seventh basic training course in Vienna from 20 January to 7 February for 59 selected experts from 22 countries. This brings the total number of persons trained by UNMOVIC to 380, including 49 staff members from Headquarters. They comprise 55 nationalities. Further training courses are envisaged. [. . . ]

## Non-inspection sources of information

With the commencement of inspections in Iraq on 27 November, the pace of work of the Office for Outside Information increased substantially. Countries that had supplied intelligence-related information to UNMOVIC in the previous two years were again contacted in an effort to obtain new up-to-date intelligence to assist in the inspection program. Also, additional countries were contacted in an effort to expand the base of knowledge currently available. To date, approximately a dozen countries have provided information of potential relevance to UNMOVIC's mandate. Much of that information has been utilized in conducting inspections in Iraq.

The Open Sources Officer has continued efforts to research and make available to UNMOVIC information relating to Iraq's industrial infrastructure that could be used in the production of prohibited weapons. In addition, there is a large volume of public information available suggesting procurement of items by Iraq that could have a dual-use capability.

## Communications

The inspectors were provided with the capabilities for clear and secure voice transmission from and within the mission area utilizing state-of-the-art equipment. The network is completely independent of the Iraqi public network. The telecommunications network, both voice and data, has a built-in redundancy and allows for future expansion. This redundancy is achieved by routing connections via two different satellite carriers.

The inspectors have INMARSAT devices and Thuraya satellite phones. Thurayas are used to establish communication from the field. The INMARSAT is being used for the field operations and also as a back-up in the regional offices. Each inspector was provided with a VHF radio and the VHF coverage extends about 80 kilometres around Baghdad. Long-range high-frequency stations were installed in the BOMVIC, the regional office in Mosul, the Office in Larnaca and the Al Rasheed air base. [. . . ]

## Observations

After three months of inspections, it may be legitimate to ask about results. First, has UNMOVIC come up to its full potential yet? Second, has Iraq cooperated, as required, and has disarmament been achieved?

The paragraphs above provide a description of the more important elements in UNMOVIC's work to establish and develop an effective inspection regime to verify that Iraq is free from, or being freed from, all weapons of mass destruction and other proscribed items—disarmament.

UNMOVIC has, in most areas, more resources and more advanced tools at its disposal than did UNSCOM and, in several respects, UNMOVIC has developed a capacity that goes beyond what was contemplated in its initial planning, e.g., in the number of personnel, number of teams in the field, number of sites visited. Yet, it could certainly further expand and strengthen its activity, e.g., in some form of controls of vehicles. Member States could also provide further support and assistance, notably in the field of information.

UNMOVIC is presently finalizing an internal document of some importance, namely, a list of the disarmament issues, which it considers currently unresolved, and of the measures which Iraq could take to resolve them, either by presenting proscribed stocks and items or by providing convincing evidence that such stocks or items no longer exist. The list, which in condensed form traces the history of clusters of weapons issues, has been prepared with a view to allowing UNMOVIC to perform its tasks under resolution 1284 (1999) to "address unresolved disarmament issues" and to identify "key remaining disarmament tasks". It could also serve as a yardstick against which Iraq's disarmament actions under resolution 1441 (2002) may be measured.

The paragraphs above further describe the actions taken by Iraq to respond to the obligations laid upon it in the relevant resolutions. Several of these are specific, as the obligation under resolution 1441 (2002) to provide a declaration 30 days after the adoption of the resolution. However, there is further the general obligation, prescribed in that resolution, to cooperate "immediately, unconditionally and actively" and the similar earlier requirement, in resolution 1284 (1999), for "cooperation in all respects". Has Iraq provided such cooperation and has it led to disarmament?

In comments on this question, a distinction has been made between cooperation on "process" and cooperation on "substance". UNMOVIC has reported that, in general, Iraq has been helpful on "process", meaning, first of all, that Iraq has from the outset satisfied the demand for prompt access to any site, whether or not it had been previously declared or inspected. There have thus been no sanctuaries in space. Nor have there been any sanctuaries in time, as inspections have taken place on holidays as on weekdays. While such cooperation should be a matter of course, it must be recalled that UNSCOM frequently met with a different Iraqi attitude.

Iraq has further been helpful in getting UNMOVIC established on the ground, in developing the necessary infrastructure for communications, transport and accommodation. Help has been given by the Iraqi side when needed for excavation and other operations. Iraqi staff has been provided, sometimes in excessive numbers, as escorts for the inspection teams. There have been minor frictions, e.g., demonstrations against inspectors and Iraqi criticism of some questions put by inspectors in the field.

A number of other actions might be discussed under the heading "cooperation on process":

A. After some initial difficulties with Iraq relating to escorting flights into the no-fly zones, UNMOVIC helicopters have been able to operate as requested both for transport and inspection purposes;

B. After some initial difficulties raised by Iraq, UNMOVIC has been able to send surveillance aircraft over the entire territory of Iraq in a manner similar to that of UNSCOM;

C. The Iraqi commission established to search for and present any proscribed items is potentially a mechanism of importance. It should, indeed, do the job that inspectors should not have to do, namely, tracing any remaining stocks or pieces of proscribed items anywhere in Iraq. Although appointed around 20 January, it has so far reported only a few findings: four empty 122-mm chemical munitions and, recently, two BW aerial bombs and some associated components;

D. The second Iraqi commission established to search for relevant documents could also be of importance, as lack of documentation or other evidence is the most common reason why quantities of items are deemed unaccounted for. Iraq has recently reported to UNMOVIC that the Commission had found documents concerning Iraq's unilateral destruction of proscribed items. As of the submission of this report, the documents are being examined;

E. The list of names of personnel reported to have taken part in the unilateral destruction of biological and chemical weapons and missiles in 1991 will open the possibility for interviews, which, if credible, might shed light on the scope of the unilateral actions. Such interviews will soon be organized. Before this has occurred and an evaluation is made of the results, it is not possible to know whether they will prove to be a successful way to reduce uncertainty about the quantities unilaterally destroyed;

F. Iraq has proposed a scientific technical procedure to measure quantities of proscribed liquid items disposed of in 1991. UNMOVIC experts are not very hopeful that these methods will bring meaningful results and will discuss this matter with Iraq in early March in Baghdad;

G. It has not yet proved possible to obtain interviews with Iraqi scientists, managers or others believed to have knowledge relevant to the disarmament tasks in circumstances that give satisfactory credibility. The Iraqi side reports that it encourages interviewees to accept such interviews, but the reality is that, so far, no persons not nominated by the Iraqi side have been willing to be interviewed without a tape recorder running or an Iraqi witness present.

Cooperation on substance:

A. The declaration of 7 December, despite the hopes attached to it and despite its large volume, has not been found to provide new evidence or data that may help to resolve outstanding disarmament issues. As has been mentioned above, it did, however, usefully shed light on the developments in the missile sector and in the sector of non-proscribed biological activities in the period 1998–2002;

B. The destruction of some items, e.g., small known quantities of mustard, is taking place under UNMOVIC supervision and further such action will take place, e.g., as regards the empty 122-mm chemical munitions;

C. Iraq has identified two aerial R–400 bombs, as well as remnants of what it states to be 118 R–400 bombs, at Azzizziyah;

D. The destruction of Al Samoud 2 missiles and related items declared by Iraq but found proscribed under the relevant resolutions has been requested and is due to commence on 1 March. Iraqi cooperation is essential;

E. The presidential decree, which was issued on 14 February and which prohibits private Iraqi citizens and mixed companies from engaging in work relating to weapons of mass destruction, standing alone, is not adequate to meet the United Nations requirements. UNMOVIC has enquired whether a comprehensive regulation is being prepared in line with several years of discussions between Iraq and UNSCOM/UNMOVIC.

Under resolution 1284 (1999), Iraq is to provide "cooperation in all respects" to UNMOVIC and the IAEA. While the objective of the cooperation under this resolution, as under resolution 1441

(2002), is evidently the attainment, without delay, of verified disarmament, it is the cooperation that must be immediate, unconditional and active. Without the required cooperation, disarmament and its verification will be problematic. However, even with the requisite cooperation it will inevitably require some time.

During the period of time covered by the present report, Iraq could have made greater efforts to find any remaining proscribed items or provide credible evidence showing the absence of such items. The results in terms of disarmament have been very limited so far. The destruction of missiles, which is an important operation, has not yet begun. Iraq could have made full use of the declaration, which was submitted on 7 December. It is hard to understand why a number of the measures, which are now being taken, could not have been initiated earlier. If they had been taken earlier, they might have borne fruit by now. It is only by the middle of January and thereafter that Iraq has taken a number of steps, which have the potential of resulting either in the presentation for destruction of stocks or items that are proscribed or the presentation of relevant evidence solving long-standing unresolved disarmament issues.

# President George W. Bush Discusses Iraq in National Press Conference, The East Room

•

## March 6, 2003

THE PRESIDENT: ... This has been an important week on two fronts on our war against terror. First, thanks to the hard work of American and Pakistani officials, we captured the mastermind of the September the 11th attacks against our nation. Khalid Sheikh Mohammed conceived and planned the hijackings and directed the actions of the hijackers. We believe his capture will further disrupt the terror network and their planning for additional attacks.

Second, we have arrived at an important moment in confronting the threat posed to our nation and to peace by Saddam Hussein and his weapons of terror. In New York tomorrow, the United Nations Security Council will receive an update from the chief weapons inspector. The world needs him to answer a single question: Has the Iraqi regime fully and unconditionally disarmed, as required by Resolution 1441, or has it not?

Iraq's dictator has made a public show of producing and destroying a few missiles—missiles that violate the restrictions set out more than 10 years ago. Yet, our intelligence shows that even as he is destroying these few missiles, he has ordered the continued production of the very same type of missiles.

Iraqi operatives continue to hide biological and chemical agents to avoid detection by inspectors. In some cases, these materials have been moved to different locations every 12 to 24 hours, or placed in vehicles that are in residential neighborhoods.

We know from multiple intelligence sources that Iraqi weapons scientists continue to be threatened with harm should they cooperate with U.N. inspectors. Scientists are required by Iraqi intelligence to wear concealed recording devices during interviews, and hotels where interviews take place are bugged by the regime.

These are not the actions of a regime that is disarming. These are the actions of a regime engaged in a willful charade. These are the actions of a regime that systematically and deliberately is defying the world. If the Iraqi regime were disarming, we would know it, because we would see it. Iraq's weapons would be presented to inspectors, and the world would witness their destruction. Instead, with the world demanding disarmament, and more than 200,000 troops positioned near his country, Saddam Hussein's response is to produce a few weapons for show, while he hides the rest and builds even more.

Inspection teams do not need more time, or more personnel. All they need is what they have never received—the full cooperation of the Iraqi regime. Token gestures are not acceptable. The only acceptable outcome is the one already defined by a unanimous vote of the Security Council—total disarmament.

Great Britain, Spain, and the United States have introduced a new resolution stating that Iraq has failed to meet the requirements of Resolution 1441. Saddam Hussein is not disarming. This is a fact. It cannot be denied.

Saddam Hussein has a long history of reckless aggression and terrible crimes. He possesses weapons of terror. He provides funding and training and safe haven to terrorists—terrorists who would willingly use weapons of mass destruction against America and other peace-loving countries. Saddam Hussein and his weapons are a direct threat to this country, to our people, and to all free people.

If the world fails to confront the threat posed by the Iraqi regime, refusing to use force, even as a last resort, free nations would assume immense and unacceptable risks. The attacks of September the 11th, 2001 showed what the enemies of America did with four airplanes. We will not wait to see what terrorists or terrorist states could do with weapons of mass destruction.

We are determined to confront threats wherever they arise. I will not leave the American people at the mercy of the Iraqi dictator and his weapons.

In the event of conflict, America also accepts our responsibility to protect innocent lives in every way possible. We'll bring food and medicine to the Iraqi people. We'll help that nation to build a just government, after decades of brutal dictatorship. The form and leadership of that government is for the Iraqi people to choose. Anything they choose will be better than the misery and torture and murder they have known under Saddam Hussein.

Across the world and in every part of America, people of good-will are hoping and praying for peace. Our goal is peace—for our nation, for our friends and allies, for the people of the Middle East. People of goodwill must also recognize that allowing a dangerous dictator to defy the world and harbor weapons of mass murder and terror is not peace at all; it is pretense. The cause of peace will be advanced only when the terrorists lose a wealthy patron and protector, and when the dictator is fully and finally disarmed.

Tonight I thank the men and women of our armed services and their families. I know their deployment so far from home is causing hardship for many military families. Our nation is deeply grateful to all who serve in uniform. We appreciate your commitment, your idealism, and your sacrifice. We support you, and we know that if peace must be defended, you are ready.

Ron Fournier.

Q:. . . Are we just days away from the point of which you decide whether or not we go to war? And what harm would it do to give Saddam a final ultimatum? A two- or three-day deadline to disarm or face force?

THE PRESIDENT: Well, we're still in the final stages of diplomacy. I'm spending a lot of time on the phone, talking to fellow leaders about the need for the United Nations Security Council to state the facts, which is Saddam Hussein hasn't disarmed. Fourteen forty-one, the Security Council resolution passed unanimously last fall, said clearly that Saddam Hussein has one last chance to disarm. He hasn't disarmed. And so we're working with Security Council members to resolve this issue at the Security Council.

This is not only an important moment for the security of our nation, I believe it's an important moment for the Security Council, itself. And the reason I say that is because this issue has been before the Security Council—the issue of disarmament of Iraq—for 12 long years. And the fundamental question facing the Security Council is, will its words mean anything? When the Security Council speaks, will the words have merit and weight?

I think it's important for those words to have merit and weight, because I understand that in order to win the war against terror there must be a united effort to do so; we must work together to defeat terror.

Iraq is a part of the war on terror. Iraq is a country that has got terrorist ties. It's a country with wealth. It's a country that trains terrorists, a country that could arm terrorists. And our fellow Americans must understand in this new war against terror, that we not only must chase down al Qaeda terrorists, we must deal with weapons of mass destruction, as well.

That's what the United Nations Security Council has been talking about for 12 long years. It's now time for this issue to come to a head at the Security Council, and it will. As far as ultimatums and all the speculation about what may or may not happen, after next week, we'll just wait and see. [. . . ]

Q: Thank you. Another hot spot is North Korea. If North Korea restarts their plutonium plant, will that change your thinking about how to handle this crisis, or are you resigned to North Korea becoming a nuclear power?

THE PRESIDENT: This is a regional issue. I say a regional issue because there's a lot of countries that have got a direct stake into whether or not North Korea has nuclear weapons. We've got a stake as to whether North Korea has a nuclear weapon. China clearly has a stake as to whether or not North Korea has a nuclear weapon. South Korea, of course, has a stake. Japan has got a significant stake as to whether or not North Korea has a nuclear weapon. Russia has a stake.

So, therefore, I think the best way to deal with this is in multilateral fashion, by convincing those nations they must stand up to their responsibility, along with the United States, to convince

Kim Jong-il that the development of a nuclear arsenal is not in his nation's interest; and that should he want help in easing the suffering of the North Korean people, the best way to achieve that help is to not proceed forward.

We've tried bilateral negotiations with North Korea. My predecessor, in a good-faith effort, entered into a framework agreement. The United States honored its side of the agreement; North Korea didn't. While we felt the agreement was in force, North Korea was enriching uranium.

In my judgment, the best way to deal with North Korea is convince parties to assume their responsibility. I was heartened by the fact that Jiang Zemin, when he came to Crawford, Texas, made it very clear to me and publicly, as well, that a nuclear weapons-free peninsula was in China's interest. And so we're working with China and the other nations I mentioned to bring a multilateral pressure and to convince Kim Jong-il that the development of a nuclear arsenal is not in his interests.

Dick.

Q: Mr. President, you have, and your top advisors—notably, Secretary of State Powell—have repeatedly said that we have shared with our allies all the current, up-to-date intelligence information that proves the imminence of the threat we face from Saddam Hussein, and that they have been sharing their intelligence with us, as well. If all these nations, all of them our normal allies, have access to the same intelligence information, why is it that they are reluctant to think that the threat is so real, so imminent that we need to move to the brink of war now? [ . . . ]

THE PRESIDENT: We, of course, are consulting with our allies at the United Nations. But I meant what I said, this is the last phase of diplomacy. A little bit more time? Saddam Hussein has had 12 years to disarm. He is deceiving people. This is what's important for our fellow citizens to realize; that if he really intended to disarm, like the world has asked him to do, we would know whether he was disarming. He's trying to buy time. I can understand why—he's been successful with these tactics for 12 years.

Saddam Hussein is a threat to our nation. September the 11th changed the strategic thinking, at least, as far as I was concerned, for how to protect our country. My job is to protect the American people. It used to be that we could think that you could contain a person like Saddam Hussein, that oceans would protect us from his type of terror. September the 11th should say to the American people that we're now a battlefield, that weapons of mass destruction in the hands of a terrorist organization could be deployed here at home.

So, therefore, I think the threat is real. And so do a lot of other people in my government. And since I believe the threat is real, and since my most important job is to protect the security of the American people, that's precisely what we'll do.

Our demands are that Saddam Hussein disarm. We hope he does. We have worked with the international community to convince him to disarm. If he doesn't disarm, we'll disarm him. [. . . ]

Jim Angle.

Q. Thank you, Mr. President. Sir, if you haven't already made the choice to go to war, can you tell us what you are waiting to hear or see before you do make that decision? And if I may, during the recent demonstrations, many of the protestors suggested that the U.S. was a threat to peace, which prompted you to wonder out loud why they didn't see Saddam Hussein as a threat to peace.[. . . ]

THE PRESIDENT: . . . I appreciate societies in which people can express their opinion. That society—free speech stands in stark contrast to Iraq.

Secondly, I've seen all kinds of protests since I've been the President. [. . . ]

I recognize there are people who—who don't like war. I don't like war. I wish that Saddam Hussein had listened to the demands of the world and disarmed. That was my hope. That's why I first went to the United Nations to begin with, on September the 12th, 2002, to address this issue as forthrightly as I knew how. That's why, months later, we went to the Security Council to get another resolution, called 1441, which was unanimously approved by the Security Council, demanding that Saddam Hussein disarm.

I'm hopeful that he does disarm. But, in the name of peace and the security of our people, if he won't do so voluntarily, we will disarm him. And other nations will join him—join us in disarming him.

And that creates a certain sense of anxiety; I understand that. Nobody likes war. The only thing I can do is assure the loved ones of those who wear our uniform that if we have to go to war, if war is upon us because Saddam Hussein has made that choice, we will have the best equipment available for our troops, the best plan available for victory, and we will respect innocent life in Iraq.

The risk of doing nothing, the risk of hoping that Saddam Hussein changes his mind and becomes a gentle soul, the risk that somehow—that inaction will make the world safer, is a risk I'm not willing to take for the American people. [ . . . ]

Q: Thank you, Mr. President. How would—sir, how would you answer your critics who say that they think this is somehow personal? As Senator Kennedy put it tonight, he said your fixation with Saddam Hussein is making the world a more dangerous place. [ . . . ]

THE PRESIDENT: My job is to protect America, and that is exactly what I'm going to do. People can ascribe all kinds of intentions. I swore to protect and defend the Constitution; that's what I swore to do. I put my hand on the Bible and took that oath, and that's exactly what I am going to do.

I believe Saddam Hussein is a threat to the American people. I believe he's a threat to the neighborhood in which he lives. And I've got a good evidence to believe that. He has weapons of mass destruction, and he has used weapons of mass destruction, in his neighborhood and on his own people. He's invaded countries in his neighborhood. He tortures his own people. He's a murderer. He has trained and financed al Qaeda-type organizations before, al Qaeda and other terrorist organizations. I take the threat seriously, and I'll deal with the threat. I hope it can be done peacefully. [ . . . ]

The price of doing nothing exceeds the price of taking action, if we have to. We'll do everything we can to minimize the loss of life. The price of the attacks on America, the cost of the attacks on America on September the 11th were enormous. They were significant. And I am not willing to take that chance again, John.

Terry Moran.

Q: Thank you, sir. May I follow up on Jim Angle's question? In the past several weeks, your policy on Iraq has generated opposition from the governments of France, Russia, China, Germany, Turkey, the Arab League and many other countries, opened a rift at NATO and at the U.N., and drawn millions of ordinary citizens around the world into the streets in anti-war protests. May I ask, what went wrong that so many governments and people around the world now not only disagree with you very strongly, but see the U.S. under your leadership as an arrogant power?

THE PRESIDENT:[ . . . ]I think you'll see when it's all said and done, if we have to use force, a lot of nations will be with us.

You clearly named some that—France and Germany expressed their opinions. We have a disagreement over how best to deal with Saddam Hussein. I understand that. Having said that, they're still our friends and we will deal with them as friends. We've got a lot of common interests. Our transatlantic relationships are very important. While they may disagree with how we deal with Saddam Hussein and his weapons of mass destruction, there's no disagreement when it came time to vote on 1441, at least as far as France was concerned. They joined us. They said Saddam Hussein has one last chance of disarming. If they think more time will cause him to disarm, I disagree with that.

He's a master at deception. He has no intention of disarming—otherwise, we would have known. There's a lot of talk about inspectors. It really would have taken a handful of inspectors to determine whether he was disarming—they could have showed up at a parking lot and he could have brought his weapons and destroyed them. That's not what he chose to do.

Secondly, I make my decisions based upon the oath I took, the one I just described to you. I believe Saddam Hussein is a threat—is a threat to the American people. He's a threat to people in his neighborhood. He's also a threat to the Iraqi people.

One of the things we love in America is freedom. If I may, I'd like to remind you what I said at the State of the Union: liberty is not America's gift to the world, it is God's gift to each and every person. And that's what I believe. I believe that when we see totalitarianism, that we must deal with it. We don't have to do it always militarily. But this is a unique circumstance, because of 12 years of denial and defiance, because of terrorist connections, because of past history.

I'm convinced that a liberated Iraq will be—will be important for that troubled part of the world. The Iraqi people are plenty capable of governing themselves. Iraq is a sophisticated society. Iraq's got money. Iraq will provide a place where people can see that the Shia and the Sunni and the Kurds can get along in a federation. Iraq will serve as a catalyst for change, positive change.

So there's a lot more at stake than just American security, and the security of people close by Saddam Hussein. Freedom is at stake, as well, and I take that very seriously.

[. . .]

Q: Sir, I'm sorry, is success contingent upon capturing or killing Saddam Hussein, in your mind?

THE PRESIDENT: We will be changing the regime of Iraq, for the good of the Iraqi people.

Bill Plante.

Q: Mr. President, to a lot of people, it seems that war is probably inevitable, because many people doubt—most people, I would guess—that Saddam Hussein will ever do what we are demanding that he do, which is disarm. And if war is inevitable, there are a lot of people in this country—as much as half, by polling standards— who agree that he should be disarmed, who listen to you say that you have the evidence, but who feel they haven't seen it, and who still wonder why blood has to be shed if he hasn't attacked us.

THE PRESIDENT: Well, Bill, if they believe he should be disarmed, and he's not going to disarm, there's only one way to disarm him. And that happens to be my last choice—the use of force.

Secondly, the American people know that Saddam Hussein has weapons of mass destruction. By the way, he declared he didn't have any—1441 insisted that he have a complete declaration of his weapons; he said he didn't have any weapons. Secondly, he's used these weapons before. I mean, this is—we're not speculating about the nature of the man. We know the nature of the man. [. . .]

Let's see here. Elizabeth.

Q: Thank you, Mr. President. As you said, the Security Council faces a vote next week on a resolution implicitly authorizing an attack on Iraq. Will you call for a vote on that resolution, even if you aren't sure you have the vote?

THE PRESIDENT: Well, first, I don't think—it basically says that he's in defiance of 1441. That's what the resolution says. And it's hard to believe anybody is saying he isn't in defiance of 1441, because 1441 said he must disarm. And, yes, we'll call for a vote.

Q: No matter what?

THE PRESIDENT: No matter what the whip count is, we're calling for the vote. We want to see people stand up and say what their opinion is about Saddam Hussein and the utility of the United Nations Security Council. And so, you bet. It's time for people to show their cards, to let the world know where they stand when it comes to Saddam.

Mark Knoller.

Q: Mr. President, are you worried that the United States might be viewed as defiant of the United Nations if you went ahead with military action without specific and explicit authorization from the U.N.?

THE PRESIDENT: No, I'm not worried about that. As a matter of fact, it's hard to say the United States is defiant about the United Nations, when I was the person that took the issue to the United Nations, September the 12th, 2002. We've been working with the United Nations. We've been working through the United Nations.

Secondly, I'm confident the American people understand that when it comes to our security, if we need to act, we will act, and we really don't need United Nations approval to do so. I want to work—I want the United Nations to be effective. It's important for it to be a robust, capable body. It's important for it's words to mean what they say, and as we head into the 21st century, Mark, when it comes to our security, we really don't need anybody's permission. [. . . ]

Hutch.

Q: Thank you, Mr. President. As you know, not everyone shares your optimistic vision of how this might play out. Do you ever worry, maybe in the wee, small hours, that you might be wrong and they might be right in thinking that this could lead to more terrorism, more anti-American sentiment, more instability in the Middle East?

THE PRESIDENT: Hutch, I think, first of all, it's hard to envision more terror on America than September the 11th, 2001. We did nothing to provoke that terrorist attack. It came upon us because there's an enemy which hates America. They hate what we stand for. We love freedom and we're not changing. And, therefore, so long as there's a terrorist network like al Qaeda, and others willing to fund them, finance them, equip them—we're at war.

And so I—you know, obviously, I've thought long and hard about the use of troops. I think about it all the time. It is my responsibility to commit the troops. I believe we'll prevail—I know we'll prevail. And out of that disarmament of Saddam will come a better world, particularly for the people who live in Iraq.

This is a society, Ron, who—which has been decimated by his murderous ways, his torture. He doesn't allow dissent. He doesn't believe in the values we believe in. I believe this society, the Iraqi society can develop in a much better way. I think of the risks, calculated the cost of inaction versus the cost of action. And I'm firmly convinced, if we have to, we will act, in the name of peace and in the name of freedom. [. . . ]

It makes no sense to allow this issue to continue on and on, in the hopes that Saddam Hussein disarms. The whole purpose of the debate is for Saddam to disarm. We gave him a chance. As a matter of fact, we gave him 12 years of chances. But, recently, we gave him a chance, starting last fall. And it said, last chance to disarm. The resolution said that. And had he chosen to do so, it would be evident that he's disarmed.

So more time, more inspectors, more process, in our judgment, is not going to affect the peace of the world. So whatever is resolved is going to have some finality to it, so that Saddam Hussein will take us seriously.

I want to remind you that it's his choice to make as to whether or not we go to war. It's Saddam's choice. He's the person that can make the choice of war and peace. Thus far, he's made the wrong choice. If we have to, for the sake of the security of the American people, for the sake of peace in the world, and for freedom to the Iraqi people, we will disarm Saddam Hussein. And by we, it's more than America. A lot of nations will join us.

Thank you for your questions. Good night.

# UNMOVIC and IAEA Briefings to the Security Council

•

# March 7, 2003

## Hans Blix, executive chairman of UNMOVIC

Mr. President,

For nearly three years, I have been coming to the Security Council presenting the quarterly reports of UNMOVIC. They have described our many preparations for the resumption of inspections in Iraq. The 12th quarterly report is the first that describes three months of inspections. They come after four years without inspections. The report was finalized ten days ago and a number of relevant events have taken place since then. Today's statement will supplement the circulated report on these points to bring the Council up-to-date.

*Inspection process*

Inspections in Iraq resumed on 27 November 2002. In matters relating to process, notably prompt access to sites, we have faced relatively few difficulties and certainly much less than those that were faced by UNSCOM in the period 1991 to 1998. This may well be due to the strong outside pressure.

Some practical matters, which were not settled by the talks, Dr. ElBaradei and I had with the Iraqi side in Vienna prior to inspections or in resolution 1441 (2002), have been resolved at meetings, which we have had in Baghdad. Initial difficulties raised by the Iraqi side about helicopters and aerial surveillance planes operating in the no-fly zones were overcome. This is not to say that the operation of inspections is free from frictions, but at this juncture we are able to perform professional no-notice inspections all over Iraq and to increase aerial surveillance.

American U–2 and French Mirage surveillance aircraft already give us valuable imagery, supplementing satellite pictures and we would expect soon to be able to add night vision capability through an aircraft offered to us by the Russian Federation. We also expect to add low-level, close area surveillance through drones provided by Germany. We are grateful not only to the countries, which place these valuable tools at our disposal, but also to the States, most recently Cyprus, which has agreed to the stationing of aircraft on their territory.

## *Documents and interviews*

Iraq, with a highly developed administrative system, should be able to provide more documentary evidence about its proscribed weapons programs. Only a few new such documents have come to light so far and been handed over since we began inspections. It was a disappointment that Iraq's Declaration of 7 December did not bring new documentary evidence. I hope that efforts in this respect, including the appointment of a governmental commission, will give significant results. When proscribed items are deemed unaccounted for it is above all credible accounts that is needed—or the proscribed items, if they exist.

Where authentic documents do not become available, interviews with persons, who may have relevant knowledge and experience, may be another way of obtaining evidence. UNMOVIC has names of such persons in its records and they are among the people whom we seek to interview. In the last month, Iraq has provided us with the names of many persons, who may be relevant sources of information, in particular, persons who took part in various phases of the unilateral destruction of biological and chemical weapons, and proscribed missiles in 1991. The provision of names prompts two reflections:

The first is that with such detailed information existing regarding those who took part in the unilateral destruction, surely there must also remain records regarding the quantities and other data concerning the various items destroyed.

The second reflection is that with relevant witnesses available it becomes even more important to be able to conduct interviews in modes and locations which allow us to be confident that the testimony is given without outside influence. While the Iraqi side seems to have encouraged interviewees not to request the presence of Iraqi officials (so-called minders) or the taping of the interviews, conditions ensuring the absence of undue influences are difficult to attain inside Iraq. Interviews outside the country might provide such assurance. It is our intention to request such interviews shortly. Nevertheless, despite remaining shortcomings, interviews are useful. Since we started requesting interviews, 38 individuals were asked for private interviews, of which 10 accepted under our terms, 7 of these during the last week.

As I noted on 14 February, intelligence authorities have claimed that weapons of mass destruction are moved around Iraq by trucks and, in particular, that there are mobile production units for biological weapons. The Iraqi side states that such activities do not exist. Several inspections have taken place at declared and undeclared sites in relation to mobile production facilities. Food testing mobile laboratories and mobile workshops have been seen, as well as large containers with seed processing equipment. No evidence of proscribed activities have so far been found. Iraq is expected to assist in the development of credible ways to conduct random checks of ground transportation.

Inspectors are also engaged in examining Iraq's program for Remotely Piloted Vehicles (RPVs). A number of sites have been inspected with data being collected to assess the range and other capabilities of the various models found. Inspections are continuing in this area.

There have been reports, denied from the Iraqi side, that proscribed activities are conducted underground. Iraq should provide information on any underground structure suitable for the production or storage of WMD. During inspections of declared or undeclared facilities, inspection teams have examined building structures for any possible underground facilities. In addition, ground penetrating radar equipment was used in several specific locations. No underground facilities for chemical or biological production or storage were found so far.

I should add that, both for the monitoring of ground transportation and for the inspection of underground facilities, we would need to increase our staff in Iraq. I am not talking about a doubling of the staff. I would rather have twice the amount of high quality information about sites to inspect than twice the number of expert inspectors to send.

## Recent developments

On 14 February, I reported to the Council that the Iraqi side had become more active in taking and proposing steps, which potentially might shed new light on unresolved disarmament issues. Even a week ago, when the current quarterly report was finalized, there was still relatively little tangible progress to note. Hence, the cautious formulations in the report before you.

As of today, there is more. While during our meetings in Baghdad, the Iraqi side tried to persuade us that the Al Samoud 2 missiles they have declared fall within the permissible range set by the Security Council, the calculations of an international panel of experts led us to the opposite conclusion. Iraq has since accepted that these missiles and associated items be destroyed and has started the process of destruction under our supervision. The destruction undertaken constitutes a substantial measure of disarmament—indeed, the first since the middle of the 1990s. We are not watching the breaking of toothpicks. Lethal weapons are being destroyed. However, I must add that no destruction has happened today. I hope it's a temporary break.

To date, 34 Al Samoud 2 missiles, including 4 training missiles, 2 combat warheads, 1 launcher and 5 engines have been destroyed under UNMOVIC supervision. Work is continuing to identify and inventory the parts and equipment associated with the Al Samoud 2 programme.

Two 'reconstituted' casting chambers used in the production of solid propellant missiles have been destroyed and the remnants melted or encased in concrete.

The legality of the Al Fatah missile is still under review, pending further investigation and measurement of various parameters of that missile.

More papers on anthrax, VX and missiles have recently been provided. Many have been found to restate what Iraq had already declared, some will require further study and discussion.

There is a significant Iraqi effort underway to clarify a major source of uncertainty as to the quantities of biological and chemical weapons which were unilaterally destroyed in 1991. A part of this effort concerns a disposal site, which was deemed too dangerous for full investigation in the past. It is now being re-excavated. To date, Iraq has unearthed eight complete bombs comprising two liquid-filled intact R–400 bombs and six other complete bombs. Bomb fragments were also found. Samples have been taken. The investigation of the destruction site could, in the best case, allow the determination of the number of bombs destroyed at that site. It should be followed by a serious and credible effort to determine the separate issue of how many R–400 type bombs were produced. In this, as in other matters, inspection work is moving on and may yield results.

Iraq proposed an investigation using advanced technology to quantify the amount of unilaterally destroyed anthrax dumped at a site. However, even if the use of advanced technology could quantify the amount of anthrax, said to be dumped at the site, the results would still be open to interpretation. Defining the quantity of anthrax destroyed must, of course, be followed by efforts to establish what quantity was actually produced.

With respect to VX, Iraq has recently suggested a similar method to quantify a VX precursor stated to have been unilaterally destroyed in the summer of 1991.

Iraq has also recently informed us that, following the adoption of the presidential decree prohibiting private individuals and mixed companies from engaging in work related to WMD, further legislation on the subject is to be enacted. This appears to be in response to a letter from UNMOVIC requesting clarification of the issue.

What are we to make of these activities? One can hardly avoid the impression that, after a period of somewhat reluctant cooperation, there has been an acceleration of initiatives from the Iraqi side since the end of January.

This is welcome, but the value of these measures must be soberly judged by how many question marks they actually succeed in straightening out. This is not yet clear.

Against this background, the question is now asked whether Iraq has cooperated "immediately, unconditionally and actively" with UNMOVIC, as required under paragraph 9 of resolution 1441 (2002). The answers can be seen from the factual descriptions I have provided. However, if more direct answers are desired, I would say the following:

The Iraqi side has tried on occasion to attach conditions, as it did regarding helicopters and U–2 planes. Iraq has not, however, so far persisted in these or other conditions for the exercise of any of our inspection rights. If it did, we would report it.

It is obvious that, while the numerous initiatives, which are now taken by the Iraqi side with a view to resolving some long-standing open disarmament issues, can be seen as "active", or even "proactive", these initiatives 3–4 months into the new resolution cannot be said to constitute "immediate" cooperation. Nor do they necessarily cover all areas of relevance. They are nevertheless welcome and UNMOVIC is responding to them in the hope of solving presently unresolved disarmament issues.

Members of the Council may relate most of what I have said to resolution 1441 (2002), but UNMOVIC is performing work under several resolutions of the Security Council. The quarterly report before you is submitted in accordance with resolution 1284 (1999), which not only created UNMOVIC but also continues to guide much of our work. Under the time lines set by the resolution, the results of some of this work is to be reported to the Council before the end of this month. Let me be more specific.

Resolution 1284 (1999) instructs UNMOVIC to "address unresolved disarmament issues" and to identify "key remaining disarmament tasks" and the latter are to be submitted for approval by the Council in the context of a work program. UNMOVIC will be ready to submit a draft work program this month as required.

UNSCOM and the Amorim Panel did valuable work to identify the disarmament issues, which were still open at the end of
1998. UNMOVIC has used this material as starting points but
analyzed the data behind it and data and documents post 1998 up
to the present time to compile its own list of "unresolved disarmament issues" or, rather, clustered issues. It is the answers to these
issues which we seek through our inspection activities.

It is from the list of these clustered issues that UNMOVIC will
identify the "key remaining disarmament tasks". As noted in the
report before you, this list of clustered issues is ready.

UNMOVIC is only required to submit the work program with
the "key remaining disarmament tasks" to the Council. As I understand that several Council members are interested in the
working document with the complete clusters of disarmament issues, we have declassified it and are ready to make it available to
members of the Council on request. In this working document,
which may still be adjusted in the light of new information, members will get a more up-to-date review of the outstanding issues
than in the documents of 1999, which members usually refer to.
Each cluster in the working document ends with a number of
points indicating what Iraq could do to solve the issue. Hence,
Iraq's cooperation could be measured against the successful resolution of issues.

I should note that the working document contains much information and discussion about the issues which existed at the end of
1998—including information which has come to light after 1998.
It contains much less information and discussion about the period
after 1998, primarily because of paucity of information. Nevertheless, intelligence agencies have expressed the view that proscribed programs have continued or restarted in this period. It is
further contended that proscribed programs and items are located
in underground facilities, as I mentioned, and that proscribed
items are being moved around Iraq. The working document contains some suggestions on how these concerns may be tackled.

Mr. President,

Let me conclude by telling you that UNMOVIC is currently
drafting the work program, which resolution 1284 (1999) requires us to submit this month. It will obviously contain our pro-

posed list of key remaining disarmament tasks; it will describe the reinforced system of ongoing monitoring and verification that the Council has asked us to implement; it will also describe the various subsystems which constitute the program, e.g. for aerial surveillance, for information from governments and suppliers, for sampling, for the checking of road traffic, etc.

How much time would it take to resolve the key remaining disarmament tasks? While cooperation can and is to be immediate, disarmament and at any rate the verification of it cannot be instant. Even with a proactive Iraqi attitude, induced by continued outside pressure, it would still take some time to verify sites and items, analyze documents, interview relevant persons, and draw conclusions. It would not take years, nor weeks, but months. Neither governments nor inspectors would want disarmament inspection to go on forever. However, it must be remembered that in accordance with the governing resolutions, a sustained inspection and monitoring system is to remain in place after verified disarmament to give confidence and to strike an alarm, if signs were seen of the revival of any proscribed weapons programs.

## Mohamed ElBaradci, director general of IAEA:

Mr. President,

My report to the council today is an update on the status of the International Atomic Energy Agency's nuclear verification activities in Iraq pursuant to Security Council Resolution 1441 and other relevant resolutions.

When I reported last to the council on February 14, I explained that the agency's inspection activities has moved well beyond the reconnaissance phase—that is, re-establishing our knowledge base regarding Iraq nuclear capabilities—into the investigative phase, which focuses on the central question before the IAEA relevant to disarmament—whether Iraq has revived or attempted to revive its defunct nuclear weapons program over the last four years.

At the outset, let me state on general observation, namely that during the past four years at the majority of Iraqi sites industrial capacity has deteriorated substantially due to the departure of the foreign support that was often present in the late '80s, the departure of large numbers of skilled Iraqi personnel in the past decade and the lack of consistent maintenance by Iraq of sophisticated equipment.

At only a few inspected sites involved in industrial research, development and manufacturing have the facilities been improved and new personnel been taken on.

This overall deterioration in industrial capacity is naturally of direct relevance to Iraq's capability for resuming a nuclear weapons program.

The IAEA has now conducted a total of 218 nuclear inspections at 141 sites, including 21 that have not been inspected before. In addition, the agency experts have taken part in many joint UNMOVIC -IAEA inspections. Technical support for nuclear inspections has continued to expand. The three operational air samplers have collected from key locations in Iraq weekly air particulate samples that are being sent to laboratories for analysis. Additional results of water, sediment, vegetation and material sample analysis have been received from the relevant laboratories.

Our vehicle-borne radiation survey team has covered some 2,000 kilometers over the past three weeks. Survey access has been gained to over 75 facilities, including military garrisons and camps, weapons factories, truck parks and manufacturing facilities and residential areas.

Interviews have continued with relevant Iraqi personnel, at times with individuals and groups in the workplace during the course of unannounced inspections, and on other occasions in pre-arranged meetings with key scientists and other specialists known to have been involved with Iraq's past nuclear program.

The IAEA has continued to conduct interviews, even when the conditions were not in accordance with the IAEA-preferred modalities, with a view to gaining as much information as possible—information that could be cross-checked for validity with other sources and which could be helpful in our assessment of areas under investigation.

As you may recall, when we first began to request private, unescorted interviews, the Iraqi interviewees insisted on taping the interviews and keeping the recorded tapes. Recently, upon our insistence, individuals have been consenting to being interviewed without escort and without a taped record. The IAEA has conducted two such private interviews in the last 10 days, and hope that its ability to conduct private interviews will continue unhindered, including possibly interviews outside Iraq.

I should add that we are looking into further refining the modalities for conducting interviews to ensure that they are conducted freely and to alleviate concerns that interviews are being listened to by other Iraqi parties. In our view, interviews outside Iraq may be the best way to ensure that interviews are free, and we intend therefore to request such interviews shortly.

We are also asking other states to enable us to conduct interviews with former Iraqi scientists that now reside in those states.

Mr. President, in the last few weeks, Iraq has provided a considerable volume of documentation relevant to the issues I reported earlier as being of particular concern, including Iraq's efforts to procure aluminum tubes, its attempted procurement of magnets and magnets-production capabilities and its reported attempt to import uranium.

I will touch briefly on the progress made on each of these issues.

Since my last update to the council, the primary technical focus of IAEA field activities in Iraq has been on resolving several outstanding issues related to the possible resumption of efforts by Iraq to enrich uranium through the use of centrifuge. For that purpose, the IAEA assembled a specially qualified team of international centrifuge manufacturing experts.

With regard to the aluminum tubes, the IAEA has conducted a thorough investigation of Iraq's attempt to purchase large quantities of high-strength aluminum tubes. As previously reported, Iraq has maintained that these aluminum tubes were sold for rocket production.

Extensive field investigation and document analysis have failed to uncover any evidence that Iraq intended to use these 81-millimeter tubes for any project other than the reverse engineering of rockets.

The Iraqi decision-making process with regard to the design of these rockets was well-documented. Iraq has provided copies of design documents, procurement records, minutes of committee meetings and supporting data and samples.

A thorough analysis of this information, together with information gathered from interviews with Iraqi personnel, has allowed the IAEA to develop a coherent picture of attempted purchase and intended usage of the 81-millimeter aluminum tubes as well as the rationale behind the changes in the tolerance.

Drawing on this information, the IAEA has learned that the original tolerance for the 81-millimeter tubes were set prior to 1987 and were based on physical measurements taken from a small number of imported rockets in Iraq's possession.

Initial attempts to reverse-engineer the rockets met with little success. Tolerance were adjusted during the following years as part of ongoing efforts to revitalize a project and improve operational efficiency. The project language for a long period during this time became the subject of several committees, which resulted in the specification and tolerance changes on each occasion.

Based on available evidence, the IAEA team has concluded that Iraq efforts to import these aluminum tubes were not likely to have been related to the manufacture of centrifuge, and moreover that it was highly unlikely that Iraq could have achieved the considerable redesign needed to use them in a revived centrifuge program.

However, this issue will continue to be scrutinized and investigated.

With respect to reports about Iraq efforts to import high-strength permanent magnets or to achieve the capability for producing such magnets for use in a centrifuge enrichment program, I should note that since 1998 Iraq has purchased high-strength magnets for various uses.

Iraq has declared inventories of magnets of 12 different designs. The IAEA has verified that previously acquired magnets have been used for missile guidance systems, industrial machinery, electricity meters and field telephones.

Through visits to research and production sites, review of engineering drawings and analysis of sample magnets, the IAEA experts familiar with the use of such magnets in centrifuge enrichment have verified that none of the magnets that Iraq has declared could be used directly for centrifuge magnetic bearings.

In June 2001, Iraq signed a contract for a new magnet production line for delivery and installation in 2003. The delivery has not yet occurred, and Iraqi documentations and interviews of Iraqi personnel indicate that this contract will not be executed.

However, they have concluded that the replacement of foreign procurement with domestic magnet production seems reasonable from an economic point of view.

In addition, the training and experience acquired by Iraq in pre–1991 period make it likely that Iraq possesses the expertise to manufacture high-strength permanent magnets suitable for use in enrichment centrifuges. The IAEA will continue, therefore, to monitor and inspect equipment and materials that could be used to make magnets for enrichment centrifuges.

With regard to uranium acquisition, the IAEA has made progress in its investigation into reports that Iraq sought to buy uranium from Niger in recent years. The investigation was centered on documents provided by a number of states that pointed to an agreement between Niger and Iraq for the sale of uranium between 1999 and 2001.

The IAEA has discussed these reports with the governments of Iraq and Israel, both of which have denied that any such activity took place.

For its part, Iraq has provided the IAEA with a comprehensive explanation of its relations with Niger and has described a visit by an Iraqi official to a number of African countries, including Niger in February 1999, which Iraq thought might have given rise to the reports.

The IAEA was able to review correspondence coming from various bodies of the government of Niger and to compare the form, format, contents and signature of that correspondence with those of the alleged procurement-related documentation.

Based on thorough analysis, the IAEA has concluded with the concurrence of outside experts that these documents which formed the basis for the report of recent uranium transaction between Iraq and Niger are in fact not authentic. We have therefore concluded that these specific allegations are unfounded. However, we will continue to follow up any additional evidence if it emerges relevant to efforts by Iraq to illicitly import nuclear materials.

Many concerns regarding Iraq's possible intention to resume its nuclear program have arisen from Iraq's procurement efforts reported by a number of states. In addition, many of Iraq's efforts to procure commodities and products, including magnets and aluminum tubes, have been conducted in contravention of the sanctions specified under Security Council Resolution 661 and other relevant resolutions.

The issue of procurement efforts remains under thorough investigation, and further verification will be forthcoming. In fact, an IAEA team of technical experts is currently in Iraq, composed of custom investigators and computer forensics specialists, to conduct a—which is conducting a series of investigations [through] inspection of trading companies and commercial organizations aimed at understanding Iraq's pattern of procurement.

Mr. President, in conclusion, I am able to report today that in the area of nuclear weapons, the most lethal weapons of mass destruction, inspections in Iraq are moving forward.

Since the resumption of inspection a little over three months ago, and particularly during the three weeks since my last ordered report to the council, the IAEA has made important progress in identifying what nuclear-related capabilities remain in Iraq and in its assessment of whether Iraq has made any effort to revive its past nuclear program during the intervening four years since inspections were brought to a halt.

At this stage, the following can be stated:

One, there is no indication of resumed nuclear activities in those buildings that were identified through the use of satellite imagery as being reconstructed or newly erected since 1998, nor any indication of nuclear-related prohibited activities at any inspected sites.

Second, there is no indication that Iraq has attempted to import uranium since 1990.

Three, there is no indication that Iraq has attempted to import aluminum tubes for use in centrifuge enrichment. Moreover, even had Iraq pursued such a plan, it would have encountered practical difficulties in manufacturing centrifuge out of the aluminum tubes in question.

Fourth, although we are still reviewing issues related to magnets and magnet-production, there is no indication to date that Iraq imported magnets for use in centrifuge enrichment program.

As I stated above, the IAEA will naturally continue further to scrutinize and investigate all of the above issues.

After three months of intrusive inspections, we have to date found no evidence or plausible indication of the revival of a nuclear weapon program in Iraq.

We intend to continue our inspection activities, making use of all additional rights granted to us by Resolution 1441 and all additional tools that might be available to us, including reconnaissance platforms and all relevant technologies.

We also hope to continue to receive from states actionable information relevant to our mandate.

I should note that in the past three weeks, possibly as a result of ever-increasing pressure by the international community, Iraq has been forthcoming in its cooperation, particularly with regard to the conduct of private interviews and in making available evidence that could contribute to the resolution of matters of IAEA concern. I do hope that Iraq will continue to expand the scope and accelerate the pace of its cooperation.

The detailed knowledge of Iraq capabilities that IAEA experts have accumulated since 1991, combined with the extended rights provided by Resolution 1441, the active commitment by all states to help us fulfill our mandate and the recently increased level of Iraqi cooperation should enable us in the near future to provide the Security Council with an objective and thorough assessment of Iraq's nuclear-related capabilities.

However, credible this assessment may be, we will endeavor, in view of the inherent uncertainties associated with any verification process, and particularly in the light of Iraq past record of cooperation, to evaluate Iraq capabilities on a continuous basis as part of our long-term monitoring and verification program in order to provide the international community with ongoing and real-time assurances. Thank you, Mr. President.

# President George W. Bush
# Addresses the Nation on Iraq

•

# March 17, 2003

My fellow citizens, events in Iraq have now reached the final days of decision. For more than a decade, the United States and other nations have pursued patient and honorable efforts to disarm the Iraqi regime without war. That regime pledged to reveal and destroy all its weapons of mass destruction as a condition for ending the Persian Gulf War in 1991.

Since then, the world has engaged in 12 years of diplomacy. We have passed more than a dozen resolutions in the United Nations Security Council. We have sent hundreds of weapons inspectors to oversee the disarmament of Iraq. Our good faith has not been returned.

The Iraqi regime has used diplomacy as a ploy to gain time and advantage. It has uniformly defied Security Council resolutions demanding full disarmament. Over the years, U.N. weapon inspectors have been threatened by Iraqi officials, electronically bugged, and systematically deceived. Peaceful efforts to disarm the Iraqi regime have failed again and again—because we are not dealing with peaceful men.

Intelligence gathered by this and other governments leaves no doubt that the Iraq regime continues to possess and conceal some of the most lethal weapons ever devised. This regime has already used weapons of mass destruction against Iraq's neighbors and against Iraq's people.

The regime has a history of reckless aggression in the Middle East. It has a deep hatred of America and our friends. And it has aided, trained and harbored terrorists, including operatives of al Qaeda.

The danger is clear: using chemical, biological or, one day, nuclear weapons, obtained with the help of Iraq, the terrorists could fulfill their stated ambitions and kill thousands or hundreds of thousands of innocent people in our country, or any other.

The United States and other nations did nothing to deserve or invite this threat. But we will do everything to defeat it. Instead of drifting along toward tragedy, we will set a course toward safety. Before the day of horror can come, before it is too late to act, this danger will be removed.

The United States of America has the sovereign authority to use force in assuring its own national security. That duty falls to me, as Commander-in-Chief, by the oath I have sworn, by the oath I will keep.

Recognizing the threat to our country, the United States Congress voted overwhelmingly last year to support the use of force against Iraq. America tried to work with the United Nations to address this threat because we wanted to resolve the issue peacefully. We believe in the mission of the United Nations. One reason the U.N. was founded after the second world war was to confront aggressive dictators, actively and early, before they can attack the innocent and destroy the peace.

In the case of Iraq, the Security Council did act, in the early 1990s. Under Resolutions 678 and 687—both still in effect—the United States and our allies are authorized to use force in ridding Iraq of weapons of mass destruction. This is not a question of authority, it is a question of will.

Last September, I went to the U.N. General Assembly and urged the nations of the world to unite and bring an end to this danger. On November 8th, the Security Council unanimously passed Resolution 1441, finding Iraq in material breach of its obligations, and vowing serious consequences if Iraq did not fully and immediately disarm.

Today, no nation can possibly claim that Iraq has disarmed. And it will not disarm so long as Saddam Hussein holds power. For the last four-and-a-half months, the United States and our allies have worked within the Security Council to enforce that Council's long-standing demands. Yet, some permanent members of the Security Council have publicly announced they will veto any resolution that compels the disarmament of Iraq. These governments share our assessment of the danger, but not our resolve to meet it. Many nations, however, do have the resolve and fortitude to act against this threat to peace, and a broad coalition is now gathering to enforce the just demands of the world. The United Nations Security Council has not lived up to its responsibilities, so we will rise to ours.

In recent days, some governments in the Middle East have been doing their part. They have delivered public and private messages urging the dictator to leave Iraq, so that disarmament can proceed peacefully. He has thus far refused. All the decades of deceit and cruelty have now reached an end. Saddam Hussein and his sons must leave Iraq within 48 hours. Their refusal to do so will result in military conflict, commenced at a time of our choosing. For their own safety, all foreign nationals—including journalists and inspectors—should leave Iraq immediately.

Many Iraqis can hear me tonight in a translated radio broadcast, and I have a message for them. If we must begin a military campaign, it will be directed against the lawless men who rule your country and not against you. As our coalition takes away their power, we will deliver the food and medicine you need. We will tear down the apparatus of terror and we will help you to build a new Iraq that is prosperous and free. In a free Iraq, there will be no more wars of aggression against your neighbors, no more poison factories, no more executions of dissidents, no more torture chambers and rape rooms. The tyrant will soon be gone. The day of your liberation is near.

It is too late for Saddam Hussein to remain in power. It is not too late for the Iraqi military to act with honor and protect your country by permitting the peaceful entry of coalition forces to eliminate weapons of mass destruction. Our forces will give Iraqi military units clear instructions on actions they can take to avoid being attacked and destroyed. I urge every member of the Iraqi military and intelligence services, if war comes, do not fight for a dying regime that is not worth your own life.

And all Iraqi military and civilian personnel should listen carefully to this warning. In any conflict, your fate will depend on your action. Do not destroy oil wells, a source of wealth that belongs to the Iraqi people. Do not obey any command to use weapons of mass destruction against anyone, including the Iraqi people. War crimes will be prosecuted. War criminals will be punished. And it will be no defense to say, "I was just following orders."

Should Saddam Hussein choose confrontation, the American people can know that every measure has been taken to avoid war, and every measure will be taken to win it. Americans understand the costs of conflict because we have paid them in the past. War has no certainty, except the certainty of sacrifice.

Yet, the only way to reduce the harm and duration of war is to apply the full force and might of our military, and we are prepared to do so. If Saddam Hussein attempts to cling to power, he will remain a deadly foe until the end. In desperation, he and terrorists groups might try to conduct terrorist operations against the American people and our friends. These attacks are not inevitable. They are, however, possible. And this very fact underscores the reason we cannot live under the threat of blackmail. The terrorist threat to America and the world will be diminished the moment that Saddam Hussein is disarmed.

Our government is on heightened watch against these dangers. Just as we are preparing to ensure victory in Iraq, we are taking further actions to protect our homeland. In recent days, American authorities have expelled from the country certain individuals with ties to Iraqi intelligence services. Among other measures, I have directed additional security of our airports, and increased Coast Guard patrols of major seaports. The Department of Homeland Security is working closely with the nation's governors to increase armed security at critical facilities across America.

Should enemies strike our country, they would be attempting to shift our attention with panic and weaken our morale with fear. In this, they would fail. No act of theirs can alter the course or shake the resolve of this country. We are a peaceful people—yet we're not a fragile people, and we will not be intimidated by thugs and killers. If our enemies dare to strike us, they and all who have aided them, will face fearful consequences.

We are now acting because the risks of inaction would be far greater. In one year, or five years, the power of Iraq to inflict harm on all free nations would be multiplied many times over. With these capabilities, Saddam Hussein and his terrorist allies could choose the moment of deadly conflict when they are strongest. We choose to meet that threat now, where it arises, before it can appear suddenly in our skies and cities.

The cause of peace requires all free nations to recognize new and undeniable realities. In the 20th century, some chose to appease murderous dictators, whose threats were allowed to grow into genocide and global war. In this century, when evil men plot chemical, biological and nuclear terror, a policy of appeasement could bring destruction of a kind never before seen on this earth.

Terrorists and terror states do not reveal these threats with fair notice, in formal declarations—and responding to such enemies only after they have struck first is not self-defense, it is suicide. The security of the world requires disarming Saddam Hussein now.

As we enforce the just demands of the world, we will also honor the deepest commitments of our country. Unlike Saddam Hussein, we believe the Iraqi people are deserving and capable of human liberty. And when the dictator has departed, they can set an example to all the Middle East of a vital and peaceful and self-governing nation.

The United States, with other countries, will work to advance liberty and peace in that region. Our goal will not be achieved overnight, but it can come over time. The power and appeal of human liberty is felt in every life and every land. And the greatest power of freedom is to overcome hatred and violence, and turn the creative gifts of men and women to the pursuits of peace.

That is the future we choose. Free nations have a duty to defend our people by uniting against the violent. And tonight, as we have done before, America and our allies accept that responsibility.

Good night, and may God continue to bless America.

# President George W. Bush
# Addresses the Nation

•

# March 19, 2003

My fellow citizens, at this hour, American and coalition forces are in the early stages of military operations to disarm Iraq, to free its people and to defend the world from grave danger.

On my orders, coalition forces have begun striking selected targets of military importance to undermine Saddam Hussein's ability to wage war. These are opening stages of what will be a broad and concerted campaign. More than 35 countries are giving crucial support—from the use of naval and air bases, to help with intelligence and logistics, to the deployment of combat units. Every nation in this coalition has chosen to bear the duty and share the honor of serving in our common defense.

To all the men and women of the United States Armed Forces now in the Middle East, the peace of a troubled world and the hopes of an oppressed people now depend on you. That trust is well placed.

The enemies you confront will come to know your skill and bravery. The people you liberate will witness the honorable and decent spirit of the American military. In this conflict, America faces an enemy who has no regard for conventions of war or rules of morality. Saddam Hussein has placed Iraqi troops and equipment in civilian areas, attempting to use innocent men, women and children as shields for his own military—a final atrocity against his people.

I want Americans and all the world to know that coalition forces will make every effort to spare innocent civilians from harm. A campaign on the harsh terrain of a nation as large as California could be longer and more difficult than some predict. And helping Iraqis achieve a united, stable and free country will require our sustained commitment.

We come to Iraq with respect for its citizens, for their great civilization and for the religious faiths they practice. We have no ambition in Iraq, except to remove a threat and restore control of that country to its own people.

I know that the families of our military are praying that all those who serve will return safely and soon. Millions of Americans are praying with you for the safety of your loved ones and for the protection of the innocent. For your sacrifice, you have the gratitude and respect of the American people. And you can know that our forces will be coming home as soon as their work is done.

Our nation enters this conflict reluctantly—yet, our purpose is sure. The people of the United States and our friends and allies will not live at the mercy of an outlaw regime that threatens the peace with weapons of mass murder. We will meet that threat now, with our Army, Air Force, Navy, Coast Guard and Marines, so that we do not have to meet it later with armies of fire fighters and police and doctors on the streets of our cities.

Now that conflict has come, the only way to limit its duration is to apply decisive force. And I assure you, this will not be a campaign of half measures, and we will accept no outcome but victory.

My fellow citizens, the dangers to our country and the world will be overcome. We will pass through this time of peril and carry on the work of peace. We will defend our freedom. We will bring freedom to others and we will prevail.

May God bless our country and all who defend her.

# PART IV

"We have begun the search for hidden chemical and biological weapons, and already know of hundreds of sites that will be investigated," President Bush told cheering sailors and marines aboard the U.S.S. *Abraham Lincoln* on May 1, 2003, after American and British forces quickly routed the Iraqis and Saddam slinked away into hiding. "We have removed an ally of Al Qaeda, and cut off a source of terrorist funding. And this much is certain: No terrorist network will gain weapons of mass destruction from the Iraqi regime, because that regime is no more," the president said.

"Operation Iraqi Freedom" won a lightning victory, but it turned out to be only the prelude to a protracted military conflict. The American attempt to bring freedom and democracy in Iraq, the ultimate objective of the war even if not the main premise for it in 2003, met growing, fierce resistance from hard-line Baathists. Jihadists recruited from around the Islamic world flocked to fight the infidel occupiers under the banner of Abu Musaab al-Zarqawi, the Jordanian-born terrorist the administration had accused Saddam of allowing to operate freely in Iraqi territory before the war.

But the hunt for Saddam's forbidden weapons of mass destruction turned up nothing. In June 2003, the director of central intelligence, George Tenet, appointed David Kay, a University of Texas graduate with a master's degree in international relations and a Ph.D. from Columbia University who had been the IAEA's chief nuclear weapons inspector in Iraq in the early 1990s, to head a new search. Kay also headed a new organization, the Iraq Survey Group, with 1,400 members including supporting military forces, with the assignment of combing the entire country for the weapons the administration still assumed to be hidden somewhere in the desert sands.

Kay's credentials with Washington were impeccable. He had

been aggressive and resourceful in his United Nations job, and before Operation Iraqi Freedom had agreed publicly that Saddam had been hiding illicit arms and that only an American invasion could unearth the truth.

Four months after his appointment, it fell to him to report to Congress that up to then, the Iraq Survey Group had still not found anything. "Empirical reality on the ground is, and has always been, different from intelligence judgments," he warned in an interim report, and soon he began sounding more like Hans Blix than Bush and Powell. Much of his testimony to congressional intelligence committees on October 2, 2003, could almost have come from one of Blix's pre-war inspection reports. The ISG had not yet found stocks of weapons, Kay said, but it was too early to say there were none. The group had turned up no evidence of "steps to actually build nuclear weapons," and had determined that Iraq "did not have a large, ongoing, centrally controlled chemical weapons program after 1991." But Saddam had all along tried to hide what he was doing, and according to some of his scientists the survey group had interviewed, he remained "firmly committed to acquiring nuclear weapons." Kay was confident that his inspectors, unlike their United Nations predecessors, would unravel the mystery.

By 2004, Kay had learned enough to tell Congress on January 28, "We were almost all wrong." Saddam had no stocks of chemical and biological weapons to use against American invaders or to turn over to terrorists, he had no nuclear weapons or uranium centrifuges. All he had—and that in abundance—were evil intentions.

What was the difference? President Bush and others asked. The difference, as American intelligence before the war failed completely to make clear, was that intentions are one thing and capabilities are quite another. Saddam may have been a long-term threat because of his murderous intentions, but the short-term threat the United States had gone to war to eliminate did not exist.

As Kay saw it, the problem was not that the president or his cabinet or anyone else had pressured government agencies to feed them only the intelligence they wanted to hear. "Almost in a perverse way, I wish it had been undue influence because we know how to correct that," he said. "We get rid of the people who, in fact, were exercising that. The fact that it wasn't tells me that we've got a much more fundamental problem of understanding what went wrong, and we've got to figure out what was there. And that's what I call fundamental fault analysis."

The problem was systemic, Kay said. "And like I say, I think we've got other cases other than Iraq. I do not think the problem of global proliferation of weapons technology of mass destruction is going to go away, and that's why I think it is an urgent issue."

Kay was leaving the Iraq Survey Group that January because, he told the Reuters news agency then, some members of the Iraq Survey Group had been diverted from searching for weapons to fighting the growing insurgency and he would be unable to complete the job by the end of June 2004, when the United States returned sovereignty to the Iraqis. Tenet named Charles A. Duelfer, another American expert on Iraq's weapons programs who had been deputy executive chairman of UNSCOM from 1993 to 2000, as Kay's successor.

Duelfer's "Comprehensive Report," issued in October 2004 and updated later, lived up to its title, with hundreds of pages of information gathered by the Iraq Survey Group in inspections of suspect weapons sites all over Iraq. It also drew conclusions about Saddam's intentions from interviews with him and some of his leading deputies in captivity. The report covered weapons programs during the entire quarter century of Saddam's regime, not just the months leading up to the war.

Like the excerpts published here, the full report detailed the Survey Group's findings and reported what they had learned about the regime's attempts to deceive U.N. inspectors (and Iraq's external enemies, primarily Iran and Israel). The picture that emerged was at once an indictment of intelligence failures and a confirmation of the Bush administration's portrayal of Saddam's regime as an evil system with even more evil intentions.

Some also read Duelfer's report as a vindication of the United Nations inspections whose leaders and apparent shortcomings had so often been denounced as failures by officials in Washington. The Iraq Security Group showed how Saddam had manipulated the sanctions and the Oil for Food program and tried to trick the inspectors over the years. But it also showed that what few weapons of mass destruction Saddam had left after Operation Desert Storm had themselves been destroyed, either by the inspectors while they were there or by Saddam himself because he knew that was the only way he could ever persuade the United Nations to lift economic sanctions.

While the chaos that followed Operation Iraqi Freedom led to widespread looting of weapons factories and storage sites, Duelfer's investigations did not find significant indications that weapons or materials to make them had been systematically spirited away to hiding places or to neighboring states like Iran or Syria (though parts of destroyed missiles did turn up later in scrapyards in Jordan).

So Saddam lied and cheated and bided his time, and if he could ever persuade the United Nations to lift sanctions and permanently remove the inspectors, he hoped to rebuild his arsenal some day. But in early 2003 he was not the armed menace the United States said he was

By the end of the year, he was also in custody in Iraq. The serious long-term issue for the United States was what to do to try to ensure that intelligence would be more accurate next time, after the disasters of September 11 and a war on a false premise in Iraq.

The National Commission on Terrorist Attacks Upon the United States, the "9/11 Commission," found systemic problems that had neutralized American intelligence on the terrorist plots that day. The commission made recommendations that resulted in the sweeping reorganization of U.S. intelligence enacted at the end of 2004.

The bipartisan Senate Select Committee on Intelligence investigation into why the intelligence on Iraq had also been so badly wrong produced its report, a unanimous one, on July 7, 2004. The report went back to the original sources for the assertions about weapons of mass destruction in Iraq by the intelligence community. The committee, nine Republicans and eight Democrats, found that almost all the assertions were overstated or not supported by the underlying intelligence, produced by analysts whose managers did not challenge their assumptions and shaped by an agency, the CIA, that was supposed to be an honest broker among competing agencies but instead had a vested interest in promoting its own views.

The president, his secretary of state, and Congress itself were the victims of these failures, not contributors to them, in the committee's view. "In the end, what the president and the Congress used to send the country to war was information provided by the intelligence community, and that information was flawed," said Republican Senator Pat Roberts of Kansas, who was the committee chairman and had supported the war.

About a fifth of the Senate committee's report was left classified. Government censors blacked out entire pages on grounds of national security or the need to protect sources, gutting many of the committee's explanations of its conclusions.

And as part of a political deal between the parties, the Senate committee did not devote much of its report to answering the question Kay had raised about how much or how little pressure the administration had put on the intelligence agencies to produce findings to justify going to war.

That and other questions about the use the administration had made of intelligence to justify the war were left to a separate panel of members of both parties named by the White House, the Commission on the Intelligence Capabilities of the United States Regarding Weapons of Mass Destruction.

By mutual consent, it was to submit its report only after the presidential elections, in March 2005.

# Interim Progress Report by David Kay on the Iraq Survey Group before the House Permanent Select Committee on Intelligence, the House Committee on Appropriations Subcommittee on Defense, and Senate Select Committee on Intelligence

•

## October 2, 2003

I welcome this opportunity to discuss with the Committee the progress that the Iraq Survey Group has made in its initial three months of its investigation into Iraq's Weapons of Mass Destruction (WMD) programs.

I cannot emphasize too strongly that the Interim Progress Report, which has been made available to you, is a snapshot, in the context of an on-going investigation, of where we are after our first three months of work. The report does not represent a final reckoning of Iraq's WMD programs, nor are we at the point where we are prepared to close the file on any of these programs. While solid progress—I would say even remarkable progress considering the conditions that the ISG has had to work under—has been made in this initial period of operations, much remains to be done. We are still very much in the collection and analysis mode, still seeking the information and evidence that will allow us to confidently draw comprehensive conclusions to the actual objectives, scope, and dimensions of Iraq's WMD activities at the time of Operation Iraqi Freedom. Iraq's WMD programs spanned more than two decades, involved thousands of people, billions of dollars, and were elaborately shielded by security and deception operations that continued even beyond the end of Operation Iraqi Freedom. The very scale of this program when coupled with the conditions in Iraq that have prevailed since the end of Operation Iraqi Freedom dictate the speed at which we can move to a comprehensive understanding of Iraq's WMD activities.

We need to recall that in the 1991–2003 period the intelligence community and the UN/IAEA inspectors had to draw conclusions as to the status of Iraq's WMD program in the face of incomplete, and often false, data supplied by Iraq or data collected either by UN/IAEA inspectors operating within the severe constraints that Iraqi security and deception actions imposed or by national intelligence collection systems with their own inherent limitations. The result was that our understanding of the status of Iraq's WMD program was always bounded by large uncertainties and had to be heavily caveated. With the regime of Saddam Hussein at an end, ISG has the opportunity for the first time of drawing together all the evidence that can still be found in Iraq—much evidence is irretrievably lost—to reach definitive conclusions concerning the true state of Iraq's WMD program. It is far too early to reach any definitive conclusions and, in some areas, we may never reach that goal. The unique nature of this opportunity, however, requires that we take great care to ensure that the conclusions we draw reflect the truth to the maximum extent possible given the conditions in post-conflict Iraq.

We have not yet found stocks of weapons, but we are not yet at the point where we can say definitively either that such weapon stocks do not exist or that they existed before the war and our only task is to find where they have gone. We are actively engaged in searching for such weapons based on information being supplied to us by Iraqis.

Why are we having such difficulty in finding weapons or in reaching a confident conclusion that they do not exist or that they once existed but have been removed? Our search efforts are being hindered by six principal factors:

1. From birth all of Iraq's WMD activities were highly compart-

mentalized within a regime that ruled and kept its secrets through fear and terror and with deception and denial built into each program;

2. Deliberate dispersal and destruction of material and documentation related to weapons programs began pre-conflict and ran trans-to-post conflict;

3. Post-OIF [Operation Iraqi Freedom] looting destroyed or dispersed important and easily collectable material and forensic evidence concerning Iraq's WMD program. As the report covers in detail, significant elements of this looting were carried out in a systematic and deliberate manner, with the clear aim of concealing pre-OIF activities of Saddam's regime;

4. Some WMD personnel crossed borders in the pre/trans conflict period and may have taken evidence and even weapons-related materials with them;

5. Any actual WMD weapons or material is likely to be small in relation to the total conventional armaments footprint and difficult to near impossible to identify with normal search procedures. It is important to keep in mind that even the bulkiest materials we are searching for, in the quantities we would expect to find, can be concealed in spaces not much larger than a two car garage;

6. The environment in Iraq remains far from permissive for our activities, with many Iraqis that we talk to reporting threats and overt acts of intimidation and our own personnel being the subject of threats and attacks. In September alone we have had three attacks on ISG facilities or teams: The ISG base in Irbil was bombed and four staff injured, two very seriously; a two person team had their vehicle blocked by gunmen and only escaped by firing back through their own windshield; and on Wednesday, 24 September, the ISG Headquarters in Baghdad again was subject to mortar attack.

What have we found and what have we not found in the first 3 months of our work?

We have discovered dozens of WMD-related program activities and significant amounts of equipment that Iraq concealed from the United Nations during the inspections that began in late 2002. The discovery of these deliberate concealment efforts have come about both through the admissions of Iraqi scientists and officials concerning information they deliberately withheld and through physical evidence of equipment and activities that ISG has discovered that should have been declared to the UN. Let me just give you a few examples of these concealment efforts, some of which I will elaborate on later:

- A clandestine network of laboratories and safehouses within the Iraqi Intelligence Service that contained equipment subject to UN monitoring and suitable for continuing CBW research.

- A prison laboratory complex, possibly used in human testing of BW agents, that Iraqi officials working to prepare for UN inspections were explicitly ordered not to declare to the UN.

- Reference strains of biological organisms concealed in a scientist's home, one of which can be used to produce biological weapons.

- New research on BW-applicable agents, Brucella and Congo Crimean Hemorrhagic Fever (CCHF), and continuing work on ricin and aflatoxin were not declared to the UN.

- Documents and equipment, hidden in scientists' homes, that would have been useful in resuming uranium enrichment by centrifuge and electromagnetic isotope separation (EMIS).

- A line of UAVs not fully declared at an undeclared production facility and an admission that they had tested one of their declared UAVs out to a range of 500 km, 350 km beyond the permissible limit.

- Continuing covert capability to manufacture fuel propellant useful only for prohibited SCUD variant missiles, a capability that was maintained at least until the end of 2001 and that co-operating Iraqi scientists have said they were told to conceal from the UN.

- Plans and advanced design work for new long-range missiles with ranges up to at least 1000 km—well beyond the 150 km range limit imposed by the UN. Missiles of a 1000 km range would have allowed Iraq to threaten targets through out the Middle East, including Ankara, Cairo, and Abu Dhabi.

- Clandestine attempts between late–1999 and 2002 to obtain from North Korea technology related to 1,300 km range ballistic missiles—probably the No Dong—300 km range anti-ship cruise missiles, and other prohibited military equipment.

In addition to the discovery of extensive concealment efforts, we have been faced with a systematic sanitization of documentary and computer evidence in a wide range of offices, laboratories, and companies suspected of WMD work. The pattern of these efforts to erase evidence—hard drives destroyed, specific files burned, equipment cleaned of all traces of use—are ones of deliberate, rather than random, acts. For example,

- On 10 July 2003 an ISG team exploited the Revolutionary Command Council (RCC) Headquarters in Baghdad. The basement of the main building contained an archive of documents situated on well-organized rows of metal shelving. The basement suffered no fire damage despite the total destruction of the upper floors from coalition air strikes. Upon arrival the exploitation team encountered small piles of ash where individual documents or binders of documents were intentionally destroyed. Computer hard drives had been deliberately destroyed. Computers would have had financial value to a random looter; their destruction, rather than removal for resale or reuse, indicates a targeted effort to prevent Coalition forces from gaining access to their contents.

- All IIS laboratories visited by IIS exploitation teams have been clearly sanitized, including removal of much equipment, shredding and burning of documents, and even the removal of nameplates from office doors.

- Although much of the deliberate destruction and sanitization of documents and records probably occurred during the height of OIF combat operations, indications of significant continuing destruction efforts have been found after the end of major combat operations, including entry in May 2003 of the locked gated vaults of the Ba'ath party intelligence building in Baghdad and highly selective destruction of computer hard drives and data storage equipment along with the burning of a small number of specific binders that appear to have contained financial and intelligence records, and in July 2003 a site exploitation team at the Abu Ghurayb Prison found one pile of the smoldering ashes from documents that was still warm to the touch.

I would now like to review our efforts in each of the major lines of enquiry that ISG has pursued during this initial phase of its work.

With regard to biological warfare activities, which has been one of our two initial areas of focus, ISG teams are uncovering significant information—including research and development of BW-applicable organisms, the involvement of Iraqi Intelligence Service (IIS) in possible BW activities, and deliberate concealment activities. All of this suggests Iraq after 1996 further compartmentalized its program and focused on maintaining smaller, covert capabilities that could be activated quickly to surge the production of BW agents.

Debriefings of IIS officials and site visits have begun to unravel a clandestine network of laboratories and facilities within the security service apparatus. This network was never declared to the UN and was previously unknown. We are still working on determining the extent to which this network was tied to large-scale military efforts or BW terror weapons, but this clandestine capability was suitable for preserving BW expertise, BW capable facilities and continuing R&D—all key elements for maintaining a capability for resuming BW production. The IIS also played a prominent role in sponsoring students for overseas graduate studies in the biological sciences, according to Iraqi scientists and IIS sources, providing an important avenue for furthering BW-applicable research. This was the only area of graduate work that the IIS appeared to sponsor.

Discussions with Iraqi scientists uncovered agent R&D work that paired overt work with nonpathogenic organisms serving as surrogates for prohibited investigation with pathogenic agents. Examples include: *B. Thurengiensis* (Bt) with *B. anthracis* (anthrax), and medicinal plants with ricin. In a similar vein, two key former BW scientists, confirmed that Iraq under the guise of legitimate activity developed refinements of processes and products relevant to BW agents. The scientists discussed the development of improved, simplified fermentation and spray drying capabilities for the simulant Bt that would have been directly applicable to anthrax, and one scientist confirmed that the production line for Bt could be switched to produce anthrax in one week if the seed stock were available.

A very large body of information has been developed through debriefings, site visits, and exploitation of captured Iraqi documents that confirms that Iraq concealed equipment and materials from UN inspectors when they returned in 2002. One noteworthy example is a collection of reference strains that ought to have been declared to the UN. Among them was a vial of live C. botulinum Okra B. from which a biological agent can be produced. This discovery—hidden in the home of a BW scientist—illustrates the point I made earlier about the difficulty of locating small stocks of material that can be used to covertly surge production of deadly weapons. The scientist who concealed the vials containing this agent has identified a large cache of agents that he was asked, but refused, to conceal. ISG is actively searching for this second cache.

Additional information is beginning to corroborate reporting since 1996 about human testing activities using chemical and biological substances, but progress in this area is slow given the concern of knowledgeable Iraqi personnel about their being prosecuted for crimes against humanity.

We have not yet been able to corroborate the existence of a mobile BW production effort. Investigation into the origin of and intended use for the two trailers found in northern Iraq in April has yielded a number of explanations, including hydrogen, missile propellant, and BW production, but technical limitations would prevent any of these processes from being ideally suited to these trailers. That said, nothing we have discovered rules out their potential use in BW production.

We have made significant progress in identifying and locating individuals who were reportedly involved in a mobile program, and we are confident that we will be able to get an answer to the questions as to whether there was a mobile program and whether the trailers that have been discovered so far were part of such a program.

Let me turn now to chemical weapons (CW). In searching for retained stocks of chemical munitions, ISG has had to contend with the almost unbelievable scale of Iraq's conventional weapons armory, which dwarfs by orders of magnitude the physical size of any conceivable stock of chemical weapons. For example, there are approximately 130 known Iraqi Ammunition Storage Points (ASP), many of which exceed 50 square miles in size and hold an estimated 600,000 tons of artillery shells, rockets, aviation bombs and other ordinance. Of these 130 ASPs, approximately 120 still remain unexamined. As Iraqi practice was not to mark much of their chemical ordinance and to store it at the same ASPs that held conventional rounds, the size of the required search effort is enormous.

While searching for retained weapons, ISG teams have developed multiple sources that indicate that Iraq explored the possibility of CW production in recent years, possibly as late as 2003. When Saddam had asked a senior military official in either 2001 or 2002 how long it would take to produce new chemical agent and weapons, he told ISG that after he consulted with CW experts in OMI he responded it would take six months for mustard. Another senior Iraqi chemical weapons expert in responding to a request in mid–2002 from Uday Hussein for CW for the Fedayeen Saddam estimated that it would take two months to produce mustard and two years for Sarin.

We are starting to survey parts of Iraq's chemical industry to determine if suitable equipment and bulk chemicals were available for chemical weapons production. We have been struck that two senior Iraqi officials volunteered that if they had been ordered to resume CW production Iraq would have been willing to use stainless steel systems that would be disposed of after a few production runs, in place of corrosive-resistant equipment which they did not have.

We continue to follow leads on Iraq's acquisition of equipment and bulk precursors suitable for a CW program. Several possibilities have emerged and are now being exploited. One example involves a foreign company with offices in Baghdad, that imported in the past into Iraq dual-use equipment and maintained active contracts through 2002. Its Baghdad office was found looted in August 2003, but we are pursuing other locations and associates of the company.

Information obtained since OIF has identified several key areas in which Iraq may have engaged in proscribed or undeclared activity since 1991, including research on a possible VX stabilizer, research and development for CW-capable munitions, and procurement/concealment of dual-use materials and equipment.

Multiple sources with varied access and reliability have told ISG that Iraq did not have a large, ongoing, centrally controlled CW program after 1991. Information found to date suggests that Iraq's large-scale capability to develop, produce, and fill new CW munitions was reduced—if not entirely destroyed—during Operations Desert Storm and Desert Fox, 13 years of UN sanctions and UN inspections. We are carefully examining dual-use, commercial chemical facilities to determine whether these were used or planned as alternative production sites.

We have also acquired information related to Iraq's CW doctrine and Iraq's war plans for OIF, but we have not yet found evidence to confirm pre-war reporting that Iraqi military units were prepared to use CW against Coalition forces. Our efforts to collect and exploit intelligence on Iraq's chemical weapons program have thus far yielded little reliable information on post–1991 CW stocks and CW agent production, although we continue to receive and follow leads related to such stocks. We have multiple reports that Iraq retained CW munitions made prior to 1991, possibly including mustard—a long-lasting chemical agent—but we have to date been unable to locate any such munitions.

With regard to Iraq's nuclear program, the testimony we have obtained from Iraqi scientists and senior government officials should clear up any doubts about whether Saddam still wanted to obtain nuclear weapons. They have told ISG that Saddam Hussein remained firmly committed to acquiring nuclear weapons. These officials assert that Saddam would have resumed nuclear weapons development at some future point. Some indicated a resumption after Iraq was free of sanctions. At least one senior Iraqi official believed that by 2000 Saddam had run out of patience with waiting for sanctions to end and wanted to restart the nuclear program. The Iraqi Atomic Energy Commission (IAEC) beginning around 1999 expanded its laboratories and research activities and increased its overall funding levels. This expansion may have been in initial preparation for renewed nuclear weapons research, although documentary evidence of this has not been found, and this is the subject of continuing investigation by ISG.

Starting around 2000, the senior Iraqi Atomic Energy Commission (IAEC) and high-level Ba'ath Party official Dr. Khalid Ibrahim Sa'id began several small and relatively unsophisticated research initiatives that could be applied to nuclear weapons development. These initiatives did not in-and-of themselves constitute a resumption of the nuclear weapons program, but could have been useful in developing a weapons-relevant science base for the long-term. We do not yet have information indicating whether a higher government authority directed Sa'id to initiate this research and, regretfully, Dr. Said was killed on April 8th during the fall of Baghdad when the car he was riding in attempted to run a Coalition roadblock.

Despite evidence of Saddam's continued ambition to acquire nuclear weapons, to date we have not uncovered evidence that Iraq undertook significant post–1998 steps to actually build nuclear weapons or produce fissile material. However, Iraq did take steps to preserve some technological capability from the pre–1991 nuclear weapons program.

- According to documents and testimony of Iraqi scientists, some of the key technical groups from the pre–1991 nuclear weapons program remained largely intact, performing work on nuclear-relevant dual-use technologies within the Military Industrial Commission (MIC). Some scientists from the pre–1991 nuclear weapons program have told ISG that they believed that these working groups were preserved in order to allow a reconstitution of the nuclear weapons program, but none of the scientists could produce official orders or plans to support their belief.

- In some cases, these groups performed work which could help preserve the science base and core skills that would be needed for any future fissile material production or nuclear weapons development.

- Several scientists—at the direction of senior Iraqi government officials—preserved documents and equipment from their pre–1991 nuclear weapon-related research and did not reveal this to the UN/IAEA. One Iraqi scientist recently stated in an interview with ISG that it was a "common understanding" among the scientists that material was being preserved for reconstitution of nuclear weapons-related work.

The ISG nuclear team has found indications that there was interest, beginning in 2002, in reconstituting a centrifuge enrichment program. Most of this activity centered on activities of Dr. Sa'id that caused some of his former colleagues in the pre–1991 nuclear program to suspect that Dr. Sa'id, at least, was considering a restart of the centrifuge program. We do not yet fully understand Iraqi intentions, and the evidence does not tie any activity directly to centrifuge research or development.

Exploitation of additional documents may shed light on the projects and program plans of Dr. Khalid Ibrahim Sa'id. There may be more projects to be discovered in research placed at universities and private companies. Iraqi interest in reconstitution of a uranium enrichment program needs to be better understood through the analysis of procurement records and additional interviews.

With regard to delivery systems, the ISG team has discovered sufficient evidence to date to conclude that the Iraqi regime was committed to delivery system improvements that would have, if OIF had not occurred, dramatically breached UN restrictions placed on Iraq after the 1991 Gulf War.

Detainees and co-operative sources indicate that beginning in 2000 Saddam ordered the development of ballistic missiles with ranges of at least 400km and up to 1000km and that measures to conceal these projects from UNMOVIC were initiated in late–2002, ahead of the arrival of inspectors. Work was also underway for a clustered engine liquid propellant missile, and it appears the work had progressed to a point to support initial prototype production of some parts and assemblies. According to a cooperating senior detainee, Saddam concluded that the proposals from both the liquid-propellant and solid-propellant missile design centers would take too long. For instance, the liquid-propellant missile project team forecast first delivery in six years. Saddam countered in 2000 that he wanted the missile designed and built inside of six months. On the other hand several sources contend that Saddam's range requirements for the missiles grew from 400–500km in 2000 to 600–1000km in 2002.

ISG has gathered testimony from missile designers at Al Kindi State Company that Iraq has reinitiated work on converting SA–2 Surface-to-Air Missiles into ballistic missiles with a range goal of about 250km. Engineering work was reportedly underway in early 2003, despite the presence of UNMOVIC. This program was not declared to the UN. ISG is presently seeking additional confirmation and details on this project. A second co-operative source has stated that the program actually began in 2001, but that it received added impetus in the run-up to OIF, and that missiles from this project were transferred to a facility north of Baghdad. This source also provided documentary evidence of instructions to convert SA–2s into surface-to-surface missiles.

ISG has obtained testimony from both detainees and cooperative sources that indicate that proscribed-range solid-propellant missile design studies were initiated, or already underway, at the time when work on the clustered liquid-propellant missile designs began. The motor diameter was to be 800 to 1000mm, i.e. much greater than the 500-mm Ababil–100. The range goals cited for this system vary from over 400km up to 1000km, depending on the source and the payload mass.

A cooperative source, involved in the 2001–2002 deliberations on the long-range solid propellant project, provided ISG with a set of concept designs for a launcher designed to accommodate a 1m diameter by 9m length missile. The limited detail in the drawings suggest there was some way to go before launcher fabrication. The source believes that these drawings would not have been requested until the missile progress was relatively advanced, normally beyond the design state. The drawing are in CAD format, with files dated 09/01/02.

While we have obtained enough information to make us confident that this design effort was underway, we are not yet confident which accounts of the timeline and project progress are accurate and are now seeking to better understand this program and its actual progress at the time of OIF.

One cooperative source has said that he suspected that the new large-diameter solid-propellant missile was intended to have a CW-filled warhead, but no detainee has admitted any actual knowledge of plans for unconventional warheads for any current or planned ballistic missile. The suspicion expressed by the one source about a CW warhead was based on his assessment of the unavailability of nuclear warheads and potential survivability problems of biological warfare agent in ballistic missile warheads. This is an area of great interest and we are seeking additional information on warhead designs.

While I have spoken so far of planned missile systems, one high-level detainee has recently claimed that Iraq retained a small quantity of Scud-variant missiles until at least 2001, although he subsequently recanted these claims, work continues to determine the truth. Two other sources contend that Iraq continued to produce until 2001 liquid fuel and oxidizer specific to Scud-type systems. The cooperating source claims that the al Tariq Factory was used to manufacture Scud oxidizer (IRFNA) from 1996 to 2001, and that nitrogen tetroxide, a chief ingredient of IRFNA was collected from a bleed port on the production equipment, was reserved, and then mixed with highly concentrated nitric acid plus an inhibitor to produce Scud oxidizer. Iraq never declared its pre-Gulf War capability to manufacture Scud IRFNA out of fear, multiple sources have stated, that the al Tariq Factory would be destroyed, leaving Baghdad without the ability to produce highly concentrated nitric acid, explosives and munitions. To date we have not discovered documentary or material evidence to corroborate these claims, but continued efforts are underway to clarify and confirm this information with additional Iraqi sources and to locate corroborating physical evidence. If we can confirm that the fuel was produced as late as 2001, and given that Scud fuel can only be used in Scud-variant missiles, we will have strong evidence that the missiles must have been retained until that date. This would, of course, be yet another example of a failure to declare prohibited activities to the UN.

Iraq was continuing to develop a variety of UAV platforms and maintained two UAV programs that were working in parallel, one at Ibn Fernas and one at al-Rashid Air Force Base. Ibn Fernas worked on the development of smaller, more traditional types of UAVs in addition to the conversion of manned aircraft into UAVs. This program was not declared to the UN until the 2002 CAFCD in which Iraq declared the RPV–20, RPV–30 and Pigeon RPV systems to the UN. All these systems had declared ranges of less than 150km. Several Iraqi officials stated that the RPV–20 flew over 500km on autopilot in 2002, contradicting Iraq's declaration on the system's range. The al-Rashid group was developing a competing line of UAVs. This program was never fully declared to the UN and is the subject of on-going work by ISG. Additional work is also focusing on the payloads and intended use for these UAVs. Surveillance and use as decoys are uses mentioned by some of those interviewed. Given Iraq's interest before the Gulf War in attempting to convert a MIG–21 into an unmanned aerial vehicle to carry spray tanks capable of dispensing chemical or biological agents, attention is being paid to whether any of the newer generation of UAVs were intended to have a similar purpose. This remains an open question.

ISG has discovered evidence of two primary cruise missile programs. The first appears to have been successfully implemented, whereas the second had not yet reached maturity at the time of OIF.

The first involved upgrades to the HY–2 coastal-defense cruise missile. ISG has developed multiple sources of testimony, which is corroborated in part by a captured document, that Iraq undertook a program aimed at increasing the HY–2's range and permitting its use as a land-attack missile. These efforts extended the HY–2's range from its original 100km to 150–180km. Ten modified missiles were delivered to the military prior to OIF and two of these were fired from Umm Qasr during OIF—one was shot down and one hit Kuwait.

The second program, called the Jenin, was a much more ambitious effort to convert the HY–2 into a 1000km range land-attack cruise missile. The Jenin concept was presented to Saddam on 23 November 2001 and received what cooperative sources called an "unusually quick response" in little more than a week. The essence of the concept was to take an HY–2, strip it of its liquid rocket engine, and put in its place a turbine engine from a Russian helicopter—the TV–2–117 or TV3–117 from a Mi–8 or Mi–17helicopter. To prevent discovery by the UN, Iraq halted engine development and testing and disassembled the test stand in late 2002 before the design criteria had been met.

In addition to the activities detailed here on Iraq's attempts to develop delivery systems beyond the permitted UN 150km, ISG has also developed information on Iraqi attempts to purchase proscribed missiles and missile technology. Documents found by ISG describe a high level dialogue between Iraq and North Korea that began in December 1999 and included an October 2000 meeting in Baghdad. These documents indicate Iraqi interest in the transfer of technology for surface-to-surface missiles with a range of 1300km (probably No Dong) and land-to-sea missiles with a range of 300km. The document quotes the North Koreans as understanding the limitations imposed by the UN, but being prepared "to cooperate with Iraq on the items it specified". At the time of OIF, these discussions had not led to any missiles being transferred to Iraq. A high level co-operating source has reported that in late 2002 at Saddam's behest a delegation of Iraqi officials was sent to meet with foreign export companies, including one that dealt with missiles. Iraq was interested in buying an advanced ballistic missile with 270km and 500km ranges.

The ISG has also identified a large volume of material and testimony by cooperating Iraq officials on Iraq's effort to illicitly procure parts and foreign assistance for its missile program. These include:

- Significant level of assistance from a foreign company and its network of affiliates in supplying and supporting the development of production capabilities for solid rocket propellant and dual-use chemicals.

- Entities from another foreign country were involved in supplying guidance and control systems for use in the Al-Fat'h (Ababil–100). The contract was incomplete by the time of OIF due to technical problems with the few systems delivered and a financial dispute.

- A group of foreign experts operating in a private capacity were helping to develop Iraq's liquid propellant ballistic missile RDT&E and production infrastructure. They worked in Baghdad for about three months in late 1998 and subsequently continued work on the project from abroad. An actual contract valued at $10 million for machinery and equipment was signed in June 2001, initially for 18 months, but later extended. This cooperation continued right up until the war.

- A different group of foreign experts traveled to Iraq in 1999 to conduct a technical review that resulted in what became the Al Samoud 2 design, and a contract was signed in 2001 for the provision of rigs, fixtures and control equipment for the redesigned missile.

- Detainees and cooperative sources have described the role of a foreign expert in negotiations on the development of Iraq's liquid and solid propellant production infrastructure. This could have had applications in existing and planned longer range systems, although it is reported that nothing had actually been implemented before OIF.

Uncertainty remains about the full extent of foreign assistance to Iraq's planned expansion of its missile systems and work is continuing to gain a full resolution of this issue. However, there is little doubt from the evidence already gathered that there was substantial illegal procurement for all aspects of the missile programs.

I have covered a lot of ground today, much of it highly technical. Although we are resisting drawing conclusions in this first interim report, a number of things have become clearer already as a result of our investigation, among them:

1. Saddam, at least as judged by those scientists and other insiders who worked in his military-industrial programs, had not given up his aspirations and intentions to continue to acquire weapons of mass destruction. Even those senior officials we have interviewed who claim no direct knowledge of any on-going prohibited activities readily acknowledge that Saddam intended to resume these programs whenever the external restrictions were removed. Several of these officials acknowledge receiving inquiries since 2000 from Saddam or his sons about how long it would take to either restart CW production or make available chemical weapons.

2. In the delivery systems area there were already well advanced, but undeclared, on-going activities that, if OIF had not intervened, would have resulted in the production of missiles with ranges at least up to 1000 km, well in excess of the UN permitted range of 150 km. These missile activities were supported by a serious clandestine procurement program about which we have much still to learn.

3. In the chemical and biological weapons area we have confidence that there were at a minimum clandestine on-going research and development activities that were embedded in the Iraqi Intelligence Service. While we have much yet to learn about the exact work programs and capabilities of these activi-

ties, it is already apparent that these undeclared activities would have at a minimum facilitated chemical and biological weapons activities and provided a technically trained cadre.

Let me conclude by returning to something I began with today. We face a unique but challenging opportunity in our efforts to unravel the exact status of Iraq's WMD program. The good news is that we do not have to rely for the first time in over a decade on

- the incomplete, and often false, data that Iraq supplied the UN/IAEA;

- data collected by UN inspectors operating with the severe constraints that Iraqi security and deception actions imposed;

- information supplied by defectors, some of whom certainly fabricated much that they supplied and perhaps were under the direct control of the IIS;

- data collected by national technical collections systems with their own limitations.

The bad news is that we have to do this under conditions that ensure that our work will take time and impose serious physical dangers on those who are asked to carry it out.

Why should we take the time and run the risk to ensure that our conclusions reflect the truth to the maximum extent that is possible given the conditions in post-conflict Iraq? For those of us that are carrying out this search, there are two reasons that drive us to want to complete this effort.

First, whatever we find will probably differ from pre-war intelligence. Empirical reality on the ground is, and has always been, different from intelligence judgments that must be made under serious constraints of time, distance and information. It is, however, only by understanding precisely what those difference are that the quality of future intelligence and investment decisions concerning future intelligence systems can be improved. Proliferation of weapons of mass destruction is such a continuing threat to global society that learning those lessons has a high imperative.

Second, we have found people, technical information and illicit procurement networks that if allowed to flow to other countries and regions could accelerate global proliferation. Even in the area of actual weapons there is no doubt that Iraq had at one time chemical and biological weapons. Even if there were only a remote possibility that these pre–1991 weapons still exist, we have an obligation to American troops who are now there and the Iraqi population to ensure that none of these remain to be used against them in the ongoing insurgency activity.

Mr. Chairman and Members I appreciate this opportunity to share with you the initial results of the first 3 months of the activities of the Iraqi Survey Group. I am certain that I speak for Major General Keith Dayton, who commands the Iraqi Survey Group, when I say how proud we are of the men and women from across the Government and from our Coalition partners, Australia and the United Kingdom, who have gone to Iraq and are carrying out this important mission.

Thank you.

# David Kay's Opening Statement to the Senate Armed Services Committee

•

# January 28, 2004

[. . . ]

Let me begin by saying, we were almost all wrong, and I certainly include myself here.

Senator [Edward] Kennedy knows very directly. Senator Kennedy and I talked on several occasions prior to the war that my view was that the best evidence that I had seen was that Iraq indeed had weapons of mass destruction.

I would also point out that many governments that chose not to support this war—certainly, the French president, [Jacques] Chirac, as I recall in April of last year, referred to Iraq's possession of WMD.

The Germans certainly—the intelligence service believed that there were WMD.

It turns out that we were all wrong, probably in my judgment, and that is most disturbing.

We're also in a period in which we've had intelligence surprises in the proliferation area that go the other way. The case of Iran, a nuclear program that the Iranians admit was 18 years on, that we underestimated. And, in fact, we didn't discover it. It was discovered by a group of Iranian dissidents outside the country who pointed the international community at the location.

The Libyan program recently discovered was far more extensive than was assessed prior to that.

There's a long record here of being wrong. There's a good reason for it. There are probably multiple reasons. Certainly proliferation is a hard thing to track, particularly in countries that deny easy and free access and don't have free and open societies.

In my judgment, based on the work that has been done to this point of the Iraq Survey Group, and in fact, that I reported to you in October, Iraq was in clear violation of the terms of [U.N.] Resolution 1441. Resolution 1441 required that Iraq report all of its activities—one last chance to come clean about what it had.

We have discovered hundreds of cases, based on both documents, physical evidence and the testimony of Iraqis, of activities that were prohibited under the initial U.N. Resolution 687 and that should have been reported under 1441, with Iraqi testimony that not only did they not tell the U.N. about this, they were instructed not to do it and they hid material.

I think the aim—and certainly the aim of what I've tried to do since leaving—is not political and certainly not a witch hunt at individuals. It's to try to direct our attention at what I believe is a fundamental fault analysis that we must now examine.

And let me take one of the explanations most commonly given: Analysts were pressured to reach conclusions that would fit the political agenda of one or another administration. I deeply think that is a wrong explanation.

As leader of the effort of the Iraqi Survey Group, I spent most of my days not out in the field leading inspections. It's typically what you do at that level. I was trying to motivate, direct, find strategies.

In the course of doing that, I had innumerable analysts who came to me in apology that the world that we were finding was not the world that they had thought existed and that they had estimated. Reality on the ground differed in advance.

And never—not in a single case—was the explanation, "I was pressured to do this." The explanation was very often, "The limited data we had led one to reasonably conclude this. I now see that there's another explanation for it."

And each case was different, but the conversations were sufficiently in depth and our relationship was sufficiently frank that I'm convinced that, at least to the analysts I dealt with, I did not come across a single one that felt it had been, in the military term, "inappropriate command influence" that led them to take that position.

It was not that. It was the honest difficulty based on the intelligence that had—the information that had been collected that led the analysts to that conclusion.

And you know, almost in a perverse way, I wish it had been undue influence because we know how to correct that.

We get rid of the people who, in fact, were exercising that.

The fact that it wasn't tells me that we've got a much more fundamental problem of understanding what went wrong, and we've got to figure out what was there. And that's what I call fundamental fault analysis.

And like I say, I think we've got other cases other than Iraq. I do not think the problem of global proliferation of weapons technology of mass destruction is going to go away, and that's why I think it is an urgent issue.

And let me really wrap up here with just a brief summary of what I think we are now facing in Iraq. I regret to say that I think at the end of the work of the [Iraq Survey Group] there's still going to be an unresolvable ambiguity about what happened.

A lot of that traces to the failure on April 9 to establish immediately physical security in Iraq—the unparalleled looting and destruction, a lot of which was directly intentional, designed by the security services to cover the tracks of the Iraq WMD program and their other programs as well, a lot of which was what we simply called Ali Baba looting. "It had been the regime's. The regime is gone. I'm going to go take the gold toilet fixtures and everything else imaginable."

I've seen looting around the world and thought I knew the best looters in the world. The Iraqis excel at that.

The result is—document destruction—we're really not going to be able to prove beyond a truth the negatives and some of the positive conclusions that we're going to come to. There will be always unresolved ambiguity here.

But I do think the survey group—and I think Charlie Duelfer is a great leader. I have the utmost confidence in Charles. I think you will get as full an answer as you can possibly get. And let me just conclude by my own personal tribute, both to the president and to [CIA Director] George Tenet, for having the courage to select me to do this, and my successor, Charlie Duelfer, as well.

Both of us are known for probably at times regrettable streak of independence. I came not from within the administration, and it was clear and clear in our discussions and no one asked otherwise that I would lead this the way I thought best and I would speak the truth as we found it. I have had absolutely no pressure prior, during the course of the work at the [Iraq Survey Group], or after I left to do anything otherwise.

I think that shows a level of maturity and understanding that I think bodes well for getting to the bottom of this. But it is really up to you and your staff, on behalf of the American people, to take on that challenge. It's not something that anyone from the outside can do. So I look forward to these hearings and other hearings at how you will get to the conclusions.

I do believe we have to understand why reality turned out to be different than expectations and estimates. But you have more public service—certainly many of you—than I have ever had, and you recognize that this is not unusual.

[ . . . ]

# Senate Select Committee on Intelligence Report on the U.S. Intelligence Community's Prewar Intelligence Assessments on Iraq

*[The entire report, 521 pages released on July 9, 2004, is available at http://intelligence.senate.gov/iraqreport2.pdf. Classified portions deleted by government agencies before the report was cleared for release are indicated as BLACKED OUT in the text, which includes only the conclusions from the 18 sections of the report.]*

## Conclusions

*Overall Conclusions—Weapons of Mass Destruction*

Conclusion 1. Most of the major key judgments in the Intelligence Community's October 2002 National Intelligence Estimate (NIE), Iraq's Continuing Programs for Weapons of Mass Destruction, either overstated, or were not supported by, the underlying intelligence reporting. A series of failures, particularly in analytic trade craft, led to the mischaracterization of the intelligence.

The major key judgments in the NIE, particularly that Iraq "is reconstituting its nuclear program," "has chemical and biological weapons," was developing an unmanned aerial vehicle (UAV) "probably intended to deliver biological warfare agents," and that "all key aspects—research & development (R&D), production, and weaponization—of Iraq's offensive biological weapons (BW) program are active and that most elements are larger and more advanced than they were before the Gulf War," either overstated, or were not supported by, the underlying intelligence reporting provided to the Committee. The assessments regarding Iraq's continued development of prohibited ballistic missiles were reasonable and did accurately describe the underlying intelligence.

The assessment that Iraq "is reconstituting its nuclear program" was not supported by the intelligence provided to the Committee. The intelligence reporting did show that Iraq was procuring dual-use equipment that had potential nuclear applications, but all of the equipment had conventional military or industrial applications. In addition, none of the intelligence reporting indicated that the equipment was being procured for suspect nuclear facilities. Intelligence reporting also showed that former Iraqi nuclear scientists continued to work at former nuclear facilities and organizations, but the reporting did not show that this cadre of nuclear personnel had recently been regrouped or enhanced as stated in the NIE, nor did it suggest that they were engaged in work related to a nuclear weapons program.

The statement in the key judgments of the NIE that "Baghdad has chemical and biological weapons" overstated both what was known and what intelligence analysts judged about Iraq's chemical and biological weapons holdings. The intelligence reporting did support the conclusion that chemical and biological weapons were within Iraq's technological capability, that Iraq was trying to procure dual-use materials that could have been used to produce these weapons, and that uncertainties existed about whether Iraq had fully destroyed its pre-Gulf War stocks of weapons and precursors. Iraq's efforts to deceive and evade United Nations weapons inspectors and its inability or unwillingness to fully account for pre-Gulf War chemical and biological weapons and precursors could have led analysts to the reasonable conclusion that Iraq may have retained those materials, but intelligence analysts did not have enough information to state with certainty that Iraq "has" these weapons.

Similarly, the assessment that "all key aspects—R&D, production, and weaponization—of Iraq's offensive BW program are active and that most elements are larger and more advanced than they were before the Gulf War" was not supported by the underlying intelligence provided to the Committee. Intelligence showed that Iraq was renovating or expanding facilities that had been associated with Iraq's past BW program and was engaged in research that had BW applications, but few reports suggested specifically that the activity was related to BW. Intelligence reports did indicate that Iraq may have had a mobile biological weapons program, but most of the reporting was from a single human intelligence (HUMINT) source to whom the Intelligence Community (IC) never had direct access. It was reasonable for intelligence analysts to be concerned about the potential weapons applications of Iraq's dual use activities and capabilities. The intelligence reporting did not substantiate an assessment that all aspects of Iraq's BW program "are" larger and more advanced than before the Gulf War, however.

The key judgment in the NIE that Iraq was developing a UAV "probably intended to deliver biological warfare agents" also overstated what the intelligence reporting indicated about the mission of Iraq's small UAVs. Numerous intelligence reports confirmed that Iraq was developing a small UAV program BLACKED OUT , but none of the reports provided to the Committee said that Iraq intended to use the small UAVs to deliver chemical or biological weapons. The Air Force footnote, which stated that biological weapons delivery was a possible mission for the small UAVs, though other missions were more likely, more accurately reflected the body of intelligence reporting.

The failure of the IC to accurately analyze and describe the intelligence in the NIE was the result of a combination of systemic weaknesses, primarily in analytic trade craft, compounded by a lack of information sharing, poor management, and inadequate intelligence collection. Many of these weaknesses, which are described in detail below, have not yet been fully addressed, despite having been identified previously by other inquiry panels, including the Joint Inquiry into Intelligence Community Activities Before and After the Terrorist Attacks of September 11, 2002 (2002), The Intelligence Community's Performance on the Indian Nuclear Tests (The Jeremiah Report, 1998), and the Report of the Commission to Assess the Ballistic Missile Threat to the United States (The Rumsfeld Commission, 1998). The Committee found no evidence that the IC's mischaracterization or exaggeration of the intelligence on Iraq's weapons of mass destruction (WMD) capabilities was the result of political pressure.

Conclusion 2. The Intelligence Community did not accurately or adequately explain to policymakers the uncertainties behind the judgments in the October 2002 National Intelligence Estimate.

One of the key failures in analytic trade craft of the National Intelligence Estimate (NIE) was the failure of the Intelligence Community (IC) to explain the details of the reporting and the uncertainties of both the reliability of some key sources and of intelligence judgments. Intelligence analysts are not only charged with interpreting and assessing the intelligence reporting, but with clearly conveying to policymakers the difference between what intelligence analysts know, what they don't know, what they think, and to make sure that policymakers understand the difference. This articulation of the IC's responsibility to policymakers is widely attributed to Colin Powell when he was serving as the Chairman of the Joint Chiefs of Staff, but the effective communication of judgments has been accepted as a primary analytic function for decades. For example, in 1964, Sherman Kent, considered the founder of intelligence analysis as a profession, wrote about the importance of using appropriate words of estimative probability to "set forth the community's findings in such a way as to make clear to the reader what is certain knowledge and what is reasoned judgment, and within this large realm of judgment what varying degrees of certitude lie behind each key statement."' ¹Sherman Kent and the Board of National Estimates: Collected Essays, Http://www.odci.gov/csi/books/shermanken-Vinst.html). From 1952 to 1967, Sherman Kent was the Chairman of the Board of National Estimates, which would later become the National Intelligence Council.

At the time the IC drafted and coordinated the NIE on Iraq's weapons of mass destruction (WMD) programs in September 2002, most of what intelligence analysts actually "knew" about Iraq's weapons programs pre-dated the 1991 Gulf War, leaving them with very little direct knowledge about the current state of those programs. Analysts knew that Iraq had active nuclear, chemical, biological, and delivery programs before 1991, and had previously lied to, and was still not forthcoming with, UN weapons inspectors about those programs. The analysts also knew that the United Nations was not satisfied with Iraq's efforts to account for its destruction of all of its pre-Gulf War weapons, precursors, and equipment. Additionally, the analysts knew that Iraq was trying to import dual-use materials and equipment and had rebuilt or was continuing to use facilities that had been associated with Iraq's pre-Gulf War weapons programs, and knew that WMD were likely within Iraq's technological capabilities.

The IC did not know whether Iraq had retained its pre-Gulf War weapons, whether Iraq was intending to use those dual-use materials and facilities for weapons or for legitimate purposes, or even if Iraq's attempts to obtain many of the dual-use goods it had been trying to procure were successful. The IC thought that Iraq had retained its pre-Gulf War weapons and that Iraq was using dual-use materials and facilities to manufacture weapons. While this was a reasonable assessment, considering Iraq's past behavior, statements in the 2002 NIE that Iraq "has chemical and biological weapons," "Iraq has maintained its chemical weapons effort," and "is reconstituting its nuclear weapons program," did not accurately portray the uncertainty of the information. The NIE failed in that it portrayed what intelligence analysts thought and assessed as what they knew and failed to explain the large gaps in the information on which the assessments were based.

In the cases in the NTE where the IC did express uncertainty about its assessments concerning Iraq's WMD capabilities, those explanations suggested, in some cases, that Iraq's capabilities were even greater than the NIE judged. For example, the key judgments of the NIE said "we judge that we are seeing only a portion of Iraq's WMD efforts, owing to Baghdad's vigorous denial and deception efforts. Revelations after the Gulf War starkly demonstrate the extensive efforts undertaken by Iraq to deny information. BLACKED OUT" [sic—ed.] While this did explain that key information on Iraq's programs was lacking, it suggested that Iraq's weapons programs were probably bigger and more advanced than the IC had judged and did not explain that BLACKED OUT analysts did not have enough information to determine whether Iraq was hiding activity or whether Iraq's weapons programs may have been dormant.

Accurately and clearly describing the gaps in intelligence knowledge is not only important for policymakers to folly understand the basis for and gaps in analytic assessments, but is essential for policymakers in both the executive and legislative branches to make informed decisions about how and where to allocate Intelligence Community resources to fill those gaps.

Conclusion 3. The Intelligence Community (IC) suffered from a collective presumption that Iraq had an active and growing weapons of mass destruction (WMD) program. This "group think" dynamic led Intelligence Community analysts, collectors and managers to both interpret ambiguous evidence as conclusively indicative of a WMD program as well as ignore or minimize evidence that Iraq did not have active and expanding weapons of mass destruction programs. This presumption was so strong that formalized IC mechanisms established to challenge assumptions and group think were not utilized.

The Intelligence Community (IC) has long struggled with the need for analysts to overcome analytic biases, that is, to resist the tendency to see what they would expect to see in the intelligence reporting. In the case of Iraq's weapons of mass destruction (WMD) capabilities, the Committee found that intelligence analysts, in many cases, based then- analysis more on their expectations than on an objective evaluation of the information in the intelligence reporting. Analysts expected to see evidence that Iraq had retained prohibited weapons and that Iraq would resume prohibited WMD activities once United Nations' (UN) inspections ended. This bias that pervaded both the IC's analytic and collection communities represents "group think," a term coined by psychologist Irving Janis in the 1970's to describe a process in which a group can make bad or irrational decisions as each member of the group attempts to conform their opinions to what they believe to be the consensus of the group. IC personnel involved in the Iraq WMD issue demonstrated several aspects of group think: examining few alternatives, selective gathering of information, pressure to conform within the group or withhold criticism, and collective rationalization.

The roots of the IC's bias stretch back to Iraq's pre–1991 efforts to build WMD and its efforts to hide those programs. The fact that Iraq had repeatedly lied about its pre–1991 WMD programs, its continued deceptive behavior, and its failure to fully cooperate with UN inspectors left the IC with a predisposition to believe the Iraqis were continuing to lie about their WMD efforts. This was compounded by the fact that Iraq's pre–1991 progress on its nuclear weapons program had surprised the 1C. The role this knowledge played in analysts' thinking is evident in the 2002 National Intelligence Estimate's (NIE) introduction which said, "revelations after the Gulf War starkly demonstrate the extensive efforts undertaken by Iraq to deny information. The revelations also underscore the extent to which limited information fostered underestimates by the Intelligence Community of Saddam's capabilities at that time." This bias was likely further reinforced by the IC's failure to detect the September 11th terrorist plot and the criticism that the Community had not done all it could to "connect the dots."

The IC had long assessed that Iraq maintained its ambitions to obtain WMD, and would seek to resume full WMD efforts once UN sanctions and inspections ended. Accordingly, after UN inspectors left Iraq in 1998, 1C analysts began to look for evidence that Iraq was expanding WMD programs. Analysts interpreted ambiguous data as indicative of the active and expanded WMD effort they expected to see. The presumption that Iraq would take advantage of the departure of inspectors to restart its WMD efforts essentially became a hypothesis in search of evidence.

The IC's bias was compounded by the fact that prior to 1998, the IC had become heavily dependent on UN information on the state of Iraq's WMD programs. When the IC lost this important information, analysts were forced to rely on less reliable and less detailed sources. For example, BLACKED OUT reporting during UN inspections often described the BLACKED OUT. These reports provided IC analysts with much insight BLACKED OUT. Intelligence reporting after inspectors departed relied on less direct sources of information such as satellite imagery of activity at suspect facilities, fragmentary and ambiguous reports of Iraqi dual-use procurement efforts, and reporting of suspicious or prohibited activity from human sources who were no longer in the country. These indirect sources left the IC with few ways to determine the exact nature of suspicious Iraqi activity. The expectation, however, that Iraq would take advantage of the departure of inspectors to resume and expand its WMD programs led analysts to downplay or ignore the increased uncertainty that came with these less detailed and less reliable sources.

The Committee found that the IC had a tendency to accept information which supported the presumption that Iraq had active and expanded WMD programs more readily than information which contradicted it. This was evident in analysts' assessments of Iraq's attempts to procure dual-use materials and activities at dual-use facilities. Dual-use materials and facilities are those which could be used in a WMD program, but which also have conventional military or legitimate civilian applications. The IC properly noted the potential threat embodied in these dual use capabilities, should they be fumed toward WMD purposes, and did an effective job of analyzing BLACKED OUT Iraq's attempts to purchase dual-use equipment and materials to show how they could advance Iraq's WMD capability. But, the IC fell short by accepting most reporting of dual-use material imports or capabilities as intended for WMD programs. Information that contradicted the IC's presumption that Iraq had WMD programs, such as indications in the intelligence reporting that the dual-use materials were intended for conventional or civilian programs, was often ignored. The IC's bias that Iraq had active WMD programs led analysts to presume, in the absence of evidence, that if Iraq could do something to advance its WMD capabilities, it would.

Another example of the IC's tendency to reject information that contradicted the presumption that Iraq had active and expanded WMD programs was the return of UN inspectors to Iraq in November 2002. BLACKED OUT When these inspections did not find evidence of active Iraqi WMD programs and in fact, even refuted some aspects of the IC's nuclear and biological assessments, many analysts did not regard this information as significant. For example, the 2002 NIE cited BLACKED OUT Iraq's Amiriyah Serum and Vaccine institute as BLACKED OUT reasons the IC believed the facility was a "fixed dual-use BW agent production" facility. When UN inspectors visited Amiriyah after their return to Iraq in November 2002, however, they did not find any evidence of BW work at the facility, BLACKED OUT. Analysts discounted the UN's findings as the result of the inspectors relative inexperience in the face of Iraqi denial and deception. Similarly, when International Atomic Energy Agency (IAEA) inspectors returned to Iraq in late 2002, one of their key lines of work was to investigate Iraq's claims that aluminum tubes it was trying to procure were intended for artillery rockets. The IAEA found that Iraq's claims that the aluminum tubes were intended for artillery rockets was completely consistent with the evidence on the ground in Iraq. The Central Intelligence Agency (CIA) responded to the IAEA's analysis by producing intelligence reports which rejected the IAEA's conclusions. Without giving many details of the IAEA's findings, CIA's analysis suggested that the IAEA was being fooled by Iraq, and reiterated CIA's assessment that the tubes were to be used in uranium centrifuges.

Intelligence analysts' presumption that all dual-use activity was intended for WMD programs recurs throughout the 2002 NIE. Analysts believed that the fact that Iraq often attempted to obtain dual-use materials surreptitiously, through front companies and other illicit means in violation of UN sanctions, indicated that Iraq intended to use those materials for WMD. Analysts argued that Iraq would have no reason to hide itself as the end user of these materials if they were intended for legitimate purposes. However, analysts ignored the fact that Iraq typically used front companies and evaded UN sanctions for imports of purely legitimate goods. Analysts who monitored Iraq's compliance with the Oil for Food Program noted several reasons that Iraq wanted to avoid legitimate channels for imports including 1) the UN often denied materials needed for legitimate purposes because the materials had WMD applications, 2) using the UN's bureaucratic process was more cumbersome and tune consuming than using illicit channels, and 3) transactions using front companies were less transparent, making corruption and profit taking easier for Iraqi managers and officials.

Likewise, analysts were predisposed to identify as suspect any activity by scientists and officials involved in Iraq's pre–1991 WMD programs. While the IC should not have ignored the activity of these people, IC analysts failed to fully consider the possibility that Iraq, having spent significant national resources developing their capabilities, might have been seeking non-WMD purposes to fully employ the idle expertise left over from closed WMD programs.

The presumption that Iraq had active WMD programs affected intelligence collectors as well. None of the guidance given to human intelligence collectors suggested that collection be focused on determining whether Iraq had WMD. Instead, the requirements assumed that Iraq had WMD, and focused on uncovering those activities and collecting against the extent of Iraq's WMD production and the locations of hidden stocks of weapons. A former manager in the CIA's Iraq WMD Task Force also told Committee staff that, in retrospect, he believes that the CIA tended to discount human intelligence (HUMINT) sources that denied the existence of Iraqi WMD programs as just repeating the Iraqi party line. In fact, numerous interviews with intelligence analysts and documents provided to the Committee indicate that analysts and collectors assumed that sources who denied the existence or continuation of WMD programs and stocks were either lying or not knowledgeable about Iraq's programs, while those sources who reported ongoing WMD activities were seen as having provided valuable information.

The presumption that Iraq had active WMD programs was so strong that formalized IC mechanisms established to challenge assumptions and "group think," such as "red teams," "devil's advocacy," and other types of alternative or competitive analysis, were not utilized. The Committee found no evidence that IC analysts, collectors, or managers made any effort to question the fundamental assumptions that Iraq had active and expanded WMD programs, nor did they give serious consideration to other possible explanations for Iraq's failure to satisfy its WMD accounting discrepancies, other than that it was hiding and preserving WMD. The fact that no one in the IC saw a need for such tools is indicative of the strength of the bias that Iraq had active and expanded WMD programs. The Committee does not regard the BLACKED OUT analysis on Iraq's aluminum tubes performed by CIA contractors as an attempt to challenge assumptions, but rather as an example of the collective rationalization that is indicative of "group think."

The contractors were only provided with information by CIA, did not question agencies about their analysis, were not briefed by other agencies about their analysis, and performed their analysis of a complex intelligence issue in only one day.

The IC's failure to find unambiguous intelligence reporting of Iraqi WMD activities should have encouraged analysts to question their presumption that Iraq had WMD. Instead, analysts rationalized the lack of evidence as the result of "vigorous" Iraqi denial and deception (D&D) efforts to hide the WMD programs that analysts were certain existed. The 2002 NIE's introduction stated that "we judge that we are only seeing a portion of Iraq's WMD efforts owing to Baghdad's vigorous D&D efforts." The intelligence provided to the Committee showed that Iraq was making efforts to hide some activity, but the reporting was not clear about what activity was being hidden or why it was being hidden. Although the IC lacked unambiguous reporting of either active WMD programs or a vigorous D'&D effort to hide WMD programs, the assumptions that Iraq was engaged in both were tied together into a self-reinforcing premise that explained away the lack of strong evidence of either.


Conclusion 4. In a few significant instances, the analysis in the National Intelligence Estimate suffers from a "layering" effect whereby assessments were built based on previous judgments without carrying forward the uncertainties of the underlying judgments.

The Committee defines "layering" as the process of building an intelligence assessment primarily using previous judgments without substantial new intelligence reporting. While this process is a legitimate and often useful analytic tool in making logical connections between intelligence reports and in understanding complex analytic problems, the process can lose its legitimacy when the cumulative uncertainties of the underlying assessments are not factored into or conveyed through the new assessments.

In discussions with the Committee about his experience running the Iraq Survey Group, Dr. David Kay suggested that the IC's mind set before Operation Iraqi Freedom concerning Iraq's weapons of mass destruction (WMD) programs was a train that seemed "to always be going in the same direction." The IC drew on very few pieces of new evidence to reach large conclusions in which new pieces of evidence would accrete to the previous conclusion and pieces that did not fit tended to be thrown aside.

One example of this layering effect occurred in the IC's analysis of Iraq's chemical weapons program. The NIE assessed that Iraq had renewed production of chemical weapons agents and stockpiled as much as 500 metric tons of chemical agent, much of it added in the last year. These assessments were largely based on another assessment, that Iraq may have been engaged in chemical weapons transshipment activity in the spring of 2002. This assessment was largely based on yet another assessment, that the presence of a specific tanker truck was a possible indicator that chemical or biological weapons related activities were occurring. The IC did not make it clear in its latter assessments that its judgments were based on layer upon layer of previous analytic judgments. This gave the reader of the NIE the impression that Iraq's chemical weapons program was advancing and growing, but did not convey that the assessment was based on very little direct or credible intelligence reporting.

Similarly, the IC based its judgment that "all key aspects—research & development (R&D), production, and weaponization—of Iraq's offensive biological weapons (BW) program are active and that most elements are larger and more advanced than they were before the Gulf War" primarily on its assessment that Iraq had mobile biological production vans. While this assessment was based on direct intelligence that indicated Iraq had mobile biological production units, the reporting was largely from a single source to whom the Intelligence Community did not have direct access. The Committee believes that the IC's expectation that Iraq would move to mobile biological weapons production, focused their attention on reporting that supported that contention and led them to disregard information that contradicted it. This exemplifies Dr. Kay's concerns that the IC made large new conclusions based on only a few pieces of new evidence that were joined to previous conclusions and that pieces that did not fulfill its expectations tended to be thrown aside.

These are just two, of many, examples of this layering effect the Committee found in the IC's analysis of Iraq's weapons of mass destruction programs. The Committee recognizes the importance of analysts' ability to perform this type of analytic extrapolation, particularly in trying to "connect the dots" of sometimes seemingly disparate pieces of intelligence. Incorporating and accurately explaining the cumulative underlying uncertainties inherent in that process is equally important, however.

Conclusion 5. In each instance where the Committee found an analytic or collection failure, it resulted in part from a failure of Intelligence Community managers throughout their leadership chains to adequately supervise the work of their analysts and collectors. They did not encourage analysts to challenge their assumptions, fully consider alternative arguments, accurately characterize the intelligence reporting, or counsel analysts who lost their objectivity.

This report describes a variety of serious analytical and collection failures in the Intelligence Community's (IC) work on Iraq's weapons of mass destruction programs. While not in any way diminishing the responsibility of the analysts and collectors that were directly involved, the Committee believes that blame for these failures can not be laid at their feet alone. hi each instance, the analysts' and collectors' chains of command in their respective agencies, from immediate supervisors up to the National Intelligence Council and the Director of Central Intelligence, all share responsibility for not encouraging analysts to challenge their assumptions, fully consider alternative arguments or accurately characterize the intelligence reporting. They failed to adequately question and challenge analysts about their assessments, and, most importantly, to recognize when analysts had lost their objectivity and take corrective action. It seems likely that these failures of management and leadership resulted at least in part as a result of the fact that the Intelligence Community's chain of command shared with its analysts and collectors the same "group think" presumption that Iraq had active and expanded weapons of mass destruction programs.

Conclusion 6. The Committee found significant short-comings in almost every aspect of the Intelligence Community's human intelligence collection efforts against Iraq's weapons of mass destruction activities, in particular that the Community had no sources collecting against weapons of mass destruction in Iraq after 1998. Most, if not all, of these problems stem from a broken corporate culture and poor management, and will not be solved by additional funding and personnel.

The Committee's review into the prewar intelligence concerning Iraq's weapons of mass destruction programs has entailed an unprecedented outside examination of a broad range of the Intelligence Community's (IC) human intelligence (HUMINT) operations. The Committee found significant short-comings in almost every aspect of these operations.

From 1991 to 1998, the IC relied too heavily on United Nations (UN) inspectors to collect information about Iraq's weapons of mass destruction programs and did not develop a sufficient unilateral HUMINT collection effort targeting Iraq to supplement UN-collected information and to take its place upon the departure of the UN inspectors. While the UN inspection process provided a valuable source of information, the IC should have used the time when inspectors were in Iraq to plan for the possibility that inspectors would leave and to develop sources who could continue to report after inspectors left.

Because the United States lacked an official presence inside Iraq, the Intelligence Community depended too heavily on defectors and foreign government services to obtain HUMINT information on Iraq's weapons of mass destruction activities. While these sources had the potential to provide some valuable information, they had a limited ability to provide the kind of detailed intelligence about current Iraqi weapons of mass destruction efforts sought by U.S. policymakers. Moreover, because the Intelligence Community did not have direct access to many of these sources, their credibility was difficult to assess and was often left to the foreign government services to judge. Intelligence Community HUMINT efforts against a closed society like Iraq prior to Operation Iraqi Freedom were hobbled by the Intelligence Community's dependence on having an official U.S. presence in-country to mount clandestine HUMINT collection efforts.

When UN inspectors departed Iraq, the placement of HUMINT agents and the development of unilateral sources inside Iraq were not top priorities for the Intelligence Community. The Intelligence Community did not have a single HUMINT source collecting against Iraq's weapons of mass destruction programs in Iraq after 1998. The Intelligence Community appears to have decided that the difficulty and risks inherent in developing sources or inserting operations officers into Iraq outweighed the potential benefits. The Committee found no evidence that a lack of resources significantly prevented the Intelligence Community from developing sources or inserting operations officers into Iraq.

BLACKED OUT. When Committee staff asked why the CIA had not considered placing a CIA officer in Iraq years before Operation Iraqi Freedom to investigate Iraq's weapons of mass destruction programs, a CIA officer said, "because it's very hard to sustain . . . it takes a rare officer who can go in . . . and survive scrutiny BLACKED OUT for a long time." The Committee agrees that such operations are difficult and dangerous, but they should be within the norm of the CIA's activities and capabilities. Senior CIA officials have repeatedly told the Committee that a significant increase in funding and personnel will be required to enable to the CIA to penetrate difficult HUMINT targets similar to prewar Iraq. The Committee believes, however, that if an officer willing and able to take such an assignment really is "rare" at the CIA, the problem is less a question of resources than a need for dramatic changes in a risk averse corporate culture.

Problems with the Intelligence Community's HUMINT efforts were also evident in the Intelligence Community's handling of Iraq's alleged efforts to acquire uranium from Niger. The Committee does not fault the CIA for exploiting the access enjoyed by the spouse of a CIA employee traveling to Niger. The Committee believes, however, that it is unfortunate, considering the significant resources available to the CIA, that this was the only option available. Given the nature of rapidly evolving global threats such as terrorism and the proliferation of weapons and weapons technology, the Intelligence Community must develop means to quickly respond to fleeting collection opportunities outside the Community's established operating areas. The Committee also found other problems with the Intelligence Community's follow-up on the Iraq-Niger uranium issue, including a half-hearted investigation of the reported storage of uranium in a warehouse in Benin, and a failure, to this day, to call a telephone number, provided by the Navy, of an individual who claimed to have information about Iraq's alleged efforts to acquire uranium from Niger.

The Committee also found that the Defense HUMINT Service (DHS) demonstrated serious lapses in its handling of the HUMINT source code named CURVE BALL, who was the principle source behind the Intelligence Community's assessments that Iraq had a mobile biological weapons program. The DHS had primary responsibility for handling the Intelligence Community's interaction with the BLACKED OUT debriefers that were handling CURVE BALL, but the DHS officers that were involved in CURVE ball's case limited themselves to a largely administrative role, translating and passing along reports BLACKED OUT analysts do not have the benefit of the regular interaction with sources or, in this case, CURVE ball's debriefers, that could have allowed them to make judgments about the reliability of source reporting.

Another significant problem found by the Committee is the fact that the CIA continues to excessively compartment sensitive HUMINT reporting and fails to share important information about HUMINT reporting and sources with Intelligence Community analysts who have a need to know. In the years before Operation Iraqi Freedom, the CIA protected its Iraq weapons of mass destruction sources so well that some of the information they provided was kept from the majority of analysts with a legitimate need to know. The biological weapons and delivery sections of this report discuss at length the CIA's failure to share important information about source reporting on Iraq's alleged mobile biological weapons program and unmanned aerial vehicle (UAV) program that left analysts and policymakers with an incomplete and, at times, misleading picture of these issues.

The process by which the Intelligence Community calculates

the benefits and risks of sharing sensitive human intelligence is skewed too heavily toward withholding information. This issue has been raised repeatedly with the Intelligence Community, particularly after the lack of information sharing was found to have played a key role in the intelligence failures of 9/11. The Committee believes that the Intelligence Community must reconsider whether the risks of expanding access to cleared analysts are truly greater than the risks of keeping information so tightly compartmented that the analysts who need it to make informed judgments are kept in the dark.

Conclusion 7. The Central Intelligence Agency (CIA), in several significant instances, abused its unique position in the Intelligence Community, particularly in terms of information sharing, to the detriment of the Intelligence Community's prewar analysis concerning Iraq's weapons of mass destruction programs.

The Intelligence Community is not a level playing field when it comes to the competition of ideas in intelligence analysis. The Director of Central Intelligence's (DCI's) responsibility, established by the National Security Act of 1947, to coordinate the nation's intelligence activities and correlate, evaluate, and disseminate intelligence that affects national security, provides the CIA with a unique position in the Intelligence Community. The fact that the DCI is the head of the CIA and head of the Intelligence Community, the principal intelligence advisor to the President, and is responsible for protecting intelligence sources and methods, provides the CIA with unique access to policymakers and unique control of intelligence reporting. This arrangement was intended to coordinate the disparate elements of the Intelligence Community in order to provide the most accurate and objective analysis to policymakers. The Committee found that in practice, however, in the case of the Intelligence Community's analysis of Iraq's weapons of mass destruction programs, this arrangement actually undermined the provision of accurate and objective analysis by hampering intelligence sharing and allowing CIA analysts to control the presentation of information to policymakers, and exclude analysis from other agencies.

The Committee found in a number of cases that significant reportable intelligence was sequestered in CIA Directorate of Operations (DO) cables, distribution of sensitive intelligence reports was excessively restricted, and CIA analysts were often provided with "sensitive" information that was not made available to analysts who worked the same issues at other all-source analysis agencies. These restrictions, in several cases, kept information from analysts that was essential to their ability to make fully informed judgments. Analysts cannot be expected to formulate and present their best analysis to policymakers while having only partial knowledge of an issue.

For example, important information concerning the reliability of two of the main sources on Iraq's alleged mobile biological weapons program was not available to most Iraq biological weapons analysts outside the CIA. Some analysts at other agencies were aware of some of the credibility concerns about the sources, but the CIA's DO did not disseminate cables throughout the Intelligence Community that would have provided this information to all Iraq biological weapons analysts.

BLACKED OUT

The CIA also failed to share important information about Iraq's UAV software procurement efforts with other intelligence analysts. The CIA did share sensitive information that indicated Iraq BLACKED OUT was trying to obtain mapping software that could only be used for mapping in the U.S. This suggested to many analysts that Iraq may have been intending to use the software to target the U.S. The CIA failed to pass on additional information, until well after the coordination and publication of the National Intelligence Estimate (NIE), BLACKED OUT. This information was essential for analysts to make fully informed judgments about Iraq's intentions to target the U.S.

In some cases CIA analysts were not open to fully considering information and opinions from other intelligence analysts or creating a level playing field in which outside analysts fully participated in meetings or analytic efforts. This problem was particularly evident in the case of the CIA's analysis of Iraq's procurement of aluminum tubes during which the Committee believes the agency lost objectivity and in several cases took action that improperly excluded useful expertise from the intelligence debate. For example, the CIA performed testing of the tubes without inviting experts from the Department of Energy (DOE) to participate. A CIA analyst told Committee staff that the DOE was not invited "because we funded it. It was our testing. We were trying to prove some things that we wanted to prove with the testing. It wasn't a joint effort." The Committee believes that such an effort should never have been intended to prove what the CIA wanted to prove, but should have been a Community effort to get to the truth about Iraq's intended use for the tubes. By excluding DOE analysts, the Intelligence Community's nuclear experts, the CIA was not able to take advantage of their potentially valuable analytic insights. In another instance, an independent Department of Defense (DOD) rocket expert told the Committee that he did not think the CIA analysts came to him for an objective opinion, but were trying "to encourage us to come up with [the] answer" that the tubes were not intended to be used for a rocket program.

The Committee also found that while the DCI was supposed to function as both the head of the CIA and the head of the Intelligence Community, in many instances he only acted as head of the CIA. For example, the DCI told the Committee that he was not aware that there were dissenting opinions within the Intelligence Community on whether Iraq intended use the aluminum tubes for a nuclear program until the NIE was drafted in September 2002, despite the fact that intelligence agencies had been fervently debating the issue since the spring of 2001. While the DCI, as the President's principal intelligence advisor, should provide policymakers, in particular the President, with the best analysis available from throughout the Intelligence Community, the DCI told Committee staff that he does not even expect to learn of dissenting opinions "until the issue gets joined" through interagency coordination of an NIE. This means that contentious debate about significant national security issues can go on at the analytic level for months, or years, without the DCI or senior policymakers being informed of any opinions other than those of CIA analysts. In addition, the Presidential Daily Briefs (PDBs) are prepared by CIA analysts and are presented by CIA briefers who may or may not include an explanation of alternative views from other intelligence agencies. Other Intelligence Community agencies essentially must rely on the analysts who disagree with their positions to accurately convey their analysis to the nation's most senior policymakers.

These factors worked together to allow CIA analysts and officials to provide the agency's intelligence analysis to senior policymakers without having to explain dissenting views or defend their analysis from potential challenges from other Intelligence Community agencies. The Committee believes that policymakers at all levels of government and in both the executive and legislative branches would benefit from understanding the full range of analytic opinions directly from the agencies who hold those views, or from truly impartial representatives of the entire Intelligence Community.

*Overall Conclusions—Terrorism*

Conclusion 8. Intelligence Community analysts lack a consistent post-September 11 approach to analyzing and reporting on terrorist threats.

Though analysts have been wrong on major issues in the past, no previous intelligence failure has been so costly as the September 11 attacks. As the Deputy Director of Intelligence (DDI) explained during an interview with Committee staff, terrorist threat analysts now use a different type of trade craft than generally employed by political, leadership or regional analysts. Threat analysts are encouraged to "push the envelope" and look at various possible threat scenarios that can be drawn from limited and often fragmentary information. As a result, analysts can no longer dismiss a threat as incredible because they cannot corroborate it. They cannot dismiss what may appear to be the rantings of a walk-in until additional vetting shows those stories to be fabricated.

To compensate for the fragmentary nature of the reporting on Iraq's potential links to al-Qaida, Intelligence Community (IC) analysts included as much detail as they could about the nature of the sources and went to great lengths to describe their analytic approach to the problem. For example, where information was limited to a single or untested source or to a foreign government service, a source description was provided. As discussed in more detail in the body of this report, a "Scope Note" was incorporated in each product to describe the analytic approach the drafters had taken to address the issue. In Iraq and al-Qaida: Interpreting a Murky Relationship, the Scope Note explained that the authors had purposefully taken an aggressive approach to interpreting the available data. In both the September 2002 and January 2003 versions of Iraqi Support for Terrorism, the Scope Note did not describe an analytic approach, but rather it highlighted the gaps in information and described the analysts' understanding of the Iraq-al-Qaida relationship as "evolving."

Though the Committee understands the need for different analytical approaches and expressions of competing viewpoints, the IC should have considered that their readership would not necessarily understand the nuance between the first "purposely aggressive" approach and a return, in Iraqi Support /or Terrorism, to a more traditional analysis of the reporting concerning Iraq's links to al-Qaida. A consistent approach in both assessments which carefully explained the intelligence reports and then provided a spectrum of possible conclusions would have been more useful and would have assisted policymakers in their public characterizations of the intelligence.

Conclusion 9. Source protection policies within the Intelligence Community direct or encourage reports officers to exclude relevant detail about the nature of their sources. As a result, analysts community-wide are unable to make fully informed judgments about the information they receive, relying instead on nonspecific source lines to reach their assessments. Moreover, relevant operational data is nearly always withheld from analysts, putting them at a further analytical disadvantage.

A significant portion of the intelligence reporting that was used to evaluate whether Iraq's interactions with al-Qaida operatives constituted a relationship was stripped of details prior to being made available to analysts community-wide. Source information and operational detail was provided only to Central Intelligence Agency (CIA) analysts. This lack of information sharing limited the level of discussion and debate that should have taken place across the Community on this critical issue. While in the case of Iraq's links to terrorism, the final analysis has proven, thus far, to have been accurate and not affected by a lack of relevant source or operational detail, we cannot rely on this system in the future. Until changes are made concerning how and when source information is made available to analysts, we run the risk of missing critical data that might provide early warning.

The absence of source and operational detail affects not only analysts, but policymakers as well. The Committee found that policymakers took an active role by personally examining individual intelligence reports for themselves. If this trend continues, it is even more important that such relevant detail be provided.

Conclusion 10. The Intelligence Community relies too heavily on foreign government services and third party reporting, thereby increasing the potential for manipulation of U.S. policy by foreign interests.

Due to the lack of unilateral sources on Iraq's links to terrorist groups like al-Qaida BLACKED OUT, the Intelligence Community (IC) relied too heavily on foreign government service reporting and sources to whom it did not have direct access to determine the relationship between Iraq and BLACKED OUT terrorist groups. While much of this reporting was credible, the IC left itself open to possible manipulation by foreign governments and other parties interested in influencing U.S. policy. The Intelligence Community's collectors must develop and recruit unilateral sources with direct access to terrorist groups to confirm, complement or confront foreign government service reporting on these critical targets.

Conclusion 11. Several of the allegations of pressure on Intelligence Community (IC) analysts involved repeated questioning. The Committee believes that IC analysts should expect difficult and repeated questions regarding threat information. Just as the post 9/11 environment lowered the Intelligence Community's reporting threshold, it has also affected the intensity with which policymakers will review and question threat information.

A number of the individuals interviewed by the Committee in conducting its review stated that Administration officials questioned analysts repeatedly on the potential for cooperation between Saddam Hussein's regime and al-Qaida. Though these allegations appeared repeatedly in the press and in other public reporting on the lead-up to the war, no analyst questioned by the Committee stated that the questions were unreasonable, or that they were encouraged by the questioning to alter their conclusions regarding Iraq's links to al-Qaida.

In some cases, those interviewed stated that the questions had forced them to go back and review the intelligence reporting and that during this exercise they came across information they had overlooked in initial readings. The Committee found that this process—the policymakers' probing questions—actually improved the Central Intelligence Agency's (CIA) products. The review revealed that the CIA analysts who prepared Iraqi Support for Terrorism made careful, measured assessments which did not overstate or mischaracterize the intelligence reporting upon which it was based.

The Committee also found that CIA analysts are trained to expect questions from policymakers, and to tailor their analysis into a product that is useful to them. [. . . ]If policymakers did not respond to analysts' caveated judgments with pointed, probing questions, and did not require them to produce the most complete assessments possible, they would not be doing their jobs.

## Niger Conclusions

Conclusion 12. Until October 2002 when the Intelligence Community obtained the forged foreign language documents[2] on the Iraq-Niger uranium deal, it was reasonable for analysts to assess that Iraq may have been seeking uranium from Africa based on Central Intelligence Agency (CIA) reporting and other available intelligence. In March 2003, the Vice Chairman of the Committee, Senator Rockefeller, requested that the Federal Bureau of Investigation (FBI) investigate the source of the documents, BLACKED OUT the motivation of those responsible for the forgeries, and the extent to which the forgeries were part of a disinformation campaign. Because of the FBI's current investigation into this matter, the Committee did not examine these issues.

Conclusion 13. The report on the former ambassador's trip to Niger, disseminated in March 2002, did not change any analysts' assessments of the Iraq-Niger uranium deal. For most analysts, the information in the report lent more credibility to the original Central Intelligence Agency (CIA) reports on the uranium deal, but State Department Bureau of Intelligence and Research (INR) analysts believed that the report supported their assessment that Niger was unlikely to be willing or able to sell uranium to Iraq.

Conclusion 14. The Central Intelligence Agency should have told the Vice President and other senior policymakers that it had sent someone to Niger to look into the alleged Iraq-Niger uranium deal and should have briefed the Vice President on the former ambassador's findings.

Conclusion 15. The Central Intelligence Agency's (CIA) Directorate of Operations should have taken precautions not to discuss the credibility of reporting with a potential source when it arranged a meeting with the former ambassador and Intelligence Community analysts.

Conclusion 16. The language in the October 2002 National Intelligence Estimate that "Iraq also began vigorously trying to procure uranium ore and yellowcake" overstated what the Intelligence Community knew about Iraq's possible procurement attempts.

Conclusion 17. The State Department's Bureau of Intelligence and Research (INR) dissent on the uranium reporting was accidentally included in the aluminum tube section of the National Intelligence Estimate (NIE), due in part to the speed with which the NIE was drafted and coordinated.

Conclusion 18. When documents regarding the Iraq-Niger uranium reporting became available to the Intelligence Community in October 2002, Central Intelligence Agency (CIA) analysts and operations officers should have made an effort to obtain copies. As a result of not obtaining the documents, CIA Iraq nuclear analysts continued to report on Iraqi efforts to procure uranium from Africa and continued to approve the use of such language in Administration publications and speeches.

Conclusion 19. Even after obtaining the forged documents and being alerted by a State Department Bureau of Intelligence and Research (INR) analyst about problems with them, analysts at both the Central Intelligence Agency (CIA) and Defense Intelligence Agency (DIA) did not examine them carefully enough to see the obvious problems with the documents. Both agencies continued to publish assessments that Iraq may have been seeking uranium from Africa. In addition, CIA continued to approve the use of similar language in Administration publications and speeches, including the State of the Union.

Conclusion 20. The Central Intelligence Agency's (CIA) comments and assessments about the Iraq-Niger uranium reporting were inconsistent and, at times contradictory. These inconsistencies were based in part on a misunderstanding of a CIA Weapons Intelligence, Nonproliferation, and Arms Control Center (WINPAC) Iraq analyst's assessment of the reporting. The CIA should have had a mechanism in place to ensure that agency assessments and information passed to policymakers were consistent.

Conclusion 21. When coordinating the State of the Union, no Central Intelligence Agency (CIA) analysts or officials told the National Security Council (NSC) to remove the "16 words" or that there were concerns about the credibility of the Iraq-Niger uranium reporting. A CIA official's original testimony to the Committee that he told an NSC official to remove the words "Niger" and "500 tons" from the speech, is incorrect.

Conclusion 22. The Director of Central Intelligence (DCI) should have taken the time to read the State of the Union speech and fact check it himself. Had he done so, he would have been able to alert the National Security Council (NSC) if he still had concerns about the use of the Iraq-Niger uranium reporting in a Presidential speech.

Conclusion 23. The Central Intelligence Agency (CIA), Defense Humint Service (DHS), or the Navy should have followed up with a West African businessman, mentioned in a Navy report, who indicated he was willing to provide information about an alleged uranium transaction between Niger and Iraq in November 2002.

Conclusion 24. In responding to a letter from Senator Carl Levin on behalf of the Intelligence Community in February 2003, the Central Intelligence Agency (CIA) should not have said that " BLACKED OUT of reporting suggest Iraq had attempted to acquire uranium from Niger," without indicating that State Department's Bureau of Intelligence and Research (INR) believed the reporting was based on forged documents, or that the CIA was reviewing the Niger reporting.

Conclusion 25. The Niger reporting was never in any of the drafts of Secretary Powell's United Nations (UN) speech and the Committee has not uncovered any information that showed anyone tried to insert the information into the speech.

Conclusion 26. To date, the Intelligence Community has not published an assessment to clarify or correct its position on whether or not Iraq was trying to purchase uranium from Africa as stated in the National Intelligence Estimate (NIE). Likewise, neither the Central Intelligence Agency (CIA) nor the Defense Intelligence Agency (DIA), which both published assessments on possible Iraqi efforts to acquire uranium, have ever published assessments outside of their agencies which correct their previous positions.

## Nuclear Conclusions

Conclusion 27. After reviewing all of the intelligence provided by the Intelligence Community and additional information requested by the Committee, the Committee believes that the judgment in the National Intelligence Estimate (NIE), that Iraq was reconstituting its nuclear program, was not supported by the intelligence. The Committee agrees with the State Department's Bureau of Intelligence and Research (INR) alternative view that the available intelligence "does not add up to a compelling case for reconstitution."

Conclusion 28. The assessments in the National Intelligence Estimate (NIE) regarding the timing of when Iraq had begun reconstituting its nuclear program are unclear and confusing.

Conclusion 29. Numerous intelligence reports provided to the Committee showed that Iraq was trying to procure high-strength aluminum tubes. The Committee believes that the information available to the Intelligence Community indicated that these tubes were intended to be used for an Iraqi conventional rocket program and not a nuclear program.

Conclusion 30. The Central Intelligence Agency's (CIA) intelligence assessment on July 2, 2001 that the dimensions of the aluminum tubes "match those of a publicly available gas centrifuge design from the 1950s, known as the Zippe centrifuge" is incorrect. Similar information was repeated by the CIA in its assessments, including its input to the National Intelligence Estimate (NIE), and by the Defense Intelligence Agency (DIA) over the next year and a half.

Conclusion 31. The Intelligence Community's position in the National Intelligence Estimate (NIE) that the composition and dimensions of the aluminum tubes exceeded the requirements for non nuclear applications, is incorrect.

Conclusion 32. The BLACKED OUT intelligence report on Saddam Hussein's personal interest in the aluminum tubes, if credible, did suggest that the tube procurement was a high priority, but it did not necessarily suggest that the high priority was Iraq's nuclear program.

Conclusion 33. The suggestion in the National Intelligence Estimate (NIE) that Iraq was paying excessively high costs for the aluminum tubes is incorrect. In addition, 7075-T6 aluminum is not considerably more expensive than other more readily available materials for rockets as alleged in the NIE.

Conclusion 34. The National Ground Intelligence Center's (NGIC) analysis that the material composition of the tubes was unusual for rocket motor cases was incorrect, contradicted information the NGIC later provided to the Committee, and represented a serious lapse for the agency with primary responsibility for conventional ground forces intelligence analysis.

Conclusion 35. Information obtained by the Committee shows

that the tubes were BLACKED OUT to be manufactured to tolerances tighter than typically requested for rocket systems. The request for tight tolerances had several equally likely explanations other than that the tubes were intended for a centrifuge program, however.

Conclusion 36. Iraq's attempts to procure the tubes through intermediary countries did appear intended to conceal Iraq as the ultimate end user of the tubes, as suggested in the National Intelligence Estimate (NIE). Because Iraq was prohibited from importing any military items, it would have had to conceal itself as the end user whether the tubes were intended for a nuclear program or a conventional weapons program, however.

Conclusion 37. Iraq's persistence in seeking numerous foreign sources for the aluminum tubes was not "inconsistent" with procurement practices as alleged in the National Intelligence Estimate (NIE). Furthermore, such persistence BLACKED OUT was more indicative of procurement for a conventional weapons program than a covert nuclear program.

Conclusion 38. The Central Intelligence Agency's (CIA) initial reporting on its aluminum tube spin tests was, at a minimum, misleading and, in some cases, incorrect. The fact that these tests were not coordinated with other Intelligence Community agencies is an example of continuing problems with information sharing within the Intelligence Community.

Conclusion 39. Iraq's performance of hydrostatic pressure tests on the tubes was more indicative of their likely use for a rocket program than a centrifuge program.

Conclusion 40. Intelligence reports which showed BLACKED

OUT were portrayed in the National Intelligence Estimate as more definitive than the reporting showed.

Conclusion 41. BLACKED OUT in that it was only presented with analysis that supported the CIA's conclusions. The team did not discuss the issues with Department of Energy officials and performed its work in only one day.

Conclusion 42. The Director of Central Intelligence was not aware of the views of all intelligence agencies on the aluminum tubes prior to September 2002 and, as a result, could only have passed the Central Intelligence Agency's view along to the President until that time.

Conclusion 43. Intelligence provided to the Committee did show that Iraq was trying to procure magnets, high-speed balancing machines and machine tools, but this intelligence did not suggest that the materials were intended to be used in a nuclear program.

Conclusion 44. The statement in the National Intelligence Estimate that "a large number of personnel for the new [magnet] production facility, worked in Iraq's pre-Gulf War centrifuge program," was incorrect.

Conclusion 45. The statement in the National Intelligence Estimate that the Iraqi Atomic Energy Commission was "expanding the infrastructure—research laboratories, production facilities, and procurement networks—to produce nuclear weapons," is not supported by the intelligence provided to the Committee.

Conclusion 46. The intelligence provided to the Committee which showed that Iraq had kept its cadre of nuclear weapons personnel trained and in positions that could keep their skills intact for eventual use in a reconstituted nuclear program was compelling, but this intelligence did not show that there was a recent increase in activity that would have been indicative of recent or impending reconstitution of Iraq's nuclear program as was suggested in the National Intelligence Estimate.

Conclusion 47. Intelligence information provided to the Committee did show that Saddam Hussein met with Iraqi Atomic Energy Commission personnel and that some security improvements were taking place, but none of the reporting indicated the IAEC was engaged in nuclear weapons related work.

## Biological Conclusions

Conclusion 48. The assessment in the October 2002 National Intelligence Estimate that, "[W]e judge that all key aspects—research & development, production, and weaponization—of Iraq's offensive biological weapons program are active and that most elements are larger and more advanced than they were before the Gulf War" is not supported by the intelligence provided to the Committee.

Conclusion 49. The statement in the key judgments of the October 2002 National Intelligence Estimate (NIE) that "Baghdad has biological weapons" overstated what was known about Iraq's biological weapons holdings. The NIE did not explain the uncertainties underlying this statement.

Conclusion 50. The statement in the National Intelligence Estimate that "Baghdad has mobile transportable facilities for producing bacterial and toxin biological weapons agents," overstated what the intelligence reporting suggested about an Iraqi mobile biological weapons effort and did not accurately convey to readers the uncertainties behind the source reporting.

Conclusion 51. The Central Intelligence Agency withheld important information concerning both CURVE ball's reliability and BLACKED OUT reporting from many Intelligence Community analysts with a need to know the information.

Conclusion 52. The Defense Human Intelligence Service, which had primary responsibility for handling the Intelligence Community's interaction with CURVE ball's BLACKED OUT debriefers, demonstrated serious lapses in handling such an important source.

Conclusion 53. The statement in the key judgments of the National Intelligence Estimate that "[C]hances are even that smallpox is part of Iraq's offensive biological weapons program" is not supported by the intelligence provided to the Committee.

Conclusion 54. The assessments in the National Intelligence Estimate concerning Iraq's capability to produce and weaponize biological weapons agents are, for the most part, supported by the intelligence provided to the Committee, but the NIE did not explain that the research discussed could have been very limited in nature, been abandoned years ago, or represented legitimate activity.

Conclusion 55. The National Intelligence Estimate misrepresented the United Nations Special Commission's (UNSCOM) 1999 assessment concerning Iraq's biological research capability.

Conclusion 56. The statement in the key judgments of the National Intelligence Estimate that "Baghdad probably has developed genetically engineered biological weapons agents" overstated both the intelligence reporting and analysts assessments of Iraq's development of genetically engineered biological agents.

Conclusion 57. The assessment in the National Intelligence Estimate that "Iraq has . . . dry biological weapons (BW) agents in its arsenal" is not supported by the intelligence information provided to the Committee.

## Chemical Conclusions

Conclusion 58. The statement in the key judgments of the October 2002 Iraq Weapons of Mass Destruction National Intelligence Estimate that "Baghdad has . . . chemical weapons" overstated both what was known about Iraq's chemical weapons holdings and what intelligence analysts judged about Iraq's chemical weapons holdings.

Conclusion 59. The judgment in the October 2002 Iraq Weapons of Mass Destruction National Intelligence Estimate that Iraq was expanding its chemical industry primarily to support chemical weapons production overstated both what was known about expansion of Iraq's chemical industry and what intelligence analysts judged about expansion of Iraq's chemical industry.

Conclusion 60. It was not clearly explained in the National Intelligence Estimate that the basis for several of the Intelligence Community's assessments about Iraq's chemical weapons capabilities and activities were not based directly on intelligence reporting of those capabilities and activities, but were based on layers of analysis regarding BLACKED OUT intelligence reporting.

Conclusion 61. The Intelligence Community's assessment that "Saddam probably has stocked at least 100 metric tons and possibly as much as 500 metric tons of chemical weapons agents— much of it added in the last year," was an analytical judgment and not based on intelligence reporting that indicated the existence of an Iraqi chemical weapons stockpile of this size.

Conclusion 62. The Intelligence Community's assessment that Iraq had experience in manufacturing chemical weapons bombs, artillery rockets and projectiles was reasonable based on intelligence derived from Iraqi declarations.

Conclusion 63. The National Intelligence Estimate assessment that "Baghdad has procured covertly the types and quantities of chemicals and equipment sufficient to allow limited chemical weapons production hidden within Iraq's legitimate chemical industry" was not substantiated by the intelligence provided to the Committee.

Conclusion 64. The National Intelligence Estimate accurately represented information known about Iraq's procurement of defensive equipment.

*Delivery Conclusions*

Conclusion 65. The Intelligence Community assessment that Iraq retains a small force of Scud-type ballistic missiles was reasonable based on the information provided to the Committee. The estimate that Iraq retained "up to a few dozen Scud-variant missiles," was clearly explained in the body of the National Intelligence Estimate to be an assessment based "on no direct evidence" and was explained in the key judgments to be based on "gaps in Iraqi accounting to the United Nations Special Commission (UNSCOM)."

Conclusion 66. The assessments that Iraq was in the final stages of development of the al Samoud missile, may be preparing to deploy the al Samoud and was deploying the al Samoud and Ababil–100 short-range ballistic missile, both which exceed the 150-km United Nations range limit, evolved in a logical progression over time, had a clear foundation in the intelligence reporting, and were reasonable judgments based on the intelligence available to the Committee.

Conclusion 67. The assessment that Iraq was developing medium-range ballistic missile (MRBM) capabilities was a reasonable judgment based on the intelligence provided to the Committee.

Conclusion 68. The Intelligence Community assessment in the key judgments section of the National Intelligence Estimate that Iraq was developing an unmanned aerial vehicle (UAV) "probably intended to deliver biological warfare agents" overstated both what was known about the mission of Iraq's small UAVs and what intelligence analysts judged about the likely mission of Iraq's small UAVs. The Air Force footnote which indicated that biological weapons (BW) delivery was a possible, though unlikely, mission more accurately reflected the body of intelligence reporting.

Conclusion 69. Other than the Air Force's dissenting footnote, the Intelligence Community failed to discuss possible conventional missions for Iraq's unmanned aerial vehicles (UAV) which were clearly noted in the intelligence reporting and which most analysts believed were the UAVs primary missions.

Conclusion 70. The Intelligence Community's assessment that Iraq's procurement of United States specific mapping software for its unmanned aerial vehicles (UAV) "strongly suggests that Iraq is investigating the use of these UAVs for missions targeting the United States" was not supported by the intelligence provided to the Committee.

Conclusion 71. The Central Intelligence Agency's failure to share all of the intelligence reporting regarding Iraq's attempts to acquire United States mapping software with other Intelligence Community agencies left those analysts with an incomplete understanding of the issue. This lack of information sharing may have led some analysts to agree to a position that they otherwise would not have supported.

Conclusion 72. Much of the information provided or cleared by the Central Intelligence Agency (CIA) for inclusion in Secretary Powell's speech was overstated, misleading, or incorrect.

Conclusion 73. Some of the information supplied by the Central Intelligence Agency (CIA), but not used in Secretary Powell's speech, was incorrect. This information should never have been provided for use in a public speech.

Conclusion 74. The Central Intelligence Agency (CIA) should have alerted Secretary Powell to the problems with the biological weapons-related sources cited in the speech concerning Iraq's al leged mobile biological weapons program.

Conclusion 75. The National Imagery and Mapping Agency (NIMA) [NIMA has recently been renamed the National Geospatial-Intelligence Agency (NGA)] should have alerted Secretary Powell to the fact that there was an analytical disagreement within the NIMA concerning the meaning of activity observed at Iraq's Amiriyah Serum and Vaccine Institute in November 2002. Moreover, agencies like the NIMA should have mechanisms in place for evaluating such analytical disagreements.

Conclusion 76. Human intelligence (HUMINT) gathered after the production of the National Intelligence Estimate (NIE), did indicate that Iraqi commanders had been authorized to use chemical weapons as noted in Secretary Powell's speech.

*Weapons of Mass Destruction (WMD) Collection Conclusions*

Conclusion 77. The Intelligence Community relied too heavily on United Nations (UN) BLACKED OUT information about Iraq's programs and did not develop a sufficient unilateral collection effort targeting Iraq's weapons of mass destruction programs and related activities to supplement UN-collected information and to take its place upon the departure of the UN inspectors.

Conclusion 78. The Intelligence Community depended too heavily on defectors and foreign government services to obtain human intelligence (HUMINT) information on Iraq's weapons of mass destruction activities. Because the Intelligence Community did not have direct access to many of these sources, it was exceedingly difficult to determine source credibility.

Conclusion 79. The Intelligence Community waited too long after inspectors departed Iraq to increase collection against Iraq's weapons of mass destruction programs.

Conclusion 80. Even after the departure of United Nations (UN) inspectors, placement of human intelligence (HUMINT) agents and development of unilateral sources inside Iraq were not top priorities for the Intelligence Community.

Conclusion 81. The Central Intelligence Agency (CIA) continues to excessively compartment sensitive human intelligence (HUMINT) reporting and fails to share important information about HUMINT reporting and sources with Intelligence Community analysts who have a need to know.

Conclusion 82. BLACKED OUT. The lack of in-country human intelligence (HUMINT) collection assets contributed to this collection gap.

*Weapons of Mass Destruction (WMD) Pressure Conclusions*

Conclusion 83. The Committee did not find any evidence that Administration officials attempted to coerce, influence or pressure analysts to change their judgments related to Iraq's weapons of mass destruction capabilities.

Conclusion 84. The Committee found no evidence that the Vice President's visits to the Central Intelligence Agency were attempts to pressure analysts, were perceived as intended to pressure analysts by those who participated in the briefings on Iraq's weapons of mass destruction programs, or did pressure analysts to change their assessments.

*White Paper Conclusions*

Conclusion 85. The Intelligence Community's elimination of the caveats from the unclassified White Paper misrepresented their judgments to the public which did not have access to the classified National Intelligence Estimate containing the more carefully worded assessments.

Conclusion 86. The names of agencies which had dissenting opinions in the classified National Intelligence Estimate were not included in the unclassified white paper and in the case of the unmanned aerial vehicles (UAVs), the dissenting opinion was excluded completely. In both cases in which there were dissenting opinions, the dissenting agencies were widely regarded as the primary subject matter experts on the issues in question. Excluding the names of the agencies provided readers with an incomplete picture of the nature and extent of the debate within the Intelligence Community regarding these issues.

Conclusion 87. The key judgment in the unclassified October 2002 White Paper on Iraq's potential to deliver biological agents conveyed a level of threat to the United States homeland inconsistent with the classified National Intelligence Estimate.

## Rapid Production of the National Intelligence Estimate Conclusions

Conclusion 88. The Intelligence Community should have been more aggressive in identifying Iraq as an issue that warranted the production of a National Intelligence Estimate (NIE) and should have initiated the production of such an Estimate prior to the request from Members of the Senate Select Committee on Intelligence.

Conclusion 89. While more time may have afforded analysts the opportunity to correct some minor inaccuracies in the National Intelligence Estimate (NIE), the Committee does not believe that any of the fundamental analytical flaws contained in the NIE were the result of the limited time available to the Intelligence Community to complete the Estimate.

## Iraqi Links to Terrorism Conclusions

Conclusion 90. The Central Intelligence Agency's assessment that Saddam Hussein was most likely to use his own intelligence service operatives to conduct attacks was reasonable, and turned out to be accurate.

Conclusion 91. The Central Intelligence Agency's (CIA) assessment that Iraq had maintained ties to several secular Palestinian terrorist groups and with the Mujahidin e-Khalq was supported by the intelligence. The CIA was also reasonable in judging that Iraq appeared to have been reaching out to more effective terrorist groups, such as Hizballah and Hamas, and might have intended to employ such surrogates in the event of war.

Conclusion 92. The Central Intelligence Agency's examination of contacts, training, safehaven and operational cooperation as indicators of a possible Iraq-al-Qaida relationship was a reasonable and objective approach to the question.

Conclusion 93. The Central Intelligence Agency reasonably assessed that there were likely several instances of contacts between Iraq and al-Qaida throughout the 1990s, but that these contacts did not add up to an established formal relationship.

Conclusion 94. The Central Intelligence Agency reasonably and objectively assessed in Iraqi Support/or Terrorism that the most problematic area of contact between Iraq and al-Qaida were the reports of training in the use of non-conventional weapons, specifically chemical and biological weapons. BLACKED OUT

Conclusion 95. The Central Intelligence Agency's assessment on safehaven—that al-Qaida or associated operatives were present in Baghdad and in northeastern Iraq in an area under Kurdish control—was reasonable.

Conclusion 96. The Central Intelligence Agency's assessment that to date there was no evidence proving Iraqi complicity or assistance in an al-Qaida attack was reasonable and objective. No additional information has emerged to suggest otherwise.

Conclusion 97. The Central Intelligence Agency's judgment that Saddam Hussein, if sufficiently desperate, might employ terrorists with a global reach—al-Qaida—to conduct terrorist attacks in the event of war, was reasonable. No information has emerged thus far to suggest that Saddam did try to employ al-Qaida in conducting terrorist attacks.

Conclusion 98. The Central Intelligence Agency's (CIA) assessments on Iraq's links to terrorism were widely disseminated, though an early version of a key CIA assessment was disseminated only to a limited list of cabinet members and some subcabinet officials in the Administration.

## *Terrorism Collection Conclusions*

Conclusion 99. Despite four decades of intelligence reporting on Iraq, there was little useful intelligence collected that helped analysts determine the Iraqi regime's possible links to al-Qaida.

Conclusion 100. The Central Intelligence Agency (CIA) did not have a focused human intelligence (HUMINT) collection strategy targeting Iraq's links to terrorism until 2002. The CIA had no BLACKED OUT sources on the ground in Iraq reporting specifically on terrorism. The lack of an official BLACKED OUT U.S. presence in the country BLACKED OUT curtailed the Intelligence Community's HUMINT collection capabilities.

Conclusion 101. BLACKED OUT

## *Terrorism Pressure Conclusions*

Conclusion 102. The Committee found that none of the analysts or other people interviewed by the Committee said that they were pressured to change their conclusions related to Iraq's links to terrorism. After 9/11, however, analysts were under tremendous pressure to make correct assessments, to avoid missing a credible threat, and to avoid an intelligence failure on the scale of 9/11. As a result, the Intelligence Community's assessments were bold and assertive in pointing out potential terrorist links. For instance, the June 2002 Central Intelligence Agency assessment Iraq and al-Qaida: Interpreting a Murky Relationship was, according to its

Scope Note, "purposefully aggressive" in drawing connections between Iraq and al-Qaida in an effort to inform policymakers of the potential that such a relationship existed. All of the participants in the August 2002 coordination meeting on the September 2002 version of Iraqi Support/or Terrorism interviewed by the Committee agreed that while some changes were made to the paper as a result of the participation of two Office of the Under Secretary of Defense for Policy staffers, their presence did not result in changes to their analytical judgments.

## *Powell Speech Conclusions—Terrorism Portion*

Conclusion 103. The information provided by the Central Intelligence Agency for the terrorism portion of Secretary Powell's speech was carefully vetted by both terrorism and regional analysts.

Conclusion 104. None of the portrayals of the intelligence reporting included in Secretary Powell's speech differed in any significant way from earlier assessments published by the Central Intelligence Agency.

Conclusion 105. Because the Director of Central Intelligence refused to provide all working drafts of the speech, the Committee could not determine whether anything was added to or removed from the speech prior to its delivery.

## *Iraqi Threat to Regional Stability and Security Conclusions*

Conclusion 106. The Intelligence Community (IC) did not take steps to clearly characterize changes in Iraq's threat to regional stability and security, taking account of the fact that its conventional military forces steadily degraded after 1990.

Conclusion 107. The quality and quantity of Human Intelligence (HUMINT) reporting on issues related to regional stability and security, particularly on the subject of regime intentions, was deficient and did not adequately support policymaker requirements.

Conclusion 108. Subject to the limitations described in conclusions 106 and 107, the Intelligence Community (IC) objectively assessed a diverse body of intelligence regarding Saddam Hussein's threat to regional stability and security, producing a wide range of high quality analytical documents on various topics. The IC's judgments about Iraq's military capabilities were reasonable and balanced, based on three factors: the size and capabilities of its military forces in relation to neighboring countries; its history of aggressive behavior prior to the first Gulf War; and, its patterns of behavior between 1991 and 2003.

Conclusion 109. The Intelligence Community should have produced a National Intelligence Estimate-level assessment of the overall threat posed by Iraq in the region prior to the start of Operation Iraqi Freedom. Such a document would have outlined—in one place and in a systematic fashion—the complete range of factors comprising Iraq's threat to regional stability and security.

## Saddam Hussein's Human Rights Record Conclusions

Conclusion 110. Between 1991 and 2003 analysis of Saddam Hussein's human rights record was limited in volume, but provided an accurate depiction of the scope of abuses under his regime. The limited body of analysis was reasonable, given the difficulty of intelligence collection inside Iraq and the demands on collection resources that were primarily targeted on other priorities. Those competing priorities included weapons of mass destruction, terrorism, regime stability and regional security. There was no indication that the Intelligence Community's (IC) analysis was shaped or manipulated in regards to analysis of human rights abuses.

Conclusion 111. The Intelligence Community's development of a systematic analytical method—the "mosaic approach," which grew out of approaches to "atrocities intelligence" in the Balkans—was an innovation for gaining a better understanding of the human rights situation in Iraq. The environment was a denied and hostile arena that thwarted most intelligence collection by organizations following human rights issues.

*The Intelligence Community's Sharing of Intelligence on Iraqi Suspect Weapons Of Mass Destruction Sites with United Nations Inspectors Conclusions*

Conclusion 112. The Intelligence Community had limited actionable intelligence on suspect Iraqi weapons of mass destruction sites.

Conclusion 113. The Central Intelligence Agency fulfilled the intent of the Administration's policy on the sharing of intelligence information.

Conclusion 114. Public pronouncements by Administration officials that the Central Intelligence Agency had shared information on all high and moderate priority suspect sites with United Nations inspectors were factually incorrect.

Conclusion 115. The rationale used by the Central Intelligence Agency for deciding what information to share with the United Nations was inherently subjective, inconsistently applied, and not well-documented.

Conclusion 116. The multiple Intelligence Community Weapons of Mass Destruction (WMD) site lists lack coherency.

Conclusion 117. The information the Central Intelligence Agency provided to Senator Levin in reply to his letters on the sharing of intelligence information with the United Nations was, in some cases, unresponsive, incomplete and inconsistent.

BLACKED OUT

# Excerpts from the Comprehensive Report of Charles A. Duelfer, Special Advisor to the DCI and Leader of the Iraq Survey Group, on Iraq's WMD

•

## October 2004

*[The entire report, more than 1,000 pages, is available at http:// www.cia.gov/cia/reports/iraq_wmd_2004/. Spellings of some proper names have been changed to conform to those in other texts of this book.]*

## Volume I :Regime Strategic Intent

*Key Findings*

Saddam Hussein so dominated the Iraqi Regime that its strategic intent was his alone. He wanted to end sanctions while preserving the capability to reconstitute his weapons of mass destruction (WMD) when sanctions were lifted.

- *Saddam totally dominated the Regime's strategic decision making.* He initiated most of the strategic thinking upon which decisions were made, whether in matters of war and peace (such as invading Kuwait), maintaining WMD as a national strategic goal, or on how Iraq was to position itself in the international community. Loyal dissent was discouraged and constructive variations to the implementation of his wishes on strategic issues were rare. Saddam was the Regime in a strategic sense and his intent became Iraq's strategic policy.

- *Saddam's primary goal from 1991 to 2003 was to have UN sanctions lifted, while maintaining the security of the Regime.* He sought to balance the need to cooperate with UN inspections—to gain support for lifting sanctions—with his intention to preserve Iraq's intellectual capital for WMD with a minimum of foreign intrusiveness and loss of face. Indeed, this remained the goal to the end of the Regime, as the starting of any WMD program, conspicuous or otherwise, risked undoing the progress achieved in eroding sanctions and jeopardizing a political end to the embargo and international monitoring.

- *The introduction of the Oil-For-Food program (OFF) in late 1996 was a key turning point for the Regime.* OFF rescued Baghdad's economy from a terminal decline created by sanctions. The Regime quickly came to see that OFF could be corrupted to acquire foreign exchange both to further undermine sanctions and to provide the means to enhance dual-use infrastructure and potential WMD-related development.

- *By 2000–2001, Saddam had managed to mitigate many of the effects of sanctions and undermine their international support.* Iraq was within striking distance of a *de facto* end to the sanctions regime, both in terms of oil exports and the trade embargo, by the end of 1999.

Saddam wanted to recreate Iraq's WMD capability—which was essentially destroyed in 1991—after sanctions were removed and Iraq's economy stabilized, but probably with a different mix of capabilities to that which previously existed. Saddam aspired to develop a nuclear capability—in an incremental fashion, irrespective of international pressure and the resulting economic risks—but he intended to focus on ballistic missile and tactical chemical warfare (CW) capabilities.

- *Iran was the pre-eminent motivator of this policy.* All senior level Iraqi officials considered Iran to be Iraq's principal enemy in the region. The wish to balance Israel and acquire status and influence in the Arab world were also considerations, but secondary.

- *Iraq Survey Group (ISG) judges that events in the 1980s and early 1990s shaped Saddam's belief in the value of WMD.* In Saddam's view, WMD helped to save the Regime multiple times. He believed that during the Iran-Iraq war chemical weapons had halted Iranian ground offensives and that ballistic missile attacks on Tehran had broken its political will. Similarly, during Desert Storm, Saddam believed WMD had deterred Coalition Forces from pressing their attack beyond the goal of freeing Kuwait. WMD had even played a role in crushing the Shi'a revolt in the south following the 1991 cease-fire.

- *The former Regime had no formal written strategy or plan for the revival of WMD after sanctions.* Neither was there an identifiable group of WMD policy makers or planners separate from Saddam. Instead, his lieutenants understood WMD revival was his goal from their long association with Saddam and his infrequent, but firm, verbal comments and directions to them.

[. . . ]

# What Saddam Thought:
# The Perceived Successes of WMD

The former Regime viewed the four WMD areas (nuclear, chemical, biological, and missiles) differently. Differences between the views are explained by a complex web of historical military significance, level of prestige it afforded Iraq, capability as a deterrent or a coercive tool, and technical factors such as cost and difficulty of production. We would expect to see varying levels of attention to the four programs and varying efforts to prepare for, or engage in, actions to restart them.

Saddam concluded that Iraq's use of CW prevented Iran, with its much greater population and tolerance for casualties, from completely overrunning Iraqi forces, according to former vice president Ramadan. Iraq used CW extensively in the Iran-Iraq war (1980–88) to repel the Iranian army.

- Iraq suffered from a quantitative imbalance between its conventional forces and those of Iran.

- Saddam's subordinates realized that the tactical use of WMD had beaten Iran. Even Taha Yasin Ramadan, one of Saddam's more independent-minded underlings, acknowledged that the use of CW saved Iraq during ground fighting in the Iran-Iraq war.

- Saddam announced at the end of the war that the Iranian army's backbone had been shattered by the war, according to the presidential secretary. Saddam stated that Iran would be unable to confront Iraq for a decade. Political divisions in Iran, weaknesses in Iranian military capabilities, and Iran's inability to sustain long-term offensive operations also reduced the risk of attack, according to the former chief-of-staff.

- Hamid Yusif Hammadi, former Secretary of the President and presidential office director (1982–1991), said that after the Iran-Iraq War, Saddam was intoxicated with conceit. He believed he was unbeatable. He spoke of this to the Iraqi Government officials and to visiting dignitaries from other Arab countries."

[ . . . ]

Saddam concluded that missile strikes on Tehran, late in the Iran-Iraq war, along with the Al Faw ground offensive had forced Iran to agree to a cease-fire, according to the former Minister of Military Industrialization.

- Saddam's logic was that the "war of the cities"—when Al Hussein missiles were fired at Iranian targets from February to April 1988—had shown that Tehran was more vulnerable to missiles because its population density was greater than Baghdad's. This gave Iraq a strategic incentive to maintain ballistic-missile capabilities.

- According to Saddam, Iraq accelerated its missile development after Iran demonstrated the range capability of its imported ballistic missiles in the 1980s. Saddam said missile technology had been important to Iraq because Iraq could build its own ballistic missiles whereas Iran could not.

[ . . . ]

# WMD Possession—Real or Imagined—Acts as a Deterrent

The Iran-Iraq war and the ongoing suppression of internal unrest taught Saddam the importance of WMD to the dominance and survival of the Regime. Following the destruction of much of the Iraqi WMD infrastructure during Desert Storm, however, the threats to the Regime remained; especially his perception of the overarching danger from Iran. In order to counter these threats, Saddam continued with his public posture of retaining the WMD capability. This led to a difficult balancing act between the need to disarm to achieve sanctions relief while at the same time retaining a strategic deterrent. The Regime never resolved the contradiction inherent in this approach. Ultimately, foreign perceptions of these tensions contributed to the destruction of the Regime.

- Saddam never discussed using deception as a policy, but he used to say privately that the "better part of war was deceiving," according to 'Ali Hasan Al Majid. He stated that Saddam wanted to avoid appearing weak and did not reveal he was deceiving the world about the presence of WMD.

- The UN's inconclusive assessment of Iraq's possession of WMD, in Saddam's view, gave pause to Iran. Saddam was concerned that the UN inspection process would expose Iraq's vulnerability, thereby magnifying the effect of Iran's own capability. Saddam compared the analogy of a warrior striking the wrist of another, with the potential effect of the UN inspection process. He clarified by saying that, despite the strength of the arm, striking the wrist or elbow can be a more decisive blow to incapacitate the entire arm; knowledge of your opponents' weaknesses is a weapon in itself.

[ . . . ]

## Preserving and Restoring
## WMD Infrastructure and Expertise

There is an extensive, yet fragmentary and circumstantial, body of evidence suggesting that Saddam pursued a strategy to maintain a capability to return to WMD after sanctions were lifted by preserving assets and expertise. In addition to preserved capability, we have clear evidence of his intent to resume WMD as soon as sanctions were lifted. The infrequent and uninformed questions ascribed to him by former senior Iraqis may betray a lack of deep background knowledge and suggest that he had not been following the efforts closely. Alternatively, Saddam may not have fully trusted those with whom he was discussing these programs. Both factors were probably at play. All sources, however, suggest that Saddam encouraged compartmentalization and would have discussed something as sensitive as WMD with as few people as possible.

- Between 1996 and 2002, the overall MIC [Military Industrialization Committee] budget increased over forty-fold from ID 15.5 billion to ID 700 billion. By 2003 it had grown to ID 1 trillion. MIC's hard currency allocations in 2002 amounted to approximately $364 million. MIC sponsorship of technical research projects at Iraqi universities skyrocketed from about 40 projects in 1997 to 3,200 in 2002. MIC workforce expanded by fifty percent in three years, from 42,000 employees in 1999 to 63,000 in 2002.

- According to a mid-level IIS official, the IIS successfully targeted scientists from Russia, Belarus, Poland, Bulgaria, Yugoslavia, China, and several other countries to acquire new military and defense-related technologies for Iraq. Payments were made in US dollars. The Iraqi Government also recruited foreign scientists to work in Iraq as freelance consultants. Presumably these scientists, plus their Iraqi colleagues, provided the resident "know how" to reconstitute WMD within two years once sanctions were over, as one former high-ranking Iraqi official said was possible.

- Saddam met with his senior nuclear scientists in 1999 and offered to provide them with whatever they needed, and increased funding began to flow to the IAEC in 2001, according to the former Minister of Military Industrialization. Saddam directed a large budget increase for IAEC and increased salaries tenfold from 2001 to 2003. He also directed the head of the IAEC to keep nuclear scientists together, instituted new laws and regulations to increase privileges for IAEC scientists and invested in numerous new projects. He also convened frequent meetings with the IAEC to highlight new achievements.

- Saddam asked in 1999 how long it would take to build a production line for CW agents, according to the former Minister of Military Industrialization. Huwaysh ['Abd-al-Tawab 'Abdullah Al Mullah Huwaysh, Director of the MIC] investigated and responded that experts could readily prepare a production line for mustard, which could be produced within six months. VX and Sarin production was more complicated and would take longer. Huwaysh relayed this answer to Saddam, who never requested follow-up information. An Iraqi CW expert separately estimated Iraq would require only a few days to start producing mustard—if it was prepared to sacrifice the production equipment.

- Imad Hussein 'Ali Al 'Ani, closely tied to Iraq's VX program, alleged that Saddam had been looking for chemical weapons scientists in 2000 to begin production in a second location, according to reporting.

- Huwaysh stated that in 2001 Saddam approached him after a

ministers' meeting and asked, "Do you have any programs going on that I don't know about," implying chemical or biological weapons programs. Huwaysh answered no, absolutely not. He assumed that Saddam was testing him, so Huwaysh added that because these programs were prohibited by the UN, he could not pursue them unless Saddam ordered it. Huwaysh said Saddam seemed satisfied, asked no further questions, and directed no follow-up actions. The incident was perplexing to Huwaysh, because he wondered why Saddam would ask him this question. While he had no evidence of WMD programs outside MIC, Huwaysh speculated that Qusay had the ability within the SSO to compartmentalize projects and select individuals to do special work.

- Saddam stated to his ministers that he did not consider ballistic missiles to be WMD, according to Huwaysh. Saddam had never accepted missile range restrictions and assessed that if he could convince the UN inspectors he was in compliance regarding nuclear, chemical and biological weapons then he could negotiate with the UNSC over missile ranges.

- Saddam stated publicly in early 2001 that "we are not at all seeking to build up weapons or look for the most harmful weapons . . . however, we will never hesitate to possess the weapons to defend Iraq and the Arab nation".

- Purported design work done in 2000 on ballistic and land attack cruise missiles with ranges extending to 1000 km suggests interest in long-range delivery systems.

- In 2002, Iraq began serial production of the Al Samud II, a short-range ballistic missile that violated UN range limits—text firings had reached 183 km—and exceeded UN prescribed diameter limitations of 600mm. Iraq's production of 76 al Samud IIs, even under sanctions conditions, illustrates that Iraq sought more than a handful of ballistic missiles, but was deterred by the existing trade restrictions.

- Saddam directed design and production of a 650 to 750 km range missile in early 2002, according to Huwaysh. Saddam wanted the missile within half a year. Huwaysh informed him, later that year, that Dr. Muzhir Sadiq Saba' Al Tamimi's twin Volga engine, liquid-propellant design would reach only 550 km and would take three to five years to produce. Saddam seemed profoundly disappointed, left the room without comment, and never raised the subject again.

- Other reports suggest work on a ballistic missile designed to exceed UN restrictions began earlier. A high-level missile official of Al Karamahh State Company said that in 1997 Huwaysh requested him to convert a Volga (SA–2) air defense missile into a surface-to-surface missile. When the official briefed Huwaysh on the results, however, he said Huwaysh told him to stop work immediately and destroy all documentary evidence of the tests. In mid–1998, another missile official said Huwaysh ordered 'Abd-al-Daqi Rashid Shi'a, general director at the Al Rashid State Company to develop a solid-propellant missile capable of a range of 1,000 to 1,200 km. The missile official speculated Huwaysh's order came directly from Saddam. A senior level official at Al Karamahh, alleged that in 2000 Huwaysh ordered two computer designs be done to extend the range of the al Samud, one for 500 km and the other for 1000 km, which were provided him in late 2000. Huwaysh disputes all these accounts.

- As late as 2003, Iraq's leadership discussed no WMD aspirations other than advancing the country's overall scientific and engineering expertise, which potentially included dual-use research and development, according to the former Minister of Military Industrialization. He recalled no discussions among Regime members about how to preserve WMD expertise per se, but he observed there were clear efforts to maintain knowledge and skills in the nuclear field.

## Pumping Up Key Revenue Streams

Baghdad made little overall progress in lifting sanctions between December 1998 and November 2002, despite Russia's pressure to include language in UNSCR 1284 that provided for the end of sanctions. The former Regime, however, was able to increase revenue substantially from several legitimate and illicit sources. Iraq started to receive the revenues of [Oil-for-Food] in January 1997. Revenues from this program increased from $4.2 billion in 1997 to a peak of $17.87 billion in 2000 [. . . ]

## Miscalculation (2002–2003)

The Miscalculation phase was marked by a series of poor strategic decisions that left Saddam isolated and exposed internationally. This period was triggered by the ill-considered reaction of the Regime—driven personally by Saddam—to the 9/11 terrorist attack.

This refusal to publicly condemn the terrorist action led to further international isolation and opprobrium. This was the first of several miscalculations that inexorably led to Operation Iraqi Freedom in 2003.

Following President George W. Bush's State of the Union speech on 29 January 2002, senior members of the Iraqi Government were nervous about both Iraq's inclusion in the "Axis of Evil," and the promise that "the United States of America will not permit the world's most dangerous regimes to threaten us with the world's most destructive weapons." Some ministers recognized that the United States intended to take direct unilateral action, if it perceived that its national security was endangered, and argued that the best course of action was to "step forward and have a talk with the Americans." Also concerned with the assertion of a connection between Iraq and its "terrorist allies," they felt they must "clarify" to the Americans that "we are not with the terrorists." Saddam's attitude, however, toward rapprochement with the UN was well known and remained unchanged. He had posed to his ministers on numerous occasions the following rhetorical question: "We can have sanctions with inspectors or sanctions without inspectors; which do you want?" The implied answer was "we're going to have sanctions one way or the other for a long time because of the hostile attitude of the United States and Great Britain."

Iraqi statements on renewing cooperation with the UN varied, perhaps indicating a clash between the private views of some officials and Saddam's policy. Vice President Ramadan on 10 February 2002 told journalists at the opening of the Syrian Products Exhibition in Baghdad that Iraq was ready to entertain a dialogue with the UN Secretary General for "return of international inspectors to Iraq without any preconditions." Four days later Iraqi Foreign Minister Naji Sabri "ruled out that Iraq would send any signals to the UN regarding its readiness to agree on the return of international inspectors."

Dialogue, however, did begin between Iraq and the UN. Senior-level talks occurred in March and May 2002 at UN Headquarters in New York among Secretary-General Kofi Annan, UNMOVIC Executive Chairman Hans Blix, IAEA Director General Mohammed El-Baradei and an Iraqi delegation headed by Naji Sabri. The results of these meetings were mixed, although both Naji Sabri and Annan agreed that the talks had been a positive and constructive exchange of views on the Iraq-UN relationship. In July 2002, Naji Sabri and Annan met again for talks in Vienna, and Naji Sabri noted that it would take a while to reach agreement on issues where there had been "12 years of lack of contact" and "12 years of conflict." Despite the positive tone of these meetings, very little substantive progress was made: Iraq still refused to accept UNSCR 1284 or to allow UN weapons inspectors to return. As a result, UNSCR 1441 imposed sanctions more harsh than those of UNSCR 1284.

President Bush's speech to the UN General Assembly on 12 September 2002, emphasizing the threat Iraq's WMD posed to global peace and security, unsettled Saddam and the former Regime's leadership.

Most chilling to them was the promise that "the purposes of the United States should not be doubted. The Security Council resolutions will be enforced—the just demands of peace and security will be met—or action will be unavoidable." According to

'Abd-al-Tawab 'Abdallah Al Mullah Huwaysh, Saddam was "very stiff" when he discussed this situation with his ministers some three weeks later, and was obviously still "feeling the pressure." Collectively, there was an even greater fear among the Regime's ministers that the United States unilaterally would attack Iraq, than when Bush made his "Axis of Evil" speech in January 2002. Saddam told them, "What can they discover, when we have nothing?" But some of the ministers were not as sure. Huwaysh said he began to wonder whether Saddam had hidden something: "I knew a lot, but wondered why Bush believed that we had these weapons," he said. Huwaysh could not understand why the United States would challenge Iraq in such stark and threatening terms, unless it had irrefutable information.

The Security Council's unanimous decision on 8 November 2002 to adopt Resolution 1441, which found Iraq in "material breach of all its obligations under relevant resolutions," clearly demonstrated the seriousness of the international community. Resolution 1441 required that Iraq "provide UNMOVIC and the IAEA immediate, unimpeded, unconditional, and unrestricted access to any and all, including underground, areas, facilities, buildings, equipment, records, and means of transport which they wished to inspect, as well as immediate, unimpeded and private access to all officials and other persons whom UNMOVIC or the IAEA chose to interview in the mode or location of UNMOVIC's or the IAEA's choice pursuant to any aspect of their mandates." UNMOVIC and IAEA were instructed "to resume inspections no later than 45 days following adoption of this resolution and to update the Council 60 days thereafter."

Having held out for so long, Saddam initially did not accept much of what UNSCR 1441 required. Although Russia and France were putting pressure on Iraq, Saddam felt the risk of war and even invasion warranted re-acceptance of inspections. According to Vice President Ramadan, Saddam eventually permitted UNMOVIC greater latitude than he had initially intended. Military leaders were instructed at a meeting in December 2002 to "cooperate completely" with the inspectors, believing full cooperation was Iraq's best hope for sanctions relief in the face of US provocation. According to a former [National Monitoring

Directorate] official, one of the Regime's main concerns prior to UNMOVIC inspections was interviews of scientists. When asked why the former Regime was so worried if there was nothing to hide, the source stated that any such meeting with foreigners was seen as a threat to the security of the Regime.

Iraq's cooperation with UN inspectors was typically uneven, and ultimately the Coalition considered the Regime's efforts to be too little, too late. By January 2003, Saddam believed military action was inevitable. He also felt that Iraqi forces were prepared to hold off the invaders for at least a month, even without WMD, and that they would not penetrate as far as Baghdad. He failed to consult advisors who believed otherwise, and his inner circle reinforced his misperceptions. Consequently, when Operation Iraqi Freedom began, the Iraqi armed forces had no effective military response. Saddam was surprised by the swiftness of Iraq's defeat. The quick end to Saddam's Regime brought a similarly rapid end to its pursuit of sanctions relief, a goal it had been palpably close to achieving.

# Renewing UN Inspections

Iraq allowed the IAEA and UNMOVIC to resume inspections in November 2002 in the face of growing international pressure while apparently calculating a surge of cooperation might bring sanctions to an end.

- As it was during the period of the UNSCOM inspections, the Higher Committee was re-established in 2002, this time headed by Vice-President Ramadan, in order to prepare for the UNMOVIC missions. According to Tariq 'Aziz, Saddam believed that the goal of these inspections was to deprive Iraq of any scientific, chemical or advanced technology. Saddam said, "These people are playing a game with us—we'll play a game with them."

- Saddam assembled senior officials in December 2002 and directed them to cooperate completely with inspectors, according to a former senior officer. Saddam stated that the UN would submit a report on 27 January 2003, and that this report would indicate that Iraq was cooperating fully. He stated that all Iraqi organizations should open themselves entirely to UN-MOVIC inspectors. The Republican Guard should make all records and even battle plans available to inspectors, if they requested. The Guard was to be prepared to have an "open house" day or night for the UNMOVIC inspectors. Husam Amin met with military leaders again on 20 January 2003 and conveyed the same directives. During this timeframe Russia and France were also encouraging Saddam to accept UN resolutions and to allow inspections without hindering them.

- The Higher Committee gradually addressed UN concerns as Ramadan relaxed Baghdad's original opposition to the UN resuming U–2 flights and conducting private, unmonitored interviews with Iraqi scientists. These actions eliminated major stumbling blocks in potential Iraqi cooperation with UN-MOVIC.

- Saddam hoped to get sanctions lifted in return for hosting a set of UN inspections that found no evidence of WMD, according to statements ascribed to him by a former senior officer. The government directed key military units to conduct special inspections to ensure they possessed no WMD-associated equipment.

- Upon the direction of UNMOVIC, Baghdad started destroying its al Samud II ballistic missiles 1 March 2003 despite disagreements over the actual operational range of the missile.

- Beginning on 27 November 2002 until United Nations withdrew all its personnel on 18 March 2003, UNMOVIC completed 731 inspections at 411 sites, including 88 sites it had visited for the first time.

- The NMD published the *Currently Accurate, Full, and Complete Declaration* on 7 December 2002, and it attempted to resolve the pending issues of the UN's *Unresolved Disarmament Issues: Iraq's Proscribed Weapons Programs* until the beginning of the war.

Iraqi military industries several times required scientists to sign statements acknowledging the prohibition on conducting WMD research. At a minimum, the forms would have provided documents to offer the UN, but they may also have stopped "free lancing" and thereby ensured that any WMD research underway was tightly controlled to avoid inadvertent disclosures.

• MIC on 20 January 2003 ordered the general directors of its companies to relinquish all WMD to the NMD and threatened severe penalties against those who failed to comply, according to documentary evidence.

• The NMD director met with Republican Guard military leaders on 25 January 2003 and advised them they were to sign documents saying that there was no WMD in their units, according to a former Iraqi senior officer. Husam Amin told them that the government would hold them responsible if UNMOVIC found any WMD in their units or areas, or if there was anything that cast doubt on Iraq's cooperation with UNMOVIC. Commanders established committees to ensure their units retained no evidence of old WMD.

Iraq's National Assembly passed a law banning WMD, a measure that had been required under paragraph 23 of the Ongoing Monitoring and Verification Plan approved under UNSCR 715—and one Iraq had refused to pass despite UN requests since 1991. On 14 February 2003, Saddam issued a presidential directive prohibiting private sector companies and individuals from importing or producing biological, chemical, and nuclear weapons or material, according to documentary evidence. The directive did not mention government organizations.

[ . . . ]

# Sorting Out Whether Iraq Had WMD Before Operation Iraqi Freedom

ISG has not found evidence that Saddam Hussein possessed WMD stocks in 2003, but the available evidence from its investigation—including detainee interviews and document exploitation—leaves open the possibility that some weapons existed in Iraq although not of a militarily significant capability. Several senior officers asserted that if Saddam had WMD available when the 2003 war began, he would have used them to avoid being overrun by Coalition forces.

# Regime Finance and Procurement— Key Findings

Throughout the 1990s and up to [Operation Iraqi Freedom] (March 2003), Saddam focused on one set of objectives: the survival of himself, his Regime, and his legacy. To secure those objectives, Saddam needed to exploit Iraqi oil assets, to portray a strong military capability to deter internal and external threats, and to foster his image as an Arab leader. Saddam recognized that the reconstitution of Iraqi WMD enhanced both his security and image. Consequently, Saddam needed to end UN-imposed sanctions to fulfill his goals.

Saddam severely underestimated the economic and military costs of invading Iran in 1980 and Kuwait in 1990, as well as underestimating the subsequent international condemnation of his invasion of Kuwait. He did not anticipate this condemnation, nor the subsequent imposition, comprehensiveness, severity, and longevity of UN sanctions. His initial belief that UN sanctions would not last, resulting in his country's economic decline, changed by 1998 when the UNSC did not lift sanctions after he believed resolutions were fulfilled. Although Saddam had reluctantly accepted the UN's Oil for Food (OFF) program by 1996, he soon recognized its economic value and additional opportunities for further manipulation and influence of the UNSC Iraq 661

Sanctions Committee member states. Therefore, he resigned himself to the continuation of UN sanctions understanding that they would become a "paper tiger" regardless of continued US resolve to maintain them.

Throughout sanctions, Saddam continually directed his advisors to formulate and implement strategies, policies, and methods to terminate the UN's sanctions regime established by UNSCR 661. The Regime devised an effective diplomatic and economic strategy of generating revenue and procuring illicit goods utilizing the Iraqi intelligence, banking, industrial, and military apparatus that eroded United Nations' member states and other international players' resolve to enforce compliance, while capitalizing politically on its humanitarian crisis.

- From Saddam's perspective, UN sanctions hindered his ability to rule Iraq with complete authority and autonomy. In the long run, UN sanctions also interfered with his efforts to establish a historic legacy. *According to Saddam and his senior advisors, the UN, at the behest of the US, placed an economic strangle hold on Iraq.* The UN controlled Saddam's main source of revenue (oil exports) and determined what Iraq could import.

- UN sanctions curbed Saddam's ability to import weapons, technology, and expertise into Iraq. Sanctions also limited his ability to finance his military, intelligence, and security forces to deal with his perceived and real external threats.

- In short, Saddam considered UN sanctions as a form of economic war and the UN's OFF program and Northern and Southern Watch Operations as campaigns of that larger economic war orchestrated by the US and UK. His evolving strategy centered on breaking free of UN sanctions in order to liberate his economy from the economic strangle-hold so he could continue to pursue his political and personal objectives.

One aspect of Saddam's strategy of unhinging the UN's sanctions against Iraq, centered on Saddam's efforts to influence certain UN SC permanent members, such as Russia, France, and China and some nonpermanent (Syria, Ukraine) members to end UN sanctions. Under Saddam's orders, the Ministry of Foreign Affairs (MFA) formulated and implemented a strategy aimed at these UNSC members and international public opinion with the purpose of ending UN sanctions and undermining its subsequent OFF program by diplomatic and economic means. At a minimum, Saddam wanted to divide the five permanent members and foment international public support of Iraq at the UN and throughout the world by a savvy public relations campaign and an extensive diplomatic effort.

Another element of this strategy involved circumventing UN sanctions and the OFF program by means of "Protocols" or government-to-government economic trade agreements. Protocols allowed Saddam to generate a large amount of revenue outside the purview of the UN. The successful implementation of the Protocols, continued oil smuggling efforts, and the manipulation of UN OFF contracts emboldened Saddam to pursue his military reconstitution efforts starting in 1997 and peaking in 2001. These efforts covered conventional arms, dual-use goods acquisition, and some WMD-related programs.

- Once money began to flow into Iraq, the Regime's authorities, aided by foreign companies and some foreign governments, devised and implemented methods and techniques to procure illicit goods from foreign suppliers.

- To implement its procurement efforts, Iraq under Saddam, created a network of Iraqi front companies, some with close relationships to high-ranking foreign government officials. These foreign government officials, in turn, worked through their respective ministries, state-run companies and ministry-sponsored front companies, to procure illicit goods, services, and technologies for Iraq's WMD-related, conventional arms, and/or dual-use goods programs.

- *The Regime financed these government-sanctioned programs by several illicit revenue streams that amassed more that $11 billion from* *the early 1990s to OIF outside the UN-approved methods.* The most profitable stream concerned Protocols or government-to-government agreements that generated over $7.5 billion for Saddam. Iraq earned an additional $2 billion from kickbacks or surcharges associated with the UN's OFF program; $990 million from oil "cash sales" or smuggling; and another $230 million from other surcharge impositions.

[. . .]

Saddam directed the Regime's key ministries and governmental agencies to devise and implement strategies, policies, and techniques to discredit the UN sanctions, harass UN personnel in Iraq, and discredit the US. At the same time, according to reporting, he also wanted to obfuscate Iraq's refusal to reveal the nature of its WMD and WMD-related programs, their capabilities, and his intentions.

- *Saddam used the IIS to undertake the most sensitive procurement missions. Consequently, the IIS facilitated the import of UN sanctioned and dual-use goods into Iraq through countries like Syria, Jordan, Belarus and Turkey.*

- The IIS had representatives in most of Iraq's embassies in these foreign countries using a variety of official covers. One type of cover was the "commercial attaches" that were sent to make contacts with foreign businesses. The attaches set up front companies, facilitated the banking process and transfers of funds as determined, and approved by the senior officials within the Government.

- The MFA played a critical role in facilitating Iraq's procurement of military goods, dual-use goods pertaining to WMD, transporting cash and other valuable goods earned by illicit oil revenue, and forming and implementing a diplomatic strategy to end UN sanctions and the subsequent UN OFF program by nefarious means.

- Saddam used the Ministry of Higher Education and Scientific

Research (MHESR) through its universities and research programs to maintain, develop, and acquire expertise, to advance
or preserve existent research projects and developments, and to
procure goods prohibited by UN SC sanctions.

- The Ministry of Oil (MoO) controlled the oil voucher distribution program that used oil to influence UN members to
support Iraq's goals. *Saddam personally approved and removed
all names of voucher recipients. He made all modifications to the
list, adding or deleting names at will.* Other senior Iraqi leaders
could nominate or recommend an individual or organization
to be added or subtracted from the voucher list, and ad hoc
allocation committees met to review and update the allocations.

Iraq under Saddam successfully devised various methods to acquire and import items prohibited under UN sanctions. Numerous Iraqi and foreign trade intermediaries disguised illicit items,
hid the identity of the end user, and/or changed the final destination of the commodity to get it to the region. For a cut of the
profits, these trade intermediaries moved, and in many cases
smuggled, the prohibited items through land, sea, and air entry
points along the Iraqi border.

By mid–2000 the exponential growth of Iraq's illicit revenue,
increased international sympathy for Iraq's humanitarian plight,
and increased complicity by Iraqi's neighbors led elements within
Saddam's Regime to boast that the UN sanctions were slowly
eroding. In July 2000, the ruling Iraqi Ba'athist paper, Al-
Thawrah, claimed victory over UN sanctions, stating that Iraq
was accelerating its pace to develop its national economy despite
the UN "blockade." In August 2001, Iraqi Foreign Minister Sabri
stated in an Al-Jazirah TV interview that UN sanctions efforts
had collapsed at the same time Baghdad had been making steady
progress on its economic, military, Arab relations, and international affairs.

- Companies in Syria, Jordan, Lebanon, Turkey, UAE, and
Yemen assisted Saddam with the acquisition of prohibited

items through deceptive trade practices. In the case of Syria and Yemen, this included support from agencies or personnel within the government itself.

- Numerous ministries in Saddam's Regime facilitated the smuggling of illicit goods through Iraq's borders, ports, and airports. The Iraqi Intelligence Service (IIS) and the Military Industrialization Commission (MIC), however, were directly responsible for skirting UN monitoring and importing prohibited items for Saddam.

[. . .]

# Financing Iraq's Illicit Procurement

*Overview*

Iraq developed four major mechanisms for raising illicit funds outside the legitimate UN OFF program. These included the sale of Iraqi oil to neighboring and regional states via trade Protocols, the imposition of surcharges on oil sold through the UN OFF program, and the receipt of kickbacks on UN-approved contracts for goods purchased under the UN OFF program, and so-called "cash-sales" or smuggling.

- From 1996 through 2000 a combination of the UN OFF Program, bilateral trade, and illicit oil profiteering allowed the Iraqi economy to recover from the post–1990 depression. This recovery ended the threat of economically induced Regime instability and provided Saddam with sufficient resources to pursue costly procurement programs.

- After the economic recovery waned in 2000, Saddam's revenues continued to amass via increasingly efficient kickback schemes and illicit oil sales. *ISG estimates Saddam generated $10.9 billion in hard currency through illicit means from 1990 to 2003.*

The 1996–2003 UN OFF Program opened many opportunities for Saddam's Regime:

- It provided $31 billion in needed goods for the people of Iraq, relieving the economic pressure on Regime stability.

- *Saddam was able to subvert the UN OFF program to generate an estimated $1.7 billion in revenue outside of UN control from 1997–2003.*

- The UN OFF oil voucher program provided Saddam with a useful method of rewarding countries, organizations and individuals willing to co-operate with Iraq to subvert UN sanctions.

[. . .]

## Economic Recovery (1997–99)

We judge that the harsh economic conditions from 1995 to 1996 were the primary factors in Saddam's decision to reluctantly accept the UNSCR 986 (see United Nations OFF Program section).

- Saddam wanted to perpetuate the image that his people were suffering as "hostages" to the international community under the UN sanctions.

UN-approved oil exports from Iraq began in December 1996. The trade fostered under the UN OFF program opened the door for Iraq to develop numerous kickback and illicit money earning schemes, possibly beginning as early as 1998. These legitimate and illegitimate revenue streams bolstered the Iraqi economy enough to raise it out of depression, at least for the Iraqi leadership and the elite.

- In the 1996 to 2000 period, Iraq's GDP increased from $10.6 billion to $33 billion.

- According to the UN International Children's Emergency

Fund (UNICEF), Iraq's chronic malnutrition rate dropped from 32 percent in 1996 to just over 20 percent in 1999.

- Iraqi oil production jumped from under 1 million barrels per day (bbl/d) in 1997 to 2.5 million bbl/d in mid–2000.

## Economic Transition and Miscalculation (1999–2003)

After 2000, Iraq's economic growth slowed for a number of reasons, most involving the production and sale of oil. As the Iraqi economy improved, Saddam began to restrict oil production to influence the price of oil in the world market and to leverage political influence. Additionally, Iraq's oil sector could not meet demand because of years of poor reservoir management, corrosion problems at various oil facilities, deterioration of water injection facilities, lack of spare parts, and damage to oil storage and pumping facilities. These petroleum infrastructure problems limited Saddam's ability to export oil and hampered the Regime's ability to sustain the economic growth shown in 1997 to 2000.

- Iraq's GDP slipped from a peak of $33 billion in 2000 to $29 billion in 2001.

- Iraqi oil production dropped from 2.5 million bbl/d in mid–2000 to under 2 million bbl/d in 2002.

Nevertheless, from the late 1990s until Operation Iraqi Freedom, Saddam steadily strengthened the fiscal position of the Regime while investing, as he wished, in development, technology, industry, and defense. Saddam also had enough revenue at his disposal to keep his loyalists in the Regime well paid. In short, *after 1996 the state of the Iraqi economy no longer threatened Saddam's hold on power in Iraq.*

- The budget for the MIC, a key illicit procurement organization, grew from $7.8 million in 1996 to $500 million in 2003.

- Despite Iraq's economic problems, MIC Director Abd al-Tawab Mullah Huwaysh stated that Saddam went on a palace and mosque building spree in the late 1990s that employed 7,000 construction workers.

## Iraq's Revenue Sources

During UN sanctions on Iraq, from August 1990 until OIF in March 2003, Saddam's Regime earned an estimated $10.9 billion utilizing four primary illicit sources of hard currency income. The UN OFF program became Saddam's sole legitimate means to generate revenue outside of Iraq:

- Illicit barrel surcharges on oil sold through the UN OFF program, hereafter referred to as surcharges.

- Ten-percent kickbacks from imports authorized under the UN OFF program, hereafter referred to as kickbacks.

- Exports, primarily petroleum, to private-sector buyers outside the Protocol and UN systems, hereafter referred to as private-sector exports.

The Regime filtered the majority of the illicitly earned monies through foreign bank accounts in the name of Iraqi banks, ministries, or agencies in violation of UN sanctions. According to senior Iraqi officials at SOMO, oil suppliers and traders, who sometimes brought large suitcases full of hard currency to embassies and Iraqi Ministry offices, so that the payments would be untraceable, filled these illegal bank accounts.

During 1997 to 2003, Saddam generated enough revenue to procure sanctioned military goods and equipment, dual-use industrial material, and technology as well as some legitimate uses. These sanctioned goods transactions will be described in detail in later sections. He used those funds to slow the erosion of his conventional military capability in contravention of UN SC resolutions. Available information also indicates Iraq used trade Protocols with various countries to facilitate the delivery of some dual-use items that could be used in the development and production of WMD.

[. . .]

## Oil Vouchers and Allocations

Throughout the UN OFF Program, Iraq used a clandestine oil allocation voucher program that involved the granting of oil certificates to certain individuals or organizations to compensate them for their services or efforts in undermining the resolve of the international community to enforce UNSC resolutions. Saddam also used the voucher program as a means of influencing people and organizations that might help the Regime. By the end of the final phase (13) of the UN OFF Program, Iraq had allocated 4.4 billion barrels of oil to approved rec1pients. However, only 3.1 billion barrels were actually lifted (loaded and exported)—the same figure reported by the UN.

• The oil allocation program was implemented through an opaque voucher program overseen and approved by Saddam and managed at the most senior levels of the Iraqi Regime.

• Starting in Phase 3 of the UN OFF program, until OIF, the Iraqi Regime began to politicize the allocations process by giving quantities of oil to individuals and political parties it favored.

• According to Tariq Aziz, Taha Yasin Ramadan al-Jizrawi, and Hikmat Mizban Ibrahim al-Azzawi, the oil voucher program was managed on an ad hoc basis by . . . Regime officials [. . .].

• The Iraqi Intelligence Service, Ambassadors, and other senior Iraqi officials also commonly made nominations for oil allocations.

## Oil Voucher Process

The MoO normally distributed the secret oil allocations in six-month cycles, which occurred in synchronization with the UN OFF phases. Senior Iraqi leaders could nominate or recommend an individual or organization to be added or subtracted from the voucher list and an ad hoc allocation committee met to review and update the allocations [. . . ] However, *Saddam personally approved and removed all names on the voucher recipient lists.*

This voucher program was documented in detail in a complete listing maintained by Vice President Taha Yasin Ramadan al-Jizrawi and the Minister for Oil, Amir Muhammed Rashid Tikriti Al Ubaydi. If a change was requested by telephone by Saddam or any other top official, either the MoO or SOMO rendered a detailed memo for the record of the conversation. A senior Iraqi official, ambassador, the IIS, or Saddam himself would recommend a specific recipient (i.e. company, individual, or organization) and the recommended amount of the allocation. That recommendation was then considered by the ad hoc committee and balanced against the total amount of oil available for export under the UN program disbursement. When former Vice President Ramadan finalized the recipient list, it was sent to Al Ubaydi. The official at SOMO in charge of issuing the final allocation vouchers (making the disbursements) stated that Tariq Aziz would give the final list to him. He believed that it was Aziz that finalized the list upon the direction of Saddam.

## Secret Voucher Recipients

In general, secret oil allocations were awarded to:

- Traditional oil companies that owned refineries.

- Different personalities and parties, which were labeled "special allocations" or "gifts." This group included Benon Sevan, the former UN Chief of the Office of Iraq Program (OIP), numerous individuals including Russian, Yugoslav, Ukrainian, and French citizens.

- "The Russian State" with specific recipients identified

Recipients could collect their allocation vouchers in person at SOMO or designate someone to collect them on their behalf. The oil voucher was a negotiable instrument. Recipients, especially those not in the petroleum business, could sell or trade the allocations at a discount to international oil buyers or companies at a 10 to 35 cent per barrel profit. Frequent buyers of these large allocations included companies in the UAE as well as Elf Total, Royal Dutch Shell and others.

[. . . ]The top three countries with companies or entities receiving vouchers were Russia (30%), France (15%), and China (10%)—three of the five permanent members of the UNSC, other than the US and UK.

[. . . ]

# Banking and the Transfer of Financial Assets for Procurement

Iraq manipulated its national banking structure to finance the illicit procurement of dual-use goods and WMD-related goods, as well as other military goods and services prohibited by the UN. Through its national banking system, Iraq established international accounts to finance its illegal procurement network. Iraq's international accounts, mainly located in Jordan, Lebanon and Syria, were instrumental in Iraq's ability to successfully transfer billions of dollars of its illicitly earned oil revenues from its various global accounts to international suppliers, front companies, domestic government and business entities, and foreign governments
[. . . ]

# Ministry of Foreign Affairs's UN Sanctions Counter-Strategy

The MFA formulated and implemented a strategy aimed at ending the UN sanctions and breaching its subsequent UN OFF program by diplomatic and economic means. Iraq pursued its related goals of ending UN sanctions and the UN OFF program by enlisting the help of three permanent UNSC members: Russia, France and China. Iraq believed it managed to varying degrees of success to influence these permanent UNSC members from strictly enforcing previously agreed UN resolutions and from initiating additional resolutions that further debilitated the Iraqi economy. By offering permanent and non-permanent Security Council members economic "carrots and sticks," Iraq believed it managed to partially influence voting at the UNSC. Iraq's economic "carrots" included offering companies from those countries lucrative oil, reconstruction, agricultural and commercial goods, and weapon systems contracts. In contrast, the Iraqi "sticks" included not only redirecting those contracts to other more "pro-Iraqi" companies, but held the threat of forfeiture of foreign debts—totaling between approximately $116–250 billion. Saddam expressed confidence that France and Russia would support Iraq's efforts to further erode the UN sanctions Regime.

- According to one source, using "semi-diplomatic cover," the IIS attempted to recruit agents from the UN headquarters in New York to provide information or influence public opinion and their national policy toward Iraq.

- Besides attempting to co-opt certain permanent UNSC members, under cover of MFA sponsored international conferences, Iraq tried to recruit sympathetic eastern European politicians by publicly lauding their pro-Iraqi sentiments and support in the UN.

Iraqi-Russian Relations. Saddam's Regime needed both Moscow's political clout in the UN and its economic expertise and resources to sustain his Regime from the 1990s until OIF. Numerous trips taken by then Iraqi Deputy Prime Minister Tariq Aziz to Moscow served as a good indicator of the Russians' opinion of Iraq's dependence on Russia.

- According to news reports, in July 2001, Tariq Aziz expressed gratitude to Russia for its efforts to pass UNSCR 1360 which continued the UN's OFF program for a tenth phase. Moreover, Iraq promised to economically reward Russia's support by placing it at the head of the list for receiving UN contracts under the UN OFF program.

Iraqi-Chinese Relations. ISG judges throughout the 1990s, the PRC consistently advocated lifting Iraqi sanctions while privately advising Baghdad to strengthen cooperation with the UN. In October 2000, Baghdad continued to seek Chinese support for the removal of UN imposed economic sanctions. By November 2000, Chinese Vice Premier Qian Qichen stated that China would support Iraq's efforts to end the sanctions, and work for an early resolution to the Iraqi issue according to press reporting.

[. . .]

Iraqi-France Relations. Unlike the relatively predictable relationships with China and Russia, the Iraqi-French relationship was more tumultuous. Saddam recognized the important role that France played on the international stage, and in particular in the UNSC. Consequently, Saddam ordered the MFA and other ministries to improve relations with France, according to recovered documents. The documents revealed that the IIS developed a strategy to improve Iraqi-Franco relations that encompassed inviting French delegations to Baghdad; giving economic favors to key French diplomats or individuals that have access to key French leaders; increasing Iraqi embassy staff in Paris; and assessing possibilities for financially supporting one of the candidates in an upcoming French presidential election.

Moreover, the IIS paper targeted a number of French individuals that the Iraqis thought had close relations to French President Jacques Chirac, including, according to the Iraqi assessment, the official spokesperson of President Chirac's re-election campaign, two reported "counselors" of President Chirac, and two well-known French businessmen. In May 2002, IIS correspondence addressed to Saddam stated that a MFA (quite possibly an IIS officer under diplomatic cover) met with French parliamentarian to discuss Iraq-Franco relations. The French politician assured the Iraqi that France would use its veto in the UNSC against any American decision to attack Iraq, according to the IIS memo.

From Baghdad's perspective, the MFA concluded that the primary motive for French continued support and cooperation with Iraq in the UN was economic. According to Tariq Aziz, French oil companies wanted to secure two large oil contracts; Russian companies not only wanted to secure (or lock in) oil contracts, but also sought other commercial contracts covering agricultural, electricity, machinery, food, and automobiles and trucks products.
[ . . . ]

## Ministry of Defense

UN sanctions after Operation Desert Storm severely hindered the MoD's overt procurement of weapons, ammunition, and other military goods. *The Regime, however, did not abandon conventional military procurement, developing instead an illicit procurement program based on supplemental budgeting, the MIC, and the use of other ministries to conceal the procurement of dual-use goods.*

- The Presidential Diwan, Presidential Secretary, and Saddam Hussein developed a supplemental process to fund numerous programs outside of the state budget, including the MoD's illicit conventional procurement.

- Saddam empowered the MIC to pursue his continuing illicit procurement, using front companies and trade intermediaries to avoid international scrutiny.

- As the UN OFF program opened additional trade opportunities, non-security ministries would purchase dual-use items and redirect them to the MoD.

[ . . . ]

# Military Industrialization Commission

By the late 1990s, Iraq was eagerly trying to acquire foreign military by goods and technical expertise for its conventional military and missile programs using a network of Iraqi front companies, some with close relationships to high-ranking foreign government officials. The billions of dollars of revenue generated by the various protocols, illicit surcharges, and oil smuggling schemes drove the explosive growth in military imports. This allowed MIC to smuggle millions of dollars worth of military equipment into Iraq in contravention of UN sanctions.

[. . . ]

# Iraqi Intelligence Service

Saddam used the IIS to undertake the most sensitive procurement missions. Consequently, the IIS facilitated the import of restricted dual-use and military goods into Iraq through Syria, Jordan, Belarus, and Turkey. The IIS had representatives in most of Iraq's embassies in these foreign countries using a variety of official covers. One type of cover was the "commercial attaches" that were sent to make contacts with foreign businesses, set up front companies, and facilitate the banking process and transfers of funds as determined and approved by the senior officials within the government. . . .

[. . . ]

## Items Procured by the IIS

In accordance with Saddam's instructions to MIC Director Abd al-Tawab Mullah Huwaysh, the MIC-IIS relationship was formed to support to Iraq's various missile programs. Although missile programs may have been the reason for the cooperative effort, the IIS also procured for the telecommunications industry, scientific research and development community, and the military. The following are examples of IIS deals that involved the procurement of such items:

- In February 2003, Saddam ordered Al-Basha'ir Head Munir Mamduh Awad al-Qubaysi, Al-Milad Company Director General Sa'ad Abbass, and IIS M4/4/5 procurement officer for Syria and Bulgaria Majid Ibrahim Salman al-Jabburi to travel to Damascus, Syria to negotiate the purchase of SA–11 and Igla surface-to-air missiles, according to a source with good access. This team negotiated with 'Abd al-Qadir Nurallah, manager of the Nurallah Company, to purchase the missiles from a Bulgarian firm, to provide end-user certificates, and to ship the weapons to Iraq.

- In mid–2001, the Technology Transfer Department of the IIS procured between 10 and 20 gyros and 20 accelerometers from a Chinese firm for use in the Al-Samud ballistic missile, according to a former high-ranking official in the MIC. At approximately the end of 2001, the IIS also arranged for Mr. Shokovan from China to teach a course on laser and night-vision technology.

- The IIS completely controlled all procurement from North Korea, according to a senior MIC official. Iraq signed a contract with North Korea to add an infrared-homing capability to the Volga missile to provide jamming resistance in 1999. Iraq also sought to improve the accuracy of its Al-Samud and Al-Fat'h ballistic missiles by obtaining inertial navigation systems, gyros, and accelerometers from North Korea. The IIS also completely controlled procurement via a Russian and Ukrainian company named Yulis that supplied small arms, Kornet antitank guided missiles, and night-vision equipment between 1999 and 2000.

- Iraq sought assistance from the Russian company Technomash in developing a test bench for missile engines, missile guidance and control systems, and aerodynamic structures. The AR-MOS Company signed a contract with a company in Poland to obtain Volga missile engines. The IIS completely controlled this transaction, which sought approximately 250 Volga engines.

- The IIS facilitated a visit by a delegation from the South Korean company Armitel, and contracts were signed to procure fiber-optic equipment for military communications between 1997 and OIF, according to a former MIC senior executive. The contracts were valued at $75 million, and Iraq received more than 30 containers during two shipments, the first via Syria and the second via Lebanon. Middle companies in Syria and the UAE covered these contracts.

- From 2000 until OIF, the IIS used the MIC Al-Basha'ir front company to facilitate a deal with the Bulgarian JEFF Company to obtain T–72 tank parts and Igla MANPADS, according to a former MIC senior executive.

[. . .]

## Ministry of Transport and Communication

The Ministry of Transportation and Communication (MoTC) also facilitated and participated in the procurement of prohibited items for the former Regime. The MoTC transshipped sensitive commodities into Iraq using a range of deceptive practices designed to foil international monitoring efforts. The MoTC also served as a benign cover end user for the acquisition of dual-use items for the MoD and other Iraqi security services. The MoTC procured prohibited fiber-optic materials to improve the Iraqi telecommunications infrastructure. By evaluating these contributions, we judge that the MoTC played a small but important role in Iraq's illicit procurement programs.

[. . .]

## Supplying Iraq With Prohibited Commodities

*Overview*

Despite UN sanctions, many countries and companies en-

gaged in prohibited procurement with the Iraqi regime throughout the 1990s, largely because of the profitability of such trade.

* Private companies from Jordan, India, France, Italy, Romania,
  and Turkey seem to have engaged in possible WMD-related
  trade with Iraq.

* The Governments of Syria, Belarus, North Korea, former Federal Republic of Yugoslavia, Yemen, and possibly Russia directly
  supported or endorsed private company efforts to aid Iraq with
  conventional arms procurement, in breach of UN sanctions.

* In addition, companies based out of the following 14 countries
  supported Iraq's conventional arms procurement programs:
  Jordan, the People's Republic of China, India, South Korea,
  Bulgaria, Ukraine, Cyprus, Egypt, Lebanon, Georgia, France,
  Poland, Romania, and Taiwan.

* The number of countries and companies supporting Saddam's
  schemes to undermine UN sanctions increased dramatically
  over time from 1995 to 2003.

* A few neighboring countries such as Jordan, Syria, Turkey,
  Egypt, and Yemen, entered into bilateral trade agreements
  with Iraq. These agreements provided an avenue for increasing
  trade coordination and eventually led to sanctions violations.

The countries supporting Iraq's illicit procurement changed
over time. These changes reflected trends based on Saddam Hussein's ability to generate hard currency to buy items and the willingness of the international community to criticize those
countries selling prohibited goods to the Regime.
  [. . . ]

# Procurement Suppliers in the Transition and Miscalculation Phases, 1998 to 2003

For the final two phases in Saddam's Regime, "Transition" and "Miscalculation," ISG has identified eight new procurement partners. From the supply side, companies from Russia, North Korea, Poland, India, Belarus, Taiwan, and Egypt have become key trading partners in military or dual-use goods. Like Syria and Turkey in earlier phases, Yemen has become a transshipment facilitator for Saddam's procurement programs

[. . . [

## North Korea

From 1999 through 2002, Iraq pursued an illicit procurement relationship with North Korea for military equipment and long-range missile technology. The quantity and type of contracts entered between North Korea and Iraq clearly demonstrates Saddam's intent to rebuild his conventional military force, missile-delivery system capabilities, and indigenous missile production capacity. There is no evidence, however, to confirm that North Korea delivered longer-range missiles, such as Scud or Scud-variants.

North Korean and Iraqi procurement relations began in 1999 when the MIC requested permission from the Presidential Secretary to initiate negotiations with North Korea. In a recovered memo the Secretary approved the plan and directed the MIC to coordinate negotiations with both the IIS and MoD. Recovered documents further suggest that orders for negotiations were also passed from Saddam directly to the Technology Transfer Office at the IIS. Related documents from this time period reveal that the North Koreans understood the limitations imposed by the UN but were willing "to cooperate with Iraq on the items it specified."

The Director of the MIC formally invited a North Korean delegation to visit Iraq in late 1999. The Director of North Korea's Defense Industry Department of the Korean Worker's Party eventually visited Baghdad in October 2000, working through a

Jordanian intermediary. Multiple sources suggest Iraq's initial procurement goal with North Korea was to obtain long-range missile technology. [. . . ]

As with its other suppliers, Iraq used its accustomed methods to obtain illicit goods from North Korea. In short, North Korea's illicit procurement relationship with Iraq was concealed behind a network of front companies, trade intermediaries, and diplomatic communications.

[. . . ]

# Importing Prohibited Commodities

*Overview*

Iraq under Saddam Hussein used various methods to acquire and import items prohibited under UN sanctions. Numerous Iraqi and foreign trade intermediaries disguised illicit items, hid the identity of the end user, obtained false end-user certificates, and/or changed the final destination of the commodity to get it to the region. For a cut of the profits, these trade intermediaries moved, and in many cases smuggled, the prohibited items to land, sea, and air border entry points along the Iraqi border.

- Companies in Syria, Jordan, Lebanon, Turkey, UAE, and Yemen assisted Saddam with the acquisition of prohibited items through deceptive trade practices. In the case of Syria and Yemen, this included support from agencies or personnel within the government itself.

- Numerous ministries in Saddam's Regime facilitated the smuggling of illicit goods through Iraq's borders, ports, and airports. The IIS and MIC, however, were directly responsible for skirting UN monitoring and importing prohibited items for Saddam.

# Volume II: Delivery Systems

## Key Findings

Since the early 1970s, Iraq has consistently sought to acquire an effective long-range weapons delivery capability, and by 1991 Baghdad had purchased the missiles and infrastructure that would form the basis for nearly all of its future missile system developments. The Soviet Union was a key supplier of missile hardware and provided 819 Scud-B missiles and ground support equipment.

Iraq's experiences with long-range delivery systems in the Iran/Iraq war were a vital lesson to Iraqi President Saddam Hussein. The successful Iraqi response to the Iranian long range bombardment of Baghdad, leading to the War of the Cities, probably saved Saddam.

By 1991, Iraq had successfully demonstrated its ability to modify some of its delivery systems to increase their range and to develop WMD dissemination options, with the Al Hussein being a first step in this direction. The next few years of learning and experiments confirmed that the Regime's goal was for an effective long-range WMD delivery capability and demonstrated the resourcefulness of Iraq's scientists and technicians.

Iraq failed in its efforts to acquire longer-range delivery systems to replace inventory exhausted in the Iran/Iraq war. This was a forcing function that drove Iraq to develop indigenous delivery system production capabilities.

Desert Storm and subsequent UN resolutions and inspections brought many of Iraq's delivery system programs to a halt. While much of Iraq's long-range missile inventory and production infrastructure was eliminated, Iraq until late 1991 kept some items hidden to assist future reconstitution of the force. This decision and Iraq's intransigence during years of inspection left many UN questions unresolved.

- Coalition airstrikes effectively targeted much of Iraq's delivery systems infrastructure, and UN inspections dramatically impeded further developments of long-range ballistic missiles.

- *It appears to have taken time, but Iraq eventually realized that sanctions were not going to end quickly.* This forced Iraq to sacrifice its long-range delivery force in an attempt to bring about a quick end to the sanctions.

- After the flight of Hussein Kamil in 1995, Iraq admitted that it had hidden Scud-variant missiles and components to aid future reconstitution but asserted that these items had been unilaterally destroyed by late 1991. The UN could not verify these claims and thereafter became more wary of Iraq's admissions and instituted a Regime of more intrusive inspections.

- *The Iraq Survey Group (ISG) has uncovered no evidence Iraq retained Scud-variant missiles, and debriefings of Iraqi officials in addition to some documentation suggest that Iraq did not retain such missiles after 1991.*

While other WMD programs were strictly prohibited, the UN permitted Iraq to develop and possess delivery systems provided their range did not exceed 150 km. This freedom allowed Iraq to keep its scientists and technicians employed and to keep its infrastructure and manufacturing base largely intact by pursuing programs nominally in compliance with the UN limitations. *This positioned Iraq for a potential breakout capability.*

- Between 1991 and 1998, Iraq had declared development programs underway for liquid- and solid-propellant ballistic missiles and unmanned aerial vehicles (UAVs).

*Iraq's decisions in 1996 to accept the Oil-For-Food program (OFF) and later in 1998 to cease cooperation with UNSCOM and IAEA spurred a period of increased activity in delivery systems development.* The pace of ongoing missile programs accelerated, and the Regime authorized its scientists to design missiles with ranges in excess of 150 km that, if developed, would have been clear violations of UNSCR 687.

- By 2002, Iraq had provided the liquid-propellant Al Samud

II—a program started in 2001—and the solid-propellant Al Fat'h to the military and was pursuing a series of new small UAV systems.

- *ISG uncovered Iraqi plans or designs for three long-range ballistic missiles with ranges from 400 to 1,000 km and for a 1,000-km-range cruise missile, although none of these systems progressed to production and only one reportedly passed the design phase. ISG assesses that these plans demonstrate Saddam's continuing desire—up to the beginning of Operation Iraqi Freedom (OIF)—for a long-range delivery capability.*

Procurements supporting delivery system programs expanded after the 1998 departure of the UN inspectors. Iraq also hired outside expertise to assist its development programs.

- ISG uncovered evidence that technicians and engineers from Russia reviewed the designs and assisted development of the Al Samud II during its rapid evolution. ISG also found that Iraq had entered into negotiations with North Korean and Russian entities for more capable missile systems.

- According to contract information exploited by ISG, Iraq imported at least 380 SA–2/Volga liquid-propellant engines from Poland and possibly Russia or Belarus. While Iraq claims these engines were for the Al Samud II program, the numbers involved appear in excess of immediate requirements, suggesting they could have supported the longer range missiles using clusters of SA–2 engines. Iraq also imported missile guidance and control systems from entities in countries like Belarus, Russia and Federal Republic of Yugoslavia (FRY). (Note: FRY is currently known as Serbia and Montenegro but is referred to as FRY in this section.)

In late 2002 Iraq was under increasing pressure from the international community to allow UN inspectors to return. Iraq in November accepted UNSCR 1441 and invited inspectors back into the country. In December Iraq presented to the UN its Currently Accurate, Full, and Complete Declaration (CAFCD) in response to UNSCR 1441.

- While the CAFCD was judged to be incomplete and a rehash of old information, it did provide details on the Al Samud II, Al Fat'h, new missile-related facilities, and new small UAV designs.

- In February 2003 the UN convened an expert panel to discuss the Al Samud II and Al Fat'h programs, which resulted in the UN's decision to prohibit the Al Samud II and order its destruction. Missile destruction began in early March but was incomplete when the inspectors were withdrawn later that month.

The CAFCD and United Nations Monitoring, Verification, and Inspection Commission (UNMOVIC) inspections provided a brief glimpse into what Iraq had accomplished in four years without an international presence on the ground.

Given Iraq's investments in technology and infrastructure improvements, an effective procurement network, skilled scientists, and designs already on the books for longer range missiles, ISG assesses that Saddam clearly intended to reconstitute long-range delivery systems and that the systems potentially were for WMD.

- Iraq built a new and larger liquid-rocket engine test stand capable, with some modification, of supporting engines or engine clusters larger than the single SA–2 engine used in the Al Samud II.

- Iraq built or refurbished solid-propellant facilities and equipment, including a large propellant mixer, an aging oven, and a casting pit that could support large diameter motors.

- Iraq's investing in studies into new propellants and manufacturing technologies demonstrated its desire for more capable or effective delivery systems.

[ . . . ]

## Undeclared Activities

Several former high-level Regime officials and scientists directly affiliated with Iraq's military industries have indicated that Iraq intentionally withheld information from the UN regarding its delivery systems programs, to include research into delivery systems with design ranges well in excess of 150 km.

- According to one former high-ranking government official, Huwaysh [director of the Military Industrialization Committee] restricted the [National Monitoring Directorate's] access to MIC when the NMD was preparing the 2002 [complete declaration]. As a result, some MIC work was omitted, which violated UNSCR 1441.

- Several sources have admitted their direct involvement in the destruction of documents related to delivery systems programs to prevent divulging them to the UN.

This pattern of activity occurred at all levels and indicates a widespread effort to protect certain activities and to deceive the international community. According to numerous sources, Iraq worked on several delivery system projects that were never declared to the UN, violating UNSCR 1441. Some of these projects were designed to achieve ranges beyond 150 km and if developed would have violated UNSCR 687 and 715. Many missile specialists directly involved in these projects have admitted to destroying documents related to these programs to prevent the UN from discovering them, which violates UNSCR 707.

- *Through a series of interviews with former MIC and NMD officials, ISG has discovered that Iraq since 1991 did not disclose the IRFNA production capability at Al Qa'qa'a to the UN.* One NMD official claimed that Hussein Kamil had passed an order not to declare this capability to the UN and this order was observed even after Hussein Kamil's death. Other officials claim that Iraq decided to withhold the IRFNA production capability of Al

Qa'qa'a for fear that the UN would destroy the plant, virtually closing Iraq's extensive munitions industries.

- Former high-ranking MIC officials and scientists in the Iraqi missile program claim that, between 2000 and 2002, Huwaysh ordered Dr. Muzhir of Al Karamah to design a long-range liquid-propellant missile (see the Long-Range Missile chapter for more information). Huwaysh retained all the hardcopy evidence of this project and later destroyed it to prevent detection by the UN, although ISG has been able to uncover some design drawings for two long-range missile projects—the two- and five-engine clustered engine designs.

- An engineer associated with the Iraqi missile program claimed that, in early 2001, Huwaysh directed 'Abd-al-Baqi Rashid Shia' of the Al Rashid General Company to pursue a long-range solid-propellant missile. The engineer also provided a diagram for a launcher for a long-range solid-propellant missile, that Al Fida' engineers had been working on. The engineer claimed that research into this missile project ceased upon the arrival of UNMOVIC in late 2002 (see the Long-Range Missile chapter for more information).

- Much of Iraq's work on SA–2 conversion projects was never disclosed to the UN, according to officials associated with these projects. MIC officials decided to withhold all information from the UN about the Sa'd project, headed by Al Kindi, in part because it had not yet reached the prototype stage. Ra'ad Isma'il Jamil Al Adhami's SA–2 conversion efforts were not declared to the UN although the flight tests were manipulated so that the missiles would not exceed 150 km.

- Iraq withheld information about its efforts to extend the range of its HY–2 cruise missiles. Two individuals within MIC claimed that the 1,000 km Jinin cruise missile project ceased at the end of 2002 before the resumption of UNMOVIC inspections. One source said that the airframes were transferred from Al Karamah where the modifications were being made to a storage warehouse before UNMOVIC arrived for fear of the project being discovered. Iraq's attempts to extend the range of the HY–2 anti-ship cruise missile to beyond 150 km in a land-attack role were not declared to the UN (see Cruise Missile chapter for more information).

- A few sources have admitted that at least one Iraqi UAV flew beyond 150 km, and Huwaysh claimed that Iraq had tested UAVs to a range of only 100 km but that the range could easily be increased to 500 km by adding a larger fuel tank. [ . . . ]

A high-level official within the Iraqi missile program claimed that, in an effort to make Iraq's missile infrastructure less dependent upon foreign suppliers, MIC directed university projects to research ingredients used in solid and liquid propellants. Because of the sensitivity of this research, Iraq never disclosed these efforts to the UN. [ . . . ]

ISG has exploited dozens of contracts that confirm the requests, orders, and deliveries of UN-restricted components and equipment involving facilities associated with Iraq's missile and UAV programs. Iraq's use of the Iraqi Intelligence Service, front companies, and false end user certificates indicate Iraq knew these activities violated international sanctions. Iraq also negotiated with other countries for complete missile systems, but there is no evidence any shipments were ever made.

[ . . . ]

- Former high-level officials admit MIC procured ballistic missile engineering assistance, gyroscopes, SA–2/Volga missile engines, and SA–2 batteries from companies in Eastern Europe. ISG has recovered contracts and other documents to corroborate these admissions.

- Huwaysh admitted that Iraq had imported hundreds of SA–2/Volga liquid-propellant engines from companies in Poland—activities that were disclosed to UNMOVIC. ISG has exploited several official documents containing the contractual details (e.g., serial numbers of these engines).

- Former high-level MIC officials disclosed that Iraq received missile components such as gyroscopes and accelerometers from China.

- Huwaysh and an Iraqi scientist both asserted that Iraq received assistance and materials for missile propellants from Indian firms, particularly NEC.

- Several documents have been recovered that include information about Iraqi negotiations with North Korea for missile materials and long-range missile systems, probably including the 1,300-km-range No Dong. *There is no evidence to confirm the delivery of any ballistic missile systems.*

- Statements from former high-level Regime officials and documentation indicate Russian entities provided assistance to Iraq's missile programs. Russian entities exported numerous key pieces of equipment to Iraq through illegal channels and also supplied technical experts. Iraq also negotiated for complete Iskander-E missiles systems, although no missiles were ever purchased or delivered, according to Huwaysh.

- Captured documents show Iraq's reliance on FRY assistance to develop a domestic G&C design, manufacture, calibration, and test capability. Iraq also imported guidance instruments from FRY.

- Former high-level MIC officials provided information about Iraq's procurement efforts through Ukraine. Iraq received missile and UAV components as well as technical assistance from the Ukraine.

[. . . ]

The Iraqi missile and UAV programs benefited from Iraq's defiance of UN sanctions because they were able to obtain material and technical expertise they otherwise could not have developed. Several sources and documentary evidence confirm that Iraq participated in such activities. The measures taken to conceal these activities from the UN are evidence that Iraq was well aware these activities were illegal.

# Nuclear

## Key Findings

Iraq Survey Group (ISG) discovered further evidence of the maturity and significance of the pre–1991 Iraqi Nuclear Program but found that Iraq's ability to reconstitute a nuclear weapons program progressively decayed after that date.

- Saddam Hussein ended the nuclear program in 1991 following the Gulf war. ISG found no evidence to suggest concerted efforts to restart the program.

- Although Saddam clearly assigned a high value to the nuclear progress and talent that had been developed up to the 1991 war, the program ended and the intellectual capital decayed in the succeeding years.

Nevertheless, after 1991, Saddam did express his intent to retain the intellectual capital developed during the Iraqi Nuclear Program. Senior Iraqis—several of them from the Regime's inner circle—told ISG they assumed Saddam would restart a nuclear program once UN sanctions ended.

- Saddam indicated that he would develop the weapons necessary to counter any Iranian threat.

Initially, Saddam chose to conceal his nuclear program in its entirety, as he did with Iraq's BW program. Aggressive UN inspections after Desert Storm forced Saddam to admit the existence of the program and destroy or surrender components of the program.

In the wake of Desert Storm, Iraq took steps to conceal key elements of its program and to preserve what it could of the professional capabilities of its nuclear scientific community.

- Baghdad undertook a variety of measures to conceal key elements of its nuclear program from successive UN inspectors, including specific direction by Saddam Hussein to hide and preserve documentation associated with Iraq's nuclear program.

- ISG, for example, uncovered two specific instances in which scientists involved in uranium enrichment kept documents and technology. Although apparently acting on their own, they did so with the belief and anticipation of resuming uranium enrichment efforts in the future.

- Starting around 1992, in a bid to retain the intellectual core of the former weapons program, Baghdad transferred many nuclear scientists to related jobs in the Military Industrial Commission (MIC). The work undertaken by these scientists at the MIC helped them maintain their weapons knowledge base.

As with other WMD areas, Saddam's ambitions in the nuclear area were secondary to his prime objective of ending UN sanctions.

- Iraq, especially after the defection of Hussein Kamil in 1995, sought to persuade the IAEA that Iraq had met the UN's disarmament requirements so sanctions would be lifted.

ISG found a limited number of post–1995 activities that would have aided the reconstitution of the nuclear weapons program once sanctions were lifted.

- The activities of the Iraqi Atomic Energy Commission sustained some talent and limited research with potential relevance to a reconstituted nuclear program.

- Specific projects, with significant development, such as the efforts to build a rail gun and a copper vapor laser could have been useful in a future effort to restart a nuclear weapons program, but ISG found no indications of such purpose. As funding for the MIC and the IAEC increased after the introduction of the Oil-for-Food program, there was some growth in programs that involved former nuclear weapons scientists and engineers.

- The Regime prevented scientists from the former nuclear weapons program from leaving either their jobs or Iraq. Moreover, in the late 1990s, personnel from both MIC and the IAEC received significant pay raises in a bid to retain them, and the Regime undertook new investments in university research in a bid to ensure that Iraq retained technical knowledge.

# Evolution of the Nuclear Weapons Program

[. . . ]

*The Early Years: Ambition*

Saddam demonstrated his commitment to obtain a nuclear weapon over two decades. Saddam's close association with the Iraqi Atomic Energy Commission (IAEC) stems from his service as Vice President of the Republic from 1968 until 1979 when he became President of Iraq. From 1973 to 1979, he also served as President of the IAEC and sponsored its acquisition of foreign-supplied facilities with which to support a nuclear weapons program.

In 1968, Iraq commissioned a Russian supplied IRT–2000 research reactor and commissioned a number of other facilities that could be used for radioisotope production at the Tuwaitha Nuclear Research Center, home of the IAEC. In the 1970s, through contracts with French and Italian firms, the IAEC built facilities at Tuwaitha that, if operational, could have allowed Iraq to attempt to produce plutonium for a weapons program. The Israeli destruction of the Tammuz 1 (Osirak) research reactor on 7 June 1981 and Iraq's subsequent failure to replace or rebuild it compelled the Iraqis to pursue a more clandestine uranium enrichment program for a nuclear weapon by the mid–1980s.

Between 1979 and 1982, Iraq bought large quantities of uranium in various forms including yellowcake and uranium dioxide from several countries. Some of the purchases were reported to the IAEA and some were not. Iraq's uranium purchases are detailed in its CAFCD in 2002 and in other, earlier disclosures.

Not long after the start of the Iraq-Iran war, Iraq began to formally pursue uranium enrichment. In January 1982, the Office of Studies and Development (OSD) was established in the IAEC to conduct research and development in uranium enrichment. The staff of OSD was drawn largely from the staff of IAEC and numbered no more than several hundred. In late 1982, the IAEC was restructured and OSD became known as Office 3000.

During the Iraq-Iran war, Iraq studied a variety of uranium enrichment techniques. It was not until near the last year of the war in the late 1980s that Iraq began to make decisions and take serious steps to develop a nuclear infrastructure.

In April 1987, the IAEC created a group structure that assigned responsibility for gaseous diffusion research projects to Group 1, EMIS research and development to Group 2, and support activities to Group 3 in the Office of Studies and Development, or Office 3000.

Also in April 1987 a program, codenamed the Al-Hussein project (HP), was formed under Hussein Kamil, supervisor of the State Organization for Technical Industries at the time, to study the steps required to start a nuclear weapons program in Iraq. The finished report outlined a range of projects and served as the basis of a formally constituted nuclear weapons program. In November 1987, the project team was transferred to the IAEC and in April 1988 became Group 4 in Office 3000. The program was implemented in June 1987 and construction began on a nuclear weapon research, development, and production complex at Al Athir in August 1988.

In August 1987, Group 1 formally left the IAEC and Tuwaitha to act independently as the Engineering Design Directorate (EDD) in the Ar Rashidiyah District of Baghdad. At that time the EDD began to develop centrifuge enrichment technology and throughout its existence was directly responsible to Hussein Kamil.

Nearly all avenues of uranium enrichment were considered,

but by late 1987 Iraq began construction of a large electromagnetic isotope separation (EMIS) plant at Tarmiya. To support the large investment in EMIS technology, a network of facilities was created to concentrate uranium, convert uranium to feed materials, fabricate EMIS equipment, and chemically recover product.

As the Iraq-Iran war drew to a close, further changes were made in the Iraqi Nuclear Program structure that would ultimately place the nuclear weapons program under Hussein Kamil. In May 1988, when the Ministry of Industry and Military Industrialization (MIMI) was officially established, EDD, renamed the Engineering Design Center (EDC), became one of the institutions of the Military Industrialization Commission (MIC), under MIMI. In November 1988, Office 3000 (Groups 2, 3, and 4) was transferred to the MIMI and in January 1989 officially given the name Petrochemical Project 3 (PC-3) under Dr. Ja'far Diya' Ja'far. Hussein Kamil, Director of MIC and MIMI, assumed control of the Iraqi Nuclear Program.

In August 1988, German engineers traveled to Baghdad and presented European centrifuge design data that EDC immediately copied to advance its otherwise slow progress in developing centrifuge enrichment. In the years before the 1991 Gulf war, several more German engineers became involved, and centrifuge design documents based on technology developed for the European enrichment consortium URENCO were transferred to EDC. Contracts were signed with a number of European firms to acquire key component manufacturing technology and critical equipment for the centrifuge program.

After the invasion of Kuwait and the UN economic embargo, Iraq initiated an accelerated, or "crash program." to produce a nuclear weapon that called for the diversion of IAEA-safeguarded research reactor fuel at Tuwaitha. Iraq planned to further enrich some research reactor fuels using an envisioned 50-machine centrifuge cascade to produce enough weapon-grade uranium for one nuclear weapon. There were numerous obstacles—such as deficiencies in cascade development, uranium recovery capability, and weapons design and development—that prevented the Iraqis from succeeding.

At the time the program ended in early 1991, the Iraqi Nuclear

Program (INP) had several thousand personnel, and Iraq was commissioning EMIS equipment at Tarmiya and producing micrograms of enriched uranium. The centrifuge enrichment program was successfully operating a single machine in a test stand and building facilities for a small enrichment cascade. The Iraqis were working on a first-generation nuclear weapon design, which they intended to make into a device deliverable by missile.

## Decline (1991–96)

Following the invasion of Kuwait, nearly all of the key nuclear facilities—those involved in the processing of nuclear material or weapons research—were bombed during Desert Storm. Many of the facilities located at Tuwaitha were devastated, and the EMIS enrichment plants at Tarmiya and Ash Sharqat were largely destroyed. Iraq's yellowcake recovery plant at Al-Qa'im and feed material production plant at Mosul (Al Jazira) also were bombed during the war. Al-Athir—a high-explosives testing site revealed after the war to be Iraq's planned nuclear weapons development and assembly site—was also damaged. Iraq' s centrifuge research and development site at Rashdiya and the planned centrifuge production and operations site at Al Furat were neither found nor targeted in the 1991 war, but industrial sites, found after the war to be supporting nuclear weapons efforts, were attacked and damaged.

The Iraqis first chose not to disclose the extent of their clandestine nuclear program in their April 1991 declaration. As part of a denial and deception effort at the end of May 1991, Kamil issued orders to collect all documents and equipment indicating Non-Proliferation Treaty violations. Equipment and documentation were moved to a variety of locations to hide program elements from the IAEA. Iraqi researchers were instructed by their managers to dispose of their laboratories, some of which were then set up in universities and institutes. In addition, Kamil ordered that at least one set of all nuclear-related documents and some equipment be retained by a senior scientist.

It was not until the Iraqis were confronted with evidence and

IAEA successfully seized EMIS components in June/July 1991 that the Iraqis admitted to the large enrichment program. Large quantities of EMIS equipment were unburied and delivered to IAEA for destruction later that year.

Even though the existence of their centrifuge enrichment program was known before 1991, the Iraqis did not fully declare its extent and maintained that it was only a limited research and development activity located at Tuwaitha, rather than Ar Rashidiyah. In 1991 the Iraqis also declared the planned centrifuge facility at Al Furat as under construction.

• After the seizure of documents pertaining to Iraq's nuclear weapons program in late September 1991, the Iraqis admitted to the existence of the Al Athir. The facility was destroyed by IAEA in April-June 1992.

Starting in 1992, MIC Director Hussein Kamil distributed PC–3 and EDC personnel and work centers around various military research and production facilities. The intention, according to one scientist from the pre–1991 nuclear program, was to keep researchers together in anticipation of a reconstituted nuclear weapon program.

Former PC–3 or EDC personnel working at the Pulse Power Research Center, which became Al Tahadi State Establishment in 1995, created an ion implantation lab with components from former IAEC and PC–3 projects (1994) and a rail gun experiment for air defense, which also used equipment from IAEC and PC–3 (1993–95).

Iraq resisted a more comprehensive disclosure of its nuclear program until after the defection of Hussein Kamil in August 1995, when a large collection of centrifuge and nuclear program documents and equipment was given to UNSCOM and IAEA. From that point onwards, the Iraqis appear to have cooperated and provided more complete information. The centrifuge program appears to have largely been declared, though a full set of documents delivered by German engineers was not supplied to IAEA inspectors.

Efforts that could preserve the progress and talent that had been developed up to the 1991 war included keeping the nuclear cadre engaged in a variety of projects, such as rebuilding of Iraq's infrastructure. However, the nuclear program was ended and the intellectual capital decayed in the succeeding years. The economy had declined, and the talent had been focused on rebuilding the country as well as other military priorities. In some cases, extraordinary measures had to be taken to retain scientists, such as restricting foreign travel or seeking other jobs.

## Recovery and Transition (1996–2002)

Iraq collaborated with the International Atomic Energy Agency (IAEA) to produce a series of Full, Final, and Complete Disclosure (FFCD) statements, including a "final" presented to the IAEA in September 1996, which reported its review findings to the UN Security Council in October 1997. The IAEA concluded that it had a technically coherent picture of the pre–1999 nuclear weapons program, although it was troubled by the absence of centrifuge program documentation and there were gaps in knowledge about nuclear weapon design and development activities and the role of foreign assistance—the latter point also a reference to a pre–1991 offer by a representative of Pakistan's A. Q. Khan to assist Iraq in developing nuclear weapons.

'Abd-al-Tawab 'Abdallah Al Mullah Huwaysh became director of the MIC in 1997 and appeared to bear no loyalty to the former nuclear program and IAEC personnel. He standardized salaries, eliminating the preferential pay differential given former PC–3 workers, and instituted measures to emphasize and monitor performance throughout MIC.

With the influx of funds from the Oil For Food (OFF) Program and later the suspension of cooperation with UNSCOM, Saddam's attention began to return to the former employees of the Iraqi Nuclear Program. In the late 1990s, raises in salaries were given to the employees of both the MIC and the IAEC. New programs were initiated, which would employ the talent of former Iraqi Nuclear Program employees, and both the MIC and IAEC expanded. Joint programs with universities were started not only to support a deteriorating university system but also to encourage involvement in MIC and IAEC efforts, offering the opportunity to pass knowledge on to new generations of scientists.

After 1998, interest by Saddam in air defense stimulated projects involving a former nuclear researcher—including one project that had the prospect of supporting a renewed nuclear weapons effort. The IAEC started a rail gun project in 1999, and the MIC was sponsoring a rail gun project at Al Tahadi in 2000. Both projects, and other air defense projects at IAEC, had poor prospects for success as weapons. The IAEC rail gun effort—led by the former head of the pre–1991 nuclear weapons design and development effort, Khalid Ibrahim Sa'id—could, with significant further development, be useful for future nuclear weapons design and development research.

New departments were established in the Physics Department of the IAEC. While primarily supporting the IAEC rail gun project, a Technical Research Branch—with laboratories for high-speed imaging, flash X-ray, impact studies, electronics, and computing—was established in 2001 in newly created laboratories outside the gates of Tuwaitha. A new laser division was created in 1999, and other departments were modernized through purchases of new equipment. Efforts were made to expand ties to universities and train more students at IAEC. Procurements were made through MIC to improve the equipment at IAEC's machine tool workshop.

## Miscalculation (2002–2003)

In the year prior to Operation Iraqi Freedom (OIF), MIC undertook improvements to technology in several areas that could have been applied to a renewed centrifuge program for uranium enrichment. These dual-use technologies included projects to acquire a magnet production line at Al Tahadi, carbon fiber filament winding equipment for missile fabrication at al Karama, and the creation of a new Department of Rotating Machinery at Ibn Yunis. All of these projects were created to improve specific military or commercial products, but the technologies could have help

support a centrifuge development project. ISG, however, has uncovered no indication that Iraq had resumed fissile material or
nuclear weapon research and development activities since 1991.

## Results of ISG's Investigation on Nuclear Issues

Iraq did not possess a nuclear device, nor had it tried to reconstitute a capability to produce nuclear weapons after 1991.

ISG has uncovered no information to support allegations of
Iraqi pursuit of uranium from abroad in the post-Operation
Desert Storm era.

[. . . ]

Iraq did not reconstitute its indigenous ability to produce yellowcake. As a result of Desert Storm and IAEA inspection efforts,
Iraq's indigenous yellowcake production capability appears to
have been eliminated. Bomb damage in 1991 destroyed the uranium extraction facility at the Al Qaim Superphosphate Fertilizer
Plant. During the years of intrusive inspections, the IAEA also
closed and sealed the Abu Skhair mine to curtail Iraq's secondary
pilot plant production capability for acquiring uranium. [. . . ]

Post–1991, Iraq had neither rebuilt any capability to convert
uranium ore into a form suitable for enrichment nor reestablished
other chemical processes related to handling fissile material for a
weapons program. Prior to the 1991 war, Iraq had established
uranium conversion and feed material capabilities at the Tuwaitha
Nuclear Research Center—Baghdad's premier nuclear center—as
well as a feed material plant near Mosul called Al-Jazira. Iraq also
was establishing chemical processes at Tarmiya, and Al-Sharqat—
its two primary sites for uranium enrichment using the electromagnetic isotope separation (EMIS) technique. Baghdad also
planned to produce feed materials for its centrifuge program at its
main centrifuge research site Rashidiyah and planned a pilot plant
at Al Furat. Uranium metal production planned for the pre–1991
program was planned for the Al-Athir nuclear weapons assembly
facility.[. . . ]

Available evidence leads ISG to judge that Iraq's development
of gas centrifuges for uranium enrichment essentially ended in

1991. Prior to 1991, gas centrifuge technology was one of the primary methods being pursued for uranium enrichment, with emphasis being placed on carbon-fiber composite centrifuge rotors.

- According to Iraq's disclosures to IAEA, ISG interviews and documentary evidence, Iraq's centrifuge program by June 1990 had built—with foreign assistance—two magnetic-bearing centrifuges, one of which was tested with uranium hexafluoride (UF6) feed. Two oil-bearing centrifuges had also been built by the Iraqis as of June 1989.

- ISG believes a reconstituted program for the purpose of producing material for nuclear weapons would have required redevelopment and testing of centrifuge manufacturing technology, the manufacture of thousands of machines required for a production plant, effort to gain experience in enrichment operations, and production of metric-ton quantities of uranium hexafluoride (UF6) feed. However, the initial research and development stages might use only a single centrifuge.

- Former Presidential Scientific Advisor Amir Hamudi Hasan al-Sadi stated that he neither received nor issued orders to resume any centrifuge-related work and could not have done so because the war had destroyed the equipment and facilities.

- The head of design implementation in the former centrifuge program, Faris 'Abd Al 'Aziz Al Samarra'i, did not believe that there was a reconstituted nuclear weapons program in Iraq after 1991. He stated that he did not believe that the universities had the resources or ability to undertake weapon-related research. Since 1992, Dr. Faris had worked for MIC, in Studies and Planning, and as Director General of the Al-Shaheen Company since 1996 and of the al Samud State Company since 2002.

- Jamal Ja'far, the designer of the pre–1991 magnetic centrifuge program, stated in an interview that he also did not believe that it was possible, given the conditions in Iraq in 2002, to reconstitute such a complicated and serious effort.

- Additional details on ISG's investigation into centrifuge-related issues can be found in sections dealing with aluminum tubes, carbon fiber, flow forming, magnet production, potential centrifuge-related facilities, and rotating machinery.

ISG also judges that Iraq continued work on none of the many other uranium enrichment programs explored or developed prior to 1991, such as EMIS or lasers. However, many of the former EMIS engineers and scientists continued to work for either the Iraqi Atomic Energy Commission (IAEC) or the Military Industrialization Commission (MIC) in roles that could preserve their technical skills.

- Since Operation Iraqi Freedom, significant looting and damage have occurred at most of the dual-use manufacturing facilities that supported the pre–1991 EMIS program. ISG has not been able to confirm that the Iraqi Regime attempted to preserve the EMIS technology, although one scientist with this pre–1991 program kept documents and components that would have been useful to restarting such an effort.[ . . . ]

It does not appear that Iraq took steps to advance its pre–1991 work in nuclear weapons design and development. ISG has not identified a materials research and fissile component manufacturing capability that would be required to reconstitute a nuclear weapons program. Working with molten highly enriched uranium requires special consideration for criticality during the melting and solidification process. ISG found no evidence that Iraq had acquired or developed the technology dealing with casting and machining issues of highly enriched uranium.

- While ISG has not identified any explosive lens development effort in Iraq that was associated with a renewed nuclear weapons program, we do believe that the Al Quds Company—a MIC establishment created in 2002—had a technical department, which built a facility capable of conducting research. *Such a facility appears well suited for types of explosives research that could be applicable to conventional military and nuclear weapons research.*

- ISG obtained evidence from recovered documents and from debriefings of Iraqi scientists that Iraq utilized high-speed switches—like those of potential interest for nuclear weapons development—in support of rail-gun projects that we believe were intended for air defense. *ISG has found no links between Iraq's interest in special high-speed switches after 1991 and a nuclear weapons program.* [. . . ]

ISG has uncovered two instances in which scientists linked to Iraq's pre–1991 uranium enrichment programs kept documentation and technology in anticipation of renewing these efforts—actions that they contend were officially sanctioned.

- A former engineer in the pre–1991 EMIS program claimed he was told by the head of MIC in 1997 to continue his work with ion implantation at his Al Tahaddi lab as a way to preserve EMIS technology.

- The former head of Iraq's pre–1991 centrifuge program also retained prohibited documents and components in apparent violation of the Regime's directives. Though this activity was isolated, it also had the potential to contribute to a possible restart of Iraq's uranium enrichment programs. [. . . ]

Furthermore, although all of the officials interviewed by ISG indicated Iraq had ended its pursuit of nuclear weapons in 1991, some suggested Saddam remained interested in reconstitution of the nuclear program after sanctions were lifted. [. . . ]

# Volume III: Iraq's Chemical Warfare Program

## Key Findings

Saddam never abandoned his intentions to resume a CW effort when sanctions were lifted and conditions were judged favorable:

- Saddam and many Iraqis regarded CW as a proven weapon

against an enemy's superior numerical strength, a weapon that had saved the nation at least once already—during the Iran-Iraq war—and contributed to deterring the Coalition in 1991 from advancing to Baghdad.

While a small number of old, abandoned chemical munitions have been discovered, ISG judges that Iraq unilaterally destroyed its undeclared chemical weapons stockpile in 1991. There are no credible indications that Baghdad resumed production of chemical munitions thereafter, a policy ISG attributes to Baghdad's desire to see sanctions lifted, or rendered ineffectual, or its fear of force against it should WMD be discovered.

- The scale of the Iraqi conventional munitions stockpile, among other factors, precluded an examination of the entire stockpile; however, ISG inspected sites judged most likely associated with possible storage or deployment of chemical weapons.

Iraq's CW program was crippled by the Gulf war and the legitimate chemical industry, which suffered under sanctions, only began to recover in the mid–1990s. Subsequent changes in the management of key military and civilian organizations, followed by an influx of funding and resources, provided Iraq with the ability to reinvigorate its industrial base.

- Poor policies and management in the early 1990s left the Military Industrial Commission (MIC) financially unsound and in a state of almost complete disarray.

- Saddam implemented a number of changes to the Regime's organizational and programmatic structures after the departure of Hussein Kamil.

- Iraq's acceptance of the Oil-for-Food (OFF) program was the foundation of Iraq's economic recovery and sparked a flow of illicitly diverted funds that could be applied to projects for Iraq's chemical industry.

The way Iraq organized its chemical industry after the mid–1990s allowed it to conserve the knowledge-base needed to restart a CW program, conduct a modest amount of dual-use research, and partially recover from the decline of its production capability caused by the effects of the Gulf war and UN-sponsored destruction and sanctions. Iraq implemented a rigorous and formalized system of nationwide research and production of chemicals, but ISG will not be able to resolve whether Iraq intended the system to underpin any CW-related efforts.

• The Regime employed a cadre of trained and experienced researchers, production managers, and weaponization experts from the former CW program.

• Iraq began implementing a range of indigenous chemical production projects in 1995 and 1996. Many of these projects, while not weapons-related, were designed to improve Iraq's infrastructure, which would have enhanced Iraq's ability to produce CW agents if the scaled-up production processes were implemented.

• Iraq had an effective system for the procurement of items that Iraq was not allowed to acquire due to sanctions. ISG found no evidence that this system was used to acquire precursor chemicals in bulk; however documents indicate that dual-use laboratory equipment and chemicals were acquired through this system.

Iraq constructed a number of new plants starting in the mid–1990s that enhanced its chemical infrastructure, although its overall industry had not fully recovered from the effects of sanctions, and had not regained pre–1991 technical sophistication or production capabilities prior to Operation Iraqi Freedom (OIF).

• ISG did not discover chemical process or production units configured to produce key precursors or CW agents. However, site visits and debriefs revealed that Iraq maintained its ability for reconfiguring and 'making-do' with available equipment as substitutes for sanctioned items.

- ISG judges, based on available chemicals, infrastructure, and scientist debriefings, that Iraq at OIF probably had a capability to produce large quantities of sulfur mustard within three to six months.

- A former nerve agent expert indicated that Iraq retained the capability to produce nerve agent in significant quantities within two years, given the import of required phosphorous precursors. However, we have no credible indications that Iraq acquired or attempted to acquire large quantities of these chemicals through its existing procurement networks for sanctioned items.

In addition to new investment in its industry, Iraq was able to monitor the location and use of all existing dual-use process equipment. This provided Iraq the ability to rapidly reallocate key equipment for proscribed activities, if required by the Regime.

- One effect of UN monitoring was to implement a national level control system for important dual-use process plants.

Iraq's historical ability to implement simple solutions to weaponization challenges allowed Iraq to retain the capability to weaponize CW agent when the need arose. Because of the risk of discovery and consequences for ending UN sanctions, Iraq would have significantly jeopardized its chances of having sanctions lifted or no longer enforced if the UN or foreign entity had discovered that Iraq had undertaken any weaponization activities.

- ISG has uncovered hardware at a few military depots, which suggests that Iraq may have prototyped experimental CW rounds. The available evidence is insufficient to determine the nature of the effort or the timeframe of activities.

- Iraq could indigenously produce a range of conventional munitions, throughout the 1990s, many of which had previously been adapted for filling with CW agent. However, ISG has found ambiguous evidence of weaponization activities.

Saddam's Leadership Defense Plan consisted of a tactical doctrine taught to all Iraqi officers and included the concept of a "red-line" or last line of defense. However, ISG has no information that the plan ever included a trigger for CW use.

- Despite reported high-level discussions about the use of chemical weapons in the defense of Iraq, information acquired after OIF does not confirm the inclusion of CW in Iraq's tactical planning for OIF. We believe these were mostly theoretical discussions and do not imply the existence of undiscovered CW munitions.

Discussions concerning WMD, particularly leading up to [Operation Iraqi Freedom], would have been highly compartmentalized within the Regime. ISG found no credible evidence that any field elements knew about plans for CW use during Operation Iraqi Freedom.

[. . .]

ISG uncovered information that the Iraqi Intelligence Service (IIS) maintained throughout 1991 to 2003 a set of undeclared covert laboratories to research and test various chemicals and poisons, primarily for intelligence operations. The network of laboratories could have provided an ideal, compartmented platform from which to continue CW agent R&D or small-scale production efforts, but we have no indications this was planned.

[. . .]

- ISG has no evidence that IIS Directorate of Criminology (M16) scientists were producing CW or BW agents in these laboratories. However, sources indicate that M16 was planning to produce several CW agents including sulfur mustard, nitrogen mustard, and Sarin.

- Exploitations of IIS laboratories, safe houses, and disposal sites revealed no evidence of CW-related research or production, however many of these sites were either sanitized by the Regime or looted prior to OIF. Interviews with key IIS officials within and outside of M16 yielded very little information about the IIS' activities in this area.

- The existence, function, and purpose of the laboratories were never declared to the UN.

- The IIS program included the use of human subjects for testing purposes.

ISG investigated a series of key pre-OIF indicators involving the possible movement and storage of chemical weapons, focusing on 11 major depots assessed to have possible links to CW. A review of documents, interviews, available reporting, and site exploitations revealed alternate, plausible explanations for activities noted prior to OIF which, at the time, were believed to be CW-related.

- ISG investigated pre-OIF activities at Musayyib Ammunition Storage Depot—the storage site that was judged to have the strongest link to CW. An extensive investigation of the facility revealed that there was no CW activity, unlike previously assessed.

# Evolution of the Chemical Warfare Program

Over a period of twenty years, beginning with a laboratory operated by the intelligence services, Iraq was able to begin and successfully undertake an offensive CW program which helped ensure the Regime's internal and external security. By 1984, Iraq was operating a number of CW agent production plants, producing hundreds of tons of a range of weaponized agents annually, for use against external and internal enemies of the Regime. The program was supported by a complex web of international procurement, R&D, weaponization and indigenous precursor production efforts. Iraq fired or dropped over 100,000 chemical munitions against Iranian forces and its own Kurdish population during the Iran-Iraq war and then later to help put down the Shi'a rebellion in March 1991.

[. . .]

- By 1991, Iraq had amassed a sizable CW arsenal, comprising thousands of short range rockets, artillery shells, and bombs, and hundreds of tons of bulk agent. It also had produced 50 nerve agent warheads for the 650 km-range al Hussein missile.

Despite the provisions of UN Security Council Resolution (UNSCR) 687 in April 1991, which called for Iraq to disarm, Iraq initially chose to retain CW weapons, precursors and associated equipment, making false declarations to the UN. Even when Iraq claimed to have complied with UNSCR 687 and its successors, Saddam retained components vital to restarting a CW program.

[. . .]

## Regime Strategy and WMD Timeline

[. . .]

Iraq had acquired sufficient expertise during the 1970s. . . to begin agent production immediately on completion of the first pilot-scale production line in the early 1980s. For example, 85 tons of mustard agent were produced at al-Rashad from 1981 to 1982. After Project 922 came on line, both facilities produced agent.

- 150 tons of mustard were produced in 1983.

- About 60 tons of Tabun were produced in 1984.

- Pilot-scale production of Sarin began in 1984.

Work at the Project 922 site did not pass unnoticed:

- During the summer of 1985, Iranian F–4 aircraft attacked the Samarra' site;

- This was followed in October 1986 with a SCUD attack.

As a result, Iraq moved a significant portion of its Roland Air Defense System to the Samarra' area to protect the project.

As production increased, Baghdad recognized that its dependence on foreign suppliers for precursors was a program weakness and took immediate steps towards self-reliance for precursor production. Iraq made plans to build three precursor production plants, starting in 1985, near the town of Fallujah, 50 kilometers west of Baghdad.

- Iraq began constructing Fallujah I, II and III between 1986 and 1988 to produce precursors.

- The decision to construct the precursor production plants was the beginning of a significant commitment of resources to a long-term CW program. In 1987, Hussein Kamil, assisted by Amer al-Sa'adi, created the MIC and renamed the CW complex the Al Muthanna State Establishment (MSE). [ . . . ]

- Between 1989 and 1990, during which time Iraq interrupted CW production because there was no longer an immediate need for agent, the MSE CW infrastructure produced civilian goods, including shampoos, disinfectants, and simple pesticides.

*Early Weaponization: Simple Solutions*

Against the background of the Iran-Iraq war and the pressure to halt the Iranians, Al Muthanna took every available shortcut in developing chemical weapons. To avoid the delays of developing indigenous delivery systems, Iraq purchased conventional bombs from Spain that easily could be modified for CW fill. Later, using reverse-engineering, Al Muthanna built the infrastructure to manufacture its own weapons.

- According to Iraq's declaration to the UN in 1996, from 1981 to 1984 Iraq purchased 40,000 artillery shells, and 7,500 bomb casings from various countries that were to be modified for delivery of CW.

• Iraq also declared that by 1989, it had manufactured 10,000 CW bomb casings and 18,500 rocket warheads, all reverse engineered from imported munitions.

## CW—A Permanent and Pivotal Strategic Weapon

The work underway at Al Muthanna State Enterprise by the late 1980s was an indication Saddam intended Iraq's CW effort to be a significant, large-scale program. From its inception, MSE's Research and Development (R&D) Directorate investigated a broad assortment of agents. Iraqi CW scientists understood that they would gain the greatest battlefield impact by developing a range of CW agents with different characteristics for different situations.

• MSE's R&D Directorate had individual departments dedicated to the development of mustard agents, nerve agents, and psychomimetic compounds according to Iraq's declaration to the UN in 1996. Reporting from various sources indicates Iraq investigated more than 40 potential CW compounds.

Saddam believed Iraqi WMD capabilities had played a central role in the winning of the Iran-Iraq war and were vital to Iraq's national security strategy. [ . . . ]

A speech by Saddam on 2 April 1990 publicly identified Iraq's CW research and production efforts in anticipation of the next war. Saddam claimed Iraq had a binary agent capability, an assertion that caught MSE scientists off guard, according to Iraqi declaration corroborated by documents the UN discovered at Al Muthanna.

• In less than a month after Saddam's speech, Iraq restarted its CW production lines, tested CW warheads for al Hussein missiles, and reverse-engineered special parachute-retarded bombs. [According to the FFCD, Iraq did not import any aerial bombs in 1990.]

Al Muthanna filled the al-Hussein warheads and aerial bombs with a binary nerve agent component. These weapons were accompanied by Jerry cans containing the second component, a chemical that, when mixed with the weapons' contents, produced nerve agent. This was the mix-before-flight Iraqi 'binary' system. Iraq deployed 1,000 binary bombs and 50 al-Hussein warheads—binary and unitary—by August 1990.

- In the subsequent first Gulf war, it is assessed that Saddam believed that the deployment of CW, and the delegated authority to use them, contributed to the US not driving on to Baghdad.

## The Decline, 1991–1996

### Destroying Iraqi Weapons

During the Gulf war in early 1991, Coalition Forces destroyed or extensively damaged most of Iraq's CW infrastructure, including many of the agent and precursor production facilities at Al Muthanna. Then, in April 1991, the UN adopted Security Council Resolution 687, which established a ceasefire in the Gulf war. Iraq was required to verifiably disarm as a prerequisite to lifting of the oil embargo imposed by UNSCR 660 of August 1990. [ . . . ]

Iraq initially chose not to fully declare its CW weapons and infrastructure, a decision usually attributed to Hussein Kamil and implemented by senior personnel including his senior deputy, Amer al-Sa'adi.

- Anticipating that inspections would be an ineffective and short-lived inconvenience, Iraqi leaders decided in early April 1991 to hide significant components of the CW program, including weapons, precursors, and equipment.

- Following a particularly invasive IAEA inspection in late-June

1991, Saddam ordered Dr. Mahmud Faraj Bilal, former deputy of the CW program, to destroy all hidden CW and BW materials, according to an interview with Bilal after OIF.

- *Available evidence indicates Iraq destroyed its hidden CW weapons and precursors,* but key documentation and dual-use equipment were retained and were later discovered by inspectors.

For the next five years, Iraq maintained the hidden items useful for a CW program restart but did not renew its major CW efforts out of fear the UN sanctions would not be removed. UN sanctions severely limited Iraq's financial resources. Raw materials, precursors, equipment, and expertise became increasingly scarce. The crippling of Iraq's CW infrastructure by the war, and the subsequent destruction and UN monitoring of much of the remaining materials and equipment limited Iraq's ability to rebuild or restart a CW program.

- The effects of sanctions reverberated throughout the scientific community and affected all aspects of industry within Iraq. Many scientists were underemployed or had access to neither research and production materials nor professional development.

In August 1995, shortly after Iraq revealed its production of bulk BW agent, Saddam's son-in-law and head of Iraq's WMD programs, Hussein Kamil, fled the country. Saddam made a decision at that time to declare virtually all hidden information and material they felt was significant on Iraq's programs, turning over WMD documentation, including 12 trunks of CW documents.

- The documentation turned over by Iraq, allegedly hidden by Hussein Kamil, included results of Iraqi research material up to 1988 that indicated more extensive research on VX than previously admitted.

- The documents also included papers related to new agent research, mix-in-flight binary munitions development, and previously undisclosed involvement of other organizations in CW research.

ISG believes that none of these events weakened Saddam's resolve to possess a robust CW capability. Baghdad believed its need for chemical weapons was justified, based on its fear of hostilities with Iran and Israel. The Regime, we judge, was also motivated by an unstated desire to elevate its status among Arab nations. ISG believes that Saddam deferred but did not abandon his CW ambitions.

- *Saddam implied, according to the former Presidential Secretary, that Iraq would resume WMD programs after sanctions in order to restore the "strategic balance" within the region and, particularly, against Israel.*

[. . . ]

## Recovery and Transition, 1996–2003

Iraq's CW program was crippled by the Gulf war and the legitimate chemical industry, which suffered under sanctions, and only began to recover in the mid–1990s. Subsequent changes in the management of key military and civilian organizations, followed by an influx of funding and resources, provided Iraq with the ability to reinvigorate its industrial base. Iraq's acceptance of the UN OFF program in 1996 was the foundation of Iraq's economic recovery and sparked a flow of illicitly diverted funds.

Iraq's chemical industry surged in the late 1990s, when more financial resources became available to the Regime. Although Iraq still lagged behind its pre–Gulf war capabilities, it was able to divert a portion of its revenue to purchase new plants and renovate existing ones to renew its basic chemical industry.

- Iraq was successful in procuring, constructing, and commissioning a complete state-of-the-art chemical facility for ammonium perchlorate through the Indian company NEC. Ammonium perchlorate is a key chemical for missile propellants.

- Iraq began refurbishing, and in some cases expanding, existing chemical facilities with foreign assistance. For example, the Al Tariq complex renovated its chlorine and phenol lines and restarted them in March 2000, according to reporting.

Between 1996 and 2003, the IIC coordinated large and important projects for the indigenous production of chemicals.

- A written order from Saddam established the National Project for Pharmaceuticals and Pesticides (NPPP). NPPP focused on the synthesis of drugs and pesticides, for which Iraq in the past relied heavily on foreign suppliers.

- The IIC examined over *1,000 chemicals for initial R&D* to determine the feasibility of scaled-up production. ISG notes that two chemicals on this list were compounds that are consistent with an experimental VX pathway.

- The process for vetting the 1,000 chemicals for economic feasibility and large-scale production was intensive and formalized. The IIC leadership built in several layers of review, research, and justification before compounds were selected for scale-up, *raising further suspicion about the three compounds, particularly dicyclocarbodiimide (DCC)—a dehydrating agent that can be used as a VX stabilizer*

- Dr. Ja'far Dhia Ja'far, and IIC member, could not recall which projects were accepted for scale-up but he knew that some compounds were dual-use and declarable to the UN, and that the National Monitoring Directorate (NMD) did not declare all of the chemicals.

Reports of an unexplained discovery of VX traces on missile warhead fragments in April 1997 led to further tension between UNSCOM and Iraq. [. . .]The uneasy relationship escalated with the discovery of [a document] . . . in July 1998 which indicated further Iraqi deception and obfuscation over its CW disclosures. Iraq's anger about these two major issues was a contributing factor to Saddam's decisions to suspend cooperation with UNSCOM and IAEA.

• *The lack of inspectors allowed further dual-use infrastructure to be developed. The lack of effective monitoring emboldened Saddam and his illicit procurement activities.*

[. . .]

There is an extensive, yet fragmentary and circumstantial body of evidence suggesting that Saddam pursued a strategy to maintain a capability to return to WMD production after sanctions were lifted by preserving assets and expertise. In addition to preserved capability, we have clear evidence of his intent to resume WMD production as soon as sanctions were lifted. All sources suggest that Saddam encouraged compartmentalization and would have discussed something as sensitive as WMD with as few people as possible.

• Huwaysh claimed that in 1999 Saddam asked how long it would take to build a production line for CW agents. Huwaysh tasked four officials to investigate, and they responded that experts could readily prepare a production line for mustard within six months. VX and Sarin production were more complicated and would take longer. Huwaysh relayed this answer to Saddam, who never requested follow-up information. An Iraqi CW expert separately estimated Iraq would require only a few days to start producing mustard—if it were prepared to sacrifice the production equipment.

## Miscalculation, 2002–2003

As the reality of the UN's impending return sank in, Iraq rapidly initiated steps to prepare for inspectors. Committees and groups were formed to ensure sites and key scientists were ready to receive the inspectors.

- As had often occurred in the past, individual scientists, heads of departments and security officials examined their plans of work for items or documents that would be subject to inspections. In every relevant location in Iraq, to some extent, normal work was disrupted in the effort to ensure Iraq was not suspected of undertaking proscribed activities.

- According to a senior chemist at the MIC, Huwaysh in October 2002, issued an order—the same order issued several times in the past—which held scientists personally responsible for any materials, equipment, or other prohibited items found by the UN.

- Vice President Taha Ramadan chaired a meeting of over 400 scientists before the inspectors returned, threatening scientists with dire consequences if the inspectors found anything that interfered with Iraq's progress towards the lifting of sanctions.

- When inspections resumed, foreign experts were hidden from the inspection teams.

In the final days of his Regime, Saddam continued to pursue efforts to enhance Iraq's industrial base, with plans underway for the construction of a multipurpose chemical plant, and nine oil refineries in Southern and Northern Iraq. The plans for this chemical plant were the result of years of the IIC's efforts to coordinate research into the indigenous production of chemicals.

- The Ministry of Industry and Minerals (MIM) owned a plot of land west of Baghdad that it set aside for construction of this multipurpose production facility, which was designed to produce a year's supply of 100 chemicals using only 10 independent pilot-scale production lines. (For more information, see Iraq's Infrastructure: Production Capability).

- Construction was scheduled to begin in March 2003, but was halted just prior to OIF. The plant would have provided Iraq with an indigenous multi-purpose production facility capable of producing large quantities of chemicals, in a relatively short time.

[. . . ]

# Biological Warfare

## *Key Findings*

The Biological Warfare (BW) program was born of the Iraqi Intelligence Service (IIS) and this service retained its connections with the program either directly or indirectly throughout its existence.

• The IIS provided the BW program with security and participated in biological research, probably for its own purposes, from the beginning of Iraq's BW effort in the early 1970s until the final days of Saddam Hussein's Regime.

In 1991, Saddam Hussein regarded BW as an integral element of his arsenal of WMD weapons, and would have used it if the need arose.

• At a meeting of the Iraqi leadership immediately prior to the Gulf war in 1991, Saddam Hussein personally authorized the use of BW weapons against Israel, Saudi Arabia and US forces. Although the exact nature of the circumstances that would trigger use was not spelled out, they would appear to be a threat to the leadership itself or the US resorting to "*unconventional harmful types of weapons.*"

• Saddam envisaged all-out use. For example, all Israeli cities were to be struck and all the BW weapons at his disposal were to be used. Saddam specified that the "*many years*" agents, presumably anthrax spores, were to be employed against his foes.

ISG judges that Iraq's actions between 1991 and 1996 demonstrate that the state intended to preserve its BW capability and return to a steady, methodical progress toward a mature BW program when and if the opportunity arose.

- ISG assesses that in 1991, Iraq clung to the objective of gaining war-winning weapons with the strategic intention of achieving the ability to project its power over much of the Middle East and beyond. Biological weapons were part of that plan. With an eye to the future and aiming to preserve some measure of its BW capability, Baghdad in the years immediately after Desert Storm sought to save what it could of its BW infrastructure and covertly continue BW research, hide evidence of that and earlier efforts, and dispose of its existing weapons stocks.

- From 1992 to 1994, Iraq greatly expanded the capability of its Al Hakam facility. Indigenously produced 5 cubic meter fermentors were installed, electrical and water utilities were expanded, and massive new construction to house its desired 50 cubic meter fermentors were completed.

- With the economy at rock bottom in late 1995, ISG judges that Baghdad abandoned its existing BW program in the belief that it constituted a potential embarrassment, whose discovery would undercut Baghdad's ability to reach its overarching goal of obtaining relief from UN sanctions.

In practical terms, with the destruction of the Al Hakam facility, Iraq abandoned its ambition to obtain advanced BW weapons quickly. ISG found no direct evidence that Iraq, after 1996, had plans for a new BW program or was conducting BW-specific work for military purposes. Indeed, from the mid–1990s, despite evidence of continuing interest in nuclear and chemical weapons, there appears to be a complete absence of discussion or even interest in BW at the Presidential level.

Iraq would have faced great difficulty in re-establishing an effective BW agent production capability. Nevertheless, after 1996 Iraq still had a significant dual-use capability—some declared—readily useful for BW if the Regime chose to use it to pursue a

BW program. Moreover, Iraq still possessed its most important BW asset, the scientific know-how of its BW cadre.

• Any attempt to create a new BW program after 1996 would have encountered a range of major hurdles. The years following Desert Storm wrought a steady degradation of Iraq's industrial base: new equipment and spare parts for existing machinery became difficult and expensive to obtain, standards of maintenance declined, staff could not receive training abroad, and foreign technical assistance was almost impossible to get. Additionally, Iraq's infrastructure and public utilities were crumbling. New large projects, particularly if they required special foreign equipment and expertise, would attract international attention. UN monitoring of dual-use facilities up to the end of 1998, made their use for clandestine purpose complicated and risk laden. [. . . ]

• *ISG judges that in 1991 and 1992, Iraq appears to have destroyed its undeclared stocks of BW weapons and probably destroyed remaining holdings of bulk BW agent. However ISG lacks evidence to document complete destruction. Iraq retained some BW-related seed stocks until their discovery after Operation Iraqi Freedom (OIF).*

• After the passage of UN Security Council Resolution (UNSCR) 687 in April 1991, Iraqi leaders decided not to declare the offensive BW program and in consequence ordered all evidence of the program erased. Iraq declared that BW program personnel sanitized the facilities and destroyed the weapons and their contents.

• Iraq declared the possession of 157 aerial bombs and 25 missile warheads containing BW agent. ISG assesses that the evidence for the original number of bombs is uncertain. ISG judges that Iraq clandestinely destroyed at least 132 bombs and 25 missiles. ISG continued the efforts of the UN at the destruction site but found no remnants of further weapons. This leaves the possibility that the fragments of up to 25 bombs may remain undiscovered. Of these, any that escaped destruction would probably now only contain degraded agent.

- ISG does not have a clear account of bulk agent destruction. Official Iraqi sources and BW personnel, state that Al Hakam staff destroyed stocks of bulk agent in mid 1991. However, the same personnel admit concealing details of the movement and destruction of bulk BW agent in the first half of 1991. Iraq continued to present information known to be untrue to the UN up to OIF. Those involved did not reveal this until several months after the conflict.

- Dr. Rihab Rashid Taha Al 'Azzawi, head of the bacterial program claims she retained BW seed stocks until early 1992 when she destroyed them. ISG has not found a means of verifying this. Some seed stocks were retained by another Iraqi official until 2003 when they were recovered by ISG.

ISG is aware of BW-applicable research since 1996, but ISG judges it was not conducted in connection with a BW program.

- ISG has uncovered no evidence of illicit research conducted into BW agents by universities or research organizations.

- The work conducted on a biopesticide (*Bacillus thuringiensis*) at Al Hakam until 1995 would serve to maintain the basic skills required by scientists to produce and dry anthrax spores (*Bacillus anthracis*) but ISG has not discovered evidence suggesting this was the Regime's intention. However in 1991, research and production on biopesticide and single cell protein (SCP) was selected by Iraq to provide cover for Al Hakam's role in Iraq's BW program. Similar work conducted at the Tuwaitha Agricultural and Biological Research Center (TABRC) up to OIF also maintained skills that were applicable to BW, but again, ISG found no evidence to suggest that this was the intention.

- Similarly, ISG found no information to indicate that the work carried out by TABRC into Single Cell Protein (SCP) was a cover story for continuing research into the production of BW agents, such as *C. botulinum* and *B. anthracis*, after the destruction of Al Hakam through to OIF.

- TABRC conducted research and development (R&D) programs to enable indigenous manufacture of bacterial growth media. Although these media are suitable for the bulk production of BW agents, ISG has found no evidence to indicate that their development and testing were specifically for this purpose.

- Although Iraq had the basic capability to work with variola major (smallpox), ISG found no evidence that it retained any stocks of smallpox or actively conducted research into this agent for BW intentions.

The IIS had a series of laboratories that conducted biological work including research into BW agents for assassination purposes until the mid–1990s. ISG has not been able to establish the scope and nature of the work at these laboratories or determine whether any of the work was related to military development of BW agent.

- The security services operated a series of laboratories in the Baghdad area. Iraq should have declared these facilities and their equipment to the UN, but they did not. Neither the UN Special Commission (UNSCOM) nor the UN Monitoring, Verification, and Inspection Commission (UNMOVIC) were aware of their existence or inspected them.

- Some of the laboratories possessed equipment capable of supporting research into BW agents for military purposes, but ISG does not know whether this occurred although there is no evidence of it. The laboratories were probably the successors of the Al Salman facility, located three kilometers south of Salman Pak, which was destroyed in 1991, and they carried on many of the same activities, including forensic work.

- Under the aegis of the intelligence service, a secretive team developed assassination instruments using poisons or toxins for the Iraqi state. A small group of scientists, doctors and technicians conducted secret experiments on human beings, resulting in their deaths. The aim was probably the development of poisons, including ricin and aflatoxin to eliminate or debilitate the Regime's opponents. It appears that testing on humans continued until the mid 1990s. There is no evidence to link these tests with the development of BW agents for military use.

In spite of exhaustive investigation, ISG found no evidence that Iraq possessed, or was developing BW agent production systems mounted on road vehicles or railway wagons.

- Prior to [Operation Iraqi Freedom] there was information indicating Iraq had planned and built a breakout BW capability, in the form of a set of mobile production units, capable of producing BW agent at short notice in sufficient quantities to weaponize. Although ISG has conducted a thorough investigation of every aspect of this information, it has not found any equipment suitable for such a program, nor has ISG positively identified any sites. No documents have been uncovered. Interviews with individuals suspected of involvement have all proved negative.

- ISG harbors severe doubts about the source's credibility in regards to the breakout program.

- ISG thoroughly examined two trailers captured in 2003, suspected of being mobile BW agent production units, and investigated the associated evidence. ISG judges that its Iraqi makers almost certainly designed and built the equipment exclusively for the generation of hydrogen. It is impractical to use the equipment for the production and weaponization of BW agent. ISG judges that it cannot therefore be part of any BW program.

[ . . . ]

## Research and Development

ISG judges that Iraq maintained the expertise and equipment necessary for R&D of bacteria, fungi, viruses, and toxins that could be used as BW agents up until Operation Iraqi Freedom (OIF) in March 2003

• ISG assesses that Iraq's bacterial and toxin BW agents were adequately researched and developed at the advent of the first Gulf war in 1991, and that Iraq had an extensive BW R&D program in the years prior to that. By the time of Desert Storm, Iraq had weaponized *Clostridium botulinum* ('Agent A'), *Bacillus anthracis* ('Agent B') and Aflatoxin ('Agent C') by filling liquid forms of these agents into munitions, although these munitions were not the most effective or efficient for BW dispersal.

Despite evidence of Iraq's intent to develop more dangerous biological agents after Desert Storm, ISG uncovered no indications that biological agents were researched for BW purposes post–1991, even though Iraq maintained—and in some cases improved—research capabilities that could have easily been applied to BW agents. ISG's investigations found no direct evidence that the expertise or equipment were being used specifically for BW work. That said, ISG judges that further R&D on the agents weaponized pre–1991 was probably not required. Additional agents would have required extensive R&D, in ISG's judgement, but despite concerns that surrounded the possible addition of other, more pathogenic, agents into the viral BW program, no evidence has been found by ISG.

• ISG conducted site visits and multiple interviews investigating Iraq's possible possession of smallpox and collected fragmentary and circumstantial information. A definitive conclusion is impossible, but, based on the available evidence, ISG concludes that Iraq intended to develop smallpox and possibly other viral pathogens like CCHF as potential BW weapons. In December 1990, Dr. Rihab informed Dr. Hazim 'Ali that Hussein Kamil wanted him to work on "more dangerous" viruses.

According to a source, Dr. Hazim 'Ali was willing to work on other viral agents if Dr. Rihab provided him with the materials. No additional materials were provided. Iraq had the basic capability to work with variola major (smallpox) and may have conducted some preliminary basic research. However, ISG has found no conclusive evidence that Iraq retained or acquired any stocks of smallpox or conducted advance R&D of pathogenic viruses.

ISG uncovered troubling information about post–1991 BW-related endeavours that raise concerns about the legitimacy of Iraq's activities and that suggest to ISG Baghdad aimed at some future time to resume its BW program.

[. . . ]

# Weaponization

Between the late 1980s and the start of Desert Storm in 1991, Iraq attempted to develop a range of systems for the dispersion of BW agent. In the dash to field viable BW weapons the workers in the program adapted robust bombs capable of mounting on many types of aircraft and warheads, including the Al Hussein missile. They also worked furiously to ready an aircraft spray system.

* The scientists and engineers conducted weapons trials over some three years with both simulants and BW agents, on occasion using living animals as targets. Delivery systems tested included a helicopter-borne spray system, aerial bombs, artillery shells, multi-barrel rocket launchers, long-range missile warheads and an aircraft mounting of an adapted auxiliary fuel tank.

* In the haste to prepare for the 1991 conflict, systems tried and tested with CW agents were preferred; the R–400 aerial bomb and the Al Hussein warhead, charged with anthrax, botulinum toxin and aflatoxin. Additionally, engineers at Al Muthanna rushed the auxiliary fuel tank, modified into a spray system, of the Mirage F1 aircraft into service[. . . ]

- Prior to Desert Storm, Iraq had dedicated complimentary programs to develop spray technology that could effectively disseminate either CW or BW agents. These spray dispersal systems were intended for use in conjunction with various developmental unmanned aerial vehicles (UAV) programs. Initial testing was quickly beginning to show progress by the time of Desert Storm. Since that time however, while their desire for these systems remained, their developmental work shifted focus. Due to the attention of the UNSCOM inspectors, the developmental effort shifted away from the more controversial spray technologies toward completing the longer range UAV goals.

ISG judges—with important reservations—that the former Regime clandestinely destroyed almost all of Iraq's biological WMD and long-range missiles in 1991. Numerous interviews with high-ranking Iraqi political figures, WMD scientists, and military and security officers indicate that after a brief period of concealment in 1991, Iraqi leaders decided to destroy Iraq's undeclared weapons stockpile in secret.

- Shortly after the passage of Security Council Resolution 687 in early April 1991, Iraqi leaders also decided to erase all traces of the offensive BW program.

- By the autumn of 1991, Iraq probably accomplished both the destruction of the weapons stockpile and surviving evidence of the BW program.

- Interviews conducted by ISG have produced a reasonably coherent picture of this unilateral destruction, with few conflicting details, although important questions about the disposition of bulk BW agent and bacterial reference strains remain.

- ISG judges that the former Regime destroyed most of its hidden stockpile of BW weapons. A few pre–1991 weapons probably either escaped destruction in 1991 or suffered only partial damage. It is thus possible that a few more will be found in the months and years ahead.

ISG bases its reservations on the following factors:

- The security situation in Iraq has limited the physical verification of Iraq's unilateral destruction claims—by excavating and counting weapon fragments, for example.

- Many of the officials interviewed by ISG had previously lied–or told half-truths–to UNSCOM, and they may have lied to ISG as well, though ISG assesses that most were being open and truthful.

- The continuing exploitation of Iraqi documents may produce evidence that contradicts the assertions of the Iraqi officials.

- The efforts of the Iraqi Interim Government and Coalition forces may yet result in the discovery of unacknowledged WMD stockpiles left by the former Regime, though ISG judges this to be very unlikely.

ISG has not discovered any evidence that Iraq has conducted research or trials dedicated to the dispersion of BW agents since declaring its offensive program in 1995. Iraq pursued some delivery systems projects until OIF that could have provided some BW utility and whose origins lay in the development of BW and CW dispersion systems.

[ . . . ]

PART V

The main premise of the war against Saddam Hussein was false. But it is clear from all the evidence that he was far from an innocent victim of flawed American policy. Saddam's demonstrated malevolence made him a threat to his people and to the peace of the world, and it was one of the reasons President Bush and his administration gave for going to war against him. That democracy would end the suffering of the Iraqi people under the dictator's cruelty and stimulate needed change throughout the Middle East was another.

If the United States had tried to convince recalcitrant allies that war was justified on these grounds alone, it might even have succeeded. Instead, the Bush administration had relied primarily on what had proved to be "one of the most public—and most damaging—intelligence failures in recent American history," in the words of an investigatory body named by the president himself, the Commission on the Intelligence Capabilities of the United States Regarding Weapons of Mass Destruction.

Under pressure from Congress, the president reluctantly agreed in early 2004 to form this panel, headed by a Democratic former governor and senator from Virginia, Charles S. Robb, and a Republican retired Federal appeals court judge, Laurence H. Silberman, to look into WMD intelligence failures in Iraq. But Congress agreed to let it delay its report until well after the 2004 election. The WMD commission submitted its 692-page classified report on the deadline, March 31, 2005, but left important sections out of the 601-page unclassified version it published then. Much of the unclassified version released by the commission follows here.

Intelligence had produced successes in Libya, which gave up its nuclear weapons programs as a result, and in Afghanistan, where Al Qaeda and the Taliban were uprooted. But, building on the earlier Senate investigation and Charles Duelfer's report, the WMD commission, like the Senate Intelligence Committee before it, found that the 2002 National Intelligence Estimate on Iraq had been based on information that it described as "nearly worthless." With inadequate human sources inside Iraq, misinformation from Iraqi exiles with overactive imaginations like "Curve Ball" who were eager to see Saddam Hussein removed under any pretext, and a vested interest in confirming its own past assessments, the CIA did not present policymakers with a complete account of what all 15 government intelligence agencies knew and did not know about Iraq. Instead, it warned of chemical weapons programs and mobile biological weapons factories that did not exist, the aluminum tubes supposedly designed for uranium centrifuges that were in fact intended for rocket engines. President Bush and Vice President Dick Cheney may have been predisposed to believe the worst anyway—and had been hearing "disastrously one-sided" intelligence reports in the Presidential Daily Brief for months before the October 2002 National Intelligence Estimate—but even administration officials like Powell who asked tough questions about the intelligence were wrongly assured by the agencies that the information was accurate, the commission found, and it saw no indication that pressure from top administration officials had led them to distort their findings. The intelligence structure in 2002 did not do justice to views inside the intelligence community that challenged the conventional wisdom, the flawed "consensus" the agency put forward to the president.

The sweeping reorganization of intelligence agencies at the end of 2004 was intended to correct such flaws. Yet, in the WMD commission's view, even that reorganization was not enough to prevent similar policy misjudgments in the future.

American intelligence on Iran was so skimpy that no firm conclusions could be reached about the existence of weapons of mass destruction programs there, the commission said in its classified report, according to an article published in *The New York Times* on March 9. The commission's conclusions about the reliability of intelligence on North Korea also remain classified.

The commission recommended a reorganization of national security intelligence activities within the Federal Bureau of Investigation, under the authority of the new director of national intelligence, and a strengthening of the relationship between the

Department of Homeland Security and the intelligence community. It asked the president to create a new national nonproliferation center, a small but powerful group that would coordinate WMD reports from all branches of government and make sure that all views, including dissents, were presented to decision makers, to guard against the kind of rush to judgment that had swept aside any doubt that Saddam had amassed a deadly arsenal in Iraq. Equally important, it called for more "human intelligence"—flesh and blood spies and informants on the ground—to reinforce and cross-check information gathered by technological means.

In receiving the report at the White House March 31, President Bush said the administration would "correct what needs to be fixed." But some listeners may well have thought he had missed one of the main lessons of Iraq, that intelligence had malfunctioned to exaggerate the threat, not underestimate it:

"Our collection and analysis of intelligence will never be perfect, but in an age where our margin for error is getting smaller, in an age in which we are at war, the consequences of underestimating a threat could be tens of thousands of innocent lives," he said. "And my administration will continue to make intelligence reforms that will allow us to identify threats before they fully emerge so we can take effective action to protect the American people."

.    .    .

What the American people were left with after the war was a difficult choice. They could stay the course to make a success of the replacement of dictatorship with democracy in a long struggle the president had led them to believe would never be necessary; or they could withdraw and leave the Iraqis on their own to deal with the Saddamites and their terrorist allies. The president had made a historic gamble, one filled with potential promise but also with great risk, and at a high cost in human life and treasure.

As to the war that he waged to eliminate the weapons of mass destruction that were already gone before it started, President Bush had this to say, to *The Washington Post* on January 16, 2005: "We had an accountability moment, and that's called the 2004 elections. And the American people listened to different assessments made about what was taking place in Iraq, and they looked at the two candidates, and chose me, for which I'm grateful."

But the war in Iraq did not eliminate the threats from weapons of mass destruction in the hands of undemocratic regimes and terrorists, nor the Bush administration's determination to eliminate those threats. As the second term began, North Korea declared publicly that it had actually developed nuclear weapons—"nukes for self-defense," it called them, saying also that it was suspending its participation in disarmament talks with the United States and its neighbors. American intelligence reported that North Korea had sent missile technology to Libya, raising fears that it could offer expertise on deadly warheads to those willing to pay enough money for it as well.

Iran, America's remaining nemesis in the Middle East, claimed off and on that it had suspended uranium enrichment activities, after trying for decades to hide them. When public disclosures of what it was up to forced Iran to open up to inspections by the IAEA in 2003, Teheran insisted its programs were all for peaceful purposes only. United States intelligence, this time including the State Department, suspected that it was secretly trying to develop nuclear weapons and rockets to carry them. But after Iraq, the world was less inclined than ever to take Washington's word for it.

In early 2005, Washington wrangled with its European allies over the best approach to use to persuade Iran to cooperate and forego all weapons of mass destruction. The Bush administration agreed to try a carrot and stick approach for a while, leaving it mainly to Cheney to point out that if that did not work, the United States would press for stronger action.

"At some point, if the Iranians don't live up to their commitments, the next step will be to take it to the U.N. Security Council, and seek the imposition of international sanctions," the vice president told Don Imus on his MSNBC show in January. "If, in fact, the Israelis became convinced the Iranians had a significant nuclear capability, given the fact that Iran has a stated policy that their objective is the destruction of Israel, the Israelis might well decide to act first, and let the rest of the world worry about cleaning up the diplomatic mess afterwards." The Israeli foreign minister, Silvan Shalom, said later that an Iranian atomic bomb would be a "nightmare" for Israel. "In our view, they are very close, they are too close, to having the knowledge to develop this kind of bomb and that's why we should be in a hurry," he said.

The United States did not want a war in the Middle East if it could avoid one, Cheney said, but "at the end of the day if the Iranians don't live up to their obligations and their international commitments to forego a nuclear program, then obviously we'll have to take stronger action."

Mohamed ElBaradei, whose IAEA had been so effective in eliminating Saddam Hussein's nuclear weapons program, told Lally Weymouth in *The Washington Post* at the end of January: "The results in Iran are something I am quite proud of. Eighteen months ago, Iran was a black box—we didn't know much about what was happening. . . . Iran has clearly cheated in the past—that is something we reported. Corrective action was taken. Now, they say they are embarking on a new path of cooperation and since then they are cooperating. If they are still cheating, we haven't seen any evidence of that. . . . When they cheated, we said so. When they are cooperating, we say so. We have been supervising their suspension of fuel cycle activities. Recently, we got access to a partial military site."

If Iran resumed its fuel cycle activities, ElBaradei warned, "they are a year away from a weapon."

The Bush administration was opposing ElBaradei's candidacy for a third term as director-general of the IAEA.

"North Korea has plutonium for sure," he told the *Post*, "enough to make at least six to eight bombs. Like Iran, we should discuss their security concerns and their sense of isolation and bring a generous offer which would enable them to give up their nuclear ambitions."

The National Intelligence Council was producing a National Intelligence Estimate on Iran in early 2005. Many lives, and not just American lives, may depend on the quality and reliability of the American intelligence about North Korea and Iran, and on the uses the Bush administration makes of that intelligence. About both, as this book went to press, the American public could do little more than guess.

# Commission on the Intelligence Capabilities of the United States Regarding Weapons of Mass Destruction

*[The complete text is available at http://www.wmd.gov.]*

March 31, 2005

Mr. President:

With this letter, we transmit the report of the Commission on the Intelligence Capabilities of the United States Regarding Weapons of Mass Destruction. Our unanimous report is based on a lengthy investigation, during which we interviewed hundreds of experts from inside and outside the Intelligence Community and reviewed thousands of documents. Our report offers 74 recommendations for improving the U.S. Intelligence Community (all but a handful of which we believe can be implemented without statutory change). But among these recommendations a few points merit special emphasis.

We conclude that the Intelligence Community was dead wrong in almost all of its pre-war judgments about Iraq's weapons of mass destruction. This was a major intelligence failure. Its principal causes were the Intelligence Community's inability to collect good information about Iraq's WMD programs, serious errors in analyzing what information it could gather, and a failure to make clear just how much of its analysis was based on assumptions, rather than good evidence. On a matter of this importance, we simply cannot afford failures of this magnitude.

After a thorough review, the Commission found no indication that the Intelligence Community distorted the evidence regarding Iraq's weapons of mass destruction. What the intelligence professionals told you about Saddam Hussein's programs was what they believed. They were simply wrong.

As you asked, we looked as well beyond Iraq in our review of the Intelligence Community's capabilities. We conducted case studies of our intelligence agencies' recent performance assessing the risk of WMD in Libya and Afghanistan, and our current capabilities with respect to several of the world's most dangerous state and non-state proliferation threats. Out of this more comprehensive review, we report both bad news and good news. The bad news is that we still know disturbingly little about the weapons programs and even less about the intentions of many of our most dangerous adversaries. The good news is that we have had some solid intelligence successes—thanks largely to innovative and multi-agency collection techniques.

Our review has convinced us that the best hope for preventing future failures is dramatic change. We need an Intelligence Community that is truly integrated, far more imaginative and willing to run risks, open to a new generation of Americans, and receptive to new technologies.

We have summarized our principal recommendations for the entire Intelligence Community in the Overview of the report. Here, we focus on recommendations that we believe only you can effect if you choose to implement them:

• Give the DNI powers—and backing—to match his responsibilities.

In your public statement accompanying the announcement of Ambassador Negroponte's nomination as Director of National Intelligence (DNI), you have already moved in this direction. The new intelligence law makes the DNI responsible for integrating the 15 independent members of the Intelligence Community. But it gives him powers that are only relatively broader than before. The DNI cannot make this work unless he takes his legal authorities over budget, programs, personnel, and priorities to the limit. It won't be easy to provide this leadership to the intelligence components of the Defense Department, or to the CIA. They are some of the government's most headstrong agencies. Sooner or later, they will try to run around—or over-the DNI. Then, only your determined backing will convince them that we cannot return to the old ways.

- Bring the FBI all the way into the Intelligence Community.

The FBI is one of the proudest and most independent agencies in the United States Government. It is on its way to becoming an effective intelligence agency, but it will never arrive if it insists on using only its own map. We recommend that you order an organizational reform of the Bureau that pulls all of its intelligence capabilities into one place and subjects them to the coordinating authority of the DNI—the same authority that the DNI exercises over Defense Department intelligence agencies. Under this recommendation, the counterterrorism and counterintelligence resources of the Bureau would become a single National Security Service inside the FBI. It would of course still be subject to the Attorney General's oversight and to current legal rules. The intelligence reform act almost accomplishes this task, but at crucial points it retreats into ambiguity. Without leadership from the DNI, the FBI is likely to continue escaping effective integration into the Intelligence Community.

- Demand more of the Intelligence Community.

The Intelligence Community needs to be pushed. It will not do its best unless it is pressed by policymakers—sometimes to the point of discomfort. Analysts must be pressed to explain how much they don't know; the collection agencies must be pressed to explain why they don't have better information on key topics. While policymakers must be prepared to credit intelligence that doesn't fit their preferences, no important intelligence assessment should be accepted without sharp questioning that forces the community to explain exactly how it came to that assessment and what alternatives might also be true. This is not "politicization"; it is a necessary part of the intelligence process. And in the end, it is the key to getting the best from an Intelligence Community that, at its best, knows how to do astonishing things.

- Rethink the President's Daily Brief.

The daily intelligence briefings given to you before the Iraq war were flawed. Through attention-grabbing headlines and repetition of questionable data, these briefings overstated the case that Iraq was rebuilding its WMD programs. There are many other aspects of the daily brief that deserve to be reconsidered as well, but we are reluctant to make categorical recommendations on a process that in the end must meet your needs, not our theories. On one point, however, we want to be specific: while the DNI must be ultimately responsible for the content of your daily briefing, we do not believe that the DNI ought to prepare, deliver, or even attend every briefing. For if the DNI is consumed by current intelligence, the long-term needs of the Intelligence Community will suffer. There is no more important intelligence mission than understanding the worst weapons that our enemies possess, and how they intend to use them against us. These are their deepest secrets, and unlocking them must be our highest priority. So far, despite some successes, our Intelligence Community has not been agile and innovative enough to provide the information that the nation needs. Other commissions and observers have said the same. We should not wait for another commission or another Administration to force widespread change in the Intelligence Community.

Very respectfully,

*(Signed by)*
LAURENCE H. SILBERMAN (Co-Chairman)
CHARLES S. ROBB (Co-Chairman)
RICHARD C. LEVIN
JOHN MCCAIN
HENRY S. ROWEN
WALTER B. SLOCOMBE
WILLIAM O. STUDEMAN
PATRICIA M. WALD
CHARLES M. VEST
LLOYD CUTLER (Of Counsel)

# List of Findings and Recommendations

## Part One: Looking Back

### *Iraq*

*Overall Commission Finding:* The Intelligence Community's performance in assessing Iraq's pre-war weapons of mass destruction programs was a major intelligence failure. The failure was not merely that the Intelligence Community's assessments were wrong. There were also serious shortcomings in the way these assessments were made and communicated to policymakers.

*Nuclear Weapons Summary Finding:* The Intelligence Community seriously misjudged the status of Iraq's alleged nuclear weapons program in the 2002 NIE and other pre-Iraq war intelligence products. This misjudgment stemmed chiefly from the Community's failure to analyze correctly Iraq's reasons for attempting to procure high-strength aluminum tubes.

1. The Intelligence Community's judgment about Iraq's nuclear program hinged chiefly on an assessment about Iraq's intended use for high-strength aluminum tubes it was seeking to procure. Most of the agencies in the Intelligence Community erroneously concluded these tubes were intended for use in centrifuges in a nuclear program rather than in conventional rockets. This error was, at the bottom, the result of poor analytical tradecraft—namely, the failure to do proper technical analysis informed by thorough knowledge of the relevant weapons technology and practices.

2. In addition to citing the aluminum tubes, the NIE's judgment

that Iraq was attempting to reconstitute its nuclear weapons program also referred to additional streams of intelligence. These other streams, however, were very thin, and the limited value of that supporting intelligence was inadequately conveyed in the October 2002 NIE and in other Intelligence Community products.

3. The other indications of reconstitution—aside from the aluminum tubes—did not themselves amount to a persuasive case for a reconstituted Iraqi nuclear program. In light of the tenuousness of this other information, DOE's argument that the aluminum tubes were not for centrifuges but that Iraq was, based on these other streams of information, reconstituting its nuclear program was a flawed analytical position.

4. The Intelligence Community failed to authenticate in a timely fashion transparently forged documents purporting to show that Iraq had attempted to procure uranium from Niger.

*Biological Warfare Summary Finding:* The Intelligence Community seriously misjudged the status of Iraq's biological weapons program in the 2002 NIE and other pre-war intelligence products. The primary reason for this misjudgment was the Intelligence Community's heavy reliance on a human source—codenamed "Curveball"—whose information later proved to be unreliable.

1. The DIA's Defense HUMINT Service's failure even to attempt to validate Curveball's reporting was a major failure in operational tradecraft.

2. Indications of possible problems with Curveball began to emerge well before the 2002 NIE. These early indications of problems—which suggested unstable behavior more than a lack of credibility—were discounted by the analysts working the Iraq WMD account. But given these warning signs, analysts should have viewed Curveball's information with greater skepticism and should have conveyed this skepticism in the NIE. The analysts' resistance to any information that could

undermine Curveball's reliability suggests that the analysts were unduly wedded to a source that supported their assumptions about Iraq's BW programs.

3. The October 2002 NIE failed to communicate adequately to policymakers both the Community's near-total reliance on Curveball for its BW judgments, and the serious problems that characterized Curveball as a source.

4. Beginning in late 2002, some operations officers within the regional division of the CIA's Directorate of Operations that was responsible for relations with the liaison service handling Curveball expressed serious concerns about Curveball's reliability to senior officials at the CIA, but these views were either (1) not thought to outweigh analytic assessments that Curveball's information was reliable or (2) disregarded because of managers' assessments that those views were not sufficiently convincing to warrant further elevation.

5. CIA management stood by Curveball's reporting long after post-war investigators in Iraq had established that he was lying about crucial issues.

6. In addition to the problems with Curveball, the Intelligence Community—and, particularly, the Defense HUMINT Service—failed to keep reporting from a known fabricator out of finished intelligence on Iraq's BW program in 2002 and 2003.

*Chemical Warfare Summary Finding:* The Intelligence Community erred in its 2002 NIE assessment of Iraq's alleged chemical warfare program. The Community's substantial overestimation of Iraq's chemical warfare program was due chiefly to flaws in analysis and the paucity of quality information collected.

1. The Intelligence Community relied too heavily on ambiguous imagery indicators identified at suspect Iraqi facilities for its broad judgment about Iraq's chemical warfare program. In particular, analysts leaned too much on the judgment that the

presence of "Samarra-type" trucks (and related activity) indicated that Iraq had resumed its chemical weapons program.

2. Analysts failed to understand, and collectors did not adequately communicate, the limitations of imagery collection. Specifically, analysts did not realize that the observed increase in activity at suspected Iraqi chemical facilities may have been the result of increased imagery collection rather than an increase in Iraqi activity.

3. Human intelligence collection against Iraq's chemical activities was paltry, and much has subsequently proved problematic.

4. Signals intelligence collection against Iraq's chemical activities was minimal, and much was of questionable value.

*Delivery Summary Finding 1:* The Intelligence Community incorrectly assessed that Iraq was developing unmanned aerial vehicles for the purpose of delivering biological weapons strikes against U.S. interests.

*Delivery Summary Finding 2:* The Intelligence Community correctly judged that Iraq was developing ballistic missile systems that violated United Nations strictures, but was incorrect in assessing that Iraq had preserved its Scud missile force.

1. The Intelligence Community made too much of an inferential leap, based on very little hard evidence, in judging that Iraq's unmanned aerial vehicles were being designed for use as biological warfare delivery vehicles and that they might be used against the U.S. homeland.

2. The Intelligence Community failed to communicate adequately to policymakers the weak foundations upon which its conclusions were based.

3. The Intelligence Community failed to give adequate consideration to other possible uses for Iraq's UAVs or to give due credence to countervailing evidence.

4. The Intelligence Community was generally correct in assessing that Iraq was continuing ballistic missile work that violated United Nations restrictions, but erred in many of the specifics.

*Regime Decisionmaking Summary Finding:* The Intelligence Community, because of a lack of analytical imagination, failed even to consider the possibility that Saddam Hussein would decide to destroy his chemical and biological weapons and to halt work on his nuclear program after the first Gulf War.

IRAQ CONCLUSIONS

1. Saddam Hussein's Iraq was a hard target for human intelligence, but it will not be the last that we face. When faced with such targets in the future, the United States needs to supplement its traditional methodologies with more innovative approaches.

2. Rewarding CIA and DIA case officers based on how many assets they recruit impedes the recruitment of quality assets.

3. The CIA, and even more so the DIA, must do a better job of testing the veracity of crucial human sources.

4. Iraq's denial and deception efforts successfully hampered U.S. intelligence collection.

5. In the case of Iraq, collectors of intelligence absorbed the prevailing analytic consensus and tended to reject or ignore contrary information. The result was "tunnel vision" focusing on the Intelligence Community's existing assumptions.

6. Intercepted communications identified some procurement efforts, but such intelligence was of only marginal utility because most procurements were of dual-use materials.

7. Signals intelligence against Iraq was seriously hampered by technical barriers.

8. Other difficulties relating to the security and counterintelligence methods of the Iraqi regime hampered NSA collection.

9. Traditional imagery intelligence has limited utility in assessing chemical and biological weapons programs.

10. Measurements and signatures intelligence (MASINT) collection was severely hampered by problems similar to those faced by other intelligence methods. Analysts' lack of familiarity with MASINT also reduced its role in analysts' assessments of Iraq's WMD programs.

11. Recognizing that it was having problems collecting quality intelligence against Iraq, the Intelligence Community launched an effort to study ways to improve its collection performance. This process was hampered by haphazard follow-up by some agencies; in particular, NSA failed to follow-up promptly on the Intelligence Community's recommendations.

12. Analysts skewed the analytical process by requiring proof that Iraq did not have WMD.

13. Analysts did not question the hypotheses underlying their conclusions, and tended to discount evidence that cut against those hypotheses.

14. The Community made serious mistakes in its technical analysis of Iraq's unconventional weapons program. The National Ground Intelligence Center in particular displayed a disturbing lack of diligence and technical expertise.

15. Analysis of Iraqi weapons programs was also flawed by "layering," with one individual assessment forming the basis for additional, broader assessments that did not carry forward the uncertainties underlying each "layer."

16. Analysis of Iraq's weapons programs took little account of Iraq's political and social context. While such a consideration

would probably not have changed the Community's judgments about Iraq's WMD, the failure even to consider whether Saddam Hussein had elected to abandon his banned weapons programs precluded that possibility.

17. The Community did not adequately communicate uncertainties about either its sources or its analytic judgments to policymakers.

18. The Community failed to explain adequately to consumers the fundamental assumptions and premises of its analytic judgments.

19. Relevant information known to intelligence collectors was not provided to Community analysts.

20. Relevant information known to intelligence analysts was not provided to Community collectors.

21. Inability to obtain information from foreign liaison services hampered the Community's ability to assess the credibility of crucial information.

22. The President's Daily Brief (PDB) likely conveyed a greater sense of certainty about analytic judgments than warranted.

23. The National Intelligence Estimate process is subject to flaws as well, and the Iraq NIE displays some of them. The length of the NIE encourages policymakers to rely on the less caveated Key Judgments. And the language of consensus ("most agencies believe") may obscure situations in which the dissenting agency has more expertise than the majority.

24. The Iraq NIE was produced to meet a very short deadline. The time pressure was unfortunate and perhaps avoidable, but it did not substantially affect the judgments reached in the NIE.

25. The shortened NIE coordination process did not unfairly

suppress the National Ground Intelligence Center's slightly more cautious estimates of Iraq's CW stockpile.

26. The Intelligence Community did not make or change any analytic judgments in response to political pressure to reach a particular conclusion, but the pervasive conventional wisdom that Saddam retained WMD affected the analytic process.

27. The CIA took too long to admit error in Iraq, and its Weapons Intelligence, Nonproliferation, and Arms Control Center actively discouraged analysts from investigating errors.

IRAQ RECOMMENDATION

The Director of National Intelligence should hold accountable the organizations that contributed to the flawed assessments of Iraq's WMD programs.

## Chapter 2: Libya Findings

1. The Intelligence Community accurately assessed what nuclear-related equipment and material had been obtained by Libya, but it was less successful in judging how well Libya was able to exploit what it possessed.

2. The Intelligence Community's central judgment that Libya possessed chemical weapons agents and chemical weapons aerial bombs was correct, but Libya's actual chemical agent stockpile proved to be smaller in quantity than the Intelligence Community estimated.

3. The Intelligence Community's assessment that Libya maintained the desire for an offensive biological weapons program, and was pursuing at least a small-scale research and development effort, remains unconfirmed.

4. The Intelligence Community's assessments of Libya's missile

programs appear to have been generally accurate, but it is not yet possible to evaluate them fully because of limited Libyan disclosures.

5. The Intelligence Community's penetration of the A.Q. Khan proliferation network provided invaluable intelligence on Libya's nuclear efforts.

6. The Intelligence Community's performance with regard to Libya's chemical and biological programs was more modest, due in part to the limited effectiveness of technical collection techniques against these targets.

7. The Intelligence Community gathered valuable information on Libya's missile program.

8. Analysts generally demonstrated a commendable willingness to question and reconsider their assessments in light of new information.

9. Analysts tracking proliferation program developments sometimes inappropriately equated procurement activity with technical capabilities, and many analysts did not receive the necessary training to avoid such failings.

10. Analytic products sometimes provided limited effective warning to intelligence consumers, and tended to separate WMD issues from broader discussions of political and economic forces.

11. Shifting priorities and the dominance of current intelligence production leave little time for considering important unanswered questions on Libya, or for working small problems that might prove to have an impact on reducing surprise over the long term.

*Chapter 3: Al-Qa'ida in Afghanistan Findings*

1. Information obtained through the war in Afghanistan and in its aftermath indicated that al-Qa'ida's biological weapons program was further along than analysts had previously assessed.

2. Analytic judgments regarding al-Qa'ida's chemical weapons capabilities did not change significantly as a result of the war.

3. The war in Afghanistan brought to light detailed and revealing information about the direction and progress of al-Qa'ida's radiological and nuclear ambitions.

4. Intelligence gaps prior to the war in Afghanistan prevented the Intelligence Community from being able to assess with much certainty the extent of al-Qa'ida's weapons of mass destruction capabilities.

5. Analysis on al-Qa'ida's potential weapons of mass destruction development in Afghanistan did not benefit from leveraging different analytic disciplines.

6. Analysts writing on al-Qa'ida's potential weapons of mass destruction efforts in Afghanistan did not adequately state the basis for or the assumptions underlying their most critical judgments. This analytic shortcoming is one that we have seen in our other studies as well, such as Iraq, and it points to the need to develop routine analytic practices for quantifying uncertainty and managing limited collection.

*Chapter 4: Terrorism Findings*

1. Although terrorism information sharing has improved significantly since September 11, major change is still required to institute effective information sharing across the Intelligence Community and with state, local, and tribal governments.

2. Ambiguities in the respective roles and authorities of the NCTC and CTC have not been resolved, and the two agencies continue to fight bureaucratic battles to define their place in the war on terror. The result has been unnecessary duplication of effort and the promotion of unproductive competition between the two organizations.

3. Persisting ambiguities and conflicts in the roles, missions, and authorities of counterterrorism organizations hamper effective warning.

4. Persistent ambiguities and conflicts in the roles, missions, and authorities of counterterrorism organizations with regard to analysis and warning have led to redundant efforts across the Community and inefficient use of limited resources.

5. The failure to manage counterterrorism resources from a Community perspective has limited the Intelligence Community's ability to understand and warn against terrorist use of weapons of mass destruction.

*Chapter 5: Iran and North Korea*

*The eleven findings in this chapter are classified.*

# Part Two: Looking Forward

*The Recommendations*

CHAPTER 6: LEADERSHIP AND MANAGEMENT

1. We recommend that the DNI bring a mission focus to the management of Community resources for high-priority intelligence issues by creating a group of "Mission Managers" on the DNI staff, responsible for all aspects of the intelligence process relating to those issues.

2. We recommend that the DNI create a management structure that effectively coordinates Community target development. This new target development process would be supported by an integrated, end-to-end "collection enterprise."

3. We recommend that the new DNI overhaul the Community's information management system to facilitate real and effective information sharing.

4. We recommend that the DNI use his human resources authorities to: establish a central human resources authority for the Intelligence Community; create a uniform system for performance evaluations and compensation; develop a more comprehensive and creative set of performance incentives; direct a "joint" personnel rotation system; and establish a National Intelligence University.

5. We recommend that the DNI take an active role in equipping the Intelligence Community to develop new technologies.

6. We recommend that the President establish a National Counter Proliferation Center (NCPC) that is relatively small (i.e., fewer than 100 people) and that manages and coordinates analysis and collection on nuclear, biological, and chemical weapons across the Intelligence Community. Although government-wide "strategic operational planning" is clearly required to confront proliferation threats, we advise that such planning not be directed by the NCPC.

7. We recommend that the Executive Branch improve its mechanisms for watching over the Intelligence Community in order to ensure that intelligence reform does not falter. To this end, we suggest that the Joint Intelligence Community Council serve as a standing Intelligence Community "customer council" and that a strengthened President's Foreign Intelligence Advisory Board assume a more vigorous role in keeping watch over the progress of reform in the Community.

8. We recommend that the President suggest that Congress take steps to improve its structure for intelligence oversight.

9. The Intelligence Community should improve its internal processes for self-examination, including increasing the use of formal "lessons learned" studies.

CHAPTER 7: COLLECTION

1. The DNI should create a new management structure within the Office of the DNI that manages collection as an "integrated collection enterprise." Such an integrated approach should include coordinated target development, collection management, data management, strategic planning and investment, and the development of new collection techniques.

2. Target Development Boards, which would be chaired by the Mission Managers, should develop collection requirements and strategies and evaluate collectors' responsiveness to these needs.

3. Strengthen the CIA's authority to manage and coordinate overseas human intelligence operations across the Intelligence Community by creating a Human Intelligence Directorate outside the Directorate of Operations.

4. The CIA should develop and manage a range of new overt and covert human intelligence capabilities. In particular, a "Human Intelligence Innovation Center," independent of the CIA's Directorate of Operations, should be established to facilitate the development of new and innovative mechanisms for collecting human intelligence.

5. The CIA should take the lead in systematizing and standardizing the Intelligence Community's asset validation procedures, and integrating them with all information gathering activities across the human intelligence spectrum.

6. The Intelligence Community should train more human intelligence operators and collectors, and its training programs should be modified to support the full spectrum of human intelligence collection methods.

7. The President should seek to have the Foreign Intelligence Surveillance Act amended to extend the duration of electronic surveillance and "pen registers" in cases involving agents of foreign powers who are not U.S. persons.

8. The DNI should appoint an authority responsible for managing and overseeing innovative technologies, including the use of technologies often referred to as "MASINT."

9. The DNI should create an Open Source Directorate in the CIA to use the Internet and modern information processing tools to greatly enhance the availability of open source information to analysts, collectors, and users of intelligence.

10. Efforts should be taken to significantly reduce damaging losses in collection capability that result from authorized disclosures of classified information related to protection of sources and methods.

11. The DNI should ensure that all Inspectors General in the Intelligence Community are prepared to conduct leak investigations for their agencies; this responsibility can be coordinated by a Community-wide Inspector General in the Office of the DNI, if such an office is established.

CHAPTER 8: ANALYSIS

1. Mission Managers should be the DNI's designees for ensuring that the analytic community adequately addresses key intelligence needs on high priority topics.

2. The DNI should create a small cadre of all-source analysts—perhaps 50—who would be experts in finding and using unclassified, open source information.

3. The DNI should establish a program office within the CIA's Open Source Directorate to acquire, or develop when necessary, information technologies to permit prioritization and exploitation of large volumes of textual data without the need for prior human translation or transcription.

4. The Intelligence Community should expand its contacts with those outside the realm of intelligence by creating at least one not-for-profit "sponsored research institute."

5. The Community must develop and integrate into regular use new tools that can assist analysts in filtering and correlating the vast quantities of information that threaten to overwhelm the analytic process. Moreover, data from all sources of information should be processed and correlated Community-wide before being conveyed to analysts.

6. A new long-term research and analysis unit, under the mantle of the National Intelligence Council, should wall off all-source analysts from the press of daily demands and serve as the lead organization for interagency projects involving in-depth analysis.

7. The DNI should encourage diverse and independent analysis throughout the Intelligence Community by encouraging alternative hypothesis generation as part of the analytic process and by forming offices dedicated to independent analysis.

8. The Intelligence Community must develop a Community program for training analysts, and both analysts and managers must prioritize this career-long training.

9. The Intelligence Community must develop a Community program for training managers, both when they first assume managerial positions and throughout their careers.

10. Finished intelligence should include careful sourcing for all analytic assessments and conclusions, and these materials

should—whenever possible in light of legitimate security concerns—be made easily available to intelligence customers.

11. The analytic community should create and store sourced copies of all analytic pieces to allow readers to locate and review the intelligence upon which analysis is based, and to allow for easy identification of analysis that is based on intelligence reports that are later modified.

12. The DNI should develop and implement strategies for improving the Intelligence Community's science and technology and weapons analysis capabilities.

13. The DNI should explore ways to make finished intelligence available to customers in a way that enables them—to the extent they desire—to more easily find pieces of interest, link to related materials, and communicate with analysts.

14. The President's Daily Brief should be restructured. The DNI should oversee the process and ensure a fair representation of divergent views. Reporting on terrorism intelligence should be combined and coordinated by the DNI to eliminate redundancies and material that does not merit Presidential action.

15. The Intelligence Community should expand the use of nonmonetary incentives that remind analysts of the importance of their work and the value of their contributions to national security.

16. Examinations of finished intelligence should be routine and ongoing, and the lessons learned from the "post mortems" should be incorporated into the intelligence education and training program.

## Chapter 9: Information Sharing

1. The confused lines of authority over information sharing cre-

ated by the intelligence reform act should be resolved. In particular:

- The Information Sharing Environment should be expanded to encompass all intelligence information, not just terrorism intelligence;

- The Director of the National Counterterrorism Center should report to the DNI on all matters relating to information sharing; and

- The overlapping authorities of the DNI and the Program Manager should be reconciled and coordinated—a result most likely to be achieved by requiring the Program Manager to report to the DNI.

2. The DNI should give responsibility for information sharing, information technology, and information security within the Intelligence Community to an office reporting directly to the DNI or to the Principal Deputy DNI.

3. In designing an Information Sharing Environment, the DNI should, to the extent possible, learn from and build on the capabilities of existing Intelligence Community networks. These lessons include:

- The limitations of "need to know" in a networked environment;

- The importance of developing mechanisms that can protect sources and methods in new ways;

- Biometrics and other user authentication (identification) methods, along with user activity auditing tools, can promote accountability and enhance counterintelligence capabilities;

- System-wide encryption of data can greatly reduce the risks of network penetration by outsiders; and

- Where sensitive information is restricted to a limited group of users, the Information Sharing Environment should ensure that others searching for such information are aware of its existence and provided with a point of contact who can decide quickly whether to grant access.

4. Primary institutional responsibility within the Intelligence Community for establishing clear and consistent "U.S. persons" rules should be shifted from individual collection agencies to the Director of National Intelligence. These rules would continue to be subject to the Attorney General's review and approval. To the extent possible, the same rules should apply across the Intelligence Community.

5. The DNI should set uniform information management policies, practices, and procedures for all members of the Intelligence Community.

6. All users of the Information Sharing Environment should be registered in a directory that identifies skills, clearances, and assigned responsibilities of each individual (using aliases rather than true names when necessary). The environment should enable users to make a "call for assistance" that assembles a virtual community of specialists to address a particular task, and all data should be catalogued within the Information Sharing Environment in a way that enables the underlying network to compare user privileges with data sensitivity.

7. The DNI should propose standards to simplify and modernize the information classification system with particular attention to implementation in a network-centric Information Sharing Environment.

8. We recommend several parallel efforts to keep the Information Sharing Environment on track:

   - *Collection of metrics.* The chief information management officer should introduce performance metrics for the Information Sharing Environment and automate their collection. These metrics should include the number and origination of postings to the shared environment, data on how often and by whom each item was accessed, and statistics on the use of collaborative tools and communications channels, among others. Such performance data can help to define milestones and to determine rewards and penalties.

- *Self-enforcing milestones.* Milestones should include specific and quantifiable performance criteria for the sharing environment, as well as rewards and penalties for succeeding or failing to meet them. The DNI should empower the chief information management officer to use the DNI's budget, mission-assignment, and personnel authorities to penalize poor agency performance.

- *Incentives.* The DNI should ensure that collectors and analysts receive honors or monetary prizes for intelligence products that receive widespread use or acclaim. Users should post comments or rate the value of individual reports or analytic products, and periodic user surveys can serve as peer review mechanisms.

- *Training.* The DNI should promote the training of all users in the Information Sharing Environment, with extended training for analysts, managers, and other users of the environment.

## CHAPTER 10: INTELLIGENCE AT HOME

1. To ensure that the FBI's intelligence elements are responsive to the Director of National Intelligence, and to capitalize on the FBI's progress, we recommend the creation of a new National Security Service within the FBI under a single Executive Assistant Director. This service would include the Bureau's Counterterrorism and Counterintelligence Divisions and the Directorate of Intelligence. The service would be subject to

the coordination and budget authorities of the DNI as well as to the same Attorney General authorities that apply to other Bureau divisions.

2. The DNI should ensure that there are effective mechanisms for preventing conflicts and encouraging coordination among intelligence agencies in the United States.

3. The Department of Justice's primary national security elements—the Office of Intelligence Policy and Review, and the Counterterrorism and Counterespionage sections—should be placed under a new Assistant Attorney General for National Security.

4. The Secretary of Homeland Security should rescind Treasury Order 113–01 as it applies to Department of Homeland Security elements.

CHAPTER 11: COUNTERINTELLIGENCE

1. The National Counterintelligence Executive should become the DNI's Mission Manager for counterintelligence, providing strategic direction for the whole range of counterintelligence activities across the government.

2. The National Counterintelligence Executive should work closely with agencies responsible for protecting U.S. information infrastructure in order to enhance the United States' technical counterintelligence capabilities.

3. The CIA should create a new capability dedicated to mounting offensive counterintelligence activities abroad.

4. The Department of Defense's Counterintelligence Field Activity should have operational and investigative authority to coordinate and conduct counterintelligence activities throughout the Defense Department.

5. The FBI should create a National Security Service that includes the Bureau's Counterintelligence Division, Counterterrorism Division, and the Directorate of Intelligence. A single Executive Assistant Director would lead the Service subject to the coordination and budget authorities of the DNI.

CHAPTER 12: COVERT ACTION

*The four recommendations in this chapter are classified.*

CHAPTER 13: THE CHANGING PROLIFERATION THREAT AND THE INTELLIGENCE RESPONSE

1. The DNI should create a Community-wide National Biodefense Initiative to include a Biological Science Advisory Group, a government service program for biologists and health professionals, a post-doctoral fellowship program in biodefense and intelligence, and a scholarship program for graduate students in biological weapons-relevant fields.

2. The DNI should use the Joint Intelligence Community Council to form a Biological Weapons Working Group. This Working Group would serve as the principal coordination venue for the Intelligence Community and biodefense agencies, including the Department of Homeland Security's National Biodefense and Countermeasures Center, NIH, CDC, the Department of Agriculture, and USAMRIID.

3. The DNI should create a deputy within the National Counter Proliferation Center that is specifically responsible for biological weapons; this deputy would be responsible to the Proliferation Mission Manager to ensure the implementation of a comprehensive biological weapons targeting strategy and direct new collection initiatives.

4. The National Security Council should form a Joint Interagency Task Force to develop a counter-biological weapons plan

within 90 days that draws upon all elements of national power, including law enforcement and the regulatory capabilities of the Departments of Homeland Security, Health and Human Services, Commerce, and State.

5. The State Department should aggressively support foreign criminalization of biological weapons development and the establishment of biosafety and biosecurity regulations under the framework of the United Nations Security Council Resolution 1540. U.S. law enforcement and intelligence agencies should jointly sponsor biological weapons information sharing events with foreign police forces.

6. The United States should remain actively engaged in designing and implementing both international and regulatory inspection regimes. It should consider extending its existing biosecurity and biosafety regulations to foreign institutions with commercial ties to the United States, using the possibility of increased liability, reduced patent protection, or more burdensome and costly inspections to encourage compliance with appropriate safeguards.

7. The President should establish a Counterproliferation Joint Interagency Task Force to conduct counterproliferation interdiction operations; to detect, monitor, and handoff suspected proliferation targets; and to coordinate interagency and partner nations' counterproliferation activities.

8. The DNI should designate the National Counter Proliferation Center as the Intelligence Community's leader for interdiction-related issues and direct the Center to support the all-source intelligence needs of the Counterproliferation Joint Interagency Task Force, the National Security Council, and other customers.

9. The President should establish, probably through a National Security Presidential Directive, a real-time, interagency decisionmaking process for counterproliferation interdiction oper-

ations, borrowing from Presidential Directive 27, the interagency decisionmaking process that supports counternarcotics interdictions.

10. The State Department should enter into additional bilateral ship-boarding agreements that also help to meet the tagging, tracking, and locating requirements of the Intelligence Community and its users.

11. The DNI should ensure that Customs and Border Protection has the most up-to-date terrorism and proliferation intelligence. In turn, Customs and Border Protection should ensure that the National Counterterrorism Center and National Counter Proliferation Center have real-time access to its databases.

12. The DNI and Secretary of Homeland Security should undertake a research and development program to develop better sensors capable of detecting nuclear-related materials. The effort should be part of a larger border defense initiative to foster greater intelligence support to law enforcement at our nation's borders.

13. *This recommendation is classified.*

14. *This recommendation is classified.*

15. The President should expand the scope of Executive Order 13224 beyond terrorism to enable the Department of the Treasury to block the assets of persons and entities who provide financial support to proliferation.

16. The President should seek to have Congress amend Section 311 of the USA PATRIOT Act in order to give the Department of the Treasury the authority to designate foreign business entities involved in proliferation as "primary money laundering concerns."

# Overview of the Report

## Introduction

On the brink of war, and in front of the whole world, the United States government asserted that Saddam Hussein had reconstituted his nuclear weapons program, had biological weapons and mobile biological weapon production facilities, and had stockpiled and was producing chemical weapons. All of this was based on the assessments of the U.S. Intelligence Community. And not one bit of it could be confirmed when the war was over.

While the intelligence services of many other nations also thought that Iraq had weapons of mass destruction, in the end it was the United States that put its credibility on the line, making this one of the most public—and most damaging—intelligence failures in recent American history.

This failure was in large part the result of analytical shortcomings; intelligence analysts were too wedded to their assumptions about Saddam's intentions. But it was also a failure on the part of those who collect intelligence—CIA's and the Defense Intelligence Agency's (DIA) spies, the National Security Agency's (NSA) eavesdroppers, and the National Geospatial-Intelligence Agency's (NGA) imagery experts. In the end, those agencies collected precious little intelligence for the analysts to analyze, and much of what they did collect was either worthless or misleading. Finally, it was a failure to communicate effectively with policymakers; the Intelligence Community didn't adequately explain just how little good intelligence it had—or how much its assessments were driven by assumptions and inferences rather than concrete evidence.

Was the failure in Iraq typical of the Community's performance? Or was Iraq, as one senior intelligence official told the Commission, a sort of "perfect storm"—a one-time breakdown caused by a rare confluence of events that conspired to create a bad result? In our view, it was neither.

The failures we found in Iraq are not repeated everywhere. The Intelligence Community played a key role, for example, in getting Libya to renounce weapons of mass destruction and in exposing the long-running A.Q. Khan nuclear proliferation network. It is engaged in imaginative, successful (and highly classified) operations in many parts of the world. Tactical support to counterterrorism efforts is excellent, and there are signs of a boldness that would have been unimaginable before September 11, 2001.

But neither was Iraq a "perfect storm." The flaws we found in the Intelligence Community's Iraq performance are still all too common. Across the board, the Intelligence Community knows disturbingly little about the nuclear programs of many of the world's most dangerous actors. In some cases, it knows less now than it did five or ten years ago. As for biological weapons, despite years of Presidential concern, the Intelligence Community has struggled to address this threat.

To be sure, the Intelligence Community is full of talented, dedicated people. But they seem to be working harder and harder just to maintain a status quo that is increasingly irrelevant to the new challenges presented by weapons of mass destruction. Our collection agencies are often unable to gather intelligence on the very things we care the most about. Too often, analysts simply accept these gaps; they do little to help collectors identify new opportunities, and they do not always tell decisionmakers just how limited their knowledge really is.

Taken together, these shortcomings reflect the Intelligence Community's struggle to confront an environment that has changed radically over the past decade. For almost 50 years after the passage of the National Security Act of 1947, the Intelligence Community's resources were overwhelmingly trained on a single threat—the Soviet Union, its nuclear arsenal, its massive conventional forces, and its activities around the world. By comparison, today's priority intelligence targets are greater in number (there are dozens of entities that could strike a devastating blow against the United States) and are often more diffuse in character (they include not only states but also nebulous transnational terror and proliferation networks). What's more, some of the weapons that would be most dangerous in the hands of terrorists or rogue nations are difficult to detect. Much of the technology, equipment, and materials necessary to develop biological and chemical weapons, for example, also has legitimate commercial applications. Biological weapons themselves can be built in small-scale facilities that are easy to conceal, and weapons-grade uranium can be effectively shielded from traditional detection techniques. At the same time, advances in technology have made the job of technical intelligence collection exceedingly difficult.

The demands of this new environment can only be met by broad and deep change in the Intelligence Community. The Intelligence Community we have today is buried beneath an avalanche of demands for "current intelligence"—the pressing need to meet the tactical requirements of the day. Current intelligence in support of military and other action is necessary, of course. But we also need an Intelligence Community with *strategic* capabilities: it must be equipped to develop long-term plans for penetrating today's difficult targets, and to identify political and social trends shaping the threats that lie over the horizon. We can imagine no threat that demands greater strategic focus from the Intelligence Community than that posed by nuclear, biological, and chemical weapons.

The Intelligence Community is also fragmented, loosely managed, and poorly coordinated; the 15 intelligence organizations are a "Community" in name only and rarely act with a unity of purpose. What we need is an Intelligence Community that is *integrated*: the Community's leadership must be capable of allocating and directing the Community's resources in a coordinated way. The strengths of our distinct collection agencies must be brought to bear together on the most difficult intelligence problems. At the same time we need a Community that preserves diversity of analysis, and that encourages structured debate among agencies and analysts over the interpretation of information.

Perhaps above all, the Intelligence Community is too slow to change the way it does business. It is reluctant to use new human and technical collection methods; it is behind the curve in apply-

ing cutting-edge technologies; and it has not adapted its personnel practices and incentives structures to fit the needs of a new job
market. What we need is an Intelligence Community that is flexible—able to respond nimbly to an ever-shifting threat environment and to the rapid pace of today's technological changes.

In short, to succeed in confronting today's and tomorrow's
threats, the Intelligence Community must be transformed—a goal
that would be difficult to meet even in the best of all possible
worlds. And we do not live in the best of worlds. The CIA and
NSA may be sleek and omniscient in the movies, but in real life
they and other intelligence agencies are vast government bureaucracies. They are bureaucracies filled with talented people and
armed with sophisticated technological tools, but talent and tools
do not suspend the iron laws of bureaucratic behavior. Like government bodies everywhere, intelligence agencies are prone to develop self-reinforcing, risk averse cultures that take outside advice
badly. While laudable steps were taken to improve our intelligence
agencies after September 11, 2001, the agencies have done less in
response to the failures over Iraq, and we believe that many within
those agencies do not accept the conclusion that we reached after
our year of study: that the Community needs fundamental change
if it is to successfully confront the threats of the 21st century.

We are not the first to say this. Indeed, commission after commission has identified some of the same fundamental failings we
see in the Intelligence Community, usually to little effect. The Intelligence Community is a closed world, and many insiders admitted to us that *it has an almost perfect record of resisting external
recommendations.*

But the present moment offers an unprecedented opportunity
to overcome this resistance. About halfway through our inquiry,
Congress passed the *Intelligence Reform and Terrorism Prevention
Act of 2004*, which became a sort of a deus ex machina in our deliberations. The act created a Director of National Intelligence
(DNI). The DNI's role could have been a purely coordinating position, with a limited staff and authority to match. Or it could
have been something closer to a "Secretary of Intelligence," with
full authority over the principal intelligence agencies and clear responsibility for their actions—which also might well have been

consistent with a small bureaucratic superstructure. In the end, the DNI created by the intelligence reform legislation was neither of these things; the office is given broad responsibilities but only ambiguous authorities. While we might have chosen a different solution, we are not writing on a blank slate. So our focus has been in large part on how to make the new intelligence structure work, and in particular on giving the DNI tools (and support staff) to match his large responsibilities.

We are mindful, however, that there is a serious risk in creating too large a bureaucratic structure to serve the DNI: the risk that decisionmaking in the field, which sometimes requires quick action, will be improperly delayed. Balancing these two imperatives—necessary agility of operational execution and thoughtful coordination of intelligence activities—is, in our view, the DNI's greatest challenge.

In considering organizational issues, we did not delude ourselves that organizational structure alone can solve problems. More than many parts of government, the culture of the Intelligence Community is formed in the field, where organizational changes at headquarters are felt only lightly. We understand the limits of organizational change, and many of our recommendations go beyond organizational issues and would, if enacted, directly affect the way that intelligence is collected and analyzed. But we regret that we were not able to make such detailed proposals for some of the most important technical collection agencies, such as NSA and NGA. For those agencies, and for the many other issues that we could only touch upon, we must trust that our broader institutional recommendations will enable necessary reform. The DNI that we envision will have the budget and management tools to dig deep into the culture of each agency and to force changes where needed.

This Overview—and, in far more detail, the report that follows—offers our conclusions on what needs to be done. We begin by describing the results of our case studies—which include Iraq, Libya, Afghanistan, and others—and the lessons they teach about the Intelligence Community's current capabilities and weaknesses. We then offer our recommendations for reform based upon those lessons.

Three final notes before proceeding. First, our main tasks were to find out how the Intelligence Community erred in Iraq and to recommend changes to avoid such errors in the future. This is a task that often lends itself to hubris and to second-guessing, and we have been humbled by the difficult judgements that had to be made about Iraq and its weapons programs. We are humbled too by the complexity of the management and technical challenges intelligence professionals face today. We recommend substantial changes, and we believe deeply that such changes are necessary, but we recognize that other reasonable observers could come to a different view on some of these questions.

Second, no matter how much we improve the Intelligence Community, weapons of mass destruction will continue to pose an enormous threat. Intelligence will always be imperfect and, as history persuades us, surprise can never be completely prevented. Moreover, we cannot expect spies, satellites, and analysts to constitute our only defense. As our biological weapons recommendations make abundantly clear, all national capabilities   regulatory, military, and diplomatic—must be used to combat proliferation.

Finally, we emphasize two points about the scope of this Commission's charter, particularly with respect to the Iraq question. First, we were not asked to determine whether Saddam Hussein had weapons of mass destruction. That was the mandate of the Iraq Survey Group; our mission is to investigate the reasons why the Intelligence Community's pre-war assessments were so different from what the Iraq Survey Group found after the war. Second, we were not authorized to investigate how policymakers used the intelligence assessments they received from the Intelligence Community. Accordingly, while we interviewed a host of current and former policymakers during the course of our investigation, the purpose of those interviews was to learn about how the Intelligence Community reached and communicated its judgments about Iraq's weapons programs—not to review how policymakers subsequently used that information.

# Looking Back:
# Case Studies in Failure and Success

Our first task was to evaluate the Intelligence Community's performance in assessing the nuclear, biological, and chemical weapons activities of three countries: Iraq, Afghanistan, and Libya. In addition, we studied U.S. capabilities against other pressing intelligence problems—including Iran, North Korea, Russia, China, and terrorism. We wanted a range of studies so we would not judge the Intelligence Community solely on its handling of Iraq, which was—however important—a single intelligence target. In all, the studies paint a representative picture. It is the picture of an Intelligence Community that urgently needs to be changed.

## *Iraq: An Overview*

In October 2002, at the request of members of Congress, the National Intelligence Council produced a National Intelligence Estimate (NIE)—the most authoritative intelligence assessment produced by the Intelligence Community—which concluded that Iraq was reconstituting its nuclear weapons program and was actively pursuing a nuclear device. According to the exhaustive study of the Iraq Survey Group, this assessment was almost completely wrong. The NIE said that Iraq's biological weapons capability was larger and more advanced than before the Gulf War and that Iraq possessed mobile biological weapons production facilities. This was wrong. The NIE further stated that Iraq had renewed production of chemical weapons, including mustard, sarin, GF, and VX, and that it had accumulated chemical stockpiles of between 100 and 500 metric tons. All of this was also wrong. Finally, the NIE concluded that Iraq had unmanned aerial vehicles that were probably intended for the delivery of biological weapons, and ballistic missiles that had ranges greater than the United Nations' permitted 150 kilometer range. In truth, the aerial vehicles were not for biological weapons; some of Iraq's missiles were, however, capable of traveling more than 150 kilometers. The Intelligence Community's Iraq assessments were, in short, riddled with errors.

Contrary to what some defenders of the Intelligence Community have since asserted, these errors were not the result of a few harried months in 2002. Most of the fundamental errors were made and communicated to policymakers well before the now-infamous NIE of October 2002, and were not corrected in the months between the NIE and the start of the war. They were not isolated or random failings. Iraq had been an intelligence challenge at the forefront of U.S. attention for over a decade. It was a known adversary that had already fought one war with the United States and seemed increasingly likely to fight another. But, after ten years of effort, the Intelligence Community still had no good intelligence on the status of Iraq's weapons programs. Our full report examines these issues in detail. Here we limit our discussion to the central lessons to be learned from this episode.

The first lesson is that the Intelligence Community cannot analyze and disseminate information that it does not have. The Community's Iraq assessment was crippled by its inability to collect meaningful intelligence on Iraq's nuclear, biological, and chemical weapons programs. The second lesson follows from the first: lacking good intelligence, analysts and collectors fell back on old assumptions and inferences drawn from Iraq's past behavior and intentions.

The Intelligence Community had learned a hard lesson after the 1991 Gulf War, which revealed that the Intelligence Community's pre-war assessments had underestimated Iraq's nuclear program and had failed to identify all of its chemical weapons storage sites. Shaken by the magnitude of their errors, intelligence analysts were determined not to fall victim again to the same mistake. This tendency was only reinforced by later events. Saddam acted to the very end like a man with much to hide. And the dangers of underestimating our enemies were deeply underscored by the attacks of September 11, 2001.

Throughout the 1990s, therefore, the Intelligence Community assumed that Saddam's Iraq was up to no good—that Baghdad had maintained its nuclear, biological, and chemical technical expertise, had kept its biological and chemical weapons production capabilities, and possessed significant stockpiles of chemical agents and weapons precursors. Since Iraq's leadership had not changed since 1991, the Intelligence Community also believed that these capabilities would be further revved up as soon as inspectors left Iraq. Saddam's continuing cat-and-mouse parrying with international inspectors only hardened these assumptions.

These experiences contributed decisively to the Intelligence Community's erroneous National Intelligence Estimate of October 2002. That is not to say that its fears and assumptions were foolish or even unreasonable. At some point, however, these premises stopped being working hypotheses and became more or less unrebuttable conclusions; worse, the intelligence system became too willing to find confirmations of them in evidence that should have been recognized at the time to be of dubious reliability. Collectors and analysts too readily accepted any evidence that supported their theory that Iraq had stockpiles and was developing weapons programs, and they explained away or simply disregarded evidence that pointed in the other direction.

Even in hindsight, those assumptions have a powerful air of common sense. If the Intelligence Community's estimate and other pre-war intelligence had relied principally and explicitly on inferences the Community drew from Iraq's past conduct, the estimate would still have been wrong, but it would have been far more defensible. For good reason, it was hard to conclude that Saddam Hussein had indeed abandoned his weapons programs. But a central flaw of the NIE is that it took these defensible assumptions and swathed them in the mystique of intelligence, providing secret information that seemed to support them but was in fact nearly worthless, if not misleading. The NIE simply didn't communicate how weak the underlying intelligence was.

This was, moreover, a problem that was not limited to the NIE. Our review found that after the publication of the October 2002 NIE but before Secretary of State Colin Powell's February 2003 address to the United Nations, intelligence officials within the CIA failed to convey to policymakers new information casting serious doubt on the reliability of a human intelligence source known as "Curveball." This occurred despite the pivotal role

Curveball's information played in the Intelligence Community's assessment of Iraq's biological weapons programs, and in spite of Secretary Powell's efforts to strip every dubious piece of information out of his proposed speech. In this instance, once again, the Intelligence Community failed to give policymakers a full understanding of the frailties of the intelligence on which they were relying.

Finally, we closely examined the possibility that intelligence analysts were pressured by policymakers to change their judgments about Iraq's nuclear, biological, and chemical weapons programs. The analysts who worked Iraqi weapons issues universally agreed that in no instance did political pressure cause them to skew or alter any of their analytical judgments. That said, it is hard to deny the conclusion that intelligence analysts worked in an environment that did not encourage skepticism about the conventional wisdom.

## Other Case Studies: An Overview

Our remaining case studies present a more mixed picture. On the positive side, Libya is fundamentally a success story. The Intelligence Community assessed correctly the state of Libya's nuclear and chemical weapons programs, and the Intelligence Community's use of new techniques to penetrate the A.Q. Khan network allowed the U.S. government to pressure Libya into dismantling those programs. In counterterrorism, the Intelligence Community has made great strides since September 11, in particular with respect to tactical operations overseas. These successes stemmed from isolated efforts that need to be replicated in other areas of intelligence; in the case of Libya, from innovative collection techniques and, in the case of terrorism, from an impressive fusion of interagency intelligence capabilities.

But we also reviewed the state of the Intelligence Community's knowledge about the unconventional weapons programs of several countries that pose current proliferation threats, including Iran, North Korea, China, and Russia. We cannot discuss many of our findings from these studies in our unclassified report, but we can say here that we found that we have only limited access to critical information about several of these high-priority intelligence targets.

## Lessons Learned from the Case Studies

Our case studies revealed failures and successes that ran the gamut of the intelligence process. Although each of these studies is covered in far greater detail in the report itself, we include here a summary of the central lessons we drew from them.

*Poor target development: not getting intelligence on the issues we care about most.* You can't analyze intelligence that you don't have—and our case studies resoundingly demonstrate how little we know about some of our highest priority intelligence targets. It is clear that in today's context the traditional collection techniques employed by individual collection agencies have lost much of their power to surprise our adversaries. The successful penetrations of "hard targets" that we did find were usually the result either of an innovative collection technique or of a creative integration of collection capabilities across agencies. In general, however, the Intelligence Community has not developed the long-term, coordinated collection strategies that are necessary to penetrate today's intelligence targets.

*Lack of rigorous analysis.* Long after the Community's assessment of Iraq had begun to fall apart, one of the main drafters of the NIE told us that, if he had to grade it, he would still give the NIE an "A." By that, he presumably meant that the NIE fully met the standards for analysis that the Community had set for itself. That is the problem. The scope and quality of analysis has eroded badly in the Intelligence Community and it must be restored. In part, this is a matter of tradecraft and training; in part, too, it is a matter of expertise.

Analytic "tradecraft"—the way analysts think, research, evaluate evidence, write, and communicate—must be strengthened. In many instances, we found finished intelligence that was loosely reasoned, ill-supported, and poorly communicated. Perhaps most worrisome, we found too many analytic products that obscured how little the Intelligence Community actually knew about an issue and how much their conclusions rested on inference and assumptions. We believe these tendencies must be reversed if decisionmakers are to have confidence in the intelligence they receive. And equally important, analysts must be willing to admit what they don't know in order to focus future collection efforts. Conversely, policymakers must be prepared to accept uncertainties and qualifications in intelligence judgments and not expect greater precision than the evaluated data permits.

Good "tradecraft" without expertise, however, will only get you so far. Our case studies identified areas in which the Community's level of expertise was far below what it should be. In several instances, the Iraq assessments rested on failures of technical analysis that should have been obvious at the time—failure to understand facts about weapons technology, for example, or failures to detect obvious forgeries. Technical expertise, particularly relating to weapons systems, has fallen sharply in the past ten years. And in other areas, such as biotechnology, the Intelligence Community is well behind the private sector.

But the problem of expertise goes well beyond technical knowledge. During the Cold War, the Intelligence Community built up an impressive body of expertise on Soviet society, organization, and ideology, as well as on the Soviet threat. Regrettably, no equivalent talent pool exists today for the study of Islamic extremism. In some cases, the security clearance process limits the Intelligence Community's ability to recruit analysts with contacts among relevant groups and with experience living overseas. Similarly, some security rules limit the ways in which analysts can develop substantive expertise. Finally, poor training or bad habits lead analysts to rely too much on secret information and to use non-clandestine and public information too little. Non-clandestine sources of information are critical to understanding societal, cultural, and political trends, but they are insufficiently utilized.

*Lack of political context—and imagination.* The October 2002 NIE contained an extensive technical analysis of Iraq's suspected weapons programs but little serious analysis of the socio-political situation in Iraq, or the motives and intentions of Iraqi leadership—which, in a dictatorship like Iraq, really meant understanding Saddam. It seems unlikely to us that weapons experts used to combing reports for tidbits on technical programs would ever have asked: "Is Saddam bluffing?" or "Could he have decided to suspend his weapons programs until sanctions are lifted?" But an analyst steeped in Iraq's politics and culture at least might have asked those questions, and, of course, those turn out to be the questions that could have led the Intelligence Community closer to the truth. In that respect, the analysts displayed a lack of imagination. The Iraq example also reflects the Intelligence Community's increasing tendency to separate regional, technical, and (now) terrorism analysis—a trend that is being exacerbated by the gravitational pull toward centers like the National Counterterrorism Center (NCTC).

*Overemphasis on and underperformance in daily intelligence products.* As problematic as the October 2002 NIE was, it was not the Community's biggest analytic failure on Iraq. Even more misleading was the river of intelligence that flowed from the CIA to top policymakers over long periods of time—in the President's Daily Brief (PDB) and in its more widely distributed companion, the Senior Executive Intelligence Brief (SEIB). These daily reports were, if anything, more alarmist and less nuanced than the NIE. It was not that the intelligence was markedly different. Rather, it was that the PDBs and SEIBs, with their attention-grabbing headlines and drumbeat of repetition, left an impression of many corroborating reports where in fact there were very few sources. And in other instances, intelligence suggesting the existence of weapons programs was conveyed to senior policymakers, but later information casting doubt upon the validity of that intelligence was not. In ways both subtle and not so subtle, the daily reports seemed to be "selling" intelligence—in order to keep its customers, or at least the First Customer, interested.

*Inadequate information sharing.* There is little doubt that, at least in the context of counterterrorism, information sharing has improved substantially since September 11. This is in no small part due to the creation of the Terrorist Threat Integration Center (now NCTC) and the increased practice of housing collectors and analysts together, which provides a real-world solution to some of the bureaucratic and institutional barriers that exist between the big intelligence-collecting agencies. But in the three and a half years since September 11, this push to share information has not spread to other areas, including counterproliferation, where sharing is also badly needed. Furthermore, even in the counterterrorism context, information sharing still depends too much on physical co-location and personal relationships as opposed to integrated, Community-wide information networks. Equally problematic, individual departments and agencies continue to act as though they own the information they collect, forcing other agencies to pry information from them. Similarly, much information deemed "operational" by the CIA and FBI isn't routinely shared, even though analysts have repeatedly stressed its importance. All of this reveals that extensive work remains yet to be done.

*Poor human intelligence.* When the October 2002 NIE was written the United States had little human intelligence on Iraq's nuclear, biological, and chemical weapons programs and virtually no human intelligence on leadership intentions. While classification prevents us from getting into the details, the picture is much the same with respect to other dangerous threats. We recognize that espionage is always chancy at best; 50 years of pounding away at the Soviet Union resulted in only a handful of truly important human sources. Still, we have no choice but to do better. Old approaches to human intelligence alone are not the answer. Countries that threaten us are well aware of our human intelligence services' modus operandi and they know how to counter it. More of the same is unlikely to work. Innovation is needed. The CIA deserves credit for its efforts to discover and penetrate the A.Q. Khan network, and it needs to put more emphasis on other innovative human intelligence methods.

Worse than having no human sources is being seduced by a human source who is telling lies. In fact, the Community's position on Iraq's biological weapons program was largely determined by sources who were telling lies—most notably a source provided by a foreign intelligence service through the Defense Intelligence Agency. Why DIA and the rest of the Community didn't find out that the source was lying is a story of poor asset validation practices and the problems inherent in relying on semi-cooperative liaison services. That the NIE (and other reporting) didn't make clear to policymakers how heavily it relied on a single source that no American intelligence officer had ever met, and about whose reliability several intelligence professionals had expressed serious concern, is a damning comment on the Intelligence Community's practices.

*The challenge to traditional signals intelligence.* Signals intelligence—the interception of radio, telephone, and computer communications—has historically been a primary source of good intelligence. But changes in telecommunications technology have brought new challenges. This was the case in Iraq, where the Intelligence Community lost access to important aspects of Iraqi communications, and it remains the case elsewhere. We offer a brief additional discussion of some of the modern challenges facing signals intelligence in our classified report, but we cannot discuss this information in an unclassified format.

Regaining signals intelligence access must be a top priority. The collection agencies are working hard to restore some of the access that they have lost; and they've had some successes. And again, many of these recent steps in the right direction are the result of innovative examples of cross-agency cooperation. In addition, successful signals intelligence will require a sustained research and development effort to bring cutting-edge technology to operators and analysts. Success on this front will require greater willingness to accept financial costs, political risks, and even human casualties.

*Declining utility of traditional imagery intelligence against unconventional weapons programs.* The imagery collection systems that were designed largely to work against the Soviet Union's military didn't work very well against Iraq's unconventional weapons program, and our review found that they aren't working very well against other priority targets, either. That's because our adversaries are getting better at denial and deception, and because the threat is changing. Again, we offer details about the challenges to imagery intelligence in our classified report that we cannot provide here.

Making the problem even more difficult, there is little that traditional imagery can tell us about chemical and biological facilities. Biological and chemical weapons programs for the most part can exist inside commercial buildings with no suspicious signatures. This means that we can get piles of incredibly sharp photos of an adversary's chemical factories, and we still will not know much about its chemical weapons programs. We can still see a lot—and imagery intelligence remains valuable in many contexts, including support to military operations and when used in conjunction with other collection disciplines—but too often what we can see doesn't tell us what we need to know about nuclear, biological, and chemical weapons.

*Measurement and signature intelligence (MASINT) is not sufficiently developed.* The collection of technologies known as MASINT, which includes a virtual grab bag of advanced collection and analytic methods, is not yet making a significant contribution to our intelligence efforts. In Iraq, MASINT played a negligible role. As in other contexts, we believe that the Intelligence Community should continue to pursue new technology aggressively—whether it is called MASINT, imagery, or signals intelligence. Innovation will be necessary to defeat our adversaries' denial and deception.

*An absence of strong leadership.* For over a year, despite unambiguous presidential direction, a turf battle raged between CIA's Counterterrorist Center (CTC) and the Terrorist Threat Integration Center (now NCTC). The two organizations fought over roles, responsibilities, and resources, and the Intelligence Community's leadership was unable to solve the problem. The intelligence reform act may put an end to this particular conflict, but we believe that the story reflects a larger, more pervasive problem within the Intelligence Community: the difficulty of making a decision and imposing the consequences on all agencies throughout the Community. Time and time again we have uncovered instances like this, where powerful agencies fight to a debilitating stalemate masked as consensus, because no one in the Community has been able to make a decision and then make it stick. The best hope for filling this gap is an empowered DNI.

# Looking Forward:
# Our Recommendations For Change

Our case studies collectively paint a picture of an Intelligence Community with serious deficiencies that span the intelligence process. Stated succinctly, it has too little integration and too little innovation to succeed in the 21st century. It rarely adopts integrated strategies for penetrating high-priority targets; decision-makers lack authority to resolve agency disputes; and it develops too few innovative ways of gathering intelligence.

This section summarizes our major recommendations on how to change this state of affairs so that full value can be derived from the many bright, dedicated, and deeply committed professionals within the Intelligence Community. We begin at the top, and suggest how to use the opportunity presented by the new intelligence reform legislation to bring better integration and management to the Intelligence Community. Our management recommendations are developed in greater detail in Chapter Six of our report. We next offer recommendations that would improve intelligence collection (Chapter 7) and analysis (Chapter 8). Then we examine several specific and important intelligence challenges—improving information sharing (Chapter 9); integrating domestic and foreign intelligence in a way that both satisfies national security imperatives and safeguards civil liberties (Chapter 10); organizing the Community's counterintelligence mission (Chapter 11); and a largely classified chapter on managing covert action (Chapter 12). We then devote a stand-alone chapter to examining the most dangerous unconventional weapons challenges the Intelligence Community faces today and offer specific prescriptions for improving our intelligence capabilities against these threats (Chapter 13).

*Leadership and Management:*
*Forging an Integrated Intelligence Community*

A former senior Defense Department official described today's Intelligence Community as "not so much poorly managed as unmanaged." We agree. Everywhere we looked, we found important (and obvious) issues of interagency coordination that went unattended, sensible Community-wide proposals blocked by pockets of resistance, and critical disputes left to fester. Strong interagency cooperation was more likely to result from bilateral "treaties" between big agencies than from Community-level management. This ground was well-plowed by the 9/11 Commission and by several other important assessments of the Intelligence Community over the past decade.

In the chapter of our report devoted to management (Chapter 6), we offer detailed recommendations that we believe will equip the new Director of National Intelligence to forge today's loose confederation of 15 separate intelligence operations into a real, integrated Intelligence Community. A short summary of our more important management recommendations follows:

- *Strong leadership and management of the Intelligence Community are indispensable.* Virtually every senior intelligence official acknowledged the difficulty of leading and managing the Intelligence Community. Along with acting as the President's principal intelligence advisor, this will be the DNI's main job. His success in that job will determine the fate of many other necessary reforms. We thus recommend ways in which the DNI can use his limited, but not insignificant, authorities over money and people. No matter what, the DNI will not be able to run the Intelligence Community alone. He will need to create a management structure that allows him to see deep into the Intelligence Community's component agencies, and he will need to work closely with the other cabinet secretaries—especially the Secretary of Defense—for whom several Intelligence Community agencies also work. New procedures are particularly needed in the budget area, where today's Intelligence Community has a wholly inadequate Planning, Programming, and Budgeting System.

- *Organize around missions.* One of the most significant problems we identified in today's Intelligence Community is a lack of cross-Community focus on priority intelligence missions. By this, we mean that in most cases there is not one office, or one individual, who is responsible for making sure the Intelligence Community is doing all it can to collect and analyze intelligence on a subject like proliferation, or a country like Iran. Instead, intelligence agencies allocate their scarce resources among intelligence priorities in ways that seem sensible to them but are not optimal from a Community-wide perspective. The DNI needs management structures and processes that ensure a strategic, Community-level focus on priority intelligence missions. The specific device we propose is the creation of several "Mission Managers" on the DNI staff who are responsible for developing strategies for all aspects of intelligence relating to a priority intelligence target: the Mission Manager for China, for instance, would be responsible for driving collection on the China target, watching over China analysis, and serving as a clearinghouse for senior policymakers seeking China expertise.

- *Establish a National Counter Proliferation Center.* The new intelligence legislation creates one "national center"—the National Counterterrorism Center (NCTC)—and suggests the creation of a second, similar center devoted to counterproliferation issues. We agree that a National Counter Proliferation Center (NCPC) should be established but believe that it should be fundamentally different in character from the NCTC. The NCTC is practically a separate agency; its large staff is responsible not only for conducting counterterrorism analysis and intelligence gathering but also for "strategic operational planning" in support of counterterrorism policy. In contrast, we believe that the NCPC should be a relatively small center (i.e., fewer than 100 people); it should primarily play a *management and coordination* function by overseeing analysis and collection on nuclear, biological, and chemical weapons across the Intelligence Community. In addition, although we agree that government-wide strategic planning is required to confront proliferation threats, we believe that entities other than the NCPC—such as a Joint Interagency Task Force we propose to coordinate interdiction efforts—should perform this function.

- *Build a modern workforce.* The intelligence reform legislation grants the DNI substantial personnel authorities. In our view, these authorities come none too soon. The Intelligence Community has difficulty recruiting and retaining individuals with critically important skill sets—such as technical and scientific expertise, and facility with foreign languages—and has not adapted well to the diverse cultures and settings in which today's intelligence experts must operate. We propose the creation of a new human resources authority in the Office of the DNI to develop Community-wide personnel policies and overcome these systemic shortcomings. We also offer specific proposals aimed at encouraging "joint" assignments between intelligence agencies, improving job training at all stages of an intelligence professional's career, and building a better personnel incentive structure.

- *Create mechanisms for sustained oversight from outside the Intelligence Community—and for self-examination from the inside.* Many sound past proposals for intelligence reform have withered on the vine. Either the Intelligence Community is inherently resistant to outside recommendations, or it lacks the institutional capacity to implement them. In either case, sustained external oversight is necessary. We recommend using the new Joint Intelligence Community Council—which comprises the DNI and the cabinet secretaries with intelligence responsibilities—as a high-level "consumer council." We also recommend the President's Foreign Intelligence Advisory Board play a more substantial advisory role. Like others before us, we suggest that the President urge Congress to reform its own procedures to provide better oversight. In particular, we recommend that the House and Senate intelligence committees create focused oversight subcommittees, that the Congress create an intelligence appropriations subcommittee and reduce the Intelligence Community's reliance on supplemental funding, and that the Senate intelligence committee be given the same authority over joint military intelligence programs and tactical intelligence programs that the House intelligence committee now exercises. Finally—and perhaps most importantly—we recommend that the DNI create mechanisms to ensure that the Intelligence Community conducts "lessons learned" and after-action studies so that it will be better equipped to identify its own strengths and weaknesses.

## Additional Leadership and Management Recommendations

In addition to those described above, Chapter Six of our report offers recommendations concerning:

- How to build a coordinated process for "target development"—that is, the directing of collection resources toward priority intelligence subjects;

- How to spur innovation outside individual collection agencies;

- How the DNI might handle the difficult challenges of integrating intelligence from at home and abroad, and of coordinating activities and procedures with the Department of Defense; and

- How the DNI might organize the office of the DNI to fit needed leadership and management functions into the framework created by the intelligence reform legislation.

## Integrated and Innovative Collection

The intelligence failure in Iraq did not begin with faulty analysis. It began with a sweeping collection failure. The Intelligence Community simply couldn't collect good information about Iraq's nuclear, biological, or chemical programs. Regrettably, the same can be said today about other important targets, none of which will ever be easy targets—but we can and should do better.

Urging each individual collection agency to do a better job is not the answer. Where progress has been made against such targets, the key has usually been more integration and more innovation in collecting intelligence. As a result, we recommend the following:

- *Create a new Intelligence Community process for managing collection as an "integrated enterprise."* In order to gather intelligence effectively, the Intelligence Community must develop and buy sophisticated technical collection systems, create strategies for focusing those systems on priority targets, process and exploit the data that these systems collect, and plan for the acquisition of future systems. Today, each of these functions is performed primarily within individual collection agencies, often with little or no Community-level direction or interagency coordination. We propose that the DNI create what we call an "integrated collection enterprise" for the Intelligence Community that is, a management structure in which the Community's decentralized collection capabilities are harmonized with intelligence priorities and deployed in a coordinated way.

- *Create a new Human Intelligence Directorate.* Both the Defense Department and the FBI are substantially increasing their human intelligence activities abroad, which heightens the risk that intelligence operations will not be properly coordinated with the CIA's human espionage operations, run by its Directorate of Operations (DO). The human intelligence activities of the Defense Department and the FBI should continue, but in the world of foreign espionage, a lack of coordination can have dangerous, even fatal, consequences. To address this pressing problem, we suggest the creation of a new Human Intelligence Directorate within the CIA, to which the present DO would be subordinate, to ensure the coordination of all U.S. agencies conducting human intelligence operations overseas. In addition to this coordination role, the Human Intelligence Directorate would serve as the focal point for Community-wide human intelligence issues, including helping to develop a national human intelligence strategy, broadening the scope of human intelligence activities, integrating (where appropriate) collection and reporting systems, and establishing Community-wide standards for training and tradecraft.

- *Develop innovative human intelligence techniques.* The CIA's Directorate of Operations is one of the Intelligence Community's elite and storied organizations. However, the DO has remained largely wedded to the traditional model—a model that does not meet the challenges posed by terrorist organizations and nations that are "denied areas" for U.S. personnel. Accordingly, we recommend the establishment of an "Innovation Center" within the CIA's new Human Intelligence Directorate—but not within the DO. This center would spur the use of new and non-traditional methods of collecting human intelligence. In the collection chapter of our report, we also detail several new methods for collecting human intelligence that in our judgment should either be explored or used more extensively.

- *Create an Open Source Directorate within the CIA.* We are convinced that analysts who use open source information can be more effective than those who don't. Regrettably, however, the Intelligence Community does not have an entity that collects, processes, and makes available to analysts the mass of open source information that is available in the world today. We therefore recommend the creation of an Open Source Directorate at the CIA. The directorate's mission would be to deploy sophisticated information technology to make open source information available across the Community. This would, at a minimum, mean gathering and storing digital newspapers and periodicals that are available only temporarily on the Internet and giving Intelligence Community staff easy (and secure) access to Internet materials. In addition, because we believe that part of the problem is analyst resistance, not lack of collection, we recommend that some of the new analysts allocated to CIA be specially trained to use open sources and then to act as open source "evange-analysts" who can jumpstart the open source initiative by showing its value in addressing particular analytic problems. All of this, we believe, will help improve the Intelligence Community's surprisingly poor "feel" for cultural and political issues in the countries that concern policymakers most. The Open Source Directorate should also be the primary test bed for new information technology because the security constraints—while substantial—are lower for open source than for classified material.

• *Reconsider MASINT. Measurements and signatures can offer important intelligence about nuclear, biological, and chemical weapons.* But the tools we use to collect these measurements and signatures—tools collectively referred to within the intelligence community as "MASINT"—do not obviously constitute a single discipline. In a world of specialized collection agencies, there is reason to suspect that these orphaned technologies may have been under-funded and under-utilized. We recommend that the DNI take responsibility for developing and coordinating new intelligence technologies, including those that now go under the title MASINT. This could be done by a special coordinator, or as part of the DNI's Office of Science and Technology. The DNI's office does not need to directly control MASINT collection. Rather, we recommend that individual collection agencies assume responsibility for aspects of MASINT that fall naturally into their bailiwicks. At the same time, the DNI's designated representative would promote and monitor the status of new technical intelligence programs throughout the Intelligence Community to ensure that they are fully implemented and given the necessary attention.

## Additional Collection Recommendations

In addition to those described above, Chapter Seven of our report offers recommendations concerning:

• Developing new human and technical collection methods;

• Professionalizing human intelligence across the Intelligence Community;

• Creating a larger and better-trained human intelligence officer cadre;

- Amending the Foreign Intelligence Surveillance Act to extend the duration of certain forms of electronic surveillance against non-U.S. persons, to ease administrative burdens on NSA and the Department of Justice; and

- Improving the protection of sources and methods by reducing authorized and unauthorized disclosures.

## Transforming Analysis

Integrated, innovative collection is just the beginning of what the Intelligence Community needs. Some of the reforms already discussed, particularly the DNI-level "Mission Managers," will improve analysis. But much more is needed. In particular, analytic expertise must be deepened, intelligence gaps reduced, and existing information made more usable—all of which would improve the quality of intelligence.

As an overarching point, however, the Intelligence Community must recognize the central role of analysts in the intelligence process. Needless to say, analysts are the people who analyze intelligence, put it in context, and communicate the intelligence to the people who need it. But in addition, analysts are the repositories for what the Intelligence Community doesn't know, and they must clearly convey these gaps to decisionmakers—as well as to collectors so that the Intelligence Community does everything it can to fill the holes. (Analysts will also play an increasingly prominent role in information security, as they "translate" intelligence from the most sensitive of sources to a variety of consumers, ranging from state and local first responders to senior policymakers.) To enable analysts to fulfill these roles, we recommend the following:

- *Empower Mission Managers to coordinate analytic efforts on a given topic.* The Mission Managers we propose would serve as the focal point for all aspects of the intelligence effort on a particular issue. They would be aware of the analytic expertise in various intelligence agencies, assess the quality of analytic products, identify strategic questions receiving inadequate attention, encourage alternative analysis, and ensure that dissenting views are expressed to intelligence users. When necessary, they would recommend that the DNI use his personnel authorities to move analysts to priority intelligence topics. At the same time, Mission Managers should not be responsible for providing a single, homogenized analytic product to decisionmakers; rather, Mission Managers should be responsible for encouraging alternative analysis and for ensuring that dissenting views are expressed to intelligence customers. In sum, Mission Managers should be able to find the right people and expertise and make sure that the right analysis, including alternative analysis, is getting done.

• Strengthen long-term and strategic analysis. The most common complaint we heard from analysts in the Intelligence Community was that the pressing demand for current intelligence "eats up everything else." Analysts cannot maintain their expertise if they cannot conduct long-term and strategic analysis. Because this malady is so pervasive and has proven so resistant to conventional solutions, we recommend establishing an organization to perform only long-term and strategic analysis under the National Intelligence Council, the Community's existing focal point for interagency long-term analytic efforts. The new unit could serve as a focal point for Community-wide alternative analysis, thereby complementing agency-specific efforts at independent analysis. And although some analysts in this organization would be permanently assigned, at least half would serve only temporarily and would come from all intelligence agencies, including NGA and NSA, as well as from outside the government. Such rotations would reinforce good tradecraft habits, as well as foster a greater sense of Community among analysts and spur collaboration on other projects.

• *Encourage diverse and independent analysis.* We believe that diverse and independent analysis—often referred to as "competitive analysis"—should come from many sources. As we have just noted, we recommend that our proposed long-term research and analysis unit, as well as the National Intelligence Council, conduct extensive independent analysis. In some circumstances there is also a place for a "devil's advocate"—someone appointed to challenge the consensus view. We also think it important that a not-for-profit "sponsored research institute" be created outside the Intelligence Community; such an institute would serve as a critical window into outside expertise, conduct its own research, and reach out to specialists, including academics and technical experts, business and industry leaders, and representatives from the nonprofit sector. Finally, the Intelligence Community should encourage independent analysis throughout its analytic ranks. In our view, this can best be accomplished through the preservation of dispersed analytic resources (as opposed to consolidation in large "centers"), active efforts by Mission Managers to promote independent analysis, and Community-wide training that instills the importance of such analysis.

- *Improve the rigor and "tradecraft" of analysis.* Our studies, and many observers, point to a decline in analytic rigor within the Intelligence Community. Analysts have suffered from weak leadership, insufficient training, and budget cutbacks that led to the loss of our best, most senior analysts. There is no quick fix for tradecraft problems. However, we recommend several steps: increasing analyst training; ensuring that managers and budget-writers allot time and resources for analysts to actually get trained; standardizing good tradecraft practices through the use of a National Intelligence University; creating structures and practices that increase competitive analysis; increasing managerial training for Intelligence Community supervisors; enabling joint and rotational assignment opportunities; ensuring that finished intelligence products are sufficiently transparent so that an analyst's reasoning is visible to intelligence customers; and implementing other changes in human resource policies—such as merit-based-pay—so that the best analysts are encouraged to stay in government service.

- *Communicating intelligence to policymakers.* The best intelligence in the world is worthless unless it is effectively and accurately communicated to those who need it. The Iraq weapons of mass destruction case is a stark example. The daily reports sent to the President and senior policymakers discussing Iraq over many months proved to be disastrously one-sided. We thus offer recommendations on ways in which intelligence products can be enhanced, including how the President's Daily Brief (PDB) might be improved. In this regard, we suggest the elimination of the inherently misleading "headline" summaries in PDBs and other senior policymaker briefs, and that the DNI oversee production of the PDB. To accomplish this, we recommend the DNI create an analytic staff too small to routinely undertake drafting itself, but large enough to have background on many of the issues that are covered by the PDB. The goal would be to enable the DNI to coordinate and oversee the process, without requiring him to take on the heavy—and almost overwhelming—mantle of daily intelligence support to the President. Critically, the DNI's staff would also ensure that the PDB reflects alternative views from the Community to the greatest extent feasible.

We also recommend that the DNI take responsibility, with the President's concurrence, for the three primary sources of intelligence that now reach the President: the PDB, the President's Terrorism Threat Report—a companion publication produced by the NCTC and focused solely on terrorism-related issues—and the briefing by the Director of the FBI. We suggest that the DNI coordinate this intelligence in a manner that eliminates redundancies and ensures that only material that is necessary for the President be included. We think this last point is especially important because we have observed a disturbing trend whereby intelligence is passed to the President (as well as other senior policymakers) not because it requires high-level attention, but because passing the information "up the chain" provides individuals and organizations with bureaucratic cover.

- Demand more from analysts. We urge that policymakers actively probe and question analysts. In our view, such interaction is not "politicization." Analysts should expect such demanding and aggressive testing without—as a matter of principle and professionalism—allowing it to subvert their judgment.

## Additional Analysis Recommendations

In addition to those described above, Chapter Eight of our report offers recommendations concerning:

- Developing technologies capable of exploiting large volumes of foreign language data without the need for human translations;

- Improving career-long analytical and managerial training;

- Creating a database for all finished intelligence, as well as adopting technology to update analysts and decisionmakers when intelligence judgments change;

- Improving the Intelligence Community's science, technology, and weapons expertise;

- Changing the way analysts are hired, promoted, and rewarded; and

- Institutionalizing "lessons learned" procedures to learn from past analytical successes and failures.

## Information Sharing

While the new intelligence reform legislation correctly identifies information sharing as an area where major reforms are necessary, the steps it takes to address the problem raise as many questions as they answer. The legislation creates a new position— a "Program Manager" who sits outside of the Intelligence Community and reports directly to the President—responsible for creating an integrated, government-wide Information Sharing Environment for all "terrorism information." At the same time, the Director of National Intelligence is given responsibility for facilitating information sharing for all intelligence information within the Intelligence Community.

We believe that these two separate statutory information sharing efforts should be harmonized. We are less confident that any particular mechanism is optimal. Perhaps the least bad solution to this tricky problem—short of new legislation—is to require that the Program Manager report to the President through the DNI, and that the Information Sharing Environment be expanded to include all intelligence information, not just intelligence related to terrorism. In recommending this solution, however, we emphasize that information sharing cannot be understood merely as an Intelligence Community endeavor; whoever leads the effort to build the Information Sharing Environment must be sensitive to the importance of distributing necessary information to those who need it both in the non-intelligence components of the federal government, and to relevant state, local, and tribal authorities.

We also make specific recommendations concerning how best to implement the information sharing effort. Among these recommendations are: designating a single official under the DNI who will be responsible for both information sharing and information security, in order to break down cultural and policy barriers that have impeded the development of a shared information space; applying advanced technologies to the Information Sharing Environment to permit more expansive sharing with far greater security protections than currently exist in the Intelligence Community; and establishing clear and consistent Community-wide information sharing and security policies. Last but not least, we recommend that the DNI jettison the phrase "information sharing" itself, which merely reinforces the (incorrect) notion that information is the property of individual intelligence agencies, rather than of the government as a whole.

Finally, we believe it is essential to note the importance of protecting civil liberties in the context of information sharing. We believe that the intelligence reform act provides the framework for appropriate protection of civil liberties in this area, and that all information sharing must be done in accordance with Attorney General guidelines relating to "U.S. persons" information. At the same time, in our view the pursuit of privacy and national security is not a zero-sum game. In fact, as we describe in our report, many of the very same tools that provide counterintelligence protection can be equally valuable in protecting privacy.

## Intelligence at Home: the FBI, Justice, and Homeland Security

Although the FBI has made strides in turning itself into a true collector and analyst of intelligence, it still has a long way to go. The Bureau, among other things, has set up Field Intelligence Groups in each of its 56 field offices and created an Executive Assistant Director for Intelligence with broad responsibility for the FBI's intelligence mission. Yet even FBI officials acknowledge that its collection and analysis capabilities will be a work in progress until at least 2010.

In our view, the biggest challenge is to make the FBI a full participant in the Intelligence Community. This is not just a matter of giving the Bureau new resources and new authority. It must also mean integrating the FBI into a Community that is subject to the DNI's coordination and leadership. Unfortunately, the intelligence reform legislation leaves the FBI's relationship to the DNI especially murky. We recommend that the President make clear that the FBI's intelligence activities are to be fully coordinated with the DNI and the rest of the Community.

- *Create a separate National Security Service within the FBI that includes the Bureau's Counterintelligence and Counterterrorism Divisions, as well as the Directorate of Intelligence.* The intelligence reform act empowers the DNI to lead the Intelligence Community, which includes the FBI's "intelligence elements." Although the statute leaves the term ambiguous, we believe that "elements" must include all of the Bureau's national security-related components—the Intelligence Directorate *and* the Counterterrorism and Counterintelligence Divisions. Anything less and the DNI's ability to coordinate intelligence across our nation's borders will be dangerously inadequate.

Simply granting the DNI authority over the Bureau's current Directorate of Intelligence is, we believe, insufficient. We say this because the Directorate of Intelligence has surprisingly little operational, personnel, and budgetary authority. Currently the directorate has no authority to initiate, terminate, or re-direct any collection or investigative operation in any of the FBI's 56 regional field offices that are scattered throughout the nation or within any of the four operational divisions (Counterintelligence, Counterterrorism, Cyber, and Criminal) at FBI Headquarters. Although the Directorate of Intelligence may "task" the field offices to collect against certain requirements, it has no direct authority to ensure that FBI resources actually carry out these requirements. Its "taskings" are really "askings." Nor does the directorate contain the great bulk of the FBI's intelligence analysts. And the directorate has no clear control over the Bureau's portion of the National Intelligence Program budget, which is largely spent by the Counterterrorism and Counterintelligence Divisions. In short, the intelligence directorate has few, if any, mechanisms for exercising direct authorities over FBI's intelligence collectors or analytic products. With a direct line of authority only to the Bureau's Directorate of Intelligence, the DNI cannot be ensured influence over the Bureau's national security functions, and the FBI will not be fully integrated into the Intelligence Community.

We therefore recommend the creation of a separate National Security Service *within the FBI* that has full authority to manage, direct, and control all Headquarters and Field Office resources engaged in counterintelligence, counterterrorism, and foreign intelligence collection, investigations, operations, and analysis. Critically, this division would then be subject to the same DNI authorities as apply to such Defense agencies as NSA and NGA. Of equal importance, this structure would maintain the Attorney General's oversight of the FBI's activities to ensure the Bureau's compliance with U.S. law. In this sense, the Attorney General's role would be similar to that of the Secretary of Defense, who—even with the appointment of the DNI—continues to oversee Defense Department agencies within the Intelligence Community, like NSA and NGA.

- *Ensure better mechanisms for coordination and cooperation on foreign intelligence collection in the United States.* The expansion of the FBI's intelligence collection and reporting activities over the past few years has engendered turf battles between the CIA and the FBI that have already caused counterproductive conflicts both within and outside of the United States. In particular, the two agencies have clashed over the domestic collection of foreign intelligence—an area in which they have long shared responsibilities. We see no reason to change the status quo dramatically or to expand the FBI's authority over foreign intelligence gathering inside the United States. If unanticipated conflicts emerge, both agencies should be instructed to take their differences to the DNI for resolution. The two agencies' capabilities should complement, rather than compete with, one another. We also expect that such an integrated approach would continue to rely on the existing Attorney General guidelines, which carefully limit the way both agencies operate within the United States, and with regard to U.S. persons overseas. We believe that strong CIA/FBI cooperation and clear guidelines are essential for protection of civil liberties as well as for effective intelligence gathering.

- *Reorient the Department of Justice.* Every agency that has major responsibility for terrorism and intelligence has been overhauled in the past four years. With one exception: at the Department of Justice, the famous "wall" between intelligence and criminal law still lingers, at least on the organization charts. On one side is the Office of Intelligence Policy and Review, which handles Foreign Intelligence Surveillance Court orders—those court orders that permit wiretaps and physical searches for national security reasons. On the other side are two separate sections of the Criminal Division (Counterterrorism and Counterespionage), reporting to two separate Deputy Assistant Attorneys General. This organizational throwback to the 1990s scatters intelligence expertise throughout the Department and in some cases has contributed to errors that hampered intelligence gathering. A single office with responsibility for counterterrorism, counterintelligence, and intelligence investigations would ensure better communication and reduce the tendency to rebuild the wall along bureaucratic lines.

We recommend that these three components (perhaps joined by a fourth Justice Department component that coordinates issues related to transnational crimes) be placed together under the authority of an Assistant Attorney General for National Security who would, like the Assistant Attorney General for the Criminal Division, report either directly to the Deputy Attorney General, or to a newly created Associate Attorney General responsible for both the National Security and Criminal Divisions.

- *Strengthen the Department of Homeland Security's relationship with the Intelligence Community.* The Department of Homeland Security is the primary repository of information about what passes in and out of the country—a critical participant in safeguarding the United States from nuclear, biological, or chemical attack. Yet, since its inception, Homeland Security has faced immense challenges in collecting information effectively, making it available to analysts and users both inside and outside the Department, and bringing intelligence support to law enforcement and first responders who seek to act on such information. We did not conduct a detailed study of Homeland Security's capabilities, but it is clear to us that the department faces challenges in all four roles it plays in the intelligence community— as collector, analyst, disseminator, and customer.

  Among the obstacles confronting Homeland Security, we found during the course of our study that the Department's Immigration and Customs Enforcement still operates under an order inherited from the Treasury Department in the 1980s. The order requires high-level approval for virtually all information sharing and assistance to the Intelligence Community. We think this order should be rescinded, and we believe the DNI should carefully examine how Homeland Security works with the rest of the Intelligence Community.

### Counterintelligence

Every intelligence service on the planet wants to steal secrets from the last remaining superpower. But as other nations increase their intelligence operations against the United States, U.S. counterintelligence has been in a defensive crouch—fractured, narrowly focused, and lacking national direction. This may change as a result of the President's newly announced counterintelligence strategy. The good ideas in the strategy must, however, still be put into practice.

CIA does counterintelligence abroad, but its capabilities are limited. The FBI's counterintelligence efforts within the United States are well-staffed, but hardly strategic in their nature. Finally, the Defense Department's counterintelligence capabilities lack effective cross-department integration and direction. To address these concerns, we recommend four steps to strengthen counterintelligence: the empowerment of the nation's chief counterintelligence officer, the National Counterintelligence Executive (NCIX); the development of a new CIA capability for enhancing counterintelligence abroad; the centralization of the Defense Department's counterintelligence functions; and, as suggested earlier, bringing the FBI into the Intelligence Community to ensure that its robust counterintelligence capabilities are employed in line with the DNI's priorities. Moreover, all of these efforts must focus greater attention on the technical aspects of counterintelligence, as our adversaries shift from human spying to attempting to penetrate our information infrastructure.

### Covert Action

If used in a careful and limited way, covert action can serve as a more subtle and surgical tool than forms of acknowledged employment of U.S. power and influence. As part of our overall review of the Intelligence Community, we conducted a careful study of U.S. covert action capabilities. Our findings were included in a short, separate chapter of our classified report. Regrettably, this area is so heavily classified that we could not include a chapter on the subject in our unclassified report.

We will, however, state here—at a necessarily high level of generality—some of our overall conclusions on covert action. At the outset, we note that we found current covert action programs in the counterproliferation and counterterrorism areas to be energetic, innovative, and well-executed within the limits of their authority and funding. Yet some critically important programs are hobbled by lack of sustained strategic planning, insufficient commitment of resources on a long-term basis, and a disjointed management structure. In our classified report we suggest organizational changes that we believe would consolidate support functions for covert action and improve the management of covert action programs within the Intelligence Community; we are unable to provide further details on these recommendations, however, in this unclassified format.

## *Addressing Proliferation*

So far, we have focused on improving the Intelligence Community writ large—on the theory that only a redesigned Community can substantially improve its performance in assessing the threat posed by weapons of mass destruction. But quite apart from the structural changes we have already recommended, the Intelligence Community also needs to change the way it approaches two of the greatest threats—biological weapons and new forms of nuclear proliferation.

### BIOLOGICAL WEAPONS

The 2001 anthrax attacks on the United States killed five people, crippled mail delivery in several cities for a year, and imposed more than a billion dollars in decontamination costs. For all that, we were lucky. Biological weapons are cheaper and easier to acquire than nuclear weapons—and they could be more deadly. The threat is deeply troubling today; it will be more so tomorrow, when genetic modification techniques will allow the creation of even worse biological weapons. Most of the traditional Intelligence Community collection tools are of little or no use in tackling biological weapons. In our classified report, we discuss some of the specific challenges

that confront our intelligence effort against the biological threat—
but regrettably we cannot discuss them here.

Faced with a high-priority problem that does not yield to traditional methods, large parts of the Intelligence Community seem
to have lowered their expectations and focused on other priorities. This is unacceptable. The Intelligence Community, and the
government as a whole, needs to approach the problem with a
new urgency and new strategies:

- *Work with the biological sciences community.* The Intelligence
  Community simply does not have the in-depth technical
  knowledge about biological weapons that it has about nuclear
  weapons. To close the expertise gap, the Community cannot
  rely on hiring biologists, whose knowledge and skills are extremely important, but whose depth and timeliness of expertise
  begins eroding as soon as they move from the laboratory to the
  intelligence profession. Instead, the DNI should create a Community Biodefense Initiative to institutionalize outreach to
  technical experts inside and outside of government. We describe specific components of this initiative in the body of our
  report.

- *Make targeted collection of biological weapons intelligence a priority
  within the Intelligence Community.* The Intelligence Community's collection woes starkly illustrate the need for more aggressive, targeted approaches to collection on biological
  threats. We recommend that the DNI create a deputy within
  the National Counter Proliferation Center who is specifically
  responsible for biological weapons; this deputy would ensure
  the implementation of a comprehensive biological weapons
  targeting strategy, which would entail gaining real-time access
  to non-traditional sources of information, filtering open source
  data, and devising specific collection initiatives directed at the
  resulting targets.

- *Leverage regulation for biological weapons intelligence.* The United
  States should look outside of intelligence channels for enforcement mechanisms that can provide new avenues of interna-

tional cooperation and resulting opportunities for intelligence collection on biological threats. In the corresponding chapter of our report, we recommend encouraging foreign criminalization of biological weapons development and establishing biosafety and biosecurity regulations under United Nations Security Council Resolution 1540. We also propose extending biosecurity and biosafety regulations to foreign institutions with commercial ties to the United States.

## NUCLEAR WEAPONS

The intelligence challenge posed by nuclear weapons continues to evolve. The Intelligence Community must continue to monitor established nuclear states such as Russia and China, and at the same time face newer and potentially more daunting challenges like terrorist use of a nuclear weapon. But the focus of the U.S. Intelligence Community has historically been on the capabilities of large nation states. When applied to the problem of terrorist organizations and smaller states, many of our intelligence capabilities are inadequate.

The challenges posed by the new environment are well-illustrated by two aspects of nuclear proliferation. The first is the continuing challenge of monitoring insecure nuclear weapons and materials, or "loose nukes"—mainly in the former Soviet Union but also potentially in other nations. The second aspect is the appearance of non-state nuclear "brokers," such as the private proliferation network run by the Pakistani scientist A.Q. Khan. In Khan's case, innovative human intelligence efforts gave the United States access to this proliferation web. However, not only does the full scope of Khan's work remain unknown, but senior officials readily acknowledge that the Intelligence Community must know more about the private networks that support proliferation. The Intelligence Community must adapt to the changing threat.

## INTELLIGENCE SUPPORT TO INTERDICTION

So far, the Intelligence Community has enjoyed a number of

successes intercepting materials related to nuclear, biological, and chemical weapons (and their related delivery systems)—the process commonly referred to as "interdiction." But success has come at a cost. The Intelligence Community has focused so much energy on its own efforts that the Community shows less ambition and imagination in supporting other agencies that should play a large role in interdiction. Many other federal agencies could do more to interdict precursors, weapons components, and dangerous agents if they had effective intelligence support. We recommend several mechanisms to improve intelligence support to these agencies, most particularly the creation of a counterproliferation Joint Interagency Task Force modeled on similar entities that have proved successful in the counternarcotics context.

Moreover, since it may not be possible in all cases to identify proliferation shipments before they reach the United States, our last line of defense is detecting and stopping these shipments before they reach our border. Yet new sensor technologies have faced challenges. In the corresponding chapter of this report, we suggest how the Intelligence Community and Department of Homeland Security can work together on this issue.

## LEVERAGING LEGAL AND REGULATORY MECHANISMS

Intelligence alone cannot solve the proliferation threat. But it may not have to. Information that spies and eavesdroppers would spend millions for and risk their lives to steal can sometimes be easily obtained by the right Customs, Treasury, or export control officials. The industries that support proliferation are subject to a host of regulatory regimes. But the agencies that regulate industry in these areas—Treasury, State, Homeland Security, and Commerce—do not think of themselves as engaged in the collection of intelligence, and the Intelligence Community only rarely appreciates the authorities and opportunities presented by regulatory regimes.

Given the challenges presented by quasi-governmental proliferation, the United States must leverage all of its capabilities to flag potential proliferators, gain insight into their activities, and interdict them, where appropriate. We therefore recommend a series of possible changes to existing regulatory regimes, all de-signed to improve insight into nuclear, biological, or chemical proliferation and enhance our ability to take action. These changes include negotiating ship boarding agreements that in-clude tagging and tracking provisions to facilitate the surveillance of suspect vessels, taking steps to facilitate greater coordination between the Commerce Department (and Immigrations and Customs Enforcement) and the Intelligence Community, using Commerce Department and Customs and Border Protection regulations to facilitate information sharing about suspect cargo and persons and to justify related interdictions, and expanding the Treasury Department's authority to block assets of proliferators.

## Conclusion

The harm done to American credibility by our all too public intelligence failings in Iraq will take years to undo. If there is good news it is this: without actually suffering a massive nuclear or biological attack, we have learned how badly the Intelligence Community can fail in struggling to understand the most important threats we face. We must use the lessons from those failings, and from our successes as well, to improve our intelligence for the future, and do so with a sense of urgency. We already have thousands of dedicated officers and many of the tools needed to do the job. With that in mind, we now turn first to what went wrong in Iraq, then to other intelligence cases, and finally to our detailed recommendations for action.

# Case Study: Iraq

## Introduction

As war loomed, the U.S. Intelligence Community was charged with telling policymakers what it knew about Iraq's nuclear, biological, and chemical weapons programs. The Community's best assessments were set out in an October 2002 National Intelligence Estimate, or NIE, a summation of the Community's views. The title, *Iraq's Continuing Programs for Weapons of Mass Destruction*, foretells the conclusion: that Iraq was still pursuing its programs for weapons of mass destruction (WMD). Specifically, the NIE assessed that Iraq had reconstituted its nuclear weapons program and could assemble a device by the end of the decade; that Iraq had biological weapons and mobile facilities for producing biological warfare (BW) agent; that Iraq had both renewed production of chemical weapons, and probably had chemical weapons stockpiles of up to 500 metric tons; and that Iraq was developing unmanned aerial vehicles (UAVs) probably intended to deliver BW agent.

These assessments were all wrong.

This became clear as U.S. forces searched without success for the WMD that the Intelligence Community had predicted. Extensive post-war investigations were carried out by the Iraq Survey Group (ISG). The ISG found no evidence that Iraq had tried to reconstitute its capability to produce nuclear weapons after 1991; no evidence of BW agent stockpiles or of mobile biological weapons production facilities; and no substantial chemical warfare (CW) stockpiles or credible indications that Baghdad had resumed production of CW after 1991. Just about the only thing that the Intelligence Community got right was its pre-war conclusion that Iraq had deployed missiles with ranges exceeding United Nations limitations.

How could the Intelligence Community have been so mistaken? That is the question the President charged this Commission with answering.

We received great cooperation from the U.S. Intelligence Community. We had unfettered access to all documents used by the Intelligence Community in reaching its judgments about Iraq's WMD programs; we had the same access to all of the Intelligence Community's reports on the subject—including the articles in the President's Daily Brief that concerned Iraq's weapons programs. During the course of our investigation, we and our staff reviewed thousands of pages of documents—ranging from raw operational traffic produced by intelligence operators to finished intelligence products—and interviewed hundreds of current and former Intelligence Community officials.

We also drew on the labors of others. The Butler Commission report on the quality of British intelligence was an important resource for us, as was the work of Australian and Israeli commissions. The careful and well-researched July 2004 report of the Senate Select Committee on Intelligence on this topic was particularly valuable.

This report sets out our findings. For each weapons category, it tells how the Intelligence Community reached the assessments in the October 2002 NIE. It also offers a detailed set of conclusions. But before beginning, we offer a few broader observations.

## An "Intelligence Failure"

For commissions of this sort, 20/20 hindsight is an occupational hazard. It is easy to forget just how difficult a business intelligence is. Nations and terrorist groups do not easily part with their secrets—and they guard nothing more jealously than secrets related to nuclear, biological, and chemical weapons. Stealing those secrets, particularly from closed and repressive regimes like Saddam Hussein's Iraq, is no easy task, and failure is more common than success. Intelligence analysts will often be forced to make do with limited, ambiguous data; extrapolations from thin streams of information will be the norm.

Indeed, defenders of the Intelligence Community have asked

whether it would be fair to expect the Community to get the Iraq WMD question absolutely right. How, they ask, could our intelligence agencies have concluded that Saddam Hussein *did not* have weapons of mass destruction—given his history of using them, his previous deceptions, and his repeated efforts to obstruct United Nations inspectors? And after all, the United States was not alone in error; other major intelligence services also thought that Iraq had weapons of mass destruction.

We agree, but only in part. We do not fault the Intelligence Community for formulating the hypothesis, based on Saddam Hussein's conduct, that Iraq had retained an unconventional weapons capability and was working to augment this capability. Nor do we fault the Intelligence Community for failing to uncover what few Iraqis knew; according to the Iraq Survey Group only a handful of Saddam Hussein's closest advisors were aware of some of his decisions to halt work on his nuclear program and to destroy his stocks of chemical and biological weapons. Even if an extraordinary intelligence effort had gained access to one of these confidants, doubts would have lingered.

But with all that said, we conclude that the Intelligence Community could and should have come much closer to assessing the true state of Iraq's weapons programs than it did. It should have been less wrong—and, more importantly, it should have been more candid about what it did not know. In particular, it should have recognized the serious—and knowable—weaknesses in the evidence it accepted as providing hard confirmation that Iraq had retained WMD capabilities and programs.

## How It Happened

The Intelligence Community's errors were not the result of simple bad luck, or a once-in-a-lifetime "perfect storm," as some would have it. Rather, they were the product of poor intelligence collection, an analytical process that was driven by assumptions and inferences rather than data, inadequate validation and vetting of dubious intelligence sources, and numerous other breakdowns in the various processes that Intelligence Community professionals collectively describe as intelligence "tradecraft." In many ways, the Intelligence Community simply did not do the job that it exists to do.

Our review revealed failings at each stage of the intelligence process. Many past discussions of the Iraq intelligence failure have focused on intelligence analysis, and we indeed will have much to say about how analysts tackled the Iraq WMD question. But they could not analyze data that they did not have, so we begin by addressing the failure of the Intelligence Community to collect more useful intelligence in Iraq.

There is no question that collecting intelligence on Iraq's weapons programs was difficult. Saddam Hussein's regime had a robust and ruthless security system and engaged in sophisticated efforts to conceal or disguise its activities from outside intelligence services—efforts referred to within the Intelligence Community as "denial and deception." The United States had no Iraq embassy or official in-country presence; human intelligence operations were often conducted at a distance. And much of what we wanted to know was concealed in compartmented corners of the Iraqi regime to which few even at high levels in the Iraqi government had access.

Still, Iraq was a high-priority target for years, and the Intelligence Community should have done better. It collected precious little information about Iraq's weapons programs in the years before the Iraq war. And not only did the Community collect too little, but much of what it managed to collect had grave defects that should have been clear to analysts and policymakers at the time. Indeed, one of the most serious failures by the Intelligence Community was its failure to apply sufficiently rigorous tests to the evidence it collected. This failure touched all the most salient pieces of evidence relied on by our intelligence agencies, including the aluminum tubes, reporting on mobile BW, uranium from Niger, and assertions about UAVs.

One of the most painful errors, however, concerned Iraq's biological weapons programs. Virtually all of the Intelligence Community's information on Iraq's alleged mobile biological weapons facilities was supplied by a source, codenamed "Curveball," who was a fabricator. We discuss at length how Curveball came to play so prominent a role in the Intelligence Community's biological weapons assessments. It is, at bottom, a story of Defense Department collectors who abdicated their responsibility to vet a critical source; of Central Intelligence Agency (CIA) analysts who placed undue emphasis on the source's reporting because the tales he told were consistent with what they already believed; and, ultimately, of Intelligence Community leaders who failed to tell policymakers about Curveball's flaws in the weeks before war.

Curveball was not the only bad source the Intelligence Community used. Even more indefensibly, information from a source who was *already known* to be a fabricator found its way into finished pre-war intelligence products, including the October 2002 NIE. This intelligence was also allowed into Secretary of State Colin Powell's speech to the United Nations Security Council, despite the source having been officially discredited almost a year earlier. This communications breakdown could have been avoided if the Intelligence Community had a uniform requirement to reissue or recall reporting from a source whose information turns out to be fabricated, so that analysts do not continue to rely on an unreliable report. In the absence of such a system, however, the Defense Intelligence Agency (DIA), which disseminated the report in the first place, had a responsibility to make sure that its bad source did not continue to pollute policy judgments; DIA did not fulfill this obligation.

Lacking reliable data about Iraq's programs, analysts' starting point was Iraq's history—its past use of chemical weapons, its successful concealment of WMD programs both before and after the Gulf War, and its failure to account for previously declared stockpiles. The analysts' operating hypothesis, therefore, was that Iraq probably still possessed hidden chemical and biological weapons, was still seeking to rebuild its nuclear weapons program, and was seeking to increase its capability to produce and deliver chemical and biological weapons. This hypothesis was not unreasonable; the problem was that, over time, it hardened into a presumption. This hard and fast presumption then contributed to analysts' readiness to accept pieces of evidence that, even at the time, they should have seen as seriously flawed.

In essence, analysts shifted the burden of proof, requiring evidence that Iraq did not have WMD. More troubling, some analysts started to disregard evidence that did not support their premise. Chastened by the effectiveness of Iraq's deceptions before the Gulf War, they viewed contradictory information not as evidence that their premise might be mistaken, but as evidence that Iraq was continuing to conceal its weapons programs.

The Intelligence Community's analysis of the high-strength aluminum tubes offers an illustration of these problems. Most agencies in the Intelligence Community assessed—incorrectly— that these were intended for use in a uranium enrichment program. The reasoning that supported this position was, first, that the tubes *could* be used in centrifuges and, second, that Iraq was good at hiding its nuclear program.

By focusing on whether the tubes could be used for centrifuges, analysts effectively set aside evidence that the tubes were better suited for use in rockets, such as the fact that the tubes had precisely the same dimensions and were made of the same material as tubes used in the conventional rockets that Iraq had declared to international inspectors in 1996. And Iraq's denial and deception capabilities allowed analysts to find support for their view even from information that seemed to contradict it. Thus, Iraqi claims that the tubes were for rockets were described as an Iraqi "cover story" designed to conceal the nuclear end-use for the tubes. In short, analysts erected a theory that almost could not be disproved—both confirming and contradictory facts were construed as support for the theory that the tubes were destined for use in centrifuges.

In the absence of direct evidence, premises and inferences must do. Analysts cannot be faulted for failures of collection. But they can be faulted for not telling policymakers just how little evidence they had to back up their inferences and how uncertain even that evidence itself was. The October 2002 NIE and other pre-war intelligence assessments failed to articulate the thinness of the intelligence upon which critical judgments about Iraq's weapons programs hinged.

Our study also revealed deficiencies in particular intelligence products that are used to convey intelligence information to senior policymakers. As noted above, during the course of its investigation the Commission reviewed a number of articles from the President's Daily Brief (PDB) relating to Iraq's WMD programs. Not surprisingly, many of the flaws in other intelligence products can also be found in the PDBs. But we found some flaws that were inherent in the format of the PDBs—a series of short "articles" often based on current intelligence reporting that are presented to the President each morning. Their brevity leaves little room for doubts or nuance—and their "headlines" designed to grab the reader's attention leave no room at all. Also, a daily drumbeat of reports on the same topic gives an impression of confirming evidence, even when the reports all come from the same source.

The Commission also learned that, on the eve of war, the Intelligence Community failed to convey important information to policymakers. After the October 2002 NIE was published, but before Secretary of State Powell made his address about Iraq's WMD programs to the United Nations, serious doubts became known within the Intelligence Community about Curveball, the aforementioned human intelligence source whose reporting was so critical to the Intelligence Community's pre-war biological warfare assessments. These doubts never found their way to Secretary Powell, who was at that time attempting to strip questionable information from his speech.

These are errors—serious errors. But these errors stem from poor tradecraft and poor management. The Commission found no evidence of political pressure to influence the Intelligence Community's pre-war assessments of Iraq's weapons programs. As we discuss in detail in the body of our report, analysts universally asserted that in no instance did political pressure cause them to skew or alter any of their analytical judgments. We conclude that it was the paucity of intelligence and poor analytical tradecraft, rather than political pressure, that produced the inaccurate pre-war intelligence assessments.

## The Iraq Study

This case study proceeds in two parts. The study first details the stream of pre-war intelligence assessments, from the Gulf

War to Operation Iraqi Freedom, and compares those to the post-war findings of the Iraq Survey Group. That comparison is provided for each weapons type—nuclear, biological, chemical, and their delivery systems—and also for the political context in Iraq during this time period. For each of these sections, the report also offers the Commission's findings, which often identify specific flaws that led to the inaccuracies in the assessments. The study then identifies the overarching conclusions about the collection, analysis, and dissemination of intelligence that we drew from our examination of the Intelligence Community's performance on the Iraq WMD question.

## Nuclear Weapons

The pre-war estimate of Iraq's nuclear program, as reflected in the October 2002 NIE *Iraq's Continuing Programs for Weapons of Mass Destruction*, was that, in the view of most agencies, Baghdad was "reconstituting its nuclear weapons program" and "if left unchecked, [would] probably . . . have a nuclear weapon during this decade," although it would be unlikely before 2007 to 2009. The NIE explained that, in the view of most agencies, "compelling evidence" of reconstitution was provided by Iraq's "aggressive pursuit of high-strength aluminum tubes." The NIE also pointed to additional indicators, such as other dual-use procurement activity, supporting reconstitution. The assessment that Iraq was reconstituting its nuclear program and could therefore have a weapon by the end of the decade was made with "moderate confidence."

Based on its post-war investigations, the Iraq Survey Group (ISG) concluded—contrary to the Intelligence Community's pre-war assessments—that Iraq had not tried to reconstitute a capability to produce nuclear weapons after 1991. Moreover, the ISG judged that Iraq's work on uranium enrichment, including development of gas centrifuges, essentially ended in 1991, and that its ability to reconstitute its enrichment program progressively decayed after that time. With respect to the aluminum tubes, the ISG concluded that Iraq's effort to procure the tubes is "best explained by its efforts to produce 81-mm rockets," and the ISG uncovered no evidence that the tubes were intended for use in a gas centrifuge.

The Community was, in brief, decidedly wrong on what many would view as the single most important judgment it made. The reasons why the Community was so wrong are not particularly glamorous—failures of analysts to question assumptions and apply their tradecraft correctly, errors in technical and factual analysis, a paucity of collection, and failure by the Community to authenticate relevant documents. But these seemingly workaday shortcomings collectively led to a major mis-estimation of a critical intelligence question.

This chapter details our review of the Intelligence Community's performance on the nuclear issue. This chapter is divided into three sections. First, we review the Intelligence Community's pre-war assessments of Iraq's nuclear program. We then summarize the findings of the ISG regarding Iraq's nuclear efforts and how those findings compare to the Intelligence Community's assessments. The final section contains our findings concerning the causes of the Intelligence Community's failures on the aluminum tubes issue and the now-infamous Niger story.

## The Intelligence Community's Pre-War Assessments

The Intelligence Community's assessments of Iraq's pre-war nuclear program were not made in a vacuum. Rather, as the Intelligence Community later explained, its assessments were informed by its analysis of Iraq's nuclear ambitions and capabilities spanning the preceding fifteen years, as well as by "lessons learned from over a decade of dealing with Iraqi intransigence on this issue." Thus the proper starting point for an evaluation of the Intelligence Community's assessments lies at the conclusion of the first Gulf War—when the Intelligence Community reviewed the state of Saddam Hussein's nuclear programs and was surprised by what it found.

*Post-Gulf War.* Following the Gulf War, based on a variety of sources of intelligence including reporting from defectors, the Intelligence Community learned that Iraq's nuclear weapons program went "far beyond what had been assessed by any intelligence organization" in 1990–1991. Before the Gulf War, in November 1990, the Community had assessed that, because analysts had not detected a formal, coordinated nuclear weapons program, Iraq likely would not have a nuclear weapon until the late 1990s. Thus after the war the Intelligence Community was surprised to discover the breadth of Iraq's nuclear weapons program, including the wide range of technologies Iraq had been pursuing for uranium enrichment, which in turn indicated that Iraq "had been much closer to a weapon than virtually anyone expected." This humbling discovery that Iraq had successfully concealed a sophisticated nuclear program from the U.S. Intelligence Community exercised a major influence on the Intelligence Community's assessments throughout the early 1990s and afterwards.

Iraq's subsequent and continuing attempts to evade and deceive international inspectors heightened analysts' concerns. In a 1994 Joint Atomic Energy Intelligence Committee (JAEIC) assessment, *Iraq's Nuclear Weapons Program: Elements of Reconstitution*, the Intelligence Community agreed that the "Iraqi government is determined to covertly reconstitute its nuclear weapons program," and that, although Iraq had not yet begun reconstitution, it "would most likely choose the gas centrifuge route" and would "invest a great deal of time and effort" to "conceal its efforts from long-term monitoring."

*Mid–1990s.* Still, through the mid–1990s, analysts continued to assess that Iraq had not yet reconstituted its nuclear program. Most agencies judged in a 1993 NIE that "if sanctions are lifted and especially if inspections cease, Baghdad will rapidly accelerate its effort" to produce nuclear weapons. And all agencies agreed in a September 1994 JAEIC assessment that Iraq "still seems to be pursuing" its former program. The Intelligence Community believed that if Iraq were able to mount a dedicated centrifuge program, it would probably take the Iraqis five to seven years to produce enough fissile material for a nuclear weapon. This consensus was best reflected by an October 1997 assessment by the JAEIC, which reaffirmed its previous judgments that Iraq would need five to seven years to produce fissile material indigenously, assuming some availability of foreign technical assistance and supplies. Whether that five to seven year clock had started to run, however, was unclear: this assessment noted that although there was "no firm evidence that reconstitution had begun, six years had passed since the Gulf War and the Community could not be certain whether the starting point for the five to seven year timeline was in the past or future."

During this period, the lack of specific intelligence on the subject continued to complicate analysts' abilities to assess Iraq's ability to reconstitute its nuclear program. The Intelligence Community noted in a 1998 assessment, for instance, that there was limited and often contradictory human intelligence reporting on Iraqi nuclear efforts, with some human intelligence sources indicating that Iraq was continuing "low-level theoretical research for a weapons program" while other sources reported that "all nuclear-related activity [had been] halted." The Intelligence Community acknowledged that it had an "incomplete picture of the Iraqi nuclear program."

*Post–1998.* The end of international inspections in 1998, prompted by Saddam Hussein's preventing the inspectors from doing their work, increased concern among analysts that Iraq would use that opportunity to reconstitute its nuclear program. Accordingly, in 1999, the JAEIC noted that although it still had no specific evidence that reconstitution had begun, the absence of inspectors gave Iraq greater *opportunity* to conduct covert research and development. As of December 2000, however, an Intelligence Community Assessment noted that Iraq still did not appear to have taken major steps toward reconstitution. Thus, after the departure of inspectors, the Intelligence Community assumed that Iraq had the opportunity and the desire to jumpstart its covert nuclear weapons program; by the end of 2000, however, the Community had seen no firm evidence that this was actually happening.

This judgment began to shift in early 2001 as a result of a discovery that, in hindsight, was the critical moment in the development of the Intelligence Community's assessment of Iraq's nuclear program. In March 2001, intelligence reporting indicated that Iraq was seeking high-strength tubes made of 7075 T6 aluminum alloy. The Intelligence Community obtained samples of the tubes when a shipment bound for Iraq was seized overseas.

At this point, a debate began within the Intelligence Community about the reason why Iraq had procured the tubes. The CIA assessed that the tubes were most likely for gas centrifuges for enriching uranium and believed that the tubes provided compelling evidence that Iraq had renewed its gas centrifuge uranium enrichment program. CIA subsequently identified possible non-nuclear applications for the tubes, but continued to judge that the tubes were destined for use in Iraqi gas centrifuges—even while acknowledging that the Intelligence Community had very little information on Iraq's WMD programs to corroborate this assessment.

This judgment concerning the tubes' likely intended use was echoed by another expert technical entity within the Intelligence Community. Analysts from the National Ground Intelligence Center (NGIC), a component of the U.S. Army recognized as the national experts on conventional military systems, judged that while it could "not totally rule out the possibility" that the tubes could be used for rockets and thus were not destined for a nuclear-related use, the tubes were, technically speaking, poor choices for rocket bodies. NGIC's expert judgment was therefore that there was a very low probability the tubes were designed for conventional use in rockets. Because of NGIC's expertise on conventional weapons systems such as rockets, NGIC's view that the tubes were poor choices for rocket bodies gave CIA analysts greater confidence in their own judgment that the tubes were likely for use in centrifuges.

Other entities took a different view, however. The Department of Energy (DOE), the U.S. government's primary repository of expertise on nuclear matters, assessed that the tubes—although they "could be used to manufacture centrifuge rotors"—were "not well-suited for a centrifuge application" and were more likely intended for use in Iraq's Nasser 81 millimeter Multiple Rocket Launcher (MRL) program. The International Atomic Energy Agency (IAEA) agreed with DOE's assessment, concluding that the tubes were usable in a gas centrifuge application but that they were not directly suited to that use.

Despite this disagreement, the CIA informed senior policymakers that it believed the tubes were destined for use in Iraqi gas centrifuges. While noting that there was disagreement within the Intelligence Community concerning the most likely use for the tubes, the CIA pointed out that there was also interagency consensus that the tubes could be used for centrifuge enrichment. This consensus on capability led many analysts at both CIA and DIA to think that the tubes supplied the evidence that Iraq was starting to "reconstitute" its nuclear program.

Other streams of evidence also raised flags. At about the same time, analysts began to see indications that Iraq was seeking procurement of other dual-use items that would be consistent with a possible renewed effort at developing centrifuges. This activity concerned even DOE, which had expressed skepticism that the intercepted tubes had centrifuge applications. These concerns were affected by the Intelligence Community's history of underestimating Iraq's nuclear program; as the National Intelligence Council (NIC) would later observe, analysts became concerned during 2002 that "they may again be facing a surprise similar to the one in 1991."

In the months before the October 2002 NIE, the CIA continued to assess that the tubes were intended for use in gas centrifuges, albeit with slight variations in the strength of that formulation, pointing out that Iraq's interest in the tubes was "key" to the assessment that Iraq was "reconstituting its centrifuge program." CIA presented this view in an Intelligence Assessment, entitled *Iraq's Hunt for Aluminum Tubes: Evidence of a Renewed Uranium Enrichment Program*, in which CIA concluded that the aluminum tubes "are most likely for gas centrifuges for enriching uranium" and that Iraq's pursuit of such tubes provided "compelling evidence that Iraq has renewed its gas centrifuge uranium enrichment program." The assessment noted that "some" in the Intelligence Community believed conventional armament applications, such as multiple rocket launchers, were "more likely end-uses," but the assessment noted that NGIC, the "national experts on conventional military systems," had found such uses "highly unlikely." At the same time, DOE disseminated a separate assessment arguing that, while the tubes could be modified for use as centrifuge rotors, "other conventional military uses [we]re more plausible." The Department of State's Bureau of Intelligence and Research (INR) agreed with DOE's assessment.

*October 2002 NIE.* The Intelligence Community judged in the NIE with moderate confidence that "Baghdad ha[d] reconstituted its nuclear weapons program." Only INR dissented from this assessment, although INR judged in the President's Summary of the NIE that the overall evidence "indicates, at most, a limited Iraqi nuclear reconstitution effort." By reconstitution, the Intelligence Community meant that Iraq was in the "process of restoring [its] uranium enrichment capability." To the relevant CIA and DIA analysts, the pursuit of aluminum tubes provided "compelling evidence" of reconstitution. In particular, the composition, dimensions, cost, and tight manufacturing tolerances for the tubes were assessed by CIA and DIA to exceed by far those needed for non-nuclear purposes, thus demonstrating that the tubes were intended for a nuclear-related use. At the interagency coordination meeting for the NIE, both NSA and the National Geospatial-Intelligence Agency (NGA) agreed with the CIA/DIA position on the tubes. DOE and INR dissented from the tubes judgment, assessing that the tubes were more likely for use in tactical rockets.

The NIE stated that the conclusion that the tubes indicated reconstitution was bolstered by additional evidence that suggested Iraq could be rebuilding its nuclear program:

1. Other Dual-Use Procurements. Reporting indicated that Iraq was attempting to procure other dual-use items that would be required to build a gas centrifuge plant, such as magnets, "high-speed balancing machines," and machine tools. These items are all dual-use materials, however, and the reporting provided no direct indication that the materials were intended for use in a nuclear program, as indicated in the NIE.

2. Nuclear Cadre. The NIE also pointed to evidence that Iraq was making efforts to preserve, and in some cases re-establish and enhance, its cadre of weapons personnel. Reporting indicated that some scientists had been reassigned to the Iraqi Atomic Energy Commission (IAEC) and that Iraq had "re-

assembled" many scientists, engineers, and managers from Iraq's previous nuclear program.

3. Activity at Suspect Sites. Sources indicated that Iraq was trying to procure a magnet production line in 1999–2001 and one report indicated the plant would be located at Al-Tahadi, where analysis suggested construction of buildings in late 2000 that could have housed a magnet production line. Both sources indicated, however, that magnet procurements were likely affiliated with Iraq's missile program, rather than with nuclear applications, though some reporting noted that the cadre of scientists and technicians at the site formerly worked in the nuclear program.

*Uranium from Niger.* Although the NIE did not include uranium acquisition in the list of elements bolstering its conclusion about reconstitution, it did note that Iraq was "vigorously trying to procure uranium ore and yellowcake" from Africa. This statement was based largely on reporting from a foreign government intelligence service that Niger planned to send up to 500 tons of yellowcake uranium to Iraq. The status of the arrangement was unclear, however, at the time of the coordination of the Estimate and the NIE therefore noted that the Intelligence Community could not confirm whether Iraq succeeded in acquiring the uranium. 60 Iraq's alleged pursuit of uranium from Africa was thus not included among the NIE's Key Judgments. For reasons discussed at length below, several months after the NIE, the reporting that Iraq was seeking uranium from Niger was judged to be based on forged documents and was recalled.

In short, all of the coordinating agencies, with the exception of INR, agreed that Iraq was reconstituting its nuclear program. Of those agencies that agreed on reconstitution, all but DOE agreed that the tubes provided "compelling evidence" for that conclusion. DOE reaffirmed its previous assessments that, while the tubes could be modified for use in a gas centrifuge, they were poorly suited for such a function and were most likely designed for use in conventional rockets. On the question of reconstitution, DOE believed that the other factors—the attempted pro-

curement of magnets and balancing machines, efforts to reconstitute the nuclear cadre, activity at suspect sites, and evidence of
Iraqi efforts to obtain uranium from Africa—justified the conclusion that Iraq was reconstituting its nuclear program. None of the
other agencies placed significant weight on reporting about attempts to procure uranium from Africa to support their conclusion of reconstitution.

*Post-NIE.* The publication of the NIE did not settle the dispute
about the aluminum tubes and so, in the period between the NIE
and the invasion of Iraq, debate within the Intelligence Community over their significance continued. INR, for its part, continued to see "no compelling reason to judge that Iraq ha[d] entered"
the timeframe of at least five to seven years that the Intelligence
Community agreed Baghdad would need to produce sufficient
fissile material for a nuclear weapon. DOE, meanwhile, continued to believe that reconstitution was underway but that the
"tubes probably were not part of the program," assessing instead
that the tubes were intended for use in conventional rockets. On
the other side of the dispute, NGIC and CIA continued to assess
that the tubes were destined for use in gas centrifuges. Outside
the Intelligence Community, the IAEA, after inspections resumed
in fall 2002, also weighed in on the dispute, concluding with DOE
and INR that the tubes were likely intended for use in Iraq's 81
millimeter rocket program.

During this time the CIA continued to explain to senior policymakers that the Intelligence Community was not of one view on
the most likely use for the tubes, but CIA offered its own view that
the "alternative explanation" for the tubes' intended use—that
they would be used for rockets—was likely an Iraqi "cover story."
The CIA also noted the overall paucity of information on Iraq's
programs, but suggested that the lack of information was due in
part to Iraq's successful efforts to hide its illicit activity.

Other countries' intelligence agencies views of the tubes were,
on balance, somewhat more circumspect than that of the majority
in the NIE. For its part, the British Joint Intelligence Committee
assessed, as did the NIE, that the aluminum tubes, with some
modifications, would be suitable for use in a centrifuge, but noted
that there was no definitive intelligence that the tubes were des-

tined for the nuclear program. The views of the Australian Office of National Assessments on the relevance of the tubes to Iraq's nuclear program were "inconsistent and changeable."

## Post-War Findings of the Iraq Survey Group

The Iraq Survey Group concluded that Iraq had not tried to reconstitute a capability to produce nuclear weapons after 1991. It concluded that Iraq's efforts to develop gas centrifuges for uranium enrichment ended in 1991, as did Iraq's work on other uranium enrichment programs, which Iraq had explored prior to the Gulf War. The ISG also found no evidence that Iraq had taken steps to advance its pre–1991 work in nuclear weapons design and development. Although the ISG did find indications that Saddam remained interested in reconstitution of the nuclear program after sanctions were lifted, it concluded that Iraq's ability to reconstitute its program progressively decayed after 1991.

Not long after the start of the Iran-Iraq war in 1980, Iraq started to pursue formally a uranium enrichment program using a variety of uranium enrichment techniques. By 1990, Iraq had built two magnetic-bearing centrifuges (with foreign assistance) using imported carbon fiber rotors and two oil-bearing centrifuges. During the first Gulf War, however, nearly all of the key nuclear facilities in Iraq—those involved in the processing of nuclear material or weapons research—were bombed and many of the facilities were largely destroyed.

After the Gulf War, Iraq initially chose not to disclose the extent of its nuclear program and instead sought to hide any evidence of it. Accordingly, the director of Iraq's Military Industrialization Commission, Hussein Kamil, ordered the collection of all inculpatory documents and equipment. The equipment and documentation were then moved to a variety of locations to hide them from the IAEA. Hussein Kamil ordered at least one set of all nuclear-related documents and some equipment to be retained by a senior scientist.

Despite Iraqi efforts, in early summer 1991 the IAEA confronted Baghdad with evidence of uranium enrichment components during the course of its inspections. At that point Baghdad admitted to its large pre-war enrichment programs, but still did not fully declare the extent of its centrifuge program.

Indeed, Iraq continued to resist more comprehensive disclosure of its pre–1991 nuclear program until after the defection of Hussein Kamil in 1995, when a large number of documents and equipment fell into the hands of UNSCOM and the IAEA. From this point forward, according to the ISG, the Iraqis appear to have been more cooperative and provided more complete information. For example, the Iraqis largely declared their pre–1991 centrifuge program, although a full set of documents obtained by Iraq from German engineers in the 1980s was not supplied to IAEA inspectors.

Although the Iraqis did not make more comprehensive disclosures about their nuclear program until 1995, the Iraq Survey Group concluded that Iraq had actually ended its nuclear program in 1991. More specifically, the ISG assessed that Iraq's development of gas centrifuges essentially ended in 1991 and that Iraq did not continue work on any of the other pre–1991 enrichment methods it had explored, including electromagnetic isotope separation (EMIS). The ISG did point out, however, that many of the former EMIS engineers and scientists continued to work for either the Iraqi Atomic Energy Commission or the Military Industrialization Commission in roles that could preserve their technical skills.

Despite these efforts to preserve the skills and talent of the nuclear cadre, the intellectual capital underlying Iraq's nuclear program decayed in the years after 1991. For example, starting around 1992, the Director of Iraq's Military Industrialization Commission transferred personnel from the former nuclear program to various military research and production facilities. Some of the work performed by these former nuclear scientists by its nature preserved for Iraq capabilities that would be needed for a reconstituted nuclear program. Still, the ISG noted that the overall decline of the Iraqi economy made it very difficult to retain scientists, many of whom departed for better prospects abroad.

With the influx of funds from the Oil-for-Food program and later the suspension of cooperation with UNSCOM, Saddam began to pay renewed attention to former members of the Iraq nuclear program. In the late 1990s, for instance, he raised salaries for those in the Military Industrialization and Iraqi Atomic Energy Commissions, and new programs, such as joint programs with universities, were initiated to employ the talent of former nuclear program employees. In the year before Operation Iraqi Freedom, Iraq's Military Industrialization Commission also took steps to improve capabilities that could have been applied to a renewed centrifuge program for uranium enrichment. But the ISG did not uncover information indicating that the technologies being pursued were intended to support such a program.

With respect to Iraq's interest in procuring high-strength aluminum tubes, the ISG concluded that the Iraqi attempt to procure the tubes is best explained by Iraq's efforts to produce effective 81 millimeter rockets; the ISG uncovered no evidence that the tubes were intended for use in a gas centrifuge. The ISG arrived at this conclusion only after investigating the key indicators that suggested a possible centrifuge end-use for the tubes—for example, the tubes' dimensions and tight manufacturing tolerances—and found no evidence of a program to design or develop an 81 millimeter aluminum rotor centrifuge.

What the ISG found instead was that, with respect to the dimensions of the tubes, Iraqi nuclear scientists thought it was at best impractical for Iraq to have made a centrifuge with 81 millimeter rotors. For example, Ja'far Diya Ja'far, the head of Iraq's pre–1991 uranium enrichment program, stated in post-war debriefings that, while it was possible to make a rotor from the tubes, he thought it would be impractical to do so. He also said that using 81 millimeter rockets as a "cover story" for a centrifuge project would not have been very useful, because Iraq had difficulty importing any goods. Ja'far similarly did not consider it reasonable that Iraq could have pursued a centrifuge program based on 81 millimeter aluminum tubes, judging the technical challenges to doing so were too great.

Conversely, the Iraq Survey Group investigation did uncover what it judged to be plausible accounts that linked the tubes to 81 millimeter rockets, and which answered questions about why the Iraqis had sought such tight manufacturing specifications for the tubes. For example, some sources indicated to the ISG that the tight tolerance requests were driven by a desire to improve the accuracy of the rockets. Inconsistencies among rockets had resulted in past variations in range and accuracy, according to these sources, and the Iraqis chose to address this problem by tightening specifications. Another explanation was that the engineering drawings for the Iraqi 81 millimeter rocket, which was originally reverse-engineered from an Italian air-to-ground rocket (the Medusa), had undergone many ad hoc revisions over the years because the Iraqis were using their 81 millimeter rockets as ground-to-ground rockets. An Iraqi military committee was convened to return the design to the original Italian-based design, according to the ISG report, and that military committee then set new, and more strict, specifications. The ISG also learned that misfires sometimes resulted from pitting in the tubes caused by improper storage and corrosion, a problem that could explain the requirement that the tubes be anodized and shipped carefully.

Though ultimately concluding that the evidence did not show that the Iraqis intended a nuclear end-use for the tubes, the Iraq Survey Group did note some inconsistencies in the explanation that the tubes were intended for use in tactical rockets. For example, the ISG found technical drawings that showed that Iraq's 81 millimeter rocket program had a history of using tubes that fell short of the strict manufacturing standards demanded in the procurement attempts before the war. Also, the ISG found evidence that, in the months just before the war, the Iraqis accepted lower-quality, indigenously produced aluminum tubes for its 81 millimeter rockets, despite the continuing efforts to procure high-specification tubes from abroad. Iraq also explored the possibility (about a year before the war) of using steel for the rocket bodies. This approach was rejected, however, because it would have required significant design modifications for the existing 81 millimeter rocket design. The ISG noted that these efforts raise questions about whether high-specification tubes were really needed for rockets.

The ISG reconciled this evidence by judging that Iraq's continued efforts to obtain tubes from abroad, even while simultaneously accepting some indigenously produced tubes for use in rockets, could be explained in large measure by bureaucratic inefficiencies and fear of senior officials in the ranks of the Iraqi government. For example, Dr. Huwaysh, the head of the Military Industrialization Commission, "exhibited a rigid managerial style" and frequently made unreasonable production demands. The fear of being held responsible for rejected tubes or components affected the lead production engineer and he therefore decided to tighten specifications for the rocket program. Similarly, a report from the rocket program noted that some engineers requested tight specifications in order to appear effective in addressing problems. Also, because Huwaysh demanded results quickly, the engineers did not have time to attempt a detailed analysis of the causes for rocket scatter and inaccuracy; instead, the engineers simply tightened some specifications in the hope that that would improve accuracy. Other factors influencing the continuing efforts to procure tubes from abroad included the "lack of sufficient indigenous manufacturing capabilities"—an effort that Iraq only began in 2002—the high costs of production, and the "pressure of the impending war."

The ISG noted that one other factor that the Intelligence Community had cited as evidence that the tubes were intended for use in a centrifuge was that the potential supplier was asked to provide 84 millimeter tubes—a change that would have meant the tubes could not be used in an 81 millimeter rocket. But the ISG found no clear indication that it was Iraq (or an Iraqi entity) that was making these inquiries about 84 millimeter tubes. In any event, the ISG concluded that, although a larger diameter tube would be better for use in a centrifuge, Iraq already had 500 tons of 120 millimeter diameter aluminum shafts which it had imported before sanctions were imposed in 1990. And, furthermore, Iraq was using those shafts in the months before Operation Iraqi Freedom to support the flow-forming operations related to the 81 millimeter rocket program.

With respect to alleged "high-level interest" in tubes by Iraqi leaders, the ISG concluded that such interest in the tubes appears to have focused on efforts to produce 81 millimeter rockets rather than on any element of a nuclear program.

The Iraq Survey Group also found no evidence that Iraq

sought uranium from abroad after 1991. With respect to the reports that Iraq sought uranium from Niger, ISG interviews with Ja'far Diya Ja'far, the head of Iraq's pre–1991 enrichment programs, indicated that Iraq had only two contacts with the Nigerian government after 1998—neither of which was related to uranium. One such contact was a visit to Niger by the Iraqi Ambassador to the Vatican Wissam Zahawie, the purpose of which Ja'far said was to invite the Nigerian President to visit Iraq (a story told publicly by Zahawie). The second contact was a visit to Iraq by a Nigerian minister to discuss Nigerian purchases of oil from Iraq—with no mention of "any kind of payment, quid pro quo, or offer to provide Iraq with uranium ore, other than cash in exchange for petroleum." The use of the last method of payment is supported by a crude oil contract, dated June 26, 2001, recovered by the ISG.

The ISG found only one offer of uranium to Baghdad since 1991—an offer that Iraq appears to have turned down. The ISG found a document in the headquarters of the Iraqi Intelligence Service that reveals that a Ugandan businessman had approached the Iraqi Embassy in Nairobi with an offer to sell uranium, reportedly from the Congo. The Iraqi Embassy in Nairobi, reporting back to Baghdad on the matter on May 20, 2001, indicated that the Embassy told the Ugandan that Iraq did not deal with "these materials" because of the sanctions.

Finally, and on a broader plane, even if an order to reconstitute had been given, Iraq Survey Group interviews with former senior officials indicated that Iraq would not have been able to do so given the conditions inside the country in 2002. Unsurprisingly, therefore, the ISG found no indication that Iraq had resumed fissile material or nuclear weapon research and development activities after 1991.

## Analysis of the Intelligence Community's Pre-War Assessments

This marked disjuncture between the Intelligence Community's assessments and the findings of the Iraq Survey Group about Iraq's purported nuclear weapons program was not solely the product of bad luck or the inherent difficulties of making intelligence judgments. It arose out of fundamental flaws in the way the Intelligence Community approached its business.

Above all, the Intelligence Community's failure on the nuclear issue was a failure of analysis. To be sure, the paucity of intelligence contributed to that failure. Although signals intelligence played a key role in some respects that we cannot discuss in an unclassified format, on the whole it was not useful. Similarly, though imagery intelligence showed some construction at a possible suspect nuclear site in or around 2000, imagery provided little helpful insight into the purpose of that activity and nothing beyond that. And, other than information on the alleged uranium deal that was later determined to be unreliable, very little human intelligence was available to provide insight into Iraq's intentions. The time pressures of the October 2002 NIE also may have hampered the normal thorough review before dissemination.

But on the crucial question of whether the aluminum tubes were for use in a gas centrifuge or in tactical rockets—an analytical question—the Intelligence Community got it wrong. And, notably, it was not one of the difficult and inherently speculative questions intelligence analysts often confront; it was not a question that required the Intelligence Community to make a prediction about future events or to draw conclusions about the state of the world based upon limited information. Rather, the critical question was, at bottom, largely a technical one, where the critical facts were known or knowable: namely, how well-suited were the aluminum tubes for tactical rockets and centrifuges, respectively? An even-handed assessment of the evidence should have led the Intelligence Community to conclude that the tubes were more likely destined for tactical rockets. This section examines this analytic failure and other issues uncovered by our review of the Intelligence Community's performance.

The judgment of most agencies that Baghdad's pursuit of aluminum tubes "provide[d] compelling evidence" that Iraq was reconstituting its weapons turned upon two separate but related analytical determinations. The first was that the tubes would not have been well-suited for use in Iraq's conventional military arsenal—in particular, as a conventional rocket casing. The second was that the tubes were a suitable fit for centrifuges in a nuclear program.

This section addresses the soundness of each of these conclusions in turn. We find that the Intelligence Community—and in particular, conventional weapons analysts at the National Ground Intelligence Center (NGIC) in the Defense Department—got the first of these two questions completely wrong; the intercepted tubes were not only well-suited, but were in fact a precise fit, for Iraq's conventional rockets, and the Intelligence Community should have recognized as much at the time. The second question—whether the tubes would have been well-suited for centrifuge applications—was a closer one, but we conclude that certain agencies were more wedded to the analytical position that the tubes were destined for a nuclear program than was justified by the technical evidence. We also conclude that these misjudgments, while reflecting lapses in basic tradecraft, ultimately stemmed from a deeper source: analysts' willingness to accept that a superficially enticing piece of evidence confirmed the prevailing assumption—that Iraq was attempting to reconstitute its nuclear program—was wrong. That CIA and DIA reached this conclusion was a product of, in our view, an effort to fit the evidence to the prevailing assumptions.

*Suitability of the tubes for conventional rockets.* The most egregious failure regarding the aluminum tubes was the inability of certain agencies to assess correctly their suitability for a conventional weapons system. While the CIA and DIA acknowledged that the tubes could be used for rockets, these agencies believed it was highly unlikely that the tubes had been intended for such a use. But these agencies' basis for believing this was wrong. Iraq had been seeking tubes composed of a particular material—high-strength 7075-T6 aluminum—which CIA and DIA viewed as suggestive of a nuclear end-use. But that material is wholly consistent with a non-nuclear end-use. This same material in fact has been used in rockets manufactured by Russia, Switzerland, and twelve other countries, according to Department of Defense rocket design engineers. Indeed, Iraq itself had used this kind of aluminum in its Nasser 81 rocket program and had declared that use in its 1996 declaration to the IAEA.

Yet NGIC, the national experts on conventional military systems, assessed in September 2002 that the material and tolerances of the tubes sought by Iraq were "highly unlikely" to be intended for rocket motor cases. That assessment was clearly mistaken and should have been recognized as such at the time. NGIC later conceded, in written testimony to the Senate Select Committee on Intelligence, that "lightweight rockets, such as those originally developed for air-to-ground systems, typically use 7075-T6 aluminum for the motor casing." As the experts on such systems, NGIC should have been aware of these facts. Similarly, although NGIC assessed that the tolerances of the tubes Iraq was seeking were "excessive" for rockets, NGIC was not aware at that time of the tolerances required for the Iraqi Nasser 81 rockets, for the Italian Medusa rocket on which the Nasser 81 was based, or for comparable U.S. rockets.

NGIC also believed that the tubes would make poor choices for rocket motor bodies because the walls of the tubes were too thick. But the tubes Iraq was seeking had precisely the same dimensions—including the same wall thickness—as the tubes that Iraq itself used in its Nasser 81 rockets in 1996. This fact also should not have come as a revelation to NGIC analysts, as DOE had published detailed assessments of the tubes used in the Nasser 81 rocket—including their dimensions—in August 2001, and as the IAEA had noted Iraq's use of the Nasser 81 rocket in its earlier catalogs of Iraq's weapons programs. Yet the two primary NGIC rocket analysts said that they did not know the dimensions of the Nasser 81 rockets at that time. While these analysts assert that they had no access to IAEA information and did not receive the DOE reporting in question, we believe that NGIC could and should have conducted a more exhaustive examination of the question. We agree with the conclusion of the Senate Select Committee on Intelligence that NGIC's performance represents a "serious lapse" in analytical tradecraft.

CIA and DIA's confidence in their conclusions also led them to fail to pursue additional, easily obtainable data on the tubes that would have pointed them in the direction of conventional weapons applications. For example, though elements of the Intelligence Community were aware that the Nasser 81 millimeter rocket was likely reverse-engineered from the Italian Medusa air-to-ground rocket, neither DIA nor CIA—the two most vociferous proponents of a nuclear end-use—obtained the specifications for the Medusa rocket until well after the commencement of Operation Iraqi Freedom. Indeed, CIA appears to have consciously bypassed attempts to gather this crucial data. A CIA officer had actually suggested that CIA track down the precise dimensions and specifications of the Medusa rocket in order to evaluate the possibility that the tubes Iraq was seeking were in fact intended for rockets. CIA rejected the request in early September 2002, however, on the basis that such information was not needed because CIA judged the tubes to be destined for use in centrifuges— a textbook example of an agency prematurely closing off an avenue of investigation because of its confidence in its conclusions.

*Suitability of tubes for nuclear centrifuges.* As discussed above, a debate raged within the Intelligence Community in the months preceding the Iraq war on a second question as well: namely, whether the intercepted aluminum tubes were well-suited for use in nuclear centrifuges. According to both DOE and CIA centrifuge experts, the resolution of this issue depended primarily on the answer to two highly technical questions: first, whether the tubes had a sufficiently large internal diameter (and hence could allow the requisite gas flow) to enrich uranium effectively, and whether the walls of the tubes were too thick for use as centrifuge rotors. While generally the analytical issue of the tubes' suitability for centrifuges was more technically complex than that of their fit for conventional rocket applications, the manner in which certain agencies answered these two technical questions about centrifuge-suitability suggests that their analysis was driven more by their underlying assumptions than by the available scientific evidence.

For example, to answer the first question, analysts from CIA's Weapons Intelligence, Non-Proliferation, and Arms Control Center (WINPAC) sought the assistance of the DOE National Laboratories—specifically, Oak Ridge National Laboratory—to test the tubes. The Oak Ridge laboratory concluded that, while it was technically possible to enrich uranium using tubes of the diameter the Iraqis were seeking, it would be suboptimal to do so. The prototype design unit that Iraq built before the Gulf War—which used carbon fiber rotors and was built with the assistance of German engineers using the European Urenco design—had a separative capability four to five times greater than would a centrifuge built using the 81 millimeter tubes for rotors. Accordingly, to support a program that could produce one nuclear device per year, Iraq would need to manufacture and deploy 10,000 to 14,000 such machines. The number of tubes Iraq was seeking, however, would be enough to manufacture 100,000 to 150,000 of these machines, which could produce 170–260 kg of highly enriched uranium per year (enough for 8–10 nuclear devices per year). But DOE pointed out that no proliferator has ever operated such a large number of centrifuges. In other words, the tubes Iraq was seeking were so suboptimal for uranium enrichment that it would have taken many thousands of them to produce enough uranium for a weapon—and although Iraq was in fact seeking thousands of tubes, DOE assessed it would have been highly unlikely for a proliferator to choose a route that would require such a large number of machines.

With respect to the second suitability question—whether the walls of the tubes were too thick for centrifuge use—CIA's WIN-PAC sought the assistance of a contractor to perform separate tests (a "spin test") of the tubes in order to determine if they were strong enough to withstand the extremely high speeds at which centrifuge rotors must spin. The initial test performed by the contractor was reported to have resulted in successfully spinning a tube at 60,000 revolutions per minute (rpm). The NIE included these test results and explained that this test provided only a rough indication that the tubes were suitable as centrifuge rotors. The NIE noted, however, that additional tests would be performed at higher speeds to determine whether the tubes were suitable for operations under conditions that replicated gas centrifuge operations.

Unfortunately, these subsequent tests—performed by CIA contractors in January 2003—only clouded an already murky picture. The contractors' initial findings gave the appearance that the tubes were of insufficient strength for use in centrifuge equipment. The CIA, however, questioned the methodology used by its contractors, asserting that the test results had failed to distinguish between the failures of the *tubes* and failures of the *test equipment* itself. The contractors then provided a "correction" with new test data, which, the CIA believed, demonstrated that the tubes had sufficient strength to be spun at speeds of 90,000 rpm. But DOE was unpersuaded by the corrected findings and argued that the CIA's conclusions were not supported by the test results. At bottom, the ineptly handled spin tests did little more than deepen the divisions between CIA and DOE over the tubes' intended use; in the words of one former senior Intelligence Community official, the tests were "like throwing a lighted match into gasoline."

In any event, the initial technical tests led all agencies to agree that the tubes *could* be used to build gas centrifuges for uranium enrichment. DOE, however, did not believe that tubes were *intended* for such use, a view with which INR agreed. DOE's view was based on disagreement with CIA's view on both counts— DOE argued that the diameter of the tubes was too small and the walls were too thick for centrifuge use. The tubes, in DOE's judgment, were therefore "not favorable for direct use as centrifuge rotors."

CIA countered that the dimensions of the tubes were "similar" to Iraq's pre-war Beams gas centrifuge design and "nearly matched" the tube size used in another type of gas centrifuge, the Zippe design. Nuclear analysts from WINPAC explained that prior to the Gulf War Iraq had pursued the development of a Beams centrifuge with aluminum rotors that had a wall thickness in excess of 3.0 millimeters, and that Iraq had built an oil centrifuge with aluminum rotors in excess of 6.0 millimeters. CIA also asserted that the unclassified document describing Zippe's design could be interpreted as using rotors with wall thicknesses that ranged from 1.0 millimeter to 2.8 millimeters. WINPAC reasoned that, although these dated models for centrifuges were not ideal, Iraq was likely to build what it *could* rather than what would be the optimal design. Specifically, old centrifuge designs using aluminum rotors were the only ones Iraq had successfully built in the past without extensive assistance from foreign experts. Similarly, DIA assessed that "[a]lternative uses" for the tubes were "possible," but that such alternatives were "less likely because the specifications [of the tubes] are consistent with late 1980s Iraqi gas centrifuge rotor designs."

DOE disputed this analysis on several grounds. From the outset, DOE believed that Iraq would pursue a more advanced design, such as the Urenco-style centrifuge that Iraq had pursued with the covert assistance of German engineers before the Gulf War. DOE also disagreed with CIA's technical conclusion that the tubes were a plausible match for the Zippe design; it asserted that the optimum Zippe design required a wall thickness no greater than a certain figure (the figure itself is classified). Finally, DOE noted that the Beams design had never been successfully used to enrich uranium—Beams himself could never get his design to work beyond pilot-plant operation. As DOE subsequently explained, in DOE's view it was therefore irrelevant, and misleading, to point to similarities with this design as evidence the tubes were intended for use in a centrifuge.

In sum, although even DOE agreed that the tubes *could* be used for centrifuges, DOE's assessment that such use was unlikely proved closer to the mark. DIA and CIA analysts overestimated the likelihood that the tubes were intended for use in centrifuges, an erroneous judgment that resulted largely from the unwillingness of many analysts to question—or rigorously test—the underlying assumption that Iraq would try to reconstitute its nuclear program.

*The influence of assumptions on the analytical process.* As we have seen, the majority of intelligence agencies—and in particular, CIA and DIA—were simply wrong on the question of whether the aluminum tubes were suitable for conventional rocket applications. A similar dynamic emerged during the intra-Community debate on whether the tubes were a good fit for centrifuge designs; while the judgments were in this case more defensible, CIA and DIA consistently construed quite ambiguous technical data as supporting the conclusion that the aluminum tubes were well-suited for use as centrifuges. A consistent pattern emerges: certain analysts, and certain agencies, were clearly inclined to view evidence— even exceedingly technical evidence—through the prism of their assumptions that Iraq was reconstituting its nuclear program.

This tendency is reflected in the way these analysts interpreted other information about the tubes as well. For instance, CIA and DIA assessed that the tight manufacturing tolerances that Iraq required for the tubes pointed towards centrifuge use, because of the increased cost and manufacturing challenges that would result from these stringent requirements. But as DOE pointed out, although the specifications did seem excessive for use in conventional rockets, the tolerances were also a peculiar requirement if they were destined for centrifuges; the specifications were neither as tight as those previously used by Iraq for centrifuges nor as tight as those typically desired for high-speed rotating equipment. Moreover, the tubes would have required substantial modifications to make them suitable for centrifuge use, and the required modifications would have been inconsistent with the tight manufacturing tolerances demanded. Finally, the tight specifications were not inconsistent with conventional rocket applications; as DOE pointed out to the Senate Select Committee on Intelligence, it is in fact quite common for inexperienced engineers to over-specify tolerances when trying to reverse-engineer equipment.

The focus of certain intelligence agencies on the cost of the tubes offers another example of analysts straining to fit the data into their prevailing theories. The NIE cites reporting indicating that Iraq paid "up to" $17.50 for the tubes, and noted that the willingness to pay this "high" price was indicative of the high priority of the purchase—a fact which, it is suggested, supports the view that the tubes had nuclear application. But in fact this price was not unusually elevated. DOE obtained a price quote from a U.S. manufacturer—without the tight tolerances—of $19.27 per tube.

Adherence to prevailing assumptions also led analysts to discount contrary evidence. Both CIA and DIA were quick to dismiss evidence which tended to show that the tubes were intended for use in Iraq's rocket program, instead attributing such contrary evidence to Iraq's "deception" efforts. Analysts were well aware that Iraq historically had been very successful in "denial and deception" activities, and that, at least in part because of such activities, the Intelligence Community had underestimated the scope of Iraq's pre-Gulf War nuclear program. So analysts, in order to ensure that they were not fooled again, systematically discounted the possibility that the tubes were for rockets.

Indeed, in some instances, analysts went even further, interpreting information that contradicted the prevailing analytical line as intentional deception, and therefore as support for the prevailing analytical view. For example, NGIC characterized the Iraqi claim that the tubes were for use in tactical rockets as "a poorly disguised cover story," reasoning that Iraq was claiming such an end-use for the tubes because Iraq was aware that its intentions to use the tubes in a nuclear centrifuge application "have been compromised." CIA also noted in a Senior Executive Memorandum that Iraq "has established a cover story . . . to disguise the true nuclear end use" for the aluminum tubes, explaining that Iraq may be exploiting press reports regarding the disagreement within the Intelligence Community about the tubes. In some quarters, then, the thesis that the tubes were destined for centrifuges took on the quality of a hypothesis that literally could not be disproved: both confirming and contradictory facts were construed as supporting evidence.

The unwillingness to question prevailing assumptions that Iraq was attempting to reconstitute its nuclear program therefore resulted in faulty analysis of the aluminum tubes. While CIA analysts now agree with the ISG position that the tubes were most likely intended for use in rockets rather than in centrifuge applications, as of March 2005, CIA had still not published a reassessment of its position on the tubes.

Until now, this review has focused on flaws in the Intelligence Community's assessment concerning the likely uses of the aluminum tubes—the central basis for the overall judgment that Iraq was reconstituting. But the Intelligence Community also identified in the NIE other evidence to support this conclusion, including Iraq's attempts to procure other dual-use items needed for a gas centrifuge such as magnets and balancing machines, efforts to reconstitute its nuclear cadre, and activity at suspect sites. This evidence, however, was based on thin streams of reporting (and indeed, as will be shown, the NIE's recitation of this evidence was also marred by inaccuracies). Analysts are of course often called upon to make judgments based on limited information, particularly on difficult targets such as Iraq's nuclear program. With that said, the NIE too often failed to communicate the paucity of intelligence supporting its assessments and also contained several inaccurate statements.

For example, the NIE indicated that according to sensitive reporting, Saddam Hussein was "personally interested in the procurement of aluminum tubes." This sensitive reporting was a single report from a liaison service which reported that Saddam was "closely following" the purchase of the tubes. Yet even this single report was under dispute. According to one CIA officer, it was the service's intelligence officer who said Saddam was following the purchase, although another CIA officer at the meeting remembered the exchange differently. Even though fundamental doubts existed about the validity and ultimate source of this information, CIA was not able to clarify this point (which was understandable, given the uncertainties inherent in working with liaison services) and allowed the NIE to use the information without reflecting this uncertainty (which was not understandable).

In other places, the NIE's assertions concerning Iraq's nuclear program were simply factually incorrect. First, the NIE pointed to Iraq's attempts to procure a permanent magnet production capability as evidence that Iraq was reconstituting its uranium enrichment program. It noted that "a large number of personnel for the new production facility worked in Iraq's pre-Gulf War centrifuge program." This, however, was a mistake; the National Intelligence Officer (NIO) for Strategic and Nuclear Programs subsequently noted that the workers had not been associated with Iraq's centrifuge program but with the former EMIS program. And the NIE misidentified a front company involved in procurement efforts and the items being procured; the company involved in the initial aluminum tube procurement was seeking high-speed spin testing machines, while another company, also involved in tube procurement, was seeking balancing machines.

In light of this, DOE's position on Iraqi nuclear reconstitution appears rather dubious. DOE was alone in its view that these other procurement attempts, combined with the later-recalled reporting regarding uranium from Africa, provided sufficient evidence to conclude that Iraq was reconstituting. Leaving aside the factual errors noted above, there was no evidence that Iraq had actually obtained the dual-use items it was seeking, and DOE conceded that there was no evidence that the magnets Iraq was seeking were intended for the nuclear program. With respect to the alleged uranium enrichment procurement efforts in Africa, DOE reasoned that any indication that Iraq was attempting to procure uranium covertly would be a significant indication of Iraq's intention to pursue a nuclear program.

The gossamer nature of the evidence relied upon by DOE, and the doubts expressed about the attempts to procure uranium from Africa long before the reporting was recalled (more in a moment about this) had led senior officials in other agencies to question the substantive coherence of DOE's position. The former NIO for Strategic and Nuclear Programs, for one, said that he had not fully understood the logic supporting DOE's conclusion that Iraq was reconstituting despite specifically questioning DOE on this point during the NIE coordination meeting. Similarly, a former senior intelligence officer remarked in November 2004 that DOE's position had "made sense politically but not substantively." In fact, the DOE intelligence analyst who participated in the coordination meetings for the NIE—while maintaining that there was no political pressure on DOE, direct or indirect, to agree with the reconstitution conclusion at the NIE coordination meeting—conceded to this Commission that "DOE didn't want to come out before the war and say [Iraq] wasn't reconstituting."

As mentioned above, DOE's position rested in part on a piece of evidence not relied upon by any of the other intelligence agencies in the NIE—that of Iraq's attempts to procure uranium from Niger. This evidence was unconfirmed at the time of the NIE and subsequently shelved because of severe doubts about its veracity. As will be shown in the next section, the Intelligence Community was right to have its doubts about this story, and DOE was wrong to rely on it as an alternative piece of evidence confirming Iraq's interest in reconstitution.

Intelligence Community agencies did not effectively authenticate the documents regarding an alleged agreement for the sale of uranium yellowcake from Niger to Iraq. The President referred to this alleged agreement in his State of the Union address on January 28, 2003—evidence for which the Intelligence Community later concluded was based on forged documents.

To illustrate the failures involved in vetting this information, some details about its collection require elaboration. The October 2002 NIE included the statement that Iraq was "trying to procure uranium ore and yellowcake" and that "a foreign government service" had reported that "Niger planned to send several tons" of yellowcake to Iraq. The statement about Niger was based primarily on three reports provided by a liaison intelligence service to CIA in late 2001 and early 2002. One of these reports explained that, as of early 1999, the Iraqi Ambassador to the Vatican planned to visit Niger on an official mission. The report noted that subsequently, during meetings on July 5–6, 2000, Niger and Iraq had signed an agreement for the sale of 500 tons of uranium. This report stated that it was providing the "verbatim text" of the agreement. The information was consistent with reporting from 1999 showing that a visit to Niger was being arranged for the Iraqi Ambassador to the Vatican.

Subsequently, Vice President Cheney requested follow-up information from CIA on this alleged deal. CIA decided to contact the former U.S. ambassador to Gabon, Ambassador Joseph Wilson, who had been posted to Niger early in his career and maintained contacts there, to see if he would be amenable to traveling to Niger. Ambassador Wilson agreed to do so and, armed with CIA talking points, traveled to Niger in late February 2002 and met with former Nigerian officials.

Following the trip, CIA disseminated an intelligence report in March 2002 based on its debriefing of Ambassador Wilson. The report carried the caveat that the individuals from whom the Ambassador obtained the information were aware that their remarks could reach the U.S. government and "may have intended to influence as well as to inform." According to this report, the former Prime Minister of Niger said that he was not aware of any contracts for uranium that had been signed between Niger and any rogue states. He noted that if there had been such an agreement, he would have been aware of it. He said, however, that in June 1999 he met with an Iraqi delegation to discuss "expanding commercial relations" between Niger and Iraq, which the Prime Minister interpreted as meaning the delegation wanted to discuss yellowcake sales. The Prime Minister let the matter drop, however, because of the United Nations sanctions on Iraq.

The British Government weighed in officially on the Niger subject on September 24, 2002, when it disseminated a white paper on Iraq's WMD programs stating that "there is intelligence that Iraq has sought the supply of significant quantities of uranium from Africa."

The story grew more complicated when, on October 9, 2002, several days after the NIE was published, an Italian journalist provided a package of documents to the U.S. Embassy in Rome, including documents related to the alleged agreement for the sale of uranium from Niger to Iraq. The State Department passed these documents on to elements of the CIA. Although the documents provided to the Embassy by the Italian journalist related to the purported agreement, these elements of the CIA did not retain copies of the documents or forward them to CIA Headquarters because they had been forwarded through Embassy channels to the State Department.

WINPAC analysts, for their part, only requested and obtained copies of the documents several months later—after State's INR had alerted the Intelligence Community in October 2002 that it had serious doubts about the authenticity of the documents. And, even after this point, CIA continued to respond to policymakers' requests for follow-up on the uranium deal with its established line of analysis, without attempting to authenticate the documents and without noting INR's doubts about the authenticity of the information—despite not having looked at the documents with a critical eye.

For example, in mid-January 2003, the Chairman of the Joint Chiefs of Staff requested information—other than information about the aluminum tubes—about why analysts thought Iraq was reconstituting its nuclear program. In response, WINPAC published a current intelligence paper pointing to Iraqi attempts to procure uranium from several African countries, citing "fragmentary reporting," and making no reference to questions about the authenticity of the source documents. Shortly thereafter, the National Security Council and Office of the Secretary of Defense requested information from the NIO for Strategic and Nuclear Programs and from DIA, respectively, on the uranium deal. The responses included information based on the original reporting, without any mention of the questions about the authenticity of the information.

The CIA had still not evaluated the authenticity of the documents when it coordinated on the State of the Union address, in which the President noted that the "British government has learned that Saddam Hussein recently sought significant quantities of uranium from Africa." Although there is some disagreement about the details of the coordination process, no one in the Intelligence Community had asked that the line be removed. At the time of the State of the Union speech, CIA analysts continued to believe that Iraq probably was seeking uranium from Africa, although there was growing concern among some CIA analysts that there were problems with the reporting.

The IAEA, after receiving copies of the documents from the United States, reviewed them and immediately concluded that they were forgeries. As the IAEA found, the documents contained numerous indications of forgery—flaws in the letterhead, forged signatures, misspelled words, incorrect titles for individuals and government entities, and anomalies in the documents' stamps. The documents also contained serious errors in content. For example, the document describing the agreement made reference to the legal authority for the agreement, but referenced an out-of-date statutory provision. The document also referred to a meeting that took place on "Wednesday, July 7, 2000" even though July 7, 2000 was a Friday.

When it finally got around to reviewing the documents during the same time period, the CIA agreed that they were not authentic. Moreover, the CIA concluded that the original reporting was based on the forged documents and was thus itself unreliable. CIA subsequently issued a recall notice at the beginning of April, 2003 for the three original reports, noting that "the foreign government service may have been provided with fraudulent reporting." On June 17, 2003, CIA produced a memorandum for the Director of Central Intelligence (DCI) stating that "since learning that the Iraq-Niger uranium deal was based on false documents earlier this spring we no longer believe that there is sufficient other reporting to conclude that Iraq pursued uranium from abroad." The NIO for Strategic and Nuclear Programs also briefed the Senate and House Intelligence Committees, on June 18 and 19, respectively, on the CIA's conclusions in this regard.

Given that there were already doubts about the reliability of the reporting on the uranium deal, the Intelligence Community should have reviewed the documents to evaluate their authenticity as soon as they were made available in early October 2002, rather than waiting over six months to do so. The failure to review these documents caused the Intelligence Community to rely on dubious information when providing highly important assessments to policymakers about the likelihood that Iraq was reconstituting its nuclear program. The Community's failure to undertake a real review of the documents—even though their validity was the subject of serious doubts—was a major failure of the intelligence system.

## Biological Warfare

The Intelligence Community assessed with "high confidence" in the fall of 2002 that Iraq "has" biological weapons, and that "all key aspects" of Iraq's offensive BW program "are active and that most elements are larger and more advanced than they were before the Gulf War." These conclusions were based largely on the Intelligence Community's judgment that Iraq had "transportable facilities for producing" BW agents. That assessment, in turn, was based largely on reporting from a single human source.

Contrary to the Intelligence Community's pre-war assessments, the ISG's post-war investigations concluded that Iraq had unilaterally destroyed its biological weapons stocks and probably destroyed its remaining holdings of bulk BW agent in 1991 and 1992. Moreover, the ISG concluded that Iraq had conducted no research on BW agents since that time, although Iraq had retained some dual-use equipment and intellectual capital. The ISG found no evidence of a mobile BW program.

That Iraq was cooking up biological agents in mobile facilities designed to elude the prying eyes of international inspectors and Western intelligence services was, along with the aluminum tubes, the most important and alarming assessment in the October 2002 NIE. This judgment, as it turns out, was based almost exclusively on information obtained from a single human source—code-named "Curveball"—whose credibility came into question around the time of the publication of the NIE and collapsed under scrutiny in the months following the war. This section discusses how this ultimately unreliable reporting came to play such a critical role in the Intelligence Community's pre-war assessments about Iraq's BW program. We begin by discussing the evolution of the Intelligence Community's judgments on this issue in the years preceding the second Iraq war; compare these pre-war assessments with what the ISG found; and, finally, offer our conclusions about the Intelligence Community's performance against the Iraqi BW target, focusing in particular on Curveball and the handling of his information by the Intelligence Community.

We note at the outset that this section includes new information about the failure of the Intelligence Community—and particularly of Intelligence Community management—to convey to policymakers serious concerns about Curveball that arose in the months preceding the invasion of Iraq. Although these findings are significant, we believe that other lessons about the Intelligence Community's assessments of Iraq's purported BW programs are the more critical ones. At bottom, the story of the Intelligence Community's performance on BW is one of poor tradecraft by our human intelligence collection agencies; of our intelligence analysts allowing reasonable suspicions about Iraqi BW activity to turn into near certainty; and of the Intelligence Community failing to communicate adequately the limited nature of their intelligence on Iraq's BW programs to policymakers, in both the October 2002 NIE and other contemporaneous intelligence assessments.

*The Intelligence Community's Pre-War Assessments*

The Intelligence Community's assessment of Iraq's BW program—like its judgments about Iraq's other WMD programs—evolved over time. The October 2002 NIE reflected a shift, however, in the Community's judgments about the state of Iraq's BW program. Previous Community estimates had assessed that Iraq could have biological weapons; the October 2002 estimate, in contrast, assessed with "high confidence" that Iraq "has" biological weapons. This shift in view, which began in 2000 and culminated in the October 2002 NIE, was based largely on information from a single source—Curveball—who indicated that Iraq had mobile facilities for producing BW agents.

*Background.* In the early 1990s, the Intelligence Community knew little about Iraq's BW program. Prior to the Gulf War, the Intelligence Community judged that Iraq was developing several BW agents, including anthrax and botulinum toxin, at a number of facilities. The Intelligence Community further assessed that Iraq might have produced up to 1,000 liters of BW agent, and that Iraq had used some of it to fill aerial bombs and artillery shells. At that time, however, the Community judged that it had insufficient information to make assessments about BW agent testing and deployment of filled munitions. Between 1991 and 1995, the Intelligence Community learned little more about Iraq's BW program. However, there was some additional human intelligence reporting indicating that pre-Gulf War assessments of Iraq's BW program had substantially underestimated the quantities of biological weapons that Iraq had produced. Moreover, this reporting suggested that the Intelligence Community was unaware of some Iraqi BW facilities.

It was not until 1995—when UNSCOM presented the Iraqis with evidence of continuing BW-related imports and Saddam Hussein's son-in-law, Hussein Kamil, defected—that Iraq made substantial declarations to the United Nations about its activities prior to the Gulf War, admitting that it had produced and weaponized BW agents. These declarations confirmed that the Intelligence Community had substantially underestimated the scale and maturity of Iraq's pre-Desert Storm BW program. Iraq had, before the Gulf War, weaponized several agents, including anthrax, botulinum toxin, and aflatoxin; produced 30,165 liters of BW agent; and deployed some of its 157 bombs and 25 missile warheads armed with BW agents to locations throughout Iraq. Following these declarations, the Intelligence Community estimated in 1997 that Iraq was still concealing elements of its BW program, and it assessed that Iraq would likely wait until either sanctions were lifted or the UNSCOM presence was reduced before restarting agent production.

After 1998, the Intelligence Community found it difficult to determine whether activity at known dual-use facilities was related to WMD production. The departed inspectors had never been able to confirm what might be happening at Iraq's suspect facilities. Accordingly, the Intelligence Community noted that it had no reliable intelligence to indicate resumed production of biological weapons, but assessed that in the absence of inspectors Iraq probably would expand its BW activities. These assessments were colored by the Community's earlier underestimation of Iraq's programs, its lack of reliable intelligence, and its realization that previous underestimates were due in part to effective deception by the Iraqis. By 1999, the CIA assessed that there was some Iraqi research and development on BW and that Iraq could restart production of biological weapons within a short period of time. The 1999 NIE on Worldwide BW Programs judged that Iraq was "revitalizing its BW program" and was "probably continuing work to develop and produce BW agents."

*Growing concern.* The Intelligence Community's concern about Iraq's BW program increased in early 2000, and the Community began to adjust upward its estimates of the Iraq BW threat, based on a "substantial volume" of "new information" regarding mobile BW facilities in Iraq. This information came from an Iraqi chemical engineer, subsequently codenamed Curveball, who came to the attention of the Intelligence Community through a foreign liaison service. That liaison service debriefed Curveball and then shared the debriefing results with the United States. The foreign liaison service would not, however, provide the United States with direct access to Curveball. Instead, information about Curveball was passed from the liaison service to DIA's Defense

HUMINT Service, which in turn disseminated information about Curveball throughout the Intelligence Community.

Between January 2000 and September 2001, DIA's Defense HUMINT Service disseminated almost 100 reports from Curveball regarding mobile BW facilities in Iraq. These reports claimed that Iraq had several mobile production units and that one of those units had begun production of BW agents as early as 1997.

Shortly after Curveball started reporting, in the spring of 2000, his information was provided to senior policymakers. It was also incorporated into an update to a 1999 NIE on Worldwide BW Programs. The update reported that "new intelligence acquired in 2000 . . . causes [the IC] to adjust our assessment upward of the BW threat posed by Iraq . . . The new information suggests that Baghdad has expanded its offensive BW program by establishing a large-scale, redundant, and concealed BW agent production capability." In December 2000, the Intelligence Community produced a Special Intelligence Report that was based on reporting from Curveball, noting that "credible reporting from a single source suggests" that Iraq has produced biological agents, but cautioned that "[w]e cannot confirm whether Iraq has produced . . . biological agents."

By 2001, however, the assessments became more assertive. A WINPAC report in October 2001, also based on Curveball's reporting about mobile facilities, judged "that Iraq continues to produce at least . . . three BW agents" and possibly two others. This assessment also concluded that "the establishment of mobile BW agent production plants and continued delivery system development provide Baghdad with BW capabilities surpassing the pre-Gulf War era." Similar assessments were provided to senior policymakers. In late September 2002, DCI Tenet told the Senate's Intelligence and Armed Services Committees (and subsequently the Senate Foreign Relations Committee) that "we know Iraq has developed a redundant capability to produce biological warfare agents using mobile production units."

*October 2002 NIE.* The October 2002 NIE reflected this upward assessment of the Iraqi BW threat that had developed since Curveball began reporting in January 2000. The October 2002 NIE reflected the shift from the late–1990s assessments that Iraq *could* have biological weapons to the definitive conclusion that Iraq "has" biological weapons, and that its BW program was larger and more advanced than before the Gulf War. Information about Iraq's dual-use facilities and its failure to account fully for previously declared stockpiles contributed to this shift in assessments. The information that Iraq had mobile BW production units, however, was instrumental in adjusting upward the assessment of Iraq's BW threat. And for this conclusion, the NIE relied primarily on reporting from Curveball, who, as noted, provided a large volume of reporting through Defense HUMINT channels regarding mobile BW production facilities in Iraq. Only in May 2004, more than a year after the commencement of Operation Iraqi Freedom, did CIA formally deem Curveball's reporting fabricated and recall it. At the time of the NIE, however, reporting from three other human sources—who provided one report each on mobile BW facilities—was thought to have corroborated Curveball's information about the mobile facilities. These three sources also proved problematic, however, as discussed below.

Another asylum seeker (hereinafter "the second source") reporting through Defense HUMINT channels provided one report in June 2001 that Iraq had transportable facilities for the production of BW. This second source recanted in October 2003, however, and the recantation was reflected in a Defense HUMINT report in which the source flatly contradicted his June 2001 statements about transportable facilities. Though CIA analysts told Commission staff that they had requested that Defense HUMINT follow-up with this second source to ascertain the reasons for his recantation, DIA's Defense HUMINT Service has provided no further information on this issue. Nor, for that matter, was the report ever recalled or corrected.

Another source, associated with the Iraqi National Congress (INC) (hereinafter "the INC source"), was brought to the attention of DIA by Washington-based representatives of the INC. Like Curveball, his reporting was handled by Defense HUMINT. He provided one report that Iraq had decided in 1996 to establish mobile laboratories for BW agents to evade inspectors. Shortly after Defense HUMINT's initial debriefing of the INC source in February 2002, however, a foreign liaison service and the CIA's

Directorate of Operations (DO) judged him to be a fabricator and recommended that Defense HUMINT issue a notice to that effect, which Defense HUMINT did in May 2002. Senior policymakers were informed that the INC source and his reporting were unreliable. The INC source's information, however, began to be used again in finished intelligence in July 2002, including the October 2002 NIE, because, although a fabrication notice had been issued several months earlier, Defense HUMINT had failed to recall the reporting.

The classified report here discusses a fourth source (hereinafter "the fourth source") who provided a single report that Iraq had mobile fermentation units mounted on trucks and railway cars.

*Post-NIE.* After publication of the NIE in October 2002, the Intelligence Community continued to assert that Baghdad's biological weapons program was active and posed a threat, relying on the same set of sources upon which the NIE's judgments were based. For example, a November 2002 paper produced by CIA's Directorate of Intelligence (DI) reiterated the NIE's assessment that Iraq had a "broad range of lethal and incapacitating agents" and that the "BW program is more robust than it was prior to the Gulf War." The piece contended that Iraq was capable of producing an array of agents and probably retained strains of the smallpox virus. It further argued that technological advances increased the potential Iraqi BW threat to U.S. interests. And a February 2003 CIA Intelligence Assessment anticipated Iraqi options for BW (and CW) use against the United States and other members of the Coalition; the report stated that Iraq "maintains a wide range of . . . biological agents and delivery systems" and enumerated 21 BW agents which it judged Iraq could employ.

Statements about biological weapons also appeared in Administration statements about Iraq in the months preceding the war. Secretary of State Colin Powell's speech to the United Nations Security Council on February 5, 2003, relied on the same human sources relied upon in the NIE. Secretary Powell was not informed that one of these sources—the INC source—had been judged a fabricator almost a year earlier. And as will be discussed at length below, serious doubts about Curveball had also surfaced within CIA's Directorate of Operations at the time of the speech—but these doubts also were not communicated to Secretary Powell before his United Nations address.

Reliance on Curveball's reporting also affected post-war assessments of Iraq's BW program. A May 2003 CIA Intelligence Assessment pointed to the post-invasion discovery of "two probable mobile BW agent productions plants" by Coalition forces in Iraq as evidence that "Iraq was hiding a biological warfare program." Curveball, when shown photos of the trailers, identified components that he said were similar to those on the mobile BW production facilities that he had described in his earlier reporting.

## Post-War Findings of the Iraq Survey Group

The Iraq Survey Group found that the Intelligence Community's pre-war assessments about Iraq's BW program were almost entirely wrong. The ISG concluded that "Iraq appears to have destroyed its undeclared stocks of BW weapons and probably destroyed remaining holdings of bulk BW agent" shortly after the Gulf War. According to the ISG, Iraq initially intended to retain elements of its biological weapons program after the Gulf War. UNSCOM inspections proved unexpectedly intrusive, however, and to avoid detection, Saddam Hussein ordered his son-in-law and Minister of the Military Industrial Commission Hussein Kamil to destroy, unilaterally, Iraq's stocks of BW agents. This took place in either the late spring or summer of 1991. But Iraq retained a physical plant at Al-Hakam and the intellectual capital necessary to resuscitate the BW program. Simultaneously, Iraq embarked on an effort to hide this remaining infrastructure and to conceal its pre-war BW-related activities.

In early 1995, however, UNSCOM inspectors confronted Iraqi officials with evidence of 1988 imports of bacterial growth media in quantities that had no civilian use within Iraq's limited biotechnology industry. This confrontation, followed by the defection of Hussein Kamil in August 1995, prompted Iraq to admit that it had produced large quantities of bulk BW agent before the Gulf War. Iraq also released a large cache of documents and issued the first of several "Full, Final and Complete Declaration[s]" on June 22, 1996, further detailing its BW program. UNSCOM subsequently supervised the destruction of BW-related facilities at Al-Hakam in 1996.

The Iraq Survey Group found that the destruction of the Al-Hakam facility effectively marked the end of Iraq's large-scale BW ambitions. The ISG did judge that after 1996 Iraq "continued small-scale BW-related efforts" under the auspices of the Iraqi Intelligence Service, and also retained a trained cadre of scientists who could work on BW programs and some dual-use facilities capable of conversion to small-scale BW agent production. Nevertheless, the ISG "found no direct evidence that Iraq, after 1996, had plans for a new BW program or was conducting BW-specific work for military purposes."

With respect to mobile BW production facilities, the "ISG found no evidence that Iraq possessed or was developing production systems on road vehicles or railway wagons." The ISG's "exhaustive investigation" of the two trailers captured by Coalition forces in spring 2003 revealed that the trailers were "almost certainly designed and built exclusively for the generation of hydrogen." The ISG judged that the trailers "cannot . . . be part of any BW program."

## Analysis of the Intelligence Community's Pre-War Assessments

The Intelligence Community fundamentally misjudged the status of Iraq's BW programs. As the above discussion demonstrates, the central basis for the Intelligence Community's pre-war assessments about Iraq's BW program was the reporting of a single human source, Curveball. This single source, whose reporting came into question in late 2002, later proved to be a fabricator.

Our intelligence agencies get burned by human sources sometimes—it is a fact of life in the murky world of espionage. If our investigation revealed merely that our Intelligence Community had a source who later turned out to be lying, despite the best tradecraft practices designed to ferret out such liars, that would be one thing. But Curveball's reporting became a central part of the Intelligence Community's pre-war assessments through a serious breakdown in several aspects of the intelligence process. The Curveball story is at the same time one of poor asset validation by our human collection agencies; of a tendency of analysts to believe that which fits their theories; of inadequate communication between the Intelligence Community and the policymakers it serves; and, ultimately, of poor leadership and management. This section thus focuses primarily on our investigation of the Curveball episode, and the findings we drew from it.

The problems with the Intelligence Community's performance on Curveball began almost immediately after the source first became known to the U.S. government in early 2000. As noted above, Curveball was not a source who worked directly with the United States; rather, the Intelligence Community obtained information about Curveball through a foreign service. The foreign service would not provide the United States with direct access to Curveball, claiming that Curveball would refuse to speak to Americans. Instead, the foreign intelligence service debriefed Curveball and passed the debriefing information to DIA's Defense HUMINT Service, the human intelligence collection agency of the Department of Defense.

The lack of direct access to Curveball made it more difficult to assess his veracity. But such lack of access does not preclude the Intelligence Community from attempting to assess the source's bona fides and the credibility of the source's reporting. Indeed, it is incumbent upon professional intelligence officers to attempt to do so, through a process referred to within the Intelligence Community as "vetting" or "asset validation."

Defense HUMINT, however, did not even attempt to determine Curveball's veracity. A Defense HUMINT official explained to Commission staff that Defense HUMINT believed that it was just a "conduit" for Curveball's reporting—that it had no responsibility for vetting Curveball or validating his information. In Defense HUMINT's view, asset validation is solely the responsibility of analysts—in their judgment if the analysts believe the information is credible, then the source is validated. This line echoes what Defense HUMINT officials responsible for disseminating

Curveball's reporting told the Senate Select Committee on Intelligence; they told the Committee that it was not their responsibility to assess the source's credibility, but that it instead was up to the analysts who read the reports to judge the accuracy of the contents.

The Senate Select Committee on Intelligence concluded that this view represents a "serious lapse" in tradecraft, and we agree. Analysts obviously play a crucial role in validating sources by evaluating the credibility of their reporting, corroborating that reporting, and reviewing the body of reporting to ensure that it is consistent with the source's access. But analysts' validation can only extend to whether what a source says is internally consistent, technically plausible, and credible given the source's claimed access. The process of validation also must include efforts by the operational elements to confirm the source's bona fides (i.e., authenticating that the source has the access he claims), to test the source's reliability and motivations, and to ensure that the source is free from hostile control. To be sure, these steps are particularly difficult for a source such as Curveball, to whom the collection agency has no direct access. But human intelligence collectors can often obtain valuable information weighing on even a liaison source's credibility, and the CIA's DO routinely attempts to determine the credibility even of sources to whom it has no direct access. In light of this, we are surprised by the Defense HUMINT's apparent position that it had no responsibility even to attempt to validate Curveball.

As a footnote to this episode, while DIA's Defense HUMINT Service felt no obligation to vet Curveball or validate his veracity, it would later appear affronted that another agency—CIA— would try to do so. On February 11, 2003, after questions about Curveball's credibility had begun to emerge, an element of the DO sent a message to Defense HUMINT officials expressing concern that Curveball had not been vetted. The next day the Defense HUMINT division chief who received that message forwarded it by electronic mail to a subordinate, requesting input to answer CIA's query. In that electronic mail message, the Defense HUMINT division chief said he was "shocked" by CIA's suggestion that Curveball might be unreliable. The reply—which the

Defense HUMINT official intended for Defense HUMINT recipients only but which was inadvertently sent to CIA as well—observed that "CIA is up to their old tricks" and that CIA did not "have a clue" about the process by which Curveball's information was passed from the foreign service.

As we have discussed, when information from Curveball first surfaced in early 2000, Defense HUMINT did nothing to validate Curveball's reporting. Analysts within the Intelligence Community, however, did make efforts to assess the credibility of the information provided by Curveball. In early 2000, when Curveball's reporting first surfaced, WINPAC analysts researched previous reporting and concluded that Curveball's information was plausible based upon previous intelligence, including imagery reporting, and the detailed, technical descriptions of the mobile facilities he provided. As a WINPAC BW analyst later told us, there was nothing "obviously wrong" with Curveball's information, and his story—that Iraq had moved to a mobile capability for its BW program in 1995 in order to evade inspectors— was logical in light of other known information.

At about the same time, however, traffic in the CIA's Directorate of Operations began to suggest some possible problems with Curveball. The first CIA concerns about Curveball's reliability arose within the DO in May 2000, when a Department of Defense detailee assigned to the DO met Curveball. The purpose of the meeting was to evaluate Curveball's claim that he had been present during a BW accident that killed several of his coworkers by seeing whether Curveball had been exposed to, or vaccinated against, a BW agent. Although the evaluation was ultimately inconclusive, the detailee raised several concerns about Curveball based on their interaction.

First, the detailee observed that Curveball spoke excellent English during their meeting. This was significant to the detailee because the foreign service had, on several earlier occasions, told U.S. intelligence officials that one reason a meeting with Curveball was impossible was that Curveball did not speak English. Second, the detailee was concerned by Curveball's apparent "hangover" during their meeting. The detailee conveyed these impressions of Curveball informally to CIA officials, and WIN-

PAC BW analysts told Commission staff that they were aware that the detailee was concerned that Curveball might be an alcoholic. This message was eventually re-conveyed to Directorate of Operations supervisors via electronic mail on February 4, 2003— literally on the eve of Secretary Powell's speech to the United Nations. The electronic mail stated, in part:

> I do have a concern with the validity of the information based on Curveball having a terrible hangover the morning of [the meeting]. I agree, it was only a one time interaction, however, he knew he was to have a [meeting] on that particular morning but tied one on anyway. What underlying issues could this be a problem with and how in depth has he been vetted by the [foreign liaison service]?

By early 2001, the DO was receiving operational messages about the foreign service's difficulties in handling Curveball, whom the foreign service reported to be "out of control," and whom the service could not locate. This operational traffic regarding Curveball was shared with WINPAC's Iraq BW analysts because, according to WINPAC analysts, the primary BW analyst who worked on the Iraq issue had close relations with the DO's Counterproliferation Division (the division through which the operational traffic was primarily handled). This and other operational information was not, however, shared with analysts outside CIA.

A second warning on Curveball came in April 2002, when a foreign intelligence service, which was also receiving reporting from Curveball, told the CIA that, in its view, there were a variety of problems with Curveball. The foreign service began by noting that they were "inclined to believe that a significant part of [Curveball's] reporting is true" in light of his detailed technical descriptions. In this same message, however, the foreign service noted that it was "not convinced that Curveball is a wholly reliable source," and that "elements of [Curveball's] behavior strike us as typical of individuals we would normally assess as fabricators." Even more specifically, the foreign service noted several inconsistencies in Curveball's reporting which caused the foreign service "to have doubts about Curveball's reliability." It should be noted here that, like the handling foreign service, this other service continued officially to back Curveball's reporting throughout this period.

Again, these concerns about Curveball were shared with CIA analysts working on the BW issue. But none of the expressed concerns overcame analysts' ultimate confidence in the accuracy of his information. Specifically, analysts continued to judge his information credible based on their assessment of its detail and technical accuracy, corroborating documents, confirmation of the technical feasibility of the production facility designs described by Curveball, and reporting from another human source, the fourth source mentioned above. But it should be noted that during the pre-NIE period—in addition to the more general questions about Curveball's credibility discussed above—at least some evidence had emerged calling into question the substance of Curveball's reporting about Iraq's BW program as well.

Specifically, a WINPAC BW analyst told us that two foreign services had both noted in 2001 that Curveball's description of the facility he claimed was involved in the mobile BW program was contradicted by imagery of the site, which showed a wall across the path that Curveball said the mobile trailers traversed. Intelligence Community analysts "set that information aside," however, because it could not be reconciled with the rest of Curveball's information, which appeared plausible. Analysts also explained away this discrepancy by noting that Iraq had historically been very successful in "denial and deception" activities and speculated that the wall spotted by imagery might be a temporary structure put up by the Iraqis to deceive U.S. intelligence efforts.

Analysts' use of denial and deception to explain away discordant evidence about Iraq's BW programs was a recurring theme in our review of the Community's performance on the BW question. Burned by the experience of being wrong on Iraq's WMD in 1991 and convinced that Iraq was restarting its programs, analysts dismissed indications that Iraq had actually abandoned its prohibited programs by chalking these indicators up to Iraq's well-known denial and deception efforts. In one instance, for example, WINPAC analysts described reporting from the second source indicating Iraq was filling BW warheads at a transportable facility near Baghdad. When imagery was unable to locate the transportable BW systems at the reported site, analysts assumed this was not because the activity was not taking place, but rather because Iraq was hiding activities from U.S. satellite overflights. This tendency was best encapsulated by a comment in a memorandum prepared by the CIA for a senior policymaker: "Mobile BW information comes from [several] sources, one of whom is credible and the other is of undetermined reliability. We have raised our collection posture in a bid to locate these production units, but years of fruitless searches by UNSCOM indicate they are well hidden." Again, the analysts appear never to have considered the idea that the searches were fruitless because the weapons were not there.

The Community erred in failing to highlight its overwhelming reliance on Curveball for its BW assessments. The NIE judged that Iraq "has transportable facilities for producing bacterial and toxin BW agents" and attributed this judgment to multiple sources. In reality, however, on the topic of mobile BW facilities Curveball provided approximately 100 detailed reports on the subject, while the second and fourth sources each provided a single report. (As will be discussed in greater detail below, the reporting of another source—the INC source—had been deemed a fabrication months earlier, but nonetheless found its way into the October 2002 NIE.) The presentation of the material as attributable to "multiple sensitive sources," however, gave the impression that the support for the BW assessments was more broadly based than was in fact the case. A more accurate presentation would have allowed senior officials to see just how narrow the evidentiary base for the judgments on Iraq's BW programs actually was.

Other contemporaneous assessments about Iraq's BW program also reflect this problem. For example, the Intelligence Community informed senior policymakers in July 2002 that CIA judged that "Baghdad has transportable production facilities for BW agents . . . according to defectors." Again, while three "defector" sources (Curveball, the second source, and the INC source) are cited in this report, Curveball's reporting was the overwhelmingly predominant source of the information.

And the NIE should not only have emphasized its reliance on Curveball for its BW judgments; it should also have communicated the limitations of the source himself. The NIE, for instance, described him as "an Iraqi defector deemed credible by the [Intelligence Community]." The use of the term "credible" was apparently meant to imply only that Curveball's reporting was technically plausible. To a lay reader, however, it implied a broader judgment as to the source's general reliability. This description obscured a number of salient facts that, given the Community's heavy reliance upon his reporting, would have been highly important for policymakers to know—including the fact that the Community had never gained direct access to the source and that he was known at the time to have serious handling problems. While policymakers may still have credited his reporting, they would at least have been warned about the risks in doing so.

After the NIE was published, but before Secretary Powell's speech to the United Nations, more serious concerns surfaced about Curveball's reliability. These concerns were never brought to Secretary Powell's attention, however. Precisely how and why this lapse occurred is the subject of dispute and conflicting memories. This section provides only a brief summary of the key events in this complicated saga.

The NIE went to press in early October 2002, but its publication did not end the need to scrutinize Curveball's reliability. To improve the CIA's confidence in Curveball, the CIA's Deputy Director for Operations (DDO), James Pavitt, sought to press the foreign intelligence service for access to Curveball. Mr. Pavitt's office accordingly asked the chief ("the division chief") of the DO's regional division responsible for relations with the liaison service ("the division") to meet with a representative of the foreign intelligence service to make the request for access. According to the division chief, he met with the representative in late September or early October 2002.

At the lunch, the division chief raised the issue of U.S. intelligence officials speaking to Curveball directly. According to the division chief, the representative of the foreign intelligence service responded with words to the effect of "You don't want to see him [Curveball] because he's crazy." Speaking to him would be, in the representative of the foreign service's words, "a waste of time." The representative, who said that he had been present for debriefings of Curveball, continued that his intelligence service was not sure whether Curveball was actually telling the truth and, in addition, that he had serious doubts about Curveball's mental stability and reliability; Curveball, according to the representative, had had a nervous breakdown. Further, the representative said that he worried that Curveball was "a fabricator." The representative cautioned the division chief, however, that the foreign service would publicly and officially deny these views if pressed. The representative told the division chief that the rationale for such a public denial would be that the foreign service did not wish to be embarrassed. According to the division chief, he passed the information to three offices: up the line to the office of CIA's Deputy Director for Operations; down the line to his staff, specifically the division's group chief ("the group chief") responsible for the liaison country's region; and across the agency to WINPAC. At the time, the division chief thought that the information was "no big deal" because he did not realize how critical Curveball's reporting was to the overall case for Iraqi possession of a biological weapons program. He assumed there were other streams of reporting to buttress the Intelligence Community's assessments. He could not imagine, he said, that Curveball was "it."

Several months later, prompted by indications that the President or a senior U.S. official would soon be making a speech on Iraq's WMD programs, one of the executive assistants for the then-Deputy Director of Central Intelligence (DDCI) John McLaughlin met with the group chief to look into the Curveball information. This meeting took place on December 18, 2002. Although the executive assistant did not specifically recall the meeting when he spoke with Commission staff, an electronic mail follow-up from the meeting—which was sent to the division chief and the group chief—makes clear that the meeting was called to discuss Curveball and the public use of his information.

As a result of this meeting, the division sent a message that same afternoon to the CIA's station in the relevant country again asking that the foreign intelligence service permit the United States to debrief Curveball. The message stressed the importance of gaining access to Curveball, and noted the U.S. government's desire to use Curveball's reporting publicly. On December 20, the foreign service refused the request for access, but concurred with the request to use Curveball's information publicly—"with the expectation of source protection."

By this point, it was clear that the division believed there was a serious problem with Curveball that required attention. A second meeting was scheduled on December 19 at the invitation of DDCI McLaughlin's same executive assistant. According to the executive assistant, he called the meeting because it had become apparent to DDCI McLaughlin that Curveball's reporting was significant to the Intelligence Community's judgments on Iraq's mobile BW capability. The invitation for the meeting stated that the purpose was to "resolve precisely how we judge Curveball's reporting on mobile BW labs," and that the executive assistant hoped that after the meeting he could "summarize [the] conclusions in a short note to the DDCI." The meeting was attended by the executive assistant, a WINPAC BW analyst, an operations officer from the DO's Counterproliferation Division, and the regional division's group chief. Mr. McLaughlin, who did not attend this meeting, told this Commission that he was not given a written summary of the meeting and did not recall whether any such meeting was held.

Although individuals' recollections of the meeting vary somewhat, there is little disagreement on the meeting's substance. The group chief argued that Curveball had not been adequately "vetted" and that his information should therefore not be relied upon. In preparation for the meeting, the group chief had outlined her concerns in an electronic mail to several officers within the Directorate of Operations—including Stephen Kappes, the then-Associate Deputy Director for Operations. The electronic mail opened with the following (in bold type):

Although no one asked, it is my assessment that Curve Ball had some access to some of this information and was more forthcoming and cooperative when he needed resettlement assistance; now that he does not need it, he is less helpful, possibly because when he was being helpful, he was embellishing, a bit. The [foreign service] ha[s] developed some doubts about him. We have been unable to vet him operationally and know very little about him. The intelligence community has corroborated portions of his reporting with open source information . . . and some intelligence (which appears to confirm that things are where he said they were).

At the meeting, the group chief stated that she told the attendees that the division's concerns were based on the foreign service representative's statements to the division chief, the CIA's inability to get access to Curveball, the significant "improvement" in Curveball's reporting over time, the decline of Curveball's reporting after he received the equivalent of a green card, among other reasons. She also recalled telling the attendees the details of the foreign service representative 's statements to the division chief. In the group chief's view, she made it clear to all the attendees that the division did not believe that Curveball's information should be relied upon.

With equal vigor, the WINPAC representative argued that Curveball's reporting was fundamentally reliable. According to the WINPAC analyst, Curveball's information was reliable because it was detailed, technically accurate, and corroborated by another source's reporting.

Both the group chief and the WINPAC analyst characterized the exchange as fairly heated. Both of the two primary participants also recalled providing reasons why the other's arguments should not carry the day. Specifically, the group chief says she argued, adamantly, that the supposedly corroborating information was of dubious significance because it merely established that Curveball had been to the location, not that he had any knowledge of BW activities being conducted there. In addition, the group chief questioned whether some of Curveball's knowledge could have come from readily available, open source materials. Conversely, the WINPAC BW analyst says that she questioned whether the group chief had sufficient knowledge of Curveball's reporting to be able to make an accurate assessment of his reliability.

It appears that WINPAC prevailed in this argument. Looking back, the executive assistant who had called the meeting offered his view that the WINPAC BW analyst was the "master of [the Curveball] case," and that he "look[ed] to her for answers." He also noted that the group chief clearly expressed her skepticism about Curveball during the meeting, and that she fundamentally took the position that Curveball's reporting did not "hold up." The executive assistant further said that while the foreign service officially assessed that Curveball was reliable, they also described him as a "handling problem." According to the executive assistant, the foreign service said Curveball was a handling problem because he was a drinker, unstable, and generally difficult to manage. In the executive assistant's view, however, it was impossible to know whether the foreign service's description of Curveball was accurate. Finally, the executive assistant said that he fully recognized Curveball's significance at the time of the meeting; that Curveball "was clearly the most significant source" on BW; and that if Curveball were removed, the BW assessment was left with one other human source, "but not much more."

The following day, the executive assistant circulated a memorandum to the WINPAC BW analyst intended to summarize the prior day's meeting. Perhaps in keeping with his reliance on the WINPAC BW analyst as the "master of the case," the executive assistant's "summary" of the draft of the memorandum, titled "Reliability of Human Reporting on Iraqi Mobile BW Capability," played down the doubts raised by the DO division:

The primary source of this information is an Iraqi émigré (vice defector) . . . After an exhaustive review, the U.S. Intelligence Community—[as well as several liaison services] . . . judged him credible. This judgment was based on:

- The detailed, technical nature of his reporting;

- [Technical intelligence] confirming the existence/configuration of facilities he described (one Baghdad office building is known to house administrative offices linked to WMD programs);

- UNSCOM's discovery of military documents discussing "mobile fermentation" capability;

- Confirmation/replication of the described design by U.S. contractors (it works); and

- Reporting from a second émigré that munitions were loaded with BW agent from a mobile facility parked within an armaments center south of Baghdad.

The memorandum then continued on to note that "[w]e are handicapped in efforts to resolve legitimate questions that remain about the source's veracity and reporting because the [foreign service] refuses to grant direct access to the source." Later, in the "Questions/Answers" section, the memorandum stated:

> *How/when was the source's reliability evaluated*—[One foreign service] hosted a . . . meeting in 2001, over the course of which all the participating services judged the core reporting as "reliable." [One of the other services] recently affirmed that view— although the [service] ha[s] declined to provide details of sources who might provide corroboration. Operational traffic . . . indicates the [hosting foreign service] may now be downgrading its own evaluation of the source's reliability.

It does not appear that this memorandum was circulated further; rather, the executive assistant explained that he would have used the memorandum to brief the DDCI at their daily staff meeting.

Former DDCI McLaughlin, however, said that he did not remember being apprised of this meeting. Mr. McLaughlin told the Commission that, although he remembered his executive assistant at some point making a passing reference to the effect that the executive assistant had heard about some issues with Curveball, he (Mr. McLaughlin) did not remember having ever been told in any specificity about the DO division's doubts about Curveball. Mr. McLaughlin added that, at the same time, he was receiving assurances from the relevant analysts to the effect that Curveball's information appeared good.

At about the same time, the division apparently tried another route to the top. Within a day or so after the December 19 meeting, the division's group chief said that she and the division chief met with James Pavitt (the Deputy Director for Operations) and Stephen Kappes (the Associate Deputy Director for Operations). At this meeting, according to the group chief , she repeated the Division's concerns about Curveball. But according to the group chief , Mr. Pavitt told her that she was not qualified to make a judgment about Curveball, and that judgments about Curveball should be made by analysts.

When asked about this meeting by Commission staff, Mr. Pavitt said that although he knew there were handling problems with Curveball, he did not recall any such meeting with the division chief or the group chief. Mr. Pavitt added, however, that he would have agreed that the call was one for the analysts to make. He also noted that he does not recall being aware, in December 2002, that Curveball was such a central source of information for the Intelligence Community's mobile BW judgments. For his part, Mr. Kappes does not specifically recall this meeting, although he said that the concerns about Curveball were generally known within the CIA. He also said that he did not become aware of the extensive reliance on Curveball until after the war.

That is where matters stood for about a month. But the issue arose once again in January 2003. During December and January, it became clear that the Secretary of State would be making an address on Iraq to the United Nations Security Council and that presenting American intelligence on Iraq's WMD programs would be a major part of the speech. In late January, the Secretary began "vetting" the intelligence in a series of long meetings at the CIA's Langley headquarters. In connection with those preparations, a copy of the speech was circulated so that various offices within CIA could check it for accuracy and ensure that material could be used without inappropriately disclosing sources and methods. As part of that process, the group chief received a copy. According to the group chief , she said that she "couldn't believe" the speech relied on Curveball's reporting, and immediately told the division chief about the situation. The group chief also said that she edited the language in a way that made the speech more appropriate.

According to the division chief , he was given the draft speech by an assistant, and he immediately redacted material based on Curveball's reporting. He then called the DDCI's executive assistant and asked to speak to the DDCI about the speech. When interviewed by Commission staff, the executive assistant did not recall having any such conversation with the division chief , nor did he remember seeing a redacted copy of the speech. However, another Directorate of Operations officer, who was responsible for evaluating the possible damage to DO sources from the release of information in the speech, remembers being approached during this time by the division chief. According to this officer, the division chief said he was concerned about the proposed inclusion of Curveball's information in the Powell speech and that the handling service itself thought Curveball was a "flake."

The DO officer responsible for sources and methods protection summarized these concerns in an electronic mail which he sent to another of the DDCI's aides for passage to the DDCI. The DO officer responsible for sources and methods did not recall that the division chief made any specific redactions of language from the draft. The DDCI's executive assistant has no recollection of such an electronic mail or of any concerns expressed about Curveball.

Later that afternoon, according to the division chief, he met with the DDCI to discuss the speech. The division chief recounted that he told the DDCI that there was a problem with the speech because it relied on information from Curveball, and that—based on his meeting with the foreign intelligence service representative—the division chief thought that Curveball could be a fabricator. Although the division chief told the Commission that he could not remember the DDCI's exact response, he got the impression that this was the first time that the DDCI had heard of a problem with Curveball. Specifically, the division chief recalled that the DDCI, on hearing that Curveball might be a fabricator, responded to the effect of: "Oh my! I hope that's not true." It was also at this time, according to the division chief, that he ( the division chief ) first learned that Curveball provided the primary support for the Intelligence Community's judgments on BW.

The group chief provided indirect confirmation of the exchange; she remembered the division chief telling her about this exchange shortly after it occurred. Similarly, former DDO James Pavitt told the Commission that he remembered the division chief subsequently relating to him that the division chief had raised concerns about Curveball to the DDCI around the time of the Secretary of State's speech.

By contrast, former DDCI McLaughlin told the Commission that he did not remember any such meeting with the division chief. Specifically, the former DDCI said that he was not aware of the division chief contacting his (Mr. McLaughlin's) executive assistant to set up a meeting about Curveball; there was no such meeting on his official calendar; he could not recall ever talking to the division chief about Curveball; and he was not aware of any recommended redactions of sections of the draft speech based on Curveball's reporting. Moreover, Mr. McLaughlin told the Commission that the division chief never told him that Curveball might be a fabricator. The former DDCI added that it is inconceivable that he would have permitted information to be used in Secretary Powell's speech if reservations had been raised about it.

On January 24, 2003, the CIA sent another message to the CIA's relevant station asking for the foreign intelligence service's "transcripts of actual questions asked of, and response given by, Curveball concerning Iraq's BW program not later than . . . COB [close of business], 27 January 2003." The message further noted that the CIA had "learned that [the President] intend[ed] to refer to the Curveball information in a planned United Nations General Assembly (UNGA) speech on 29 January 2003." According to the division chief, this message was sent on behalf of the DCI's office, but was "released" by the group chief.

Three days later, on January 27, 2003, the relevant station responded and said that they were still attempting to obtain the transcripts. The message then noted:

> [The foreign liaison service handling Curveball] has not been able to verify his reporting. [This foreign service] has discussed Curveball with US [and others], but no one has been able to verify this information. . . . The source himself is problematical. Defer to headquarters but to use information from another liaison service's source whose information cannot be verified on

such an important, key topic should take the most serious consideration.

Shortly after these messages were exchanged with the relevant station, the division chief told the DDCI's executive assistant that the foreign service would still not provide the CIA with access to Curveball. The division chief also sent an electronic mail—the text of which was prepared by the group chief—to the DDCI's executive assistant from the DO, which noted (in part):

In response to your note, and in addition to your conversation with [ the division chief ], we have spoken with [the relevant] Station on Curve Ball:

- We are not certain that we know where Curve Ball is . . .

- Curve Ball has a history of being uncooperative. He is seeing the [handling foreign service soon] for more questions. The [handling foreign service] cannot move the meeting up, we have asked.

- [The foreign service] ha[s] agreed to our using the information publicly, but do[es] not want it sourced back to them. Neither the [foreign service] nor, per [the foreign service's] assessment, Curve Ball, will refute their information if it is made public and is not attributed. Per Station, and us, we should be careful to conceal the origin of the information since if Curve Ball is exposed, the family he left in Iraq will be killed.

- The [handling foreign service] cannot vouch for the validity of the information. They are concerned that he may not have had direct access, and that much of what he reported was not secret. (per WINPAC, the information they could corroborate was in open source literature or was imagery of locations that may not have been restricted.)

- [A magazine says that the handling foreign service has] intelligence information on the mobile poison capabilities of the Iraqis, but that they will not share it.

As a result, according to the division chief, the executive assistant told the division chief that the DDCI would speak to the analysts about the issue. Although the executive assistant did not remember such a conversation, former DDCI McLaughlin told the Commission that he remembered talking to the WINPAC BW analyst responsible for Iraq about Curveball in January or February 2003. Mr. McLaughlin said that he received strong assurances from the WINPAC analyst that the reporting was credible.

By this time, there was less than a week left before Secretary Powell's February 5 speech, and the vetting process was going full-bore. On February 3, 2003, the DDCI's executive assistant who had previously participated in meetings about Curveball sent a memorandum titled " [Foreign service] BW Source" to the division chief. The memorandum, addressed to the division chief, read:

[T]his will confirm the DDCI's informal request to touch base w/ the [relevant] stations once more on the current status/whereabouts of the émigré who reported on the mobile BW labs. A great deal of effort is being expended to vet the intelligence that underlies SecState's upcoming UN presentation. Similarly, we want to take every precaution against unwelcome surprises that might emerge concerning the intel case; clearly, public statements by this émigré, press accounts of his reporting or credibility, or even direct press access to him would cause a number of potential concerns. The DDCI would be grateful for the [Chief of Station's] view on the immediate 'days-after' reaction in [the handling foreign service country] surrounding source of this key BW reporting.

Preparations for the United Nations address culminated with Secretary Powell, Director of Central Intelligence George Tenet, and support staff going to New York City prior to the speech, which was to be delivered on February 5, 2003. Until late in the night on February 4, Secretary Powell and Mr. Tenet continued to finalize aspects of the speech.

According to the division chief, at about midnight on the night before the speech, he was called at home by Mr. Tenet. As the division chief recalls the conversation, Mr. Tenet asked whether the division chief had a contact number for another foreign intelligence service (not the service handling Curveball) so Mr. Tenet could get clearance to use information from a source of that service. The division chief told the Commission that he took the opportunity to ask the DCI about the " [foreign service country] reporting" from the liaison service handling Curveball. Although he did not remember his exact words, the division chief says that he told Mr. Tenet something to the effect of "you know that the [foreign service] reporting has problems." According to the division chief , Mr. Tenet replied with words to the effect of "yeah, yeah," and that he was "exhausted." The division chief said that when he listened to the speech the next day, he was surprised that the information from Curveball had been included.

In contrast to the division chief's version of events, Mr. Tenet stated that while he had in fact called the division chief on the night before Secretary Powell's speech to obtain the telephone number (albeit in the early evening as opposed to midnight) there had been no discussion of Curveball or his reporting. Nor was there any indication that any information in the speech might be suspect. Mr. Tenet noted that it is inconceivable that he would have failed to raise with Secretary Powell any concerns about information in the speech about which Mr. Tenet had been made aware. Moreover, he noted that he had never been made aware of any concerns about Curveball until well after the cessation of major hostilities in Iraq.

In sum, there were concerns within the CIA—and most specifically the Directorate of Operations' division responsible for relations with the handling liaison service—about Curveball and his reporting. On several occasions, operations officers within this division expressed doubts about Curveball's credibility, the adequacy of his vetting, and the wisdom of relying so heavily on his information.

These views were expressed to CIA leadership, including at least the Associate Deputy Director for Operations and the executive assistant to the Deputy Director of Central Intelligence, and likely the Deputy Director for Operations and even—to some degree—mentioned to the Deputy Director of Central Intelligence himself. It would appear, however, that the criticism of Curveball grew less pointed when expressed in writing and as the issue rose through the CIA's chain of command. In other words, although we are confident that doubts about Curveball were expressed in one way or another to the Deputy Director for Central Intelligence, it is less clear whether those doubts were accompanied by the full, detailed panoply of information calling into question Curveball's reliability that was presented to more junior supervisors. We found no evidence that the doubts were conveyed by CIA leadership to policymakers in general—or Secretary Powell in particular.

As the discussion above illustrates, it is unclear precisely how and why these serious concerns about Curveball never reached Secretary Powell, despite his and his staff's vigorous efforts over several days in February 2003 to strip out every dubious piece of information in his proposed speech to the United Nations. It is clear, however, that serious concerns about Curveball were widely known at CIA in the months leading up to Secretary Powell's speech. In our view, the failure to convey these concerns to senior management, or, if such concerns were in fact raised to senior management, the failure to pass that information to Secretary Powell, represents a serious failure of management and leadership.

A team of Intelligence Community analysts was dispatched to Iraq in early summer 2003 to investigate the details of Iraq's BW program. The analysts were, in particular, investigating two trailers that had been discovered by Coalition forces in April and May 2003, which at the time were thought to be the mobile BW facilities described by Curveball. As the summer wore on, however, at least one WINPAC analyst who had traveled to Iraq, as well as some DIA and INR analysts, became increasingly doubtful that the trailers were BW-related.

The investigation also called into question other aspects of Curveball's reporting. According to one WINPAC BW analyst who was involved in the investigations, those individuals whom Curveball had identified as having been involved in the mobile BW program "all consistently denied knowing anything about this project." Furthermore, none of the supposed project designers even knew who Curveball was, which contradicted Curveball's claim that he had been involved with those individuals in developing the mobile BW program.

Additional research into Curveball's background in September 2003 revealed further discrepancies in his claims. For example, WINPAC analysts interviewed several of Curveball's supervisors at the government office where he had worked in Iraq. Curveball had claimed that this office had commenced a secret mobile BW program in 1995. But interviews with his supervisors, as well as friends and family members, confirmed that Curveball had been fired from his position in 1995. Moreover, one of Curveball's family members noted that he had been out of Iraq for substantial periods between 1995 and 1999, times during which Curveball had claimed he had been working on BW projects. In particular, Curveball claimed to have been present at the site of a BW production run when an accident occurred in 1998, killing 12 workers. But Curveball was not even in Iraq at that time, according to information supplied by family members and later confirmed by travel records.

By the end of October 2003, the WINPAC analysts conducting these investigations reported to the head of the ISG that they believed Curveball was a fabricator and that his reporting was "all false." But other WINPAC analysts, as well as CIA headquarters management, continued to support Curveball. By January 2004, however, when CIA obtained travel records confirming that Curveball had been out of Iraq during the time he claimed to have been working on the mobile BW program, most analysts became convinced that Curveball had fabricated his reporting.

Mr. Tenet was briefed on these findings on February 4, 2004. CIA management, however, was still reluctant to "go down the road" of admitting that Curveball was a fabricator. According to WINPAC analysts, CIA's DI management was slow in retreating from Curveball's information because of political concerns about how this would look to the "Seventh Floor," the floor at Langley where CIA management have their offices, and to "downtown." CIA's Inspector General, in his post-war Inspection Report on WINPAC, concluded that "the process [of retreating from intelligence products derived from Curveball reporting] was drawn out principally due to three factors: (1) senior managers were determined to let the ISG in Iraq complete its work before correcting the mobile labs analysis; (2) the CIA was in the midst of trying to gain direct access to Curveball; and (3) WINPAC Biological and Chemical Group (BCG) management was struggling to reconcile strong differences among their BW analysts." Senior managers did not want to disavow Curveball only to find that his story stood up upon direct examination, or to find that "the ISG uncovered further evidence that would require additional adjustments to the story."

Any remaining doubts, however, were removed when the CIA was finally given access to Curveball himself in March 2004. At that time, Curveball's inability to explain discrepancies in his reporting, his description of facilities and events, and his general demeanor led to the conclusion that his information was unreliable. In particular, the CIA interviewers pressed Curveball to explain "discrepancies" between his aforementioned description of the site at Djerf al-Naddaf, which he had alleged was a key locus for transportable BW, and satellite imagery of the site which showed marked differences in layout from that which Curveball described. Specifically, there was a six foot high wall that would have precluded mobile BW trailers from moving into and out of the facility as Curveball had claimed. Curveball was completely unable or unwilling to explain these discrepancies. The CIA concluded that Curveball had fabricated his reporting, and CIA and Defense HUMINT recalled all of it.

The CIA also hypothesized that Curveball was motivated to provide fabricated information by his desire to gain permanent asylum. Despite speculation that Curveball was encouraged to lie by the Iraqi National Congress (INC), the CIA's post-war investigations were unable to uncover any evidence that the INC or any other organization was directing Curveball to feed misleading information to the Intelligence Community. Instead, the post-war investigations concluded that Curveball's reporting was not influenced by, controlled by, or connected to, the INC.

In fact, over all, CIA's post-war investigations revealed that INC-related sources had a minimal impact on pre-war assessments. The October 2002 NIE relied on reporting from two INC sources, both of whom were later deemed to be fabricators. One source—the INC source—provided fabricated reporting on the existence of mobile BW facilities in Iraq. The other source, whose information was provided in a text box in the NIE and sourced to a "defector," reported on the possible construction of a new nuclear facility in Iraq. The CIA concluded that this source was being "directed" by the INC to provide information to the U.S. Intelligence Community. Reporting from these two INC sources had a "negligible" impact on the overall assessments, however.

Another serious flaw affecting the Intelligence Community's pre-war assessments was its inability to keep reporting from a known fabricator out of finished intelligence. Specifically, the INC source, handled by DIA's Defense HUMINT Service, provided information on Iraqi mobile BW facilities that was initially thought to corroborate Curveball's reporting. The INC source was quickly deemed a fabricator in May 2002, however, and Defense HUMINT issued a fabrication notice but did not recall the reporting on mobile BW facilities in Iraq. Despite the fabrication notice, reporting from the INC source regarding Iraqi mobile BW facilities started to be used again several months later in finished intelligence—eventually ending up in the October 2002 NIE and in Secretary Powell's February 2003 speech to the United Nations Security Council.

This inability to prevent information known to be unreliable from making its way to policymakers was due to flawed processes at DIA's Defense HUMINT Service. Specifically, Defense HUMINT did not have in place a protocol to ensure that once a fabrication notice is issued, all previous reporting from that source is reissued with either a warning that the source might be a fabricator or a notice that the report is being recalled. Though a fabrication notice was sent out, the reporting was never recalled, nor was the fabrication notice electronically attached to the original report. Analysts were thus forced to rely on their memory that a fabrication notice was issued for that source's reporting—a difficult task especially when they must be able to recognize that a particular report is from that source, which is not always obvious from the face of the report.

Some steps have been taken to remedy this procedural problem. First, DIA's Defense HUMINT Service has now taken steps to ensure that reporting from a fabricating source is reissued with either the fabrication notice or recall notice electronically attached, rather than simply issuing a fabrication notice. Second, the Director of the Central Intelligence Agency is currently working to establish Community-wide procedures to ensure that the information technology system links original reports, fabrication notices, and any subsequent recalls or corrections. Unfortunately, however, the Intelligence Community continues to lack a mechanism that electronically tracks the sources for finished intelligence materials or briefings. This makes "walking back" intelligence papers or briefings to policymakers difficult, as there is no way to know which pieces relied upon what information.

This failure properly to inform others that the INC source's reporting was not valid, however, was not merely a technical problem. DIA's Defense HUMINT Service also allowed Secretary Powell to use information from the INC source in his speech to the United Nations Security Council—even though a Defense HUMINT official was present at the coordination session at CIA held before the speech. A Defense HUMINT Division Chief, who was aware of the fabrication notice on the INC source, attended both of the February 2 and 3 coordination meetings for the Powell speech yet failed to alert the Secretary that one of the sources the speech relied upon was a fabricator. That Defense HUMINT official said that he was not aware that the information being discussed came from the INC source , indicating that Defense HUMINT had not adequately prepared itself for the meeting by reviewing the information Secretary Powell was considering using in the speech.

## Conclusion

This section has revealed that Intelligence Community management was remiss in not taking action based on expressed concerns about Curveball's reliability. In retrospect, we conclude that the Intelligence Community's leadership should have more aggressively investigated Curveball's bona fides, rather than seeing the confidence of the analysts and the responsible liaison service as sufficient reason to dismiss the rival concerns of the operators and other liaison services. These leaders also should have pushed harder for access to Curveball—even at the cost of significant inter-liaison capital—given that the source's reporting was so critical to the judgment that Iraq was developing a mobile BW capability. After the NIE, CIA leadership should have paid closer heed to mounting concerns from the DO and, at the very least, informed senior policymakers about these concerns.

This said, the Community's failure to get the Iraq BW question right was not at its core the result of these managerial shortcomings. We need more and better human intelligence, but all such sources are inherently uncertain. Even if there had not been—as there was—affirmative reason to doubt Curveball's reporting, it is questionable whether such a broad conclusion (that Iraq had an active biological weapons production capability) should have been based almost entirely on the evidence of a single source to whom the U.S. Intelligence Community had never gained access. The Intelligence Community's failure to get the BW question right stemmed, first and foremost, from the strong prevailing assumptions about Iraq's intentions and behavior that led the Intelligence Community to conclude that Curveball's reporting was sufficient evidence to judge with "high confidence" that Iraq's offensive BW program was active and more advanced than it had been before the first Gulf War. The Intelligence Community placed too much weight on one source to whom the Community lacked direct access—and did so without making clear to policymakers the extent of the judgment's reliance on this single, unvetted source.

## Chemical Warfare

In the fall of 2002, the Intelligence Community concluded with "high confidence" that Iraq had chemical warfare agents (CW), and further assessed that it had "begun renewed production of mustard, sarin, GF (cyclosarin), and VX." Although the NIE autioned that the Intelligence Community had "little specific information on Iraq's CW stockpile," it estimated that "Saddam probably [had] stocked at least 100 metric tons (MT) and possibly as much as 500 MT of CW agents." The Community further judged that "much of" Iraq's CW stockpiles had been produced in the past year, and that Iraq had "rebuilt key portions of its CW infrastructure."

After the war, the ISG concluded—contrary to the Intelligence Community's pre-war assessments—that Iraq had unilaterally destroyed its undeclared CW stockpile in 1991 and that there were no credible indications that Baghdad had resumed production of CW thereafter. The ISG further found that Iraq had not regained its pre–1991 CW technical sophistication or production capabilities. Further, the ISG found that pre-war concerns of Iraqi plans to use CW if Coalition forces crossed certain defensive "red lines" were groundless; the "red lines" referred to conventional military planning only. Finally, the ISG noted that the only CW it recovered were weapons manufactured before the first Gulf War, and that after 1991 only small, covert labs were maintained to research chemicals and poisons, primarily for intelligence operations. The ISG did conclude, however, that "Saddam never abandoned his intentions to resume a CW effort when sanctions were lifted and conditions were judged favorable," and that Iraq's post–1995 infrastructure improvements "would have enhanced Iraq's ability to produce CW" if it chose to do so.

The Intelligence Community's errors on Iraq's chemical weapons were, not unlike its errors on Iraq's nuclear and biological programs, heavily influenced by a single factor. In the case of chemical weapons, the factor was the Community's over-reliance on dubious imagery indicators. At the same time, the Community's chemical weapons assessment was further led astray by breakdowns in communication between collectors and analysts and a paucity of supporting human and signals intelligence. All of this played a part in leading the Community to assess, incorrectly, that Iraq was stockpiling and producing chemical agents. And while a chemical warfare program is difficult to distinguish from a legitimate chemical infrastructure, the roots of the Community's failures reached well beyond such difficulties.

This section opens with a careful look at the Intelligence Community's assessments of Iraq's chemical program dating back to the end of the first Gulf War and reaching forward to the beginning of Operation Iraqi Freedom. The chapter then shifts to a detailed summary of the findings of the ISG regarding Iraq's alleged chemical warfare program. It then offers the Commission's findings from its in-depth study of the performance of the Intelligence Community on this subject, focusing especially on over-reliance on faultily-used imagery indicators and on the poverty of human and signals intelligence.

## The Intelligence Community's Pre-War Assessments

The Intelligence Community's assessment of Iraq's CW programs and capabilities remained relatively stable during the 1990s, judging that Iraq retained a modest capability to restart a chemical warfare program. The October 2002 NIE therefore marked a shift from previous assessments in that it concluded that Iraq had actually begun renewed production of chemical agents on a sizable scale. This shift was based primarily on imagery, although analysts also saw support for their assessment in a small stream of human and signals intelligence on Iraq's CW capabilities.

*Background.* For more than ten years, the Intelligence Community believed that Iraq retained the capability to jumpstart its CW program. After Operation Desert Storm in 1991, the Community judged that Iraq retained CW munitions and CW-related materials; the Community based these judgments primarily on accounting discrepancies between Iraq's declarations about its chemical weapons program and what UNSCOM had actually discovered. As with assessments of Iraq's nuclear and biological weapons programs, the conclusion that Iraq still had CW munitions was "reinforced by Iraq's continuing efforts to frustrate" United Nations inspectors. Encapsulating this line of reasoning, in 1995 the CIA judged that Iraq could "begin producing [chemical] agent in a matter of weeks after a decision to do so," based on the assessment that Iraq had "sequestered . . . at least some tens of metric tons" of CW precursors. This assessment cautioned, however, that building Iraq's "CW program to its previous levels" would require two to three years.

*Mid–1990s: Growing concern.* The Intelligence Community's understanding of Iraq's CW program was altered with the defection in August 1995 of Hussein Kamil, the head of Iraq's Military Industrialization Committee and, as such, the head of Iraq's WMD programs. Among a host of damning revelations, Kamil released details previously unknown to the U.S. Intelligence Community about Iraq's pre–1991 production and use of VX nerve gas. More specifically, Iraq subsequently admitted that it had worked on in-flight mixing of binary CW weapons before the Gulf War, produced larger amounts of VX agent than previously admitted, and perfected long-term storage of a VX precursor. These admissions about Iraqi work on VX—a potent nerve agent and an advanced chemical weapon—all played an important role in shaping subsequent Intelligence Community assessments about Iraq's CW program.

Two further revelations about the extent of Iraq's pre–1991 CW efforts also markedly influenced the Community's view of Iraq's CW programs. First, in June 1998, U.S. tests of warhead fragments from an Iraqi al-Hussein missile yielded traces of degraded VX. This finding was noteworthy to Community analysts because it established beyond any doubt (in analysts' eyes) that Iraq, before 1991, had successfully weaponized VX—a technical advance that Iraq refused to admit in its United Nations declarations both before and after the United States became aware of the test results.

Second, in July 1998, weapons inspectors found documents—now commonly known as the "Air Force Documents"—that detailed Iraqi CW use in the Iran-Iraq War. This finding was significant because the documents indicated Iraq had expended far fewer CW munitions in the Iran-Iraq War than previously thought, thus suggesting that Iraq possessed more unexpended CW munitions than analysts believed. Analysts lent additional credence to the information because Iraqi officials refused to let inspectors actually keep the relevant document, which suggested to analysts that the documents were incriminating and important. Though both of these revelations concerned Iraq's pre–1991 CW effort, analysts saw them as lending support to the assessment that Iraq was continuing its deliberate efforts to obscure elements of its CW capabilities.

By 1998, the Intelligence Community was continuing to assess that Baghdad retained "key elements of its CW program including personnel, production data, and hidden stocks of production equipment and precursor chemicals" and that "Iraq could begin limited CW agent production within weeks after United Nations sanctions are lifted and intrusive inspections cease." The Community noted, however, that it lacked "reporting to confirm whether [CW] production [was] taking place."

*2001–2002: Little change.* The Community continued through 2001 to note that there was no evidence that Iraq had started large-scale production of CW. Though analysts continued to believe that Iraq's capability to produce CW was increasing, primarily through the development of an indigenous chemical industry, and that Iraq might have engaged in small-scale production, the Community continued to assess that Iraq had not restarted large-scale production. Even after the terrorist attacks of September 11, 2001—when the Intelligence Community detected what it determined to be the dispersal of Iraqi military units in anticipation of U.S. military strikes—the CIA found no evidence that the munitions Iraq was moving were CW-related. And additional reporting during this time did not reveal whether certain suspect sites were actively engaged in CW weapons production—although it remained impossible to determine whether dual-use precursor chemicals were being produced for illicit purposes.

With respect to possible CW stockpiles, as of 2002 the Community assessed that Iraq possessed between 10 and 100 metric tons of CW agent and that it might have had sufficient precursors to produce an additional 200 metric tons. This estimated stockpile was smaller than the stockpiles Iraq possessed before the Gulf War, as an early 2002 Senior Executive Memorandum noted. But according to a CIA analyst's mid–2002 briefing to senior officials, Iraq could restart CW production in a matter of days by using dual-use facilities and hidden precursors. These assessments, however, did not go so far as to conclude that Iraq had restarted production or, relatedly, had sizable CW stockpiles.

*The October 2002 NIE.* The October 2002 NIE reflected a shift in the Intelligence Community's judgment about Iraq's CW program in two ways: (1) the NIE assessed that Iraq had large stockpiles of CW; and (2) the NIE unequivocally stated that Iraq had restarted CW production.

Regarding stockpiles, the NIE stated that "[a]lthough we have little specific information on Iraq's CW stockpile, Saddam probably has stocked at least 100 metric tons and possibly as much as 500 metric tons of CW agents—much of it added in the last year." This judgment represented a significant increase in the Intelligence Community's estimate of the size of Iraq's CW stockpile.

This stockpile estimate rested primarily on Iraqi accounting discrepancies, Iraq's CW production capacity, estimates of Iraqi precursor stocks, and—at the upper limit (500 metric tons)—on practical considerations such as the size of pre-Gulf War stockpiles and Iraq's limited delivery options. This calculation was also informed by the Intelligence Community's assessments of Iraqi military requirements, ammunition demand, and possible changes in Iraqi use doctrine.

The lower end of this stockpile range (100 metric tons) was premised on the aforementioned 1999 estimate that Iraq possessed between 10 and 100 metric tons of CW agents and that Iraq "could" produce an additional 200 tons of agents "using unaccounted-for precursor chemicals." This 1999 estimate was itself premised on previous Iraqi CW accounting irregularities. The Community assessments of the range of Iraq's CW stockpile thus rested largely on what analysts estimated Iraq could do with unaccounted-for precursors and production capabilities.

In addition to assessing the size of the Iraqi CW stockpile, the NIE judged that "much" of the CW stockpile had been "added in the last year." This latter assessment, in turn, rested on the NIE's second major CW conclusion: that Baghdad had "begun renewed production of mustard, sarin, GF (cyclosarin), and VX."

The NIE's judgment that Iraq had restarted CW production was based primarily on imagery intelligence. As analysts subsequently explained, this imagery showed trucks transshipping materials to and from ammunition depots, including suspect CW sites, in Iraq. These transshipments began in March 2002 and continued until early 2003. At approximately 11 sites, imagery analysts saw a number of "indicators" in the imagery that suggested to them that some of the trucks were possibly moving CW munitions; then, because imagery analysts observed evidence of numerous such shipments, CW analysts in turn assessed that Iraq was moving significant volumes of CW munitions and therefore that Iraq had restarted CW production. These indicators included the presence of "Samarra-type" trucks—a distinctive type of tanker truck—which were regularly associated with CW shipments in the late 1980s and during the Gulf War; atypical security patterns "associated with" the Special Republican Guard, which was believed to be responsible for protecting parts of Iraq's WMD programs; at least at one site, the grading of the topsoil, which likewise suggested to analysts deliberate concealment of suspect activity; and other indicators.

Although the NIE's judgment that Iraq had restarted CW production was based primarily on imagery, that judgment was also supported by small streams of human and signals intelligence. The NIC subsequently explained in its Statement for the Record that this human intelligence reporting consisted of "a number of specific reports alleging that Iraq had resumed large-scale production of CW agents." None of these reports was considered "highly reliable," however, and only six were deemed "moderately reliable."

Of these reports, Community analysts identified to us several as having been most significant, although subsequent analysis of the reports revealed—in some cases—serious flaws in the reporting. The key reports were: one involving a foreign source in 1999 who reported that two Iraqi companies were involved in the production of nerve gas; reporting concerning a factory for the production of castor oil that could be used to make "sarin"; information from an Iraqi defector, who claimed to be an expert in VX production, describing the production of "tons" of nerve agents in mobile labs; reporting from a source with "good but historical access" asserting that, as of 1998, mustard and binary chemical agents were being produced in Iraq; a source who reported that Iraq was producing a binary compound and mustard as of fall 2001; and reporting on the production of CW at dual-use facilities.

Finally, a liaison service reported in September 2002 that a senior Iraqi official had indicated that Iraq was producing and stockpiling chemical weapons. Although this report was distributed to a very small group of senior officials prior to the publication of the NIE—including to the NIE's principal author—it was not made available to most analysts. In any event, as described below, the senior Iraqi official later denied having made such statements.

In addition to these imagery indicators of transshipment activity and human intelligence, the NIE also drew upon a handful of additional pieces of information—based largely on other Intelligence Community reporting—to support the assessment that Baghdad had restarted CW production. This information suggested suspect activity at dual-use sites and included: indications that Iraq was expanding its indigenous chemical industry in ways that were deemed unlikely to be for civilian purposes, specifically by increasing the indigenous production capacity for chlorine—despite the fact that Iraq's civilian chlorine needs were met through United Nations-permitted imports; the "management" of key chemical facilities by "previously identified CW personnel"; attempted procurement of nuclear, biological, and chemical weapons defensive materials; and the attempted procurement of dual-use materials associated with CW. Although the NIE noted that the Intelligence Community could not "link definitively Iraq's procurement of CW precursors, technology, and specialized equipment from foreign sources directly" to its CW program, it nevertheless assessed that "Iraq's procurements have contributed to the rebuilding of dual-use facilities that probably are adding to Iraq's overall CW agent capability." In drawing this conclusion, the NIE drew particular attention to Iraq's attempts to obtain necessary precursors for nerve agents.

Finally, reporting on other aspects of Iraq's unconventional weapons programs also influenced some analysts' CW-related conclusions. Specifically, reporting on the existence of Iraqi mobile BW production facilities—namely, reports from Curveball—buttressed some analysts' certainty in their CW judgments. As one CIA analyst put it, "much of the CW confidence [in the prewar assessments] was built on the BW confidence." In other words, although some CW analysts at times questioned the existence of significant Iraqi CW stockpiles, the reports that Iraq had a hidden, mobile BW program pushed the analysts "in the other direction" and helped convince them of their ultimate conclusion: that Iraq was hiding a CW program.

*Post-October 2002 NIE reports.* In November 2002, the NIC published a Memorandum to Holders of the October NIE entitled *Iraq's Chemical Warfare Capabilities: Potential for Dusty and Fourth-Generation Agents.* The Memorandum warned that Iraq might possess dusty agent and that it had the technical expertise to develop fourth-generation agents that could be extremely lethal. Identifying the "Key Intelligence Gaps" on Iraq's CW program, the Memorandum observed that although the Intelligence Community "assess[ed]" that Iraq was producing blister and nerve agents, the Intelligence Community had not "identified key production facilities" and did "not know the extent of indigenous production or procurement of CW precursors." But just as the NIE had cautioned that the Intelligence Community had "little specific information on Iraq's CW stockpile," the Memorandum stated that the Intelligence Community had "almost no information on the size, composition, or location of Iraq's CW stockpile." In a separate NIE published in January 2003, however, the Community reiterated its estimate that Iraq "ha[d] 100 to 500 metric tons of weaponized bulk agent."

In December 2002, CIA's WINPAC published a coordinated Intelligence Community paper that reiterated its belief that "Iraq retain[ed] an offensive CW program," but it did not specifically describe the extent of any CW stockpiles. In addition, the CIA reported the Intelligence Community had "low confidence" in its ability to monitor the Iraqi CW program due to "stringent operational security" and "successful denial and deception practices."

## Post-War Findings of the Iraq Survey Group

The Iraq Survey Group's findings undermined both the Intelligence Community's assessments about Iraq's pre-war CW program and, indeed, the very fundamental assumptions upon which those assessments were based. The ISG concluded—contrary to the Intelligence Community's pre-war assessments—that Iraq had actually unilaterally destroyed its undeclared CW stockpile in 1991 and that there were no credible indications that Baghdad resumed production of CW thereafter. Iraq had not regained its pre–1991 CW technical sophistication or production capabilities prior to the war. Further, pre-war concerns of Iraqi plans to use CW if Coalition forces crossed certain defensive "red lines" were groundless; the "red lines" referred to conventional military planning only. Finally, the only CW the Iraq Survey Group recovered were weapons manufactured before the first Gulf War; the ISG concluded that, after 1991, Iraq maintained only small, covert labs to research chemicals and poisons, primarily for intelligence operations. However, "Saddam never abandoned his intentions to resume a CW effort when sanctions were lifted and conditions were judged favorable," and Iraq's post–1996 infrastructure improvements "would have enhanced Iraq's ability to produce CW" if it had chosen to do so.

Despite having "expended considerable time and expertise searching for extant CW munitions,"—the vaunted stockpiles—the ISG concluded with "high confidence that there are no CW present in the Iraqi inventory." The ISG specifically investigated 11 sites that were associated with suspected CW transshipment activity, conducting an in-depth inspection of two of the sites, which were "assessed prior to war to have the strongest indicators of CW movement." Neither of these sites revealed any CW munitions. Further, the ISG's "review of documents, interviews, intelligence reporting, and site exploitations revealed alternate, plausible explanations" for pre-war transshipment activity that the Intelligence Community judged to have been CW-related.

Regarding Iraq's dual-use chemical infrastructure and personnel, the Iraq Survey Group found no direct link to a CW program. Instead, investigators found that, though Iraq's chemical industry began expanding after 1996, in part due to the influx of funds and resources from the Oil-for-Food program, the country's CW capabilities remained less than those which existed prior to the Gulf War. The ISG also interviewed 30 of the approximately 60 "key" Iraqi CW scientists, all of whom denied having been involved in any CW activity since 1990 and the vast majority of whom denied having any knowledge of any CW activity occurring.

The ISG also cited a number of reasons why Iraq's expansion of its chlorine capacity was not, contrary to the NIE's assessment, capable of being diverted to CW production. Specifically, Iraq experienced a "country-wide chlorine shortage," and Iraq's chlorine plants "suffered from corroded condensers and were only able to produce aqueous chlorine." Further, "[t]echnical problems and poor maintenance of aging equipment throughout the 1990s resulted in many chemical plants, including ethylene and chlorine production plants, operating at less than half capacity despite the improvements to the chemical industry."

In sum, the Iraq Survey Group found no direct link between Iraq's dual-use infrastructure and its CW program. However, "concerns" about some aspects of the infrastructure arising out of "an extensive, yet fragmentary and circumstantial body of evidence" suggested Saddam intended to maintain his CW capabilities by preserving CW-related assets and expertise.

Regarding Iraqi decisionmaking about its CW program after 1991, the ISG concluded that, in the aftermath of the Gulf War, "Iraq initially chose not to fully declare its CW" in anticipation that inspections would be short-lived and ineffective. This position changed after a particularly invasive search in late June 1991, after which Iraq destroyed its hidden CW and precursors while retaining some documents and dual-use equipment. Iraq kept these latter items for the next five years, but did not renew its CW efforts out of fear that such a move would imperil its effort to have sanctions lifted. In August 1995, however, after the defection of Hussein Kamil, Saddam relented and revealed to inspectors extensive VX research and other, more advanced, technologies.

Overall, although the vast majority of CW munitions had been destroyed, the Iraq Survey Group recognized that questions remained relating to the disposition of hundreds of pre–1991 CW munitions. Still, given that, of the dozens of CW munitions that the ISG discovered, all had been manufactured before 1991, the Intelligence Community's 2002 assessments that Iraq had restarted its CW program turned out to have been seriously off the mark.

Finally, on two ancillary issues the ISG found little or no evidence to support indications of Iraqi CW efforts. First, with respect to a "red line" defense of Baghdad, the ISG found no information that such a defense—which amounted to a multi-ring conventional defense of the city—called for the use of CW. According to a senior Iraqi military officer, the "red line" was simply the line at which Iraqi military units would no longer retreat. At the same time, both generals and high-level defense officials believed that a plan for CW use existed, even though they themselves knew nothing about it.

Second, with respect to CW work by the Iraqi Intelligence Service, there was "no evidence" of CW production in clandestine labs, other than the Service's laboratory effort to develop substances to kill or incapacitate targeted individuals.

## *Analysis of the Intelligence Community's Pre-War Assessments*

As the foregoing comparison illustrates, the Intelligence Community's pre-war assessments of Iraq's CW program were well off the mark. Iraq did not have CW stockpiles; it was not producing CW agent; and its chemical infrastructure was in far worse shape than the Intelligence Community believed. It is a daunting task in any circumstance to distinguish a normal chemical infrastructure and conventional military establishment on the one hand from a chemical warfare program on the other. But the Community made more difficult the challenges of identifying a CW program in Iraq by latching on to ambiguous imagery indicators and by failing to collect enough good intelligence to keep analytic judgments tethered to reality.

There are several reasons for the significant gap between the Intelligence Community's pre-war assessment of Iraq's CW program and the Iraq Survey Group's findings. Chief among these was the over-reliance on a single, ambiguous source (the Samarra-type tanker trucks) to support multiple judgments. Less central, although still significant, were the failure of analysts to understand fully the limitations of technical collection; the lack of quality human intelligence sources; the lack of quality signals intelligence; and, on a broader plane, the universal difficulty of establishing the existence of a CW program in light of the prevalence of dual-use technology.

As noted, the pre-war assessment that Iraq had restarted CW production relied primarily on CW analysts' assessments of imagery intelligence. This imagery showed trucks transshipping materials to and from ammunition depots, including suspect CW-sites, in Iraq. In the late spring of 2002, analysts started to believe that these shipments involved CW munitions. This belief was based on the aforementioned "indicators" seen on the imagery—that is, activity and circumstances surrounding the shipments that were thought to be indicative of CW activity. The most important of these indicators was the presence of "Samarra-type" trucks—a distinctive type of tanker truck—which had been regularly associated with Iraqi CW shipments in the late 1980s and during the Gulf War. Based on the assessment that the presence of these Samarra-type trucks (in combination with the other indicators) suggested CW shipments, CW analysts then judged that the frequency of such transshipments pointed to the assessment that "CW was already deployed with the military logistics chain," which, in turn, indicated to these analysts that Iraq had added to its CW stockpile in the last year. That assessment, in turn, indicated to analysts that Iraq had restarted CW production.

In short, the key pre-war assessments about Iraq's CW program—that Iraq was actively producing CW and had increased its stockpile of CW—rested on the following evidence and associated reasoning:

- Imagery revealed the presence of Samarra-type trucks at suspect weapons sites;

- The presence of Samarra-type trucks indicated CW activity;

- The scale of the Samarra-type trucks' involvement demonstrated Iraq had already deployed CW with their forces; and

- For CW to be deployed with Iraqi forces, Iraq had to have restarted CW production within the past year—the period during which analysts had seen Samarra-type trucks.

As this logic train illustrates, the final conclusion regarding restarted CW production was, therefore, fundamentally grounded on the single assessment that the Samarra-type trucks seen on imagery were in fact CW-related. This assessment, however, proved to be incorrect—thereby eliminating the crucial pillar on which the Community's judgment about Iraq's CW program rested.

Post-war investigation revealed how the Intelligence Community ran astray. After the war, NGA "reassessed" the imagery from one of the sites thought to bear the strongest indications of CW activity—the Al Musayyib Barracks—by incorporating information from ISG inspections and debriefings of key personnel. Contrary to pre-war assessments, NGA concluded that the activity represented "conventional maintenance and logistical activity rather than chemical weapons." NGA analysts drew this conclusion in part after reexamining imagery and in part on ISG debriefs of former commanders of the Al Musayyib site.

More detailed analysis of other imagery intelligence—in particular, surface grading—also revealed the absence of a clear link to CW. NGA assessed that grading could be associated with innocuous, routine activities. The rationales behind that assessment are discussed in the classified report.

The story is much the same with respect to pre-war assessments of other imagery evidence regarding certain security patterns. Post-war analysis by NGA could not confirm pre-war assessments that these security patterns were indicative of Special Republican Guard activity associated with security at CW-related sites. Indeed, at least one human source debriefed after the war said the security activity in question was not related to the Special Republican Guard and that it was actually related to the performance of miscellaneous jobs associated with the ammunition depot.

Finally, post-war debriefings suggested that other CW-related imagery evidence was also innocuous, although this suggestion was neither definitively confirmed nor refuted by the imagery reassessment. And NGA notes that it is generally not possible to determine from imagery whether some activities, such as certain safety measures, are intended to support the training of offensive or defensive chemical warfare troops. And NGA has noted that imagery, when used alone, may not definitely determine the intended purpose of an adversary's activity.

The Community's over-reliance on ambiguous imagery indicators thus played a pivotal role in its ultimate misjudgment that Iraq had restarted CW production and had increased its CW stockpiles. In our view analysts relied too heavily on the presence of Samarra tanker trucks—backed by other, even more ambiguous imagery indicators—to support multiple, interdependent, and wide-ranging judgments about Iraq's chemical warfare program. And the Community did so despite the truism about which NGA itself has cautioned: imagery alone can neither prove nor disprove a CW association.

Building one assessment upon another in this fashion—without carrying forward the uncertainty of each "layer" of assessment—results in a false impression of certainty for analysts' ultimate judgment. We believe, therefore, that at a minimum analysts must communicate the uncertainty of their judgments, and the degree to which they rely on narrow assessments about specific indicators. Moreover, avoiding the pitfalls of such layering requires careful consideration of alternative hypotheses, such as, in this case, the possibility that the shipments involved conventional weapons and that the trucks were for water supply or fire suppression.

We do not discount the fact that analysts must sometimes focus on seemingly mundane indicators. But at the same time analysts must always recognize, and communicate to decisionmakers, the tenuous quality of their reasoning.

Analytical flaws in assessing the significance of the imagery indicators were not the only factors leading to the misassessment of the imagery intelligence. In addition, analysts may have misperceived the significance of the imagery on Iraq's supposed CW program because they did not fully understand—and the collectors did not fully explain—the scope and nature of imagery collection against the target. Indeed, we cannot rule out the possibility that the analytic judgment that Iraq had added to its CW stockpile in the preceding year rested, at least in part, on a simple increase in *collection* and reporting rather than any rise in Iraqi *activity*.

Pre-war, analysts relied upon imagery to detect transshipment activity at suspected CW sites, and beginning in March 2002, analysts believed that they were seeing an "increase" in such activity. In reality, however, the "increase" in transshipment activity that analysts saw starting in March 2002 may have been due, at least in part, to an increased volume of imagery *collected* by U.S. satellites rather than to any increased activity by the Iraqis. To only somewhat oversimplify the matter, it wasn't that the Iraqis were using Samarra trucks more often in 2002—it was that in 2002 the United States was taking more pictures of places where the Samarra trucks were being used. And this failure to distinguish between actual increased activity at suspect CW sites and the *appearance* of increased activity due to increased imaging likely contributed to the mistaken assessment that Iraq was ramping up CW production in 2002.

This error sprung from the fact that not all Community analysts were fully cognizant of a major change in NGA collection that occurred in the spring of 2002. Until 2000, imagery collection on Iraq had been oriented primarily toward supporting military operations associated with the no-fly zones. But in 2001 and 2002, imagery collection against Iraq WMD more than doubled, prompted by recommendations that more attention be given to the target. Most significantly, the United States began "expanded imagery collection over Baghdad [and] suspect WMD sites" in March 2002—not coincidentally the same time that analysts began to "see" new activity they associated with CW transshipments.

Thus, in drawing their conclusions about the state of Iraq's CW production based on increased transshipment activity, analysts did not realize the necessity of distinguishing between the "new" activity they saw, on the one hand, at sites that had been previously imaged on a regular basis (e.g., suspect WMD sites) and, on the other, at sites that had not been previously imaged on a regular basis (e.g., ammunition depots that had not been previously associated with WMD). Whereas increased activity at the former could be attributed to changes in Iraqi behavior (since the United States had been photographing the sites prior to March 2002), the same could not be said for the latter category (since there was no "baseline" of activity with which to compare levels of activity seen from March 2002 on).

This problem extended to one of the sites that was key to analysts' conclusions about Iraqi CW production—the Al Musayyib Barracks. According to NGA, Al Musayyib had not been regularly imaged prior to the March 2002 imaging blitz because it had not been previously associated with Iraq's chemical or biological weapons programs. Unaware of this important fact, analysts confidently assessed that the Iraqis had expanded transshipment activity at Al Musayyib, as well as other sites, when they began to see more images of Samarra-type truck activity. In short, analysts attributed what they saw to nefarious Iraqi activity when it could just as easily have been attributed to changes in U.S. collection priorities. In our view, this failure is the direct result of poor communication between analysts and collectors about a crucial change in the scope and nature of collection against a vital target.

Analysts were not alone in contributing to a flawed assessment about a resuscitant Iraqi CW program. Collectors, too, were involved—but mostly by their conspicuous absence. Against Iraq's program, Intelligence Community collectors failed to produce much either in terms of quantity or, worse, validity, thus making analysts' jobs considerably harder, and influencing analysts to place more weight on the imagery intelligence than it could logically bear.

A small quantity of human source reporting supplied the bulk of the narrow band of intelligence supplementing the imagery intelligence. And the most striking fact about reporting on Iraq's CW program was, as with other elements of Iraq's weapons programs, its paucity. Yet there was more than just scarcity, for—as with sources on Iraq's supposed BW program—many of the CW sources subsequently proved unreliable. Indeed, perhaps even more so that with the BW sources, Community analysts should have been more cautious about using the CW sources' reporting, as much of it was deeply problematic on its face. In our view, prior to the war, analysts should have viewed at least three human sources more skeptically than they did. In addition, post-war, questions about the veracity of two other human sources have also surfaced.

*Sources Whose Reliability Should*
*Have Been Questioned Prior to the NIE*

One source, an Iraqi defector who had worked as a chemist in Iraq through the 1990s, reported information that made its way into the NIE. This happened even though, from the start of his relations with the U.S. Intelligence Community, the Community had deemed aspects of his reporting not credible. His information survived, despite these indications that he might be an unreliable source, because analysts simply rejected those parts of his reporting that seemed implausible and accepted the rest. For example, he claimed that Iraq had produced a combined nuclear-biological-chemical weapon, a claim that analysts recognized at the time as absurd. Analysts were also skeptical of his claim that Iraq had begun producing "tons" of VX in 1998 in mobile labs, because such labs would be very unlikely to have the capacity to produce such large amounts of agent.

Despite these highly suspect claims, analysts credited the source's reporting that Iraq had successfully stabilized VX. As one analyst reviewing his reporting after the war said of it, "half seems credible and half seems preposterous." Yet at the time the NIE was written, with substantial skepticism about the validity of much of his information, analysts nevertheless judged his reporting to be "moderately credible." In our view, given that important parts of his information were simply unbelievable and recognized as such by analysts, the Community should have approached him and his intelligence with more caution—and certainly should have been more skeptical about using selections from his reporting in the authoritative NIE.

Indeed, analytic skepticism about the source's claims was later confirmed by revelations about his operational history, revelations that led to the Intelligence Community deeming him a fabricator and recalling his reporting, although not all of his reporting was recalled until almost one year after the war started. He had initially come to the CIA's attention via a foreign intelligence service, which asked for the CIA's assistance after he had approached them. In March 2003, however, the CIA terminated contact with him, after administering an examination in February 2003 during which he was deceptive. CIA had also learned that he had—before approaching this foreign service—already been debriefed by two other intelligence services, indicating that he was something of an "information peddler." Moreover, one of these two services had concluded that although his pre–1991 information was credible, his post–1991 information was both not credible and possibly "directed" by a hostile service. CIA started to recall his reporting in March 2003, but did not recall all of it until February 2004.

Another source, who was described as a contact with "good but historical access" but lacking "an established reporting record," reported in July 2002 that, as of 1998, Iraq was producing mustard and binary chemical agents. At the same time, he also reported on a "wide range of disparate subjects," including on Iraq's missile program and nuclear and biological weapons programs. Such broad access, on its face, was inconsistent with what analysts understood to be Iraq's well-known tendency towards compartmentation of sensitive weapons programs. Yet because of the Community's *own* compartmentation—working-level analysts saw reporting on *their* area but not on others—they did not realize at the time that one source was reporting on a range of topics for which he was unlikely to have access. Moreover, although analysts did not know it at the time, the source obtained his information from unknown and undescribed sub-sources.

Finally, a third source provided information that was technically implausible on its face. His reporting claimed that Iraq had constructed a factory for the production of castor oil that could be used for the production of sarin. Although castor beans can be used to make ricin, not sarin—a fact that analysts readily understood—analysts did not discount the information. Instead, they interpreted it in a way that would cure the technical difficulty, reading it as indicating that the facility could produce both sarin and ricin. But in so doing, analysts were consciously compensating for technical errors in the reporting. This exercise of "compensating for errors" in the reporting may well be appropriate in some instances, as when the source of the report may not have the competence to report accurately on a given technical subject. But such speculative interpretation must be carefully balanced with a healthy skepticism, especially when, as in the case of Iraq's CW program, the intelligence as a whole on the subject is weak and analysts' underlying assumptions are strong. An untethered "compensating for errors" runs the risk of skewing the analysis in the direction of those assumptions, as, unfortunately, happened here.

## *Sources Whose Reliability Has Been Questioned After the NIE*

The remaining human intelligence sources relied upon to support the conclusion that Iraq had restarted CW production, while not so problematic on the surface as the sources just described, have become questionable in hindsight.

One liaison source, details about whom cannot be disclosed at this level of classification, reported on production and stocks of chemical and biological weapons and agents, based on what he learned from others in his circle of high-level contacts in Baghdad. While this source provided general information on Iraq's CW program, he provided few details. In our view, the bottom line on this source was that he had no personal knowledge of CW and provided few details of CW capabilities—factors that should have prompted caution in using his reporting as significant evidence that the Iraqis had restarted CW production.

One other human source—while unlikely to have affected the NIE because his reporting dissemination was so limited—was also called into question after the start of the war. In September 2002, a liaison service reported that a senior Iraqi official had said that Iraq was producing and stockpiling chemical weapons. The source of the information claimed to have spoken with this senior official on this topic. CIA was able to confirm at the time of the report that the senior official had been in contact with the source. After the start of the war, however, when CIA officers interviewed the senior official, he denied ever making such comments. Although the CIA's Directorate of Operations requested liaison assistance in clarifying this issue, as of March 2005 the issue remained unresolved.

Signals intelligence provided only minimal information regarding Iraq's chemical weapons programs and, due to the nature of the sources, what was provided was of dubious quality and therefore of questionable value. Although the Intelligence Community originally cited more than two dozen such intelligence reports as supporting the proposition that Iraq was attempting to reconstitute its chemical weapons program, a subsequent review revealed that only a handful of the reports provided any usable information for analysis. It is not readily apparent what caused this discrepancy, but we think it plain that the Intelligence Community should have conducted a far more careful and thoughtful prewar analysis of this signals intelligence information and treated it with greater skepticism.

## Conclusion

Similar to its assessments about Iraq's nuclear and biological efforts, the Intelligence Community's mistaken assessments about Iraq's chemical weapons program can be traced in large part to a single point of failure—the Community's over-reliance on ambiguous imagery indicators. But the Community's bottom line on Iraq's chemical weapons capabilities was further influenced by a breakdown in communication between imagery collectors and analysts; a basic paucity of quality intelligence, particularly quality signals intelligence; and the fact that much of the human and signals intelligence that was collected was bad.

It is, however, understandable that analysts assessed—as they did throughout the 1990s—that Iraq retained a chemical warfare capability. Iraq's pre-Gulf War chemical weapons stockpile was large and relatively sophisticated. Nor did Saddam's uncooperative and secretive behavior after the war encourage confidence that he had converted from the CW path. The Community's failure on CW was therefore not in thinking that Iraq had such a capability—that was, in many ways, the only sensible conclusion, given the evidence. Rather, analysts erred in their assessment—based largely on ambiguous imagery indicators that could not logically support the judgment—that Iraq had in fact resumed producing and stockpiling significant quantities of CW.

# Delivery Systems

The Intelligence Community assessed in the October 2002 NIE that Iraq was developing small Unmanned Aerial Vehicles (UAVs) capable of autonomous flight, which most agencies assessed were "probably" intended to deliver biological warfare agents. The Intelligence Community also judged that these UAVs could threaten the U.S. homeland. This latter assessment was based on an Iraqi attempt to procure commercially available civilian U.S. mapping software for its UAVs. That attempted procurement, the Intelligence Community assessed, "strongly suggest[ed] that Iraq [was] investigating the use of these UAVs for missions targeting the United States."

By January 2003, however, the Intelligence Community had pulled back from its view that Iraq intended to target the United States. This re-assessment reflected a belief among CIA analysts that the Iraqi attempt to procure U.S. mapping software may have been inadvertent. As a result, the Intelligence Community assessed in January 2003 that while the mapping software could provide the *capability* to target the United States, the purchasing attempt did not necessarily indicate an intent to do so. By early March 2003, CIA had further retreated from the view that the purchase of the mapping software evidenced an intent to target the United States and, in early March 2003, on the eve of the invasion of Iraq, CIA advised senior policymakers that it was an open question whether the attempted software procurement evinced the intent to target the United States at all.

Following its exhaustive investigation in Iraq, the Iraq Survey Group concluded that Iraq had indeed been developing small UAVs, but found no evidence that the UAVs had been designed to deliver biological agent. Instead, the ISG concluded that Iraq had been developing and had flight tested a small, autonomous UAV intended for use as a reconnaissance platform, and had developed a prototype for another small UAV for use in electronic warfare missions. Although both UAVs had the range, payload, guidance, and autonomy necessary to deliver a biological agent, the ISG found no evidence that Iraq intended to use them in such a way. With respect to the mapping software, Iraqi officials told ISG investigators that the software in question had been included as part of a package deal with autopilots they had purchased for the UAVs; the Iraqis, the ISG judged, had not actually intended to buy the mapping software.

The October 2002 NIE had also examined whether Iraq was deploying missiles capable of reaching beyond the 150 kilometer limit imposed by the United Nations. The NIE assessed that Iraq was deploying two types of short-range ballistic missiles capable of flying beyond the United Nations-authorized range limit. The NIE also assessed, based largely on Iraqi accounting discrepancies and incomplete records and record keeping, that Iraq retained a covert force of up to a few dozen Scud-variant missiles in defiance of United Nations resolutions. The ISG concluded—consistent with this assessment—that Iraq had been developing and deploying ballistic missiles that exceeded United Nations restrictions, although the ISG also found, contrary to pre-war assessments, that Iraq had not retained Scud or Scud-variant missiles after 1991.

The Intelligence Community's assessments of Iraq's delivery systems developments offered both a bright and a dark spot on its Iraq record. While far from perfect (which can never be reasonably expected in intelligence work), the Community's judgments about the progress of Iraq's ballistic missile programs were substantively accurate. As the ISG discovered, the Iraqis were indeed violating United Nations strictures by working on missiles that exceeded the 150 kilometer range limit. But on the issue of whether Iraq was developing UAVs to deliver biological agent against U.S. targets—including the U.S. homeland—the Community erred, once again attributing more to spotty intelligence than that information could bear.

This section describes the Community's analysis of Iraq's work on delivery systems between the first Gulf War and Operation Iraqi Freedom, as well as the ISG's findings concerning the same. The Commission then offers its findings based on a thorough investigation into the Community's efforts on Iraqi delivery systems, concentrating particularly on the analytical flaws apparent from the Community's products on the uses of Iraqi UAVs.

*The Intelligence Community's Pre-War Assessments*

As with other aspects of Iraq's WMD programs, the Intelligence Community's assessment of Iraq's delivery systems evolved over the course of many years and was heavily influenced by Iraq's past actions and intransigence.

*Background.* Before the Gulf War Iraq had been in the early stages of a project to convert the MiG–21 jet aircraft into UAVs for BW delivery. In addition, Iraq had experimented in 1990 on a BW spray system, designed to be used with the MiG–21 UAV. Iraq admitted to this program in 1995, after the defection of Hussein Kamil. Subsequent UNSCOM inspections discovered video showing the spray-system experiments. Also, analysts in the early 1990s had observed continued activity at Salman Pak—Iraq's primary BW research and development facility prior to the Gulf War—where, UNSCOM reported, work continued on modified commercial crop sprayers for BW delivery and the presence of UAV program personnel. Iraq claimed that, because of the war, it had abandoned the MiG–21 UAV project after conducting only one experiment in 1991, but UNSCOM inspections could not confirm this claim. In the mid–1990s Iraq also began testing another modified jet aircraft, the L–29, as a UAV, that analysts believed was a follow-on to the converted MiG–21 program.

These discoveries also cast new light, in analysts' minds, on UNSCOM's earlier discovery of 11 small-to-medium sized UAV drones at the Salman Pak compound in 1991. Although Iraq denied having developed these UAVs for BW delivery, Iraq's later admission—after an initial denial—that the MiG–21 program was for the purpose of delivering biological agents led analysts to believe, given Iraqi deception, that Iraq's small UAVs had a similar purpose. Analysts also focused on Iraqi admissions—in their 1996 declaration to the United Nations—that, in the late 1980s, senior Iraqi officials had met to discuss the feasibility of using small UAVs as BW delivery vehicles.

This history, along with evidence that Iraq had flight-tested small and medium-sized UAVs, led most Intelligence Community analysts to conclude consistently from the late 1990s through 2002 that Iraq was maintaining its UAV program for BW and CW delivery. Briefings and written products to senior policymakers in mid–2002 reflected this assessment. As with the other elements of Iraq's purported weapons programs, however, intelligence on UAVs in the years preceding 2002 was partial and ambiguous. While it was clear that Iraq did have a UAV program, the key question—whether that program was meant to be a delivery system—remained unanswered. Therefore, analysts' judgments again depended heavily upon assumptions based on Iraq's earlier behavior and Community views about Iraq's sophisticated denial and deception activities.

With respect to ballistic missiles, the Intelligence Community judged in 1992 that Iraq's ballistic missile programs were more advanced than the Community had assessed before the Gulf War. Iraq was further along in its production capability for Scud and Scud-derivative missiles and had produced more components indigenously than the Intelligence Community had assessed before the Gulf War. By 1995, the Intelligence Community judged that Iraq was developing liquid-propellant missiles with an expected range of about 150 kilometers. In 1998, the Community assessed that these missiles, named the al-Samoud, were capable of flying farther than the 150 kilometer limit imposed by the United Nations and that Iraq was also developing solid-propellant missiles. By early 2002, the Intelligence Community judged that Iraq probably still retained a small force of Scud missiles and that both its liquid-propellant and solid-propellant missiles were capable of flying over 150 kilometers.

*October 2002 NIE.* The October 2002 NIE judged, with a dissent from the Director of Air Force Intelligence, that Iraq was developing small UAVs "probably" for BW delivery which could be used against U.S. forces and allies in the region. In addition, the NIE mentioned the concern of most agencies about the possible intent to use UAVs as delivery systems against the U.S. homeland. This possible use was based on the attempted procurement of U.S. mapping software by an Iraqi procurement agent.

As noted, the Director of Air Force Intelligence dissented from the majority view. In contrast to other organizations, the Air Force judged that Iraq was developing UAVs "primarily for reconnaissance rather than [as] delivery platforms for [CW or BW] agents." The Air Force further noted that CW or BW delivery is "an inherent capability of UAVs but probably is not the impetus for Iraq's recent UAV programs."

Analysts' judgments that Iraq's small UAVs were intended for BW delivery were based on the following logic: the Iraqis had admitted that the MiG–21 program was intended for BW delivery, and analysts judged that the L–29 program, for which there was some evidence of a BW-delivery mission, was the successor to the MiG–21 program. Because the L–29 program had suffered setbacks in late 2000 after a crash, analysts then deduced that Iraq's new, small UAVs may have been designed to replace the L–29 effort, and that they were therefore also intended to deliver BW agents.

There was very little reporting, however, to support the conclusion that the small UAVs were "probably" intended for BW delivery. Only one human intelligence report indicated that small UAVs were intended for CW or BW delivery. Given the dearth of reporting on the purpose for the small UAVs, analysts instead deduced their intended purpose from Iraq's previous admissions and from what was assessed about the characteristics of Iraq's other UAV programs.

For example, analysts pointed to several human intelligence reports that suggested that Iraq's L–29 UAV program could be used to deliver CW or BW agents. Only one of those reports, however, stated explicitly that the L–29 UAV was intended for biological or chemical weapon delivery, and that early 1998 report was based on a report of unknown reliability. Analysts believed, though, that this conclusion was reinforced by separate reporting indicating that Iraq was prepared to use modified L–29 UAVs against U.S. forces in the Persian Gulf area; these UAVs, the reasoning went, would have been useless for delivery of conventional weapons and BW was therefore a likelier function.

But there were other indications that the UAVs were not intended for BW delivery. Iraq's 1996 declaration to the United Nations indicated that the drones discovered in 1991 were actually intended for reconnaissance and aerial targeting—not BW delivery. Intelligence reporting supported this view; Iraq was attempting to procure equipment for its small UAVs, which suggested the

UAVs' purpose was reconnaissance. Finally, as noted in the Air Force dissent, the small UAVs were not ideally suited for BW or CW delivery; the Air Force assessed instead that "the small size of Iraq's new UAV strongly suggests a primary role of reconnaissance, although chemical/biological weapons (CBW) delivery is an inherent capability." Although CIA's WINPAC had published an Intelligence Assessment in 2001 that discussed these possible non-BW delivery missions for Iraq's UAVs, such alternative missions were not emphasized in the October 2002 NIE because WINPAC's "focus [in] the NIE was WMD delivery systems and not the Iraqi UAV program as a whole."

In sum, the evidentiary basis for the pre-war assessment that Iraq was developing UAVs "probably intended" for BW delivery was based largely on the BW focus of Iraq's pre–1991 UAV programs and a thin stream of (primarily human intelligence) reporting that hinted at such a function for post–1991 UAVs.

As noted above, the NIE also judged that Iraq's UAVs "could threaten . . . the U.S. Homeland." This assessment was based on two streams of reporting: first, intelligence reporting indicating that the UAVs had a range of over 500 kilometers and could be launched from a truck; and, second, reporting that an Iraqi procurement agent was attempting to buy U.S. mapping software for its small UAVs. The latter piece of information was, however, the only evidence that supported Iraq's intent to target the United States. Based on this stream of reporting, the NIE reasoned that, because the mapping software would be useless outside the United States, its procurement "strongly suggest[ed]" Iraq was interested in using the UAVs to target the United States.

The procurement effort revealed by the reporting was spearheaded by an Iraqi procurement agent who had been involved in the pre-Gulf War Iraqi UAV program ("the procurement agent"). The procurement agent had subsequently emigrated to another country where he ran an illicit procurement network for Iraq. In late 2000 or early 2001, the procurement agent received a "shopping list" from an Iraqi general associated with the UAV program that included autopilots and gyroscopes. To fill this request, the procurement agent researched potential suppliers for these items, and in May 2001 he submitted requests for price quotes to a manufacturer and a distributor for the requested items, which included autopilots and gyroscopes but also included "Map Source" mapping software. The distributor responded with a price quote for the autopilot package, which included "Garmin 50 State" topographic mapping software, also sold as "Map Source." After consulting with Baghdad and soliciting a final price quote, in early 2002 the procurement agent submitted a final procurement list, which included the Garmin 50 State mapping software, to the distributor.

Although the distributor had been assured by the procurement agent that the end-user was "legitimate," the distributor remained concerned about the procurement agent's interest in these items and contacted its own country's authorities in March 2002. The distributor also removed the mapping software from its website.

Following the attempted procurement, several analytical assessments were published regarding the attempted procurement of the mapping software. An Intelligence Community Assessment titled Current and Future Air Threats to the US Homeland, published July 29, 2002, noted that Iraq was seeking route planning software and an associated topographic database "likely intended to use with its UAVs" and "almost certainly relate[d] to the United States." CIA's Office of Near Eastern and South Asian Analysis also disseminated an intelligence assessment on August 1, 2002, observing that the mapping software would "provide precise guidance, tracking, and targeting in the United States."

A liaison intelligence service subsequently approached the procurement agent to question him about the attempted procurement. In these discussions, the procurement agent claimed that he had not intended to purchase mapping software of the United States. Although he admitted that the software he had ordered had not been "bundled" with other items he ordered, he explained that he had not well understood all of the elements of the package and had not wanted to miss out on an important piece of software. He said he had been concerned that the other system pieces might not work if he did not purchase the mapping software; it was cheap; and he had thought the system would allow the user to scan maps and program them into a GPS. Asked by the liaison service to submit to a thorough examination, the procurement agent refused. Thus, by fall 2002, the CIA was still uncertain whether the procurement agent was lying.

While the October 2002 NIE was being coordinated, a CIA analyst interviewed the procurement agent in an effort to determine if his attempted procurement of the U.S. mapping software had in fact been inadvertent, as he claimed. The analyst initially concluded that the procurement agent was lying because a review of the website showed that, contrary to the procurement agent's claims, the option to purchase the mapping software was not on the page with the autopilots and gyroscopes. After further research, however, the analyst determined that the version of the website that the procurement agent had accessed in early 2001 had in fact contained the configuration and software option that the procurement agent described. This discovery led the analyst to believe that the purchase order may have indeed been inadvertent.

Although the CIA was now beginning to obtain indications that the procurement agent's attempted purchase of the U.S. mapping software may in fact have been inadvertent as the procurement agent claimed, CIA remained uncertain whether the procurement agent was lying. As the National Foreign Intelligence Board was convening to review and approve the NIE, several CIA analysts expressed concern about its use of the words "strongly suggests" and recommended that the language be toned down. But these concerns did not reach the DCI himself until the Board process had concluded. With the lengthy Board meeting finished, the DCI concluded that the word "strongly" would remain in the NIE because the coordination process was complete at that point and the new information had not been confirmed.

As noted, the NIE also stated that gaps in accounting suggested that Iraq retained a small covert Scud force, and the NIE assessed that Iraq was deploying missiles capable of flying farther than the United Nations limit of 150 kilometers.

*Post-NIE.* The Intelligence Community's assessment that the UAVs were "probably" for BW delivery remained unchanged in the run-up to the war. In a paper sent to the National Security Council in January 2003, the CIA noted that an Iraqi Ministry of Defense official had indicated that Iraq considered its UAVs to be an important strategic weapon. And in testimony before the Senate Select Committee on Intelligence in early February 2003, DCI Tenet stated that "[w]e are concerned that Iraq's UAVs can dispense chemical and biological weapons."

The Intelligence Community did, however, begin to retreat from its assessment that Iraq intended to target the U.S. homeland, though not quickly enough to prevent the charge's inclusion in the President's speech in Cincinnati in October 2002. In the immediate aftermath of the publication of the October 2002 NIE, CIA increasingly believed that the attempted purchase of the mapping software—on which this judgment was based—may have been inadvertent. Accordingly, at least one CIA analyst recommended that a reference to the UAVs targeting the United States be deleted from a draft Presidential speech. Because of persistent uncertainty within the analytical ranks about the significance of the mapping software, however, CIA and the Intelligence Community's official position remained unchanged from the NIE. The President's speech, which was delivered on October 7, 2002 in Cincinnati, therefore expressed concern "that Iraq is exploring ways of using these UAVs for missions targeting the United States."

Subsequent analytical products did begin to reflect the uncertainty over the significance of the mapping software, though. An NIE addressing the UAV question, entitled *Nontraditional Threats to the US Homeland Through 2007*, which was approved by the National Foreign Intelligence Board in November 2002, was not published for two months because of disagreement over whether the order for the U.S. mapping software indicated Iraqi intent to target the U.S. homeland. The *Nontraditional Threats* NIE ultimately addressed the UAV issue in terms of capabilities rather than intent. That is, that NIE phrased the first judgment like the October 2002 Iraq NIE, noting that Iraqi UAVs "could strike the US Homeland if transported to within a few hundred kilometers," but phrased the software judgment only in terms of capability, noting that this "[route planning] software . . . could support [the] programming of a UAV autopilot for operation in the United States." For their parts, the Air Force, DIA, and the Army assessed that the purpose of the acquisition was to obtain generic mapping capability and that that goal was "not necessarily indicative of an intent to target the US homeland."

By early March 2003, days before the March 19 invasion of Iraq, the CIA had further pulled back from its October NIE view, concluding in a memorandum to the Chairman of the House Permanent Select Committee on Intelligence that it was an open question whether the attempted procurement of the mapping software had been the result of a specific request from Baghdad or had been inadvertent. CIA also advised senior policymakers of this change in view. In the memorandum, the CIA stated that it "[had] no definite indications that Baghdad [was] planning to use WMD-armed UAVs against the U.S. mainland. . . . [Although] we cannot exclude the possibility that th[e] purchase [of mapping software] was directed by Baghdad, information acquired in October suggests that it may have been inadvertent."

With respect to ballistic missiles, CIA's position remained unchanged after the NIE. Subsequent to the NIE, the Intelligence Community confirmed from Iraq's December 2002 declaration to the United Nations that Iraq had two versions of the al-Samoud missile, as described in the NIE. The longer-range version was inefficiently designed and did not go as far as the NIE had postulated, but it did have a range in excess of 150 kilometers.

## *Post-War Findings of the Iraq Survey Group*

The Iraq Survey Group concluded that, although Iraq had pursued UAVs as BW delivery systems in the past, Iraq's pre-Operation Iraqi Freedom program to develop small, autonomous-flight UAVs had actually been intended to fulfill reconnaissance and airborne electronic warfare missions. The ISG found no evidence suggesting that Iraq had, at the time of the war, any intent to use UAVs as BW or CW delivery systems.

The ISG concluded that Iraq's purpose in converting a MiG–21 into a Remotely Piloted Vehicle (RPV) in early 1991 had been to create a CBW delivery system. After the MiG–21 RPV program failed, Iraq in 1995 resumed efforts to convert manned aircraft into RPVs, this time with an L–29 jet trainer. The ISG, however, was unable to establish whether the L–29 had an intended CBW role, although the ISG did obtain some indirect evidence that the L–29 RPV may have been intended for CBW delivery. The ISG also concluded that Iraq had the capability to develop chemical or biological spray systems for the L–29, but found no evidence of any work along these lines. The L–29 program ended in 2001.

After several crashes of the L–29s, Iraq began to pursue long-range UAV options, probably at some point in 2000. The ISG assessed, however, that these small UAVs had not been intended for use as chemical or biological delivery systems. Specifically, although these small UAVs had the range, payload, guidance, and autonomy necessary to be used as BW delivery platforms, the ISG found no evidence that Iraq had intended to use them for such a purpose, had a suitable dispenser available, or had conducted research and development activity associated with use as a BW delivery system.

The more advanced of Iraq's two UAV programs, the Al-Musayara–20, had actually been developed for use as a reconnaissance platform, according to a senior Iraqi official. An interview with an Iraqi military official after Operation Iraqi Freedom revealed that many general officers had been shot down on helicopter reconnaissance missions during the Iran-Iraq war and therefore the military was interested in developing a UAV to perform such missions. According to another official, although the Al-Musayara–20 was developed for a reconnaissance role, other roles, such as for the delivery of high explosives, were also considered.

A competing program to the Al-Musayara, the Al Quds UAV program, had been less advanced but had included prototypes of varying sizes and weights. The ISG concluded that the Al Quds program had been intended as an airborne electronic warfare platform. Like the Al-Musayara, the Al Quds UAV had the range, autonomous guidance, and payload to enable it to deliver CBW. The ISG uncovered no evidence, however, that Iraq had been developing a dispenser or had the intent to use the UAV as a BW delivery system. The Al Quds UAV was still in development when the war started.

According to the Iraq Survey Group, Iraqi officials denied deliberately seeking to acquire mapping software for the United States, but did say they received mapping software that came as part of the package with the autopilots they purchased. An official claimed to have received several autopilots for UAVs through the procurement agent, but asserted that these autopilots were never installed because they arrived on the eve of the war. The official was unaware of the current location of the autopilots.

Regarding missile systems, the Iraq Survey Group concluded that Iraq had been developing and deploying ballistic missiles that exceeded United Nations restrictions. The ISG concluded that Iraq had not possessed Scud or Scud-variant missiles after 1991, having by then either expended or unilaterally destroyed its stockpile.

## Analysis of the Intelligence Community's Pre-War Assessments

The Iraq Survey Group's uncovering of ballistic missile work that violated United Nations' restrictions affords a bright spot for the Intelligence Community's record of assessments on Iraq's unconventional weapons programs. The NIE accurately assessed that Iraq was deploying ballistic missiles with ranges exceeding United Nations restrictions. And although the NIE did not assess accurately the status of Iraq's Scud missile force, we are not especially troubled by this inaccuracy in light of the NIE's clear statement that this assessment was based merely on accounting discrepancies.

The record of the Intelligence Community's performance on the UAVs is more mixed (in part because the Intelligence Community's assessments themselves shifted during the pre-war period). While these assessments accurately described the Iraqi UAVs technical capability to deliver BW, the Intelligence Community's assessments that the UAVs were intended for this purpose—or that Iraq intended to strike the United States—were not borne out by the ISG's findings.

It is worth considering why the Intelligence Community's assessments were more correct in this area than they were with respect to other aspects of Iraq's arsenal. One possible answer is that—unlike the status of Iraq's BW and CW stockpiles—certain

questions about Iraq's delivery systems—especially missiles—
could be answered through technical means that operate from
outside of the denied area, and which are generally less subject to
questions about reliability. The intentions of a closed regime,
however, are difficult to penetrate, and the reliability of any such
information is difficult to determine. In areas of analysis that turn
largely on intent, therefore, such as whether a regime is producing BW or intends to use its UAVs for BW delivery, the quality of
the analysis will be largely dependent on the quality of the available human intelligence and on the ability of signals intelligence
to penetrate communications. This highlights the imperative for
analysts to explain the premise of their judgments, particularly
when the ultimate judgment may rest on a very thin stream of information or on a chain of assumptions about intent.

With that said, the pre-war assessments on Iraq's delivery systems reflect significant shortcomings in analysis.

The NIE went beyond what one could reasonably conclude
from the intelligence by judging that Iraq's UAVs were "probably
intended to deliver biological warfare agents." Although past
Iraqi interest in UAVs as BW vehicles was a reasonable indicator
that the interest may have continued, the paucity of subsequent
evidence should have led to a more nuanced statement in the
NIE—such as that BW delivery was a possible use, but not necessarily an intended one. That the NIE did not discuss in any detail
other possible missions for the UAVs only compounded this
problem. Moreover, most analysts discounted specific reporting
indicating that Iraq was seeking equipment suited to a reconnaissance mission for its UAVs.

The Intelligence Community's assessments about the purpose
of Iraq's UAV programs rested largely on inferences drawn from
the inherent capabilities of such UAVs and knowledge about
Iraq's past UAV programs, as discussed above. The conclusion
that the UAVs were probably intended for BW delivery, however,
reached beyond what the intelligence would reasonably bear.

Similarly, the single stream of reporting that the Iraqi procurement agent was attempting to purchase U.S. mapping software
was insufficient to justify the NIE's statement that this interest
"strongly suggest[ed]" that Iraq was investigating ways to target

the U.S. homeland with UAVs. While certain analysts took the proper steps to push the Intelligence Community back from this judgment after doubts about this reporting emerged, the Intelligence Community as a whole was slow to assimilate this new information—particularly given its critical importance.

Whether or not any statement about attacking the U.S. homeland merited inclusion in the NIE, it is clear that the rather thin foundation for these assessments was not clearly communicated to policymakers. And the NIE's assessment that the UAVs were "probably intended" for BW delivery did not make clear that this conclusion rested largely on analytical assumptions about Iraqi intent based on the history of Iraq's UAV programs and on the UAVs' inherent capabilities. Nor did the NIE explain why it focused only on a possible weapons-related role for UAVs. A WIN-PAC analyst subsequently explained that the NIE's purpose was to discuss Iraq's WMD programs, and that accordingly the UAV section addressed the UAVs' use as a BW delivery platform and not their other possible uses. The failure to explain that reasoning in the NIE, however, leaves the impression that other possible uses for the UAV had been rejected rather than simply not discussed.

Finally, once again, the UAV episode reflects the tendency of Intelligence Community analysts to view data through the lens of its overall assumptions about Saddam Hussein's behavior. As noted, the NIE itself did not discuss other possible purposes for the UAVs or explain why the Estimate focused only on a weapons-related purpose. In addition, however, the Intelligence Community was too quick to characterize evidence that contradicted the theory that UAVs were intended for BW delivery as an Iraqi "deception" or "cover story." And a Senior Executive Memorandum warned that Iraq "probably will assert that UAVs are intended as target drones or reconnaissance platforms" to counter the claim in the British and U.S. "white papers" that the UAVs have a BW delivery role.

We commend the Intelligence Community for correctly assessing that Iraq was working on ballistic missile programs that violated United Nations strictures. As the ISG's findings demonstrate, however, many of the Community's specific estimates were off the mark. The Community judged, for instance, that Iraq retained a force of "up to a few dozen Scud-variant SRBMs [short-range ballistic missiles]." The ISG concluded, however, that Iraq did not have any Scud missiles after 1991. Similarly, the Community stated in the NIE that "in January 2002, Iraq flight-tested an extended-range version of the al-Samoud that flew beyond the 150-km range limit." The Community subsequently learned that it had misidentified the missile and had incorrectly deduced the missile's range; in actuality, the missile, while it had a range that exceeded 150 kilometers, did not exceed that limit by as much as analysts initially thought because the engine was less effective than they estimated.

In short, while the Community was technically correct that Iraq's missile systems violated United Nations strictures, it erred significantly in degree.

### Conclusion

As has proven the case with other pre-war Intelligence Community judgments about Iraq's unconventional weapons programs, the assumptions held by Iraq analysts about Saddam Hussein's behavior were not unreasonable ones. These assumptions, however, drove the Intelligence Community to make overly inferential leaps about Iraq's UAV program based on thin evidence, and to fail to communicate this thin evidentiary basis to policymakers. While we fully understand that, in the wake of September 11, the Community felt obliged to report even relatively unlikely threats against the United States, the Community should have at a minimum explained more fully the uncertainties underlying its assessments.

## Regime Decisionmaking

The Intelligence Community failed to examine seriously the possibility that domestic or regional political pressures or some other factors might have prompted Saddam Hussein to destroy his stockpiles and to forswear active development of weapons of mass destruction after the first Gulf War. The Community was certainly aware of the overall political dynamics that underpinned Saddam Hussein's regime—that he was a brutal dictator who ruled Iraq through a combination of violence, secrecy, mendacity, and fear—but the Community did not seriously consider the range of possible decisions that Saddam might make regarding his weapons programs given his idiosyncratic decisionmaking processes.

Though the likelihood that one of those possible decisions was to destroy his weapons seemed very remote to almost all outside observers, it was one that Community analysts at least should have seriously considered. In truth, any assessment of the effect of Saddam's political situation on his decisions about WMD in the years from 1991 to 2003 would more likely than not have resulted—and, in point of fact, did result—in the conclusion that Saddam retained his WMD programs. But whether or not it was extraordinarily difficult (if not effectively impossible) for the Intelligence Community to have discerned Saddam Hussein's true intentions, the Community's lack of imagination about the range of strategies and tactics Saddam might adopt left the Community with an incomplete analytical picture.

Having gained access to Iraq and its leaders, the Iraq Survey Group concluded that the unlikely course of voluntary abandonment by Saddam Hussein of his weapons of mass destruction was, in fact, the reality. According to the ISG, Saddam's regime, under severe pressure from United Nations sanctions, reacted by unilaterally destroying its WMD stockpiles and halting work on its WMD programs. Saddam decided to abandon his weapons programs because the economy and infrastructure of Iraq were collapsing under the weight of the sanctions. Saddam therefore ordered the unilateral destruction of biological and chemical weapons stockpiles in 1991 and chose to focus on securing sanctions relief before resuming WMD development. At the same time, in an attempt to project power—both domestically as well as against perceived regional threats such as Iran and Israel—Iraq chose to obfuscate whether it actually possessed WMD. As a result, the U.S. Intelligence Community—and many other intelligence services around the world—believed that Iraq continued to possess unconventional weapons in large part because Iraqis were acting as if they *did* have them.

This section begins with a brief description of how the Intelligence Community assessed Baghdad's decisionmaking before the war and then compares that with the ISG's findings. We then describe the Community's lack of creative thinking about Saddam's motives that led to the failure even to consider the possibility that Saddam Hussein had decided to abandon his banned weapons programs.

## The Intelligence Community's Pre-War Assessments

The Intelligence Community's assessments of Saddam's thought processes in the decade before Operation Iraqi Freedom are reflected in two broad lines of analysis: the threats to Saddam's regime and his threat to regional security. Throughout both these areas, one aspect remained relatively constant—the Intelligence Community emphasized repeatedly that it lacked "solid information about the activities and intentions of major players in Iraq" and was, in the words of one senior intelligence official, "flying blind" on the subject.

*Regime stability and decisionmaking.* The Intelligence Community early on identified sanctions as a significant threat to Saddam's regime, but never assessed whether Saddam might address that threat by destroying his WMD. Immediately after the Gulf War, for example, the Intelligence Community prepared a Special National Intelligence Estimate assessing Saddam's prospects for survival in power. That assessment noted that economic vulnerabilities presented a threat to Saddam's regime and that the "lifting of sanctions . . . would provide relief to the regime and would strengthen Saddam's prospects for survival." The Special Estimate therefore assessed that Saddam would concentrate on getting sanctions eased or removed.

Through the mid–1990s, the Intelligence Community continued to judge that the sanctions were a threat to the regime, but that Saddam "probably believe[d]" he could "outlast" them. For example, in December 1993, the Intelligence Community produced another NIE on Saddam's prospects for survival, judging that the United Nations sanctions were "Saddam's Achilles' heel" because of their debilitating effect on the Iraqi economy. The NIE did not consider the possibility that Iraq would actually comply with United Nations resolutions. In fact, the Estimate identified as one of the assumptions underlying the analysis that "Saddam Husayn would not fully comply with U.N. Resolutions."

By June 1995, as living conditions and the economy continued to decline, the Intelligence Community assessed that Saddam's overall strategy was to seek a lifting of sanctions with the lowest possible level of compliance with UNSCOM's demands for a full accounting of Iraq's WMD programs. Laying out Saddam's options, a June 1995 Special Estimate judged that in the short term Saddam was "likely to make a gesture to UNSCOM . . . by providing limited additional information on Iraq's BW program." If that gesture failed to achieve relief from sanctions within three months, however, Saddam "probably [would] return to a confrontational mode." Such a "confrontational mode" included suspending cooperation with UNSCOM, sabotaging or obstructing UNSCOM monitoring, and expelling or taking hostage United Nations personnel. In short, the Intelligence Community judged that Saddam would choose confrontation over greater cooperation with the United Nations as a way to end sanctions.

Throughout the remainder of the 1990s, the Intelligence Community continued to assess that sanctions threatened Saddam's regime, but also that "Saddam [was] determined to maintain elements of his WMD programs and probably calculate[d] he [could] stonewall UNSCOM while wearing down the Security Council's will to maintain sanctions." Saddam's success in undermining international support for the sanctions and in repressing internal dissent also gave him greater confidence and resolve. But more importantly, the commerce allowed under the Oil-for-Food program fueled international perceptions that sanctions had weakened. This weakening, combined with the failure of UNSCOM to "uncover tangible proof of Iraqi concealment of weapons of mass destruction," bolstered domestic and international perceptions of the regime's strength.

At the same time, by the end of the decade the Community assessed that Saddam "appear[ed] to have made a strategic decision that confrontation would be necessary to gain an end to the sanctions." Saddam felt "that putting pressure on UNSCOM and the Security Council [was] the only way to achieve his goal of ending sanctions," according to the Intelligence Community, because Saddam did "not intend to fully comply with relevant Security Council resolutions."

The Intelligence Community viewed Iraq's behavior vis-à-vis the United Nations inspections during this time against the backdrop of these assessments and of Iraq's history of concealing its WMD programs. Accordingly, the Community judged that Iraq would continue to obstruct inspections "to the degree they believe[d] the inspections [would] undermine the security apparatus or uncover proscribed materials." Thus, when Iraq agreed to the resumption of inspections in 2002, the Intelligence Community judged that Iraq did so in part because of confidence in its ability to hide its weapons-related activities. The Community also assessed that Saddam was motivated to reengage with the United Nations in order to avoid U.S. military intervention. If such delaying tactics failed to divert an attack, Iraq "could make a tactical retreat by acceding to some United Nations and U.S. demands and then reneg[ing] on them at the earliest opportunity." Although Iraq had tried to open several back channels to the United States seeking improved relations, the Community viewed these moves as public relations efforts and did not consider as an option the possibility that Iraq would actually comply with United Nations resolutions.

Still, analysis of Saddam's thinking and motivations remained largely speculative. In addition to the simple lack of information on Saddam's plans and intentions, the nature of Saddam's decisionmaking process, which the Intelligence Community assessed as highly centralized and therefore difficult to penetrate, compounded analysts' difficulties. Saddam made "all key policy decisions" with little input from the bureaucracy, and he usually acted quickly and decisively. He could also be "impulsive and deceptive" about his decisions. Moreover, the Intelligence Community judged that Saddam "rule[d] primarily by fear," using his control over the military, security, and intelligence services to "impose his absolute authority and crush resistance." Saddam reinforce[d] this control through "prominent members of his Tikriti clan who oc-cup[ied] key leadership positions." As a result, "all major decisions [were] made by Saddam and a few close relatives and associates." The Intelligence Community noted that these characteristics of Saddam's leadership style made it very difficult to read his inten-tions.

*Regional security and decisionmaking.* The Intelligence Commu-nity assessed that regional supremacy for Iraq remained Saddam Hussein's fundamental goal from 1991 through 2003. The Com-munity judged, though, that to achieve that goal Saddam would need to rebuild Iraq's military might—including weapons of mass destruction.

But, according to the Intelligence Community, Iraq's conven-tional military capabilities had deteriorated significantly during this time. By 1999, after four more years of sanctions and damage inflicted by U.S. military operations, Saddam's military was "smaller and much less well-equipped than it was on the eve of his 1990 invasion of Kuwait." By 2002, the Community assessed that "Iraqi military morale and battlefield cohesion [were] more frag-ile today than in 1991."

With respect to WMD capabilities, on the other hand, the Community's assessments that Iraq "retain[ed] residual chemical and biological weapons of mass destruction" remained constant. Although cautioning that reading Saddam's intentions was diffi-cult and that "critical factors important in shaping his behavior [we]re largely hidden from us," the Community nonetheless as-sessed that Saddam was "determined to retain elements of his WMD programs so that he [would] be able to intimidate his neighbors and deter potential adversaries such as Iran, Israel, and the United States." Given Iraq's history with WMD, its desire for regional dominance, and the weaknesses in its conventional mili-tary forces, the Community did not consider the possibility that Saddam would try to achieve such intimidation and deterrence while bluffing about his possession of WMD.

*Post-War Findings of the Iraq Survey Group*

The Iraq Survey Group concluded that Saddam Hussein unilaterally destroyed his WMD stocks in 1991. Saddam apparently concluded that economic sanctions posed such a threat to his regime that, although he valued the possession of WMD, he concluded that he had to focus on sanctions relief before resuming WMD development.

*Background.* Iraq's successful use of CW to repel human-wave attacks in the Iran-Iraq war had convinced Saddam Hussein of the importance of WMD and it became an "article of faith" for Saddam that WMD and theater ballistic missiles were necessary to secure Iraqi national security. Saddam also believed that Iraq's possession of WMD and Iraq's willingness to use it "contributed substantially to deterring the United States from going to Baghdad in 1991."

*The destruction of WMD.* After the Gulf War, however, the United Nations passed resolutions explicitly linking the removal of economic sanctions with Iraq's WMD disarmament. Saddam Hussein initially judged that the sanctions would be short-lived, that Iraq could weather them by making a few limited concessions, and that Iraq could successfully hide much of its pre-existing weaponry and documentation. Accordingly, Iraq declared to the United Nations part of its ballistic missile and chemical warfare programs, but not its biological or nuclear weapons programs. But after initial inspections proved much more thorough and intrusive than Baghdad had expected, Saddam became concerned. In order to prevent discovery of his still-hidden pre–1991 WMD programs, Saddam ordered Hussein Kamil to destroy large numbers of undeclared weapons and related materials in July 1991.

According to the Iraq Survey Group, Saddam's decision to destroy Iraq's WMD stockpiles in 1991 was likely shared with only a handful of senior Iraqi officials, a decision that would have important and lasting consequences. Saddam so dominated the political structure of the Iraqi regime that his strategic policy and intent were synonymous with the regime's strategic policy and intent. Moreover, in addition to dominating the regime's decisionmaking, Saddam also maintained secrecy and compartmentalization in his decisions, relying on a few close advisors and family members. And Saddam's penchant for using violence to ensure loyalty and suppress dissent encouraged a "culture of lying" and discouraged administrative transparency. As a result, the ISG concluded that instructions to subordinates were rarely documented and often shrouded in uncertainty. The decision to destroy the WMD stockpiles was therefore confined to a very small group of people at the top of the Ba'ath pyramid.

*The sanctions bind.* By the mid–1990s, United Nations sanctions were taking a serious toll; removing them therefore became Saddam's first priority, according to the ISG. Iraq's failure to document its unilateral destruction of WMD, however, complicated this effort. Also complicating Saddam's goal of sanctions removal was his continuing concern with regional threats to his security. Although he had destroyed his militarily significant WMD stocks, his "perceived requirement to bluff about WMD capabilities made it too dangerous to clearly reveal" Iraq's lack of WMD to the international community, especially Iran. Saddam was therefore in a bind, on the one hand wanting to avoid being caught in a violation of United Nations sanctions but, on the other, not wanting his rivals to know of his weakness.

Saddam decided to strike the balance between these competing objectives, according to the ISG, by preserving Iraq's ability to reconstitute his WMD while simultaneously seeking sanctions relief through the appearance of cooperation with the IAEA, UNSCOM, and, later, the United Nations Monitoring Verification and Inspection Commission (UNMOVIC). Iraq's behavior under the sanctions reflects that the Iraqis "never got the balance right." Though Saddam repeatedly told his ministers not to participate in WMD-related activity, he at the same time was working to preserve the capability eventually to reconstitute his unconventional weapons programs. And the Iraqis continued to conceal proscribed materials from United Nations inspectors. Moreover, even when there was nothing incriminating to hide, the Iraqis did not fully cooperate with the inspectors, judging that an effective United Nations inspection process would expose Iraq's lack of WMD and therefore expose its vulnerability, especially vis-à-vis Iran.

The regime's decision to disclose long-concealed WMD documents in the wake of Hussein Kamil's defection in 1995 further eroded confidence in the credibility of Iraqi declarations. The ISG concluded that the release of these documents served only to validate UNSCOM concerns that Iraq was still concealing its WMD programs.

*Suspending cooperation with the United Nations.* Angered by the continuing sanctions, inspections, and military attacks such as Operation Desert Fox, Saddam Hussein in a secret meeting in 1998 unilaterally abrogated Iraqi compliance with all United Nations resolutions, though, according to the ISG, it is unclear if anything concrete followed from this decision. Meanwhile, Iraq continued to take advantage of the Oil-for-Food Program to augment regime revenue streams. Saddam Hussein used much of Iraq's growing reserves of hard currency to invest in Iraq's military-industrial complex, to procure dual-use materials, and to initiate military research and development projects. Sanctions remained in place, however.

With international scrutiny bearing down on Iraq in late 2002, Saddam Hussein finally revealed to his senior military officials that Iraq had no weapons of mass destruction. His generals were "surprised" to learn this fact, because Saddam's "boasting" had led many to believe Iraq had some hidden WMD capacity and because Saddam's secretive decisionmaking style fostered uncertainty. In fact, senior officials were still convinced that Iraq had WMD in March 2003 because Saddam had assured them that if the United States invades, they need only "resist one week" and then Saddam would "take over."

## Analysis of the Intelligence Community's Pre-War Assessments

Saddam Hussein's decisionmaking process was, as the Intelligence Community assessed before the war and the Iraq Survey Group confirmed, secretive and highly centralized. And in this sense, the Intelligence Community cannot be faulted for failing to penetrate this process. But we believe the Community is open to criticism for failing to appreciate the full range of Saddam's strategic and tactical decisionmaking options regarding his weapons programs. At the very least, the Community should have *considered* the possibility that Saddam had halted active pursuit of his WMD programs after 1991.

Saddam and his regime repeatedly insisted that all of Iraq's banned weapons had been destroyed and that there were no active programs to reconstitute the capability. The United Nations inspectors, after 1996, found no conclusive evidence that these claims were wrong. In retrospect, as found by the ISG, it is clear that the stockpiles and programs were not there to be found. The question therefore arises of why the Intelligence Community did not discover that fact before the war, or at least consider the possibility that, however improbably, Saddam was telling the truth.

As discussed above, the Intelligence Community made multiple—and avoidable—errors in concluding "with high confidence" that Saddam retained WMD stockpiles and programs. It is a separate question why the Community failed to conclude affirmatively that he did not have them.

In large part the explanation lies in Saddam's own behavior. He had concealed crucial facts about his WMD efforts. He did repeatedly and continually obstruct the inspectors, to the point, in 1998, of completely terminating cooperation and forcing the inspectors to conclude that they could no longer do their work. When someone acts like he is hiding something, it is hard to entertain the conclusion that he really has nothing to hide.

The failure to conclude that Saddam had abandoned his weapons programs was therefore an understandable one. And even a human source in Saddam's inner circle, or intercepts of conversations between senior Iraqi leaders, may not have been sufficient for analysts to have concluded that Saddam ordered the destruction of his WMD stockpiles in 1991—and this kind of intelligence is extremely difficult to get. According to Charles Duelfer, the Special Advisor to the Director of Central Intelligence for Iraq's Weapons of Mass Destruction and head of the Iraq Survey Group, only six or seven senior officials were likely privy to Saddam's decision to halt his WMD programs. Moreover, because of Saddam's secretive and highly centralized decisionmaking process, as well as the "culture of lies" within the Iraqi bureaucracy, even after Saddam informed his senior military leaders in December 2002 that Iraq had no WMD, there was uncertainty among these officers as to the truth, and many senior commanders evidently believed that there were chemical weapons retained for use if conventional defenses failed.

That it would have been very difficult to get such evidence is, however, not the end of the story. Failing to conclude that Saddam had ended his banned weapons programs is one thing—not even considering it as a possibility is another. The Intelligence Community did not even evaluate the possibility that Saddam would destroy his stockpiles and halt work on his nuclear program. The absence of such a discussion within the Intelligence Community is, in our view, indicative of the rut that the Community found itself in throughout the 1990s. Rather than thinking imaginatively, and considering seemingly unlikely and unpopular possibilities, the Intelligence Community instead found itself wedded to a set of assumptions about Iraq, focusing on intelligence reporting that appeared to confirm those assumptions.

Over the course of 12 years the Intelligence Community did not produce a single analytical product that examined the possibility that Saddam Hussein's desire to escape sanctions, fear of being "caught" decisively, or anything else would cause him to destroy his WMD. The National Intelligence Officer for Near East and South Asia noted that such a hypothesis was so far removed from analysts' understanding of Iraq that it would have been very difficult to get such an idea published even as a "red-team" exercise. An intellectual culture or atmosphere in which certain ideas were simply too "unrespectable" and out of synch with prevailing policy and analytic perspectives pervaded the Intelligence Community. But much of the conventional wisdom that led analysts to reject even the consideration of this alternative hypothesis was itself based largely on assumptions rather than derived from analysis of hard data. In our view, rather than relying on inherited assumptions, analysts need to test favored hypotheses even more rigorously when the paucity of intelligence forces analysts to rely, not on specific intelligence, but on a country's history, politics, and observed behavior.

*Conclusion*

Iraq's decision to abandon its unconventional weapons programs while simultaneously hiding this decision was, at the very least, a counterintuitive one. And given the nature of the regime, the Intelligence Community can hardly be blamed for not penetrating Saddam's decisionmaking process. In this light, it is worth noting that Saddam's fellow Arabs (including, evidently, his senior military leadership as well as many of the rest of the world's intelligence agencies and most inspectors) also thought he had retained his weapons programs, thus responding to charges that the Community was projecting Western thinking onto a product of a foreign culture.

What the Intelligence Community can be blamed for, however, is not considering whether Saddam might have taken this counterintuitive route. Community analysts should have been more imaginative in contemplating the range of options from which Saddam might select. While such imaginative analysis would not necessarily or even likely have ultimately led analysts to the right conclusion, serious discussion of it in finished intelligence would have at least warned policymakers of the range of possibilities, a function that is critically important in the inherently uncertain arena of political analysis.

# Causes for the Intelligence Community's Inaccurate Pre-War Assessments

The Intelligence Community fundamentally misjudged the status of Iraq's nuclear, biological, and chemical programs. While the Intelligence Community did accurately assess certain aspects of Iraq's programs, the Community's central pre-war assessments—that Iraq had biological and chemical weapons and was reconstituting its nuclear weapons program—were shown by the post-war findings to be wrong. The discrepancies between the pre-war assessments and the post-war findings can be, in part, attributed to the inherent difficulties in obtaining information in denied areas such as Iraq. But the Intelligence Community's inaccurate assessments were also the result of systemic weaknesses in the way the Community collects, analyzes, and disseminates intelligence.

## Collection

The task of collecting meaningful intelligence on Iraq's weapons programs was extraordinarily difficult. Iraq's highly effective denial and deception program (which was employed against all methods of U.S. collection), the absence of United Nations inspectors after 1998, and the lack of a U.S. diplomatic presence in-country all contributed to difficulties in gathering data on the Iraqi regime's purported nuclear, biological, and chemical programs. And these difficulties were compounded by the challenge of discerning regime intentions.

Nonetheless, we believe the Intelligence Community could have done better. We had precious little human intelligence, and virtually no useful signals intelligence, on a target that was one of the United States' top intelligence priorities. The preceding sections, which have focused on the Intelligence Community's assessments on particular aspects of Iraq's weapons programs, have tended to reflect shortcomings in what is commonly referred to as "tradecraft"; the focus has been on questions such as whether a critical human source was properly validated, or whether analysts drew unduly sweeping inferences from limited or dubious intelligence. But it should not be forgotten why these tradecraft failures took on such extraordinary importance. They were important because of how little additional information our collection agencies managed to provide on Iraq's weapons programs.

This was a problem the Intelligence Community saw coming. As early as September 1998, the Community recognized its limited collection on Iraq. The National Intelligence Council noted these limits in 1998, the specifics of which cannot be discussed in an unclassified forum. Yet the Intelligence Community was still unwilling—or unable—to take steps necessary to improve its capabilities after late 1998. In short, as one senior policymaker described it, the Intelligence Community after 1998 "was running on fumes," depending on "inference and assumptions rather than hard data."

This section examines and assesses the performance of each of the collection disciplines on Iraq's weapons programs.

## Human Intelligence

Human intelligence collection in Iraq suffered from two major flaws: too few human sources, and the questionable reliability of those few sources the Intelligence Community had. After 1998, the CIA had no dedicated unilateral sources in Iraq reporting on Iraq's nuclear, biological, and chemical programs; indeed, the CIA had only a handful of Iraqi assets in total as of 2001. Furthermore, several of the liaison and defector sources relied upon by the Intelligence Community, most prominently Curveball, proved to be fabricators. Several systemic impediments to effective collection contributed to this dearth of human intelligence.

There are several reasons for the lack of quality human sources reporting on Iraqi weapons programs. At the outset, and as noted above, Iraq was an uncommonly challenging target for human intelligence. And given the highly compartmented nature of Saddam Hussein's regime, it is unclear whether even a source at the highest levels of the Iraqi government would have been able to provide true insight into Saddam's decisionmaking. The challenges revealed by the Iraq case study suggest some inherent limitations of human intelligence collection.

But these difficulties also point to the need, not only for improving traditional human source collection, but also for exploring new methods to approach such targets. Although CIA's Directorate of Operations has a well-developed methodology for recruiting and running assets in denied areas, the nature of the WMD target, particularly as aspects of it may migrate away from centralized, state-run programs, indicates that current methodologies should be supplemented with alternative approaches. In particular, when we want information about procurement networks or non-state run proliferation activities of interest, then we may need to use non-traditional platforms. The technical complexity of the WMD target also suggests that it may require a cadre of case officers with technical backgrounds or training.

The Iraq case study also reveals the importance of liaison relationships for exploiting human sources in denied areas. Reliance on liaison sources, without any knowledge of the identity of the source or subsource(s), can be problematic, as the Curveball episode most painfully demonstrates. But liaison services can provide invaluable access to targets the U.S. Intelligence Community may find it difficult, if not impossible, to recruit or penetrate. It is thus critical to enhance our intelligence from liaison services.

This case study also suggests that current internal promotion and incentive structures are impediments to recruitment of quality assets. In practice, both CIA's Directorate of Operations (DO) and DIA's Defense HUMINT Service reward case officers based largely on the quantity rather than quality of their recruitments. While this is in part because quality is inherently difficult to measure, the "numbers game" encourages officers to focus their recruitment efforts on assets who are easier to recruit—often individuals who are themselves several steps removed from information of intelligence value. Other activities that may enhance the long-term ability to recruit quality assets—language or WMD-related technical training, for example—are also often discouraged because of the significant amount of time such training takes out of the officer's career.

Finding the right personnel incentive structures is a perennial concern, and CIA's DO has taken some positive steps in recent years. But much more needs to be done.

Another problem was the questionable reliability of the few human sources the Community had. As the Curveball and Niger experiences illustrate, asset validation and authentication are crucial to the Intelligence Community's ability to produce reliable intelligence. Although the CIA has an established asset validation system in place, the system and its use are not without flaws. As practiced, asset validation can sometimes become an exercise in "checking the boxes" rather than a serious effort to vet and validate the source.

On the other hand, at least the CIA understands the importance of asset validation. With respect to Curveball—the primary source of our intelligence on Iraq's BW program—the Defense HUMINT Service disclaimed any *responsibility* for validating the asset, arguing that credibility determinations were for analysts and that the collectors were merely "conduits" for the reporting. This abdication of operational responsibility represented a serious failure in tradecraft.

Although lack of direct physical access to the source made vetting and validating Curveball more difficult, it did not make it impossible. While Defense HUMINT neglected its validation responsibilities, elements of the CIA's DO understood the necessity of validating Curveball's information and made efforts to do so; indeed, they found indications that caused them to have doubts about Curveball's reliability. The system nonetheless "broke down" because of analysts' strong conviction about the truth of Curveball's information and because the DO's concerns were not heard outside the DO.

In that regard, although CIA was alert to the need to assess Curveball's credibility, CIA was insufficiently diligent in following up on concerns that surfaced regarding his reliability. When what had been "handling" concerns became issues that reflected more directly on Curveball's veracity, working-level CIA officials did not press these concerns early enough or with sufficient vigor to the senior-most levels of CIA and senior leaders did not pay enough attention to those concerns that were expressed.

For its part, these senior-most levels of management at CIA— including the Deputy Director for Operations and the Deputy Director of Central Intelligence—were remiss in not raising concerns about Curveball with senior policymakers before the war. Even though these concerns may not have been raised with sufficient passion to indicate a serious problem, CIA management should at a minimum have alerted policymakers that such concerns existed.

While the DO made some efforts to try to validate Curveball, its failure to authenticate the Niger reporting also reflected a tradecraft error. The CIA made no effort to authenticate the documents on which those reports were based—even though one of those reports was a "verbatim" text of a document, and even though there were doubts emerging about their authenticity.

This said, we of course do not suggest that reliance on human intelligence reporting should be limited only to those sources who have been fully vetted and validated. The Intelligence Community does, however, need to ensure that consumers of intelligence have better visibility into the Community's assessment of the integrity of a given source.

Iraq's well-developed denial and deception efforts also hampered the Intelligence Community's ability to collect reliable intelligence. On the human intelligence front, for instance, by the early 1990s the Community had identified significant Iraqi efforts to manipulate U.S. human intelligence operations. The Iraqis sought to saturate U.S. intelligence collection nodes with false and misleading information. Furthermore, Iraq's pervasive security and counterintelligence services rendered attempts to recruit Iraqi officials extremely difficult.

Iraq's denial and deception capabilities also frustrated U.S. signals and imagery collection due to Iraq's excellent security practices . The specifics of these capabilities are discussed in the classified report.

At the same time, the knowledge that Iraq's denial and deception techniques had been so successful in the past hampered efforts to develop quality human sources. For example, several human sources asserted before the war that Iraq did not retain any WMD. And one source, who may have come closer to the truth than any other, said that Iraq would never admit that it did not have WMD because it would be tantamount to suicide in the Middle East. But the pervasive influence of the conventional wisdom—that Iraq had WMD and was actively hiding it from inspectors—created a kind of intellectual "tunnel vision" that caused officers to believe that information contradicting the conventional wisdom was "disinformation." Potential sources for alternative views were denigrated or not pursued by collectors. Moreover, collectors were often responding to requirements that were geared toward supporting or confirming the prevailing analytical line. The reliance on prevailing assumptions was not just an analytical problem, therefore, but affected both the collection and analysis of information.

## Technical Intelligence Collection

Technical intelligence was able to provide very little in the way of conclusive intelligence about Iraq's purported WMD programs. This deficiency stemmed from several causes.

In the late 1990s, the Intelligence Community focused on targeting procurement networks. This approach was problematic, in part because much of the equipment and precursor materials required to produce biological and chemical weapons, and to a lesser extent nuclear weapons, can also serve other legitimate purposes. Also, attempted procurements cannot be equated with an actual weapons capability. Although evidence that a country such as Iraq was procuring dual-use items can of course be useful, such procurement activity will rarely provide unequivocal evidence of weapons activity. As such, information that Iraq was procuring industrial chemicals provided little insight into Iraq's CW programs because such purchases were consistent with the development of an indigenous chemical industry. This inherent problem was compounded by the Intelligence Community's tendency to exaggerate the nefariousness of Iraq's dual-use procurement efforts.

The National Security Agency's (NSA's) lack of access was largely the result of technical barriers to collection. As a result, NSA was unable to exploit those communications that would be most likely to provide insights into Iraq's WMD programs. The technical barriers to accessing these communications are substantial, and NSA and other signals intelligence collectors must continue efforts to develop technical solutions to such challenges. The classified report discusses these technical barriers in greater detail.

The classified report discusses further reasons why signals intelligence collection against Iraq was so challenging.

Imagery intelligence is also limited in what it can reveal about a nation's WMD programs. Imagery intelligence will rarely, if ever, provide insight into intent regarding WMD—particularly CW or BW programs. Flawed conclusions drawn from imagery of suspected Iraqi CW sites before the war, for instance, demonstrate that even precise and high-quality photographs of a target may yield little of value or, worse, positively mislead. While imagery will be a valuable tool for the Community in developing a full picture of a target country's infrastructure and overt movements, without credible human or signals intelligence imagery is of limited utility with regard to BW and CW. This said, imagery will nevertheless remain critical for satisfying requirements such as intelligence support to military operations, helping to cue other forms of collection by providing overhead images, and providing methods for corroborating or disproving information from other collection methods.

As the National Geospatial-Intelligence Agency's (NGA's) has conceded, the inherent nature of chemical and biological weapons facilities means that the infrastructure and activities of suspect WMD programs are difficult to assess even with sophisticated and expensive U.S. satellites. Imagery analysts must therefore look for "signatures" of suspicious activity. These signatures hold open the possibility of identifying suspect activity but are susceptible to error and denial and deception. As such, to answer the question whether a facility is intended for the production of biological or chemical weapons, imagery analysis must be supplemented with other kinds of intelligence.

Beyond these straightforward difficulties, suspect activity can also be deliberately concealed from overhead reconnaissance. Iraq—like many other countries with aspirations to develop nuclear, biological, and chemical weapons programs—was well aware of U.S. overhead collection capabilities and practices, and took steps to avoid detection. Imagery intelligence will therefore remain only one piece of the collection effort against WMD, and will have to be used in conjunction with information from other sources.

Despite these inherent limitations, the pre-war assessments of Iraq's chemical warfare program relied very heavily on imagery. For example, the NIE assessed that "much of" Iraq's estimated stockpile of 100 to 500 metric tons of CW was "added in the last year." Analysts explained that this assessment—which indicated not only that Iraq had large stockpiles but that it was actively producing CW agents—was based largely on imagery showing "transshipment" activity that analysts judged to be the movement of CW munitions. Post-war "reassessments" by the National

Geospatial-Intelligence Agency, however, revealed that this trans-shipment activity was likely related to conventional maintenance and logistical activity. Because of the dearth of solid reporting from signals or human intelligence on Iraq's chemical warfare program, imagery of "transshipments" was asked to carry more weight than it could logically bear.

*Measurement and signature intelligence (MASINT).* MASINT played a negligible role in intelligence collection against the Iraqi WMD target. There were several reasons for this.

MASINT collection was hampered by practical problems stemming from the difficulties inherent in collecting intelligence against a regime such as Saddam's Iraq. Furthermore, information from other intelligence collection methods is important to cue MASINT collection. The difficulties described above, which are described in greater detail in the classified report, rendered MASINT collection an even more difficult task than usual.

Second, in part because of a lack of collection and in part because of a general lack of understanding among analysts about MASINT and its capabilities, very little MASINT actually factored into Community assessments. There was MASINT reporting on WMD—the National Intelligence Collection Board noted that from June 2000 through January 2003 MASINT sources produced over 1,000 reports on Iraqi WMD (none of which provided a definitive indication of WMD activity). But the reporting did not play a significant role in forming assessments about Iraq's WMD programs. This lack of reliance was no doubt due in part to the tendency among analysts to discount information that contradicted the prevailing view that Iraq had WMD. But it was also due in part to unfamiliarity with, and lack of confidence in, MASINT.

## Collection Management

Our study of Iraq not only reveals shortcomings in (and inherent limitations of) specific collection disciplines; it also highlights the Intelligence Community's inability to harmonize and coordinate the collection process across collection systems. There are many reasons for the Community's inability to do so, including resource and personnel management issues. But another reason for the difficulty may be the simple fact that there is no institutionalized process above the various collection agencies that oversees the whole of collection. It was not until 1998 that a collection management system was established that was dedicated to "examin[ing] the [Intelligence Community]'s most intractable intelligence problems and develop[ing] new ways to improve collection." That entity, the Collection Concepts Development Center (CCDC), was established by the Assistant DCI for Collection. When the CCDC tackled the problem of collection on Iraq—in 2000—it set out a coordinated approach that sought to optimize the available collection resources. For example, the CCDC study recommended a shift of imagery collection away from military targets such as the no-fly zones and towards suspect WMD sites. The study also recommended ways for NSA to try to penetrate Iraq's communications, as discussed below. But the CCDC effort is sustained only through the force of the Assistant DCI for Collection's individual efforts. Our report will offer recommendations as to the best way that such an effort can be institutionalized within the Intelligence Community.

Such an institutionalized process would also ensure that new collection strategies are implemented by individual collection agencies. For example, as noted, the 2000 CCDC study addressed the problem presented by NSA's inability to exploit certain critical Iraqi communications. The CCDC recommended that NSA collect signals from a certain source to assess whether that source was being used for WMD-related communications. NSA failed to pursue this recommendation vigorously. Instead, NSA acknowledged that "NSA did not discover that the Iraqis had this mode of communications . . . until late 2002," at which time "NSA's limited resources were fully engaged with other priorities." This anecdote highlights the imperative for a well-managed collection system, to ensure that we do not miss valuable collection opportunities in the future.

A related problem—that of the poor quality of interagency communication—is illustrated by imagery analysis of increased collection of suspected Iraqi CW sites in 2002. In this instance, analysts fundamentally misunderstood how imagery was collected, a significant breakdown in a crucial communication link between collectors and analysts. Until 2000, imagery intelligence collection had been largely oriented toward supporting military operations such as patrolling the no-fly zones. Imagery collection operations against the Iraq WMD target more than doubled from 2001 through 2002, however, prompted largely by the aforementioned CCDC study, which recommended that more resources be focused on that target. The increased coverage included images of ammunition depots that had not previously been imaged on a regular basis. Analysts, however, were not aware of the degree to which imaging was increased during this period nor of the specifics of NGA's targeting changes. As a result, analysts interpreted this imagery as reflecting new and increased activity—when, in reality, much of the "increase" in activity may have been simply an increase in the volume of imagery collected.

## Analysis

Intelligence analysis is a tricky business. Analysts are often forced to make predictions in the absence of clear evidence—and then are pilloried after twenty-twenty hindsight reveals that they failed to paint a full picture from conflicting and scattered pieces of evidence. As we have seen, assessing the scope of an adversary's nuclear, biological, and chemical weapons programs poses an especially formidable challenge in this regard; extrapolations from past experience and thin streams of reporting are usually necessary.

Even the best analytical practices, therefore, will sometimes result in assessments that later prove inaccurate. But given the difficulties inherent in analyzing WMD programs—and the serious consequences for judging the capabilities and intentions of such programs incorrectly—it is imperative that the analysis on which such judgments are based be as rigorous, thorough, and candid as possible. In the case of Iraq, the analytical community fell short of this standard.

Analysts have indicated that their starting point for evaluating

Iraq's WMD programs was Iraq's past. Analysts' assumptions were formed based on Iraq's history of producing CW and BW, its use of CW, its history of effectively concealing its nuclear program before the Gulf War, and the regime's failure to account for its previously declared stockpiles. Thus, the analysts operated from the premise that Iraq very likely still possessed CW and BW, was still hiding it from inspectors, and was still seeking to rebuild its nuclear weapons program. The analytical flaw was not that this premise was unreasonable (for it was not); rather, it was that this premise hardened into a presumption, and analysts began to fit the facts to the theory rather than the other way around.

One consequence of this tendency was that analysts effectively shifted the burden of proof, requiring proof that Iraq did *not* have active WMD programs rather than requiring affirmative proof of their existence. Though the U.S. *policy* position was that Iraq bore the responsibility to prove that it did not have banned weapons programs, the Intelligence Community's burden of proof should have been more objective. CIA's WINPAC nuclear analysts explained that, given Iraq's history of successful deception regarding the state of its nuclear program and evidence that Iraq was attempting to procure components that *could* be used in a uranium enrichment program, they could not envision having reached the conclusion that Iraq was not reconstituting its nuclear program. The analysts noted that they could have reached such a conclusion only if they had specific information from a very well-placed, reliable human source. By raising the evidentiary burden so high, analysts artificially skewed the analytical process toward confirmation of their original hypothesis—that Iraq had active WMD programs.

Indeed, it appears that in some instances analysts' presumptions were so firm that they simply *disregarded* evidence that did not support their hypotheses. As we saw in several instances, when confronted with evidence that indicated Iraq did not have WMD, analysts tended to discount such information. Rather than weighing the evidence independently, analysts accepted information that fit the prevailing theory and rejected information that contradicted it. While analysts must adopt some frame of reference to interpret the flood of data they see, their baseline assumptions must be flexible enough to permit revision by discordant information. The analysts' frame of reference on Iraq's WMD programs—formed as it was by Iraq's previous use of such weapons, Iraq's continued efforts to conceal its activities, and Iraq's past success at hiding such programs—was so strong, however, that contradictory data was often discounted as likely false.

Analysts' discounting of contradictory information reflected, in part, an awareness of Iraq's sophisticated denial and deception efforts and of Iraq's past success in hiding the extent of its WMD programs. Reacting to that lesson, analysts understandably (if not wholly defensibly) began to view the absence of evidence of WMD as evidence of Iraq's ability to deceive the United States about its existence. For example, both CIA and the National Ground Intelligence Center simply assumed that Iraq's claims that the aluminum tubes were for rockets was a "cover story" designed to deflect attention from Iraq's nuclear program. Similarly, analysts had imagery intelligence from 2001 that contradicted Curveball's information about mobile BW facilities, but analysts believed that this discrepancy was attributable to Iraq's denial and deception capabilities.

The disciplined use of alternative hypotheses could have helped counter the natural cognitive tendency to force new information into existing paradigms. Alternative hypotheses are particularly important for assessing WMD programs, which can be easily concealed under the guise of dual-use activity. With the aluminum tubes, the "transshipment" activity at ammunition depots, and the development of small UAVs, analysts did not fully consider the alternative (and non-WMD related) explanations. Analysts set aside evidence indicating a reconnaissance mission for the UAVs, and did not fully explore the possibility that the transshipment activity involved only conventional munitions. And with respect to the aluminum tubes, CIA and DIA analysts concluded that the tubes were destined for use in a gas centrifuge largely because they could be used for such a purpose, in the process discounting evidence that the tubes were in many respects better suited for use in rockets.

The widely recognized need for alternative analysis drives many to propose organizational solutions, such as "red teams" and other formal mechanisms. Indeed, the *Intelligence Reform and Terrorism Prevention Act* mandates the establishment of such mechanisms to ensure that analysts conduct alternative analysis. Any such organs, the creation of which we encourage, must do more than just "alternative analysis," though. The Community should institute a formal system for competitive—and even explicitly contrarian—analysis. Such groups must be licensed to be troublesome. Further, they must take contrarian positions, not just ones that take a harder line (a flaw with the Team B exercise of the 1970s).

The Iraq case shows, however, that alternative analysis mechanisms offer, at best, an incomplete solution to the problem. In addition to testing fully-developed judgments with formal red team exercises, analysts must incorporate the discipline of alternative hypotheses into the foundation of their analytical tradecraft, testing and weighing each piece of evidence. It would be unrealistic to "zero-base" every assessment, or to ignore history when forming analytical judgments. But the conventional wisdom must be tested throughout the analytical process to ensure that a position is not adopted without rigorous questioning.

Competitive analysis must also take place at the institutional level. In other words, the need for individual analysts to question their hypotheses and challenge the conventional wisdom also applies to the Intelligence Community as a whole, and suggests the need to strengthen competitive analysis among agencies in the Intelligence Community.

After September 11, the Intelligence Community was criticized for its failure to communicate and share information across agency lines. That failure prevented analysts from "connecting the dots" because information known to one agency was not put together with information known to another. With each agency holding one or two pieces of the puzzle, none could see the whole picture. The logical response, therefore, was to recommend the formation of centers to bring all the relevant information together. The Iraq story, however, presents a different set of problems. As discussed, the strength of the prevailing assumptions about Iraq presented a distinct picture to analysts and pieces of the puzzle that did not fit that picture were either made to fit awkwardly or discarded. The problem, therefore, was not that analysts lacked awareness of what other analysts were thinking; rather, the problem was that most analysts were thinking the same thing.

Strengthening competitive analysis among components of the Intelligence Community could help alleviate that problem. There was of course some competitive analysis on Iraq—the NIE contained dissenting positions from State's Bureau of Intelligence and Research (INR), DOE, and the Air Force. And those dissenting positions were at least somewhat closer to the truth than the majority position. Although reasonable minds can differ as to how significant the dissents were (at least in the cases of INR and DOE), such competitive analyses in general encourage the consideration of alternative views and ensure that those independent views reach policymakers.

The problem of discounting contrary evidence was compounded by inexcusable analytical lapses. One reason that CIA analysts were confident in their conclusion that the aluminum tubes were for use in centrifuges and not rockets was that the "rocket experts" in the Intelligence Community, the National Ground Intelligence Center (NGIC), assessed that the tolerances of the tubes Iraq was seeking were "excessive" for rockets. But NGIC rocket analysts told Commission staff that at the time they made that assessment they were not aware of the tolerances required for the Iraqi Nasser 81 rockets, for the Italian Medusa rocket on which the Nasser 81 was based, or for comparable U.S. rockets. NGIC should have been aware of these facts.

The reasons for this failure of technical analysis were not particularly grand. Rather, analysts in NGIC, used to focusing almost exclusively on Soviet weapons systems, simply did not do their homework in tracking down information about Iraqi and U.S. weapons that would have shed light on the question whether the aluminum tubes could be used in conventional rockets. CIA analysts, for their part, were too quick to see confirmation of their hypothesis—that Iraq would seek to reconstitute its nuclear program at the first opportunity—based on somewhat dubious technical evidence.

A related concern is the problem of layering of analysis: the building of one judgment upon another without carrying forward the uncertainties of the earlier judgments. The judgment in the October 2002 NIE that Iraq was reconstituting its weapons programs was built on previous assessments about Iraq's weapons programs. These earlier assessments, however, were based on relatively thin streams of reporting, yet the cumulative level of uncertainty was not reflected in the Key Judgments nor in some of the NIE's discussions. In brief, previous assessments based on uncertain information formed, through repetition, a relatively unquestioned baseline for the analysis in the pre-war assessments.

The NIE's CW assessments offer an example of the phenomenon. The NIE's estimates that Iraq had up to 500 metric tons of chemical weapons were based largely on accounting discrepancies and Iraq's CW production capacity rather than positive evidence. Although the NIE conceded that "we have little specific information on Iraq's CW stockpile," it did not make clear that the baseline assumption rested largely on Iraqi accounting discrepancies. Because that baseline assumption was not made clear, the NIE gave the impression of greater certainty about the actual existence and size of stockpiles than was warranted. Similarly, the assessment that "much" of that stockpile was "added in the last year" was based largely on imagery evidence of "transshipment" in the spring of 2002. Analysts assessed that Iraq had added to its CW stockpile in the previous year because the level of transshipment activity seen on imagery indicated that "CW is already deployed with the military logistics chain." But that assessment in turn rested on whether the activity seen on imagery was CW-related. As the post-war reassessment by NGA concluded, it was not. By building one assessment on top of another without carrying forward the uncertainty from the first layer, the NIE gave the impression of greater certainty about its judgments than was warranted.

This "layering" phenomenon occurred not only with respect to one line of analysis over time, but it also occurred across analytical lines. For example, a senior CW analyst related that he and other CW analysts had been "drifting" in the direction of concluding that Iraq did not have much of a CW program. The appearance of Curveball's reporting on BW, however, "pushed [CW analysts] the other way." The analyst explained that if Iraq was producing and hiding BW, then it was probably also producing and hiding CW. In other words, "much of the CW confidence was built on the BW confidence."

Another shortcoming of the pre-war assessments of Iraq's WMD programs was the failure to analyze the state of these programs within the context of Iraq's overall political, social, cultural, and economic situation. In short, the Intelligence Community did not sufficiently understand the political dynamics of Saddam Hussein's Iraq, and as a consequence did not understand the political and economic pressures that led to his decision to destroy his WMD stockpiles while continuing to obfuscate about Iraq's possession of WMD.

As the Iraq Survey Group found, Saddam was facing two opposing pressures—the need to get relief from sanctions and the need to project strength at home and abroad. Saddam reacted to these pressures, according to the ISG, by destroying his WMD stockpiles after the Gulf War and focusing on sanctions relief before resuming WMD development. At the same time, Saddam continued to hinder the inspectors and sow confusion about Iraq's WMD programs.

Yet the weapons analysts did not consider how the political situation might have affected Baghdad's decisions regarding its weapons programs. To be sure, it is doubtful that such consideration would have changed the analytical outcome—the regional analysts were also operating under certain assumptions about Saddam's regime, and those assumptions did not allow for the possibility that Saddam would destroy his CW and BW stocks and halt work on his nuclear programs, as the ISG found. But the failure even to consider how the political dynamics in Iraq might have affected Saddam's decisions about his WMD programs was a serious shortcoming that resulted in an incomplete analytical picture. The failure by the Intelligence Community to entertain the possibility that Saddam was actually telling the truth also inclined analysts to accept deeply problematic evidence that might have been more rigorously questioned if the Community had actually considered the possibility that Saddam had abandoned his banned programs.

Several related problems contribute to the lack of context in analytical products. One, there is not yet an institutionalized, effective method to exploit open source resources that would have allowed a better understanding of developments in Iraq. Two, analysts are rarely assigned to one substantive account for any length of time (with the exception of INR analysts) and cannot therefore develop the requisite expertise to evaluate contextual influences. (Of course, longevity on one account can exacerbate the problem of over-reliance on past judgments.) And three, the pressure to respond to current intelligence needs as opposed to long-term research efforts degrades the overall level of expertise on all accounts. Given limited analytical resources, the demand for current intelligence suffocates long-term research and therefore largely precludes development of the kind of in-depth knowledge that such research fosters. A related aspect of this problem is the current system of incentives for analysts, which rewards analysts for the quantity of finished intelligence pieces produced, and therefore encourages analysts to focus on current intelligence. CIA's Directorate of Intelligence is exploring ways to provide incentives for long-term research. Also, the Directorate's creation of a Senior Analytical Service to enable analysts to continue at the working-level (instead of moving into management) and still be promoted should help build expertise.

More generally, the pre-war assessments highlight the importance of correct presentation of material to consumers, particularly regarding the uncertainties of given judgments and how these judgments were made. While finished intelligence needs to offer a bottom line to be useful to the policymaker, it should also clearly spell out how and from what its conclusions were derived. In the case of WMD programs in hard target nations like Iraq, this means that policymakers must be made aware when—as will often necessarily be the case—many of the Community's estimates rely largely on inherently ambiguous indicators such as capabilities assessments, indirect reports of intentions, deductions based on denial and deception efforts associated with suspect WMD sites, and on ambiguous or thin pieces of "confirmatory" evidence. For example, the fact that the evidence for Iraq's biological weapons program relied largely on reporting from a single source, and that the evidence for Iraq's chemical weapons program derived largely from limited signature-based evidence of "transshipment" activity, should have been more transparent.

Such context is largely absent from the daily products provided to senior policymakers, however, and the daily dose of such products may provide a cumulative level of "certainty" that is unwarranted. Moreover, with respect to NIEs, the "confidence measures" used to describe the level of certainty in the judgments are not well-explained or understood. A more detailed description, explanation, and/or display of what those confidence measures mean should be incorporated. And those measurements should be rigorously and consistently applied.

Ironically, the NIE did contain numerous caveats, but their impact was diminished by their presentation. For example, as noted, the NIE stated that "[t]oday we have less direct access and know even less about the current status of Iraq's nuclear program than we did before the Gulf War." Yet that caveat came on page 13 of the NIE, after it had twice stated that Iraq was reconstituting its program and could have enough fissile material for a nuclear weapon in the next several years.

The fundamental assumptions and logical premises on which analytical judgments are based should be clearly explained. Analysts noted that the "impending war" influenced their approach to the pre-war assessments of Iraq's WMD programs, particularly the October 2002 NIE. That is, with the knowledge that U.S. troops would soon have to face whatever WMD capabilities Iraq had, analysts adopted more of a worst-case-analysis approach. Yet that approach was not identified or explained to the reader of the NIE. By contrast, when the CIA's Counterterrorism Center prepared a paper on possible links between Iraq and al-Qa'ida, it clearly identified the analysis underlying that paper as of the aggressive, "dot-connecting" sort.

Although too many qualifications can lead to equivocal analysis, when the evidence is equivocal, the conclusion must be as well. This must especially be the case when the results of debate about intelligence data or analysis will influence important policy decisions. Flagging the logical premises and baseline assumptions for the ultimate judgment would produce a better understanding by policymakers of the possible logical weaknesses in the assessment. It also would likely improve the analytic process as well, by forcing analysts themselves to articulate clearly their operative assumptions. Similarly, analysis that relies heavily on a single source, such as on Curveball's reporting and on the presence of Samarra-type trucks to support the conclusions that Iraq had BW and CW, respectively, should be highlighted.

## Information Sharing

In addition to illuminating shortcomings in intelligence collection and analysis, our study of Iraq also highlighted a familiar challenge: that of ensuring effective sharing of information. In the Iraq case, the information sharing problem manifested itself in three specific ways: intelligence was not passed (1) from the collectors to the analysts; (2) from the analysts to the collectors; and (3) from foreign liaison services to the Intelligence Community.

The lack of an effective system for information sharing between collectors and analysts is a well-known systemic problem, but one that has proven highly resistant to resolution. Intelligence Community collectors retain a strong institutional bias against sharing operational information with analysts—CIA's Directorate of Operations is often reluctant to share relevant operational information with CIA's Directorate of Intelligence, let alone with the rest of the Community or with policymakers. Similarly, NSA is reluctant to share raw data with anyone outside of NSA. Both NSA and the DO have legitimate concerns for the protection of sources and methods, and this concern must be weighed carefully when determining whether, and in what form, to share information across the Community or even across directorates.

Our review of the Intelligence Community's performance on Iraq identified several specific shortcomings in the way that collectors share intelligence with analysts. First, the source descriptions on raw human source reporting often provided insufficient detail and clarity to allow analysts adequate insight into the source's reliability. For example, the CIA report on the alleged uranium deal that was sourced to Ambassador Wilson described him (unhelpfully) as "a contact with excellent access who does not have an established reporting record." Source descriptions that provide more explicit information on the context in which the information was obtained can significantly improve analysts' ability to gauge the credibility of that information. In September 2004, the CIA's DO implemented new source descriptions that are designed to provide additional such contextual detail. This is an important step in the right direction, but more needs to be done.

Second, with CIA reporting, analysts were often unable to determine whether a series of raw human intelligence reporting came from the same source. For most reporting, there is currently no way to determine from the face of the CIA report whether a series of reports represents one source reporting similar information several times or several different sources independently providing the same information. For obvious reasons, it is important to distinguish corroboration from repetition. The improved source descriptions should help alleviate this problem, as will increased dialogue between collectors and analysts.

Finally, analysts often obtain insufficient insights into the operational details bearing on the reliability of sources. Such information sharing is not an end in itself, of course. In the case of Curveball, for example, the DO did share operational information with DI analysts—including information that indicated possible problems with the source's reliability—but analysts' belief in Curveball's information remained unshaken. Increased dialogue, rather than simply sharing traffic, may help bridge these gaps.

It must be acknowledged that sharing operational details presents a great threat to the protection of sources and methods. Accordingly, any information sharing protocol must therefore be carefully tailored. The CIA recently conducted a DI-DO information sharing pilot program, which addressed the operational as well as technical barriers to effective information sharing within CIA. Such pilot programs, however, are of little use if the recommended protocols are not implemented across the board.

A separate, but related problem is the lack of a mechanism to ensure that information calling into question a prior piece of intelligence is swiftly communicated to those analysts (and policymakers) who received the intelligence. This problem was most acutely demonstrated in the case of the Iraqi National Congress source , in which Defense HUMINT failed to reissue the reporting (either with the fabrication notice or recall notice attached)—a failure that led analysts and senior policymakers to accept the reporting months after it was known to be worthless. Defense HUMINT has taken steps to ensure that fabricated reporting is recalled, and the Director of the CIA is currently working to establish Community-wide standards to ensure that the original reporting, the fabrication notice, and the recalled reporting are electronically linked. It remains to be seen, however, whether the information-technology hurdles involved in linking related reporting can be overcome.

The systemic lack of effective information sharing occurs in the other direction as well, however. For example, the DO was not aware that the DI was relying so heavily on reporting from Curveball in its pre-war assessments of Iraq's BW program. Similarly, although Defense HUMINT participated in the coordination sessions for Secretary Powell's speech, the Defense HUMINT participant said that he was not aware that the information being discussed came from the same Iraqi National Congress source who was known to be a fabricator.

The National Intelligence Council has taken steps to address this problem. For example, the DO and Defense HUMINT will now directly participate in the NIE coordination process and will do so from the initial stages of that process, giving the collectors a better window into the sources relied upon and therefore an enhanced opportunity to bring to the fore any concerns about those sources. Also, a new National Intelligence Officer for "Intelligence Assurance" has been established to oversee these quality control measures. Although it is still too early to tell, we hope that these steps address previous shortcomings in the NIE process.

The information sharing problem is compounded with respect to foreign liaison. Although the Intelligence Community has been criticized for over-reliance on liaison sources, such criticism is to some extent overstated. Liaison reporting can play a valuable role in opening up avenues of collection the United States would not be able to approach on its own; indeed, at times it is the only information we have. The key to its usefulness, however, is the ability to assess its reliability. That determination hinges on several factors, including effective information sharing with the liaison service.

Information sharing between intelligence services is dependent upon many factors, including diplomatic and policy factors that are beyond the Intelligence Community's ability to control. Despite constant requests from the CIA, the handling foreign service refused to provide direct access to Curveball until spring of 2004, which seriously undermined the ability to determine his reliability. And in at least two instances—the inability of the Intelligence Community to learn the identity of the individual who provided the fourth BW source's information or the identity of the source of the corroborating information the liaison service claimed for the Niger deal—the foreign liaison services refused to share crucial information with the United States because of fear of leaks. Until that systemic problem can be addressed, increased information sharing with liaison is unlikely to improve markedly.

A cautionary note: the increased sharing of intelligence reporting among liaison services—without sharing the sourcing details or identity of the source—may lead to unwitting circular reporting. When several services unknowingly rely on the same sources and then share the intelligence production from those sources, the result can be false corroboration of the reporting. In fact, one reason for the apparent unanimity among Western intelligence services that Iraq posed a more serious WMD threat than proved to be the case was the extensive sharing of intelligence information, and even analysis, among liaison services. Such sharing of information, without sharing of source information, can result in "groupthink" on an international scale.

## Dissemination

The collection, analysis, and dissemination of finished intelligence is a cycle, and many of the issues related to collection and analysis also affect dissemination of the product. But at least one issue merits separate discussion. The interface between the Intelligence Community and the policymaker—the way that intelligence analysis is conveyed to the consumer—needs reexamination.

As part of its investigation, this Commission was provided access, on a limited basis, to a number of articles from the President's Daily Brief (PDB) relating to Iraq's WMD programs. Although we saw only a limited cross-section of this product, we can make several observations about the art form. In short, many of the same problems that occurred with other intelligence products occurred with the PDBs, only in a magnified manner. For instance, the PDBs often failed to explain, or even signal, the uncertainties underlying their judgments. Information from a known fabricator was used in PDBs, despite the publication of a fabrication notice on that source months earlier. PDB articles discounted information that appeared to contradict the prevailing analytical view by characterizing, without justifications, such information as a "cover story" or purposeful deception. The PDBs attributed information to multiple sources without making clear that the information rested very heavily on only one of those sources. And the titles of PDB articles were sometimes more alarmist than the text would support.

In addition to the problems it shares with other intelligence products, the PDB format presents some unique problems as well. As discussed above, the emphasis on current intelligence can adversely affect the distribution of analytical resources and can reduce the level of expertise needed for contextual analysis. But the focus on current intelligence may also adversely affect the consumers of intelligence. In particular, the daily exposure to current intelligence products such as the PDB may create, over time, a greater perception of certainty about their judgments than is warranted. And the way these products are generated and disseminated may actually skew the way their content is perceived. For example, when senior policymakers are briefed with the President's Daily Brief or a similar product, they often levy follow-up questions on the briefer. The response to those questions is then typically disseminated in the same format. Therefore, if one policymaker has an intense interest in one area and actively seeks follow-up, that questioning can itself generate numerous PDBs or Senior Executive Memoranda. A large volume of reporting on one topic can result, and that large volume may skew the sense among other policymakers as to the topic's importance.

Long-term products such as the NIE bear reexamination as well. With respect to the October 2002 NIE on Iraq, some of the weaknesses in that product are attributable to anomalies in this particular NIE process, including the unusually short timeframe for publication (discussed further below), while others are attributable to inherent weaknesses in the NIE process itself.

One criticism of NIEs in general is that they are too long, read poorly, and are not popular with consumers. The October 2002 NIE, at 90 pages, is almost twice as long as the average NIE. One consequence of the length of the NIE—aside from discouraging its readers to look beyond the Key Judgments—is that its sheer heft suggests that there was a surfeit of evidence supporting those Key Judgments. That impression may encourage reliance on the Key Judgments alone. To the extent that intelligence judgments are often questions of degree ( e.g. , the *likelihood* that an adversary has BW), however, short summaries and Key Judgments run a serious risk of misleading readers. Moreover, to the extent that daily intelligence products to senior policymakers may have conveyed a high level of confidence on Iraq WMD previous to the publication of the NIE, policymakers may have understood the confidence levels in the NIE to be higher than actually intended. At a minimum, therefore, NIEs must be carefully caveated and the degree of uncertainty in the judgments clearly communicated.

Another criticism of the NIE process is that it is inappropriately democratic—as the Assistant DCI for Analysis and Production described it, the "FBI has the same vote as the DOE" even when one agency clearly has greater expertise on the relevant subject matter. The quest for consensus in NIEs—and the democratic process applied to reach that consensus—can produce confusing results.

For example, on the question whether Iraq was reconstituting its nuclear program, the position of CIA and DIA (with NGA and NSA in agreement) was that the tubes were for use in centrifuges, and therefore that the procurement of these tubes, along with some other procurement activity, indicated that Iraq was reconstituting its nuclear weapons program. The position of CIA and DIA was that they would not have reached a judgment of reconstitution without the tubes. DOE, on the other hand, believed that the tubes were not for centrifuges but that the other activity was sufficient to conclude that Iraq was reconstituting. While it is true that CIA and DOE agreed on the ultimate conclusion—reconstitution was underway—their respective bases for that conclusion were fundamentally at odds. The "most agencies believe" formulation glossed over this fundamental problem. A straightforward presentation of each agency's views might have better exposed the logical incompatibility of the CIA and DOE positions. Moreover, the "democratic" process diminished the weight of DOE's "expert" opinion on nuclear technology.

Finally, the Iraq story revealed another inherent weakness of the NIE. The Iraq NIE, we now know, relied to a large extent on unreliable human source reporting. Although there were many contributing factors to this problem, one significant failing was that those involved in the coordination process were not aware of the degree to which the BW assessments relied on a single source or that another source had already been deemed a fabricator. This problem is currently being addressed. Newly-instituted National Intelligence Council procedures require the collecting agency to review and verify the reliability of its sources used in the NIE.

To understand the unusual nature of the Iraq NIE process, it is necessary to understand how the National Intelligence Estimate process usually works. NIEs are produced under the auspices of the National Intelligence Council and are the "Intelligence Community's most authoritative written judgments on national security issues." NIEs are primarily "estimative," that is, they "make judgments about the likely course of future events and identify the implications for U.S. policy." Because of this "estimative" quality, NIEs are generally produced over the course of several months. In the usual process, an NIE is requested by the NIC or by senior policymakers. The first step after the NIE is requested and authorized is the preparation of the Terms of Reference, which define precisely the question the NIE will address. The National Intelligence Officer with responsibility for that subject area will generally take responsibility for overseeing the research and drafting of the NIE and its coordination. The individual agencies will appoint senior-level officers to serve as representatives for coordination sessions. These representatives will not be the drafters of the NIE but will speak for their agencies at the co-ordination meetings.

The drafting and coordination of a National Intelligence Estimate is an iterative process. After a draft NIE is produced and reviewed by the NIC, the draft is circulated to the individual agencies for review. Comments on the draft are discussed at the interagency coordination meetings and changes are incorporated. If consensus is not possible on certain points, the dissenting agency is free to draft a dissent for inclusion in the NIE. The coordinated draft is submitted to a panel of outside readers for their review. The draft is then submitted to NIC management for review and approval. The final step is review and approval by the National Foreign Intelligence Board, which is chaired by the Director of the CIA. Substantive changes occasionally are made to the NIE at this level.

Once a draft is written, the review and coordination process alone takes at least one month, according to the NIO for Strategic and Nuclear Programs. Therefore, the NIO noted that a normal timeframe to draft, coordinate, and disseminate an NIE on a topic such as Iraq's WMD programs would be "several" months.

The October 2002 NIE on Iraq, however, was requested on September 9, 2002, in a letter from Senator Richard Durbin of the Senate Select Committee on Intelligence (SSCI), for publication within three weeks. This short deadline significantly truncated the usual NIE process. Although the NIOs and the working-level analysts involved in drafting the NIE agree that this short time frame probably did not affect the overall judgments in the NIE, the rushed schedule had consequences that may have affected the quality of the product.

One consequence was that the Joint Atomic Energy Intelligence Committee (JAEIC), which often provides "expert" input on estimates involving nuclear issues, did not convene an interagency meeting to discuss the dispute over the aluminum tubes in the weeks immediately preceding the NIE coordination sessions, despite several attempts to do so. Whether input from the JAEIC would have altered the judgments in the NIE is of course an open question. The opportunity for the JAEIC to review the points of contention between the CIA and DOE on the aluminum tubes, however, may have at a minimum resulted in a clearer exposition of that debate. The short timeframe may also have compromised the quality of the overall exchange of views during the coordination process. Normally, there might be several rounds of coordination at the interagency level. In the October 2002 NIE, however, there was one marathon coordination session. According to one DOE analyst who attended the coordination meeting, the short deadline reduced the chances that the various agencies could succeed in harmonizing their positions.

The Intelligence Community might well have avoided the need to produce the NIE in such a short timeframe, however. On July 22, 2002, the Chairman of the Senate Select Committee on Intelligence sent a letter to DCI Tenet requesting that the NIC prepare a National Intelligence Estimate on covert action, to include an assessment of Iraq's WMD efforts. The CIA's Office of Congressional Affairs, however, did not pass this request to the NIOs responsible for global WMD activities. According to the NIO for Strategic and Nuclear Programs, the SSCI was informed orally that covert action activities were not a proper subject for NIEs and that such an NIE would not be prepared. A formal response was not sent to the SSCI until September 25, 2002, at which time the DCI reiterated this position but also added that he had "directed the preparation of a new NIE on Iraq's weapons of mass destruction" in response to the September 9, 2002 request from Senator Durbin. The NIO for Strategic and Nuclear Programs noted that if he had been alerted in July about the Senate Select Committee's interest in an NIE on Iraq's weapons of mass destruction, he could have started the process at that point and avoided much unnecessary time pressure.

Another anomaly in the October 2002 NIE process contributed to some of the inconsistencies between the text of the NIE on the one hand and the Key Judgments and the unclassified NIE on the other. According to the NIO for Strategic and Nuclear Programs, under normal procedures the National Intelligence Council prepares the classified NIE and then derives the unclassified summary from that NIE. In the case of Iraq, however, the NIC accepted an assignment from the White House in May 2002 to prepare an unclassified "White Paper" on Iraq WMD, without first preparing a classified NIE. When the Senate requested a classified NIE (and an unclassified version of the NIE) in September 2002, the NIO noted that the National Intelligence Council should have then folded the "White Paper" project into the NIE project, by deriving the unclassified product from the classified version. The two projects continued on parallel tracks, however. Accordingly, when attempts were later made to harmonize the two papers, caveats such as "we assess" were dropped from the Key Judgments, communicating a greater sense of certainty than was warranted.

In short, the inherent flaws in the NIE process were compounded in this situation by the particular circumstances surrounding production of the Iraq NIE.

Though the National Intelligence Estimate process in general, and the 2002 Iraq NIE process in particular, suffer from numerous flaws, in this case that process was not responsible for unduly suppressing agency views, as some have suggested. At least two analysts from one agency—NGIC—believe that NGIC's views on Iraq's CW program were not accurately represented in the October 2002 NIE. These two NGIC analysts expressed the belief that this omission was not inadvertent but was consciously and unfairly omitted by the NIO for Strategic and Nuclear Programs. While we have much to criticize about the NIE process, this is not one of them and is not supported by the facts.

According to the NGIC analysts, NGIC disagreed with the NIE's assessment that Iraq had restarted CW production and therefore could have increased its stockpiles to between 100 and 500 metric tons. NGIC believed that Iraq's stockpiles therefore remained within the previously assessed 10 to 100 metric ton range. Yet, apparently to NGIC's dismay, the 100 to 500 metric tons figure was eventually published in the NIE without an indication that NGIC disagreed with the Estimate's conclusions about Iraq's CW production and existing CW stockpiles.

NGIC's claim that its dissenting views were purposefully suppressed by the NIO is not, however, borne out by the facts. According to NGIC's line edits on the NIE draft, NGIC did indeed suggest softening the language in some places—for example, to say that Iraq had begun production of mustard agent and *possibly* nerve agents, and to say that Iraq was *attempting* to procure various chemicals and equipment covertly. NGIC also suggested that, rather than saying that Iraq had *as much as* 500 metric tons of CW stockpiled, the NIE should say that Iraq had *up to* 500 metric tons stockpiled. Even accepting that these views represented a meaningful dissenting position, NGIC's views were not purposefully suppressed. NGIC had several opportunities to make its dissent known (through DIA), including at the NIE coordination meeting on September 25, 2002; on a number of drafts of the NIE; or at the Military Intelligence Board meeting on September 30, 2002. If NGIC (or DIA, as NGIC's representative) had wanted to insert a footnote reflecting a different view, it had the opportunity to do so at that point. Yet it did not.

In fact, DIA concurred with the language in the NIE regarding the size of Iraq's CW stockpile because the language "was sufficiently caveated to indicate DIA's uncertainty in the size of the stockpile." Nor did NGIC subsequently take the opportunity between the NIE and the opening of the war to publish its dissenting view in finished intelligence.

In sum, the National Ground Intelligence Center's serious accusation that its views on Iraq's CW program were purposefully excluded from the NIE is not supported by the available evidence.

## Politicization

Many observers of the Intelligence Community have expressed concern that Intelligence Community judgments concerning Iraq's purported WMD programs may have been warped by inappropriate political pressure. To discuss whether those judgments were "politicized," that term must first be defined.

The Commission has found no evidence of "politicization" of the Intelligence Community's assessments concerning Iraq's reported WMD programs. No analytical judgments were changed in response to political pressure to reach a particular conclusion. The Commission has investigated this issue closely, querying in detail those analysts involved in formulating pre-war judgments about Iraq's WMD programs.

These analysts universally assert that in no instance did political pressure cause them to change any of their analytical judgments. Indeed, these analysts reiterated their strong belief in the validity and soundness of their pre-war judgments at the time they were made. As a former Assistant Secretary of State for Intelligence and Research put it, "policymakers never once applied any pressure on coming up with the 'right' answer on Iraq." Moreover, the CIA's Ombudsman for Politicization conducted a formal inquiry in November 2003 into the possibility of "politicization" with respect to assessments of Iraqi WMD. That inquiry involved the (perceived) delay in CIA's reassessment of its position on WMD in Iraq. The Ombudsman also found no evidence, based on numerous confidential interviews with the analysts involved, that political pressure had caused any analyst to change any judgments.

The Commission also found no evidence of "politicization" even under the broader definition used by the CIA's Ombudsman for Politicization, which is not limited solely to the case in which a policymaker applies overt pressure on an analyst to change an assessment. The definition adopted by the CIA is broader, and includes any "unprofessional manipulation of information and judgments" by intelligence officers to please what those officers perceive to be policymakers' preferences. But the definition retains the idea that circumstantial pressure to produce analysis quickly is not politicization—there must be some skewing of analytical judgments, either deliberately or unintentionally. The Ombudsman noted that in his view, analysts on Iraq worked under more "pressure" than any other analysts in CIA's history, in terms of their being required to produce so much, for so long, for such senior decisionmakers. But that circumstantial pressure did not cause analysts to alter or skew their judgments. We have found no evidence to dispute that conclusion.

There is also the issue of interaction between policymakers and other customers on the one hand and analysts on the other. According to some analysts, senior decisionmakers continually probed to assess the strength of the Intelligence Community's analysis, but did not press for changes in the Intelligence Community's analytical judgments. We conclude that good-faith efforts by intelligence consumers to understand the bases for analytic judgments, far from constituting "politicization," are entirely legitimate. This is the case even if policymakers raise questions because they do not like the conclusions or are seeking evidence to support policy preferences. Those who must use intelligence are entitled to insist that they be fully informed as to both the evidence and the analysis.

Nor is pressure to work more quickly than is ideal or normal "politicization." Iraq WMD analysts insisted to Commission staff that they faced tremendous pressure to produce finished intelligence and to respond promptly to policymakers' questions, but that such "pressure" was generated by time and analytical resource limitations, not by efforts to alter the analysts' judgments. And according to the National Intelligence Officers responsible for drafting the NIE on Iraq WMD in the fall of 2002, there was no communication with policymakers about the Estimate's conclusions beyond pressure to complete the paper within a short three-week timeframe. Furthermore, all of the Iraqi WMD analysts interviewed by the Commission staff stated that they reached their conclusions about Iraq's pursuit of WMD independently of policymaker pressure, based on the evidence at hand. In fact, given the body of evidence available, many analysts have said that they could not see how they could have reached any other conclusions about Iraq's WMD programs.

However, there is no doubt that analysts operated in an environment shaped by intense policymaker interest in Iraq. Moreover, that analysis was shaped—and distorted—by the widely shared (and not unreasonable) assumption, based on his past conduct and non-cooperation with the United Nations, that Saddam retained WMD stockpiles and programs. This strongly-held assumption contributed to a climate in which the Intelligence Community was too willing to accept dubious information as providing confirmation of that assumption. Neither analysts nor users were sufficiently open to being told that affirmative, specific evidence to support the assumption was, at best, uncertain in content or reliability.

Some analysts were affected by this "conventional wisdom" and the sense that challenges to it—or even refusals to find its confirmation—would not be welcome. For example, the National Intelligence Officer for Near East and South Asia described a "zeitgeist" or general "climate" of policymaker focus on Iraq's WMD that permeated the analytical atmosphere. This "climate" was formed in part, the NIO claimed, by the gathering conviction among analysts that war with Iraq was inevitable by the time the NIE was being prepared. But this "zeitgeist," he maintained, did not dictate the prevailing analytical view that Iraq had CW and BW and was reconstituting its nuclear program—in fact, the NIO said he did not see how analysts could have come up with a different conclusion about Iraq's WMD based on the intelligence available at the time. Similarly, the DOE analysts who participated in the NIE coordination meeting stated that there was no political pressure on DOE, direct or indirect, to agree with the NIE's conclusion that Iraq was "reconstituting" its nuclear program. At the same time, however, he said that "DOE did not want to come out before the war and say [Iraq] wasn't reconstituting."

Even in the absence of politicization, distortion can creep into the analytical product, not only through poor tradecraft, but through poor management and reliance on conventional wisdom. The general assumption that Saddam retained WMD and the backdrop of impending war, particularly in the wake of September 11, affected the way analysts approached their task of predicting the threat posed by Iraq's WMD programs. For example, this atmosphere contributed to analysts' use of a worst-case-scenario or heightened-burden-of-proof approach to analysis. This overall climate, we believe, contributed to the too-ready willingness to accept dubious information as supporting the conventional wisdom and to an unwillingness even to consider the possibility that the conventional wisdom was wrong.

But while some of the poor analytical tradecraft in the pre-war assessments was influenced by this climate of impending war, we have found no evidence to dispute that it was, as the analysts assert, their own independent judgments—flawed though they were—that led them to the conclusion that Iraq had active WMD programs.

As described above, the pre-war assessments of Iraq's WMD programs suffered from numerous other analytical failures. Primary among those analytical flaws was a failure to question assumptions or to keep an open mind about the significance of new data. Such failures are more likely if management within the Intelligence Community does not foster, or at least tolerate, dissenting views. Yet one systemic problem within the Intelligence Community works to frustrate expressions of dissent. As the former Assistant Secretary of State for Intelligence and Research described the problem, the senior leadership of the Intelligence Community is faced with an inevitable conundrum—the head of the Intelligence Community must be close to the President in order for the intelligence product to have relevance, but such closeness also risks the loss of objectivity. When this balance tips too far toward the desire for the Intelligence Community to be "part of the [Administration] team," analysts may be dissuaded from offering dissenting opinions.

The failure to pursue alternative views in forming the pre-war assessments of Iraq's WMD, however, was likely due less to the political climate than to poor analytical tradecraft, a failure of management to actively foster opposition views, and the natural bureaucratic inertia toward consensus. In the case of pre-war assessments of Iraqi WMD, working-level WINPAC analysts described an environment in which managers rewarded judgments that fit the consensus view that Iraq had active WMD programs and discouraged those that did not. To the degree that analysts judged—as we believe some of them did—that "non-consensus" conclusions would not be welcomed, vigorous debate in the analytic process was made much more difficult.

Yet these analysts insisted that they genuinely believed that consensus view, based on the evidence at hand, and we have found no evidence that this was not the case. Moreover, to the extent management at CIA or elsewhere in the government created a climate of conformity, it was not unique to the Iraq situation. For example, an employee survey in April 2004 revealed that 17 percent of WINPAC analysts said they worked "in an atmosphere in which some managers who hold strong views make it difficult to publish opposing points of views." In surveys of the CIA's Directorate of Intelligence as a whole, however, 23 percent reported working in such an environment.

A related problem is bureaucratic resistance to admitting error. Just as the Intelligence Community has an obligation to consumers to provide unvarnished intelligence assessments that are free from politicization, the Community also has an obligation to inform consumers when it learns that information on which previous judgments were based is unreliable. The Iraq experience demonstrates that the Intelligence Community is reluctant to confess error, and is even reluctant to encourage the pursuit of information that may reveal such error. In this respect, the infamous case of Curveball offers an excellent example.

After the initial phase of the war, two WINPAC analysts who had traveled to Iraq began to have doubts about the foundation of their assessments, particularly the BW assessments. Yet CIA management was resistant to this new information. The reaction of CIA management in this instance demonstrates at best a lack of encouragement for dissenting views. As described above, when analysts traveled to Iraq in the summer and fall of 2003 and began to investigate Curveball's bona fides, serious doubts arose about his truthfulness. The WINPAC BW analyst who had conducted the investigations in Iraq brought his concerns to WINPAC management. He argued that Curveball was a fabricator because he had lied about his access (in particular covering up that he had actually been fired from his government job in 1995), lied about being present during a BW accident when he had actually been out of the country at that time, and lied about the purpose for the trailers found by Coalition forces. According to the analyst, however, management was hostile to the idea of publishing a reassessment or retreating from Curveball's information, since other analysts still believed in his veracity.

By January 2004, however, travel records confirmed that Curveball had not even been in Iraq during the time he claimed to have been present at a BW facility, and this discrepancy convinced most analysts that Curveball was a fabricator. By March 2004, when CIA was able to interview Curveball and he could not explain imagery that contradicted his reporting, "any remaining doubts" about Curveball's reliability were removed, according to the former WINPAC BW analyst.

CIA management, however, was still reluctant to "go down the road" of admitting that Curveball was a fabricator. According to the former WINPAC analyst, Directorate of Intelligence management was slow in retreating from Curveball's information because of concerns about how this would look to the "Seventh Floor" and to "downtown." When Curveball's reporting was finally recalled in May 2004, the CIA alerted senior policymakers to that fact, but CIA did not publish a reassessment of its position on Iraq's BW program.

As noted, the CIA's Inspector General, in a review of WIN-PAC's performance finished in November 2004, concluded that "the process [of retreating from intelligence products derived from Curveball reporting] was drawn out principally due to three factors: (1) senior managers were determined to let the ISG in Iraq complete its work before correcting the mobile labs analysts; (2) the CIA was in the midst of [trying] to gain direct access to Curveball; and (3) WINPAC Biological and Chemical Group (BCG) management was struggling to reconcile strong differences among their BW analysts." The report went on to say that senior managers did not want to disavow Curveball only to find that his story stood up upon direct examination or to find that "the ISG uncovered further evidence that would require additional adjustments to the story."

But CIA had gained direct access to Curveball in March 2004 and his reporting had been recalled in May 2004. After May 2004, therefore, two of the Inspector General's reasons were no longer valid, and the third—waiting for the Iraq Survey Group report—would delay any reassessment for six months after the Intelligence Community had already conceded that the primary source for its pre-war BW assessment had fabricated his reporting. In any event, as of March 2005 WINPAC has still not published a reassessment of Iraq's BW program.

Moreover, the analysts who raised concerns about the need for reassessments were not rewarded for having done so but were instead forced to leave WINPAC. One analyst, after presenting his case in late 2003 that Curveball had fabricated his reporting, was "read the riot act" by his office director, who accused him of "making waves" and being "biased." The analyst told Commission staff that he was subsequently asked to leave WINPAC. Similarly, a

WINPAC CW analyst who pressed to publish a reassessment of Iraq's CW program in late 2003 was also, according to the analysts, "told to leave" WINPAC. Although managers must be able to overrule subordinates once an issue has been debated, managers must also create an atmosphere in which such debate is encouraged rather than punished.

In sum, there was no "politicization" of the intelligence product on Iraq. Poor tradecraft, exacerbated by poor management, contributed to the erroneous assessments of Iraq's WMD programs. These problems were further exacerbated by the reluctance of Intelligence Community management to foster and consider dissenting views. Finally, the Intelligence Community was unwilling to identify the errors underlying its intelligence assessments, admit those errors, and explain to consumers how those errors affected previous judgments.

## Accountability

Numerous failures within the Intelligence Community contributed to the flawed estimates on Iraq. Many of these failures are systemic—flaws in the way the Intelligence Community is managed, organized, and structured. Part Two of this report contains dozens of recommendations for systemic reform based on the lessons learned from Iraq and other case studies. But reform requires more than changing the Community's systems; it also requires accountability.

*Individuals.* There are unfortunately a number of examples in the Iraq assessments of individuals whose conduct fell short of what the Intelligence Community has a right to expect. Among these is the handling of Curveball's reporting on mobile BW. In late January of 2003, the Secretary of State was engaged in an intense personal effort to explore every flaw in the intelligence he was about to present to the United Nations Security Council. By then, a division in the CIA's Directorate of Operations had spent months pointing out Curveball's flaws with some persistence. Yet the Secretary of State never learned of those doubts.

A number of individuals stood between the two and could have made the connection. Some acknowledge knowing about Curve-ball's problems but did not understand that he was the key to the entire BW assessment. Others knew how central Curveball was to the BW case but deny knowing about Curveball's problems. Still others—particularly in CIA's WINPAC—were aware of both sides of the issue and did not present the doubts to the Secretary or other policymakers. Finally, the most senior officials of the Agency insist the serious concerns expressed about Curveball's reliability were never conveyed to them—despite assertions to the contrary.

This Commission was not established to adjudicate personal responsibility for the intelligence errors on Iraq. We are not an adjudicatory body, nor did we take testimony under oath. We were not authorized or equipped to assign blame to specific individuals, particularly when there are disputes about critical facts. We are, however, equipped to address the question of organizational accountability.

Organizations. Almost every organization in the Intelligence Community—collectors, analysts, and management—performed poorly on Iraq. But there are differences among the agencies, both in their initial performance and in how they responded when their mistakes became clear. The National Intelligence Council, for example, faltered badly in producing the flawed NIE on Iraq's WMD programs. But it also learned from its errors. It now brings the collection agencies into the NIE process to evaluate their sources, and its recent estimates are more candid about intelligence gaps, weak sources, and divergent viewpoints.

For some organizations, however, problems run deeper. Three agencies made such serious errors, or resisted admitting their errors so stubbornly, that questions may fairly be raised about the fundamental culture or capabilities of the organizations themselves.

1. The performance of the National Ground Intelligence Center (NGIC) in assessing the aluminum tubes was a gross failure. NGIC got completely wrong the question of the tubes' suitability for conventional rockets—a question that is at the core of NGIC's assigned area of expertise. And NGIC was not

aware of, and did not pursue, basic information that was critical to its assessments.

2. The Defense HUMINT Service inexcusably failed to recall reporting from a known fabricator, and compounded that error by failing to notice when its discredited reporting crept into Secretary Powell's speech. Defense HUMINT also bears heavy responsibility for the Curveball episode. Defense HUMINT disseminated Curveball's reporting while taking little or no responsibility for checking the accuracy of his reports. In fact, Defense HUMINT still calls itself merely a "conduit" for Curveball's information and resists the idea that it had any real responsibility to vet his veracity.

3. CIA's Weapons Intelligence, Nonproliferation, and Arms Control Center (WINPAC) is the Intelligence Community's center for all-source analysis on weapons of mass destruction. As such, it was at the heart of many of the errors discussed earlier, from the mobile BW case to the aluminum tubes. Just as bad, some WINPAC analysts—and WINPAC as an institution—showed great reluctance to correct these errors, even long after they had become obvious. Creating an intelligence center always carries some risk that alternative views will be sacrificed in pursuit of consensus, and we fear that a culture of enforced consensus has infected WINPAC as an organization.

In short, we have doubts that the broad reforms described in Part Two will be enough to change the organizational culture of NGIC, Defense HUMINT, and WINPAC. Yet the cultures of each contributed crucially to the Iraq WMD debacle. We therefore recommend that the Director of National Intelligence give serious consideration to whether each of these organizations should be reconstituted, substantially reorganized, or made subject to detailed oversight.

# Terrorism: Managing Today's Threat

## Summary & Findings

As part of the Commission's charter to assess whether the Intelligence Community is properly postured to support the U.S. government's efforts to respond to the threats of the 21st century, we reviewed the progress the Intelligence Community has made in strengthening its counterterrorism capabilities since the September 11 attacks. We found that, although the Community has made significant strides in configuring itself to better protect the homeland and take the fight to terrorists abroad, much remains to be done to ensure the efficient use of limited resources among agencies responsible for counterterrorism intelligence. The U.S. government has not yet successfully defined the roles, missions, authorities, and the means of sharing information among our national and homeland security organs. Specifically, we found that:

- Information flow between the federal, state, local, and tribal levels—both up and down—is not yet well coordinated;

- Ambiguities in the respective roles and authorities of the National Counterterrorism Center and the Intelligence Community-wide Counterterrorist Center have not been resolved;

- Persistent conflicts over the roles, missions, and authorities of counterterrorism organizations may limit the Community's ability to warn of potential threats;

- Confusion and conflict regarding the roles, missions, and authorities of counterterrorism organizations have led to redundant efforts across the Community and inefficient use of limited resources; and

- The failure to manage counterterrorism resources from a Community perspective has limited the Intelligence Community's ability to understand and warn against terrorist use of weapons of mass destruction.

## Introduction

Providing intelligence that facilitates the global war on terrorism and warns against terrorist use of weapons of mass destruction is currently the Intelligence Community's most vital mission. There is every reason to believe that this will remain the top priority for a generation or more. As a result, it is impossible to reach broad conclusions regarding the Intelligence Community's overall performance, and develop meaningful suggestions for improvement and reform, without an understanding of Intelligence Community capabilities with regard to countering the terrorist threat—both now and in the future.

We did not set out to study "terrorism" writ large; such an ambitious endeavor is beyond the scope and time allotted to this Commission. Rather, we chose to focus narrowly on examining several well-documented weaknesses inherent in the Intelligence Community's counterterrorism capabilities prior to the September 11 attacks, and on measures the Intelligence Community has subsequently taken to remedy those deficiencies. Our work thus focused on four primary areas:

1. The status of *information sharing* among federal agencies with foreign and domestic intelligence and law enforcement responsibilities, as well as between federal agencies and state, local, and tribal law enforcement;

2. The effectiveness of the *threat-warning* mechanism by which policymakers are kept informed of potential terror threats;

3. The ability to synthesize relevant *all-source terrorism analysis* in a timely manner; and

4. The Intelligence Community's ability to provide the intelligence necessary to interdict a planned *terrorist attack using a weapon of mass destruction.*

We conclude that although the Intelligence Community has made significant strides in each of these areas, much remains to be done. We found substantial evidence that information flows between the federal level and the state, local, and tribal levels—both upward and downward—are not yet well coordinated. The roles and responsibilities among Intelligence Community agencies charged with primary responsibility for terrorism intelligence—both tactical and strategic—are not clearly defined. Sustained bureaucratic infighting and poor coordination prevent the Community from optimizing its resources to fight terrorism and alert policymakers to terrorist threats. Moreover, Community efforts to integrate technical and regional intelligence expertise with counterterrorism analysis do not provide sufficient focus on the threat posed by weapons of mass destruction in the hands of terrorists.

Resolving complex bureaucratic issues that transcend agency and subject-matter boundaries is usually difficult. However, three and a half years removed from the September 11 attacks, the persistence of agency coordination problems and unclear definitions of responsibility suggest to us a lack of Community leadership. The intelligence entities responsible for counterterrorism, especially terrorism analysis and threat warning, must be properly aligned, supported, and integrated for the task at hand.

## Systemic Flaws as of the "Summer of Threat"

It is well-established that the Intelligence Community's structure and practices prior to the September 11 attacks were simply not up to the task of waging a global war on terror and protecting the homeland. The systemic Intelligence Community deficiencies during the "Summer of Threat" leading up to the attacks were summed up by the 9/11 Commission in two short sentences: "Information was not shared . . . Analysis was not pooled." For present purposes, we highlight three of the specific failings identified by the 9/11 Commission in its examination of the Intelligence Community before September 11.

First, prior to September 11, there was a failure to share terrorism-related information rapidly and efficiently within agencies; among entities within the Intelligence Community tasked with producing intelligence to support counterterrorism efforts, and with state, local, and tribal law enforcement. For example, the FBI lacked basic computer capabilities, and did not share information even within its own organization. The CIA and the FBI were unwilling or unable to exchange information quickly and effectively with each other. And the Immigration and Naturalization Service and FBI did not learn from the CIA which identified terrorists were entering the United States and where they might be.

Second, the Intelligence Community's analysts were ill-equipped to "connect the available dots" that might have led to advance warning of the September 11 attacks. The "dispersal of effort on too many priorities" and the "declining attention to the craft of strategic analysis" were among the shortcomings identified by the 9/11 Commission's staff. The CIA published many useful analytical reports on terrorism before the attack, but the Intelligence Community failed to produce a comprehensive, cross-cutting assessment of the threat. Analysts had difficulty carving out time to work on longer-term analyses that could have unified disparate elements of intelligence and pointed to the existence of a growing threat or particular vulnerability.

Third, there was a lack of coordinated effort among the major federal agencies tasked with counterterrorism responsibilities, and confusion as to the roles and responsibilities of those agencies. Because the CIA and FBI lacked an optimized, cooperative analytical and operational effort, they were not well configured to detect and counter a threat, like that posed by the September 11 plotters, which "fell into the void between foreign and domestic threats."

# Notable Improvements
# Since the September 11 Attacks

We found evidence that this grim picture has improved in many respects since September 11. In the information sharing arena, for example, consolidation of terrorist "watchlists" and expanded use of those lists for screening purposes have increased the likelihood of detecting known or suspected terrorists and obtaining additional information about them. Moreover, counterterrorism information sharing has increased in quantitative terms—that is, terrorism intelligence products are disseminated more broadly, and are produced by more agencies, than before September 11.

Similarly, the Intelligence Community has remedied many of the analysis-related problems it faced leading up to the September 11 attacks. In particular, the Community increased its analytic efforts on terrorism-related issues, including analytic support to operations, and at the President's direction established the Terrorist Threat Integration Center (TTIC, now the National Counterterrorism Center, or NCTC) as the Community's center for analysis on these topics. Many analysts arrive with substantial experience gained from working on terrorism accounts at the DCI's Counterterrorist Center (CTC), an organization originally based at the CIA and staffed primarily by CIA officers that also includes representatives from throughout the Community. Analysts are increasingly being assigned to the NCTC for two-year rotations instead of short-term, stop-gap stints, enabling it to develop some badly-needed depth of expertise among its analytic corps. Perhaps most significantly in light of the criticisms leveled by the 9/11 Commission, the NCTC is producing analytic products that integrate the comments and concerns of analysts across the Community.

Moreover, the President's Terrorist Threat Report, a daily analytic publication produced by the NCTC, is truly a Community effort—with five agencies regularly contributing and a production schedule established by regular interagency meetings. Prior to the September 11 attacks, it was far from clear that the intelligence resources of all the relevant agencies in the Intelligence Community were being tapped to create a complete picture of terror threats for senior policymakers. In contrast, the NCTC now hosts "ecumenical" meetings five days a week, in which managers representing CIA, FBI, DIA, NSA, and the Departments of State and Homeland Security share and discuss intelligence regarding key terror threats. The NCTC also meets five times weekly with senior representatives of CIA, FBI, DIA, and Homeland Security at a formal planning production board to divide responsibility for drafting analytical products (mainly those which will appear in the President's threat report) and to share information. This process represents a level of formal and informal interaction on the terrorist threat among the primary intelligence agencies that simply did not exist prior to September 11, and that seems to clearly represent an improvement in the identification of threats and the mechanism through which threat warning intelligence is provided to senior policymakers.

In our view the overall quality of finished analytic pieces on terrorism has also improved. Analysts in the Community now have access to substantially more information as the result of the Intelligence Community's heightened prioritization of the terrorism issue, the availability of intelligence from new collectors (particularly FBI and Homeland Security), and expanded access to information about human intelligence sources.

Perhaps most importantly, from an operational perspective it is clear that many of CTC's efforts to disrupt terrorist networks and plots—partially enabled by its in-house analytic cadre—have been extraordinary successes. Put simply, CTC has brought the fight to the terrorists.

Finally, we have found that September 11 and the subsequent anthrax attacks not only triggered an aggressive counterterrorism response throughout the U.S. government, but also prompted the Community to reconsider its approach to the possible acquisition and use of weapons of mass destruction by terrorists, which we refer to by short-hand throughout this case study as "WMD terrorism." In December 2002, in the midst of post-September 11 bureaucratic realignment, the President announced a national strategic policy on weapons of mass destruction. The President called for the application of new technologies, increased emphasis on intelligence collection and analysis, the strengthening of alliance relationships, and the establishment of new partnerships with former adversaries. The main pillars of the President's program included interdiction efforts, nonproliferation programs, and consequence management. In particular, he called for an emphasis on improving intelligence regarding weapons of mass destruction facilities and activities, expanding the interaction among U.S. intelligence, law enforcement, and military agencies, and enhancing intelligence cooperation with friends and allies.

High-level attention within the policy and intelligence communities has had an important impact on the WMD terrorism issue. Our interviews suggest that the Intelligence Community now has a more extensive operational capability dedicated to the problem, has enhanced its intelligence reporting and analysis functions, and has instituted a more robust effort to address the problem domestically. Moreover, the Community appears at least to recognize the unique characteristics of unconventional weapons in the terrorism context, as other organizations have followed the CIA's lead in placing additional although not yet sufficient—resources for WMD terrorism into the counterterrorism effort.

Since September 11, the reallocation of resources to respond to WMD terrorism has resulted in significant improvements in both foreign and domestic intelligence. We understand that within the Intelligence Community, sources have gotten better, the amount of data available has dramatically increased, and intelligence is more harmonized, consistent, and less reliant on vague "chatter." On the domestic side, there have been significant attempts to disrupt terrorist means of delivery.

Despite all of these noteworthy developments, our study found that the Community still has a long way to go before it can claim to have optimized its counterterrorism capabilities or fully fixed the serious deficiencies that existed prior to September 11. We thus turn to the areas where the picture is not as promising.

We begin by focusing on needed improvements in the sharing of terrorism information with state, local, and tribal governments. Next, we examine the more general bureaucratic "turf war" between agencies, and the pronounced lack of clarity as to the roles, responsibilities, and authorities involving various entities tasked with the counterterrorism mission—particularly the NCTC and the Counterterrorist Center. Finally, we examine the continuing coordination problems between the CIA, FBI, and Homeland Security in addressing the threat posed by WMD terrorism.

# Information Sharing: Much Room for Improvement

For a number of years before the September 11 attacks, the Intelligence Community closely followed the al-Qa'ida terrorist threat, yet failed to adequately exploit information it had concerning several individuals who were either involved in the planning of or participated in the attacks. Although the 9/11 Commission did not find that better information sharing would have prevented the attacks, at least nine of the ten "operational opportunities" that the commission identified as missed opportunities to possibly thwart the plot pertain to some form of a failure to share information. These perceived failures have made "information sharing" a mantra for intelligence reform for the three and a half years since the attacks.

We have found that as a general matter, the Intelligence Community has sought to improve terrorism information sharing by modifying the structures and processes for sharing that were in place prior to September 11—rather than establishing wholly new approaches. We agree with the recent assessment of the Intelligence Community Inter-Agency Information Sharing Working Group, which found that "[a] great deal of energy . . . is being expended across the [Intelligence Community] to improve information sharing. However, the majority of these initiatives *will not produce the enduring institutional change required to address our current threat environment."*

The importance of effective sharing of information at all levels of the Intelligence Community is discussed in several chapters of our report. In this section, we specifically address the Intelligence Community's efforts, since September 11, to improve the sharing of terrorism information across the Intelligence Community and with state, local, and tribal governments. Our specific findings are categorized in four broad areas.

First, we found substantial improvement in information sharing relating to terrorist watchlisting and screening. "Watchlisting"—the process of assembling databases of known or suspected terrorists—was not well coordinated among federal agencies prior to September 11, but several effective reforms have been implemented in the wake of the attacks. For example, the new Terrorist Screening Center—an interagency effort to consolidate terrorist watchlists and provide operational support for federal employees around the world, hours a day, seven days a week—now administers a single database that combines international and domestic terrorism data provided by the NCTC and FBI. The database also integrates information from immigration and customs offices, the Transportation Security Administration, the U.S. Marshals Service, Department of Defense, and Interpol. The Terrorist Screening Center ensures that government investigators, screeners, and agents are working from the same comprehensive information and that they have access simultaneously to information and experience that will allow them to act quickly when a suspected terrorist is screened and stopped.

Second, we have found that the sharing of counterterrorism information has increased in quantitative terms—more terrorism information is being shared with more entities both inside and outside the Intelligence Community than before the September 11 attacks. This has largely occurred through the increased use of "tearlines"—the practice of generating intelligence reports at several different classification levels so it can be shared with a cross-section of federal, state, local, and tribal officials—which has resulted in more releasable information being provided to consumers. And security-based sharing restrictions have been substantially reduced, allowing analysts and security personnel greater access to the information they need to do their jobs.

All this being said, problems remain. While the Intelligence Community has reduced its use of restrictions on further dissemination of intelligence products without the consent of the originator, inconsistent application of dissemination restrictions, such as ORCON ("originator controlled"), continue to impede the flow of useful terrorism information. In relations with state, local, and tribal authorities, more terrorism information is being shared, but federal officials continue to have difficulty establishing consistent and coordinated lines of communication with these officials. In this regard, we have found that there is no comprehensive policy or program for achieving the appropriate balance regarding what terrorism information to provide to state, local, and tribal authorities and how to provide it. Additionally, the redundant lines of communication through which terrorism-related information is passed—for example, through the Joint Terrorism Task Forces, Anti-Terrorism Advisory Councils, Homeland Security Information Network, TTIC Online, Law Enforcement Online Network, Centers for Disease Control alerts, and Public Health Advisories, to name just a few—present a deluge of information for which state, local, and tribal authorities are neither equipped nor trained to process, prioritize, and disseminate.

Our third category of findings relates to the sharing of information to ensure that analysts throughout the Intelligence Community have the widest possible access to information regardless of which agency collects the information. Today, the primary means of sharing information throughout the Community continues to be through interagency personnel exchange programs, such as the model used by the NCTC. These personnel exchanges can be quite effective, but they do nothing to improve the flow of information throughout those agencies or enable agencies to engage in competitive analysis based on access to the same set of information. Collectors of information continue to operate as though they "own" information and, in fact, collectors largely control access to the information that they generate. Decisions to withhold information are typically based on rules that are neither clearly defined nor consistently applied, with no system in place to hold collectors accountable for inappropriately withholding information.

Finally, we have found that there is currently no single entity in the Intelligence Community with the responsibility and authority to impose a centralized approach to sharing information. Although the NCTC model has certainly facilitated improved information sharing on counterterrorism issues, it lacks sufficient authority and resources necessary to provide strong leadership in this area.

# Counterterrorism Warning Analysis:
# A Struggle Between Agencies

Notwithstanding significant gains in terrorism intelligence since September 11, a number of problems remain. Our study found evidence of bitter bureaucratic "turf battles" between agencies, and a pronounced lack of clarity as to the roles, responsibilities, and authorities of various entities tasked with the counterterrorism mission. Specifically, this interagency jockeying over overlapping counterterrorism analytical responsibilities indicates that major organizational issues affecting the allocation of resources, assignment of responsibilities, coordination of analysis, and effective warning remain unresolved.

## *Who's in Charge of Counterterrorism Analysis and Warning?*

The Community's inability to implement a "one team, one fight" strategy in the terror war may be attributed both to ongoing bureaucratic battles between agencies charged with responsibility for counterterrorism analysis and warning, as well as the failure of Community leaders to effectively resolve these disputes and clearly define agency roles and authorities. The conflict and ambiguity surrounding the role of the Terrorist Threat Integration Center during its abbreviated existence starkly illustrates both points.

After the September 11 attacks, TTIC was created for the purpose of improving the sharing of terrorist threat data and the analysis of terrorism-related information. However, as the Markle Foundation has reported, "the very fact of the TTIC's creation caused confusion within the federal government and among state and local governments" about the respective roles of TTIC and other federal agencies responsible for counterterrorism analysis and terrorist threat assessments. Even today—despite being designated by the intelligence reform act as the preeminent, integrated center for threat warning and analysis—the NCTC continues to have difficulty asserting its primacy for the terrorism warning mission.

This dispute—and the potential problems to which it could lead—has been apparent since February 2003, when Senators Collins and Levin highlighted the issue in a joint letter (the "Collins-Levin Letter") to the Secretary of Homeland Security, the Director of TTIC, and the Directors of Central Intelligence and the FBI. The letter asked that the officials clarify responsibilities among counterterrorism elements of the U.S. government. In their April 2004 response, the agency heads stated that "TTIC has primary responsibility in the [U.S. government] for terrorism analysis (except analysis relating solely to purely domestic terrorism) and is responsible for the day-to-day terrorism analysis provided to the President and other senior policymakers." In order to make it possible for TTIC to achieve this mission, the letter further stated that the DCI, in consultation with the other leaders of the Intelligence Community, would determine by June 1, 2004, what additional analytic resources would be transferred to TTIC from the CTC.

Despite this unequivocal statement, TTIC was never able to fully perform its mission. Other entities, CTC in particular, differed over the level of support they should provide to TTIC and resisted supplying it with an adequate number of detailees—thus hampering TTIC's ability to assume the leading role assigned to it.

In May 2004, TTIC Director John Brennan sent correspondence to then-Director of Central Intelligence George Tenet, explaining how TTIC intended to carry out the responsibilities identified in the Collins-Levin letter. He warned that lacking significant new analytic resources, TTIC would not be able to carry out the mission of having "primary responsibility" for providing terrorism analysis to the President and senior policymakers.

The next month, Director Brennan sent the DCI a follow-up memorandum entitled "TTIC at the Breaking Point." In this memorandum, he argued that other intelligence agencies had failed to provide sufficient numbers of analysts to TTIC, and that the personnel that had been provided possessed only limited competency or a low level of experience. He further noted that these agencies continued to insist on developing their own independent counterterrorism analytical capabilities. This organizational multiplicity, Director Brennan argued, had created not only a "dangerous shortfall in TTIC's analytic resources and mission," but also "unnecessary analytic redundancy within the intelligence, law enforcement, defense, and homeland security communities." In sum, Director Brennan wrote, a general refusal by entities within the Intelligence Community to "sign on to the fundamental premise that resources and mission will migrate to TTIC" had left the Center "unable to fulfill the mission of 'primary responsibility' for terrorism analysis in the U.S. government," and had forced the U.S. government into a "retreat from the integration model" of terrorism analysis and threat warning.

Approximately one week later—on July 2, 2004—then-Deputy Director of Central Intelligence John McLaughlin attempted to address Director Brennan's concerns by outlining (at the DCI's request) a "division of resources and analytical responsibilities" between CIA and TTIC. In interviews with this Commission, Director Brennan repeatedly stated that he had not received an official answer to his urgent memos of May and June. When later asked specifically about the July 2 response, he dismissed it as failing to provide a meaningful answer to the basic questions he had raised regarding allocation of responsibilities for counterterrorism analysis and warning—despite the fact that the July 2 memorandum does in fact deal with virtually every issue highlighted by Director Brennan.

The memorandum may not have been the answer Director Brennan wanted, but it certainly constituted a clear attempt by the Community's leadership to allocate roles, responsibilities, and resources among counterterrorism organizations. Addressed to CIA's Deputy Directors for Intelligence and Operations, as well as to Director Brennan, the memorandum provided for the immediate transfer of 60 personnel to TTIC, but it did not provide the "primary responsibility" over terrorism analysis for TTIC that Director Brennan had requested. In fact, the memorandum declined to grant TTIC sole authority over analysis pertaining to international terrorist networks, instead explicitly stating that other agencies (including CTC) would continue sharing that function. The memorandum acknowledged that this would result in redundancy, but argued that "on something as important as terrorism analysis," some overlap between agencies was to be preferred.

Although we believe that excessive redundancy in Community counterterrorism efforts is wasteful of scarce resources and thus counterproductive (see our discussion below), we express no view on the overall merits of the organizational plan and division of labor outlined in the July 2, 2004 memorandum. However, it is of great significance, we think, that the Community was ultimately unable to enforce that plan—or, to date, any plan—and bring an end to the interagency squabbling between CTC and NCTC.

We have been told that the plan outlined in the July 2 memorandum fell victim to bureaucratic neglect and rapid change within the Community; shortly after its distribution there was turnover in the DCI's office, and ambiguities fostered by creation of the NCTC by executive order and, later, passage of the intelligence reform act, raised new questions about the designated roles of the nation's counterterrorism organizations. Our study suggests that there may have been another factor, as well: the entrenched opposition of both CTC and NCTC to effectively cooperating or consolidating aspects of their authorities.

The fact that Director Brennan did not regard clear direction from the DCI to be an "answer" to his pleas to resolve confusion over roles, resources, and responsibilities—presumably because it did not allocate the prerogatives to his organization that he had requested—speaks volumes about the hardened mindsets of the two organizations' leadership, and their desire to protect or expand their bureaucratic "turf." As the Director of the Counterterrorist Center characterized the relationship, the Center "is fighting a war with TTIC."

Although recent passage of the intelligence reform act may resolve issues related to responsibilities and resources, the history of the dispute tempers our optimism. Whatever the precise allocation of resources and responsibilities is to be, the DNI must act quickly to resolve the issue. Absent strong leadership, other organizations in the Intelligence Community may continue to resist providing resources to NCTC, as they did with TTIC, and may dispute its "primary" role in coordinating terrorism intelligence. Alternatively, NCTC may resist well-reasoned direction to permit CTC to continue performing several of its important functions. If so, the war between agencies that are tasked to fight the war on terror will continue. Unfortunately, such a conflict constitutes far more than a common bureaucratic dispute, the sort of administrative power struggle so common in the corridors of government. Rather, it has profound operational implications for the ability of the Intelligence Community to perform the all-important function of providing terrorism analysis and warning information to policymakers.

## *A Failure to Warn with One Voice*

The dispute between the NCTC and CTC is especially troubling in the context of threat warning—the process by which threat information is conveyed to decisionmakers in time for them to take action to manage or deter the threat. Continuing disagreements about the two offices' roles and missions have in the past led to inconsistent warning messages being conveyed to decisionmakers and—far more troubling—these warnings were conveyed in a manner that may have sowed confusion.

# What Part of "Warning" Should Be Competitive?

For present purposes, we divide warning into two components: (1) the *analytic* function that produces a warning and (2) the *process of communicating* those threat judgments to decisionmakers. As a general matter, while we strongly endorse competitive *warning analysis* ( *i.e.* , competition in the first component of warning), we believe that the process of communicating threats to decisionmakers ( *i.e.* , the second component) should be coordinated and integrated. We say this because we do not believe decisionmakers are well-served by incoherent, uncoordinated warnings of impend-

> ing threats. Rather, warning should be presented to deci-
> sionmakers in a coordinated manner that makes clear the
> level of certainty with which they are held.

According to NCTC officials, the NCTC must have primacy, if not exclusivity, in providing warning intelligence to the President and controlling the analytical resources required for this mission. NCTC principals acknowledge that CTC needs to retain analytical capability to directly support the CIA's Directorate of Operations (DO)—and to continue the spectacular successes the DO has achieved in the war on terror. However, as a general matter they assert that it is improper to "divide effort when it comes to terrorism," and have claimed as a core responsibility the "production of terrorist threat warnings, advisories, and alerts," which are to be "issued by [the NCTC] alone or as formally coordinated products of the 'Warn 7.'" Moreover, in its role as coordinator of the President's Terrorist Threat Report (PTTR), the NCTC insists that it has oversight responsibility for determining what terrorism analysis is provided to the President. In sum, the NCTC conceives its mission as providing coordinated threat warning and analytical reports—reflecting "diversity of viewpoint but coordination of common response"— to senior policymakers.

Perhaps unsurprisingly, CTC does not embrace this division of labor. CTC views itself as the preeminent counterterrorism entity within the Intelligence Community.

In CTC's view, NCTC's main contribution to the terrorism fight lies in its access to intelligence information and databases— both foreign and domestic. As a result, CTC leaders expressed to us the view that the NCTC should be responsible for generating an integrated Community view of threats, but should not have the dominant voice in counterterrorism analysis and warning. A recent example of where this theoretical disagreement had concrete consequences is discussed in our classified report, but cannot be detailed in an unclassified format.

Ideally, a single warning vehicle (such as the President's Terrorist Threat Report, now provided daily by the NCTC) should provide a forum for ensuring that policymakers do not receive inconsistent messages. But we have seen evidence that this is not always so. It is further possible that legislation creating the NCTC may obviate such interagency conflicts in the future— but we are only guardedly optimistic. In this sense, we believe that the DNI will have to create mechanisms by which competitive analysis for warning is maintained, and the dissemination of warnings is carefully coordinated. More broadly, the DNI will have to force the nation's counterterrorism organizations to concentrate more fully on fighting terrorists, rather than each other.

## Maintenance of Redundant Capabilities

An absence of clearly defined roles and authorities with regard to analysis and warning leads inevitably to competition in key capabilities, and redundant efforts across the Community. For example, we spoke with a senior analytic manager who recounted one incident in which a single raw intelligence report spurred five different agencies to write five separate pieces, all reaching the same conclusion. Not only were analysts' efforts redundant, but policymakers were then required to read through all five papers to look for subtle differences in perspective that could have been better conveyed in a single, coordinated paper.

This phenomenon is especially troubling given the scarce analytic resources available for counterterrorism efforts. Agencies expressed serious concern about their ability to engage in long-term strategic analysis given the demands generated by customer questions and daily indicators of new threats. For example, the NCTC spends roughly 70 percent of its time on immediate threats, primarily because analysts have to run each potential threat to ground, even if it seems suspect from the outset. Similarly, the FBI estimates that about percent of analysts' time is spent on direct operational support. All of these requirements tend to leave little time and resources for thoughtful, strategic work on new and emerging threats. All of this is, of course, compounded by the significant trouble agencies are experiencing in retaining qualified and experienced analysts.

Despite this serious resource issue, there is ongoing evidence of an interagency failure to cooperate and efficiently divide responsibility in counterterrorism analysis. For example, NCTC WMD analysts with whom we spoke described their willingness and capability to engage in long-term, strategic analysis on behalf of the counterterrorism community. But when a senior CTC official—who noted the need for such analysis and lamented the difficulty of allocating time and resources for it in the context of CTC's operationally-driven environment—was asked about the possibility of using NCTC resources for that purpose, he stated bluntly that "[NCTC] doesn't have those capabilities." It is unclear whether such statements reflect a lack of understanding between the two entities concerning complementary capabilities that could be mutually leveraged, institutional resentment and an unwillingness to operate collaboratively, or simply an ongoing struggle over personnel resources.

Again, although recent passage of the intelligence reform act may resolve issues related to responsibilities and resources, we are not optimistic that anything in the legislation itself resolves the dispute. We address the issues associated with managing scarce analytic resources more fully in later chapters.

## The Failure to Manage Community Resources in Response to the WMD Terrorism Threat

Recognizing that the worst terrorist attack would be one involving weapons of mass destruction, some elements within the Community have begun to incorporate analytic and collection capabilities with respect to the WMD terrorism threat into their counterterrorism organizations. At the same time, the CIA's Weapons Intelligence, Nonproliferation, and Arms Control Center provides intelligence support aimed at protecting the United States and its interests from all advanced weapons threats. Our review of the relationship among these various entities reveals that some systemic weaknesses are preventing the development of a focused, integrated, well-resourced bureaucracy that can most effectively combat the worst-case threat of a homeland terrorist attack. Specifically:

- There is no clear leadership or bureaucratic architecture defining roles and responsibilities for WMD terrorism. This adversely affects analysis, collection, and threat warning; and

- The domestic intelligence effort on WMD terrorism is lagging behind the U.S. government's foreign intelligence capabilities.

## Defining Roles and
## Responsibilities for the WMD Terrorism Threat

Notwithstanding the President's National Strategy to Combat Weapons of Mass Destruction promulgated in December 2002, the overriding concern of key officials whom we have interviewed is that, within the U.S. government, there is no overall direction and coordination on WMD terrorism. As the chief of the FBI's WMD Countermeasures Unit rhetorically asked, "[w]ho is ultimately responsible for preventing the use of a WMD?"

The most significant consequence of the lack of coordination is that each organization appears to be defining its own mission and trying to make sure it has the resources to be self-sufficient across a broad range of responsibilities. The result is predictable: duplicative roles, power vacuums where individual organizations assert their authority, and confusion within the Community. As the NCTC's head of analysis observed, it is necessary not only to clarify affirmative roles and responsibilities, but also to delineate those responsibilities for which agencies are *not* responsible.

For example, despite changes since September 11, coordination problems between the FBI and the CIA continue to disrupt analysis on WMD terrorism and operations against weapons of mass destruction targets. As the FBI has expanded its overseas operations and the CTC tries not to lose its targets when they travel to the United States, coordination is essential. However, according to the head of the CTC's WMD unit, there is no sense of "jointness," or shared mission, on the part of the FBI and CTC, despite the co-location of portions of both organizations.

It appears that coordination among domestic agencies responsible for responding to a potential WMD terrorist threat also suffers from confusion and a lack of coordination. For instance, the FBI told us that the Department of Homeland Security had, in response to a possible threat, taken the initiative to start moving radiation detection resources to New York during the Republican National Convention without coordinating with the Bureau. Subsequent to the move, the "threat" was revealed to be a legitimate movement of a medical isotope. Had even the most elemental communication and coordination taken place—in the form of a phone call from Homeland Security to the FBI—this fact might have surfaced earlier, thereby avoiding the squandering of limited counterterrorism resources.

Perhaps most alarming is the allegation that when terrorism cases move from a purely foreign focus to a domestic emphasis requiring a hand-off in primary responsibility from the CIA to the FBI, the CIA finds it difficult to obtain information from the FBI about ongoing investigations. Such gaps in cooperation, occurring at the vital fault line between foreign and domestic intelligence, are reminiscent of the "void" that the September 11 attack plotters operated in to achieve their objectives.

The stark division between the Intelligence Community's WMD terrorism programs and the Community's state-based weapons of mass destruction programs further hampers the WMD terrorism effort. As our case study of al-Qa'ida in Afghanistan also confirms, the personnel who work the WMD terrorism issue mostly coordinate with their state program counterparts on an *ad hoc* basis. Efforts have been made to remedy this problem within CIA, but we think it vital that such cooperation be greatly expanded throughout the Community.

### *The Domestic Intelligence Effort on WMD Terrorism*

While the FBI has responded to the threat posed by WMD terrorism by increasing the resources dedicated to this issue, the

FBI's efforts in this regard remain subordinated to the broader war on terror. For example, approximately a year ago, the FBI committed (on paper) to staffing its WMD Integration and Targeting Unit—the unit responsible for providing expertise on WMD terrorism—with a total of staff positions. Today, the unit has only two people—the unit chief and a single intelligence analyst.

Unsurprisingly, the FBI, like other agencies responsible for the WMD terrorism threat, is having difficulty finding people with the right expertise and has yet to develop a specific career track or program for developing expertise regarding the threat. Other agencies having responsibility for WMD terrorism are also understaffed, and the few experts that do exist are suffering from burnout. To its credit, the FBI has acknowledged its need for more resources in this area, but it is clear to us that the FBI's weaknesses are not susceptible to a quick fix.

# Conclusion

The Intelligence Community's capabilities with regard to current terror threats have improved significantly since September 11, 2001. Nevertheless, the continued lack of definitional clarity as to roles and responsibilities in the war on terrorism, and ongoing conflicts among key counterterrorism agencies, constitute an ongoing challenge—and one that we believe should be foremost on the mind of the new DNI.

# Iran and North Korea: Monitoring The Development Of Nuclear Capabilities

The Commission carefully studied the Intelligence Community's capability to assess accurately the nuclear programs of Iran and North Korea. In doing so, we reviewed numerous intelligence reports and conducted interviews with Intelligence Community analysts, collectors, and supervisors, as well as policymakers and non-governmental regional and weapons experts. Because even the most general statements about the Intelligence Community's capabilities in this area are classified, the Commission's assessments and eleven specific findings cannot be discussed in this report. The Commission has, however, incorporated the lessons learned from its study of Iran and North Korea in all of our recommendations for reform of the Intelligence Community.

# Leadership and Management: Forging an Integrated Intelligence Community

## Summary & Recommendations

Today's Intelligence Community is not a "community" in any meaningful sense. It is a loose confederation of 15 separate intelligence entities. The new intelligence reform legislation, by creating a Director of National Intelligence (DNI) with substantial new authorities, establishes the basis for the kind of leadership and management necessary to shape a truly integrated Intelligence Community. But the reform act provides merely a framework; the hard work of forging a unified Community lies ahead.

In order to surmount these challenges, the DNI will need to lead the Community; he will need to integrate a diffuse group of intelligence entities by gaining acceptance of common strategic objectives, and by pursuing those objectives with more modern management techniques and governance processes. We recommend several structures that could demonstrate the value of such collaboration.

Specifically, we recommend that the DNI:

- Bring a mission focus to the management of Community resources for high-priority intelligence issues by creating several "Mission Managers" on the DNI staff who are responsible for overseeing all aspects of intelligence relating to priority targets;

- Create a leadership structure within the Office of the DNI that manages the intelligence collection process on a Community basis, while maintaining intact existing collection agencies and their respective pockets of expertise;

- Make several changes to the Intelligence Community's personnel policies, including creating a central Intelligence Community human resources authority; developing more comprehensive and creative sets of performance incentives; directing a "joint" personnel rotation system; and establishing a National Intelligence University.

We also recommend that:

- The President establish a National Counter Proliferation Center (NCPC) that reports to the DNI. The NCPC—a relatively small organization, with approximately0 staff—would manage and coordinate analysis and collection on nuclear, biological, and chemical weapons across the Intelligence Community, but would not serve as a focal point for government-wide strategic operational planning; and

- The Executive Branch take steps to strengthen its intelligence oversight to ensure that intelligence reform does not falter, and that the Intelligence Community strengthen its own processes for self-evaluation.

## Introduction

Today's Intelligence Community is not truly a community at all, but rather a loose confederation of 15 separate entities. These entities too often act independently of each other. While a "community" management staff has long existed in the Office of the Director of Central Intelligence (DCI), it has never had the authority or resources it needed to manage all these disparate components.

The diffuse nature of the Intelligence Community does have important merits—for example, the existence of different agency cultures and ways of doing business increases the likelihood that hypotheses about key intelligence issues will be "competitively" tested, and allows for the development of diverse pockets of expertise. While such advantages should be retained, they aren't a reason to tolerate the current lack of coordination. As our case studies aptly demonstrate, the old, single-agency methods of gathering intelligence are losing ground to our adversaries. And conversely, many of our recent intelligence successes have resulted from innovative cross-agency efforts—but such laudable examples are the exception, the products of *ad hoc* efforts rather than institutionalized collaboration.

Concern about the harmful impact of disunity on national security was a major factor leading to passage of the *Intelligence Reform and Terrorism Prevention Act of 2004*. In creating a Director of National Intelligence (DNI) with substantial (though not sweeping) new authorities, the act created the framework for an integrated management structure for the United States' intelligence apparatus. However, passage of the intelligence act is merely prologue; the hard work of forging a genuine Intelligence Community, linked for the purpose of optimizing its capabilities and resources, must now begin.

We are realists. We recognize that effecting such a transformation in intelligence will take years to accomplish—and, indeed, will fall short without sustained leadership from the Director of National Intelligence and continued support from the President and Congress. This chapter offers our view on the essential tasks the new DNI might prioritize—and the challenges he will confront—as he begins this effort. We also offer, at the end of the chapter, a notional organizational structure for the new Office of the DNI, which we believe would serve the DNI well in confronting these tasks and challenges.

# Building an Integrated Intelligence Community

## *Levers of Authority: Powers and Limitations of the New DNI*

First, the good news. Under prior law, the Director of Central Intelligence had three demanding jobs—he ran the CIA, acted as the President's principal intelligence advisor, and (in theory, at least) managed the Intelligence Community. Thanks to the new intelligence legislation, the new DNI is now only responsible for two; the task of running the day-to-day operations of the CIA will be left to the Agency's own Director.

The bad news is that the DNI's remaining statutory responsibilities continue to be demanding, full-time jobs. The DNI's management responsibilities will be both critically important and exceedingly difficult, and there is a real risk that the obligation to provide current intelligence support to the President and senior policymakers will reduce or eliminate the attention the DNI can devote to the painstaking, long-term work of integrating and managing the Community. It would be unrealistic—and undesirable—to expect the Office of the DNI to neglect or abdicate its responsibility as intelligence advisor to the President. But it is not necessary in all instances for the DNI to be present at the briefings himself. We do believe that it is possible for the DNI to assume what is essentially an oversight rather than a direct role in fulfilling this function, and we suggest that the DNI interpret the obligation in this way.

The DNI's management responsibilities will be more than sufficient to occupy the DNI's time and talents. On the first day in office, the new DNI will not have much of a foundation to build upon. A former senior Defense Department official has described today's Intelligence Community as "not so much poorly managed as unmanaged." After a comprehensive study of the Community, we can't disagree. The DNI will need to create—virtually from scratch—structures, processes, and procedures for managing this notoriously sprawling, complicated, and fragmented bureaucracy. But with this "blank slate" also comes an opportunity. The new Director will be in a position to build a leadership and management staff that is suited to today's intelligence needs, rather than accommodate and modify an inherited administrative structure.

The intelligence reform legislation gives the DNI substantial new levers of authority to perform management responsibilities, but those powers are also limited in important respects. Most of the entities within the Intelligence Community—such as NSA, NGA, and the intelligence component of the FBI—continue to be part of separate executive departments. This means that the DNI will be expected to manage the Intelligence Community, but will not have direct "line" authority over all the agencies and entities he is responsible for coordinating and integrating. NSA, to cite just one example, remains with the Department of Defense, and its employees will therefore continue to be part of the Defense Department's "chain of command."

This means that the DNI will be required to manage the Community more by controlling essential resources than by command. And the new legislation does give the DNI important new budget and personnel authorities. For example, the intelligence reform act grants the DNI a substantially stronger hand in the development and execution of the overall intelligence budget, or National Intelligence Program, than that previously given to the DCI. The leverage that these budget authorities were intended to provide, however, cannot be effectively exercised without an overhaul of the Intelligence Community's notoriously opaque budget process, which obscures how resources are committed to, and spent against, various intelligence programs. The DNI could wield his budgetary authorities with far more effectiveness if he were to build an end to end budgetary process that allowed for clarity and accountability—a process similar to the Planning, Programming, and Budgeting System employed by the Department of Defense.

With that said, the DNI's "power of the purse" is far from absolute. Many important intelligence programs are funded in whole or in part from joint military and tactical intelligence budgets that are under the control of the Defense Department. In light of these overlapping responsibilities and competing budgetary authorities, it is imperative that the Office of the DNI and the Department of Defense develop parallel and closely coordinated planning, programming, and budget processes. (Indeed, the relationship between the DNI and the Secretary of Defense is of great importance and will be discussed separately in this chapter.)

Another important (and related) management tool for the DNI is the acquisition process. If the DNI builds and drives a coherent, top-down Intelligence Community acquisition structure, he will have a powerful device for Community management, and will make an important step toward developing the coherent long-term allocation of resources that the Intelligence Community sorely lacks today—particularly with respect to evaluating and acquiring large, technology-driven systems. But, as in other areas, the DNI's role in the acquisition process is not absolute. Under the new intelligence reform act, the Secretary of Defense and the DNI will have joint acquisition authorities in many instances—another factor that weighs in favor of strong Defense Department-Intelligence Community interaction on many fronts.

In addition to these budget and acquisition authorities, the intelligence act also grants the DNI significant personnel powers. The act gives the DNI a substantial staff, and it empowers the DNI to transfer personnel from one element of the Intelligence Community to another for tours of up to two years. These are important new authorities; our terrorism case study sets out the difficulties the Terrorist Threat Integration Center encountered in obtaining adequate personnel support from other agencies. However, like the DNI's budgetary authorities, these powers are not unrestricted; the intelligence reform act states that the procedures governing these personnel transfers must be developed jointly by the DNI and by the affected agencies, which could provide department and agency heads with an opportunity to impede the DNI's initiatives. We suggest that the DNI make the development of these procedures an early priority, to ensure that the required "procedures" become just that—processes for effecting the flexible transfer of personnel and minimizing negative impact on the affected agencies, and not vehicles that provide agencies with a veto over the DNI's personnel authorities.

The intelligence act also expressly directs the DNI to implement management-related reform measures that have long been neglected by Community managers. Among these are specific mandates to develop Community personnel policies; maximize the sharing of information among Community agencies; improve the quality of intelligence analysis; protect the sources and methods used to collect intelligence from disclosure; and improve operational coordination between CIA and the Department of Defense. This explicit congressional direction should significantly strengthen the DNI's hand as the work of creating a new management structure begins.

The DNI will likely need every bit of the leverage bestowed by these new powers and embodied in the statutory mandate for change. Few of the recommendations that follow can be implemented without affecting the current responsibilities of a particular agency, sometimes in ways that can be expected to leave the affected agency unhappy. For instance, if the DNI is going to manage the target development system—the process by which the Intelligence Community prioritizes information needs and develops collection strategies to fulfill those needs—he will, by necessity, be taking responsibilities away from the collection agencies. If the DNI is going to build a modern information sharing infrastructure for the Intelligence Community, he will need to override particular agencies' views about what information is and is not too sensitive to be placed in the shared information space.

Making hard decisions that adversely affect particular agencies will constitute a major departure from prior Community management practices. Former DCIs have brought the Intelligence Community together by consensus, a practice that left many difficult but important management challenges unaddressed. Indeed, over the course of our study we repeatedly came across important decisions that Community leaders were unable to resolve—a state of affairs that allows bureaucratic disputes and unhealthy ambiguities in responsibilities to fester. (The lengthy turf battle between the CIA Counterterrorist Center and the Terrorist Threat Integration Center (now NCTC), is just one example.)

While the air is thick with talk of the need for coordination within the Intelligence Community, one can expect that the DNI's new (and sometimes ambiguous) authorities will be challenged in ways both open and subtle. In order to sustain successful integration, the DNI will need to establish processes that demonstrate by their own effectiveness the value of Community-wide cooperation. This can be achieved by securing "buy-in" on common strategic objectives, developing common practices in reviewing progress toward goals (using shared metrics whenever possible), and building a common approach to human resource management. We recommend several structures—such as the "Mission Managers" that we discuss immediately below—that could be useful in demonstrating the value of collaboration, and we also encourage the DNI to seek to emulate best practices used by large organizations both within and outside government.

## Organize Around Missions

Throughout our study, we observed a lack of Community focus on intelligence missions. Each individual agency tries to allocate its scarce resources in a way that seems sensible to that particular agency, but might not be optimal if viewed from a Community perspective. The DCI's management staff is organized around intelligence functions—there are, for instance, separate Assistant DCIs for "Collection" and "Analysis"—rather than around priority intelligence targets. So while it might have been the case that an individual at the DCI level was responsible for knowing about our collection capabilities on a given country, and while it might also have been the case that an individual at the DCI level was responsible for knowing the state of *analysis* on that country, no one person or office at the DCI level was responsible for the *intelligence mission* concerning that country as a whole.

We believe it is important that the DNI develop a management structure and processes that ensure a strategic, Community focus on priority intelligence missions. The specific device we propose is the creation of "Mission Managers."

Under the current system, collectors, analysts, and supervisors throughout the Community working on a given target function largely autonomously, communicating and collaborating only episodically. The Mission Managers we propose would be responsible for designing and implementing a coordinated effort. As the DNI's point person for individual high-priority subject matter areas, Mission Managers would be responsible for knowing both what the Community knows (and what it does not know) about a particular target, and for developing strategies to optimize the Community's capabilities against that particular target. For any such target—be it a country like China, a non-state actor like al-Qa'ida, or a subject like "proliferation"— a Mission Manager would be charged with organizing and monitoring the Community's efforts, and serving as the DNI's principal advisor on the subject. Most importantly, and in contrast to the diffusion of responsibility that characterizes the current system, the Mission Manager would be the person responsible for Community efforts against the target. There would never be a question of accountability.

The Mission Manager, therefore, would have substantial responsibilities both for driving collection and identifying shortcomings in analysis in the Mission Manager's subject area. With respect to collection, Mission Managers would chair Target Development Boards, described further below. In this capacity, the Mission Managers' role would include identifying collection gaps, working with the various collection agencies to fill them, and monitoring the collection organizations' progress in that regard. They would also serve as the DNI's primary tool for focusing the Intelligence Community's analytical attention on strategic threats to national security and optimizing the Community's resources against them. While they would not directly command the analytical cadre, they could—in cases where agency heads were resistant to properly aligning resources or addressing analytic needs—recommend that the DNI's personnel powers be invoked to correct the situation or quickly re configure the Community to respond to a crisis. Because of their responsibilities for developing a coordinated approach to collection and analytic efforts, we believe that the Mission Managers would also collectively serve as an important device for achieving Community integration over time.

Some might suggest that the Mission Manager function will conflict with the role of National Intelligence Officers (NIOs) within the National Intelligence Council (NIC), the Community's focal point for long-term, interagency analysis. The NIOs are granted authority under the new legislation for "evaluating community-wide collection and production of intelligence by the Intelligence Community and the requirements and resources of such collection and production." We believe this role is complementary with that of the Mission Managers. NIOs, in our view, should continue to serve as the Community's principal senior analysts. In this position, they spearhead assembly of National Intelligence Estimates and other publications that articulate Community analytic conclusions, identify differences in agency views and why they exist, and explore gaps and weaknesses in collection. But once an Estimate on a given topic is finished, NIOs move quickly to the next, perhaps not to officially revisit the subject matter for years. They have neither the time nor the authority to craft and implement strategic plans designed to improve the Community's work on a particular issue over time. This, as we see it, will be the Mission Managers' role.

## Coordinate Target Development

The Intelligence Community's fragmented nature is perhaps best exemplified by the process in which its resources are directed to collect information on subjects of interest. One would expect that this vital aspect of intelligence—which we refer to as "target development"—would be among those where coordination and integration is most essential. Instead, the target development process is left primarily to individual collection agencies, operating from a general list of intelligence objectives called the National Intelligence Priorities Framework, in combination with *ad hoc* requirements generated by analysts and other intelligence "customers," such as policymakers and the military. This decentralized process is refined only episodically at the Community level, usually through the personal intervention of the Assistant Director of Central Intelligence for Collection.

This is an unacceptable status quo, and we recommend that the DNI make fixing it a top priority. As our case studies have shown, many of the recent penetrations of hard targets have been facilitated by fusing collection disciplines. Such cross-agency collection strategies cannot be systematically encouraged while the various collection platforms remain isolated within the confines of their individual agencies. The current system, in which individual agencies set their own collection priorities, also marginalizes the role of the intelligence "customers" and analysts for whom intelligence is collected.

As a result, we believe it is essential that the DNI develop a unified target development process that exists "above the stovepipes." We would give the Mission Managers responsibility for driving and maintaining an overarching collection strategy in their subject matter areas. In developing this strategy, each Mission Manager would chair, and be supported by, a standing DNI-level Target Development Board that would include experts from key "customers" and from each major collection agency, who could keep the Mission Manager informed of its agency's capabilities (and limitations) against the target. This approach would ensure that the target development process was both integrated and user-driven.

We also recommend that the target development process be supported by an integrated "collection enterprise": that is, a collection process that is coordinated and integrated at all stages, from collection management to data exploitation to strategic investment.

## Facilitate Information Sharing

No shortcoming of the Intelligence Community has received more attention since the September attacks than the failure to share information. There have been literally dozens of Intelligence Community initiatives in this area, with advances most apparent in the area of counterterrorism. Unfortunately, almost all of these efforts have worked around the most intractable and difficult information-sharing impediments, rather than solved them. While minor advances have been made in some areas, the ultimate objective of developing a Community-wide space for sharing intelligence information has proven elusive. In our view, the fundamental reason for the lack of success is the absence of empowered, coherent, and determined Community leadership and management.

We strongly recommend that the new DNI tackle this problem early on by overhauling the Community's information management system, including as a central component the creation of a single office responsible both for information management and information security. We also suggest that the DNI begin with a painless, but symbolically important, first step: namely, to jettison the very phrase "information sharing." To say that we must encourage agencies to "share" information implies that they have some ownership stake in it—an implication based on a fundamental (and, unfortunately, all too common) misunderstanding of individual collection agencies' obligations to the Intelligence Community, and to the government more broadly. We believe that the DNI might begin the process of building a shared information space by putting the DNI's imprimatur on a new phrase, perhaps "information access," that indicates that information within the Community is a Community asset—not the property of a particular agency. Our information sharing recommendations begin from this premise.

## *Create Real "Jointness" and Build a Modern Workforce*

Perhaps the most effective authorities the intelligence reform act grants the DNI are those pertaining to personnel. These new authorities come none too soon, as it is becoming increasingly apparent that the Intelligence Community cannot continue to manage its personnel system the way it always has. The Community still attracts large numbers of highly qualified people, but retaining them has become a real challenge. Today's most talented young people change jobs and careers frequently, are famously impatient with bureaucratic and inflexible work environments, and can often earn far more outside the government. The Community's personnel system is ill-suited to hire and retain people with these characteristics; merely getting hired can take over a year, and compensation is too often tied to time-in-grade, rather than demonstrated achievement.

Moreover, at precisely the moment when the Intelligence Community is facing the prospect of recruiting in this very different job market, the average experience level of the people in many elements of the Intelligence Community is declining. It is uncertain whether this is merely a transitory phenomenon, reflecting an ambitious post–9/11 hiring program. The analytical cadre may grow in experience and stabilize over the next few years. In the short term, however, it is clear that the Intelligence Community suffers from an eroding base of institutional wisdom, not to mention a lack of accumulated knowledge and expertise.

These overarching employment trends are, unfortunately, only the tip of the iceberg. Today's Intelligence Community has additional systemic weaknesses with regard to personnel. For example, the Community has had difficulty recruiting individuals with certain critical skill sets; has often failed to encourage the type of "joint" personnel assignments that are necessary to breaking down cultural barriers that exist among agencies; and has proven insufficiently adept at hiring and mainstreaming mid-career "lateral" hires from outside of the Intelligence Community. This section suggests reforms of the human resources system that would help equip the Community to confront these formidable challenges.

*Establish a central Human Resources Authority for the Intelligence Community.* As a threshold matter, the Intelligence Community needs a DNI-level office responsible for analyzing the workforce, developing strategies to ensure that priority intelligence missions are adequately resourced, and creating Community human resources standards and policies to accomplish these objectives. The human resources authority would also establish evaluation standards and metrics programs to assess the intelligence agencies' performance in hiring, retention, and career development.

This office would also have responsibility for developing policies to fill gaps in the Intelligence Community's workforce. Our case studies have highlighted a wide variety of these critical personnel needs. We have found that the Community has difficulty in attracting and retaining people with scientific and technical skills, diverse ethnic and religious backgrounds, management experience, and advanced language capabilities. Similarly, the Community has struggled to develop the mid-career lateral hires that will be increasingly necessary to complement a workforce that can no longer expect to depend on Intelligence Community "lifers." This authority would have responsibility for developing the Community personnel policies that can overcome these systemic shortcomings.

*Direct a personnel rotation system that develops "joint" professionals in the senior ranks of the Intelligence Community. Much has been made of the need to develop "jointness" in the Intelligence Community.* Study after study has cited the significance of the Goldwater-Nichols Act in transforming the U.S. military from four independent services to a single, unified fighting force. The Goldwater-

Nichols analogy does not apply perfectly to the Intelligence Community; as we discuss below, we do not believe that the Intelligence Community should be reorganized comprehensively around national intelligence "centers" that would serve as the equivalent to the military's joint commands. But we do believe that the personnel reforms of the Goldwater-Nichols Act, which encouraged (and in some instances required) individuals to serve "joint" tours of duty outside of their home services, should be replicated within the Intelligence Community.

We recommend, therefore, that the DNI promptly develop mechanisms to ensure that joint assignments are taken seriously within the Intelligence Community. Today, the Community's agencies vary substantially in the seriousness of their commitment to cross- and interagency assignments. It is insufficient merely to ensure that an Intelligence Community professional who works in an Intelligence Community center or at a different intelligence agency will suffer no punishment upon returning home. Instead, personnel should be affirmatively rewarded for successfully completing joint tours, and intelligence professionals should gain eligibility for promotion to senior levels only if they complete joint assignments. Jointness did not occur effortlessly in the Department of Defense. The DNI will likely find that fostering a truly "joint" culture in the Intelligence Community will require significant and persistent attention.

*Create more uniform performance evaluation and compensation systems.* Personnel systems across the Intelligence Community are in flux, with some agencies moving to new merit-based pay systems and others retaining but modifying the traditional federal General Schedule (GS) system. These differences have the effect of inhibiting the cross-agency movement of personnel that is so critical to building an integrated Intelligence Community. To avoid this problem, we recommend that the Intelligence Community's human resources authority adopt a common personnel performance evaluation and compensation plan. This plan would define core Community competencies and set evaluation criteria (for the entire workforce as well as for key segments, such as analysts), and establish a standard pay grade and compensation structure— while retaining the flexibility to allow agencies to evaluate performance factors unique to their organizations. We further recommend that such a unified compensation structure be based on a merit-based model. A merit-based approach is being used increasingly across the federal workforce, and more rationally links performance to organizational goals and strategies.

We also believe that this review of the compensation structure should focus in particular on ways for the Intelligence Community to recruit talented individuals from *outside* the government. Today, the Intelligence Community can promise the following to talented scientists, scholars, or businesspersons who wish to serve: a lengthy clearance process before they begin, a large pay and benefits cut, a work environment that has difficulty understanding or using the talents of outsiders, and ethics rules that significantly handcuff them from using their expertise when they seek to return to their chosen professions. It should come as little surprise that too few talented people from the private sector take the offer. The DNI should develop special hiring rules aimed at attracting such individuals, including special salary levels and benefits packages and streamlined clearance processes.

*Develop a stronger incentive structure within the Intelligence Community.* In addition to encouraging greater use of financial incentives, we recommend that the Community consider new techniques to motivate positive performance. A real "Intelligence Community" would reward and encourage types of behaviors that currently are not emphasized. These behaviors—a commitment to sharing information, a willingness to take risk, enthusiasm for collaborating with intelligence professionals at other agencies, and a sense of loyalty to the Intelligence Community's missions— must be reinforced if they are to become institutionalized. Government entities are severely limited in the monetary rewards they can offer to reinforce desired behavior, but there are other rewards that can serve as suitable alternatives. Advanced education and training, professional familiarization tours, coveted assignments, and opportunities to attend conferences and symposia are all rewards that might be associated with reinforcing new behaviors.

But it is not enough merely to encourage the right kinds of behavior; it is also critical that the Intelligence Community does not reward its employees for the wrong reasons. Our review found that agencies within the Intelligence Community often made personnel decisions based upon the wrong criteria. For instance, as discussed in our Iraq case study, agencies that collect human intelligence place considerable value on the number of sources they recruit—an incentive system that of course encourages its employees to recruit easier, less important sources rather than taking the time (and the risk) to develop the harder ones. A similar problem exists in the analytical community, where we were told that analysts are disproportionately rewarded for producing "current intelligence" assessments, such as articles that appear in the President's Daily Brief. If we are to expect our human intelligence collectors to take risks and our intelligence analysts to devote time to long-term, strategic thinking, agencies must have a personnel evaluation system that does not punish them for these behaviors.

*Establish a National Intelligence University.* The Intelligence Community has a number of well-founded and successful training programs. Individual organizations within the Community conduct various discipline-specific training programs. Yet there is no initial training provided to all incoming Intelligence Community personnel that instills a sense of community and shared mission— as occurs, for example, in all of the military services. Nor is there an adequate management training program —a fact that may have contributed to declining numbers in the Intelligence Community's mid-level management corps, and the low performance evaluations that this corps recently received in one major intelligence agency.

A National Intelligence University (NIU) could fill these gaps by providing Community training and education programs, setting curriculum standards, and facilitating the sharing of the Community's training resources. A progressive and structured curriculum—from entry level job-skills training to advanced education—could link to career-advancement standards for various Intelligence Community occupations and permit intelligence professionals to build skills methodically as they advance in their responsibilities. The NIU could also serve as a research center for innovative intelligence tools and a test bed for their implementation across the Intelligence Community. The development of such a university—which could be built easily and at modest expense on top of existing Intelligence Community training infrastructure—would be a relatively easy and cost-effective way to develop improved Community integration and professionalism.

## Develop New Mechanisms for Spurring Innovation

While human intelligence has always been the most romanticized of the collection disciplines, technology has driven the course of intelligence over the past century. Advanced technology and its creative application remain a comparative advantage for the United States, but we fear that the Intelligence Community is not adequately leveraging this advantage. Elements of the Intelligence Community continue to perform remarkable technical feats, but across many dimensions, Intelligence Community technology is no longer on the cutting edge. And this problem affects not only intelligence collection; we also lag in the use of technologies to support analysis. This trend may result from a recent decline in the Intelligence Community's commitment to scientific and technological research and development.

We advise the DNI to take an active role in reversing this trend. To be sure, individual agencies will continue to develop new technologies that will serve their missions. But we recommend that the DNI encourage a parallel commitment to early-stage research and development to ensure that important new technologies that might be neglected by individual collection agencies are explored. Toward this end, we recommend that the Office of the DNI have its own significant pool of research and development money at its disposal.

It is not enough, moreover, merely to develop new technologies; it is also critical to ensure that there are effective processes in place to make sure those new technologies are actually put into practice. Like many large organizations, the Intelligence Community has had difficulty "mainstreaming" new technologies (which are often developed by outside organizations like In-Q-Tel, a private, non-profit entity that identifies and invests in new technologies for the CIA). It also often fails to build programmed funding transitions from research and development to deployment. In order to ensure that new technologies actually reach the users who need them, we recommend that the DNI require the larger agencies within the Intelligence Community to establish mechanisms for integrating new technologies, and develop metrics for evaluating each agency's performance in this regard.

We recommend DNI-level management practices that would encourage the development of new technical collection technologies. But there is more to the problem than that. Research and development leaders within the Intelligence Community have told us that they cannot attract or retain the best and the brightest young scientists and engineers because career paths are unattractive, the Community's research infrastructure is poor, and the environment is too risk averse. We have seen similar shortfalls in technical and scientific expertise among the analytic corps and within the cadre of human intelligence collectors. As has been noted above, we advise the DNI to utilize personnel authorities to ensure that scientific and technical career tracks are adequately developed and rewarded by intelligence agencies.

## A Different Kind of "Center": Developing the National Counter Proliferaton Center

In the preceding section we recommended that the new Director of National Intelligence take several steps aimed at forging a better integrated Intelligence Community. In this section we address whether this objective could be further advanced through the creation of a National Counter Proliferation Center (NCPC). The recent intelligence reform legislation envisions the creation of an NCPC modeled on the newly-created National Counterterrorism Center (NCTC). But the act also gives the President the opportunity to decide not to create the center—or to modify certain characteristics—if the President believes that doing so serves the nation's security.

Although we endorse the idea of creating an NCPC, we believe it should look very different from the NCTC. The distinguishing feature of the NCTC is its hybrid character: the NCTC serves simultaneously as an integrated center for counterterrorism intelligence *analysis* and as a driver and coordinator of national interagency counterterrorism *policy* (the new intelligence legislation describes this latter responsibility, in rather confusing fashion, as "strategic operational planning"). As a result of these two roles, the Director of the NCTC has a dual-reporting relationship; he reports to the DNI on terrorism intelligence matters, and reports to the President when wearing his policy coordination hat. While we understand the motivations that may have led to these overlapping intelligence and policy functions in the counterterrorism area, we doubt that it is a good idea to replicate the model—and the mixed reporting relationships it creates—in other substantive areas.

We are also skeptical more generally about the increasingly popular idea of creating a network of "centers" organized around priority national intelligence problems. While we sympathize with the desire for better coordination that animates these proposals, centers also impose costs that often go unappreciated. As our Iraq case study aptly illustrates, centers run the risk of crowding out competitive analysis, creating new substantive "stovepipes" organized around issues, engendering turf wars over where a given center's mission begins and ends, and creating deeply rooted bureaucracies built around what may be temporary intelligence priorities. In most instances we believe that there are more flexible institutional solutions than centers, such as the national Mission Managers we propose.

So, while we recommend the creation of a National Counter Proliferation Center, the center we envision would differ substantially from both the NCTC and from the large analytical centers that some have suggested might serve as organizing units for the Intelligence Community. The NCPC we propose would serve as the DNI's Mission Manager on counterproliferation issues: it would not conduct analysis itself, but would instead be responsible for *coordinating* analysis and collection on nuclear, biological, and chemical weapons across the Intelligence Community. As such, it would be much smaller than the NCTC (it would likely require a staff of no more than 100 people) and would not perform a policy planning function. Specifically, the Director of the NCPC would:

*Develop strategies for collecting intelligence on the proliferation of nuclear, biological, and chemical weapons (and their delivery vehicles).* The Director of the NCPC would manage the target-development process for nuclear, biological, and chemical weapons. Like any Mission Manager, the NCPC would develop multi-disciplinary collection strategies to attack hard targets, and would review the performance of collection agencies in gaining access to these targets. Similarly, it would have full visibility into all compartmented intelligence programs, thus ensuring that relevant capabilities are fully employed by collectors and considered by analysts.

*Coordinate, oversee, and evaluate analytic production.* As already noted—and in contrast to the National Counterterrorism Center—the NCPC would *not* contain a large staff of analysts working on proliferation. Rather, the NCPC would coordinate decentralized analytic efforts occurring at various agencies. This would increase the likelihood of competitive analysis of proliferation issues across the Community. In some cases, the NCPC might determine that no part of the Community is addressing a proliferation-related issue sufficiently and designate a small group of resident NCPC analysts drawn from throughout the Community to work on the issue.

With these analytic oversight responsibilities, the NCPC will fulfill several critical functions, including ensuring that appropriate technical expertise is focused on state weapons programs; that gaps in the Community's knowledge about the relationship between state actors and non-state threats ( *e.g.*, black- and gray-market proliferators such as A.Q. Khan) are addressed; and that the NCTC has access to subject matter expertise on nuclear, biological, and chemical questions. We do not believe that the NCPC should take the lead on the crucial question of the terrorist procurement of unconventional weapons. That responsibility should, in our view, fall to the NCTC. But the Director of the NCPC should support the NCTC and be prepared to step in and appeal to the DNI if this crucial area is receiving insufficient resources and attention.

*Participate in setting the budget associated with nuclear, biological, and chemical weapons.* As the 9/11 Commission correctly noted, true management authority also must include some budget authority. In line with this observation, the NCPC would make recommendations regarding counterproliferation-related budget submissions for National Intelligence Program funds. The NCPC would also support the DNI in fulfilling his statutory responsibilities to "participate" in the development of counterproliferation-related program funds in other military intelligence budgets.

*Support the needs of a Counterproliferation Joint Interagency Task Force, the National Security Council, and other relevant consumers as the Intelligence Community's leader for interdiction-related issues.* Counterproliferation interdiction, in a variety of forms, will remain an important part of combating the spread of nuclear, biological, and chemical weapons. The NCPC would play a vital intelligence support role both in helping to formulate U.S. interdiction strategies and in assisting in individual interdiction operations. The NCPC would also support strategic planning for interdiction efforts pursued by other government entities, including the Departments of Defense, State, Homeland Security, Commerce, and Treasury. Developing plans for and executing interdiction operations using the full capabilities of interagency, private sector, and international partners is a role appropriately played by a new Counterproliferation Joint Interagency Task Force.

As noted above, we do not believe that, in addition to these important responsibilities, the NCPC should also be the focal point for strategic *policy* planning on countering nuclear, biological, and chemical proliferation. The Intelligence Community will inevitably be a major force in any interagency strategic planning process, but we believe it is inadvisable to "double-hat" another intelligence component with what is fundamentally a policy role, or to bifurcate the command structure overseeing it.

Nevertheless, it is self-evident that *someone* should be performing strategic interagency planning on counterproliferation issues. The task of collecting intelligence on biological weapons and other proliferation threats is notoriously difficult; and we cannot reasonably expect intelligence alone will keep us safe. A successful counterproliferation effort will require a coordinated effort across the entire U.S. government, from the Intelligence Community to the Department of Defense to the Department of Commerce to the other agencies involved in this important work. In our more comprehensive later treatment of the counterproliferation challenge, we offer several recommendations on how to build such a sustained interagency coordination process, including the creation of a joint task force for counterproliferation.

## Potential Pitfalls on the Path to Integration

Our recommendations to this point have involved management strategies and organizational structures that could support the DNI's effort to forge an integrated Intelligence Community. In this section, we briefly identify two formidable challenges that may stand in the way of this objective. They both involve potentially problematic *relationships* for the Intelligence Community's leadership: namely, with the FBI and the Department of Defense.

### *Working with the FBI:*
### *Integrating Intelligence at Home and Abroad*

Former Director of Central Intelligence James Woolsey told us that one of the most critical jobs of the new DNI will be to fuse the domestic and foreign intelligence enterprises. This objective can only be achieved if the capabilities of agencies with intelligence responsibilities in the United States, like the FBI, are both strengthened and integrated with the efforts of other intelligence agencies. The FBI has made some significant strides in creating an effective intelligence capability, and we make substantial recommendations that we believe would further strengthen those capabilities.

There may, however, be speed bumps ahead for the DNI in ensuring that the FBI's intelligence resources are managed in the same manner as those within other Intelligence Community agencies. The intelligence reform legislation is ambiguous in the extent to which it brings the FBI's analytical and operational assets into the Intelligence Community and under the DNI's leadership. We advise that this ambiguity be quickly resolved and suggest ways of making the DNI's authority over the FBI comparable to that of other intelligence agencies such as NSA and NGA—subject to, of course, the ongoing involvement of the Attorney General in ensuring the Bureau's compliance with laws designed to protect privacy and civil liberties.

## *Working with the Defense Department: Coordinating the National Intelligence Program with the Secretary of Defense*

The most controversial sections of the intelligence reform act were those relating to the relationship between the DNI and the Secretary of Defense. This is not at all surprising, given the vital importance of effective intelligence support to military operations and the fact that many of the largest components of the Intelligence Community reside in the Department of Defense. These realities create an inherent challenge for any DNI seeking to bring order and coherent management to the Intelligence Community.

Recent events have highlighted the magnitude of this challenge. Over the past few months the Department of Defense has taken several steps to bolster its own internal intelligence capabilities. These have included initiatives to remodel defense intelligence that may enable Combatant Commanders to task and control national collection assets directly; establishing the U.S. Strategic Command (STRATCOM) as the Global Intelligence, Surveillance, and Reconnaissance (ISR) manager for the Defense Department; assigning the DIA as the key intelligence organization to support STRATCOM's ISR mission; and building up the Defense Department's human intelligence capabilities to make the Defense Department less reliant on the CIA's espionage operations.

We believe that several of these Defense Department initiatives are good ones, and should be supported. However, in all instances, we think these efforts need to be closely coordinated with the DNI—and in some cases we believe steps should be taken to ensure that the Defense Department's intelligence efforts do not undermine the new DNI's ability to manage the Intelligence Community. We identify four important issues pertaining to this relationship here: the need to balance support to military operations with other intelligence requirements; the importance of ensuring that the DNI maintains collection authority over national intelligence collection assets; the need to manage Intelligence Community agencies that reside in the Department of Defense; and the importance of coordinating Defense Department and CIA human intelligence operations.

*Balancing support to military operations with other intelligence needs.* Balancing the high priority, and often competing, demands on the U.S. Intelligence Community resources will be a significant challenge. The DNI will need to develop processes for serving the military's requirements while preserving the ability to fulfill other national needs. Toward this end, we recommend the creation of a high level position within the Office of the DNI dedicated to military support. This individual would function as the principal military intelligence advisor to the DNI, serve as the Mission Manager for military support issues, and advise the DNI on issues of Defense Department-Intelligence Community coordination.

*Ensuring that the DNI maintains authority over the tasking of national intelligence collection assets.* If the Director of National Intelligence is to have any ability to build an integrated Intelligence Community, the DNI must be able effectively to manage national intelligence collection capabilities. To achieve this goal, we believe the Defense Department's requirements for national collection assets should be funneled through, not around, the DNI's integrated collection enterprise. In this process, the Defense Department's requirements for national intelligence collection in support of military operations will be represented by the DNI's principal military advisor. This individual will work closely with STRATCOM and the Combatant Commanders to ensure their needs for national intelligence support are met, and will lead the Target Development Board responsible for creating integrated collection strategies in response to U.S. military requirements. This process maintains the DNI's authority to manage national intelligence collection assets and increases the DNI's ability to effectively meet both the military's requirements and other national intelligence needs.

*Developing clear procedures for the management of Defense Department agencies within the Intelligence Community.* Many of the Intelligence Community's largest agencies reside within the Department of Defense. The new intelligence legislation's push towards unified intelligence management will further complicate the lives of the heads of these agencies, who will be uncertain whether they should answer to the Secretary of Defense or to the DNI. While some ambiguity is inevitable, there are certain steps that the DNI and the Secretary of Defense could take to add clarity in this area, including developing a joint charter that specifies each agency's reporting chain and operating authorities, and combining and coordinating management evaluations and audits to avoid needless and unproductive duplication of management oversight activities.

It is also critical that the DNI and the Secretary of Defense establish effective and coordinated protocols for exercising their acquisition authorities. As we have noted, the new legislation requires the DNI to share Milestone Decision Authority with the Secretary of Defense on all "Department of Defense programs" in the national intelligence budget. This important provision is also among the statute's more ambiguous ones, as the term "Department of Defense program" is undefined. As the success of these shared acquisition authorities is crucial to the fielding of future capabilities, we believe that the President should require the Secretary of Defense and the DNI to submit, within 90 days of the DNI's confirmation, their procedures for exercising shared Milestone Decision Authority, and a list of those acquisition programs they deem to be "Defense Department programs" under the legislation.

*Coordinating Special Operations Command and CIA activities.* The war on terrorism, and U.S. Special Operations Command's expanded role as the Defense Department's operational lead, have dramatically increased military intelligence interactions around the world. While the Defense Department has an organic human intelligence capability, the Department must closely coordinate its operations with the DNI to ensure deconfliction of operations and unity of purpose. We recommend that the DNI and the Secretary of Defense, as part of their obligation to report to Congress within 180 days on joint procedures for operational coordination between the Defense Department and CIA, address this specific issue of deconfliction with U.S. Special Operations Command.

## Another Potential Pitfall:
## Legal Myths in the Intelligence Community

Throughout our work we came across Intelligence Community leaders, operators, and analysts who claimed that they couldn't do their jobs because of a "legal issue." These "legal issues" arose in a variety of contexts, ranging from the Intelligence Community's dealings with U.S. persons to the legality of certain covert actions. And although there are, of course, very real (and necessary) legal restrictions on the Intelligence Community, quite often the cited legal impediments ended up being either myths that overcautious lawyers had never debunked or policy choices swathed in pseudo-legal justifications. Needless to say, such confusion about what the law actually requires can seriously hinder the Intelligence Community's ability to be proactive and innovative. Moreover, over time, it can breed uncertainty about *real* legal prohibitions.

We believe this problem is the result of several factors, but for present purposes we note two. First, in the past there has not been a sizable legal staff that focused on Community issues. As a result, many Community problems were addressed through *ad hoc* , interagency task forces that tended to gravitate toward lowest common denominator solutions that were based on consensus and allowed action to be stalled by the doubts of the most cautious legal shop. Second, many rules and regulations governing the Intelligence Community have existed for decades with little thought given to the legal basis for the rules, or whether circumstances have changed the rules' applicability. Under such circumstances, it is unsurprising that legal "myths" have evolved.

The recent creation of a DNI General Counsel's office will increase the probability that Community legal issues are addressed more seriously. But the existence of the office alone does not guarantee an ongoing and systematic examination of the rules and regulations that govern the Intelligence Community. We therefore recommend that the DNI General Counsel establish an internal office consisting of a small group of lawyers expressly charged with taking a forward-leaning look at legal issues that affect the Intelligence Community as a whole. By creating such an office, the DNI will help ensure that the Intelligence Community is fully able to confront the many real—and imaginary—legal issues that will arise.

# Sustained Oversight from the Outside and Improved Self-Examination from Within: Making Sure Reform Happens

Many—perhaps most—of the recommendations contained in this report have been made before. That we find ourselves proposing several sensible changes that former Secretary of Defense and Director of Central Intelligence James Schlesinger endorsed in 1971 suggests to us either that the Intelligence Community is inherently resistant to outside recommendations, or that it does not have the institutional capacity to implement them. In either case, we are left with the distinct impression that meaningful intelligence reform proposals are only likely to become reality if the Intelligence Community receives sustained, senior level attention from knowledgeable outside observers. Today the Community receives only episodic oversight from the President's Foreign Intelligence Advisory Board (PFIAB), Congress, and a thinly-stretched National Security Council. We recommend several changes to improve this state of affairs.

We recommend that the Joint Intelligence Community Council (JICC) serve as a "customer council" for the Intelligence Community. The JICC, which was created by the recent legislation, consists of the heads of each department that has a component in the Intelligence Community. Chaired by the DNI, the JICC will include the Secretaries of State, Treasury, Defense, Energy, and Homeland Security, the Attorney General, and other officers designated by the President. Although not a perfectly representative group of consumers, the JICC should provide the DNI with valuable feedback on intelligence products. We do not think, however, that the JICC is the appropriate body to perform more sustained oversight of the Intelligence Community. Since the DNI chairs the JICC, and the members of the JICC are heads of departments containing intelligence components, the body would have a "conflict of interest" that would impair its ability to play an independent oversight role.

We recommend that the President's Foreign Intelligence Advisory Board assume a more vigorous role with respect to the Intelligence Community. The PFIAB as it is currently constituted, however, is insufficiently equipped to accomplish this task. In addition to the seasoned national security policy experts now on the Board, a reinvigorated PFIAB would need more technical specialists able to assess Intelligence Community performance, as well as a larger staff to support the review and investigation tasks inherent in meaningful oversight. Such a PFIAB is not impossible to conceive, for it has existed in the past—as it should in the future.

As a commission established by the President, we tread onto the terrain of congressional reform with some trepidation. The new intelligence legislation, however, contains a provision requiring the delivery of our report to Congress. As a result, we believe that it would not be inappropriate for us to make suggestions for reform in this area that the President could, in turn, recommend that the Congress implement.

The 9/11 Commission concluded in its final report that the Congressional intelligence committees "lack the power, influence, and sustained capability" necessary to fulfill their critical oversight responsibilities. The 9/11 Commission offered two alternatives for overhauling the intelligence committees: (1) creating a bicameral committee, modeled on the Joint Atomic Energy Committee; or (2) combining intelligence authorization and appropriation authorities into a single committee in each chamber. The House and Senate have not adopted either of these options. While we echo the 9/11 Commission's support for these proposals, we also recommend a number of more modest suggestions for improving Congressional oversight of intelligence.

*Limit the activities of new intelligence oversight subcommittees to strategic oversight.* Both the House and the Senate intelligence committees have indicated their intention to establish oversight subcommittees. But these subcommittees will not improve intelligence if they simply demand additional testimony from top intelligence officials on the crisis or scandal of the day. We suggest that, if created, the oversight subcommittees limit their activities to "strategic oversight," meaning they would set an agenda at the start of the year or session of Congress, based on top priorities such as information sharing, and stick to that agenda.

*Adjust term limits.* The Senate has voted to remove term limits for the Senate Select Committee on Intelligence. While the House may consider this too large a step, it could consider alternatives that would ensure the survival of institutional memory while also bringing in "new blood" and providing more members with exposure to intelligence issues. For example, the House could lengthen or even eliminate the term limits for some of the committee slots rather than for all of the slots. We suggest making the House leadership's authority to waive term limits explicit in the rules, and specifying that some positions on the intelligence committee would be free of term limits.

*Reduce the Intelligence Community's reliance upon supplemental funding.* There were good reasons for supplemental funding requests following the September 11 attacks. But for fiscal year 2005, nearly two-thirds of the key operational needs for counterterrorism were not included in the President's budget, and instead were put in a supplemental budget request later in the year. This reduces the Intelligence Community's ability to plan operations and build programs. Instead of continuing to rely on large supplemental appropriations, we recommend that Congress and the President develop annual budgets that include the Intelligence Community's needs for the entire year and better allow planning for future years.

*Adjust budget jurisdiction.* Currently, the House and Senate oversight committees have different jurisdictions over the various components of the intelligence budget. Both committees have jurisdiction over the National Intelligence Program (NIP). The House intelligence committee also shares jurisdiction with the Armed Services Committee over the Joint Military Intelligence Program (JMIP) and Tactical Intelligence and Related Activities (TIARA) budgets. The Senate intelligence committee has no jurisdiction over JMIP or TIARA, although it provides advice to the Armed Services Committee on both budgets. This complicates conferences on the intelligence authorization bill and reduces intelligence committee input into the JMIP and TIARA budgets. We recommend broadening the Senate intelligence committee's jurisdiction to include JMIP and TIARA in order to integrate intelligence oversight from the tactical through to the national level.

*Allocate the intelligence budget by mission, rather than only by program or activity.* The DNI can also take steps to streamline and professionalize the intelligence oversight process. One impediment to Congressional evaluation of the intelligence budget is the way the budget is presented. Because line items track specific technologies or programs rather than mission areas, it is nearly impossible for Congress—or the Executive Branch—to evaluate how much money is being spent on priority targets such as terrorism or proliferation. We recommend that the DNI restructure the budget by mission areas, thus permitting greater transparency throughout the budget cycle. This mission-centered budget would permit the individual Community elements to track their expenditures by mission throughout the year, affording the DNI greater flexibility in managing the Community, and the Executive Branch and Congress an increased ability to provide effective oversight.

*Deter unauthorized disclosures.* More substantive Congressional oversight must be accompanied by a strengthened commitment to protect sensitive information from unauthorized disclosure. The Congress has rules to protect sensitive information and a process for investigating and penalizing those who violate those rules. In some instances, however, unauthorized disclosures have either been ignored or treated lightly. The Senate and House leadership should place greater emphasis on ensuring that all members understand the need to carefully protect sensitive information and the penalties for unauthorized disclosures. For example, the leadership could make clear that all unauthorized disclosures of classified information will be referred to the ethics committees. Furthermore, both Senate and House members who are read into sensitive compartments should follow the same nondisclosure procedures applicable to the Executive Branch.

*Improve committee mechanisms to encourage bipartisanship.* Partisan politics should never be allowed to threaten national security. To foster bipartisanship, we recommend that the House intelligence committee consider adopting provisions similar to those in the Senate, such as designating the ranking member as the Vice Chairman of the committee, requiring that the majority maintain no more than a one-member advantage in membership, and ensuring that the rules provide the majority and minority leaders with equal access to committee information. The committees could also take concrete steps to reinforce close, cooperative relationships among the entire staff. For example, regular joint staff meetings could be encouraged or even required. Perhaps most importantly, the staff should consist of national security professionals focused on the objectives and priorities of the committee.

*Encourage more informal discussions and collaboration between the Intelligence Community and its congressional overseers.* The Intelligence Community typically interacts with Congress in formal ways, through briefings to the intelligence committees and formal testimony. However, there also have been occasional "off sites" at which senior lawmakers and Intelligence Community leaders have met in a more informal and less adversarial setting. Both sides have stressed the value of these informal sessions, both in fostering cordial cross-branch relationships and in increasing bipartisanship among lawmakers. We encourage the expanded use of these and other informal collaborative efforts.

*Consider an intelligence appropriations subcommittee.* While the intelligence authorizing committees are well-staffed and completely focused on the Intelligence Community, the intelligence appropriations are simply a small part of the Defense and other appropriators' jurisdiction, so staffing and attention to intelligence issues are in short supply on the appropriations committees. The resulting mismatch reduces oversight and coordination of policy within Congress. While we recognize the difficulties, we suggest that serious consideration be given to the establishment of an appropriations subcommittee focused exclusively on the intelligence budget.

*Look for ways to reduce the cost of oversight in the Intelligence Community.* With so many congressional committees with jurisdiction over aspects of foreign and domestic intelligence, the oversight process—between staff requests, formal testimony, congressionally directed actions, and budget reviews—imposes great demands on the resources of the Intelligence Community. Intelligence Community professionals collectively appear before Congress in briefings or hearings over a thousand times a year, and also respond to hundreds of formal written requests from Congress annually—and the latter number will only increase in light of the recent intelligence reform legislation, which itself added 27 one-time and 16 annual reports to the DNI's annual congressional reporting requirements. While we recognize that congressional oversight inherently has costs, we encourage the Congress to look for ways to streamline their interactions with the Intelligence Community.

As important as executive and legislative oversight is, they will never be a substitute for an Intelligence Community that takes self-evaluation seriously. But the Intelligence Community has done far too little to institutionalize "lessons learned" studies and other after-action evaluations that are commonplace in the Department of Defense and other government agencies. Of course, when human resources are stretched thin, the idea of devoting good personnel to examine the past often seems a luxury that intelligence agencies cannot afford.

Understandable as it is, this view must be resisted. Over the long run, an organization with sound "lessons learned" processes will be more efficient and productive—even if those processes seem to be distracting good people and resources from the imperatives of the moment. We recommend that the DNI develop institutionalized processes for performing "lessons learned" studies and for reviewing the Intelligence Community's own capabilities, rather than waiting for commissions like ours to do the job. We offer a recommendation in this regard that is specific to analysis— but this is a problem that affects all areas of intelligence. While we think it advisable that organizations devoted to self-evaluation exist in all major intelligence agencies, the DNI must drive an independent "lessons learned" process as well—for it is the DNI who will have insight into shortcomings and failures that cut across the intelligence process. We also note that whatever entities at the DNI or agency level assume these after-action responsibilities— be they agency inspectors general or other offices—they should not conduct these reviews to justify disciplinary or other personnel action, but rather to identify shortcomings and successes and to propose improvements to aspects of the intelligence process.

## Conclusion

The creation of an integrated Intelligence Community will not happen merely by improving activities within different agencies, and it will most certainly not happen spontaneously. It will take assertive leadership by the new DNI, vigorous support from senior policymakers and Congress, and sustained oversight from outside the Intelligence Community. Provided all that, and substantial time, a Community that has resisted management reform—and often management of any sort—can emerge better configured to deal with the pressing challenges of the new century.

## Addendum: The Office of the Director of National Intelligence

In our discussion of management issues the DNI will confront, we have tried to eschew the "boxology" that often dominates discussions of government reform. While it is obviously important to consider what staff functions will be performed in the Office of the DNI, precise organizational questions about the structure of the office—such as, for instance, the number of deputies the DNI should have and their responsibilities—are questions to which there is no "right answer." Nonetheless, when considering the tasks that will need to be performed in the office of the DNI, we necessarily had to consider how the office might be organized to perform these functions. We offer here the result of these considerations, but we emphasize that the model we propose is a notional one that we offer only to facilitate further discussion.

The new legislation creates a number of positions in the Office of the Director of National Intelligence. The statute creates a Senate-confirmed principal deputy to the DNI, and empowers the DNI to appoint up to four deputy directors. In addition, the statute also states that the Office of the DNI shall contain a General Counsel, a Director of Science and Technology, a National Counterintelligence Executive, a Civil Liberties Protection Officer, and the National Intelligence Council. Finally, the legislation provides that the Office of the DNI *may* include "[s]uch other offices and officials as may be established by law or the Director may establish or designate in the office," including "national intelligence centers." Of these various mandated and discretionary offices, only one—the Civil Liberties Protection Officer—is required by the act to "report directly to" the DNI; in our view, the remainder can therefore report to the Director through one of the four Deputy DNIs (DDNI) permitted under the legislation.

The notional model described below—and depicted on the wiring chart at the end of this chapter—is structured around four Deputy Directors: a Deputy Director for Integrated Intelligence Strategies; a Deputy Director for Collection; a Deputy Director for Plans, Programs, Budgets, and Evaluation; and the Chief Information Management Officer. We also suggest the creation of two additional positions: an Assistant DNI for Support to Military Operations, and an Assistant DNI for Human Resources. The section that follows briefly describes the responsibilities of each of these subordinate offices.

## *Deputy DNI for Integrated Intelligence Strategies*

We have stressed the need for ensuring that the Intelligence

Community's management structure be focused on missions, and propose the creation of Mission Managers to ensure that intelligence collection is driven by the needs of analysts, policymakers, and other intelligence "customers." In our proposed organizational structure for the Office of the DNI, Mission Managers would be housed in the office of a Deputy DNI for "Integrated Intelligence Strategies." This office would also perform the following functions (often through the Mission Managers):

*Mission Manager coordination, support, and oversight.* The Deputy Director for Integrated Intelligence Strategies would advise the DNI on the intelligence subjects that require Mission Managers, and develop processes for the periodic review of those subjects to ensure that new priority intelligence topics are not missed. He or she would also oversee the Mission Managers and resolve disputes among them in those (we expect rare) situations where they disagree among each other over the prioritization of intelligence requirements.

*Customer support.* Mission managers will be the primary interface for customer support on their substantive topics, but the DDNI for Integrated Intelligence Strategies would establish procedures to improve customer support across the Intelligence Community and assess new ways to improve the ways in which policymakers and other users receive intelligence support.

*Analytical oversight.* The office of the Deputy Director for Integrated Intelligence Strategies would be responsible for overseeing the analytical community (often through Mission Managers), reaching out to subject-matter experts outside of the Intelligence Community (and developing procedures and processes for analysts throughout the Community to do the same), and encouraging the development and mainstreaming of new analytical tools.

*Current intelligence support to the DNI.* In fulfilling his role as principal intelligence advisor to the President, the DNI will require a support staff. This staff would be housed in the Office of the Deputy Director for Integrated Intelligence Strategies, who would serve as the DNI's principal intelligence expert.

## Deputy DNI for Collection

We emphasize the need for Community-level leadership of vital collection functions that today are not centrally managed. We would create a Deputy DNI for Collection to perform this role. One of this official's most important functions would be to oversee the customer-driven collection requirements process managed by the Mission Managers and their Target Development Boards. The Mission Managers should provide the needed analytic input directly to collection agencies, but there must be a mechanism to ensure that intelligence collectors are responding to those requirements. The Deputy DNI for Collection would also perform the following functions:

*Strategic oversight of collection.* The Office of the Deputy Director for Collection would monitor the performance of collection agencies in responding to all customer needs, including, most importantly, the requirements developed by Mission Managers and Target Development Boards and those that ensure that U.S. military commanders and forces are also appropriately supported. It would also oversee the development of the "integrated collection enterprise" we recommend.

*Development of new collection sources and methods.* When collection requirements cannot be met because of insufficient capabilities, this office would spur the development of new sources and methods to overcome the capability gap. This office would play an especially important role in sponsoring those new capabilities whose interoperability across collection agencies is critical to Community collaboration. Efforts to identify new capabilities will include outreach to U.S. government laboratories, industry, and academia, as appropriate.

*Strategic investment for Community collection.* When collection requirements cannot be met because of insufficient capability, and new technologies and systems are required, the Deputy DNI for Collection would advocate innovative science and technology for collection applications, and would ensure such capability requirements are addressed in the development of the National Intelligence Program (NIP) budget, and in the DNI's inputs to the Joint Military Intelligence Program (JMIP) and Tactical Intelligence and Related Activities (TIARA) budgets.

## Deputy DNI for Plans, Programs, Budgets, and Evaluation

As we have noted, the DNI's primary leverage will come not through "line" control of Intelligence Community agencies, but rather from his budgetary authorities. We would establish a Deputy DNI for Plans, Programs, Budgets, and Evaluation (PPBE) to ensure that this authority is exercised promptly and completely. The Deputy DNI for PPBE's most significant functional responsibilities would include:

*Plans and policy.* The DNI is responsible for developing and presenting the NIP budget and for participating in the development of the JMIP and TIARA budgets. To develop a rational investment balance to meet customer needs, the DNI will have to evaluate the capabilities of the Community, develop options for resource allocations, and propose specific programs submitted for inclusion in the NIP.

*Comptroller.* As a financial manager, the DNI is responsible for executing the NIP and reprogramming funds within limits established in the new legislation. In performing these duties, the DNI will require a staff element to fill these comptroller functions.

*Acquisition.* The reform legislation makes the DNI the Milestone Decision Authority for major acquisition systems funded in whole within the NIP and assigns the DNI responsibility to procure information technology systems for the Intelligence Community. Through the Deputy DNI for PPBE, the DNI would set acquisition policy, provide acquisition oversight, and act as program manager for all Community systems whose interoperability is essential to Community effectiveness. As we have noted, for the major systems over which the DNI and the Secretary of Defense share acquisition authority, joint procedures must be established with the Defense Department.

*Program evaluation.* The Deputy DNI for PPBE would be responsible for analyzing and evaluating plans, programs, and budgets in relation to Community objectives and requirements, and for ensuring that costs of Community programs are presented accurately and completely.

## Chief Information Management Officer

One of our major information sharing recommendations is that the DNI appoint a chief information management officer (CIMO) who would manage the information sharing environment for the Intelligence Community. Given the importance of the development of such an environment, we would make the CIMO one of the DNI's Deputies. We detail the CIMO's responsibilities in another chapter, but we emphasize here that this individual would be responsible both for information *sharing* and information *security* across the Intelligence Community. As the attached organizational chart suggests, we would have the CIMO supported by three separate component offices dedicated to information sharing, information security and protection of sources and methods, and risk management.

## Assistant DNI for Support to Military Operations

The Director of Central Intelligence (DCI) currently has an Associate DCI for Military Support—a position created in the wake of Operation Desert Storm to provide a high level military representative on the DCI's staff whose mission was to improve the Intelligence Community's support to military operations. Incumbents in this position have been three-star officers, normally with a combat-arms background. As we have noted in our management discussion, in the wake of the intelligence reform legislation the relationship between the DNI and the Secretary of Defense will assume great significance. Accordingly, we would suggest that a similar—and strengthened—military support position be created in the Office of the DNI who would act as principal advisor to the DNI on military support issues, serve as Mission Manager for intelligence support to military operations, and assist the DNI in developing joint strategies and coordination procedures between the DNI and the Secretary of Defense.

## *Assistant DNI for Human Resources*

The intelligence legislation provides the DNI with substantial personnel authorities, and we recommend earlier in this chapter that a DNI-level Human Resources Authority be established to develop and implement appropriate personnel policies and procedures for the Intelligence Community. We would propose that an Assistant DNI for Human Resources oversee this Human Resources Authority, and oversee the substantial changes in recruiting, training, and personnel policy that we believe are necessary. The Assistant DNI for Human Resources would also oversee the National Intelligence University that we recommend in this chapter.

# Counterintelligence

## Summary & Recommendations

Even as our adversaries—and many of our "friends"—ramp up their intelligence activities against the United States, our counterintelligence efforts remain fractured, myopic, and marginally effective. Our counterintelligence philosophy and practices need dramatic change, starting with centralizing counterintelligence leadership, bringing order to bureaucratic disarray, and taking our counterintelligence fight overseas to adversaries currently safe from scrutiny.

We recommend that:

- The National Counterintelligence Executive (NCIX)—the statutory head of the U.S. counterintelligence community— become the DNI's Mission Manager for counterintelligence, providing strategic direction for the full breadth of counterintelligence activities across the government. In this role, the NCIX should also focus on increasing *technical* counterintelligence efforts across the Intelligence Community;

- The CIA create a new capability dedicated to conducting a full range of counterintelligence activities outside the United States;

- The Department of Defense's Counterintelligence Field Activity assume operational and investigative authority to coordinate and conduct counterintelligence activities throughout the Defense Department; and

- The FBI create a National Security Service that includes the Bureau's Counterintelligence Division, Counterterrorism Division, and the Directorate of Intelligence. A single Executive Assistant Director would lead the service subject to the coordination and budget authorities of the DNI.

# Introduction

Enthusiasm for spying on the United States has not waned since the Cold War. Quite the reverse. The United States is almost certainly one of the top intelligence priorities for practically every government on the planet. Faced with overwhelming American military and economic might, our adversaries increasingly rely on intelligence to gain comparative advantage. A wide range of intelligence activities are used to attack systematically U.S. national security interests worldwide. Yet while our enemies are executing what amounts to a global intelligence war against the United States, we have failed to meet the challenge. U.S. counterintelligence efforts have remained fractured, myopic, and only marginally effective.

Today, we mostly wait for foreign intelligence officers to appear on our doorstep before we even take notice. The lion's share of our counterintelligence resources are expended inside the United States despite the fact that our adversaries target U.S. interests globally. Needless to say, the result is that we are extremely vulnerable outside of our borders.

The losses the United States has sustained within its borders are formidable as well. Spies such as Walker, Ames, Hanssen, and Montes have significantly weakened our intelligence and defense capabilities. Hanssen alone compromised U.S. government secrets whose cost to the nation was in the billions of dollars, not to mention the lives of numerous human sources. Our adversaries have penetrated U.S. intelligence agencies (by recruiting spies) and operations (by running double agents). The theft of some our most sensitive military and technological secrets allows states like China and Russia to reap the benefits of our research and development investments. And while our defense is lacking, our current counterintelligence posture also results in the loss of offensive opportunities to manipulate foreign intelligence activities to our strategic advantage.

Moreover, while stealing our secrets, our adversaries also learn *how* we spy, and how best to counter our efforts in the future, which in turn renders our remaining sources and methods even less effective and more liable to compromise and loss—a cycle of defeat that cannot be indefinitely sustained. As former Director of

Central Intelligence Richard Helms once said, "No intelligence service can be more effective than its counterintelligence component for very long."

We believe that U.S. counterintelligence has been plagued by a lack of policy attention and national leadership. We hope this is now coming to a close with the signing of the first national counterintelligence strategy, approved by the President on March 1, 2005. The National Counterintelligence Executive (NCIX)—the statutory head of the U.S. counterintelligence community—has characterized the new offensive counterintelligence strategy as part of the administration's policy of pre-empting threats to the security of the United States.

But a new strategy alone will not do the job. As in the old—and clearly unsuccessful—approach to homeland security, U.S. counterintelligence is bureaucratically fractured, passive (*i.e.*, focusing on the defense rather than going on the offense), and too often simply ineffective. But unlike homeland security, counterintelligence is still largely neglected by policymakers and the Intelligence Community. In fact, counterintelligence has generally *lost* stature since September 11, eclipsed by more immediate counterterrorism needs. While not denigrating it outright, our top policymakers and Intelligence Community management have traditionally paid lip service to counterintelligence. Until, that is, a major spy case breaks. Even then, bureaucratic defensiveness tends to win out. Senior officials have largely addressed counterintelligence issues *ad hoc*, reacting to specific intelligence losses by replacing them with new technologies or collection methods, without addressing the underlying counterintelligence problems.

We offer four recommendations to improve counterintelligence. First, that the NCIX serve as the planner, manager, and supervisor for all United States counterintelligence efforts. Second, that CIA create a new capability dedicated exclusively to attacking intelligence threats outside the United States—a capability our nation currently does not have. Third, that the Department of Defense's Counterintelligence Field Activity be given operational and investigative authority to execute department-wide counterintelligence activities. Fourth, that the FBI establish a National Security Service that is fully responsive to the DNI.

Counterintelligence efforts across the Intelligence Community must be better executed in support of the foreign intelligence mission. At the heart of our recommendations is the belief that an integrated and directed U.S. counterintelligence effort will take advantage of intelligence collection opportunities; protect billions of dollars of defense and intelligence-related investments, sources, and methods; and defend our country against surprise attack.

# The Counterintelligence Challenge

Spies have always existed, but currently our adversaries—and many of our "friends"—are expanding and intensifying their intelligence activities against U.S. interests worldwide. They target virtually all of our nation's levers of national power—foreign policy and diplomatic strategies, strategic weapon design and capabilities, critical infrastructure components and systems, cutting edge research and technologies, and information and intelligence systems. Our rivals use a range of sophisticated human and technical intelligence techniques, including surveillance, spies, attempts to influence the U.S. media and policymakers, economic espionage, and wholesale technology and trade secret theft . Further, there are indications that foreign intelligence services are clandestinely positioning themselves to attack, exploit, and manipulate critical U.S. information and intelligence systems.

The United States has not sufficiently responded to the scope and scale of the foreign intelligence threat. The number of foreign agents targeting the United States is disturbing—and the majority of them are targeting U.S. interests *outside* the United States. Despite this fact, a very large proportion of U.S. counterintelligence resources are deployed inside the United States—a percentage that has changed very little since the end of the Cold War.

Although we cannot discuss details at this level of classification, suffice it to say that a number of sophisticated intelligence services are aggressively targeting the United States today. These include traditional players such as China and Russia, both of whom deploy official and non-official cover officers to target American interests.

But it is not only major nation states which employ aggressive intelligence services. Terrorist groups like Hizbollah and al-Qa'ida also conduct intelligence operations within the United States. The 9/11 Commission Report, for instance, detailed how the al-Qa'ida hijackers targeted U.S. sites, cased them, and otherwise engaged in classic intelligence activities such as reconnaissance. According to a senior counterintelligence official at CIA, the Agency is only just beginning to understand the intelligence capabilities of terrorist organizations.

Then there are adversaries who attempt to undermine the United States in more subtle ways—through covert influence and perception management efforts. A 1997 Senate investigation found that as many as six individuals with ties to the People's Republic of China sought to channel Chinese money covertly into the 1996 U.S. presidential campaign in order to influence the American political process.

The sum total of these foreign intelligence efforts is striking. During the Cold War, every American national security agency—with the possible exception of the Coast Guard—was penetrated by foreign intelligence services. Moreover, in just the past 20 years CIA, FBI, NSA, DIA, NRO, and the Departments of Defense, State, and Energy have all been penetrated. Secrets stolen include nuclear weapons data, U.S. cryptographic codes and procedures, identification of U.S. intelligence sources and methods (human and technical), and war plans. Indeed, it would be difficult to exaggerate the damage that foreign intelligence penetrations have caused.

## The Status Quo

While our rivals have become ever more imaginative and aggressive, our own counterintelligence services remain fractured and reactive. Each U.S. counterintelligence agency pursues its own mission from its own vantage point, rather than working in concert guided by nationally-derived strategies. Our counterintelligence effort has no national focus, no systematic way to coordinate efforts at home and abroad.

Among United States agencies, the FBI dominates counterintelligence within the homeland. Until recently the Bureau focused its resources and operational efforts on foreign spies working out of formal diplomatic establishments—classic official-cover intelligence. The *covert* foreign intelligence presence was largely unaddressed. Today, despite bolstering its counterintelligence resources in all field offices, the FBI still has little capacity to identify, disrupt, or exploit foreign *covert* intelligence activities.

Outside the United States, the CIA has primary responsibility for counterintelligence, a task which, in practice, it defines very narrowly. CIA does not systematically or programmatically undertake the counterintelligence mission of protecting the equities of other U.S. government entities, nor does it mount significant, strategic offensive counterintelligence operations against rival intelligence services. Its focus is mostly defensive; the CIA's Counterintelligence Center and the counterintelligence elements within the Directorate of Operations aim primarily to protect CIA operations. CIA's current approach to counterintelligence is in contrast to its approach during the Cold War, when CIA case officers routinely targeted Warsaw Pact officials, an effort that led to a considerable number of successful counterespionage investigations.

The Department of Defense, with its component counterintelligence units located within the military services, principally focuses on protecting the armed forces. But no counterintelligence organization has the operational mission for the Department as a whole, leaving large swaths of unprotected areas, including highly sensitive policymaking, technology, and acquisition functions. The current system assigns each of the armed services responsibilities for counterintelligence activities in other agencies that lack their own internal capability. The services, however, do not have the range of capabilities necessary to perform this role. While the Department's Counterintelligence Field Activity (CIFA) has taken steps towards implementing a more comprehensive approach to counterintelligence, CIFA currently does not have adequate authority or resources to take on this Department-wide operational mission.

As if agency-level concerns are not enough, the absence of effective and adequately empowered national counterintelligence leadership makes the situation even worse. The National Counterintelligence Executive (NCIX) is the theoretical "head" of counterintelligence, but NCIX has little control over the scattered elements of U.S. counterintelligence. NCIX has only advisory budget authority, little visibility into individual agencies' counterintelligence operations, and no ability to assign operational responsibility or evaluate performance. The recent intelligence reform act did not alter this situation, but it did take what we believe is a useful step—placing the NCIX in the Office of the DNI.

## Institutionalizing Leadership

Organizational change is not a panacea for counterintelligence, but it is necessary. Today there is no individual or office that can impose Community-wide counterintelligence reform or hold individual agencies accountable for fulfilling national counterintelligence requirements. This should change, and we believe that the obvious candidate for leadership is an empowered NCIX.

The recent intelligence reform legislation situated the NCIX in the Office of the DNI, thereby placing counterintelligence near the Intelligence Community's levers of power. To make this more than window dressing, the NCIX needs all of the DNI's authorities for counterintelligence—particularly authority over the FBI's counterintelligence operations. As the Mission Manager for counterintelligence, the NCIX would build collection plans with prioritized targets and provide strategic direction to operational components. Unlike other Mission Managers, the NCIX would also be responsible for the production of strategic counterintelligence analysis.

To this end, we recommend that the NCIX assume the power and the responsibility to:

* Prepare the National Intelligence Program's counterintelligence budget and approve, oversee, and evaluate how agencies execute that budget;

- Produce national counterintelligence requirements and assign operational responsibilities to agencies for meeting those requirements;

- Evaluate the effectiveness of agencies within the Intelligence Community in meeting national counterintelligence requirements;

- Direct and oversee the integration of counterintelligence tradecraft throughout the Intelligence Community;

- Establish common training and education requirements for counterintelligence officers across the Community, and expand cross-agency training;

- Identify and direct the development and deployment of new and advanced counterintelligence methodologies and technologies;

- Ensure that recommendations emerging from counterintelligence damage assessments are incorporated into agency policies and procedures;

- Deconflict and coordinate operational counterintelligence activities both inside and outside of the United States; and

- Produce *strategic* counterintelligence analysis for policymakers.

These powers would bring the NCIX on par with the other Mission Managers discussed in other chapters.

One area we believe is especially critical for the NCIX to address is the absence of a systematic and integrated technical counterintelligence capability. Historically, counterintelligence has been almost exclusively devoted to countering foreign services' human intelligence efforts. At the same time, other organizations like NSA have focused on protecting the U.S. information infrastructure. We therefore recommend that the NCIX devote particular attention to working with agencies that already devote substantial resources to protection of the information infrastructure, looking beyond traditional "counterintelligence" agencies to NSA, other parts of the Department of Defense, the Department of Homeland Security's Information Analysis and Infrastructure Protection Directorate, and the National Institute of Standards and Technology.

## Inside the Agencies

Primary responsibility for carrying out counterintelligence activities should remain with CIA, FBI, and the Department of Defense. These agencies, however, need to change the way they fulfill their missions. Under stronger NCIX leadership, they must become the core of the U.S. counterintelligence community—a community with common purpose, focus, and unity of effort.

The CIA should expand its current counterintelligence focus beyond the protection of its own operations to conduct a full range of counterintelligence activities outside the United States. This will require that CIA adopt the mission of protecting the equities of other U.S. government agencies overseas and exploiting opportunities for counterintelligence collection.

We recommend that CIA pursue this mission by establishing a new capability that would—along with the Agency's existing Counterintelligence Center—report to the Associate Deputy Director of Operations for Counterintelligence. This new capability would mount counterintelligence activities outside the United States aimed at recruiting foreign sources and conducting activities to deny, deceive, and exploit foreign intelligence targeting of U.S. interests. In short, the goal would be for the counterintelligence element to track foreign intelligence officers *before* they land on U.S. soil or begin targeting U.S. interests abroad. In doing so, the new capability would complement the Agency's existing defensive operations, and would provide the Intelligence Community with a complete overseas counterintelligence capability. And as with all intelligence activity, the CIA's actions—to the extent they involved U.S. persons—would continue to be subject to the Attorney General's guidelines designed to protect civil liberties.

We must stress that our recommendation is not intended to downplay the importance of continuing to protect CIA operations. These counterintelligence activities must continue, and resources currently allocated to asset validation or other operational counterintelligence capabilities should not be diminished. In this vein, we believe that case officers devoted to the new, offensive activity should be "fenced off" so that they cannot be directed to execute other tasks.

While our intelligence foes strategically target our defense infrastructure, the Department of Defense's counterintelligence response remains hardwired to the 1947 framework in which it was created, with each armed service running its own counterintelligence component. In 2002, the Defense Department began to address this deficiency by creating the Counterintelligence Field Activity (CIFA), which has the authority to oversee Department of Defense "implementation support to the NCIX," complete counterintelligence program evaluations, conduct operational analysis, provide threat assessments, conduct counterintelligence training, and "oversee Defense-wide CI investigations."

There is, however, one very significant hole in CIFA's authority: it cannot actually carry out counterintelligence investigations and operations on behalf of the Department of Defense. Rather, Defense-wide investigations and operations are left to the responsibility of the individual services—which are, at the same time, also responsible for investigations and operations *within* their own services. Perhaps unsurprisingly, the result of this arrangement is that intra-service investigations are given priority by the services, and no entity views non-service-specific and department-wide investigations as its primary responsibility. What this means is that many Defense Department components (*e.g.*, Combatant Commands, the Defense Agencies, and the Office of the Secretary of Defense) lack effective counterintelligence protection.

We believe this serious shortcoming would be best addressed by giving CIFA the authority and responsibility to provide Department-wide counterintelligence functional support by conducting investigations, operations, collection, and analysis for the Combatant Commands, Defense Agencies, and the Office of the Secretary of Defense, both inside and outside of the United

States. The counterintelligence elements within each military service would be left in place to focus on their department's counterintelligence requirements. CIFA would acquire new counterespionage and law enforcement authorities to investigate national security matters and crimes including treason, espionage, foreign intelligence service or terrorist-directed sabotage, economic espionage, and violations of the National Information Infrastructure Protection Act. Specific authorization from the Secretary of Defense and a directive from the DNI can implement this change. And, as with the CIA and service elements, all of CIFA's activities that relate to U.S. persons should be performed in accordance with Attorney General-approved guidelines.

Giving CIFA additional operational authorities will make it a stronger organization better able to execute its current management responsibilities. Today the armed services are not constituted to perform the full range of counterintelligence functions that the Department of Defense requires. CIFA will gain greater visibility across the Department and relieve the service counterintelligence components from a responsibility that dilutes resources and effort away from their primary mission—to protect their services from foreign intelligence activities.

With respect to the FBI, we are convinced that a number of significant changes need to take place, largely as part of our recommended creation of a new National Security Service within the Bureau. We address this proposal in detail in Chapter Ten (Intelligence at Home). For current purposes, we merely identify the key reasons why this reform is especially necessary in the counterintelligence field. In our view, bringing the FBI's national security elements under a single Executive Assistant Director responsible to the DNI, and therefore also to the NCIX, would improve the overall effectiveness and strategic direction of FBI counterintelligence and effectively empower analysts to direct collections, investigations, and operations.

## Conclusion

Since the passage of the National Security Act of 1947, counterintelligence has been treated as a kind of second-class citizen in the intelligence profession. The result is that the subject is pushed to the periphery, our adversaries take advantage of our neglect, and American national security suffers. It is all too easy to forget counterintelligence because, other than periodic spy controversies, there is little public sign that we are doing it poorly. But we are. And our adversaries know it. Our recommended changes—centralizing management and planning, expanding our overseas efforts, and integrating and directing the counterintelligence components of the CIA, Department of Defense, and FBI—are long overdue and will help to stanch the hemorrhaging of our secrets and take the fight to our adversaries.

# Covert Action

Most U.S. presidents have made use of covert action as an instrument of foreign policy; under appropriate and limited circumstances, it serves as a more subtle and surgical tool than acknowledged employment of U.S. power and influence. In the future, when the threats of proliferation and terrorism loom large, covert action may play an increasingly important role. The Commission conducted a careful study of U.S. covert action capabilities, with attention to the changing national security landscape and the special category of missions that involve both CIA and U.S. Special Operations Forces. Because even the most general statements about the Intelligence Community's capabilities in this area are classified, the Commission's assessments and four specific findings cannot be discussed in this report. The Commission has, however, incorporated the lessons learned from its study of covert action in all of our recommendations for reform of the Intelligence Community.

# The Changing Proliferation Threat
# and the Intelligence Response

## Summary & Recommendations

The threat of chemical, biological, and nuclear weapons proliferation has transformed over the past two decades. The technical expertise required to produce these weapons has become increasingly widespread, while many of the materials needed to make them are widely available on the open market. Meanwhile, terrorists have expressed a growing demand for these weapons and demonstrated their willingness to use them. The Intelligence Community has not kept pace with these events.

Rather than attempt a top-to-bottom assessment of the chemical, biological, and nuclear weapons threat, here we focus on relatively new aspects of the threat that present specific intelligence challenges, and that—in our view—require additional Intelligence Community reforms beyond those discussed in our other chapters.

We recommend that:

- The DNI take several specific measures aimed at better collaboration between the intelligence and biological science communities;

- The National Counter Proliferation Center develop and ensure the implementation of a comprehensive biological weapons targeting strategy. This entails gaining real-time access to non-traditional information sources; filtering open source data; and devising specific collection initiatives directed at the resulting targets;

- The Intelligence Community, along with other relevant government bodies, support a more effective framework to interdict shipments of chemical, biological, and nuclear proliferation concern; and

- The Intelligence Community better leverage existing legal and regulatory mechanisms to improve collection and analysis on chemical, biological, and nuclear threats.

## Introduction

We live in a world where the most deadly materials created by man are more widely available than ever before. Over the past decade or so, the proliferation of nuclear, biological, and chemical materials, and the expertise to weaponize them, has become a global growth industry.

Grim evidence of this abounds. For instance, the Soviet Union may have been relegated to the dustbin of history, but its nuclear materials—under uncertain control, and sought by rogue states and terrorists alike—still imperil our present. At the same time, terrorists who have already demonstrated their intent to attack us with anthrax seek more advanced biological and nuclear weapons. Perhaps worst of all, the biotechnology revolution is rapidly making new, previously unimagined horrors possible, raising the specter of a modern-day plague, spawned from a back room or garage anywhere in the world.

There is no single strategy the Intelligence Community can pursue to counter the "proliferation" menace. As we discuss in this chapter, any weapon capable of causing mass casualties presents a unique set of challenges. Our study of this subject indicates, however, that there are themes common to all. First, the Intelligence Community's efforts with regard to the spread of nuclear, biological, and chemical weapons have not kept up with the pace of proliferation, and urgently require improvement. We believe that catching up will likely require prioritizing counterproliferation over many other competing national security issues. It will also require more aggressive and innovative collection techniques, and the devotion of resources commensurate to the seriousness of the threat and the difficulty of the collection challenge.

Second, the Intelligence Community must reach outside its own confines to tap counterproliferation information, authorities, and expertise resident in the government and nation at large. The Community cannot expect to thwart proliferators on its own; counterproliferation is a team sport, and our squad must draw on the rest of the U.S. government and the full weight of its regulatory and diplomatic powers, as well as on scientific and technical experts from academia and private enterprise.

We begin our discussion of the proliferation problem by examining these themes within the context of the threat posed by biological weapons. Of all the potentially catastrophic threats facing the United States, those related to biological substances are changing the most quickly, metastasizing in recent years to include a variety of new potential users and substances. Unlike nuclear or chemical weapons, a biological weapon has actually been used to attack the United States, in the form of the anthrax attacks of 2001. In our view, biological weapons are also the mass casualty threat the Intelligence Community is least prepared to face. We therefore have focused on developing recommendations that can immediately improve our capabilities in this area—by bringing into the Community much-needed scientific experience, sharpening collection techniques, and harnessing regulatory authorities to bolster intelligence efforts.

We then survey the threat landscape with regard to nuclear and chemical weapons, and follow this with a series of recommendations designed to improve overall Intelligence Community support to the interdiction of materials of proliferation concern. We close with recommendations that recognize the importance of more generally leveraging legal and regulatory mechanisms to aid in the service of intelligence.

The stakes for the Intelligence Community with regard to all weapons of mass destruction are self-evidently high. It is not hyperbole to suggest that the lives of millions, and the very fabric and fate of our society, may depend on the way in which the Community is configured, and the powers it can bring to bear against the challenges posed by proliferation. Our recommendations do not purport to solve the proliferation problem; no commission can claim to do that. We do hope, however, that the recommendations can help better configure the Community to cope with an increasingly fluid and volatile threat environment.

## Biological Weapons

### Introduction: "The Greatest Intelligence Challenge"

For many years, the U.S. intelligence and policy communities did not take the biological weapons threat as seriously as the dangers posed by nuclear weapons. Many felt that states might experiment with biological weapons, but would not use them against the United States for fear of nuclear retaliation. Similarly, terrorists who promised to bring "plagues" upon the United States were thought to be merely indulging in grandiose threats; they lacked the technical expertise to actually develop and deploy a biological weapon.

These views changed suddenly in September and October of 2001 when anthrax attacks in the United States killed five people, crippled mail delivery in several cities for over a year, and required decontamination efforts costing more than $1 billion. The still-unsolved attack was striking in its asymmetry: the anthrax could have been produced for less than $2,500.

Even more striking is how lucky we were. A determined terrorist group could do far worse with only a little more effort and a bit of luck. Even allowing for imperfect dissemination techniques, if a gram of the same anthrax used in the 2001 attacks had been disseminated outdoors in an urban area, between 100 and 1,000 people would likely have been infected, and many would have died. A kilogram might infect tens of thousands of people. And because biological weapons have a delayed effect, terrorists could execute multiple or campaign-style attacks before the first attack is even noticed and the warning sounded.

We are concerned that terrorist groups may be developing biological weapons and may be willing to use them. Even more worrisome, in the near future, the biotechnology revolution will make even more potent and sophisticated weapons available to small or relatively unsophisticated groups.

In response to this mounting threat, the Intelligence Community's performance has been disappointing. Its analyses of state and non-state biological weapons programs often rest on assumptions unsupported by data. This is in large part because traditional collection methods do not work well, or at all, against biological threats. Even though scientists, academics, and government officials routinely describe an attack with biological weapons as one of the most terrifying and probable disasters the United States faces, the Intelligence Community is lagging behind in looking for new collection strategies, and has not sought sufficient help outside the halls of intelligence agencies. The Community cannot defeat what one senior policymaker told us was "the greatest intelligence challenge" by itself.

We recommend three ways of changing the Intelligence Community's overall approach to biological weapons: (1) better coordination with the biological sciences community; (2) more aggressive, targeted approaches to intelligence collection; and (3) effective use of new regulatory mechanisms to create collection opportunities.

## Biological Threats*

### TERRORISM

Despite the possibility that terrorists have gained access to biological weapons, a large bioterrorist attack has not yet occurred. Why not? First, executing a large-scale biological attack is still fairly difficult as a technical matter; it requires organization and long-term planning. Second, biological agents can be highly infectious; working with them is dangerous. Finally, the war on terrorism may have derailed nascent attack plans . But these thin lines of defense are rapidly eroding. Some terrorist groups may have the financial resources to purchase scientific expertise. Even without sophisticated expertise, a crude delivery system would be

---

*The classified version of this section contains a more detailed discussion of the nature of the biological weapons threat, and also provides examples that could not be included in an unclassified report.

sufficient to inflict mass disruption and economic damage. Moreover, extremists willing to die in a suicide bombing are not likely to be deterred by the dangers of working with biological weapons. As a result, a senior intelligence official told the Commission that we should consider ourselves "lucky" we have not yet suffered a major biological attack. And the terrorist threat will only grow, as biological weapons are rapidly becoming cheaper, easier to produce, and more effective.

## STATES

States pose another biological weapons threat, and the weapons they produce are potentially more sophisticated—and therefore more lethal—than those made by terrorists. We can only speculate as to why countries have not yet used biological weapons on a large scale. In part, there is the risk of blowback—infection could spread to the state's own population. The United States may also be protected by the threat that it will respond violently to a biological attack. As President Nixon said when he terminated the United States biological weapons program and embraced an international ban, "We'll never use the damn germs, so what good is biological warfare as a deterrent? If somebody uses germs on us, we'll nuke 'em."

Covert use, however, is an entirely different matter. If the United States is attacked with biological weapons and cannot identify the attacker, the threat of nuclear retaliation will be of little use. States might attack the United States or its military installations overseas and avoid retaliation by posing as terrorists. If the spread of illness is the first sign that such an attack has taken place, the U.S. government may have difficulty responding effectively. In many attack simulations, U.S. biodefense capabilities struggle to simultaneously administer medical countermeasures, quarantine infected individuals, and decontaminate large areas.

## BIOTECHNOLOGY

A third biological weapons threat lies not far in the future. Terrorists may soon be able to cause mass casualties that are now possible only for state-run biological weapons programs. Scientists can already engineer biological weapons agents to enhance their lethality either through genetic engineering or other manipulations. Such weapons of science fiction may soon become a fact. Given the exponential growth in this field and access to its insights through the Internet, our vulnerability to the threat might be closer at hand than we suspect.

## *The Intelligence Gap: What We Don't Know*

The Intelligence Community has struggled to understand the biological weapons threat. According to a senior official in CIA's Counterproliferation Division, "We don't know more about the biological weapons threat than we did five years ago, and five years from now we will know even less."

### ANALYSIS: ASSUMPTIONS ABOUND

Assessments of state and non-state programs rely heavily on assumptions about potential biological weapons agents, biological weapons-adaptable delivery systems, and fragmentary threat reporting. Unsurprisingly, this leads to faulty assessments. For example, in October 2002, the Intelligence Community estimated with "high confidence" that Iraq had an active biological weapons program. Yet the Iraq Survey Group's post-war investigation "found no direct evidence that Iraq had plans for a new biological weapons program or was conducting biological weapons-specific work for military purposes" after 1996. In Afghanistan, the story is the reverse. Despite suspicions that al-Qa'ida had biological weapons intentions, the Intelligence Community was unaware of the ambitious scope of its efforts.

Biological weapons analysis also suffers from the litany of problems we have identified elsewhere in our report, including insufficient outreach to technical experts in the CIA's Directorate of Science and Technology and the Department of Energy's National Labs, as well as those in the business community, public heath sector, and academia. With limited interaction between technical experts and political analysts, the Intelligence Community "does a poor job of matching capabilities with intent" to develop realistic biological attack scenarios for state and non-state actors alike. As one National Intelligence Officer told us, biological weapons analysts have an "institutional bias against creative war-gaming" and rarely engage in systematic testing of alternative hypotheses.

## COLLECTION: CONTINUED FRUSTRATION AND A GLIMMER OF HOPE*

The weaknesses of analysis, however, pale beside the Intelligence Community's inability to collect against the biological weapons target. We found that the Community's biological weapons collection woes result from both the technological limits of traditional collection methods and a poorly focused collection process that is ill-equipped to gather and sort through the wealth of information that could help alert the Community to crucial indicators of biological weapons activity. In our classified report, we discuss these intelligence collection limitations at length; unfortunately, these details cannot be included in our unclassified report.

At bottom, the gap in collection on the biological threat is largely attributable to the fact that the Community is simply not well configured to monitor the large stream of information—much of it publicly available—relevant to biological weapons. In our classified report, we illustrate how considerable information about al-Qa'ida's pre-war biological weapons program in Afghanistan could have been known through public or government sources; we cannot, however, provide these details in an unclassified format. We emphasize here simply that t he Community must focus on doing a better job of collecting and connecting similar indicators of biological weapons personnel and activity in the future. Moreover, it is essential that the Community improves its access to and use of open source intelligence—the challenges posed by the biological weapons threat reinforce that conclusion.

However, before the Community can begin to effectively mon-

---

*A considerable majority of information contained in this section of our classified report could not be discussed in an unclassified format.

itor such vital indicators of biological activity, it must develop a basic understanding of the threat landscape. We were disappointed to discover that, three-and-a-half years following the anthrax attacks, the Intelligence Community has still not taken many of the most rudimentary steps necessary for this sort of collection. In our classified report, we offer examples of how particular intelligence agencies have failed to take these steps, but these details cannot be discussed in an unclassified format. We also describe a (classified) nascent effort at CIA that we believe to be worthy of praise. In all events, the Intelligence Community must ensure that any new efforts support a comprehensive collection effort across different regions, groups, and biological threats. Just as in other areas of intelligence, agencies at times jealously guard their most sought-after information. This fragmentation and parochialism highlights the importance of integrating the government's efforts against proliferators as well as the need for naming a deputy to the Proliferation Mission Manager, as recommended below, to focus exclusively on biological weapons issues.

## The United States Response: The Biodefense Shield

Although resources have flowed freely into biodefense since the 2001 anthrax attacks, only a fraction of these resources has gone to funding new intelligence collection strategies. A senior official at the National Security Council laments that, with regard to biological weapons intelligence, "there's still a sense that it's too hard to do." Although future biodefense technologies and medical countermeasures may allow the United States to neutralize the effects of biological attack, intelligence is one of the few tools today that holds out hope of avoiding attack, rather than just limiting the damage. Biodefense is critical, but it should not be our first line of defense. As a senior Centers for Disease Control and Prevention (CDC) official states, we "need to move upstream from the event"—a reactive biological weapons posture will not suffice.

One positive outgrowth of U.S. biodefense programs is that they have bred new intelligence customers, beyond the traditional military and foreign policy users. Technical experts, who include the CDC, Department of Homeland Security, the United States Army Medical Research Institute for Infectious Diseases (USAM-RIID), the National Institute for Allergies and Infectious Diseases (part of the National Institutes of Health, or NIH), and the Department of Agriculture, now need biological weapons threat information to inform their biodefense efforts. The existence of these customers presents an opportunity to encourage more focused biological weapons intelligence, and in turn to provide the Intelligence Community with much needed expertise.

Regrettably, new biodefense customers are largely unaware of what intelligence can bring to the table. A senior NIH official, for example, expressed frustration with the quality of biological weapons intelligence that NIH receives, as well as the lack of a structured venue for receiving and assessing such information. This has made the effort to set vaccine research and development priorities more difficult and, worse yet, may have divorced vaccine research from what is known about the current threat. Yet at the same time, demonstrating the cultural gap that still divides the biodefense and intelligence communities, this same official expressed immediate reluctance when told that NIH could perform its own intelligence analysis of open sources to identify the most likely biological threats.

CIA analysts observe that their agency in particular does a poor job of interacting with outside experts, but there are promising initiatives elsewhere within the Community. One effort aimed at increasing such interaction is the Defense Intelligence Agency's Bio-Chem 2020, a small-scale attempt at discussing emerging biotechnology threats with outside experts, usually at the unclassified or secret level. These scientists publish periodic papers on general biological threats rather than reviewing specific biological weapons analysis. A senior National Security Council official praises Bio-Chem 2020 but is quick to note that it is a "cottage program," not part of a broader Intelligence Community endeavor. Another useful initiative is a plan for a National Interagency Biodefense Campus at Fort Detrick, Maryland, with personnel from USAMRIID, NIH, and the Departments of Agriculture and Homeland Security. The campus, which is designed to coordinate biodefense research and serve as a central repository for expertise, will not be complete until 2008. In our view, the culture gap between the biological science and defense communities is so large that housing them together is essential to fostering a common strategy. The extent of Intelligence Community participation at the campus, however, remains undetermined.

## Going Forward:
## Improving Biological Weapons Intelligence Capabilities

If the Intelligence Community does not improve its foreign and domestic collection capabilities for biological weapons, the risk of catastrophe will only grow. We see a need for three broad changes: (1) tighter Intelligence Community coordination with the biological science community both inside government and out; (2) far more emphasis on integrated and aggressive intelligence targeting; and (3) stronger regulatory efforts to control potential biological weapons technologies, which would enable more intelligence collection than any go-it-alone effort by the Intelligence Community.

### WORKING WITH THE BIOLOGICAL SCIENCE COMMUNITY

When an intelligence analyst wants to understand a foreign nuclear weapons program, the analyst can draw on the expertise of thousands of Americans, all of whom understand how to run a nuclear program—because that is what they do, day in and day out. If an analyst wants the same insight into biological weapons programs, working bio-weaponeers are simply not available. The last offensive American biological weapons program ended 35 years ago.

The United States faced a similar dilemma in the late 1950s with regard to nuclear physics. The World War II physicists at Los Alamos were aging, and the younger generation did not have strong ties to the U.S. government. In response, the Defense Department founded the JASONs, an elite group of distinguished nuclear scientists that interacts with senior policymakers, receives intelligence briefings, and provides classified studies on pressing national security issues. Considering the number of Nobel laureates in the group, the opportunity for rising stars to interact with leading scientists in their field, and the financial compensation that members receive, membership to the JASONs remains highly coveted.

According to a CIA report summarizing a conference of life science experts, "a qualitatively different relationship between the government and life sciences communities might be needed to most effectively grapple with the future biological weapons threat." Although DIA's Bio-Chem 2020 is a successful interaction mechanism with academia and the private sector, it is insufficient compared to what is required. The Intelligence Community needs more consistent advice than that provided by unpaid professionals, and more contemporary advice than that provided by intelligence scientists who have not published research in over a decade.

We therefore recommend that the new DNI create a National Biodefense Initiative composed of several programs aimed at strengthening the Intelligence Community's biological weapons expertise. Such an initiative could be composed of the following four components:

- An elite Biological Sciences Advisory Group, administered by the DNI's Director of Science and Technology, which would be composed of the nation's leading life science experts. The group would be compensated for their work and asked to examine and advise the DNI on biological threats;

- A part-time government service program for select biologists and health professionals to review biological weapons analysis and answer Community queries;

- A post-doctoral fellowship program that funds scientists for one to two years of unclassified research relevant to biodefense and biological weapons intelligence; and

- A scholarship program that rewards graduate students in the biological weapons-relevant hard sciences in exchange for intelligence service upon completion of their degrees.

In addition to reaching *outside* the government to develop a more robust and mutually beneficial relationship with the biological science community, the Intelligence Community needs more effective links with biological experts and authorities inside the government. Nurturing this relationship will help ensure that relevant science is informing actual intelligence collection and better serving new customers. We believe that the DNI could utilize the Joint Intelligence Community Council, established by the intelligence reform legislation, to convene a working group of agencies with interest in biological weapons intelligence to serve as a kind of "consumer council." This working group would have the added benefit of helping both sides—the intelligence and biological science communities—understand the needs of the other so that they can more effectively work in parallel. The DNI might consider moving the biological weapons working group, or other biological weapons intelligence units, to the National Interagency Biodefense Campus once it is completed in 2008.

TARGETING BIOLOGICAL WEAPONS THREATS

As our previous discussion of the Community's collection woes starkly illustrates, the Intelligence Community needs more aggressive, targeted approaches to intelligence collection on biological threats. Systematic targeting of potential biological weapons personnel and programs is critical. CIA's Directorate of Science and Technology is funding some promising efforts, but they remain in their initial stages, and the Directorate lacks the authority to implement a program across the Community. Much more needs to be done.

First, the Intelligence Community needs a targeted, managed, and directed strategy for biological weapons intelligence. We strongly suggest designating an office within the NCPC to handle biological weapons specifically. It is also essential that this designee (or deputy) for biological weapons work in tandem with his or her counterparts at the National Counterterrorism Center.

With visibility across the Intelligence Community, the biological weapons deputy in the National Counter Proliferation Center (NCPC) could draw on different pockets of relevant expertise. But if CIA's Directorate of Operations (DO) is any kind of microcosm of the biological weapons intelligence world, then a daunting task lies ahead. Within the DO, the Counterterrorist Center collects against bioterrorism; the Counterproliferation Division collects against most state biological weapons programs, and the geographic area divisions collect against the remainder. Such fragmentation leaves serious potential gaps.

Devising and implementing a biological weapons targeting strategy will require not only that the Intelligence Community begin to think as a whole, but also that the Intelligence Community think beyond itself. Part of the challenge involves drawing on personnel and databases housed in non-Intelligence Community agencies such as Commerce's Bureau of Industry and Security and Homeland Security's Customs and Border Protection. Data from non-intelligence sources needs to be cross-referenced with the Intelligence Community's biological weapons databases, and filtered through a set of developed biological weapons indicators to direct intelligence collection. FBI and Homeland Security personnel need training in intelligence targeting and access to this system to identify homeland threats.

A comprehensive and strategic approach to biological weapons targeting will also involve open source exploitation to drive collection and warning strategies, and a multi-year research and development plan for the development and deployment of emerging collection technologies. In our classified report, we offer several suggestions for improving the Intelligence Community's capabilities which cannot be discussed in an unclassified format. Elements within the Community deserve praise for having taken steps to implement these suggestions.

It is our hope that through a Target Development Board, the NCPC's deputy for biological weapons can drive the Intelligence Community to pursue the necessary multifaceted collection approach. We encourage the Community to continue to explore and develop new approaches to collection, and we expect that these efforts would be dramatically furthered by the Mission Manager and Target Development Board devices.

## LEVERAGING REGULATION FOR
## BIOLOGICAL WEAPONS INTELLIGENCE

The United States should look outside of intelligence channels for enforcement mechanisms that can provide new avenues of international cooperation and resulting opportunities for intelligence collection. The National Counter Proliferation Center will be able to do a great deal to expand outreach to the biological science, biodefense, and public health sectors, but an even broader effort is required to draw on departments and agencies outside of the Intelligence Community. We believe the National Security Council or perhaps the Homeland Security Council is the most appropriate venue for convening different national security elements to devise such national-level strategies. Intelligence will be able to most effectively operate in a national security environment that is organized around and cognizant of its combined efforts to work against the biothreat.

We suggest that the Joint Interagency Task Force consider, as part of its development of a counter-biological weapons plan, the following two recommendations—which involve developing beneficial relationships with foreign states and applying regulatory powers to foreign entities that do business with the United States.

Developing close relationships with foreign governments on the biological weapons issue will be imperative if the United States is to better achieve its goals of monitoring and containing biological threats. Perhaps most importantly, the United States can bring its powers of suasion to bear on states to adopt domestic legislation that criminalizes biological weapons and establishes domestic controls to prevent proliferation—as they are obligated to do under the terms of United Nations Security Council Resolution 1540.

Criminalization will facilitate cooperation from liaison services, which are more likely to assist the United States in contexts where their domestic laws are violated. U.S. law enforcement and intelligence agencies should make cooperation with foreign officials a priority, and should establish regular information sharing events with foreign police forces to assist them in honing their awareness of the biological weapons threat and encouraging cooperation.

International inspections will—at least with respect to state programs—remain an important counterproliferation tool in the future. Arguably, designing effective inspection regimes will become all the more critical in a future where proliferation increasingly involves countries with small (and therefore difficult to detect) chemical, biological, and nuclear weapons programs. The benefits to having on-the-ground access to suspect facilities could be substantial.

There is little prospect in the near future for an international biological weapons inspection regime, however. The United States should therefore seek to obtain some of the benefits of inspections through the use of creative regulatory approaches. One such approach would involve a traditional regulatory model of imposing obligations on international businesses. The approach would build on Executive Order 12938 as amended, which directs the Secretary of Treasury to prohibit the importation into the United States of products produced by a foreign person or company who "materially contributed or attempted to contribute to" the development, production, stockpiling, or acquisition of weapons of mass destruction. More vigorous enforcement of this order would begin to reduce the biological weapons proliferation vulnerabilities that arise through lax internal controls in the private sector.

How might such a regime work? All companies that handle dangerous pathogens could be required to meet security standards and provide data about their facilities, as is already being done inside the United States. This need not be a unilateral undertaking. Objections from major trading partners could be reduced through cooperative inspection agreements with, for example, the United States, the European Union, and Japan. Compliance by individual companies could be ensured with a mix of carrot and stick—such as "fast lane" border controls, whereby companies that adhere to United States standards are granted speedier customs processing at our ports and airports; with the possibility of reduced liability protections and patent protections for the uncooperative.

## Conclusion

Improvements in intelligence are no guarantee against a successful biological attack, but they could make such an attack substantially less likely to succeed. There are no perfect solutions, but there are better solutions than the ones we have today. For now, better is all we can do. Given the potential costs of a biological weapons attack, better is what we must do.

# Nuclear Weapons

## Introduction

For the Cold War-era Intelligence Community, the challenge of nuclear proliferation was menacing but manageable. The Community focused primarily on intelligence collection against a few states seeking to join the "Nuclear Club"—with an especially watchful eye directed toward states aligned with the Soviet Union.

Although tracking proliferation developments was an important and large-scale enterprise, the world's accumulated storehouse of nuclear material and knowledge was relatively well accounted for (at least internally) by nuclear states. Moreover, the number of potential nuclear proliferators and their prospective state clients were relatively few, and the potential pathways for transferring nuclear material were reasonably well known and could be monitored—in theory at least—by traditional collection platforms.

Today's nuclear proliferation threat is much more diverse, and the challenges are more difficult. The state-based threat remains, and has been joined by the nightmarish possibility that non-state actors like terrorist groups could obtain a nuclear weapon or a "dirty bomb" and detonate it in the heart of a major American city. Simultaneously, the sources of nuclear materials and expertise have themselves dramatically proliferated. The breakup of the Soviet Union has left a large body of poorly secured, dubiously inventoried nuclear materials and weapons, about which the

Community knows precious little. Meanwhile, shadowy, non-state proliferation networks have appeared, quietly peddling their products to the highest bidder. These new nuclear proliferators and their customers operate under a veil of secrecy, including the use of front companies to mask their intentions and movements. It is the misfortune of our age to witness the globalization of trade in the ultimate weapon of mass destruction.

There are many facets to the nuclear proliferation problem; here we focus on but two of the most important—the availability of unsecured nuclear weapons and materials, or "loose nukes," and the appearance of non-state nuclear "brokers." We believe that the Intelligence Community must do much more to improve its collection capabilities with regard to both, for the purpose of halting nuclear proliferation at the *source*. That said, we recognize the inherent difficulty of both targets, as well as the limitations on our ability to contribute much in the way of concrete operational recommendations as to how the community can improve in this regard (other than the understandable, but rather unhelpful, advice, to "try harder" and "spend more" on the endeavor). Consequently, as we discuss later in this chapter, our recommendations focus on improving the process for interdicting nuclear materials once they are in transit from the proliferators or, as a last resort, on their way to the United States.

## *Loose Nukes: The Great Unknown*

The single greatest hurdle to a terrorist's fabrication of a nuclear device is the acquisition of weapons-usable nuclear material. If terrorists are able to procure such material intact, they can skip this most difficult part of the nuclear weapons development cycle. Just as Willie Sutton robbed banks "because that's where the money is," terrorist groups are most likely seeking nuclear material from the former Soviet Union because that is where the most material is available. (Additional information concerning terrorist efforts to obtain nuclear material is presented in the classified report but cannot be discussed here.) Tracking this nuclear material in the former Soviet Union is exceedingly difficult. However, we would like to emphasize that the United States has not made collection on loose nukes a high priority.

In our classified report we discuss in greater detail the reasons why our efforts to collect intelligence in this area have struggled, and we offer suggestions for improvement that cannot be discussed in an unclassified format. While we have generally shied away from simply recommending "more" effort or funding, we believe that some of these techniques may require additional funding.

The loose nukes problem is in many ways indicative of problems facing the Intelligence Community as a whole. Analysts and collectors are too consumed with daily intelligence requirements to formulate or implement new approaches. The war on terrorism and ongoing military operations have distracted the Community from longer-term threats of critical importance to national security. The perception is that there is no "crisis" until a weapon or fissile material is stolen. The problem, of course, is that we might not know this was the case until we are jolted by news of a catastrophe in Washington, D.C. or midtown Manhattan.

## Established Nuclear Powers: China & Russia

While the discussion in this section has focused on the emerging intelligence challenges resulting from the proliferation of nuclear weapons and related materials, we recognize that the traditional threat of nuclear weapons in the hands of determined state adversaries remains alive and well and requires the continued attention of policymakers and the Intelligence Community. The nuclear arsenals and emerging capabilities of China and Russia, in particular, pose a challenge to the United States—a challenge about which the Intelligence Community today knows too little. In our classified report we detail some of the struggles the Intelligence Community has had in developing information about these more traditional targets—but we cannot elaborate upon our findings in this area in this report.

## The Khan Network: "One-Stop Shopping" for Proliferation

Private proliferators and the "grey market" for nuclear trafficking pose another emerging threat. States no longer have a monopoly on sophisticated nuclear technology, materials, and expertise. The insecurity of nuclear materials, combined with diffusion of the technical knowledge necessary to construct or assemble a nuclear device, has resulted in a burgeoning industry for entrepreneurial middlemen. As demonstrated in our Libya case study, this threat requires new intelligence approaches.

Former Director of Central Intelligence George Tenet has spoken publicly about the "emerging threat" posed by private proliferators like A.Q. Khan. As the father of Pakistan's atomic bomb, Khan helped pioneer the practice of clandestine nuclear procurement. Through front companies, subsidiaries, and a network that stretched from Pakistan to Europe, Khan sought to provide countries with "one-stop shopping" for nuclear goods. We now know that Khan's network supplied nuclear equipment and expertise that "shav[ed] years off the nuclear weapons development timelines of several states including Libya." Among other things, Khan's network supplied Libya with nuclear centrifuge technology.

Working alongside British counterparts, CIA's Directorate of Operations was able to penetrate and unravel many of Khan's activities through human spies. They deserve great credit for this impressive success. However, the effort dedicated to bringing down the network demonstrates how rare and hard-fought future successes may be. It is possible, although unlikely, that Khan is unique. Private dealers, after all, control many of the materials needed for nuclear weapons production.

The A.Q. Khan achievement also suggests that the Intelligence Community will meet with limited success if it acts alone. Combating proliferation networks requires insight into the networks' modes of operation; for example, understanding the front companies through which they operate. As we discuss more fully in the interdiction section below, the Intelligence Community must reach out to non-traditional partners elsewhere in the government to augment its own capabilities.

## Conclusion

There is little more frightening than the thought of terrorists detonating a nuclear device within the United States. And events of the past decade—including the questionable security of former-Soviet nuclear material, the emergence of private proliferation threats like A.Q. Khan, and the rise of terrorist groups determined to strike U.S. territory—have added to the threat. Furthermore, there is no good reason to expect that North Korea and Iran will be the last states to try to acquire nuclear weapons. Indeed, acquisition by these two countries might set off a cascade of efforts by others in East Asia and the Middle East. (Nor is there a good reason to expect that states of concern will only be the neighbors of these two countries and others possessing nuclear weapons. It is worth remembering that South Africa, remote in many ways from the central regions of the Cold War, made them.) We believe that our recommendations for reform discussed elsewhere in the report, in combination with this chapter's discussion of intelligence support to interdiction and leveraging regulatory mechanisms for intelligence, will at least help the Intelligence Community be as prepared as it can be.

# Chemical Weapons

Even when unintentionally released, poisonous chemicals can have terrible effects. An accidental release of poisonous gas from a chemical plant in Bhopal, India, killed thousands in 1984. Deliberate chemical attacks, of course, have the potential to be even worse. In 1995, the Japanese cult Aum Shinrikyo released the chemical nerve agent sarin on the Tokyo subway, killing twelve people, sending more than 5,500 to the hospital, and sowing fear throughout the city. Commentators attributed the relatively low number of fatalities to the poor quality of the agent and Aum Shinrikyo's inefficient dispersal devices. In our classified report, we offer further examples of suspected chemical weapons plots that cannot be discussed in an unclassified format.

While biological and nuclear weapons could cause the worst

damage, terrorists could kill thousands of Americans by simply sabotaging industrial chemical facilities. And, due to the large volume and easy accessibility of toxic chemicals in the United States, a chemical attack causing mass casualties may be more likely than a nuclear or biological attack in the near term.

As with biological and nuclear threats, the Intelligence Community is poorly positioned to meet the challenges posed by chemical weapons. Historically, it has focused on state programs and has only recently turned its attention to potential uses of chemical weapons by terrorist groups. The Community's task is complicated by the ubiquity of toxic chemicals—which are available for sale across the United States and the world—and the relative ease with which other, even more deadly substances can be manufactured from common chemical precursors. Moreover, given the increasing sophistication of the chemical industry and the various dual uses of its products, the Community will face an increasingly difficult task in differentiating legitimate from potentially hostile manufacturing efforts. Finally, as is the case with biological weapons, many small-scale chemical production facilities can be concealed in nondescript facilities that are not easily detectable through conventional collection means, such as imagery.

The Intelligence Community certainly needs to do everything possible to collect on the plans and intentions of those terrorist groups that would use chemical weapons in an attack on the United States. Moreover, because of the easy accessibility of toxic chemicals and chemical precursors, it is essential that the Community develop strong links with the FBI, which may be better suited to monitor and respond to suspicious purchases of chemicals on the state and local level and to interface with local law enforcement for the same purpose.

Such traditional intelligence activities are necessary. But as our discussion about nuclear proliferation above demonstrates, traditional methods of intelligence collection have not proved particularly adept at monitoring "loose nukes," and there are serious questions as to whether the Community will be able to detect and disrupt new, diffuse proliferation networks that acquire and traffic in nuclear materials. Without admitting defeat, we must acknowledge the possibility that nuclear materials and perhaps nuclear weapons will find their way into the international transportation stream; bound for terrorists or rogue states, who will in turn attempt to bring them to the United States. A similarly disturbing state of affairs exists with regard to chemical weapons—as the sheer volume and availability of chemicals at home and abroad indicate that it is likely such weapons or materials will come into the hands of those who would do us harm.

As a result, it seems clear that in addition to improving its traditional collection capabilities, the Intelligence Community should also focus on improving its capabilities with regard to directly supporting interdiction activities, both inside and out of the United States, and to fully utilizing the regulatory and legal mechanisms at our disposal for controlling proliferators. It is to these tasks that we now turn.

# The Interdiction Challenge: Intelligence for Action

## Introduction

The United States has articulated a broad and aggressive policy that emphasizes the seizure or disruption of proliferation-related materials bound for states or individuals. However, the Intelligence Community is currently ill-equipped to support this policy. As one senior national security official told the Commission, counterproliferation interdiction requires "a whole intelligence support mechanism. . . that we don't have."

First, the Intelligence Community must collect information from a wide variety of non-traditional sources, ranging from customs officials to private parties. Second, the Community must provide information to a wide variety of non-traditional customers, ranging from foreign partners to law enforcement. But perhaps most importantly, the intelligence process—collection, analysis, and dissemination—must be much faster and more action-oriented than has traditionally been the case. If intelligence officials detect information about an illicit nuclear shipment, they cannot wait weeks for their analytical units to produce "finished intelligence," or for policy entities to approve an interdiction response. In this regard, support to interdiction must resemble counterterrorism or counternarcotics intelligence support; it must be quick, integrated, and accurate.

In this section we will address the broad theme of intelligence support to the interdiction of weapons of mass destruction, and make recommendations designed to address these basic requirements. We propose a new model for coordinating and executing interdiction, as well as several specific suggestions that could improve the Community's collection efforts and help to protect our borders.

Although the discussion below could apply to any weapon of mass destruction, in the near-term it is likely to pertain primarily to nuclear devices and chemical materials; detection and interdiction of biological substances is particularly difficult given the dual-use nature of biological equipment and the lack of discernible signatures attributed to biological materials. As was demonstrated in 2001, a biological weapon can be effectively delivered, undetected, in an envelope.

## Improving the Flow of Information

To support interdiction, the Community must tap into a wide variety of information networks that are, in many cases, outside of the Intelligence Community. Counterterrorism and counternarcotics intelligence have already taken significant steps in this regard. Counterproliferation intelligence must follow suit.

One critical information source is the Department of Homeland Security, which controls several databases that can help tip off analysts and operators looking for proliferation targets. For example, two main components of Homeland Security—Immigration and Customs Enforcement (ICE) and Customs and Border Protection (CBP)—operate a variety of databases that follow flows of people and goods across U.S. borders. These databases provide a rich source of data for relationship mapping and link-analysis among foreign companies and individuals. Yet our interviews with operators have revealed serious information sharing problems between Homeland Security and the Intelligence Community that dramatically limit their usefulness. Our classified report offers examples of these information sharing difficulties and of one successful program run by the Office of Naval Intelligence.

## Developing Tools to Do It in Real Time

Effective interdiction also requires that policymakers and operators have new analytical tools that can extract information from the Intelligence Community in real time. Ships carrying nuclear material will not wait for a lengthy analysis to run its course before delivering their cargoes.

For example, to support counternarcotics interdictions Joint Interagency Task Force-South has link-analysis tools that, if shared on a government-wide basis, would permit operators to quickly establish connections among terrorist organizations, proliferation networks, and other dubious international activities. Rather than starting with such existing assets, nearly every intelligence, law enforcement, or military entity involved in counterproliferation is also developing similar tools. A National Security Council-commissioned report by the Community's Collection Concepts Development Center concluded in November 2003 that these efforts composed a "'Balkan gaggle' of sometimes redundant programs with little coordination and incomplete operational integration." The DNI should use his authority to encourage development of these tools and coordinate agency efforts.

Carrying out effective interdictions also requires real time awareness of activities in the sea and the air. The Coast Guard's Maritime Domain Awareness program and the recent National Security Presidential Directive articulating a Maritime Security Policy are steps in the right direction. There is also an urgent need to share at least some portion of our air and maritime domain awareness information, and our computer-based tools, with international partners who will assist the United States in carrying out interdictions.

The scope of these activities demonstrates that successful interdiction requires a vision that stretches far beyond the Intelligence Community. To restate one of the primary themes we found in our study of proliferation: the Intelligence Community cannot win this battle on its own. Coordination and integration will be necessary.

## Going Forward: A Different Model

Currently, interdiction efforts are not sufficiently coordinated across agencies. This is particularly true with respect to operational planning and execution. We do not believe that the National Security Council is the proper locale for managing daily operations—counterproliferation or otherwise. Although the National Security Council plays a critical role in helping to develop government-wide counterproliferation policy, it should not become the center for interagency operations as the United States ramps up its interdiction capability.

A new Joint Interagency Task Force for counterproliferation would fill the role of planning and executing interdiction operations, drawing on the full range of military, law enforcement, and intelligence capabilities of the United States. Ideally, a Counterproliferation Joint Interagency Task Force would be flexible enough to support the operational needs of U.S. Strategic Command or any other entity tasked with stopping, seizing, or destroying a given cargo. The Task Force would contain diplomatic, military, intelligence, law enforcement, and other representatives from across the government. We recommend that it:

- Plan and execute the full range of overt and clandestine interdiction operations;

- Seek approval from the National Security Council for interdiction operational plans through the real-time decision making process described below;

- Provide tactical and operational intelligence, air, and sea support to the Department of Defense Unified Commands to carry out particular operations;

- Establish the legal basis for all interdiction operations, including through agreements with consenting private sector actors and partner nations that have signed ship-boarding agreements;

- Coordinate country team and partner nation initiatives in order to defeat the flow of materials of proliferation concern; and

- Conduct regular interdiction gaming exercises with international partners to develop new operational plans and concepts.

Our proposed National Counter Proliferation Center (NCPC) will serve a variety of functions. With regard to interdiction, the NCPC will fulfill the requirements of the Counterproliferation Joint Interagency Task Force, the National Security Council, and a growing body of counterproliferation intelligence users. Through a Target Development Board, the NCPC would prioritize and target for interdiction those proliferation networks of greatest strategic concern. Finally, the NCPC would ensure that the Intelligence Community provides the Task Force and the National Security Council with real-time proliferation intelligence support.

The National Security Council currently holds a weekly interdiction sub-Policy Coordinating Committee meeting to identify potential interdiction targets and determine courses of action. Since counterproliferation interdiction targets may often involve sensitive diplomatic and legal issues, the National Security Council will want to approve operational interdiction plans prior to execution. The time sensitivity of certain interdiction operations suggests that the National Security Council should adopt a virtual decision-making process–one in which parties can consult remotely–to accomplish this oversight function.

To streamline and clarify the counterproliferation interdiction process, we recommend a set of procedures similar to those established by Presidential Directive 27 for dealing with counternarcotics interdictions and other "types of non-military incidents."

Because interdictions may involve military operations that would conflict with covert activities, we recommend a separate National Security Presidential Directive that outlines the National Security Council process for supervising the planning and execution of interdiction operations. To make these decisions, National Security Council staff and senior policymakers will need intelligence to answer a range of questions. Unlike the existing intelligence paradigm, which is heavily reliant on the production of "finished" intelligence products, interdiction may require, for example, that military commanders or customs officials communicate directly with collectors and analysts.

The State Department is currently charged with responsibility to secure bilateral ship-boarding agreements in support of the Proliferation Security Initiative. To date, the Department has secured three important agreements. We do not believe, however, that sufficient strategic thought has been directed toward how these agreements can be structured to serve intelligence purposes.

Through such bilateral agreements or related customs regulations, the State Department could, for example, require ships and aircraft to declare their locations through GPS and satellite uplink. Failure to report location information could be viewed as the rough equivalent of driving with a broken taillight, and might establish reasonable suspicion to conduct an interdiction. Such agreements and the imposition of other tracking requirements would enable intelligence to draw on new sources of data to monitor potential cargoes, vessels, and aircraft of proliferation concern.

## Protecting our Borders:
## The Department of Homeland Security

It may not be possible in all cases to identify and halt biological, nuclear, or chemical weapons shipments before they reach the United States. In such cases, our last line of defense is detecting and stopping these shipments as they cross our border. The Department of Homeland Security, through Customs and Border Protection, collects information on incoming cargo shipments that the Intelligence Community must learn to exploit. The flip side of this equation is equally important—Customs and Border Protection needs threat information from the Intelligence Community to target shipments of concern headed to the United States. Plainly, Homeland Security and the Intelligence Community need to strengthen their relationship. A discussion of ways in which this relationship can be improved is in the classified version of our report, but cannot be discussed in an unclassified format.

If we are to increase our chances of detecting proliferation materials before they enter the United States, it is critical that Homeland Security work closely with the Intelligence Community in developing its plans for screening materials coming into the United States . Moreover, once the plans are instituted, Homeland Security and the Intelligence Community must maintain a close relationship to ensure that homeland security policies reflect the Intelligence Community's most current assessments.

The Intelligence Community's collaboration with the Department of Homeland Security should not stop at targeting cargoes. A comprehensive border defense initiative would employ an array of advanced technologies to protect our borders. For example, reconnaissance satellites, unmanned aerial vehicles, nuclear detection technologies, and biometric identification cards could all play a role in border protection.

Many critical technologies to protect the border, are still in their infancy. A senior official at the Department of Homeland Security laments that the sensors deployed at our borders are "way below ideal." Customs and Border Protection officials complain that some detectors are imprecise and prone to false alarms. A concerted research and development effort is necessary to bring these technologies to maturity. A new sense of urgency is required.

# Enlisting Commerce and Treasury to Combat Proliferation

## Introduction

The Intelligence Community will be most effective at combating chemical, biological, and nuclear threats if it works in concert with non-traditional government partners. Legal and regulatory regimes can help enable better intelligence gathering and disrupt proliferation-related activity.

On several occasions throughout our inquiry, departments and agencies outside of the Intelligence Community asked why our Commission was interested in their work. These comments illustrate the lack of connection between the Intelligence Community and large parts of the government. The Community often sees itself as a world apart, and it is viewed by outsiders as an unapproachable exotic.

In the area of proliferation in particular, such a failure to see beyond the Intelligence Community's borders—and a failure to acknowledge what intelligence can and cannot do—has deprived the country of anti-proliferation levers that it badly needs. As we saw with biological weapons, the lack of an effective (and truly reciprocal) relationship between intelligence and biological sciences has limited the Community's efforts. Similarly, the Community has not sufficiently harnessed the power of legal and regulatory regimes, and the synergies that could result from working more closely with them. While we did not seek to reach beyond the scope of our mandate, which is to study the Intelligence Community, the Commission did look at some ways in which legal and regulatory regimes might enhance intelligence collection specific to the counterproliferation issue.

We do not pretend to have weighed fully every non-intelligence interest at work in many of these regimes. For that reason, many of our recommendations only suggest areas for possible action by both the affected agency and the Intelligence Community. But regardless of whether specific regimes are instituted, we believe that closer cooperation between the Intelligence Community and the Departments of Commerce and Treasury could result in many mutually beneficial relationships and improved collection against difficult proliferation-related targets. The Intelligence Community will be most effective at combating chemical, biological, and nuclear threats if it works in concert with non-traditional government partners.

## Department of Commerce:
## Enforcing the Export Control Regime

The Department of Commerce's Bureau of Industry and Security (BIS) administers and enforces the Export Administration Regulations, which govern the export of dual-use items. BIS's law enforcement authorities place it in a position to collect large amounts of information that could be of great use to the Intelligence Community.

In order to obtain the cooperation of export control violators, however, BIS needs stronger law enforcement powers, something it has lacked in recent years, mainly because some of BIS's law enforcement authorities lapsed when the Export Administration Act expired. BIS could also assist the Intelligence Community more fully if it had authority to impose increased penalties for export violations and more authority to conduct undercover activities of potential intelligence value. The Administration has supported a renewal of the act that would confer these authorities, and congressional action on renewal would make cooperation between BIS and the Intelligence Community more productive.

The Export Administration Regulations provide additional opportunities to support counterproliferation efforts. Specifically, BIS inspections, the conditions BIS imposes on export licenses, and BIS's possible access to corporate records may provide valuable intelligence and counterproliferation opportunities. We discuss these and other related matters, including two classified recommendations, more fully in our classified report.

## Department of the Treasury: Stopping Proliferation Financiers

The Treasury Department can also provide more support to counterproliferation than it does today. The Department currently has two powerful authorities with respect to terrorism that do not now apply to proliferation. The first is the authority to freeze the assets of terrorists and their financiers; the second is the authority to take action against foreign financial institutions that allow their services to be used to support terrorism. We see no reason why these same authorities should not be enhanced to also combat proliferation.

Pursuant to the International Emergency Economic Powers Act, the President authorized the Department of the Treasury to block the assets of persons who sponsor terrorism. However, Treasury lacks a similar tool to block the assets of proliferators. To fill this gap, we recommend the President take steps to allow the Secretary of the Treasury to take the same action against persons "who provide financial or other material support to entities involved in the proliferation of weapons of mass destruction." In light of the virtually universal recognition that the greatest threat the United States faces is the intersection of terrorism and proliferation, we see no reason why Treasury's authority should extend to only half of this potentially catastrophic combination.

Currently, section 311 of the USA PATRIOT Act authorizes the Secretary of the Treasury—in consultation with other federal officers, including the Secretary of State and the Chair of the Board of Governors of the Federal Reserve System—to designate a foreign jurisdiction or financial institution a "primary money laundering concern," and to require that U.S. financial institutions take certain measures against the designee. This power can be used when the Intelligence Community determines that a foreign financial institution is involved in proliferation-related activity. And by doing so, the Department can effectively cut the foreign institution off from the U.S. banking system. This authority is limited, however to financial institutions that assist proliferation. It would be more effective if it could also be applied to *non-financial* business entities involved in proliferation.

The reason for this suggested change is simple—many aspects of proliferation involve non-financial institutions, such as pharmaceutical, petrochemical, and high-tech companies. By limiting the Treasury Department's designation authority to financial institutions, the current law effectively addresses only one part of the business-related proliferation challenge. Expanding Treasury's authority would thus allow the U.S. government to also take action against the very businesses that supply the materials that make proliferation possible.

Specifically, we believe the Secretary's authorities should extend to the designation of individual businesses involved in proliferation as "primary money laundering concerns." Once a business was so designated, U.S. financial institutions could be required by the Treasury Department to take certain steps to avoid engaging in business transactions with the designated companies. The Secretary of the Treasury might also be able to affect whether foreign financial institutions are willing to conduct business with business entities involved in proliferation. If so, the Secretary of the Treasury could help cut off proliferators from their financial lifeblood.

## Conclusion

Legal and regulatory mechanisms are valuable tools the Intelligence Community should use to their full extent. But proper use of these mechanisms requires extensive interagency cooperation. This will not be an easy task. But we believe it is a worthwhile endeavor, and one that may in the long run—prove invaluable in combating the proliferation of nuclear, biological, and chemical weapons.

# Conclusion

We have approached our task mindful of its historical context. In truth, looking to the past, we find cause for discouragement. Many of the ideas and recommendations that we have made in this report were advanced with compelling reasoning by previous commissions. After ceremonious presentations to the President and to Congress, the previous recommendations were ignored or implemented weakly. Most of them failed to take hold. The question is inescapable: why should this Commission be different from the others?

Nevertheless, we are hopeful. The Intelligence Community is at the juncture of a number of powerful historical forces: the end of the Cold War, the first catastrophic attacks in the United States by international terrorists, the proliferation of nuclear weapons, the failure of U.S. intelligence in Iraq, the broad-based demand for change by the American people, and enactment by Congress of the most sweeping legislative reform since the creation of the existing Intelligence Community in 1947. These are reasons enough to believe that our work may be put to good purpose.

Perhaps the single most prominent and recurring theme in our recommendations is a call for stronger and more centralized management of the Intelligence Community, and, in general, the creation of a genuinely integrated Community instead of a loose confederation of independent agencies. This is not a new idea, but it has never been successfully implemented.

Part of the solution is to put more power and authority in the hands of the DNI. This was a principal purpose of the intelligence reform act of 2004. As we have noted elsewhere, however, the DNI's authorities under the new legislation are far from absolute. In many instances, the DNI will require the support and concurrence of the Secretary of Defense. He will need, as well, the commitment of the Federal Bureau of Investigation to become a part of the Intelligence Community and to be subject to

DNI oversight. The DNI will need to use his new authorities swiftly to overcome the barriers that have plagued previous efforts. The new Intelligence Community leadership will also need to cross the old boundaries. The Mission Managers, as we have described them in our report, show how a new approach to management can bring together previously isolated activities and orchestrate an effort that embraces the entire Community.

But it is also incontrovertible that the Intelligence Community's flaws cannot be cured by top-down management alone. Reform must rise from the bottom too, and it must involve true cultural change within the Community. We make a number of specific suggestions along these lines in our report. To state just a few: processes to support analysts working long-term strategic topics; an innovation center to incubate new concepts in human intelligence; an open-source directorate that can freely experiment with new information technologies; a sizeable, uncommitted research and development budget that is available to quickly infuse funding; entirely new approaches to gathering intelligence on biological weapons; and incentives to promote the behaviors that lead to better intelligence (and discourage those that don't). Some of these challenges—especially support for long-term analysis, for innovative collection, and for aggressive research and development—will require greater resources. We are not in a position to make a precise estimate of the costs, but we believe that budget is less likely to be a constraint than culture and tradition. At every level, new and better ways of doing business should be encouraged, nurtured, and protected.

Throughout our work, we have been struck by the range of opinions on reform of the Intelligence Community. Some former and current leaders with impressive experience believe that most of what needs to be done has already occurred. We respectfully disagree. We have unquestionably seen a break with the past and many brave initiatives. We have heard of stunning successes, many of which are too sensitive to mention even in an unclassified report. But too many of these efforts are "more of the same," and many of those that break with past practices are only timid forays into new territory that could easily end in retreat.

There is another group of highly respected individuals, also with long and deep experience, who are fundamentally pessimistic about the recent legislative changes. They foresee new layers of bureaucracy with little value added weighing on institutions that are already overloaded with formalities. We also disagree with this group, but we understand their concern.

Every person with whom we spoke was unanimous on one point: there is nothing more important than having the best possible intelligence to combat the world's deadliest weapons and most dangerous actors. We agree, wholeheartedly; indeed, our survival may well depend upon it. Of course, even the most improved intelligence process is no guarantee against surprise or against weapons of mass destruction. Biological and nuclear weapons are becoming too easy to obtain for any intelligence reforms to provide absolute protection from catastrophe. But in the face of such staggering risks, we must do all we can to avoid danger. That means building an integrated, innovative, and agile Intelligence Community. Despite the uncertainties, we have done our best to chart a course that will take us to the Intelligence Community that our nation deserves.

# Postscript: Future Intelligence Challenges

No commission could examine every important issue facing the Intelligence Community. Our Commission encountered issues that were tangential to our mandate but that are likely to be crucial to the Intelligence Community and the DNI in coming years. We record in this postscript three of the issues that fall into this category.

## Security, Counterintelligence, and Information Assurance

This country's security policies—considered in their broadest form to include physical security, infrastructure security, personnel security, and information and cyber security—are in need of serious review. Today we face new threats and vulnerabilities that are in many ways more encompassing, complex, and subtle than those we confronted in the past century. We begin with several broad observations:

- Security is a highly decentralized government function. Today there is no single advisor to the President who deals with the full spectrum of security-related issues.

- Effectively addressing security generates costs that must be balanced against risk and threats.

- Security, as a discipline, has historically been dominated by "police" type management, processes, and enforcement approaches. Although the police function is still required, today's security vulnerabilities are increasingly technical in nature and related to information technology systems, software, and hardware.

Several contemporary security challenges threaten to undermine not only intelligence sources and methods, but also the national security at large. These include: unauthorized leaks, which are now beginning to rival espionage in frequency, scope, and cumulative damage; the deterioration of the concept of need-to-know, and an increasing need to balance security concerns against the need for more robust information sharing; the particular vulnerability of communication and information sharing systems; foreign information warfare programs; and the persistent incentives for overclassification of information. To respond to these challenges, the Intelligence Community must harness the power of digital and biometric "identity"; improve the efficiency of the investigation, clearance, and adjudication process; develop mechanisms designed to protect sources, methods, and capabilities; effectively manage compartmentation; and certify secure spaces and improve physical security for people, facilities, and critical infrastructure.

Intelligence analysts have been placed in a difficult position. On the one hand, analysts must protect new and extremely sensitive sources and methods. On the other hand, analysts are expected to facilitate the broadest possible forms of information sharing, both amongst fellow analysts and with outside customers who increasingly want direct access to raw data and want to collaborate directly with the most knowledgeable and credible analysts.

We have considered many of these issues and offer recommendations that we believe will help address aspects of the security challenge, including our recommendations on Information Sharing (Chapter 9), and on authorized and unauthorized disclosures (Chapter 7, Collection). Yet we know we have only scratched the surface of this complex problem. The issue of security writ large requires a separate inquiry. Accordingly, this Commission recommends early action to define new strategies for managing security in the 21st century.

# Rethinking Overhead Collection

Some of the most difficult issues for the Intelligence Community in the next few years concern satellite surveillance systems. These systems are extremely costly, so that cost overruns in satellite systems tend to suck resources from the rest of the intelligence budget. Increasingly, too, there are air-breathing alternatives to satellite surveillance. Satellites can sometimes gather weapons of mass destruction intelligence not available in any other way, but sometimes satellites provide little assistance in targeting other WMD activities. They also play a crucial role for the military. Choosing which satellite systems are best in this evolving environment is an enormous challenge.

The DNI will need to make tough choices about our future imagery capabilities; doing so will require a strong Planning, Programming, and Budgeting Execution System capable of comparing the marginal values of the respective collection disciplines. We did not believe that it was within our competence to make specific judgments about whether and how to overhaul future satellite intelligence plans, although we have offered recommendations that we believe will better enable the DNI to make these judgments. Given the importance of the issue, we recommend that the DNI specifically visit this issue early in his tenure.

# Maximizing Intelligence Support to Public Diplomacy and Information Warfare

We live in an information age, and the United States needs an Intelligence Community willing and able to support the demands of our public diplomacy efforts. Moreover, we need a sophisticated capability to defend our own information environments and infrastructures from attack . The Intelligence Community has already developed some capabilities of this sort, but they require further investment and attention in order to address our current weaknesses. Our computer network defense capabilities lag considerably, making us vulnerable to countries with growing offensive capabilities.

Our intelligence organizations collect information about adversaries to enable public diplomacy. They also seek information on hostile intentions and possible attacks on U.S. and allied systems. Intelligence must be able to support all of these activities. Some aspects of the Intelligence Community's capabilities in this area cannot be discussed in an unclassified format.

Although our information warfare capabilities are still evolving, this large and complex subject merits further inquiry. Many components of the discipline are also controversial. But intelligence has a major role to play in this job.

The United States, as well as the entire modern global economy, is utterly dependent on its information systems as well as the sources that move, store, and display that information. The Intelligence Community must be focused and well-postured to address any vulnerabilities to these systems.

We did not fully explore these issues; they cut across government and private sector interests, and we believe that the Intelligence Community needs to: participate in initiatives designed to define the country's information warfare policies and doctrine; fund its activities; establish appropriate oversight; and provide for better integration, coordination, and collaboration across agencies. This is an appropriate job for a Presidential Task Force.

# Glossary

## Common Abbreviations

| | |
|---|---|
| BIS | Bureau of Industry and Security (Department of Commerce) |
| BW | Biological Weapons or Biological Warfare |
| CBP | Customs and Border Protection (Department of Homeland Security) |
| CBRN | Chemical, Biological, Radiological and Nuclear Weapons |
| CCDC | Collection Concepts Development Center |
| CDC | Centers for Disease Control and Prevention |
| CIA | Central Intelligence Agency |
| CIFA | Counterintelligence Field Activity (Department of Defense) |
| CPD | Counterproliferation Division (CIA) |
| CTC | Counterterrorist Center |
| CW | Chemical Weapons or Chemical Warfare |
| D&D | Denial and Deception |
| DCI | Director of Central Intelligence |
| DCIA | Director of Central Intelligence Agency |
| DHS | Department of Homeland Security |
| DIA | Defense Intelligence Agency |
| DNI | Director of National Intelligence |
| DO | Directorate of Operations (CIA) |
| DOD | Department of Defense |
| DOE | Department of Energy |
| DOJ | Department of Justice |
| DS&T | Directorate of Science and Technology (CIA) |
| FBI | Federal Bureau of Investigation |
| FBIS | Foreign Broadcast Information Service |
| FIG | Field Intelligence Group (FBI) |
| FISA | Foreign Intelligence Surveillance Act |

| | |
|---|---|
| HPSCI | House Permanent Select Committee on Intelligence |
| HUMINT | Human Intelligence |
| IAEA | International Atomic Energy Agency |
| IAEC | Iraqi Atomic Energy Commission |
| ICE | Immigration and Customs Enforcement (Department of Homeland Security) |
| INC | Iraqi National Congress |
| INR | Bureau of Intelligence and Research (Department of State) |
| INS | Immigration and Naturalization Services |
| IRTPA | Intelligence Reform and Terrorism Prevention Act of 2004 |
| ISB | Intelligence Science Board |
| ISE | Information Sharing Environment |
| ISG | Iraq Survey Group |
| ITIC | Intelligence Technology Innovation Center |
| JAEIC | Joint Atomic Energy Intelligence Committee |
| JICC | Joint Intelligence Community Council |
| JITF-CT | Counterterrorism Joint Intelligence Task Force |
| JMIP | Joint Military Intelligence Program |
| JTTF | Joint Terrorism Task Force |
| MASINT | Measurement and Signature Intelligence |
| NCIX | National Counterintelligence Executive |
| NCPC | National Counter Proliferation Center |
| NCTC | National Counterterrorism Center |
| NGA | National Geospatial-Intelligence Agency |
| NGIC | National Ground Intelligence Center |
| NIC | National Intelligence Council |
| NIE | National Intelligence Estimate |
| NIH | National Institutes of Health |
| NIO | National Intelligence Officer |
| NIP | National Intelligence Program |
| NIU | National Intelligence University |
| NRO | National Reconnaissance Office |
| NSA | National Security Agency |
| NSC | National Security Council |
| ODNI | Office of the Director of National Intelligence |

| | |
|---|---|
| OIPR | Office of Intelligence Policy Review (Department of Justice) |
| PDB | President's Daily Brief |
| PFIAB | President's Foreign Intelligence Advisory Board |
| PTTR | President's Terrorism Threat Report |
| SEIB | Senior Executive Intelligence Brief |
| SEVIS | Student and Exchange Visitor Information System |
| SIGINT | Signals Intelligence |
| SOF | Special Operations Forces |
| SSCI | Senate Select Committee on Intelligence |
| STRATCOM | U.S. Strategic Command |
| TDB | Target Development Board |
| TIARA | Tactical Intelligence and Related Activities |
| TTIC | Terrorist Threat Integration Center |
| UAV | Unmanned Aerial Vehicles |
| UNMOVIC | United Nations Monitoring, Verification, and Inspection Commission |
| UNSCOM | United Nations Special Commission |
| USAMRIID | U.S. Army Medical Research Institute for Infectious Diseases |
| UNVIE | U.S. Mission to International Organizations in Vienna |
| WINPAC | Weapons Intelligence, Nonproliferation and Arms Control Center (CIA) |
| WMD | Weapons of Mass Destruction |

PUBLICAFFAIRS is a publishing house founded in 1997. It is a tribute to the standards, values, and flair of three persons who have served as mentors to countless reporters, writers, editors, and book people of all kinds, including me.

I. F. STONE, proprietor of *I. F. Stone's Weekly*, combined a commitment to the First Amendment with entrepreneurial zeal and reporting skill and became one of the great independent journalists in American history. At the age of eighty, Izzy published *The Trial of Socrates*, which was a national bestseller. He wrote the book after he taught himself ancient Greek.

BENJAMIN C. BRADLEE was for nearly thirty years the charismatic editorial leader of *The Washington Post*. It was Ben who gave the *Post* the range and courage to pursue such historic issues as Watergate. He supported his reporters with a tenacity that made them fearless, and it is no accident that so many became authors of influential, best-selling books.

ROBERT L. BERNSTEIN, the chief executive of Random House for more than a quarter century, guided one of the nation's premier publishing houses. Bob was personally responsible for many books of political dissent and argument that challenged tyranny around the globe. He is also the founder and was the longtime chair of Human Rights Watch, one of the most respected human rights organizations in the world.

.     .     .

For fifty years, the banner of Public Affairs Press was carried by its owner Morris B. Schnapper, who published Gandhi, Nasser, Toynbee, Truman, and about 1,500 other authors. In 1983 Schnapper was described by *The Washington Post* as "a redoubtable gadfly." His legacy will endure in the books to come.

Peter Osnos, *Publisher*